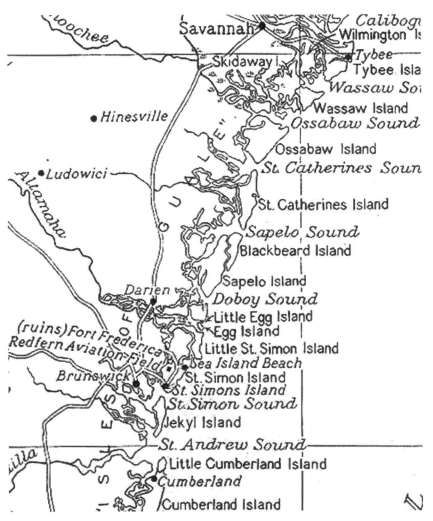

The Georgia Coast in the 1930s. (From National Geographic, February 1932).

Shrimp boats at Valona, McIntosh County, early 1960s.

Notes From Low Country Georgia

History, Ecology & Perspective

Buddy Sullivan

1734 survey of the new town of Savannah, attributed to Peter Gordon

Copyright Buddy Sullivan 2020
ISBN: 978-1-09832-215-1
Set in 11 point Goudy Oldstyle
Cover image: Katie Brown of Sapelo Island, ca. 1937 (Photograph courtesy of Malcolm Bell, III).

Contents

A Note on Methodology   7

An Ecological Overview   13
   Science & the Salt Marsh

The First Conservationists?   46
   Northern Money and Low Country Georgia

Selected Writings   87
   Researches in Coastal Ecology as History

   Ecology and Historical Archaeology   87
   Societe de Sapelo: The French in Coastal Georgia   123
   Land Use & Landscape: Antebellum Sapelo Island   146
   Roswell King, Jr. and Plantation Management   197
   Butler's Island Before and After the War   297
   Hopeton: Model Plantation of the Antebellum South   328
   Canal Building in Coastal Georgia   341
   A Rice Planter on Bryan Neck: Richard James Arnold   357
   Slaves and Religion in Low Country Georgia   390
   Land Use & Landscape: Harris Neck   397
   Postbellum Sapelo Island   486
   Racial Unrest in Darien & McIntosh County, 1899   560
   H.E. Coffin and R.J. Reynolds at Sapelo Island & After   569
   Land Use & Landscape: Ossabaw Island   627
   Henry Ford and the Great Ogeechee   654
   Clyde: A Lost Town of Coastal Georgia   668
   Maritime Notes from Coastal Georgia   688
   Land Use & Landscape: Railroads and Naval Stores   777
   The Altamaha River: A Coastal Legacy   788
   Saving a River: William G. Haynes and Ophelia Dent   798

Afterword: A Low Country Legacy   810

Index   820

Robert Cromley, last keeper of the Sapelo light station, 1932. See p. 590.

A Note on Methodology

This book may be said to be an amalgamation of my historical researches over the past forty years, offered here through a personal perspective based on an intimate and lifelong association with the Georgia low country. There is an intent here which will become apparent in the first two chapters, with discussions on the ecological uniqueness of the coast, followed by a review of the evolution of the coastal islands from antebellum plantations to private enclaves for the wealthy, and then to conserved and protected lands.

There will be much here that is familiar to readers of my other books. These papers, essays and personal observations have appeared in various forms in earlier works, though there is much that is new. The passage of time has allowed for new revelations, new perspectives, to emerge, thus the present work is a synthesis of the newest findings that build upon the foundations laid by previous books, including *Early Days on the Georgia Tidewater, From Beautiful Zion to Red Bird Creek, Environmental Influences on Life & Labor in McIntosh County, Georgia,* and "All Under Bank," among others.

The stories in this volume are a reflection of my tandem interest in, and fascination with, the ecosystems of coastal Georgia as relates to some of its most interesting history. A recurring theme in this approach to coastal history has been to recognize the important correlation between *ecology* and *history* in the ways evolving populations have lived their lives economically and culturally. The focus in the papers thus reflects how people used the land, as well as another favorite theme—the maritime legacy of coastal Georgia.

During my eight years of editing the *Darien News* (1985-93) and the following twenty years as the manager of the Sapelo Island National Estuarine Research Reserve, I was able to produce a number of publications on coastal history. There were monographs on subjects such as the Darien Presbyterian Church (1986), Sapelo Island (1988), The Darien Bank (1989) and McIntosh County (1990) that preceded the publication of the first edition of *Early Days on the Georgia Tidewater* in late 1990, a book that the critics called "definitive" and reprinted in five subsequent editions through 2001, ultimately growing to 858 pages. *Early Days* was out of print for several years before I undertook a complete revision, recasting and up-dating of the book. The finished product of 918 pages—in essence an entirely new book—was published in 2018. During my working years in state government at Sapelo, I produced a number of other books. These ranged from two edited journals of rice planters (antebellum Roswell King, Jr. and postbellum John G. Legare), an examination of Darien's post-Civil War timber industry, including the editing of the Thomas Hilton memoirs, a comprehensive history of Bryan County, similar in style, research and depth to the McIntosh County history, and a history of Georgia as a volunteer project for the Georgia Historical Society.[1]

Departing Sapelo and state government in 2013 enabled me to undertake more research and writing, including a collection of my writings in *A Georgia Tidewater Companion*; a monograph on Northern acquisition of the coastal islands after the Civil War, and how these acquisitions led to the later movement to conserve and

---

[1] *Georgia: A State History* (Charleston, SC: Tempus Publishing, 2003), in association with the Georgia Historical Society.

protect Georgia's islands; the revision of *Early Days* previously mentioned; a biography and collection of the writings of county historian Bessie Lewis; *Sapelo: People and Place on a Georgia Sea Island*, a comprehensive semi-scholarly review of the history of the island complimented by archival images and the strikingly-beautiful contemporary photographs of my colleague Benjamin Galland; and, in 2018, *Environmental Influences on Life & Labor in McIntosh County*.

The thematic approach to my published works since 2006 or so has been to relate the economic, agricultural and maritime history of the Georgia coast from an ecological perspective, i.e. how local environmental circumstances and conditions, both ashore and afloat, have shaped people's lives, and how they made their living. I have used stories of how people utilized the land in tandem with the ecosystem, stories of "land use and landscape," and of "life and labor" on the tidewater as viewed through the prism of ecology. My research instincts, and my writing and organizational skills have measurably improved over the years—particularly so since my former newspaper days when writing on pressing deadlines often compromised my preference to preserve the sanctity of the Queen's English. Some of my best works have evolved from projects upon which I entered with little or no knowledge of the subject. The best example of this is my history of Bryan County, *From Beautiful Zion to Red Bird Creek* (2000), a volume that incorporates what I still feel to this day is the best combination of research, book organization and cohesion of writing of any book I have done before or since.

My perspective on the flow of coastal history reflects this ongoing interest in *ecology as history* from several topical approaches: an understanding of the dynamics of salt marsh ecology, and the estuarine science employed in understanding it; what ecology and archaeology have told us about the way people lived a thousand years in the past; the use of the land by generations of its owners; tideflow rice cultivation utilizing fresh water and tidal systems; agriculture in a barrier island environment; the influence of waterways—fresh and salt—in the development of a coastal maritime legacy, including the commercial oyster and shrimp fisheries; ecology as history in its relevance to the interior pine flatwoods in the conduct of naval stores production; and, finally, studies relating to the twentieth century coast—uplands, islands, marshes and tidal waterways—and the evolving efforts within these systems toward attaining scientific understanding and the environmental conservation of local natural resources.

The current book is about the uniquely Southern concept of *place*. I say that because coastal Georgians, blacks and whites alike, have always had an abiding sense of "place" and "permanence" because the tidewater has represented home and stability for many generations of people who have lived and labored here. The theme of "place" is a recurring one throughout my stories.

The work here generally represents a synthesis of my more than three decades of research and investigation of the history and culture of McIntosh County and coastal Georgia. The topics covered are as diverse as the Native American influences of the coast through archaeological investigation, to the commercial shrimping industry of the mid-twentieth century; antebellum tideflow rice cultivation; the use of the land (and waters) of the tidewater in a multiplicity of ways; the nineteenth century timber economy that guided commercial fortunes in Savannah, Darien and Brunswick; and patterns of

African American settlement and land ownership, particularly in McIntosh and Liberty counties.

As noted, the essays and papers herein have as their thematic basis the fundamental symbiosis of how the people of the region have adapted to their environmental circumstances in virtually every aspect of their lives—the methods by which they planted their crops, how they built their homes and commercial buildings, how they got about from one place to another, and a myriad of other life-determining factors, almost all reliant upon the ecological and environmental conditions of where they were. This concept is not nearly as pronounced in the modern era, with the technology and scientific knowledge of the twenty-first century. Certainly the environment of coastal Georgia is of paramount concern in the present day, but in different ways than it was 150 years ago. In 1850, for example, the local ecosystem was the driving factor in practically every aspect of life. Now, we see the ecosystem more as something to be protected and conserved rather than developed or otherwise over-utilized. As responsible stewards of the coast, we are usually passionate to a fault about how we manage our barrier islands, our salt marshes, our beach and dune systems, our maritime forests. It is to be fervently hoped that we, and succeeding generations of coastal Georgians, continue along this path of conservation and careful and thoughtful stewardship of our ecological resources.

Buddy Sullivan
Cedar Point 2020

Abbreviations in Notes

GDAH	Georgia Department of Archives and History
GDNR	Georgia Department of Natural Resources, Atlanta
GHS	Georgia Historical Society, Savannah
HSP	Historical Society of Pennsylvania, Philadelphia
NARA	National Archives and Records Administration
RMCG	Records of McIntosh County, Georgia
SHC	Southern Historical Collection, Chapel Hill
SINERR	Sapelo Island National Estuarine Research Reserve
UGAMI	University of Georgia Marine Institute, Sapelo Island

An Ecological Overview:
Science & the Salt Marsh

Coastal Georgia's tidal salt marshes, with their labyrinthine network of rivers and creeks, in combination with the fresh-water river deltas to about fifteen miles upstream from the sea, comprises roughly a third of the total area of tidewater Georgia. Even through a casual look at a coastal map one can easily ascertain that the waterways and wetlands of the region command a sizeable presence. Further inland, the influences of the fresh-water rivers contribute to a large patchwork of swamps and other low-lying areas unsuitable for crop cultivation, or extended human habitation. In the aggregate, the coast, like much of the southeastern tidewater from Charleston to St. Augustine, comprises one of the most unique ecosystems in the world.

"Ecology" in the context of the previous paragraph, and for the purposes of the following discussion, entails the salt marshes and their tidal cycles, and the biological and chemical processes within those elements, along with other ecological considerations of the coast: soil types, river hydrology, weather, etc.

The present stands of the Georgia coastal marshes that form wide swaths between the barrier islands and the mainland are well developed, and have been relatively stable for the last five thousand years as *Holocene* formations. Earlier late-*Pleistocene* marshes, however, underwent frequent change, even disappearing altogether at times in response to alterations in sea level that created unstable conditions. With adequate sea level heights in the Holocene, water-borne sediments were deposited on underlying Pleistocene sediments to build new marshes and beaches over the earlier ones. Clays and fine sands make up the marsh deposits that form in the sheltered areas away from the direct impacts of the sea, accounting for the stable marsh belts between the barrier island the mainland.[2]

Another destabilizing cycle may currently be in progress in light of evidence of pronounced sea level rise along the south Atlantic shoreline. The coastal islands are drifting, albeit imperceptibly, ever southward, perhaps at the rate of an inch per year. This movement is based on a natural phenomenon known as *sand sharing,* a process that reaches back in time to the genesis of what now constitutes the Georgia coast.

The islands formed thousands of years ago as a collective movement of upland soils and sediments; they continue to alter in an ongoing natural cycle perpetuated by winds, storms, tides and ocean currents. The forces that created Sapelo began about two million years ago as the Pleistocene glaciers reached their southernmost advancement, establishing a temporary beachhead

---

[2] J.R. Hails and J.H. Hoyt, "An Appraisal of the Evolution of the Lower Atlantic Coastal Plain of Georgia," *Proceedings* of the Institute of British Geographers 46 (1969): 53-68.

eighty miles east of the present shoreline. The ice sheet began melting 18,000 years ago, depositing water into the ocean, and enabling the level of the sea to rise. Early sand ridge and beach formations were alternately flooded by seawater with a simultaneous accumulation of additional upland soil deposits washed eastward by the melting glaciers.

The age of the coastal islands is actually two-fold. Carbon 14 dating of submerged shell samples indicates the main portion of Sapelo as being 25-to-36,000 years old. Sapelo's uplands formed during several stages of the Pleistocene when the sea level was higher than at present. The seaward parts of the islands were formed 4-5,000 years ago, and are Silver Bluff barrier island formations (late Pleistocene) and modern (Holocene).[3] The Georgia islands are situated in the most recent of a series of six Pleistocene shoreline complexes that increase in age and elevation from the present shoreline. Sapelo's shoreline is composed of fine quartz sands that cumulatively build to create beaches and dunes as an extension of the shallow, gently-sloping sea bottom that extends 70-75 miles offshore as the Continental Shelf.

The Georgia coast, about one hundred miles in length, features a distinct island chain separated from the mainland by a four-to-six-mile swath of salt marsh. From east to west, the islands feature sand beaches, dune lines, and a slightly-elevated interior forest often dissected by tidal sloughs and freshwater ponds. The marshes lie

---

[3] Albert Sydney Johnson, Hilburn O. Hillestad, Sheryl Fanning Shanholtzer and G. Frederick Shanholtzer, *An Ecological Survey of the Coastal Region of Georgia* (Washington, D.C.: National Park Service Monograph Series 3, 1974), 14-16.

contiguous to the islands on their western sides. Penetrated by tidal creeks and rivers, the marshes extend westward to the coastal mainland. At its eastern edge the mainland is only slightly elevated, but is buffered from the direct effects of tropical storms by the marshes and islands that lie seaward. Freshwater rivers—the Savannah, Ogeechee, Altamaha, Satilla, and St. Marys—empty into the Atlantic Ocean through sounds that separate the islands. A sequence of salt, brackish, and freshwater marshes follow the river channels upstream into areas of decreasing salinity.

An ocean current, the longshore littoral current, evolves counter-clockwise off the Gulf Stream, flowing from north to south along the Georgia shoreline, and producing a constant movement of sand to the southward. At Sapelo Island, as an example, the littoral current then mixes with a strong outflow current moving from northwest to southeast on ebbing tides from Doboy Sound. The sandbars, beaches and dunes of Cabretta Island and Nanny Goat Beach are regularly altered by a combination of currents, tide flow and wind conditions. Simultaneously, the accretion of sands washed southward from Blackbeard accumulate on the beaches on the southern end of Sapelo with additional buildup of marsh west of the dunes and on the lighthouse tract. This natural "sand-sharing" process makes Sapelo Island one of the few remaining places on the east coast where the phenomenon is evolving with minimal interference from human activity.

These shoreline changes can be readily observed from a study of topographic maps and navigation charts of the area over the last two hundred years in which there is a progressive erosion of the north end of Blackbeard Island with a concomitant accretion of beach on

Sapelo's South End. There are sharply-eroded, truncated dune ridges on the north end of Blackbeard with much of their sediment eventually being deposited on the lower part of Sapelo where the beaches are pro-grading and the dunes are increasing in size. Both islands have shifted southward about 0.75 mile during the present Holocene high stand of the sea. At the same time, the accumulation of sand on Sapelo's South End has created natural obstacles to the Doboy Sound entrance with continually-shifting shoals and sandbars, not all of which are exposed at low tide—hence the numerous shipwrecks and ship groundings that have been recorded over the last two centuries by traffic approaching the inlet. Some of the sand from Nanny Goat Beach is also washed southward by the prevailing winds and currents. The cycle of erosion and accretion is constant, with sand eroded from one area of beach to be deposited in the offshore sandbars, then being washed back onto the beach with the resultant buildup of dunes.

The beach itself is composed of fine quartz sands mixed with small amounts of crushed shell. On Nanny Goat, the beach slopes gradually from the dune base to the water's edge, varying in width with its narrowest portion on the north across the inlet from Cabretta Island. Typical of the gently shelving southeastern shoreline, the water is very shallow for a considerable distance offshore from Sapelo, averaging only about eight feet a mile from the beach at mean low water.

The changing dynamics of the Georgia islands that are in federal or state administration, or those that remain in private ownership such as St. Catherines Island, do not affect people as there is no development on these islands near beach areas; it can, however, be detrimental to nesting areas for turtles and shorebirds such as the American Oystercatcher, Wilson's Plover, Least Tern, Gull-billed Tern, and Black Skimmer. These species rely on the stability of the beaches near the high tide line to lay their eggs.

During the summer months, marine turtles regularly nest and lay their eggs on the barrier island beaches and dunes, particularly those with minimal human use or impacts, the most prevalent species being the Atlantic loggerhead (*Caretta caretta caretta*). From May to early September the female loggerheads move to the beach at night, often during the flood stage of a spring tide, to lay from 120 to 130 eggs on dry ground close to the dune line. Most of the eggs fall victim to natural predators, but some hatchlings survive and return to the sea. Other large marine turtles may have nested on Sapelo in the past, including the Atlantic hawksbill, Atlantic green, and Atlantic leatherback.

Beach sand dunes are quite fragile; new dunes nearest the beach are the most unstable, and are under constant alteration by "blowout" from strong winds, and "washover" from a combination of storm waves and northeasterly winds. Dune buildup near the beaches typically occurs in periods of calm weather with onshore winds. As seen from the air, the lower end of Nanny Goat Beach on Sapelo Island displays dune lines in large arcs curving around the southern tip of the beach with sand accruing in the embayment washed by Doboy Sound's currents, lying just southeast of the lighthouse.

When constructed in the early nineteenth century, the lighthouse was on an island sand spit separated by a creek from the main island. Like Nanny Goat Beach, the lighthouse spit is Holocene but is positioned well behind the beaches and dunes; it is also subject to accretion, but in a different way. Nineteenth and early twentieth century maps and photographs reveal a gradual buildup of marshes projecting south of the lighthouse: a 1932 photograph of the tower places it very near the waters of Doboy Sound whereas marshes have since filled in a considerable area south of the tower, a clear illustration of the buildup of the South End through the sand-sharing system.

Sapelo Island has two distinct lines of sand dunes, with the inter-dune meadow in between. Closest to the beach are the active and back (primary) dunes that undergo frequent alteration through the effects of the littoral current, spring tides and northeasters. East of Dean Creek, less than half a mile west of Nanny Goat, is a high, wooded ridge of older dunes that are revealed as primary dunes in mid-1920s aerial photographs of the South End—further evidence of the natural accretive effects associated with barrier island sand-sharing.

Salt-spray tolerant vegetation prevalent along the coastal beaches and dunes plays an important role in the ecosystem. Natural plants that proliferate in the active dunes and the back dunes near the beach serve as stabilizers. The most prevalent of these are sea oats (*Uniola paniculata*), which serve as a binder to hold the active dunes in place. Other dune plants serving the same purpose are beach elder, beach hogwort, beach pennywort, water pennywort, beach sand-spur, panic grass, morning glory, and Spanish bayonet (*Yucca*).

In the inter-dune meadow, away from the direct effects of salt, are other stabilizing shrubs and trees, including wax myrtle, red cedar, sand live oak, buckthorn, groundsel, yaupon holly, tamarisk, Muhlenbergia, and prickly pear—a plant that can play havoc with the feet and ankles of unwary strollers through the sand. The dunes and meadow provide feeding habitat and shelter for a variety of animals, especially ghost crabs and rattlesnakes, and a variety of shorebirds.[4]

Tides have a pronounced effect on Sapelo's shoreline as well as the inshore salt marshes. There is a tidal amplitude around Sapelo ranging about seven feet up to about eleven feet on spring tides. Not surprisingly, the hydraulics of the tides affects the ecology of the marshes to a great extent. Tidal rise and fall is a key factor in the active processes that occur in the marshes, and constitute the diversity of habitats for a number of organisms in the intertidal area. Most tidal creeks lie within steep mud banks and natural levees that create a pattern for the movement of water preceding its eventual dissipation in headwaters on the marsh surface. Tidal waters flow across the low marsh levees only on the highest spring tides. There are two tidal cycles daily with about 600 square miles of marsh and creeks in coastal Georgia being inundated, drained and refilled.[5]

In an ebbtide-dominated regime tidal dynamics are most noticeably pronounced in the waters of the estuarine sounds that provide the breaks between the barrier islands along the coast. For example, off the south end of Sapelo Island, Doboy Sound has a strong outflow on the ebb tide. This tidal outflow is northwest to southeast. When combined with the input from the nearby Altamaha River, and the north-to-south emergence of water from

---

[4] Ibid., 35-40.
[5] The twenty-eight volumes of *Collected Reprints*, 1962-2004, University of Georgia Marine Institute (School of Marine Sciences, Athens), containing the published papers of UGAMI scientists, is the primary source for findings and conclusions based on forty years of scientific field investigations in the salt marsh ecosystem of Sapelo and other areas of coastal Georgia.

Old Teakettle Creek, tidal fronts are often quite distinctive, sometimes marked by narrow lines of foam running crossways to the water flow.

Depending on the wind direction, recreational boaters, and even local shrimp boat operators, universally note that Doboy Sound can be some of the roughest water on the Georgia coast. For example, if there is a prevailing southeasterly wind from offshore going against the strong outflow of current from the sound toward the ocean, the waters of the sound can be quite turbulent. The opposite effect prevails if the wind is from the northwest on a flooding tide. Doboy has a slightly lower salinity than the offshore ocean waters due to indirect freshwater inflow from the Altamaha delta just to the south. The Altamaha River system represents one of the largest watersheds in the eastern United States when including the inland Ocmulgee, Oconee and Ohoopee rivers. Substantial amounts of fresh water flow to the sea, mixing with the salt water from the Atlantic in the Altamaha delta just south of Sapelo Island. This brackish mix, occurring up to twenty-five miles inland, affects the hydrology of Doboy Sound, being more pronounced during periods of unusually high flow of fresh water from the interior.

An important component of the tidal interactions within the coastal ecosystem is the phenomena between the barrier islands and the mainland called "dividings." These are areas in which several streams meet and their tidal flows converge—tides meet from different directions and "divide." Most of the barrier islands of Georgia and South Carolina have these convergence areas, dividings, as tidal streams flow though the marshes between the islands and the mainland. Often, changing shoal areas are created at dividings at which the tides flow in different directions. Sandbars shift and the areas of shoaling can create hazards for the unwary mariner. There is one notable area of tidewater McIntosh County where this phenomenon occurs: the Dividings east of Valona is that confluence of several streams where the ebbing and flooding tides meet. If these streams were the points of a compass then Mud River would be to the east, Old Teakettle Creek to the south, Shellbluff Creek from Valona to the west, and the South Sapelo River (Crescent River) to the northwest, all meeting in the middle. Add to these a fifth waterway that has tidal influence, the lower end of Creighton Narrows just north of the Dividings where it meets the lower end of South Sapelo River.

Mud River, west of Sapelo Island and separating it from the mainland, is aptly named. It is one of coastal Georgia's most distinctive—and unusual—tidal streams. This broad, shallow river was for over a hundred years the principal connection between its confluence with Sapelo Sound on the north and New Teakettle Creek for coasting traffic between Savannah and Darien. It has always been notorious for its difficulty of navigation on anything but high tide, or very nearly high tide. Northeasterly and southwesterly winds (both are prevalent at varying times of the year) tend to practically empty Mud River on an ebbing tide. Much of the mud bottom of the river is exposed at low tide, although locals in anything smaller than a shrimp boat know how to navigate the passage through a narrow channel hugging the marsh. Tides below half-tide are the most unforgiving to those not familiar with local conditions, for the mud bottom can't be seen, yet is only a foot or less below the surface. There are numerous examples of the problems encountered with this waterway. The following account, written by a coastal traveler in 1853, is typical:

"...We passed through sounds and creeks and narrow rivers, some so narrow and shallow that two steamboats cannot pass each other, and not infrequently, the boats ground, lying in the mud over one tide. When they get fast to the soft bottom, all efforts of course are made to get them off, the most effectual being to send a boat ahead, manned by half a dozen negroes who, taking a stout rope with them, fasten it to a long pole thrust deeply down into the soft mud in a slanting position, and then attach the other end of the rope to the capstan on board the steamer; that, turned by the aid of the engines, soon drags them out of the mud. We grounded in the Mud River at half tide. For some miles the tide went out and left us high and dry as if we had been in the middle of a prairie. I tried to see for myself how far I could thrust a pole into the mud, and taking one about 20 feet long, I forced it down by my own strength from 12 to 15 feet. We were released when the water returned to half tide, and went on our way rejoicing. I truly said that this route was a novel one. Now we would be shut into a narrow stream and then we would come out again almost into the open sea..."[6]

The situation was finally rectified in 1913 with the Corps of Engineers dredging a cut, Creighton Narrows, through the marsh connecting the Dividings with Front River, thus enabling marine traffic to bypass Mud River altogether.

Perhaps the best example of a tidal waterway and its interaction with, and influence by, tidal cycles is the Duplin River which flows within Sapelo Island. The Duplin, largest of the streams lying entirely within the marshes of Sapelo, transits the western side of the island, emptying on its southern end into Doboy Sound. Except for rainfall and groundwater discharge from the nearby uplands, the Duplin

---

[6] Joseph W. Smith, *Visits to Brunswick, Georgia and Travels South* (Boston, 1907), 18-19.

receives no freshwater, and thus can be more accurately defined as a large tidal creek or embayment. Along its six-and-a-half mile length, the Duplin has three distinct sections, or tidal "prisms." The lower component ends near Pumpkin Hammock, the second extends northward to Moses Hammock, and the third comprises the several tidal creek branches of the upper Duplin.

The strong tidal currents and the lack of freshwater input generally keep the hydrological dynamics of the upper Duplin excluded from those of the lower section of the river nearer Doboy Sound. Occasionally, during especially high spring tides, water in the upper Duplin may merge with that of Mud River a short distance to the north. Conversely, the lower Duplin can sometimes have lower salinity levels than that of the upper sections during times of heavy discharge from the Altamaha River into Doboy Sound. The Duplin estuary covers 3,300 acres, about fifteen per cent of which remains submerged at mean low water with a tidal excursion of about three miles.[7]

A survey of the Duplin by University of Georgia Marine Institute scientists in the 1950s determined that the river's water surface was relatively narrow at low tide. When the water rises to six feet above mean low tide, however, it begins to leave the banks and flow in a sheet across the marsh. Small increases in tidal height impel increased volumes of water into the estuary, and as a consequence the tidal flow is turbulent. This promotes greater turbidity, though marsh flushing is incomplete with very little fresh water entering the system. Most water in the estuary merely oscillates back and forth,

---

[7] Johnson, Hillestad, et.al., *Ecological Survey of the Coastal Region of Georgia*, 91.

rather than draining away to be replaced. The sediments in the bed of the Duplin are low in mud content and contain accumulations of shell material, much of which is deposited from the oyster banks along the river. At Little Sapelo Island and Pumpkin Hammock the river is eroding sandy Pleistocene deposits.[8] The intertidal habitat of the Duplin, and its largest tributary, Barn Creek, is teeming with marine organisms that receive nutrients from the marshes, and in turn, provide food sources for saltwater fish species. The Marine Institute has conducted much of its research in these marshes, and over the last half century has made important discoveries relative to the feeding habits of subtidal species. Microalgae are productive in the river, and these and other organisms provide a food source for juvenile menhaden, a plankton feeder. Menhaden, in turn, are preyed upon by larger fish and birds. Flounder, bluefish and yellowtail are other finfish predators in the estuary; mullet are deposit feeders, and mummichog live in the shallower creeks and headwaters where they are rarely threatened by larger fish. Shrimp utilize the creeks off the Duplin throughout the year, and are especially prevalent during the summer. Larger predators, such as dolphins that feed around Marsh Landing dock on the lower Duplin, and mink and otter forage in the smaller creeks and marsh edges; birds feed in the tidal waters as well—pelicans, gulls and terns nearer the sound, and blue herons, ospreys and egrets further up the Duplin.

---

[8] R.G. Wiegert and B.J. Freeman, *Tidal Salt Marshes of the Southeast Atlantic Coast: A Community Profile* (Washington, DC: U.S. Department of the Interior, Fish and Wildlife Service, 1990); R.A. Ragotzkie and R.A. Bryson, "Hydrography of the Duplin River, Sapelo Island, Georgia," *Bulletin of Marine Science of the Gulf and Caribbean* 5 (1955): 297-314.

Eugene P. Odum, ecologist of the University of Georgia, and regarded as the "father of modern ecology," once described tidal creeks as a great circulatory system driven by the pumping "heart" of the tides. Despite a relatively short coastline, coastal Georgia has hundreds of tidal creeks that wend their way through the marshes between the islands and the mainland. The creeks mostly flow into larger tidal rivers while a few, on the islands, flow directly into the sounds. All the creeks provide new water input to the marshes on each high tide, while flushing out and removing many of the by-products of marsh growth and marsh decay—detritus—on the ebbing tide. Some of the creeks are almost bare at low tide leaving exposed mud banks that serve as habitat to a variety of consumers such as fiddler crabs, herons, egrets, and marsh hens. On a flooding tide snails become active while periwinkles and insects graze on the stems of the marsh cordgrass. Plankton and juveniles of various species enter the creeks with incoming tides, as do shrimp and fish when the water becomes deep enough.

McIntosh County's salt marshes are composed of many plant species, but the most prevalent by far is smooth cordgrass—*Spartina alterniflora*—which comprises about ninety per cent of the marsh system, and receives the greatest amount of tidal inundation. Despite its low diversity the marsh is considered to be one of the most productive natural areas on earth.[9] The basis for the marsh food chain is detritus originating from the dominant vascular plant, the cordgrass. There are differences in the *Spartina* along the creek banks,

---

[9] E.P. Odum and C.L. Schelske, "Mechanisms Maintaining High Productivity in Georgia Estuaries," *Proceedings* of the Gulf and Caribbean Fish Institute 14 (1961): 75-80.

and that of the high marsh nearer the transitional zone that is comprised of a mix of short *Spartina*, and *Salicornia* marsh. Low marsh *Spartina* is taller and more luxuriant than other marshes, and prevails along the creek and river fringes. All life requires fresh water to carry on metabolic processes, and the marshes have unique mechanisms that allow them to extract fresh water from the saline waters of the estuary.[10]

Marsh soils are anaerobic except near the surface and around the roots. Soil bacteria that breaks down accumulated organic matter require an anaerobic environment with the rate of breakdown, and that in which plant nutrients become available for new marsh growth, being related to water-flow characteristics and the dispersal of waste products.[11] Plant zonation is always subject to elevation and hydrology but there is a water table that maintains the marsh sediments in a near waterlogged state in all but the highest intertidal elevations.[12] Consequently, there is a high diversity of plant, soil, and microbial attributes between the low and high *Spartina* zones.

---

[10] The most lucid study of the *Spartina* marsh ecosystem, minus the technical jargon, is Charles Seabrook, *The World of the Salt Marsh: Appreciating and Protecting the Tidal Marshes of the Southeastern Atlantic Coast* (Athens: University of Georgia Press, 2012). See also Mildred Teal and John Teal, *Portrait of an Island* (New York: Atheneum, 1964) and Teal and Teal, *Life and Death of a Salt Marsh* (New York: Atlantic, 1969).

[11] J.R. Wadsworth, "Geomorphic Characteristics of Tidal Drainage Networks in the Duplin River System, Sapelo Island, Georgia," PhD diss., University of Georgia, 1980; R.W. Frey and P. Basan, "Coastal Salt Marshes," in R.A. Davis, Jr., ed. *Coastal Sedimentary Environments*, 2nd edit. (New York: Springer-Verlag, 1985), 225-301.

[12] Wiegert and Freeman, *Tidal Salt Marshes of the Southeast Atlantic Coast*. See also the many technical papers relating to marsh studies in *Collected Reprints*, UGAMI.

Salt marsh requires nitrogen and phosphorus as nutrients, the latter of which is abundantly available in both the soil and the tidal waters. Nitrogen availability is more complicated. The use of this common air element by *Spartina* requires its conversion to ammonia, nitrate or nitrite by the marsh through blue-green algae on the marsh surface, and bacteria within the soil.[13] Thus, the adaptability of the marsh to natural processes in a salt water environment makes it one of the more unique plant species of any ecosystem.

Twice-daily tidal cycles convey nutrients into the marshes, export detritus and nutrients back into the estuary, and provide a large surface area for phytoplankton production. Tidal flushing maintains a desirable vertical distribution of nutrients and detritus; the base of the detritus food chain is decayed *Spartina*, which is attacked by microorganisms.

Marine Institute research has determined that bacteria found in marsh mud are an important link in the food chain. In the late 1950s, John Teal found the important detritus-algae feeders to be fiddler crabs, periwinkle snails and nematodes among Sapelo's deposit feeders. The utilization of marsh organic matter accounts for about fifty-five per cent of production, leaving about forty-five per cent available for support of finfish, crabs, shrimp, oysters, and other estuarine species.[14] Further investigations found that marsh algae form a thin stratum between a dark, nutrient-rich, anaerobic sediment, and either an illuminated, aerobic, comparatively nutrient-poor water column. Thus, the algae habitat is subjected to rapid

---

[13] L.R. Pomeroy and R.G. Wiegert, *The Ecology of a Salt Marsh* (New York: Springer-Verlag, 1981).

[14] John M. Teal, "Energy Flow in the Salt Marsh Ecosystem of Georgia," *Ecology* 43 (1962): 614-24.

changes in light, temperature, pH, salinity, and nutrients that can have correspondingly rapid effects on the photosynthetic rate. Benthic productivity was found to represent about twelve per cent of the net primary production of the macrophytes in the marsh. About seventy-five per cent of this production occurs during ebbing tides, with the exposed creek banks being the most productive areas.[15]

In the higher intertidal zone between the *Spartina* and the upland, areas subjected to less frequent tidal inundation, other marsh-type plants are prevalent. Glasswort and saltgrass appear mixed with the shorter cordgrass. Black needlerush (*Juncus roemerianus*) develops as patches amid the cordgrass with its thin grey-brown stalks and sharp points. Other salt-tolerant plants mixed with the short *Spartina* in this zone are marsh bulrush and sea oxeye. Also featured in the higher zones are salt pans—barren sections of flat, packed soil that is free of vegetation because of its excessively high salinity.

Areas of vegetation lying amid *Spartina* marsh along the fringe abutting a tidal creek, or even a short distance apart from the uplands, are clumps of vegetation of varying size known as hammocks. These formations of high ground feature a mix of similar vegetation, including red cedar, sabal palm, wax myrtle, and yaupon holly. Hammock characteristics are similar, and they range in size from less than an acre to several acres. Little Sapelo Island, on the lower Duplin, is considered a large hammock even though it comprises 200 acres of upland, but about half of which is subject to occasional tidal inundation. There are several other named

---

[15] L.R. Pomeroy, W.M. Darley, E.L. Dunn, J.L. Gallagher, E.B. Haines and D.M. Whitney, "Primary Production," in Pomeroy and Wiegert, *Ecology of a Salt Marsh*, 39-67.

hammocks along the Duplin north of Little Sapelo: Mary, Fishing, Pumpkin, and Jack hammocks. Like Little Sapelo they have Pleistocene bases surrounded by their Holocene marshes.

A variety of marine organisms utilize the marshes for nutrients as decomposing *Spartina* detritus gradually dissolves and is flushed by the tides to provide food. Numerous consumer species inhabit the marsh ecosystem with the major groups being comprised of zooplankton, benthic invertebrates, insects, fishes, reptiles, birds and mammals. Benthic macro-invertebrates are the most conspicuous of the consumers, particularly fiddler crabs (*Uca* species), marsh mussel (*Geukensia demissa*), and marsh periwinkle (*Littorino irrorata*). Noticeable along some creek banks are oyster reefs. Oysters (*Crassostrea virginica*) settle on solid surfaces along the banks and subtidal water; as filter feeders they use marsh nutrients as an important food source. Oyster beds can alter tidal flow in the creeks by creating pools and small breakwaters.

In the early decades of the twentieth century, Georgia salt marshes supported a sizeable oyster industry but over-exploitation, and the failure to replace shell, led to its near-collapse by the 1950s. Another beneficiary of marsh nutrients directly related to commercial use is the Atlantic blue crab (*Callinectus sapidus*), the majority of which are taken in the sounds and the smaller rivers and creeks. Crabs use the marshes and creeks as habitat during their juvenile and sub-adult stages.

Of even greater economic significance, the marsh is critical in supporting the coastal shrimp fishery, long a multi-million dollar industry on the Georgia coast, with peak production in the middle decades of the twentieth century. While coastal shrimp (*Penaeus*) spawn in the open ocean, they migrate to the inshore waters as juveniles, and depend on marsh-produced nutrients during their growth stages before returning to the sea.

At low tide, the ubiquitous fiddler crab, particularly the sand fiddler (*Uca pugilator*), is frequently observed scuttling along the mudflats foraging for food near its burrow. Fiddlers extract food from the substrate based on differing feeding stimulants in response to levels in the food resource.[16] Gradients in biotic and abiotic factors resulting from tidal flooding affect the distribution of marsh organisms with the structural characteristics of *Spartina* providing refuge for some species from predators and submergence. The periwinkle prevalent in the marshes is a favorite of predators, particularly the blue crab.

Much of the current understanding of the salt marsh ecosystem and its attendant rivers, creeks and dividings, and the biological and chemical processes that occur within these systems, began to be formulated after 1953 with the establishment of the University of Georgia Marine Institute (UGAMI) on Sapelo Island. Most of the material in this chapter is synthesized from the research, investigations and conclusions that have evolved through the work of resident and visiting scientists at UGAMI. A young biology professor at the University of Georgia, Eugene P. Odum (1913-2002), who was laying the foundation for the first serious investigations of saltmarsh ecosystems on the southeastern coast, and several of his colleagues, worked with Sapelo owner Richard J. Reynolds, Jr. to make it

---

[16] J.R. Robertson, K. Bancroft, G. Vermeer, and K. Plaiser, "Experimental Studies on the Foraging Behavior of the Sand Fiddler Crab," *Journal of Experimental Marine Biology and Ecology* 52 (1980): 47-64.

possible for the marine biological laboratory to come to Sapelo in the summer of 1953.[17]

The ecological research at Sapelo Island in the first forty years often entailed field studies stemming from two basic considerations: determining the water flow characteristics of *Spartina alterniflora* (smooth cordgrass marsh), and the chemical and biological processes associated with *Spartina,* in concert with the marine organisms that proliferate the marsh ecosystem, or are directly affected by the marsh. Eventually, an important connection was made between the dynamics of the natural processes occurring in the salt marshes, and the sustainability of marine life in the nearshore and estuarine waters, as Emory Thomas points out:

> "This transmittal through tidal action of organic matter is primarily in the form of detritus which is mostly decomposed *Spartina.* The process by which detritus enters the ocean is called 'outwelling' and the initial hypothesis among Odum and the other scientists at the University of Georgia Marine Institute was that this outwelling from salt marshes and estuaries lay at the base of the food chain which supported the abundant marine life found off the east coast. Thus there seemed to be an empirical connection between *Spartina* and shrimp cocktail at least. In very recent years, however, scientists have challenged the assumption that 'outwelling' from salt marshes is vital to the food chain in coastal waters."[18]

Odum's research in those early years at Sapelo had important ramifications for the work of the Marine Institute in its first two decades. It also influenced his own evolving attitudes about ecology

---

[17] Betty Jean Craige, *Eugene Odum: Ecosystem Ecologist & Environmentalist* (Athens: University of Georgia Press, 2001). 54-58.
[18] Emory M. Thomas, "The South and the Sea: Some Thoughts on the Southern Maritime Tradition," *Georgia Historical Quarterly* 67 (Summer 1983).

and environmentalism. Odum expresses an almost spiritual connection to the marsh and tides:

> "We moved up tidal creeks in small outboard motor boats on ebbing tides; we found ourselves in deep canyons of golden mud banks, topped by six-foot high stands of marsh grass looking for all the world like a well-fertilized stand of sugar cane. The notion came to us in those early days that we were in the arteries of a remarkable energy-absorbing natural system whose heart was the pumping action of the tides. The entire tideland complex of barrier islands, marshes, creeks, and river mouths was a single operational unit linked together by the tide. If we were right, each part of the system would have to be dependent for its life-sustaining energy not only on the direct rays of the sun, but also on the energy of the tides...Does nature routinely exploit tidal power as men have dreamed of doing for centuries? In the past, biologists who studied estuarine and seashore organisms had been preoccupied with how such life adapts to the obvious stresses; that some of the stresses might be converted to subsidies was, and still is, something of a new theory. This germ of an idea, subsequently developed by twenty years of team research on Sapelo, will, we hope, provide the basis for man to design with, rather than against, nature on this remarkable sea coast."[19]

There evolved a direct corollary between estuarine science and maritime culture as inculcated through the field investigations of some of the world's preeminent ecologists at Sapelo's Marine Institute. Odum, along with Lawrence R. Pomeroy, Theodore Starr, Robert Ragotzkie, Donald C. Scott, John M. Teal, and Donald Kinsey, among many others, set the early parameters for establishing the conduit between the "life and death" of the salt marsh and the biological life cycle of marine organisms that habituated the

---

[19] Eugene P. Odum, "Living Marsh," in Robert Hanie, *Guale: The Golden Coast of Georgia* (San Francisco: Friends of the Earth, 1974), Introduction.

ecosystem, including major shellfish species such as oysters, shrimp and blue crabs.[20]

Relative to the evolving research, a symposium of lasting significance was held on Sapelo Island in March 1958, less than five years after the UGAMI was begun. The Salt Marsh Conference was hosted by UGAMI, with funding support from the National Science Foundation and R.J. Reynolds of Sapelo. The conference attracted fifty-five scientists from the U.S., Canada, Europe and New Zealand. This interdisciplinary workshop included discussions on geology, tidal river hydrology, physiological stresses, marsh production, and the role of saltmarshes as historical records. The conference's published proceedings represented a major contribution to the field of coastal research. The conference was important—it might be said to have been the Marine Institute's "coming out party."[21]

The 1960s and 1970s were dynamic decades for the Marine Institute. The disciplinary approaches to applied research began to have measurable ramifications for the sustainability of coastal marshes and estuaries. The realization began to emerge that the marshes, in tandem with the tides, played a critical role in the natural balance of the southeastern Atlantic ecosystem. Expanding on the earlier work by Odum and Pomeroy, Robert Reimold and Jack Gallagher employed conventional high-resolution photography to document vegetation changes, and infrared photography to map

---

[20] E.P. Odum, "A Proposal for a Marshbank and the Strategy of Ecosystem Development for the Estuarine Zone of Georgia," *The Future of the Marshlands and Sea Islands of Georgia* (Brunswick, GA: Coastal Area Planning and Development Commission, 1968), 74-85.
[21] *Proceedings of the Salt Marsh Conference Held at the Marine Institute of the University of Georgia, March 25-28, 1958* (Athens: UGAMI, 1959).

water flow patterns, tide height, and diseased areas of vegetation. Reimold's findings on phosphorous movement in *Spartina* provided useful insights into phosphorous cycling in the marsh.[22] Pomeroy and William Wiebe conducted saltmarsh detritus studies, and in the mid-1970s Pomeroy and Richard Wiegert followed a carbon model as a method of quantifying the contribution of identified subsystems to the entire ecosystem. These findings established the connection between *Spartina* and carbon, since carbon is a readily monitored variable, and is universal since all living matter is carbon-based.

Building on the success of the 1958 Salt Marsh Conference, the Marine Institute faculty, in association with scientists at the Athens campus, conducted additional conferences and symposia in the mid-to-late 1960s that were to have important consequences for the preservation of Georgia's marshlands and shoreline. In 1964, a Conference on Estuaries was held at Jekyll Island with planning underwritten by the Sapelo Island Research Foundation. Emerging from this meeting was a multidisciplinary volume, *Estuaries*, edited by George Lauff, and published in 1967. It became a primary text for coastal ecological studies for decades. Several factors merged in 1968 to produce arguably the most important conference on estuarine preservation ever conducted in coastal Georgia. Biological research at the Marine Institute had theretofore achieved the first real understanding of the interactions that occur in the saltmarsh and estuarine environment: the significance of the remnants of *Spartina* decay (detritus) to the marine food web; the excretion of organic and inorganic matter by a variety of marine organisms and plants; and the

---

[22] R.J. Reimold, "The Movement of Phosphorous Through the Salt Marsh Cordgrass," *Limnology and Oceanography* 17 (1972): 606-11.

concomitant use of excreted materials by other organisms in the food web. Thus when a proposal surfaced for large-scale industrial strip mining of the Georgia marshes for phosphate, the concretization of the fragile stability of marshes and island ecosystems through the research of Marine Institute biologists and geologists became of great importance.

In October 1968, the Conference on the Future of the Marshlands and Sea Islands was held at the Cloister Hotel on Sea Island to address the mining issue, and other problems related to potential degradation of the coastal ecosystem. The diversity of the conference participants, and the range of the topics they addressed, attested to the seriousness with which the scientific community, as well as many in the public sector, saw the threat imposed by the mining proposal.

J.H. Hoyt and Vernon J. Henry addressed barrier island geology; Charles Fairbanks the archaeological resources of coastal Georgia; Sandy Torrey West of Ossabaw on her Ossabaw Island Project; Reid W. Harris on proposed Georgia coastal wetland conservation legislation; Frederick C. Marland on "The Impending Crisis: Phosphate Mining Off the Georgia Coast"; Eugene Odum on a proposal for protected marshlands and the zoning of coastal estuaries; and John Milton of the Conservation Foundation on the future protection of the state's marshes and islands. The published proceedings of the conference, *The Future of the Marshlands and Sea Islands of Georgia*, was significant and hard-hitting in validating the criticality of coastal conservation.[23] The papers demonstrated that

---

[23] David S. Maney, Frederick C. Marland, and Clifford B. West, eds., *The Future of the Marshlands and Sea Islands of Georgia*, op. cit.

marsh mining was neither environmentally nor economically sensible for Georgia; soon thereafter, a special commission from the University System of Georgia provided Governor Lester Maddox and the state General Assembly with the academic input that resulted in the 1970 Coastal Marshlands Protection Act, a stringent protective device, and one of the most consequential pieces of public legislation ever enacted on behalf of the Georgia coast. Impelled through the legislative process by the energies of coastal state legislator Reid Harris, the Coastal Marshlands Act, and its companion piece, the Shoreline Protection Act (1979), served as models for similar legislation by other coastal states for the remainder of the twentieth century. The legislation placed Georgia's 400,000 acres of salt marshes under state ownership and oversight, excepting some tracts deeded to private owners through Crown or state grants.

* * *

The upland wooded areas contiguous to the marshes on the coastal mainland, as well as areas of the barrier islands, are characterized by a mixed maritime forest dominated by stands of mature live oak (*Quercus virginiana*), and several varieties of pine (*Pinus*). Other sections of the upland forest comprise a mixed oak-hardwood community, but with less presence of pine. Here there are live oak, laurel oak, water oak, hickory, bay, holly, magnolia, and some slash pine. The oaks with their low, spreading limbs support various vines and epiphytes (air plants), the latter dominated by Spanish moss and resurrection fern. The latter epiphyte appears dead and dried out in its dormant phase but springs to life, lush and green, during periods of rainfall. Wending their way around the gnarled thick lower trunks and limbs of the oaks are grapevines and Virginia creeper. Spanish moss is a bromeliad and features tiny green flowers, hardly visible. Moss is a distinctive feature of the oaks but can also be observed on other tree species. Often seen on or near the marsh fringes are stands of native cabbage palm (*Sabal palmetto*) with an understory dominated by wax myrtle, broomsedge and panic grass in uncleared areas.

Along the Georgia coast's tidal areas and on the larger islands, there are several distinct ecologies and forest zones: upland hardwood maritime forests, lowland hardwood forests, old and new pine plantations, and grassy savannahs. The lowland forests are typically found in wetter areas, and are comprised of live oak, water oak, loblolly pine, hickory, blackgum, sweetgum, and sweetbay, set amidst thick understorys of palmetto and wax myrtle.

Proper timber management, both on the mainland and the islands, provides open food habitat for deer and other species, and facilitates the healthy growth of the maritime forest and commercial pine plantations. Mixed stands of oak and pine are scattered in many areas of the county's uplands, with closed oak canopies beneath many of the pines. The selective cutting of pine timber results in cleared habitat for deer herds, and also hastens the regeneration of natural oak and other hardwood species in parts of the timbered areas. Large sections of the coastal maritime forest are dominated by pine-palmetto vegetation with the pine canopy rarely closed. Though pine is cut selectively, natural seeding remains effective in some areas. Saw palmetto form dense thickets four to five feet tall amid the pine forests and is often interspersed with other vegetation.

In a number of areas on the coastal mainland and islands will be observed cleared, grassy meadows, some being open grasslands, or savannahs, usually the result of manmade modifications for agriculture and cattle pasturage in the nineteenth and early twentieth centuries. Some of these areas are accentuated by thick stands of bahia grass (*Poaceae notatum*) planted earlier as forage for cattle herds. Many areas of the islands and the eastern mainland tidewater remain relatively clear and open, evidence of earlier crop cultivation.

One of the best means of exemplifying the connectedness of ecology and land use is through an understanding of coastal soil types. The soils of the islands and many sections of the mainland tidewater, are characterized by fine quartz sands that generally have high permeability, a condition that results in low water-holding capacity and rapid leaching. These soils range from deep, well-drained sands to poorly drained thick black loam surfaces and subsurface horizons of gray sands. Most of the soils, however, range from moderately well-drained to poorly-drained. These coastal soils are generally highly acidic, whether they are well-drained or poorly-drained.

Additionally, nineteenth and early-to-mid- twentieth century agriculture and cattle operations resulted in the clearing, ditching, and draining of many upland areas, thus altering both the natural hydrology as well as the soil dynamics in some areas. This is particularly true of parts of the larger islands, the deltas of the freshwater rivers as they near the sea, and areas of the western sections of the coastal counties which often feature low-lying swamps and forested timber land.

Hydrological factors especially come into play in the tidewater areas, including the islands. On the island beaches, high salt concentrations in dune sands inhibit the vertical percolation of rainwater through the dunes. This limited water supply reduces the amount of vegetation on the seaward side of the county's islands. On the inshore islands, the western sides of the larger barrier islands, and along the eastern mainland tidewater the salts exert an influence on vegetation in the intertidal zone between the marshes and the upland, and tend to limit species diversity. The abundant nutrients, however, enable the relatively few species in these areas to be highly productive. Conversely, as noted earlier, there are hard salt pans in the high marsh in some areas that are so concentrated in salts, usually two or more times that of sea water, that few vascular plants can grow there.

The most cultivable coastal soils in McIntosh County are the "fine sands" of the Galestown, St. Johns, Palm Beach and Ona-Scranton series, all of which are moderately well-drained with a sandy surface. Galestown, Ona-Scranton and pockets of Leon fine sand especially supported the cultivation of sea island cotton, sugar cane and provision crops in the nineteenth century. Palm Beach fine sand is dark and well drained, and found on level areas of sand ridges near tidal marsh. With proper fertilization, this soil was also of utility for cotton cultivation. Although it supported provision and subsistence crop cultivation in many areas, St. Johns fine sand is relatively poorly drained and is often found in damp areas, with vegetation of sabal palm, palmetto, huckleberry, gallberry, and scattered pines. Many of the Ona-Scranton and Palm Beach soils are now forested with pine, chiefly loblolly pine, with mixed stands of live oak, areas often indicative of earlier agricultural activities.

Rutledge fine sand is fairly extensive on the eastern tidewater and the islands. However, it is generally poorly drained, and is covered by water part of the year with vegetation of blackgum, cypress, and pine. With adequate drainage Rutledge is well-suited for pine plantations, but is usually too wet for most crops.

The eastern sections of the coastal counties closest to the tidelands, including those on the islands, include many areas of high-phase tidal marsh soil in zones close to the marsh that are non-cultivable but are sufficiently above the frequent influence of tidal inundation to allow vegetation of red cedar, small oaks and coarse grasses. These areas include the marsh zones of the smaller, back-barrier islands, such as Wilmington and Skidaway in Chatham County, Colonel's in Liberty County, and Creighton, Harris Neck and Little Sapelo in McIntosh, where tidal inundation occasionally occurs. Soils identified as High tidal marsh, and subject to more frequent periods of tidal inundation, such as on spring tides, fringe the upland marsh transition zones and have vegetation of wax myrtle, marsh elder, saltwort and sea oxeye. Low tidal marsh is comprised almost exclusively of smooth cordgrass (*Spartina*) with pockets of black needlerush (*Juncus*) in the higher areas. The prevailing soil on the seaward sides of the barrier islands is Coastal beach sand, a wide strip that runs along the entire easternmost edges of the barrier islands. Strips of porous Blanton and Lakeland sands are featured on the upland sand ridges on some of the islands, such as both the north and south ends of Blackbeard Island. However, on a sand ridge in Blackbeard's northwest corner there is a strip of Palm Beach fine sand, validating the use of that small section of the island for cotton cultivation in the early 1800s.

There is one other feature of the Georgia coast that should be mentioned for its soil types. In the deltas of the fresh-water rivers as they near the sea—the Savannah, Ogeechee, Altamaha and Satilla—the prevailing soil is that identified as Wet Alluvial land. These are described in some surveys as Altamaha clay soil deposits. The delta areas of the four main fresh-water rivers were the scene of extensive rice cultivation throughout the nineteenth century.

Relevant to the forgoing discussion it must be kept in mind that sizeable sections of the coast have been subjected to modification of varying degrees by human activity over the last two-and-a-half centuries, primarily for agriculture, cattle-herding, and timbering. Successive private owners in many coastal areas, including the islands, constructed irrigation canals and ditches to drain off low-lying sections, and built levees and embankments to facilitate agriculture and timbering. Irrigation ditches were dug by slave labor in the nineteenth century to facilitate crop production, particularly rice production, and the watering of livestock. For example, the ecological dynamic of the Altamaha delta is reflective of the differences from that of the tidewater and the interior pine flatwoods. The delta is an area that, prior to English settlement, was dominated by dense cypress hardwood swamps and other wetlands. After the Revolution the cypress swamps in the lower Altamaha gave way to large-scale rice production with planters utilizing the soils of the rich river bottomlands washed down to the coast from middle Georgia. Here the nineteenth century planters produced rice as a money staple, with cotton and sugar cane as rotation crops. These areas are unpopulated now, being under state administration as protected waterfowl management areas.

* * *

Wildlife and birdlife abound in coastal Georgia's marshes and beach areas. Annual counts have identified almost two hundred species of birds at varying times of the year. In the marsh, and on the sounds, and tidal creeks and rivers will be found the brown pelican, herring gulls, laughing gulls, ring-billed gulls, and double-crested cormorants. Present on the beaches are American oystercatchers, shearwaters, petrels, loons, clapper rails, plovers, and varieties of gulls, terns, and skimmers, among others. Around the tidal sloughs and marshes are black sanderlings, clapper rails, several species of herons and egrets, wood storks, and white ibis. In the forested uplands, grassy savannas, and marsh fringes it is common to observe several species of hawks, ospreys, turkey vultures, kestrels, coots, woodpeckers, mockingbirds, and varieties of ducks, including teals, scaups, canvasbacks, and mergansers; the occasional bald eagle is observed, and in the spring and summer, cattle egrets, and the spectacular painted bunting, one of the most impressive of the coast's birdlife species.

Animal species common to the islands and tidewater areas are white-tailed deer, raccoons, opossum, squirrels, otters, minks, armadillos, and feral hogs and cattle. Eastern diamondback rattlesnakes populate the uplands and beach dunes, cottonmouth water moccasins are in the wetter areas, and numerous species of non-venomous snakes are commonly encountered in the less-cleared areas. It is likely that much, perhaps most, of the flora and fauna encountered today is not the same as that of the Archaic period (10,000-3,000 B.P.). During the Archaic most of the area was covered by a climax forest, which would have reduced the available food supply in the spring and summer. There would have been browsing areas available in the shrub-herb layers of the ecosystem but it would not have supported the large deer herds, and other wildlife that prevail today with open pastures and second-and-third generation forest growth. As oak species matured in the Archaic, the fall and winter months would have produced sufficient acorn fall to support deer in greater numbers as time went along; Spanish moss and plants growing in the high marsh would have provided additional food sources. The remaining vestiges of the maritime climax forest from that period disappeared when large areas of the islands and coastal mainland were cleared for agriculture and oak timbering in the eighteenth and nineteenth centuries. If the early climax forest was not seriously depleted during the proto-historic and aboriginal agricultural eras, then it almost certainly was during the colonial period and after.

Weather is an important component of local environmental considerations. Coastal Georgia's climate is classified as sub-tropical, consisting of brief, relatively mild winters, and warm, humid summers. Cold temperatures in some winters prevent tropical or sub-tropical vegetation to persist but are sufficiently mild to allow some species characteristic of warmer areas to grow and reproduce naturally. The average date of the earliest frost is early December, with the latest being early March. Intense summer showers account for much of the annual precipitation, which averages about 52 inches. The wettest months are June, July, and August with the driest being October and November. Several hurricanes from 1989-2005 passed near the Georgia coast but none caused serious damage. Most east coast hurricanes tend to follow the warmer waters of the offshore Gulf Stream. Brunswick, Georgia, is the westernmost point from the Gulf Stream of any section of the south Atlantic coast.

Several historic hurricanes, however, have created extreme conditions that precipitated temporary economic chaos. The storms directly impacting the coast with either landfall or severe effects, occurred in 1804, 1824, 1854, 1893, 1896, 1898, 1944, 1964 (Dora), 1979 (David), 2016 (Matthew) and 2017 (Irma). The worst of these were the 1824 and 1898 cyclones.

The First Conservationists?
Northern Money and Low Country Georgia

Soon after William T. Sherman's march of destruction through Georgia there began a second Northern invasion, this time centered upon the coastal low country. While the damage to land, infrastructure, and state pride took years to heal, the precipitous arrival of Northern money to the coast that began almost immediately after the war was a circumstance much more favorably received by Georgians than Sherman's depredations. Through the prism of history, the argument can be made that the infusion of Northern capital, with the concomitant acquisition of thousands of acres of coastal lands by Northerners, had such a salutary and lasting effect that a foundation was laid a century later for the ecological preservation of much of tidewater Georgia.

The thematic intent here is twofold for it will demonstrate the duality of purpose in the postbellum use of Northern money in coastal Georgia. Some Northerners spent money to make money, with little regard for the environmental consequences. Others,

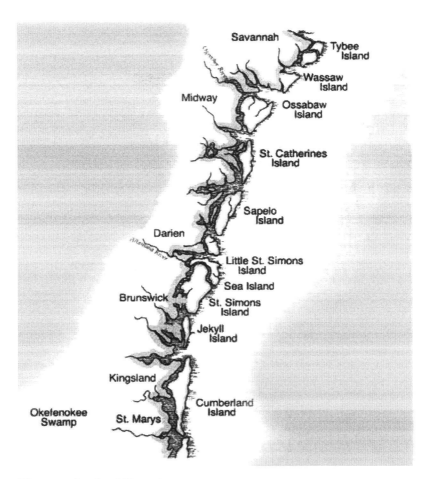

The sea islands of Georgia.

particularly on the sea islands, spent money to acquire escape, solitude and respite. It will be argued here that the latter group represented the first true conservationists of the coast, though they were largely unaware of it at the time.

It was primarily Yankee money that underwrote the rise of a prosperous lumber trade that in turn fueled a much-needed increase in employment opportunities for recently-emancipated African Americans and financially-strapped whites broken by the war. This occasioned a dramatic departure from the agrarian-based coastal economy before the war. Simultaneously, the processing and export of timber ignited a mechanized revolution that occurred almost two decades before the manifestation of Henry W. Grady's vision of a new industrialized South. Though obviously not realized at the time, the concurrent acquisition of many of Georgia's sea island and mainland properties by Northerners from 1866 to 1930 led directly or indirectly to the subsequent conservation and protection of many of the lands.[24]

It is perhaps paradoxical that many observers of regional history, often lacking important underlying facts and context, have not always acknowledged the generally responsible stewardship of the Georgia coast, particularly the barrier islands, by affluent Northerners during and after the late nineteenth century. In fact, the industrialists and financiers of that era have often received undeserved bad press. The impressions created by pervasive political attitudes have in recent times precipitated negative connotations of the industrialists and their largely positive contributions to the social, economic and material dynamics that laid the foundation for what has come to be known as "America's century" throughout the 1900s.

A combination of circumstances radically altered the antebellum

---

[24] For a scholarly treatment of the people and economy of coastal Georgia from an ecological perspective in the postbellum era see Mart A. Stewart, *"What Nature Suffers to Groe"* (Athens: University of Georgia Press, 1996), 193-242. Also useful in this regard from a more focused viewpoint on one coastal Georgia locale is Drew Swanson, *Remaking Wormsloe Plantation: The Environmental History of a Lowcountry Landscape* (Athens: University of Georgia Press, 2012). For the postbellum perspective of one family see Malcolm Bell, Jr., *Major Butler's Legacy: Five Generations of a Slaveholding Family* (Athens: University of Georgia Press, 1987), 372-482.

formula for life and economy on the coastal islands and mainland after the Civil War, the most obvious being that Yankee money and enterprise began going to places impoverished by the war. The infusion of capital to underwrite coastal interests, with the simultaneous acquisition of island properties, enabled a more rapid economic recovery from the war in the low country than in many other areas of the old Confederacy. Some of the names of those associated with this transition are readily familiar while others are obscure or forgotten. And while the Northerners were generally not overtly aware of an environmental consciousness in the manner that we are today, their contributions are essential to a broader understanding of the conservation movement that has evolved in modern coastal Georgia over the last fifty years.

The intellectual underpinning, the most visible symbol, for how Northerners consciously or unconsciously adopted a generational philosophy of conserving their coastal lands clearly began with their evolving and increasing presence on the sea islands, perhaps attaining its idealization in this respect with the Jekyll Island Club in the 1890s and early 1900s. By extension, the Jekyll Island venture may be said to be a precursor to the rapid development of south Florida by affluent Northerners a generation later—and events have shown in the last hundred years how differently that experiment turned out to be when contrasted with that of coastal Georgia.[25]

---

[25] William Barton McCash and June Hall McCash, *The Jekyll Island Club: Southern Haven for America's Millionaires* (Athens: University of Georgia Press, 1989) is the outstanding treatment of Jekyll's Club era; for environmentalism in conflict with development in Florida in the late nineteenth and early twentieth centuries see Mark Derr, *Some Kind of Paradise: A Chronicle of Man and the Land in Florida* (New York: William Morrow, 1989).

The other side of this equation of course involves the local pre-war land owners. Once enjoying the financial prosperity established upon the backs of enslaved people before the war, low country planters found themselves almost universally prostrate afterwards, their money, resources and infrastructure devastated by repeated Union naval incursions against the south Atlantic coast from Charleston to St. Marys. Their land was essentially their only remaining asset, but the former planter aristocracy was often unable to even bear the expense of property taxes on their expansive holdings. Thus the planters began to sell all or parts of their lands to outsiders—Northerners—who were flush with cash generated by an up-tempo war economy. Sometimes the land acquisitions were speculative, but more often were based on the desires of buyers to acquire isolated islands with temperate climates to serve as retreats.

In neighboring South Carolina there was a somewhat different dynamic in play in parts of the low country. While there was a desire by some Northerners for private lands for hunting, relaxation and escape, it was also about profit potential and the investing of money to make money. South Carolina locals were hungry for capital, jobs and revenue after the Civil War, and they encouraged Northerners to cut timber and build railroads. Several dozen companies, mostly financed by Northern money, clear-cut huge swaths of timber in Georgetown County and in the Ashepoo-Combahee-Edisto basin, much of it on former plantation lands. Large sections of the Carolina low country thus became a timber corridor, and about five miles on each side of the freshwater rivers were clear-cut. When the large-scale timber cutting operations moved further away from the rivers, railroads were built to extend the access to the timber. "The

[Northern timber firms] left behind a vast trail of destruction," notes Angela C. Halfacre. "They practiced a 'cut out and get out' policy that sought to maximize profits while devastating the forest."[26]

A notable exception to low country South Carolina's complicated story of land acquisition for profit, as opposed to conservation, is that of Belle W. Baruch (1899-1964). Belle Baruch was an exceedingly talented and far-sighted woman, the daughter of Bernard Baruch, a prominent American financier of the late nineteenth and early twentieth century. She befriended First Lady Edith Wilson, rode horses competitively, flew planes for pleasure, and searched for German U-boats off the coast of South Carolina. Later in her adventurous life she purchased her father's coastal estate, the 17,500-acre Hobcaw Barony in Georgetown County, then left it as a public trust for research and conservation. Hobcaw has diverse ecosystems—maritime forests, swamp, beach and great expanses of salt marsh, all habitat to an abundance of wildlife. Belle was enamored of the coastal flora and fauna, which prompted her to establish a trust to preserve the land for scientific research.[27]

Further south, closer to coastal Georgia, were the abandoned rice plantations and the ravaged timberlands of the ACE Basin, shorn of pine and hardwoods after the war, then given deliverance a generation later by Northern land buyers seeking hunting tracts. Due in part to private owners later making available these properties for

---

[26] Angela C. Halfacre, *A Delicate Balance: Constructing a Conservation Culture in the South Carolina Lowcountry* (Columbia: University of South Carolina Press, 2012), 34. See also Albert E. Cowdrey, *This Land, This South: An Environmental History* (Lexington: University Press of Kentucky, 1983), 111-14.
[27] See Mary E. Miller, *Baroness of Hobcaw: The Life of Belle W. Baruch* (Columbia: University of South Carolina Press, 2006).

conservation, coupled with a flurry of Nature Conservancy easements that shielded the old rice tracts from future development, much of the region between the Edisto River and Beaufort eventually came under a blanket of protection through state and federal acquisition of uplands and tidal wetlands to serve as wildlife refuges.[28]

All this is not to say that low country Georgia escaped the attention of profit-seeking Northern timber investors. A case in point is the town of Darien, burned in a Union army raid in 1863. Impelled by an infusion of Northern money, in combination with the energy of locals seeking work, Darien rose to industrial prosperity during Reconstruction. Their town and plantations ruined by the Union attacks, Darien's people had few residual funds for investment toward a timber economy. The sawmills, the waterfront facilities, the towboats and steamboats to move timber, and the other infrastructure associated with the newfound prosperity, were largely subsidized through the migration to Darien of Northerners who inspired a burgeoning Yankee postwar capitalism.[29] For example, the large Lower Bluff mill, operated by local interests before the war, was acquired in 1866 by the Northern partnership of James Young and Charles Langdon, both of whom became leaders in the rebuilding community. At least three other large timber firms were based on Northern interests. The importance of Darien as a timber entrepot thus went hand-in-hand with

---

[28] Useful in establishing the chains of title for all the tracts in the lower watershed of the Ashepoo, Combahee and Edisto rivers, from the eighteenth century to the end of the twentieth, is Suzanne Cameron Linder, *Historical Atlas of the Rice Plantations of the ACE River Basin* (Columbia: South Carolina Department of Archives and History and The Nature Conservancy, 1995).

[29] Hilton Papers, Collection 387, Box 1, Folders 1, 2, Georgia Historical Society, Savannah.

Northern money, and locals were not complaining. Darien people in the flush times of the 1880s and 1890s were fond of referring to their little town as "big Darien, little Savannah and no Charleston" when denoting the important seaports on the southern tidewater.

It is necessary to correlate postbellum economic developments in the Georgia low country within the greater national context. With the technological advances in the development of armaments and transportation, concomitant with the intensity of industrial production and railroad construction during the war, the United States had by 1870 become the second largest economy in the world to Great Britain, and would supersede Britain as the world leader less than twenty years later. Small wonder then that Darien, with its advantages of geography (the Altamaha River), workforce availability (the freed slaves), and the benefit of prior experience in timber, rose from the ashes of conflict with impressive rapidity. This phenomenon perfectly exemplified the fundamental dynamic that lay in the economic rebirth of the once agriculturally-oriented old Confederacy. It was just the kind of industrial impetus Henry Grady envisioned for his New South, and the lumber mills and railroads of south Georgia played as integral a role in that economic growth as the production of textiles in the cotton mills of Atlanta, Columbus, Macon and Augusta.

In 1868 William E. Dodge of New York organized the Georgia Land and Lumber Company with a capitalization of $1.5 million and the acquisition of over 300,000 acres of southeast Georgia timber land. The forerunner of this company was the New York and Georgia Mill, Land and Lumber Company which bought, then lost, the same acreage during the 1830s and 1840s. The tracts were subsequently held by several owners, including the State of Indiana from 1838 to 1849, before being acquired by Dodge. In 1870, the Georgia General Assembly created a new county from Telfair and Pulaski counties, naming it Dodge. Georgia Land and Lumber acquired tracts in these and other counties to cut pine timber, then to raft it down the Altamaha River to sawmills at Darien and St. Simons. Meanwhile, the 1866 Southern Homestead Act was repealed in 1876, freeing up for sale millions of acres of federal land originally set aside to enable freedmen, poor white farmers and sharecroppers to buy land at cheap prices. Much of the federally-administered land in the southern states was sold, including large amounts of southeast Georgia timber acreage to the Dodge interests. What ensued was ongoing controversy and litigation once the Dodge influence began to assert itself. The legal maneuverings and court battles between the so-called Northern "land barons"—the Dodge Company—and local landowners at times erupted into violence as angry land squatters demanded that "the Dodges be sent hellward." The end result was that over several decades the Dodge interests and their subsidiaries left the pine forests along the Altamaha corridor a veritable wasteland, with thousands of acres of timber stripped along the river's banks.[30]

There is a paradox here that had manifested itself with a cumulative clarity by the start of the twentieth century. While

---

[30] The definitive account of the Dodge interests, their land acquisitions and the subsequent disputes and legal battles over land ownership and occupation in southeast Georgia is Jane Walker and Chris Trowell. The Dodge Land Troubles, 1868-1923 (Fernandina, Fla.: Wolfe Publishing, 2004). See also Stephen Whigham, ed., *The Lightwood Chronicles: Murder and Greed in the Piney Woods of South Georgia, Being the True Story of Brainard Cheney's Novel Lightwood* (Charleston, S.C.: CreateSpace, 2014).

Northern timber brokers were clear-cutting the mainland forests with a pronounced disdain for conservation, their Yankee counterparts on the sea islands were reveling in the tranquil ambience of the low country ecosystem, and vowing to preserve their collective Edens for themselves and succeeding generations.

As for the locals, coastal folk were rarely averse to Northern money coming to their communities, whether on the mainland or the islands, for outside capital meant recovery, sustenance and rescue from the postwar economic doldrums. One descendant of a South Carolina planter may have summed up the prevailing local attitudes best when he succinctly stated, "Lord, please send us a rich Yankee." The prayers were frequently answered. Northern money ultimately determined the shape of much of today's low country landscape as the "rich Yankees" who acquired the islands and mainland tracts decided their properties were worth keeping for themselves, and unknowingly helped launch one of the nation's most successful conservation movements.[31]

Purchase of low country island properties on the Georgia coast began almost immediately after the war: George Parsons (1826-1907) of Kennebunk, Maine acquired Wassaw Island in 1866; the same year, John N.A. Griswold (1821-1909) of Newport, Rhode Island bought the north end of Sapelo Island from the descendants of Thomas Spalding, and the Cannon's Point tract at St. Simons Island

---

[31] See Robert B. Cuthbert and Stephen G. Hoffius, eds., *Northern Money, Southern Land: The Lowcountry Plantation Sketches of Chlotilde R. Martin*, (Columbia: University of South Carolina Press, 2009), a useful work that offers the perspective of a local observer regarding Northern acquisition of local lands.

from James H. Couper. In 1881, Thomas Carnegie (1843-1886) of the Pittsburgh steel family acquired a large portion of Cumberland Island, and Amos Sawyer (1830-1913), a soap manufacturer from Northampton, Massachusetts, bought the upper half of Sapelo. Two large acquisitions followed in 1886: Jekyll Island, by a New York consortium, and the north end of Ossabaw Island to James M. Waterbury (1852-1931) of New York, followed by the acquisition of most of Ossabaw by Philadelphia department store magnate John Wannamaker (1838-1922) starting in 1895.

All of these properties had been multi-generational holdings by long-established low country families, some since the mid-eighteenth century.[32] Meanwhile, Pierre Lorillard (1833-1901), a tobacco magnate from New York City, and charter member of the Jekyll Island Club, discovered a site in 1889 that captivated him with its beauty and privacy, the upper end of Harris Neck on the South Newport River. He bought acreage on the Neck and built two homes, eschewing his Jekyll Island membership for the greater isolation of Harris Neck.

Initially, there was a proprietary interest on the part of some buyers to profit from their island acquisitions. A case in point is that of Griswold at Sapelo and St. Simons who anticipated dividends

---

[32] June Hall McCash, *The Jekyll Island Cottage Colony* (Athens: University of Georgia Press, 1998); Mary R. Bullard, *Cumberland Island: A History* (Athens: University of Georgia Press, 2005). For Sapelo, see Buddy Sullivan, *Sapelo, People and Place on a Georgia Sea Island* (Athens: University of Georgia Press, 2017). For Ossabaw, see "Land Use and Landscape: Ossabaw Island," by the present author later in this volume. For Wassaw, see Elizabeth D. McMaster, *Wassaw: The Story of an Island* (Kennebunk, Maine: privately published, 1974).

from the revival of cotton cultivation, hopes that were dashed by the modification of labor conditions as a result of Emancipation and the Fourteenth Amendment. Griswold eventually lost his low country holdings to foreclosure.

After 1900, a second generation of Northerners established themselves in coastal Georgia, including Howard E. Coffin (1873-1937) at Sapelo Island, Henry N. Torrey (1880-1945) at Ossabaw, Clement M. Keys (1876-1952)and Edward J. Noble (1882-1958) at St. Catherines, Robert C. Roebling (1904-1983) at Skidaway, and Philip Berolzheimer (1867-1942) at Little St. Simons.[33] At Skidaway, Roebling donated Modena, his north end Black Angus cattle farm, to the state of Georgia for a marine research facility in 1968.

Others acquired mainland tracts, combining a consciousness of their local ecology while assiduously working the coastal tidelands in agriculture and commercial fishing, thus providing employment for many coastal Georgians in the midst of the Great Depression. The desire of Northerners to acquire coastal plantation properties on the mainland coincided with a gradual decline of the once-prosperous tidewater rice industry from 1880 to 1910 in South Carolina and Georgia. The effects of three hurricanes in the 1890s and two more in the first decade of the twentieth century, coupled with increased production in Louisiana and Texas, spelled the end of the south

---

[33] For St. Catherines, see George J. Armelegos and John Toby Woods, Jr., *St. Catherines Island: The Untold Story of People and Place* (privately published, 2012); for Skidaway, see V.E. Kelly, *A Short History of Skidaway Island* (privately published, 1994, 2nd edit.); for Little St. Simons, see Junius Rochester, *Little St. Simons Island on the Coast of Georgia* (privately published, 1994).

Atlantic rice industry.[34] Abandoned rice lands were converted to truck crop cultivation at Richmond Hill by Henry Ford (1863-1947) of Dearborn, Michigan, and at Butler Island by Tillinghast L. Huston (1867-1938) of New York. Both were cognizant of the ecological uniqueness of their respective river systems, the Ogeechee for Ford, and the Altamaha for Huston.[35]

Conspicuously relevant to this discussion, essentially the end to the means, is that virtually all of the above cited lands evolved from the descendants of their postwar owners to protected, or relatively protected, status in the second half of the twentieth century. An impressive extent of acreage on the Georgia coast is free of marinas, condominiums, golf courses and the assorted other trappings of the developmental art. Wassaw, Blackbeard, and Wolf islands are federally-managed wildlife refuges; most of Cumberland is a national seashore; Ossabaw, Sapelo, Jekyll and Butler islands, and most of the Altamaha River delta, are state-managed and administered properties, free from potential development, except for Jekyll, which is controlled. St. Catherines, Little St. Simons and Little Cumberland remain in private ownership with very limited, if any,

---

[34] James M. Clifton, "Twilight Comes to the Rice Kingdom: Postbellum Rice Culture on the South Atlantic Coast," *Georgia Historical Quarterly* 62 (Summer 1978), 146-54.

[35] Marty Appel, *Pinstripe Empire: The New York Yankees from Before the Babe to After the Boss* (New York: Bloomsbury USA, 2012). Huston was part owner of the New York Yankees baseball team during the height of the Babe Ruth era in the 1920s. For Henry Ford, see Buddy Sullivan, *From Beautiful Zion to Red Bird Creek A History of Bryan County, Georgia* (Pembroke, Ga.: Bryan County Commission, 2000), 297-330. Ford accumulated an aggregate of 90,000 acres on the lower Ogeechee River in Bryan and Chatham counties from 1925 to 1940.

public access. The transition of several of these island properties to protected status will be addressed later in this paper.

The acquisition of the Georgia islands by Northerners was motivated far more by aesthetics than by their profit potential. The buyers sought lands that satisfied their wish for isolation and privacy. They wanted vacation retreats with solitude and natural beauty, and not inconsequentially, they viewed the islands as comfortable havens to escape the rigors of northern winters for rest and recreation, well removed from the stresses of Wall Street. Thousands of acres of former plantation lands were bought by a Who's Who of America's entrepreneurial giants who came to Georgia and South Carolina to relax, shoot quail, play golf and otherwise bask in the semi-tropical climate from December to April.

The locals benefited as well. The use of the islands positively influenced the low country economy for several decades. The seasonal sojourns of the Northerners in the southern and coastal sections of South Carolina and Georgia provided local economic stimulus by their buying local supplies, building materials and equipment, and by employing hundreds of locals as servants, groundskeepers, off-season caretakers and watermen. "Above all, the island[s] provided a warm and salubrious refuge from the bitter northern winter they had left behind."[36] Besides privacy, and the relief from winter weather, the Northerners eagerly embraced the natural beauty of the coast and its wildlife. The inaccessibility of the island sanctuaries was paramount. June Hall McCash notes that members of the Jekyll Island Club relished the isolation of their

---

[36] McCash and McCash, *The Jekyll Island Club*, 22.

island "where strict control of arrivals and departures was possible, [making] it virtually inaccessible to any who were not authorized to be there."[37]

The Northerners generally were in agreement on the motivations for their migration to coastal Georgia. They understood the geographical and ecological uniqueness and desirability of the islands, and they were willing to invest large amounts of money into acquiring and improving their new sanctuaries. Significantly, as became evident with the passage of the years, they developed the kind of appreciation for the islands that compelled them to maintain a generational hold on the properties that evolved into the publicly and privately-held islands of a later era. It is ironic that Thomas M. Carnegie, whose family fortune was built on the productivity of heavy industry, bought Dungeness on Cumberland Island in 1881 principally because he sought healthier air to breathe in a locale comfortably distant from the smoky, smog-filled skies of Pittsburgh's iron and steel mills.[38] Lucy Coleman Carnegie, Thomas' widow, asserted unconditionally in her will that Cumberland was to be held in perpetuity as a private estate. This set a precedent continued by her heirs to keep the island within their control despite the exorbitant costs of taxes and maintaining buildings and other infrastructure.[39]

Further validation of the strong ties Thomas and Lucy Carnegie had toward their island were stipulations in their wills that any of the Carnegie children who wished to sell their interests in Cumberland

---

[37] McCash, *The Jekyll Island Cottage Colony*, 1.
[38] Bullard, *Cumberland Island*, 181.
[39] Ibid., 254-58.

could only do so with the majority consent of the other family members who had island interests. In this way, Thomas and Lucy hoped to keep their part of Cumberland in the possession of future descendants. In the 1950s and 1960s, the Carnegie heirs held two-thirds of Cumberland while the upper third of the island was owned by the Candler family of Atlanta. A later generation of Carnegie heirs eventually began seeking means of ensuring the preservation of Cumberland, to prevent development but also allowing public access to the island, but "carefully controlled access."[40]

Another aspect of Northern money equating to later conservation of coastal lands is the Jekyll Island Club. Jekyll is one of the smaller islands held by several generations of the DuBignon family from 1794 to 1886. In the latter year it was sold to New York investors in the newly-formed Club. A membership that initially included the likes of such financial luminaries as J.P. Morgan, William Vanderbilt, Joseph Pulitzer, William Rockefeller, Edwin Gould and Frank Henry Goodyear, intentionally kept their surroundings pristine and relatively free of ostentation, perhaps sub-consciously sensitive to preserving Jekyll's ecosystem and habitat. The obligatory golf course was later constructed, but the so-called "cottages" and main clubhouse were by agreement built with restraint and little pretentiousness, particularly when compared to their summer estates at Newport and Bar Harbor. There were few formal gardens and little landscaping. Jekyll's roads were kept to a minimum and intentionally

---

[40] Ibid., 245-47; Stewart, *"What Nature Suffers to Groe,"* 251. Charles Howard Candler (1878-1957) of Atlanta, eldest son of Asa G. Candler (1851-1929) of Atlanta, who built the Coca-Cola Company fortune in the early 1900s, acquired High Point, the north end of Cumberland, in 1930.

narrow. Even though hunting was a favorite pursuit for some members, there was an effort to preserve the habitat of birds and animals. The island's game populations were restocked when they neared depletion, particularly with quail and pheasants, and the responsibility of the head gamekeeper was "to take charge of the breeding, preservation, and care of game." The Club's rules included restrictions on timber cutting on Jekyll, and for protection of the island's creeks and marshes from mainlanders attempting to poach Jekyll's oyster beds.[41]

Historian Mart Stewart's assessment is that the motives of the Club's members were not entirely altruistic, feeling their ecological views were impelled more by possession than by purely environmental concerns. He notes that "these meager, and often easily attained, efforts at conservation came less from an appreciation of nature than from a desire to achieve absolute control of the island's environment."[42] Nonetheless, as frequently reflected in their letters and journals, many of the members viewed Jekyll as a place of exceptional natural uniqueness, one worthy of conservation despite their rarely ever stating that in specific terms.[43] Theirs was a seasonal "splendid isolation," and if the island was to be "developed" in any way, it would be only by their hands. Club member Stewart Maurice, an avid naturalist, "loved [Jekyll] so—he knew it so well—its birds—its flowers—its trees—its shrubs—its paths, and all its history and development." Dean Gildersleeve, a frequent visitor, waxed poetic in her memories of Jekyll, describing the island as like "a setting for

---

[41] McCash and McCash, *The Jekyll Island Club*, 22, 42; Stewart, *"What Nature Suffers to Groe,"* 221.
[42] Stewart, *"What Nature Suffers to Groe,"* 223.
[43] McCash and McCash, *The Jekyll Island Club*, 14, 17.

Shakespeare's *The Tempest* [with] long-leaved pines that formed forest aisles inland, the dull shimmer of oaks, the radiance of huge magnolias, the sun glow of wild oranges, the Cherokee roses and wisteria..."[44]

For just over a century, the Parsons family of New England owned Wassaw Island, one of Georgia's smaller barrier islands situated southeast of Savannah and just east of Skidaway Island. The sentiments of George Parsons, who bought Wassaw just after the Civil War, and several generations of his descendants reflect the passion by which Northerners came to embrace the Georgia low country. "I intensely loved Wassaw," noted Joseph Parsons, a grandson of George. "We had the island all to ourselves, and it was exactly the right place for us...The happiest of all my recollections is bound up with Wassaw." Conserving the remarkable island ecosystem must have been somewhere in Joseph Parsons' thoughts when he reflected upon his taking long walks in the maritime forest and along the salt marsh, and "rising at sunrise to see the dewy freshness of warm spring mornings, the chattering of the multitude of birds [that sounded] like a noisy aviary...the evenings that brought forth the fragrance of honeysuckle..."

A later Parsons descendant, Elizabeth McMaster, shared the similar feelings of Carnegie descendants at Cumberland further down the coast in the mid-1960s; she was determined to conserve Wassaw and prevent its commercial development. "We had tried so hard to find someone, or a group of people, who would help save Wassaw...There were politicians who wanted to seize the island, and

---

[44] McCash, *The Jekyll Island Cottage Colony*, 104, 134.

condemn it...they wanted to build a bridge from Skidaway, make the five-mile beach a public park and develop the back land." Savannah city officials, including the mayor, urged the Georgia legislature to condemn Wassaw and force its sale to the state, the result of which, if done, would be a financial tax windfall for Chatham County. These possibilities were averted when, in 1969, the family sold Wassaw to the federal Department of the Interior with the stipulation the island be made a wildlife refuge with limited public access. "We did this not because we wanted to but because we had to in order the save the island," McMaster reflected.[45]

Beyond the examples of Jekyll and Wassaw, two case studies of Georgia islands that came to be under state management, Sapelo and Ossabaw, illustrate the degree of connectivity between private ownership of the islands by Northerners and their transition to protected status as public trusts.

Howard Coffin's years at Sapelo Island had important and enduring effects on coastal Georgia. He was rather a late arrival in the cavalcade of wealthy Northerners who since the early 1880s had accrued substantial amounts of coastal property, particularly on the sea islands. Coffin continued a discrete trend of the private acquisition of coastal lands that would be held among several prominent families, or groups of families, for three generations until the 1960s and 1970s when many of the properties came under state or federal management and protection.

Coffin fit the mold perfectly; he expanded his national vision that was initially grounded in his contributions to the Detroit automotive

---

[45] McMaster, *Wassaw: The Story of an Island*, 47-48, 106.

industry directly to Sapelo, then to coastal Georgia, and beyond. By the time his efforts at Sapelo reached their apogee in 1930, it had become obvious there was an intensely intellectual underpinning behind Coffin's purpose and sagacity.

A progressive and intentional stewardship of the coast was practiced in the early twentieth century by Howard Coffin of Sapelo, one of the second generation of Northerners who became enamored of the Georgia low country. An automotive pioneer and partner in the Hudson Motor Car Company of Detroit, he exemplified the energy, expertise and innovation of American industry in the early twentieth century.[46] Coffin's purchase of Sapelo in 1912 was evocative of an era a century earlier when his predecessor, Thomas Spalding, built an island empire with energy, skill and vision. There is no ambiguity when comparing the two men who left their mark on the island so many years apart, for Coffin was to early twentieth century Sapelo almost exactly what Spalding had been to the early nineteenth. There were commonalities of purpose, intent, and philosophy between the two visionaries. Both were men of principle, intellect and wisdom. Mindful of the obvious technological progression from one century to the next, the distillation of the similarities between Coffin and Spalding is most clearly defined in

---

[46] The story of the Coffin years at Sapelo Island, 1912-34, and at Sea Island, 1926-37, is covered in Sullivan, *Sapelo, People and Place on a Georgia Sea Island*, op. cit., 213-52; Sullivan, *Early Days on the Georgia Tidewater*, all editions, 1990-2018; and Sullivan, *Twentieth Century Sapelo Island: Howard E. Coffin & Richard J. Reynolds, Jr.* (privately published, 2020), 9-106. For Coffin's career in the Detroit automotive industry, see Harold Martin, *This Happy Isle: The Story of Sea Island and the Cloister* (Sea Island, Ga.: Sea Island Company, 1978), 3-11.

their shared sense of *place* and *permanence* when it came to Sapelo and coastal Georgia.

An abiding sense of "place" is traditionally imbued in many native Southerners, and has always been especially prevalent among coastal folk in tidewater Georgia and South Carolina. Antebellum planter families and their descendants, especially on the sea islands, have long shared a collective sense of place and permanence. This characteristic is perhaps even more recognizable among the native coastal African Americans whose ancestors worked the plantations as enslaved people, then acquired their own land as freedmen and established permanent roots, often on, or in close proximity to, the lands on which their forebears labored as bondsmen. By extension it can be argued that the migrating Northerners adopted that sense of "place" from the earlier owners of the islands, which can be said to be an early catalyst for the later conservation efforts on the Georgia coast.[47]

Coffin has a place among the first true coastal conservationists based upon his astute ecological comprehension and the efficacy of his local business initiatives. He established a connection between his national vision that was initially grounded in his contributions to the automotive industry directly to Georgia, his adopted state, and to Sapelo Island. He became a localist in the strictest Spalding sense. By the time Coffin's efforts at Sapelo attained their apotheosis in 1930, it was clear there had been an intellectual conceptualization influencing his vision. It is therefore no coincidence that his

---

[47] The theme of "place" and "permanence" for the people of coastal Georgia is elaborated upon in the three books by the present author cited in note 46 above, as well as throughout the present study.

achievements at Sapelo, and later at Sea Island, represented the formulation of Coffin's own instrumentality, the most tangible attribute congenial to his own interests. His energy, inquisitiveness, and innovation were manifested through his Georgia accomplishments, and the residual concepts of his vision endured long after his death in 1937.

Coffin was a sagacious observer of the marsh and tidal ecosystem and sought ways to simultaneously conserve the estuaries and provide employment to people in McIntosh and Glynn counties in the production and harvesting of oysters. He built canneries at Sapelo and Darien, and purchased oyster-producing marshlands in Altamaha Sound between Sapelo and Little St. Simons islands, an acquisition aggregating some 35,000 acres, including Wolf and Egg islands. He began scientific oyster farming, "breaking up overcrowded beds where the oysters grew too small to harvest and planting seed oysters at carefully chosen water depths." It was a successful project, and within four years oysters became prolific in the area. However, the success was unsustainable because the initiative "attracted the attention of every oyster poacher on the coast. Short of standing guard with a shotgun over the thousands of acres of tidal marsh, Coffin had no way of protecting his oyster farms. After a few years he gave up the project."[48] However, there was a silver lining to the failed oyster effort that had beneficial consequences to coastal Georgia: Coffin sold Wolf and Egg islands to the federal government in 1929, and a year later they were designated as protected national wildlife refuges by the U.S.

---

[48] Martin, *This Happy Isle*, 28.

Department of the Interior.

Coffin also had a special interest in federally-owned Blackbeard Island, an attentiveness that was the product of his growing awareness for coastal conservation and protection, particularly of undeveloped lands. Blackbeard was endowed with a thick forest of live oak (*Quercus virginiana*), accounting for its acquisition by the U.S. Navy Department in 1800 as a timber reserve for the construction of wooden warships. From 1880-1910, the U.S. Marine Hospital Service utilized Blackbeard as a federal quarantine station to inspect transiting ships for yellow fever and other tropical diseases. In 1924, the uninhabited island was made a federal wildlife refuge with limited public access. Coffin wanted Blackbeard to be off-limits to hunters so that government-sponsored biological research might be conducted there. He became something of a self-appointed caretaker for Blackbeard and spent $20,000 of his own money to pay for security guards to protect the island from mainland game poachers and nocturnal rum smugglers. Coffin's protection of Blackbeard also provided a convenient firewall to protect Sapelo's game preserves and oyster beds from poachers.

These and a similar initiative by Coffin at Cabin Bluff in Camden County in the late 1920s and early 1930s, by which he either directly or indirectly enhanced coastal conservation, represented the amalgamation of his increased awareness of the importance of promoting the responsible stewardship of his adopted region. Blackbeard, Wolf and Egg islands all remain in the federal wildlife refuge system, while Cabin Bluff also remains a protected property. Coffin's creation of the Sea Island Company in 1926 ultimately led to the preservation of over 700 acres at Cannon's Point on the north

H.E. Coffin (l) with his cousin Alfred W. Jones, ca. 1932.

end of St. Simons Island for ecological and cultural education for the public, and research by the academic community. At Sapelo, Coffin, and later Richard J. Reynolds, Jr., laid the foundation for what became a model for coastal estuarine research and education.

In 1925, Coffin began purchasing former plantation properties on St. Simons, including the Retreat tract where he laid out the Sea Island Golf Club, followed by his acquisition the following year of a five-mile strip of beach and marsh known locally as Glynn Isle (formerly Long Island), which he renamed Sea Island Beach. There, Coffin immediately laid plans to develop the Sea Island Company, and build a resort hotel. After paving roads and laying lines for electricity, water and telephones to Sea Island, Coffin and Bill Jones engaged prominent Palm Beach architect Addison Mizner to design the new Cloister Hotel, which opened in the fall of 1928. Coffin hoped to attract wealthy northerners to the Cloister as a winter alternative to the developing south Florida resorts.

The Cloister was an instant success. To facilitate access to Sea Island, Coffin and Jones started a bus line from Jacksonville and Savannah to Brunswick. Another contribution to the coastal Georgia economy by Coffin was his support of a growing industry by which south Georgia pine trees were industrially converted to pulpwood and paper products. Coffin's association with George Mead of the Mead Paper Company played a role in the successful effort by Mead and Scott Paper Company to form the Brunswick Pulp and Paper Company in 1936. This venture (now Georgia-Pacific) evolved into one of the largest pulp-paper manufacturers in the world.

Coffin understood the significance of the low country ecosystem and the responsible development of its potential. "Two projects now well along in the making are sure to profoundly affect the economic future of this coast country," he remarked in 1935. "One is the work of Colonel Tillinghast Huston, who is blazing the way in the reclamation of the great rice fields which fringe the deltas of our rivers. The potentialities and the far-reaching effects of Colonel Huston's activities are such as to well warrant a visit to his plantation, Butler's Island on the Altamaha. Here you will feel yourself in Holland and will absorb new ideas in dairying, bulb, fruit and vegetable culture, crop rotation, etc., with frost protection and perfect freshwater irrigation through the rise and fall of the salt water tides..."[49]

Ironically, it was a Northern "outsider" to coastal Georgia, Coffin, who was among the first to realize that a healthy coastal ecosystem could work in tandem with economic development, particularly in relation to tourism and the hospitality industry, concepts that represented the framework of his creative instincts with Sapelo, Sea Island and the Cloister. "We have a bit of philanthropy, and a good deal of business tied up together in Sea Island," he noted two years after the Cloister opened in 1928. "As a matter of experience, I have had a part in the past in starting at least two semi-philanthropic projects, both of which have paid better than almost anything else I ever went into...It is the people doing things that we want here. It is the people doing things that Georgia needs, to the end that we may all take an even greater pride in Georgia as the finest [place] in the

---

[49] Howard E. Coffin, "From Indian Canoe to Airship in the Country of the Golden Isles," address before the Georgia Real Estate Association, Sea Island Beach, Ga., November 1, 1935, 10-11, printed copy in Sea Island Company archives.

whole world in which to live, to work, and to play."⁵⁰ Shortly after Coffin's death in 1937, *Atlanta Constitution* publisher Clark Howell noted that Coffin "was in some respects a greater Georgian than many of us native sons, for he had the vision to discern and develop what our state possessed when we perhaps were less observant, less audacious, and less willing to gamble on our judgement."⁵¹

    Coffin's legacy to the low country was carried forward by two other Northerners with whom he was closely associated: his young cousin, Alfred W. Jones, Sr. (1902-1982) of Akron, Ohio, whom Coffin had brought on in 1923 to manage Sapelo, and later Sea Island, and Eugene W. Lewis of Detroit, a member of the Sea Island board of directors and owner of substantial acreage on St. Simons Island. The story of Jones is one of philanthropy and coastal conservation. When the Hamilton plantation tract, the winter home of Lewis, came on the market, the Sea Island Company acquired the property. Jones made it available at minimal cost to the South Georgia Conference of the Methodist Church as an educational conference center, even signing the note himself that enabled the Church to borrow the money to buy the land. As a close friend of Richard J. Reynolds, Jr. (1906-1964), who bought Sapelo from Coffin in 1934, Jones was one of the trustees named when Reynolds created the Sapelo Island Research Foundation in 1949. As Chairman of the Board of Trustees of the Foundation in 1976, he negotiated the

---

[50] Howard E. Coffin, "Georgia's Future and Some of Her Undeveloped Resources. An Address Before the Annual Meeting of the Georgia Bar Association, The Cloister Hotel, Sea Island Beach, Ga.," 1930, transcript in Sea Island Company archives.
[51] Martin, *This Happy Isle*, 72.

transfer of the Foundation's Sapelo properties to the state of Georgia under federal designation as a protected national estuarine sanctuary, the first between Virginia and Florida, and the present-day Sapelo Island National Estuarine Research Reserve. In 2015, the 6,000-acre Altama plantation tract on the lower Altamaha River in Glynn County, owned for years by Jones and his descendants, became a state conservation property through a coordination of efforts by The Nature Conservancy and the Georgia Department of Natural Resources.

Henry Norton Torrey was of the generation of Detroit industrialists that included Coffin and Henry Ford, and was closely affiliated with both. Torrey's twenty-year association with Ossabaw Island paralleled in many ways that of Coffin with Sapelo and Ford at Richmond Hill. Two earlier Northerners were at Ossabaw, James M. Waterbury of New York City, and John Wanamaker of Philadelphia, prior to the purchase of the island by Torrey in 1924. Torrey was an industrial surgeon with Harper Hospital in Detroit. His wife Nell was the daughter of John B. Ford, founder of the Pittsburgh Plate Glass Company and the Wyandotte Chemical Company in Michigan.

With a coastal ecological awareness already established by their earlier residence on the Savannah mainland, the Torreys built a 20,000-square foot residence on Ossabaw's North End set in a natural landscape of live oaks, palms, and gardens laid out by Mrs. Torrey and the prominent landscape architect Ellen Biddle Shipman. After acquiring Ossabaw Torrey researched the records in the Georgia Historical Society pursuant to writing a monograph about the island's early history. In the document, Torrey articulated his appreciation and understanding of the island's ecology: "Ossabaw's highlands are heavily wooded, with live oak, virgin pine and palmetto predominating and the vegetation is semi-tropical and very luxuriant...The salt marshes of Ossabaw are many miles in extent and have a peculiar beauty and fascination to all lovers of the Georgia coast. Traversing these marshes and extending into the highlands are many salt rivers and creeks which afford splendid fishing...The primitive and original atmosphere of Ossabaw has always been maintained, and the property today retains its natural beauty and charm..."[52]

The process by which Ossabaw became a protected public trust began in 1961 when the Torreys' daughter, Eleanor Torrey (Sandy) West (b. 1913) and her husband Clifford West, established the Ossabaw Foundation for the preservation and educational enhancement of the island. In implementing the goals of the Foundation, the Wests initiated four ongoing programs in the 1960s and 1970s—the Ossabaw Island Project, the Genesis Project, the Professional Research Program, and the Public Use and Education Program. The Ossabaw Island Project was an interdisciplinary program through which qualified participants were invited to the island from the U.S. and abroad to pursue their research and creativity in the arts, humanities, and sciences while benefiting from the isolation and solitude of Ossabaw. The Genesis Project was begun in 1970 and was active until 1982. In it, Sandy West provided Ossabaw as a platform for people of all skills and talents to come to

---

[52] H.N. Torrey, *The Story of Ossabaw* (Savannah, Ga.: privately printed, 1926), Introduction.

the island to undertake independent projects and initiatives, usually associated with ecological, botanical, zoological and archaeological disciplines. Genesis participants lived in rustic quarters they built themselves at remote Middle Place on the west side of the island. There were few amenities and participants cultivated their own food. The Public Use and Education Program has continued to the present day in an innovative format coordinated by the Foundation. This initiative grew out of Mrs. West's desire for people to experience the natural environment of Ossabaw through camping for limited stays, and day trip programs for qualified groups coming to the island for environmental and cultural education. Educational meetings, symposia, and overnight trips to Ossabaw continue to be conducted by the Foundation the year around.

Sandy Torrey West fervently wanted to see her island preserved from overuse and commercial development. Thus in 1978, through a combination of purchase with public funds, and a donation by the Torrey and West families, the state of Georgia acquired Ossabaw and the island became a state Heritage Preserve to be used solely for "natural, scientific and cultural study, research and education and environmentally sound preservation of the ecosystem." Mrs. West retained a life estate on the North End, including the main house. She continues to be an advocate both for Ossabaw and the Georgia coast, and played a key role in the reinvigoration of the Ossabaw Foundation in 1994. At that time, Leopold Adler II of Savannah, whose wife, Emma Morel Adler, is directly descended from Ossabaw's first colonial owner, became the Foundation's president. In an interview in 2001, Sandy West tells the story that Ossabaw was actually purchased on a whim by her mother, Nell, while her father was away. Mrs. Torrey "never dreamed her offer of $150,000 would be accepted" by the sellers. Sandy West also noted that she hated the island, "with all its marsh and boggy swamps" when she first went there as an eleven-year-old child in 1924. But as time and events would prove she became the most ardent advocate for the preservation of Ossabaw the island has ever known.[53]

Clement M. Keys of New York City, who with Howard Coffin and James Willson, acquired St. Catherines Island in 1929, was another of the Northern "late arrivals" to coastal Georgia. While his sojourn in the low country was far more transitory than that of the Torreys at neighboring Ossabaw, Keys was every bit as protective of his island during the 1930s as his coastal contemporaries. Keys was a prominent aviation consultant who led the major corporate merger of what became the powerful Curtis-Wright Corporation. The isolation of St. Catherines provided a perfect retreat for his family, an ideal escape from the rigors of corporate America and Wall Street during the Great Depression. Like those before him, as well as his Northern-born coastal neighbors, Keys fully understood the uniqueness of the low country ecology and the beauty of his island, intending to conserve St. Catherines for future generations of his family. Over the mantle of the restored main house on the island's North End, Keys carved a short poem that affirmed his commitment to the island, "Come to my forest in the circle of the sea, come to my cottage and dwell a while with me, come to my garden where old

---

[53] *Savannah Morning News*, January 4, 2001. At the time of this writing in 2020 Sandy Torrey West was still living at the age of 107 in Savannah. Until the spring of 2016 she had resided, usually alone, in the Ossabaw home built by her parents ninety-one years earlier. She is a remarkable woman.

timed blossoms grow, smiles will come to you, and sighs with you go." Financial burdens led to Keys' reluctant sale of St. Catherines in 1939 to the Rauers family of Savannah, an earlier owner of the island. In 1943, Edward Noble of New York bought St. Catherines. After his death, the island was transferred to the Edward John Noble Foundation. In 1981, as research, education, and conservation programs expanded, ownership of the island was transferred to the Georgia-based St. Catherines Island Foundation. The island remains privately owned and administered by the St. Catherines Foundation to this day.[54]

The transition of many of the Georgia coastal lands from private to public ownership beginning in the late 1940s has served as a model for how states, acting in concert with environmental groups and interested members of the public and corporate sectors, can conserve ecologically sensitive properties, particularly those along the nation's coastlines.

The dissolution of the Jekyll Island Club during World War II, followed by state acquisition of the island in 1948, resulted from the turbulence of the Great Depression and two wars, along with the increased attraction for the younger generation of Club families to Palm Beach, Boca Raton and Biscayne Bay for their winter escapes. Nonetheless, the first generation had laid an important foundation for the managed conservation of Jekyll that accompanied state acquisition, and the island was the first of several to follow a similar path in succeeding decades. June Hall McCash describes the transition as evolving from "a societal shift of [great] magnitude,"

---

[54] Armelagos and Woods, *St. Catherines Island*, 71-97.

adding perceptively, "As the middle class expanded, the wealthy social elite seemed to dwindle, and such elegant leisure as they had known in places like the Jekyll Island Club began to vanish. The great fortunes that had been built by the vision of men like Pulitzer and Rockefeller…were divided among larger numbers of people…The new era toppled [the] wealthy industrialists, already profoundly shaken by the Great Depression…As a group they had frequently been described as 'robber barons.' It was an unflattering image…Few of the Jekyll [members] had ever fit the stereotype. They had been, by and large, men and women of substance with a profound sense of social responsibility. Their social and cultural philanthropies left the country as a whole richer and more stable…Indeed, the stereotype has been called into question by various [recent] scholars, and as one historian has noted, few of the so-called 'industrial buccaneers' ever fit the pattern."[55]

No defense can be made for the profit-driven timber companies that devastated large amounts of land in low country Georgia and South Carolina in the three decades after the Civil War. Their motivation was about making money and not conservation; they had no inclination to sustain the triad of coastal ecosystems embracing maritime forests, freshwater rivers and tidal salt marshes. But the hindsight of history must be kinder to the affluent Northerners who acquired the Georgia islands, as most of the newcomers became over time acutely sensitive to their locales and the need to preserve them. It can be argued that the "social awareness" embraced by them in the late nineteenth and early twentieth centuries also came to include a

---

[55] McCash, *The Jekyll Island Cottage Colony*, 269-70.

subliminal "environmental awareness," perhaps without their full comprehension at the time, and certainly long before such a concept permanently established itself upon the national conscience.

Following the state acquisition of Jekyll, and the framework established for a state Authority to manage it, the movement to conserve Georgia coastal lands gathered momentum in the 1950s and 1960s. Butler Island, once privately-owned, became a state property in 1954. Soon thereafter, most of the Altamaha River delta came under state management as a protected waterfowl area administered by the Georgia Game and Fish Commission.

The growing movement toward conservation of the coast became more pronounced than ever before in the 1960s as an assortment of real and potential threats to the low country ecosystem emerged and, for the first time, drew considerable scrutiny from proactive state legislative officials, the academic and research communities, and the general public, particularly (as would be expected) populations along the coast itself. The 1968 Marshlands Conference at Sea Island featured a broad coalition of elected officials, scientists, conservationists and citizens in response to several issues, including the proposed building of a highway transecting the coastal marshes for more than one hundred miles, connecting to each barrier island—in tandem with the construction of Interstate Highway 95 already then under development along the coast. The radical highway proposal was envisioned by developers and local county officials with profitability and development in mind, with largely unspoiled marshes and uplands being transformed into housing and resort tracts with an assortment of amenities for the anticipated influx of thousands of new residents with the consequent enhancement of the public tax rolls. An additional threat occurred when phosphate mining companies bought two small islands with plans to dredge large sections of the coast, an effort that included the proposed dumping of millions of tons of dredged spoil into the marshes to create small islands for potential development.

These threats to coastal conservation impelled the further acquisition of properties by state and federal entities in the late 1960s and during the 1970s. Wassaw Island became a national wildlife refuge in 1969. The state acquired Sapelo in two transactions in 1969 and 1976; the National Park Service designated much of Cumberland as a National Seashore in 1972; and in 1978, the state bought Ossabaw. Wolf and Blackbeard islands were already under federal management as wildlife refuges while private owners or foundations held and protected several other islands, the larger ones being St. Catherines, Little St. Simons, Little Cumberland and Creighton.

The protection of the islands fueled the spontaneous growth of estuarine and ecological scientific research beginning in the 1950s under the auspices of such well-known biologists as Eugene P. Odum, Lawrence R. Pomeroy and Robert A. Ragotzkie. The most significant contribution by Richard J. Reynolds, Jr., owner of Sapelo Island after its sale in 1934 by Howard E. Coffin, was his facilitation of what precipitated the expanded scientific understanding of the coastal ecosystem. In 1953, Reynolds provided infrastructure and marshlands on Sapelo to the University of Georgia for a marine biological research station. This had important ramifications over the next half-century relevant to the growth of academic disciplines associated with the chemical and biological processes of the salt marshes and the tidal estuary. There thus evolved a direct corollary between estuarine science and maritime culture as inculcated through the field investigations of some of the world's preeminent ecologists at Sapelo's Marine Institute. E. P. Odum, acknowledged in the academic community as the "father of modern ecology," along with Pomeroy, Ragotzkie, John Teal, and Donald Kinsey, among many others, set the early parameters for establishing the conduit between the "life and death" of the salt marsh and the biological life cycle of marine organisms that habituated the ecosystem, chiefly shellfish—oysters, shrimp and the Atlantic blue crab. It was the criticality of this ecological research that in 1976 occasioned the creation of the Sapelo Island National Estuarine Sanctuary, now Research Reserve, through a cooperative agreement between the State of Georgia and the National Oceanic and Atmospheric Administration, thus ensuring the continued integrity of Sapelo South End as a platform for scientific investigation.

The chief outgrowth of early ecological marsh study disciplines at the University of Georgia Marine Institute at Sapelo Island laid the groundwork for legislative acts of great consequence for the conservation and stewardship of coastal Georgia. Chief among these were the Georgia Coastal Marshlands Protection Act of 1970 and its companion piece, the Shore Protection Act of 1979. The growing understanding and awareness of the significance of the biological processes relating to the salt marshes and tidal estuaries is ongoing, and may thus be said to be yet another extension of the evolution of the islands from their Northern owners to protected public trusts. The publicly-owned islands, with their controlled access by state and federal administrators, also have come to serve as platforms for recreation and the projection of ecological education and coastal resource management.[56]

The transition of several of the islands from private ownership to protected status as public trusts has not been without its challenges. The example of Cumberland Island serves as a useful example in this respect starting in the mid-1950s. Ironically, the catalyst for the modern conservation efforts for low country Georgia was provided by some who were less inclined to fully appreciate the conservation of the coast, being more bent on the profit margin.

In their desire to see their island properly conserved starting in the mid-1950s, the Carnegie descendants were understandably unhappy and concerned that a proposal for the State of Georgia to acquire Cumberland from them and make the island publicly-accessible; the island would be managed by a state authority in the manner of nearby Jekyll, complete with a causeway and the ubiquitous golf courses and boat marinas. Anxious for conservation to be implemented with sensitivity and with as little impact as possible on Cumberland's natural ecosystem, members of the family

---

[56] *Proceedings of the Salt Marsh Conference Held at the Marine Institute of the University of Georgia, March 25-28, 1958* (Athens: University of Georgia Marine Institute, 1959); E. P. Odum, "A Proposal for a Marshbank and the Strategy of Ecosystem Development for the Estuarine Zone of Georgia," in *The Future of the Marshlands and Sea Islands of Georgia* (Brunswick, Ga.: Coastal Area Planning and Development Commission, 1968), 74-85. For the Coastal Marshlands Protection Act story, see Paul Bolster, *Saving the Georgia Coast: A Political History of the Coastal Marshlands Protection Act* (Athens: University of Georgia Press, 2020). For the preservation of the tidal marshes and the scientific research conducted therein, see Charles Seabrook, *The World of the Salt Marsh: Appreciating and Protecting the Tidal Marshes of the Southeastern Atlantic Coast* (Athens: University of Georgia Press, 2012), an excellent work both for its erudition and readability.

were reluctant to sell their shares of the island. In 1960, the National Park Service (NPS) proposed the establishment of a national seashore with public access, but with no bridges and no commercialization of the island. This concept put in motion what became the template for managed conservation of much of the Georgia coast in the following decades.

The Carnegie family gradually began to see the NPS as the logical alternative toward the desired goal of securing the responsible stewardship of their island. This evolution was precipitated in 1968 when Charles Fraser, a native of coastal Georgia's Liberty County and the primary developer of Sea Pines Plantation at South Carolina's Hilton Head Island, cast his eyes upon Cumberland for similar development as a beach and golf resort. "The Carnegies viewed Fraser as the arch villain and began [efforts] to oppose him, galvanized into unanimity," commented environmental writer John McPhee in the early 1970s. "Ironically it was Fraser's plans that served as the catalyst for the eventual conservation victory. The Carnegies sold their two-thirds of Cumberland to the National Park Service in 1972 [and] Fraser succumbed to the pressure of those who, in his opinion, loved trees more than people." McPhee accompanied the eminent environmentalist David Brower, founder of the Sierra Club, to Cumberland during the discussions with Fraser regarding converting the island to a residential and beach resort. Brower actually partly agreed with Fraser's proposal in the mid-1960s that the best means of protecting the island was that his development be surrounded by the National Seashore, thus buffering Cumberland against other potential developers. In other words, Brower reasoned, it was better to have one responsible land developer than many.

Nonetheless, the commercial development of Cumberland was thus averted and almost 20,000 acres came under NPS administration. The achievement of an even stronger layer of conservation and protection was established through the Wilderness Act of 1982; the same year, the Candler family at High Point sold 2,200 acres to the NPS, giving the federal administration almost complete control of Cumberland. Not everyone was happy with these developments, particularly some state legislators and local Camden County officials who supported the Fraser development proposals to convert Cumberland into a revenue-producing beach resort.[57]

The Cumberland initiative clearly contributed to the energy behind the movement to conserve Georgia's privately-held islands, and the growing influence of conservation entities such as The Nature Conservancy, the Georgia Conservancy and the Sierra Club to shield from development the state and federally-administered islands, as well as the coastal river basins of the Altamaha, Ogeechee and Satilla rivers.

The state's acquisition of Jekyll for controlled development of a state recreational beach park interspersed with small residential communities of leased properties, and the Carnegie family's "victory" over developers to protect Cumberland were among the first of a series of victories, both large and small, that evolved from later generations of Northerners that precipitated the conservation and protection of much of the Georgia coast. Others followed by which private lands became public trusts protected from commercial

---

[57] James Kilgo, "Tidewater Heritage," in *The New Georgia Guide* (Athens: University of Georgia Press, 1996), 656-57; Bullard, *Cumberland Island*, 286-87.

development.[58] And while, for example, Sapelo and Ossabaw continue to be protected and with controlled access, there remains a caveat that must be recognized and carefully considered. No one can be assured of perpetual conservation of the islands in future generations. Conservationists argue that those who care about these places must be constantly vigilant, remain steadfast, and stay the course, never wavering in their commitment to the preservation of coastal Georgia's ecological and cultural identity. It will continue to be a "top-down" commitment, for as Pulitzer Prize winning historian William McFeely so aptly expressed it in his assessment of Sapelo's future, "As long as there are governors and commissioners who respect the unique and truly valuable natural resource that the island is, real estate and recreational predators are held at bay. But governors, commissioners [and politics] can change. Some arrangement more solid than that presently existing is needed to hold the line."[59]

In the late 1960s, environmental author McPhee, an "outsider," understood the uniqueness of the Georgia coast and the threats it faced far sooner and with greater awareness than the great majority of Georgians. His essay about Cumberland was evocative, and served as a catalyst, perhaps a fire bell in the night, for those who had not yet paid attention to the then-emerging developmental threats. In closing his piece he noted, "For three days we had roamed an island

---

[58] Tonya D. Clayton, Lewis A. Taylor, William J. Cleary, Paul E. Hosier, Peter H.F. Graber, William J. Neal, and Orrin H. Pilkey, Sr., *Living with the Georgia Shore* (Durham, N.C.: Duke University Press, 1992), 3-5.
[59] William S. McFeely, *Sapelo's People* (New York: W.W. Norton, 1994), 149-50.

bigger than Manhattan and had seen no one on its beach, no one in its interior woodlands. In the late twentieth century, in this part of the world, such an experience was unbelievable, a privilege made possible in our time by private ownership. No one was ever to be as free on that wild beach in the future as we had been that day."[60]

---

[60] John McPhee, *Encounters with the Archdruid* (New York: Farrar, Straus and Giroux, 1971), quoted in Kilgo, "Tidewater Heritage," 657.

Selected Writings

Researches in Coastal Ecology as History

Ecology and Historical Archaeology

A direct consequence of the association between the local environment and its historical implications may be read in the study of the tangible fragments from the past. This aspect of the connectivity between "man and the landscape" is often at one with the soil of that landscape, either surficial or substrative—that is, the interpretation and analysis of the artifacts and detritus of past eras of human occupation and activity.

This is archaeology, of course.

Of greater salience in this regard is the melding of the conclusions drawn from the written record—history—with that of the analytical study of the tangible evidence—artifacts—to produce that happy marriage known as historical archaeology. This concatenation of academic and research disciplines has resulted in the exponential expansion of knowledge and understanding of how people lived on the Georgia coast the last four hundred years and, for the purposes of our discussion, how they facilitated the local environment in virtually every aspect of their lives.

Lower Creek peoples—Guale, Yamacraw, Timucuan—were established long before Europeans arrived on the scene. Indian shell formations on Ossabaw and Sapelo Islands, some dating at least 4,500 years B.P., were the foci of systematic archaeological investigation by Clarence B. Moore as early as 1896, work later amplified by the research of Antonio J. Waring, Gerald Milanich, Lewis Larson, and Morgan R. Crook, among many other prominent specialists. The detailed reports that accompanied their fieldwork provide a unique window into Native American life and culture on the coast.

"The Two Forgotten Centuries" is appropriately descriptive of the nearly 200 years of the Spanish interregnum on the Georgia coast. It began in 1526, when Lucas Vasquez de Ayllon, a sugar planter and magistrate from Hispaniola, attempted a short-lived Spanish colony in what became Georgia, quite possibly in the region of Sapelo Sound. This unsuccessful colony in what came to be known as "Tierra de Ayllon"—Land of Ayllon—was the first true European settlement in what became the continental United States.[61] It seems odd that the protracted Spanish influence on coastal history in the 16th and 17th centuries has only recently begun to be seriously investigated by the academic community. Perhaps one explanation is the prevalent attitude for many years that "nothing much happened"

---

[61] Paul Hoffman, A New Andalucia and a Way to the Orient (Baton Rouge: Louisiana State University Press, 1990). This is the definitive study of Ayllon's attempt at colonization on the Georgia coast. Utilizing contemporary Spanish navigational reports and other archival records, Hoffman persuasively argues for the location of the "lost" settlement of San Miguel de Gualdape as being at or near Sapelo Sound. Whatever the locale, Ayllon and the majority of his 500 colonists did not survive, succumbing to disease, cold and starvation within two months, with the remaining colonists returning to Hispaniola.

in coastal Georgia before the arrival of Oglethorpe, testimony to the "Anglicization" of early Georgia history from 1733 onward.

Some of the numbers provide clarity to the two "lost centuries". Ayllon's colony, San Miguel de Gualdape, predated the first permanent Spanish settlement at St. Augustine (1565) by thirty-nine years; it came 81 years before the first permanent English settlement at Jamestown, and 207 years before the founding of Savannah. Conversely, San Miguel was settled a mere thirty-four years after Cristoforo Colon (Columbus) accidentally stumbled upon the Western Hemisphere.

The 1981 discovery of the site of Mission Santa Catalina de Guale at St. Catherines Island in investigations led by David Hurst Thomas, and the subsequent documentation and recovery of artifacts there, represent what is arguably the most significant archaeological field project in the history of coastal Georgia. Missions at St. Catherines, Sapelo, St. Simons, Cumberland and Amelia islands flourished from ca. 1570 to 1686, and have been researched recently by Thomas, John Worth, Rebecca Saunders, and others. Their authoritative writings on this subject are detailed and definitive.[62]

Events precedent to the founding of Georgia, and certainly consequential to it later, occurred in 1670 with the establishment of Charles Town and South Carolina. These developments drastically altered the stability of the Spanish strategic position in Guale, and

---

[62] See David Hurst Thomas, *The Archaeology of Mission Santa Catalina de Guale: 1. Search and Discovery* (New York, 1987); Thomas, with Grant D. Jones, Roger S. Durham and Clark Spencer Larsen, *The Anthropology of St. Catherines Island: Vol. 1, Natural and Cultural History* (New York, 1978); John E. Worth, *The Struggle for the Georgia Coast: An Eighteenth Century Spanish Retrospective on Guale and Mocama* (New York: American Museum of Natural History, 1995).

the inevitable incursions by the English gradually pushed the Spanish southward into Florida. In 1684 the missions north of Amelia Island were abandoned and for over 35 years the so-called Guale coast lay unoccupied and uncontested by Europeans, a "Debatable Land".

Native Americans were utilizing Sapelo Island as a food-gathering source by 4,500 B.P. The predominant group of gatherers was the Guale, a Muskhogean-speaking agrarian component of the Lower Creeks that may have had initial contact with Europeans as early as 1526. In the last fifty years there has been extensive study of the Guale and their living patterns along the middle Georgia coast between the Altamaha and the Ogeechee rivers, particularly on the islands from St. Simons to Ossabaw.[63]

While the native peoples utilized the nearby islands seasonally during food-gathering periods, the prominent Guale settlements were typically on the mainland. Based on archaeological research, Sapelo was occupied during the Late Archaic (ca. 2500-1000 B.C.), a period associated in the Southeast with the production of fiber-tempered ceramics. On Sapelo, the Guale utilized vegetal fiber—usually Spanish moss—mixed with the clay of their manufactured pottery to prevent cracking during the firing process. Scattered evidence of this pottery has been found on Sapelo on the high ground abutting the Duplin and Mud rivers, and Blackbeard Creek, including areas away from shell middens.

---

[63] Two excellent interdisciplinary studies relating to the Guale are David Hurst Thomas, *Native American Landscapes of St. Catherines Island, Georgia*, in three volumes, with contributions (New York: American Museum of Natural History Anthropological Papers 88, 2008), and Victor D. Thompson and David Hurst Thomas, eds., *Life among the Tides: Recent Archaeology on the Georgia Bight* (New York: American Museum of Natural History Anthropological Papers 98, 2013).

The island was less populated in the Woodland phase (ca. 1000 B.C.-1000 A.D.), and only a few traces of artifact evidence have been documented. One Woodland phase occupation site has been identified at Moses Hammock, beneath a shell midden attributed to a later phase. Sapelo's Guale population increased during the two phases of the Late Prehistoric (Mississippian) period: Savannah phase (ca. 800-1350), and Irene (ca. 1350-1570). Sapelo's Mississippian sites are characterized by a number of large burial mounds at Kenan, Bourbon and Dumoussay fields, with additional evidence documented at Long Row Field, Moses Hammock and High Point. The Guale mounds on Sapelo were encircled by shallow ditches from which came the materials used in the mound construction. Mounds were typically the repositories for large numbers of burials.

The Guale eventually became primarily agrarian; archaeological evidence demonstrates their considerable agricultural expertise with the cultivation of beans, squash, melons, pumpkins and maize, a crop ground into flour for making flat, round cakes. With their shell hoes, the Guale women cultivated the land, growing the vegetables; they also cured and dressed the skins of deer and other animals killed by the male hunters, and manufactured the clay pots utilized for cooking and storage. Many fragments of these pots have been found in the burial mounds and middens by the archaeologists. Crops were grown based on the Guale's increased understanding of local soil and weather conditions. Guale planters adapted to the lack of adequate fertility found in the sandy coastal soils, and developed proportionality to their farming techniques, and the types of crops cultivated. Fr. Sedeno of the Santa Catalina mission on St. Catherines Island noted that "the Indians are scattered because they do not have that with which to clear trees for their fields, so they go where they find a small amount of land without forest in order to plant their maize; and the land is so miserable they move with their households from time to time to seek other lands that they can bring to productivity..."[64]

Meat was plentiful. Herds of buffalo roamed the mainland forests, and deer habituated the woods and grassy savannas. The Guale hunted white tail deer on Sapelo as a year-around dietary staple, with the skins being utilized as clothing, and for barter. The Guale men hunted the meat, utilizing bows and arrows made of reed, mulberry or cedar, and tipped with fishbone and chipped beads of flint. Other meat sources were bear, wild turkey, raccoon and rabbit.

Shellfish was another important food source for the Guale during the Archaic. Various species could easily be collected from the creek banks without the necessity of watercraft. Mussels and periwinkles abounded in the salt marsh, and since inter-tidal oysters form beds along the creek banks it was relatively easy for the Guale to harvest these shellfish. In addition to shellfish, the Guale ate large quantities of finfish. Consumable fish species included sea trout, Atlantic croaker, yellowtail, drum and shad.[65] The men travelled the tidal creeks in dugout canoes commonly made from cypress logs, hollowing them out by means of fire. The Guale used the dugouts to

---

[64] Lewis H. Larson, *Aboriginal Subsistence Technology on the Southeast Coastal Plain during the Late Pre-Historic Period* (Gainesville: University of Florida Press, 1980).
[65] Morgan R. Crook, Jr., *Mission Period Archaeology of the Georgia Coastal Zone* (Athens: University of Georgia Laboratory of Archaeology Series, No. 1, 1986), 34-42.

search the waterways for food, and to visit their neighbors on the islands and mainland.

Live oak acorns, gathered in the fall in great quantity beneath the tree canopy, were sweet and were eaten raw. Wild grapes were abundant in the fall, while berries, persimmons and grapes were available in spring and summer.

Artifact analysis based on a century of archaeological field investigation indicates considerable Guale activity on St. Simons, Sapelo, St. Catherines and Ossabaw islands during the Mississippian period. Guale settlement patterns on Sapelo were concentrated on the western and northeast sections of the island in the higher elevations contiguous to the marsh, and at points where tidal creeks offered access to the high ground.[66]

The occupational sites have been identified as Kenan Field on the Duplin River, Long Row Field south of Chocolate, the strip on the northwest portion of the island from the Shell Ring to High Point, and Dumoussay and Bourbon fields in Sapelo's northeast quadrant. Scattered shell mound evidence also points to Guale presence on the South End several hundred yards east of the Marine Institute campus.

Archaeologist Morgan R. Crook, Jr. conducted a systematic survey of Guale sites at Kenan and Bourbon fields in the mid-1970s, concluding that settlements were present at both sites. Amplifying field work at Bourbon conducted earlier by Clarence B. Moore, Crook determined that testing of ceramic and mortuary findings

---

[66] Alan E. McMichael, "A Model for Barrier Island Settlement Patterns," in Daniel P. Juengst, ed., *Sapelo Papers: Researches in the History and Prehistory of Sapelo Island, Georgia* (Carrollton, Ga.: West Georgia College Studies in the Social Sciences, 1980), 48.

from two large mounds suggested Savannah and Irene period utilization, while pottery analysis from the site further validated a Mississippian provenance.[67]

The several archaeological phases of the Mississippian period, about 800-1500 AD, were marked by changes in Guale pottery patterns such as tempering, stamping, and incising with increasingly decorative craftsmanship. These evolving techniques in ceramics were clearly identifiable from the Savannah, and subsequent Irene phases of the late Mississippian era, and continued to be developed in the mission period in the early seventeenth century. It must be understood that early investigative archaeology was quite rudimentary. There was a general absence of definition in, and a concurrent lack of appreciation for, the academic aspects of the discipline. An observation in the *Savannah Morning News* in November 1898 is typical: a reporter led his piece with a caption stating, "No Treasure Ever found in the Mounds and No Giants Either." This attitude was symptomatic of the widespread misconceptions about the theretofore undocumented aboriginal societies of pre-Columbian coastal Georgia.

In 1872, William McKinley, a Milledgeville, Georgia attorney, submitted a paper to the *Smithsonian Annual Report* based on his investigations of burial mounds on Sapelo. The document reflected his unscientific observations during a May 1871 visit to the island. He described a number of shell aggregations in addition to a detailed description of three burial mounds, noting that "great mound-circles were doubtless for councils or games." He included a reference to a

---

[67] Morgan R. Crook, Jr., "Spatial Associations and Distribution of Aggregate Village Sites," in Juengst, ed., *Sapelo Papers*, 82.

mound named "Druid Grove," or "Spalding," near the old Spalding house on Sapelo's South End, labelling it on a map accompanying his report. Regarding a mound complex situated in the center of the island, McKinley noted "These cemetery-mounds are very ancient...Sapelo Island is famous for its wonderful moss-hung live oaks; but the largest-bodied tree on the island, one over four feet in diameter at the stump, and seven feet in height, to just below the first fork, grows on top of the biggest burial mound at the place marked Kenan."[68]

The first archaeologist to employ scholarly rigor to investigative field research on Sapelo was Clarence Bloomfield Moore, a Philadelphia academic who conducted studies on the south Atlantic and Gulf coasts in the 1890s and early 1900s. His detailed field notes and drawings, when published in 1897 as *Certain Aboriginal Mounds of the Georgia Coast*, documented for the first time Native American societal life in the region. This compendium included an assessment of his work at Sapelo in 1896.[69]

While McKinley and Moore had different professional backgrounds, their common interests and didactic observations, in tandem with the validity of their notes and reports on Sapelo's mound complexes, provided later generations of researchers with critically important insights into aspects of pre-Columbian life on the island.

---

[68] William McKinley, "Mounds in Georgia," *Smithsonian Institution, Annual Report for 1872*, 27 (1873): 422-24. The visit is noted in Robert L. Humphries, ed., *The Journal of Archibald C. McKinley* (Athens: University of Georgia Press, 1991), 69.
[69] Clarence B. Moore, *Certain Aboriginal Mounds of the Georgia Coast* (Philadelphia: Journal of the Academy of Natural Sciences, 1897).

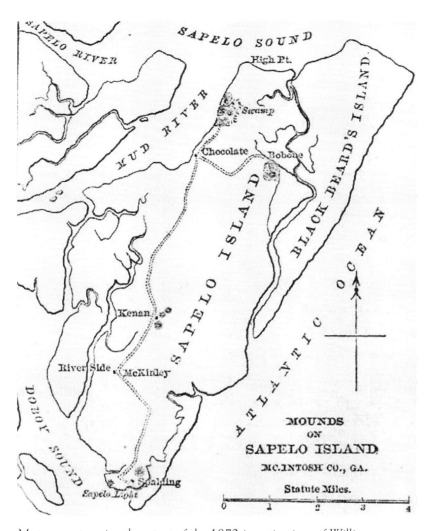

Map accompanying the report of the 1872 investigations of William McKinley on Sapelo Island, appearing in the Smithsonian Institution Annual Report.

Moore's interest in Southeastern coastal aboriginal societies was inspired by a series of articles published in the *American Naturalist* from 1892 to 1894 on the "Shell Heaps of the St. Johns River." Moore's meticulous attention to detail in the methodology of his field collection, and subsequent documentation of aboriginal sites visited between 1894 and 1918, has enabled his findings to be used continuously through the years. He and his staff traveled the Gulf of Mexico, and the southeastern Atlantic coasts, in addition to making trips along several interior rivers. The annual field work was usually conducted from October through April after which Moore returned to Philadelphia for the summer to collate and rewrite his field notes, and make public his latest research.

McKinley's 1872 Smithsonian report includes a description of a mound complex in a place he identifies as "Bobone field" a colloquial term used by the African Americans residing in that section of the island. In his 1897 report, *Certain Aboriginal Mounds*, Moore noted that "Boobone" was a small black settlement that "extending back from the landing is an extensive tract of rich land, undulating with shell deposits, long under cultivation, the property of Amos Sawyer, Esq., of Arlington, R.I. to whom we are indebted for cordial permission to make complete archaeological investigation."[70]

McKinley and Moore studied two mounds at Bourbon. In one mound "about one quarter of a mile S.E. by S. from the landing" Moore documented 192 points of human remains, including 115 skeletons.[71] His report indicated that the two mounds were 150 yards apart, the largest measuring seventy-two feet in diameter at the base, and eight feet in height, the second being thirty-eight feet in diameter at the base, and three feet, four inches in height. In the larger mound Moore recovered pottery vessels, clay tobacco pipe bowls, conch shell chisels, conch bowls, shell beads, and polished stone axes. When McKinley measured the mound earlier in 1871 he recorded the

---

[70] Ibid., 55-67.
[71] Ibid., 56-57.

largest as being seventy feet in diameter at the base, and nine feet in height, and nothing for the smaller one, adding that the "entire surface of which field is dotted and white with hundreds of shell-mounds, from two to four feet high, and from fifteen to fifty feet base."[72]

Probably the earliest of Sapelo's prehistoric sites is the Shell Ring complex in the northwest section of the island, the most prominent feature of which was often referred to as the "Spanish Fort" in the eighteenth and nineteenth centuries. This aboriginal formation is regarded as one of the largest, and most intact of the few remaining southeastern shell rings. McKinley's 1871 observations brought this unique formation to the attention of the anthropological community for the first time. He identified three rings south of High Point: the larger, most prominent one still much in evidence, and two smaller rings only three feet high "in an open field long cultivated." Of the larger ring, McKinley noted that it was

"240 feet wide; 9 feet high; base, 30 feet; no gateway; built of earth and shells, densely overgrown with live oak, palmetto, myrtle, grape-vines, which perfectly mask it; western side built along the very edge of the table land; so as to front a salt marsh and the Mud River as a wall 20 feet high; on the north, skirting a fresh water flag and bulrush marsh or stream, 150 feet wide, separating it from circle No. 2, which is 210 feet wide, in an open field long cultivated; mound now rising 3 feet on 20 feet base, composed of shell and earth; area plain. Circle No. 3 is 150 feet wide, just like No. 2. These circles are surrounded by hundreds of shell mounds, about 3 feet high, on bases of 20 to 50 feet, which crowd, without visible order, a field of one hundred acres or more, bounded on the west by salt marsh and inland salt river, and on the east by fresh-water jungle. On all these shell-mounds and over all the plain are found fragments of Indian pottery, both plain and ornamented. No funeral-mounds are nearer

---

[72] McKinley, "Mounds in Georgia," 424.

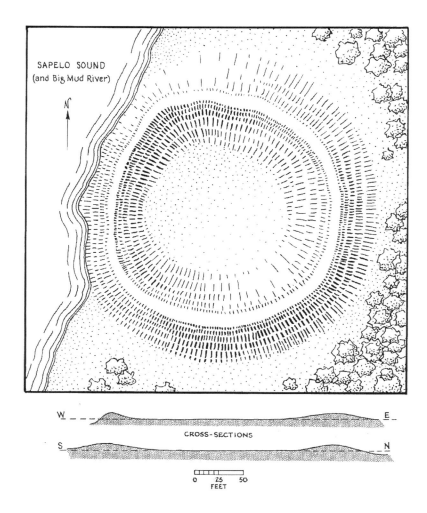

Sapelo Shell Ring, based on a 1949 sketch by Antonio J. Waring from C. B. Moore.

than three miles. The shells are all of mollusks yet living in the neighboring waters, the oyster, clam, conch, scallop, & c., which fact, and the broken pottery, show plainly that these shell-mounds, indicated by dots on the map, in countless number, are ancient camps of the Indians or mound-builders, where they dwelt, while the three great mound circles were doubtless for councils or games."[73]

McKinley's description indicates that the area was large and

---

[73] McKinley, "Mounds in Georgia," 422-23.

somewhat disturbed, probably because of the rings being utilized as a convenient source for oyster shells in the early nineteenth-century construction of tabby buildings on Sapelo Island. Moore referenced the Shell Ring in his publication as the "Aboriginal Enclosure at Sapelo High Point," noting

> "On Sapelo High Point, overlooking Sapelo Sound and at periods of storm, washed by the water of Big Mud River which has laid bare a section of the walls, is an almost circular aboriginal fortification or ceremonial enclosure. The enclosure which we examined by permission of Amos Sawyer, Esq., upon whose property it is has a diameter, including the walls, of somewhat over 300 feet. The walls have an average height of from 5 to 7 feet, and a thickness of about 50 feet at the base. They are flattened on top where at present they have an average width of from 10 to 15 feet. They are covered with forest trees, and are composed exclusively of shells, mainly those of the oyster, with the usual midden refuse intermingled, such as fragments of bone, bits of earthenware, and the like."[74]

An important dissimilarity emerged from the findings of the two archaeologists: Moore's report noted, "Earthenware in fragments, shattered bones of the deer and a fragment of a temporal bone from a human skull were met with." It appears because Moore was actually excavating at the Shell Ring site in 1896-97, and McKinley was only making visual observations a quarter-century earlier, their interpretations of the ring mounds are somewhat contradictory.

A more rigorous investigation of the site was conducted half a century after Moore by Antonio J. Waring, Jr. and Lewis H. Larson,

---

[74] Moore, *Certain Aboriginal Mounds*, 71-73.

Jr. In 1949 and 1950 they documented the largest ring as having an interior diameter of 200 feet, noting it "seemed likely that the Shell Ring was the site of many small habitations. The occupants apparently piled the rapidly accumulating shell beside their small dwellings; later they moved, and new shell was then piled on the former habitation site." Waring and Larson concluded that the area inside the ring was intentionally "kept scrupulously clean" by the Guale since it was found to be devoid of shell.[75]

Like Moore, Waring and Larson noted that the composition is largely oyster shell, with a mix of clam, mussel and whelk. Dating of fiber-tempered pottery remains indicate a Late Archaic or Early Woodland Period provenance for the site. Radiocarbon dating of oyster shell remains places the starting date of building the ring at about 3,800 years B.P., plus or minus 350 years. The construction of the ring over several thousand years by the Guale was apparently quite purposeful, a planned project spanning generations of Native Americans. Artifacts excavated in 1950 included animal bone, projectile points, fiber tempered pottery, tools and ornaments. The two nearby smaller rings observed by McKinley in 1871 have been validated by more recent investigation using advanced scientific techniques and analysis.

The research of archaeologist Victor Thompson starting in 2004 validated the findings of Waring and Larson regarding settlement patterns at the Shell Ring sites. Thompson posited that the largest formation was likely a permanent settlement during the Late Archaic

---

[75] A.J. Waring, Jr. and Lewis H. Larson, Jr., "The Shell Ring on Sapelo Island," Stephen Williams, ed., *The Waring Papers: The Collected Works of Antonio J. Waring, Jr.* (Cambridge, Mass.: Peabody Museum, 1968), 263-73.

period, ending ca. 1000 B.C. The interpretation here is that there were actual structural elements—housing—inside the circumference of the ring, while the ring itself was a gradual accumulation of waste and shell deposits by the Guale. After the Archaic the Shell Ring ceased to be a settlement, but continued to evolve as a ceremonial site. The Shell Ring settlement possibly transitioned a few miles south to Kenan Field where a substantial Guale town was in evidence through several periods, including Late Archaic, and Late Prehistoric.[76]

In addition to Sapelo Island, C.B. Moore conducted field studies at several other sites in McIntosh County, finding the north end of Creighton Island of particular interest. One of Moore's field visits in his 1896 season was to Creighton Island's north end.[77] In that era, the north end landing for Creighton was on its northwest point via a causeway through the marsh to Back River as delineated on an 1859 Coast Survey map of the island. Moore presumably accessed Creighton at this landing by way of Sutherland's Bluff across the Sapelo River, since his notes indicate investigations at sites on Bruro Neck, including Contentment, then a small African American settlement. His research vessel, the *Gopher*, could have docked at the northwest landing, or the vessel may have been moored at

---

[76] Victor D. Thompson, Matthew Reynolds, Brian Haley, Richard Jefferies, Jay Johnson and Catherine Humphries, "The Sapelo Shell Rings Site: Remote Sensing on a Georgia Sea Island," *Southeastern Archaeology* 23 (2004):192-201; Richard W. Jefferies and Victor D. Thompson, "Mission Period Native American Settlement and Interaction on Sapelo Island, Georgia," paper presented at the annual meeting of the Southeastern Archaeological Association, 2005; and Victor D. Thompson, "Questioning Complexity: The Prehistoric Hunter-Gatherers of Sapelo Island, Georgia," Ph.D. diss., University of Kentucky, 2006.
[77] Moore, *Certain Aboriginal Mounds*, op. cit., 28-43.

Sutherland's Bluff across the river. Creighton's only other access points are both on its south end on the Front River (east) and South Sapelo River (west). Otherwise, Creighton Island is completely surrounded by salt marsh penetrated by a few small tidal creeks that require a flood tide to gain access to the upland. As he did not investigate the south end of Creighton, Moore almost certainly accessed the island by utilizing the Back River landing on the island's northwest point. Moore noted he had been given permission to investigate Creighton's north end by owner George E. Atwood.[78] About a mile southeast of the Back River landing Moore reported a large archaeological site at a pasture that featured a number of shell middens reduced in size by earlier cultivation. He described this mound as having layers and pockets of oyster shell and sand with features more akin to a cemetery rather than the typical burial mounds he had found in other coastal locations. Moore estimated that 220 persons were interred within this site. There were eight urn burials located. The burial urns were described as being "a bowl of about 4 gallons capacity, with marginal incised decoration surmounting the complicated stamp." According to Lewis Larson, who inspected this mound in 1951, these embellishments were a variant of a very common rim treatment associated with Mississippi Period Irene Phase wares."[79]

Moore also investigated a mound on the banks of Shellbluff

---

[78] Moore had earlier done field work at another Atwood property, Shell Bluff. His field notes also indicate a brief investigation of a mound at Cedar Point in early 1897. Cedar Point lies about one mile directly across the marsh from Creighton's south end. See ff.
[79] Lewis Larson, *The Georgia and South Carolina Expeditions of Clarence Bloomfield Moore* (Tuscaloosa: University of Alabama Press, 1998), 19; Moore, *Certain Aboriginal Mounds*, 32, 40.

Creek at Valona, that settlement being then known as Shell Bluff, much of the tract being the property of George E. Atwood. Moore reported that the mound had been largely obliterated by cultivation and other disruptions, but he nonetheless discovered several sherds of uncomplicated stamping, and the remains of thirty-one burials. He described six of these, one of which was an urn burial contained within a checked stamped vessel, and two other pottery vessels containing calcined bone.[80] In March of 1897, Moore's field notes indicate that he investigated a mound at Cedar Point, about two miles north of Shell Bluff, though reference to this visit does not appear in his published report. Moore noted that the Cedar Point mound was "was considerably leveled at [the] top by a church for colored people (we were informed), [it is] now removed. Deep depression at portions of margin [is this a borrow pit?]"[81] Larson states in his Introduction to the 1998 edition of Moore's report, that his colleague, Antonio J. Waring, had referenced a platform mound at Cedar Point, stating that it conformed to a similar mound on the north end of Creighton Island not far away. "A mound large enough to support a church and one that might have had a top level enough for the construction of a church may well have been a platform mound," Larson observed.[82]

During the time of his Creighton Island investigation Moore visited the Walker Mound, about a mile and a half west of present-day Shellman Bluff. Based on his notes, Moore and his assistants apparently went up the Sapelo River to Belleville Point at the end of

---

[80] Ibid., 16.
[81] Ibid., 18.
[82] Ibid.

each day's field work, then returned the next morning to Shellman Bluff. There the *Gopher* was moored in the Bruro River during Moore's day trips to Creighton Island and the Walker Mound on the mainland near Shellman.

Moore described the Walker Mound as being almost six feet high with a base diameter of forty-six feet:

"The mound had previously been dug into to an inconsiderable extent. On its northern margin grew a live-oak 5 feet in diameter, 3 feet from the ground. This tree was not removed, though otherwise the mound was totally demolished...The mound was composed of rich, loamy brown sand with many local layers of oyster shells. The usual charcoal and fireplaces were present... A black layer from 3 inches to 1 foot thickness, made up of sand mingled with charcoal in minute particles, ran through the mound at about the level of the surrounding territory...the layer [being] 5 feet 9 inches below the surface."[83]

Moore discovered the remains of seventy-five individuals in thirty-six burials. Some of the burials were cremations in urns based on Moore's discovery of charred bones, in addition to the remains of bones placed in the pits that were then filled with oyster shell. Shell beads were catalogued within the mound, as were other grave goods including whelk bowls, shell ear pins and cups. Irene-incised bowls and other pottery vessels and jars were recovered, one of which yielded Irene Complicated Stamped decoration.

Larson visited the Walker Mound site in 1953 and noted that the live oak tree described by Moore a half century earlier was still standing, among other oaks. The trees were likely on the site to provide shade for cattle herds or workers cultivating the fields, a

---

[83] Moore, quoted in Larson, ibid., 23.

common practice on coastal farm tracts in the nineteenth and early twentieth centuries.[84] Larson noted that the site had disappeared and has not been relocated, largely due to the extensive planting of a pine plantation on and around the site. Large expanses of slash pine have made the Walker Mound all but impossible to find in the present-day. During this time Moore also investigated a mound near Contentment Bluff about a mile and a half mile north of Shellman Bluff on the Bruro River.

Joseph R. Caldwell (1916-1973) conducted archaeological research at the Fort King George site in 1940 hoping to determine the precise location of the 1721 fortification constructed by Colonel John Barnwell and his South Carolina Rangers as a deterrent to potential Spanish aggression from the south. Caldwell's field work, perhaps unintentionally at the time, played an important role in eventually determining for scholars that the location of Mission Santo Domingo de Talaje/Asajo was on the later site of Fort King George, and not at the site of the nineteenth century sugar mill ruins at Elizafield on the Glynn County side of the Altamaha River as had been supposed by historians in the 1920s and 1930s.[85]

---

[84] For a review of nineteenth century agriculture in northern McIntosh County, including the Shellman Bluff area, see Buddy Sullivan, *Harris Neck and Its Environs: Land Use & Landscape in North McIntosh County, Georgia* (privately published: 2020); and Sullivan, *Early Days on the Georgia Tidewater*, op. cit., all editions.

[85] Portions of the following discussion relating to early archaeological research at the Fort King George site is based on Sheila K. Caldwell, "Archaeological Excavations at the Darien Bluff Site 9MC10 1952-53," edited by Mark Williams, Richard W. Jefferies and Mary C. Scales, University of Georgia, Laboratory of Archaeology Series, Report No. 81.

Caldwell conducted limited excavation and failed to locate any evidence of the fort, but he did discover the remnants of structures dating to the Spanish mission period, along with Spanish pottery consistent with seventeenth century Guale Indian pottery. Thus, Caldwell's excavations clearly lent credence to the possibility that the section of Lower Bluff one mile east of the later Darien town site, and where Fort King George was built in 1721, was the location of Mission Santo Domingo de Talaje.

Several test pits dug on the sandy bluff overlooking the Darien River marshes divulged the remains of fifteen graves containing the skeletons of adult males. Nearby, Caldwell found fragments of an aboriginal house that had burned and collapsed, perhaps resulting from the 1661 Chichimeco attack on the mission village, as discussed in the previous chapter. Found among the residue were several clay-lined pits containing whole and broken pottery vessels, among which were fragments of Native American pottery along with a fragment of a Spanish olive jar. The all-purpose olive jar was an essential piece of equipment in Spanish missions along the Guale coast (see photo page 84). It was utilized extensively by the Spanish in the sixteenth and seventeenth centuries for containing oil, wine, and various foodstuffs. Because of the utility of the olive jar, it might accurately be called the modern-day version of the cardboard box.

Finding a burial site on the bluff containing male skeletons was significant. McIntosh County historian Bessie Lewis had been researching the story of Fort King George since the 1920s, and the discovery of a burial ground made her even more certain the fort was located at Lower Bluff a mile east of Darien. Lewis was therefore naturally pleased with the findings of Joseph Caldwell's archaeological work. Although the signature footprint of Fort King George was still missing, the fifteen burials documented by Caldwell seemed certain to be those of part of its garrison largely composed of South Carolina rangers. The state historical commission later designated Lower Bluff as a historic site and marked the graves with simple white headstones. A marble marker was placed on the site near the burial ground relating the significance of Fort King George.

In 1952-53, shortly after her graduation from the University of Georgia, Sheila Kelly Caldwell (1929-1978), the wife of Joseph R. Caldwell, conducted more extensive archaeological investigations at the site of Fort King George than the earlier work by her husband. She extended Joseph Caldwell's 1940 test excavation further north and, in the process, discovered two additional military burials, and traces of a burned structure through which they had been dug. Additional olive jar fragments were also catalogued. In her notes, Sheila Caldwell observed that

"The first two weeks of work produced aboriginal and Spanish ceramics in context, and several large square post holes that were eventually to form a part of the outlines of a large European, but pre-English structure. The original lines of military burials were also extended. This area, the western edge of the park, was labeled Trench I. Along the right-of-way extending eastward from Darien were a series of discontinuous test trenches. The tests along the roadway were called Trench 2. The findings here were spotty due mostly to widespread modern disturbances. At one time a large part of this area had been leveled for use as an airstrip. It was clear however that the Spanish / Indian materials were concentrated at the eastern end of the bluff, which was also the site of Fort King George itself."[86]

---

[86] Ibid., 23.

During her 1952 season of field work, Caldwell discovered several structures which were determined to be from the Spanish period of occupancy of the site. One of these may have been the mission church of Santo Domingo de Talaje. Spanish period ceramics were found. One of the goals of Caldwell's work—and that of the Georgia Historical Commission—was to determine the location of the Christian cemetery that would have been associated with the mission and its Guale village. It was also felt that more military burials from the British occupation of the site in 1721-27 had yet to be located.

Caldwell noted that "At the end of the 1952 season we had managed, in the face of many trials to uncover the fallen palisade of Fort King George itself. It was identified purely on the basis of its location and the actual structural remains as again there was not a shred of associated material. Lying over two of the graves from the period of Fort King George was one of the tabby blocks which had served as foundations for a structure, presumably frame, which together with others traced in this part of the site."[87]

The following year, 1953, Caldwell unearthed evidence of additional structures, in addition to pits, post-molds and artifacts, all from the Spanish period of occupation of the site. She identified two distinct concentrations of structures and pits and labeled these as East and West villages. These were set back from the edge of the bluff overlooking the marsh and slightly north of the British soldiers'

---

[87] Ibid., 17. The tabby foundation remains near the military burial ground are from a ca. 1810 dwelling built by John Hampden McIntosh (1785-1825) and his wife Charlotte Nephew McIntosh. Buddy Sullivan, *Environmental Influences on Life & Labor in McIntosh County, Georgia* (privately published, 2018), 330.

burial ground. Caldwell interpreted the remains of one structure as being those of the mission church.

Meanwhile, local historian Bessie Lewis continued to work closely with the Caldwells in tandem with her own ongoing historical research relating to Fort King George.

Lewis (1889-1983), a native of Ohio, moved to McIntosh County with her parents as a child, and at an early age became interested in the history of the low country.[88] She was teaching school in Darien as early as 1916, even though her early training was in music. In 1929, she was accorded the status of official historian of McIntosh County, a title she was to hold for more than a half century.

In the mid-1920s, there came to light the South Carolina colonial papers of Colonel John Barnwell, commander of the Carolina Rangers who established Fort King George on the lower Altamaha River in the summer of 1721, a mile east of the later site of Darien. Barnwell's Journal and Report to Governor Francis Nicholson, first Royal Governor of the South Carolina colony, had been discovered among these obscure records, and the contents of the documents were published in the October 1926 issue of the *South Carolina Historical and Genealogical Magazine*.[89] Utilizing Barnwell's Journal, and its details relating to the location and construction of Fort King

---

[88] The present author has published a biography of Lewis and a collection of her writings. See Buddy Sullivan, *A Low Country Diary: Bessie Mary Lewis and McIntosh County, Georgia* (Charleston, S.C.: CreateSpace, 2016).

[89] Joseph W. Barnwell, "Fort King George: The Journal of Col. John Barnwell in the Construction of the Fort on the Altamaha in 1721," *South Carolina Historical and Genealogical Magazine* 27 (1926): 189-203.

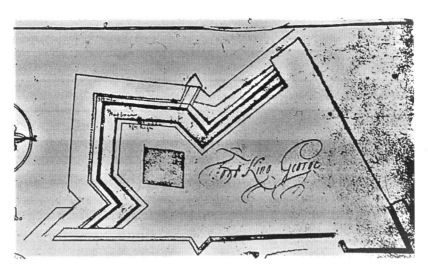

Barnwell's 1721 plan of Fort King George found in the British Public Records Office, London.

George, Lewis became the leading investigator in conducting the first serious historical research of the fort. The fort, and the subsequent early development of New Inverness (Darien), became the primary focus of her research for the rest of her long career, and made her the acknowledged authority on the two subjects for the remainder of her life.

The Barnwell papers helped Lewis definitively establish the actual site of the fort. Her continuing research probes, and her work with Joseph and Sheila Caldwell in the 1940s and 1950s, provided momentum for the archaeological field work conducted by the state at Fort King George. Plans and other documents relating to the building of a three-level cypress blockhouse were located in the British National Archives. In 1948 the Sea Island Company, though the initiative of Sea Island chief executive Alfred W. Jones, Sr., deeded the site of Fort King George to the state of Georgia for its development as a historic site.

Lewis's investigation of the Fort King George story established her as an authority on the history of colonial Georgia, and led to the publication in 1932 of her first important monograph, *The Story of Old Fort King George,* an account of Barnwell and the events surrounding the short history of the Altamaha outpost. Her persistent efforts in concert with the Georgia Historical Commission eventually led to recognition by the Commission of Fort King George as an official state historic site in the early 1960s, followed soon thereafter by the construction of a museum and interpretive center.

In 1953, partly behind the efforts of Lewis, plans were made for a paved access road to be built terminating in a parking area at the western boundary of the site. The road extended from the Darien bridge, a mile west, along the Darien River bluff to the fort site with access to the soldiers' burial ground and monument. Sheila Caldwell noted:

"Bessie Lewis felt that the planned road should be preceded by salvage archaeology along its proposed right-of-way. Salvage archaeology can be defined as archaeology done with the best methods that time permits for the purpose of rescuing historical and aboriginal material that are threatened with destruction. Bessie Lewis' willingness to verify her historical studies through archaeological methods, and her lively concern for the possible destruction of historical materials, are indications of an enlightened attitude. Many others, after the fiasco following the Ford excavations at Elizafield, felt that the work of the historian was best kept entirely separate from that of the archaeologist..."[90]

---

[90] Caldwell, "Archaeological Excavations," 22.

The tabby remains at Lower Bluff alluded to earlier added to the confusion among earlier historians and archaeologists, further fueling a controversy that had been ongoing since the 1930s over the provenance of coastal Georgia's tabby. In the 1920s and early 1930s much was written on a scholarly level about coastal tabby; one group favored the theory that the tabby ruins on Georgia's coast were those of seventeenth century Spanish missions, and another group, which subsequently proved correct, held that the ruins were those of early nineteenth century sugar houses and other plantation structures. An important scholarly treatment of the origins of Georgia tabby, and the procedure by which tabby was made and utilized in antebellum construction was published in 1937 as *Georgia's Disputed Ruins*, edited by Merton Coulter with the main evidentiary essays prepared by Savannah architectural historian Marmaduke Hamilton Floyd and Smithsonian Institution archaeologist James A. Ford. Floyd's research of ruins in McIntosh County, and Ford's archaeological field work at the tabby ruins at Elizafield plantation on the Glynn County side of the Altamaha debunked the tabby/mission theory.

Books had been published in the 1920s and early 30s that averred that the tabby ruins at Elizafield were those of the San Domingo de Talaje mission, which was subsequently determined to have been at Lower Bluff east of Darien, and that tabby remains at the Thicket, seven miles northeast of Darien overlooking Doboy Sound, were those of the Tolomato mission, which later scholarship determined was at Harris Neck. *Georgia's Disputed Ruins* was an important book, the product of significant research, particularly by Floyd whose essay proved that the coastal tabbies of McIntosh, Glynn and Camden counties were actually the remains of nineteenth century sugar mills and other plantation structures. The Thicket ruins proved beyond doubt that the "so-called" Spanish mission ruins there were actually the remains of William Carnochan's sugar mill and rum distillery which operated at the Thicket from 1816 to 1824. Some historians in the 1920s made misleading statements insisting that such ruins as those at the Thicket, at Spalding's Sapelo sugar mill, and Robert Grant's sugar mill at Elizafield on the Altamaha River, were attributable to the Spanish mission presence. The evidence presented in *Georgia's Disputed Ruins* proved otherwise. "Cherished ideas die hard; they only fade away slowly," noted Sheila Caldwell in her Lower Bluff report:

"In March of 1934 the owner of the tabby ruins at Elizafield, now widely believed to be the ruins of Santo Domingo de Talaxe, offered the 450 acre site on which the ruins stand to the state of Georgia as a state park, contingent upon a restoration. The offer was accepted, and in May, archaeologist James A. Ford, who had been recommended by the Smithsonian Institution, arrived at Elizafield to authenticate the mission and to recover anything buried there that might assist in the work of restoration. Unfortunately, Ford found nothing to indicate that the structure was of Spanish date and many finds that indicated it had been built in the period after 1825, and was a mill of some sort. These findings were available at the time a dinner given at Brunswick Georgia to announce the acceptance by the state of the ruins of Santo Domingo de Talaxe for development as a state park. The announcement was modified to read that, the ruins were now disclosed to be those of a sugar mill, but the site was indeed that of Santo Domingo. Ford was considerably annoyed because this statement was not substantiated in any way by his work at Elizafield."[91]

The findings contained in *Georgia's Disputed Ruins* received further

---

[91] Caldwell, "Archaeological Investigations," 20.

validity and substantiation three years later with the publication of Coulter's important work, *Thomas Spalding of Sapelo*. By then, the Spanish "mission myth" had completely been laid to rest.

The significance of Sheila Caldwell's excavations at Lower Bluff in 1952-53 cannot be over-stated. Her work found a portion of a Spanish mission and Guale complex that led to an increased understanding of Spanish and Native American lifeways patterns in the seventeenth century, and helped provide important clues to subsequent searches that led to the discovery of Mission Santa Catalina on St. Catherines Island, and San Joseph de Sapala on Sapelo Island.

Though Caldwell's 1950s work naturally focused on the Native American and Spanish occupation of the Lower Bluff site, her findings unavoidably dovetailed with the nineteenth and early twentieth century saw mill and lumber processing activities on the same land that once was the Spanish mission of Santo Domingo de Talaje and, later, Fort King George. Caldwell noted that "saw mill activity had been intense on this portion of the bluff, but our excavations recovered little that would be of use to any future student of industrial archaeology. We hoped in vain to located traces of a pit saw, a peculiar type said to have been in use in the Darien area perhaps as early as 1750.[92]

In 1819, a steam sawmill was constructed on the site of Fort King George at Lower Bluff, with water frontage on the Darien River.[93] It was soon after this that the two local mills came to be known

---

[92] Ibid., 17.
[93] The following discussion of saw mill activity at Lower Bluff is from Sullivan, *Early Days on the Georgia Tidewater*, op. cit., all editions.

familiarly as "Upper Bluff Mill" and "Lower Bluff Mill." In his memoir, "High Water on the Bar" (1951), Thomas Hilton noted that the Lower Bluff mill began as the "Darien Eastern Steam Saw Mill Co., incorporated Dec. 1820. John Kell, Chairman; James H. Gieke & Co., Gen. Agents; Charles McGregor, Secretary; William Carnochan and James H. Gieke as executors of William Dammett, deceased, proprietors of the Darien Eastern Steam Saw Mill, lately erected on the north branch of the river Altamaha, below the city of Darien." This sawmill was probably named "Eastern Steam Saw Mill" because of its situation on the eastern side of Darien, as opposed to the mill which had been erected earlier on the west side of town. In many respects, the Eastern Steam Saw Mill resembled the Upper Mill, its engine being of the improved Boulton & Watt English type.

Jacob H. Rokenbaugh operated the Lower Bluff sawmill before the Civil War; in 1866, the mill was mortgaged then sold to the northern firm of Young and Langdon. In 1877, Young and Langdon mortgaged the Lower Bluff mill, and in 1879 it was purchased by John W. Kimball of Boston, a transaction which led to the mill's acquisition by the Hilton Timber and Lumber Company soon thereafter.[94] In 1868, Darien's timber and lumber exports were exceeding twenty million board feet a year. By 1874, shipments surpassed 100 million feet for the first time.[95] Darien became an important factor on the international timber market, and several European consulates were established in the town. There had not been such a foreign influence since the 1830s when cotton exports reached their peak. The volume of

---

[94] The Hilton Timber & Lumber Company became the Hilton-Dodge Lumber Company in 1888 after a merger with the Dodge saw mill interests at St. Simons Island. Hilton-Dodge maintained the company's corporate headquarters in Darien.
[95] *Darien Timber Gazette*, July 18, 1874.

shipments generally increased until the all-time high was attained in 1900: 1868—20 million board feet of timber and lumber exported; 1874—100 million board feet; 1876—68 million board feet; 1881—99 million board feet; 1887—62 million board feet; 1888—83 million board feet; 1889—95 million board feet; 1897—101 million board feet; 1900—112.5 million board (peak year).

In 1895, the Darien and Western connected with the Florida Central and Peninsular Railroad in the western section of McIntosh County, and rail shipments of timber to Darien began. In 1905, timber began arriving for the first time at a new Hilton and Dodge sawmill at Lower Bluff. By then, heavy timber was in shorter supply, thus eliminating the need for large-scale steam-driven gang sawmilling. At Hilton and Dodge timber began to be processed by a smaller, circular sawmill built in 1905 alongside the old log basin.[96] The new Lower Bluff circular mill replaced the bigger gang saws since there was no longer enough available large timber. The smaller logs for the circular mill were floated into the basin and hoisted by cranes into the mill for sawing. Evidence of this activity can still be seen at the Fort King George Historic Site, although only foundations and the brick ruins of the fire-box remain amid a grove of cedars, and the log basin is filled with brackish marsh grass. A 1919 U.S. Geological Survey map of the Darien area delineates a spur track of the Georgia Coast and Piedmont Railroad leading from the main line just northeast of Darien to Lower Bluff, thus facilitating the transport of logs to the circular mill. At Lower Bluff, the G.C. & P. spur split into

---

[96] Buddy Sullivan, ed., *High Water on the Bar: An Operational Perspective on a Tidewater Timber Port with the Memoirs of Thomas Hilton* (Darien, Ga.: Downtown Development Authority, 2009), 32-33.

Circular saw mill at Lower Bluff, ca. 1905.

two tracks; one to Lower Bluff's wharves at which smaller coasting vessels continued to come for lumber; and the other by which milled lumber was shuttled from the Lower Bluff mill back along the spur to the main line.[97]

In 1913, the Savannah River Lumber Company assumed the operation of the Lower Bluff sawmill from Hilton-Dodge Lumber Company, and mill operations were continued there for ten years. Hilton-Dodge was defunct as a corporate entity by 1916.

A trickle of coastwise shipping, mostly sailing schooners, continued to load lumber at Darien during and just after World War I. A black-and-white photographic postcard of a lumber schooner moored at Lower Bluff is noted as being made in 1918. William Kelso, who conducted archaeological work at Fort King George for the Georgia Historical Commission in 1967, makes reference to the

---

[97] William M. Kelso, "Excavations at the Fort King George Historical Site, Darien, Georgia: The 1967 Survey," Georgia Historical Commission, Archaeological Research Series, No. 1, 1968.

"remaining old mill buildings at Lower Bluff being used for a short-lived handle factory" after Savannah River Lumber took over operations on the bluff. This is incorrect, as the handle mill was actually at Kell Creek a few hundred yards northeast of the Lower Bluff sawmill. A contemporary site diagram, circa 1915, delineates the Savannah River Lumber Company's circular sawmill at Lower Bluff and the log pond adjoining it (now filled with marsh) slightly northwest of the old gang sawmill. This would place the circular mill adjacent to the present-day museum building. The drawing shows the "Log Pond" contiguous to the circular mill. Ruins of the structure are adjacent to the north side of the present museum. On the same diagram, shown as a separate panel, is delineated the handle factory, known as the Altamaha Woodworking Company, "Manufacturer of Tool Handles." The diagram notes that the Savannah River Lumber sawmill at Lower Bluff was "one mile east of the McIntosh County court house" and that the handle factory was "one mile northeast of the court house." Since both facilities were shown on the same period diagram, it is easy to see how Kelso could have assumed the handle factory was also at Lower Bluff.

In 1923, Savannah River Lumber suspended operations at Lower Bluff, marking the end of lumber processing in Darien. Three years later, the Company sold the tract to the Sea Island Company. The general point of reference for the end of Darien's timber era could justifiably thus be set with the date of the 1926 sale of Lower Bluff.

Kelso's 1967 findings yielded additional evidence of Mission Santo Domingo de Talaje.[98] Kelso's excavations largely occurred in

---

[98] Ibid.

an area of the site just north of Sheila Caldwell's investigations fifteen years earlier, that is, in and around the Fort King George cemetery.

Beneath two levels of soil, Kelso found aboriginal ceramics and Spanish period artifacts, as well as structural remains. The structure was composed of several post-holes and slot trenches, and within these in the interior were found Spanish ceramics. "Specific dating of the construction and occupation [of the Guale structure] must be treated in general terms," Kelso noted in his report. "However, both the aboriginal and Spanish ceramics suggest that this particular structure was probably built an occupied sometime late in the Spanish Mission period."[99]

Kelso's analysis determined that the artifacts found, both Spanish and Native American, reflect a seventeenth century manufacture. Presumably, the artifacts would have pre-dated 1661. That was year an attack by rival Chichimeco warriors resulted in the destruction of the mission, compelling Santo Domingo de Talaje to be relocated from the mainland to the north end of nearby St. Simons Island as Mission Santo Domingo de Asajo.[100] A Spanish musket butt-plate found suggests a manufacture after 1676, after the mission site was abandoned. "Therefore, if the iron object excavated at the Fort King George site is a Spanish butt-plate then it was probably attached to a piece manufactured during the last quarter of the seventeenth century. Thus, the late seventeenth century dates of the iron objects, tenuous as they may be, combined with the dates of the San Marcos

---

[99] Ibid., 11.
[100] Worth, *Struggle for the Georgia Coast*, op. cit., 18. Worth places the probable location of the relocated mission at Cannon's Point.

ware and Spanish olive jar sherds suggest that the Indian structure [found earlier by Sheila Caldwell] was in use in the second half of the seventeenth century."[101]

Relevant to the lumber mill activity at Lower Bluff, Kelso noted that "the artifacts recovered in the [1967] survey also help to confirm the historical fact that an important industrial complex once existed at the Darien Lower Bluff. More specifically, the numerous bits of unfinished iron objects were found scattered among deposits of slag which hints that the sawmill blacksmith shop, reputed to have been included in the mill complex, did exist...Finally, the fragments of nineteenth century ceramics found at the site testify to the known fact that Americans generally relied on the importation of English pottery during this period."[102]

* * *

The original concept for Georgia was philanthropic in nature, as James E. Oglethorpe and John Percival, and their colleagues in Parliament originally envisioned a proprietary colony to assuage the problem of debtors in English prisons. But increasingly, the Georgia Trustees, established in London to oversee the affairs of the colony, entrusted Oglethorpe, with his acute military sensibilities, with the protection of the mercantile affairs of South Carolina against the increasingly resentful Spanish in Florida. Military considerations notwithstanding, Oglethorpe had an opportunity in 1733 to implement his formalized eighteenth century Savannah town plan (from the London model), based on a rigorous, preconceived layout

---

[101] Kelso report, 15. It is possible, perhaps even likely, that there was some degree of Guale presence at the Fort King George site after the mission was relocated to St. Simons in 1661.
[102] Ibid., 19.

of wards, squares and lots, the concept of which is very much in evidence today in the Savannah National Landmark Historic District.[103]

In 1734, Peter Gordon, colonial surveyor to Oglethorpe, produced a detailed survey of the new town of Savannah a year after its founding. This unique document is perfectly illustrative of the relationship between the written manuscript record and the evidence yielded from the ground—historical archaeology. Archaeologists can utilize the written record to determine with greater precision the provenance of their artifact discoveries. Conversely, the historian can learn a great deal about the people he is researching by the tangible evidence of their times, the surviving fragments of their lives.

Similar precepts may certainly be applied to our present case study, that of the historical ecology of coastal Georgia. The evidence from archaeological research conducted on Sapelo Island since 1975 has resulted in a rich yield of useful data from all eras of the human occupation of the coast, pre-Columbian and historical. Archaeologists have also surveyed former African American occupational sites throughout coastal Georgia, including extensive field investigations at such antebellum plantation sites as Butler's Island in McIntosh County, Cannon's Point at St. Simons Island, Marianna and Kings Bay in Camden County, and Julianton at Harris Neck. Some of the findings of this work will be seen in several of the essays that follow.

---

[103] The published *Collections of the Georgia Historical Society*, 21 volumes, 1840 to 1989, contain period manuscripts, account books, letters, documents and plans which detail the early years of the Georgia colony, including the development of Savannah.

Societe de Sapelo: The French in Coastal Georgia

Christophe Poulain DuBignon (1739-1825) was the son of a poor Breton aristocrat who used his involvement in the Sapelo venture as the catalyst for becoming one of the leading cotton planters in the region. DuBignon went to sea at the age of twelve, serving nearly four decades as a sailor and captain in the French India Company and Royal Navy. When the French Revolution erupted, this "bourgeois noble" was enjoying a comfortable retirement in Brittany at the age of fifty. As the trouble worsened, DuBignon looked to America as a place for his family to escape the turmoil in France.[104]

The French Sapelo Company began in February 1789, when Francois Marie Loys Dumoussay de La Vauve (1754-1794) purchased Sapelo from John McQueen for £5,000 sterling. The acquisition included the adjoining smaller islands of Blackbeard, Cabretta, and Little Sapelo. There were legal complications. McQueen filed a writ of attachment against Dumoussay for default of payment when the loss of a vessel used as partial payment for Sapelo was wrecked near Savannah. Additionally, McQueen, encumbered by debt at the time of the sale, fled to Spanish East Florida to avoid bankruptcy.

---

[104] The biography of DuBignon is Martha L. Keber, *Seas of Gold, Seas of Cotton: Christophe Poulain DuBignon of Jekyll Island* (Athens: University of Georgia Press, 2002), Keber's use of French manuscripts places the Sapelo Company in context, particularly the convoluted path taken in the formation of the Company. See also Kenneth H. Thomas, Jr., "The Sapelo Company: Five Frenchmen on the Georgia Coast, 1789-1794," *Proceedings and Papers of the Georgia Association of Historians*, 10 (1989): 37-64. Thomas' paper "de-mythologized" much of what had previously been written about the French period on Sapelo, correcting errors in the earlier literature.

McQueen's creditors subsequently filed a legal claim to Sapelo to satisfy the obligations. Dumoussay thus had no clear title to the island initially; the legalities regarding title were not resolved until 1791.[105]

Dumoussay returned to France to seek investors, and in the spring of 1790, Julien Joseph Hyacinthe Chappedelaine (1757-1794), a young nobleman and protégé of Dumoussay, became the first to join the venture. Chappedelaine subsequently reported the Sapelo possibilities to other prospective investors. "There is an enormous quantity of wild game," Chappedelaine wrote to his uncle, Picot de Boisfeillet, in July 1790. "Sapelo has a great deal of live oak and pine, immense meadows of one league and a half, and where the cattle feed always. The orange trees, lemon trees, and olive trees grow there...There is, my dear uncle, the *Eden.*" Chappedelaine then noted the primary purposes of this missive: "If you have any funds, they cannot be better employed."[106]

DuBignon was recruited by Chappedelaine, and soon thereafter, the Sapelo Company (*Societe de Sapelo*) was formalized in France in October 1790. In addition to DuBignon, Chappedelaine and Dumoussay, the consortium included Pierre Cesar Picot de Boisfeillet (1744-1800), Pierre Jacques Grandclos Mesle (1728-1806), and Francois Magon dela Villehuchet (1727-1794), the latter as a joint holder of his friend Grandclos Mesle's fifth share of Sapelo. Grandclos became important to the new Company from a financial

---

[105] The matter of finances relating to the lost vessel was resolved when McQueen returned to Georgia in 1791. See Walter C. Hartridge, ed., *The Letters of Don Juan McQueen to His Family* (Columbia, S.C., Georgia Society of the Colonial Dames of America, 1943), xxvii.
[106] Quoted in Keber, *Seas of Gold,* 149-50.

perspective—he was a wealthy shipowner from Saint-Malo, and thus gave the venture early financial stability. Grandclos did not plan to accompany the group to Georgia, preferring to remain in France to attend to his shipping business.

The Company purchased two houses in Savannah, and in February 1791, Dumoussay bought Jekyll Island from Richard Leake. Later, he acquired for the Company the southern half of St. Catherines Island. Though not a partner, another player had involvement with the Sapelo Company. Thomas Dechenaux (1767-1814), a Savannah commission merchant and fellow French émigré, came to represent the Company as a factor for marketing its agricultural commodities.

The complexities of the Company, and the precursor of its future legal and management difficulties, were manifested through the divergent personalities of its investors. In particular, Dumoussay's lack of transparency led to increasing friction, particularly on the part of DuBignon and Grand Clos. The prospects of profitability were amplified by the youth and free-spirited nature of several members of the syndicate. Dumoussay was thirty-six; Chappedelaine, at thirty-three, was the youngest, and his uncle, Boisfeillet, was forty-nine. Others of the group were older, which made the transition to a new country, particularly the inhospitable environment of Sapelo Island, more challenging. DuBignon was now fifty-one, Grandclos Mesle, who never went to Georgia, was sixty-two, and Villehuchet, who was at Sapelo only a short time was sixty-three.

Dumoussay's frequent duplicity, often leaving the investors in ignorance of what was transpiring, eventually led to animosity and a lack of trust in him. Dumoussay misled his colleagues by implying that the French navy would be the principal customer for Sapelo's live oak, with great profit to the investors. In fact, the French Revolutionary government declined to accept the Company's timber contract because it refused to incur the costs of shipping the oak from Georgia to France, information that Dumoussay neglected to report to the others.

In early 1791, Dumoussay fell delinquent on paying property taxes to Liberty County for the Company's Sapelo holdings, and to Glynn County for Jekyll, resulting in both islands being placed on public auction that spring. The collapse of the Company was only averted by the action of Villehuchet who bought Sapelo at the tax sale with his own resources, enabling the investors the opportunity to obtain separate title deeds to Sapelo by virtue of the island's resale by Villehuchet to his colleagues.[107]

By September 1793, fifteen slaves were jointly held by the investors. Others of the group purchased their own slaves—Dumoussay eventually had fifty-one slaves on Sapelo to manage his farming activities. Initially the partners owned the Sapelo land in common. A similar arrangement pertained to furniture, buildings, and a boat. The Company brought cattle to the island, and cultivated corn and sea island cotton. Hogs were raised on Sapelo's South End, but poachers from the mainland were a constant aggravation and hurt the prospects for profitability in raising livestock.

The shareholders occupied a communal house at High Point on the northern tip of Sapelo overlooking Sapelo Sound. The dwelling may have been constructed by the French in 1791, but it more likely

---

[107] Thomas, "Sapelo Company," 46-47.

was a house built ca. 1765 by island owner Patrick Mackay, and perhaps modified by the French. Sharing the house as a common residence was ill-conceived as events would prove. The arrangement was unsuitable due to the age differences of the investors, and their increasing disagreements.

Several partners planned individual houses on other parts of Sapelo. Dumoussay's dwelling was south of High Point near Spanish Fort (Shell Ring). DuBignon began "Bel Air" overlooking the ocean on the South End, a dwelling begun with two brick chimneys. DuBignon probably started this construction on or near the same plot of land in the oak grove upon which Thomas Spalding later built his South End House in 1810. DuBignon's house was never completed due to financial difficulties. DuBignon's one-fifth Sapelo share was the southern portion of the island on which he intended to cut and sell live oak timber. He also wanted to raise cattle at nearby Little Sapelo Island, a hammock across the Duplin River from Sapelo contiguous to his other South End properties, which he collectively called "Hermitage."[108] Also on the South End was Thomas Sterling, an overseer and mariner for John McQueen earlier and now possibly employed in a similar capacity by the Company. Sterling lived in a house near Marsh Landing apparently built before the French arrived. This dwelling was later utilized by Thomas Spalding and his family until the completion of South End House in 1810.

In January 1793, Boisfeillet and his family arrived at Sapelo; he began planting cotton and provision crops on a tract on the island's

---

[108] *Georgia Gazette* (Savannah), July 24, 1794. There is no site on Sapelo Island now named "Hermitage."

northeast side that later came to be called Bourbon Field. It was probably unrealistic to expect these initiatives to produce appreciable results. Boisfeillet lacked financial discipline, and his monetary commitments to the Company fell in arrears. Chappedelaine managed the day-to-day activities on the island while Dumoussay attended to the Company's tenuous financial affairs. Some useful work was accomplished: a new chimney was added to the High Point house, a salting house was built, and an east-west fence was constructed across the island.

Letters from Chappedelaine to DuBignon while the latter was visiting in France reflect the "highs and lows" of the venture: "Our crop has been extremely poor on Sapelo due to the bad weather," Chappedelaine reported in December 1791. "It is unbelievable how much fish of all kinds are in our creeks. Once we have built what is necessary we too shall take up fishing, but we must have at least 50 good negroes, [and] 4 good carpenters, to fell and bark our live oaks or green oaks for which there is a big market now..." In May 1792, Chappedelaine reported:

"Dumoussay arrived and has seen for himself the hell we live in—*nothing like experience for a teacher*. After months of patience nothing is accomplished. Grousse [Villehuchet], the old man, wants to go to Jekyl [sic], I to Blackbeard, you to Bel Air and I think Dumoussay will choose the Point or the Spanish fort. I sent Le Cou and Cabaret to Blackbeard to put up some hay...We have rearranged all your elegant kitchenware...Boiled beef and roast are what our cooking consists of—though we still do some grilling. The pans serve us as cups of which we drink plenty of beer. The small vine with little leaves of which there is a quantity around the house at the Point and which we mistook for a small creeper has many grapes, big ones in bunches of 8 or 10, well filled out. Dumoussay seems inclined to settle at the Spanish fort and to dig a small canal there for our boats. There are possibilities to make something pretty there by having by having about 10 negroes work there for 2 or 3 years. We will probably end by having our houses built at Savannah and have them brought here to use already made...The marsh near the old field of Mackay's is very good for hay. The grass which we burnt there is so thick and splendid we cannot walk there. Madame Belle's negro has finished cutting and thrashing the rice on Raccoon Bluff. We are going to Merritt's house on Blackbeard..."

"Madame Belle" may refer to Boisfeillet's wife. Le Cou and Cabaret were workers brought from France by the investors. The latter was much given to rum, and "was an ugly drunk, quarrelsome and violent, who tried to beat up the old man Villehuchet on one occasion."[109] Merritt's identity is uncertain but he was probably an overseer in the employ of the French.

Living arrangements were often unpleasant; Boisfeillet delayed in building a house at Bourbon because of title disputes with Dumoussay, a situation that caused increasing resentment on the part of the former. The relationship between Boisfeillet and Dumoussay had been acrimonious from the start, and was eventually to have serious consequences for the Company.

On their arrival in early 1793, Boisfeillet and his family moved into the Company's common house at High Point, a dwelling already occupied by Chappedelaine and Dumoussay. Because of ongoing friction with Boisfeillet Dumoussay tired of this situation, and began building another house at Spanish Fort one-and-a-half miles south of High Point. Increasing differences with his uncle compelled Chappedelaine to also depart the High Point residence several months later, and move in with Dumoussay. Dumoussay may have

---

[109] Keber, *Seas of Gold*, 171. The two letters from Chappedelaine to DuBignon quoted above were provided the author courtesy of Martha Keber in 1994.

built or utilized another house at Mackay's Old Fields (later Dumoussay Field), a 400-acre tract southeast of High Point that he acquired in the later division of property. It is more probable that a structure already existed at Old Fields, built by Patrick Mackay sometime after his 1762 acquisition of Sapelo. This dwelling may have been utilized by the Company for housing the French workers brought to Sapelo.

In the spring of 1793, DuBignon confronted Dumoussay over not having received title deeds to his Sapelo land; he renounced future financial responsibility for the Company's debts.[110] He subsequently negotiated a property exchange that enabled him to swap his share of Sapelo for the Jekyll shares of Dumoussay and Chappedelaine. By the end of 1793, DuBignon and his family had relocated to Jekyll.

Villehuchet had also become exasperated with the Company's management; embroiled in a contentious relationship with Chappedelaine, he returned to France in May 1792. Like DuBignon, Villehuchet had briefly entertained hopes of acquiring Jekyll for himself—"[B]oth Villehuchet and DuBignon may have had a heightened appreciation of Jekyll because of the therapeutic distance it afforded them from Chappedelaine and Dumoussay," DuBignon biographer Martha Keber notes perceptively.[111] A 1793 memorandum by the French consul at Charleston further validates the escalating discontent:

"I have given orders to receive the statement of Captain Dusolier, Commander, and of the crew of the little vessel from St. Domingue purchased by a French company that put in at Sapello [sic] Island.

---

[110] *Georgia Gazette* (Savannah), May 9, 1793.
[111] Keber, *Seas of Gold*, 182.

One of those who calls himself Comte de Chapeldelaine [sic] was obliged to trample the flag of this vessel under foot. His associates are named Poulain de Bignon, Marquis de Trois Feuilles [sic] and Duc Moussay [sic]. The rest of the partners live in France. Grand Clos-Mele of St. Malo is one. *They are all at daggers drawn and this establishment cannot maintain itself.*"[112]

When DuBignon left the partnership in May 1793 it precipitated the events that led to the end of the Company. Villehuchet and Grandclos Mesle also withdrew their investment, and called for a division of property. This was a serious blow since Grandclos, with considerable funds at his disposal, had theretofore provided much of the monetary support for the Company. At Dechenaux's request, the Liberty County Superior Court appointed arbiters to facilitate a Sapelo property settlement in the summer of 1793. The land, the fifteen commonly-owned slaves, livestock, equipment and furnishings were to be distributed equally among the investors once the Company's common debt had been settled. In September the investors approved the terms for the dissolution of the partnership. A formal agreement was then signed at Sapelo Island on November 18 outlining the distribution of land, cattle, and other property, with plans set for the following May to finalize the division of assets. Parenthetically, a witness to the agreement was Thomas Spalding, this apparently being the first official connection the young barrister had with the island that would be his plantation a few years later.[113]

---

[112] Richard K. Murdoch, "Correspondence of French Consuls in Charleston, South Carolina, 1793-1797," *South Carolina Historical Magazine* 74 (1973): 6-7, cited in Thomas, "Sapelo Company," 45.
[113] Superior Court Minutes, July 1793, Liberty County Records; Deed Book C (1794), 108-10, Liberty County Records; "Agreement between the Concerned in the Islands of Sapelo for the Liquidation of the Business," November 18, 1793, Record Group 21, box 116, NARA, Southeast Region,

The final disposition of assets in the spring of 1794 produced yet another argument between Dumoussay and Boisfeillet. The public sale of the Company's livestock was held at Sapelo on May 20. Furious over being left out of the auction arrangements, Boisfeillet publicly assailed Dumoussay, charging him with deliberately failing to notify him about the sale.

In June, Dumoussay sold the southern half of St. Catherines to Dechenaux for £500 but applied only his name to the deed of sale even though he and Chappedelaine had invested in the property jointly. On June 14, the final agreement was drawn up between Dumoussay, Chappedelaine, DuBignon, and Grandclos Mesle—the four investors who had shares of Jekyll Island—for the dispensation of property at Sapelo and Jekyll. Transfer deeds were signed whereby Dumoussay and Chappedelaine swapped their one-fourth shares of Jekyll to DuBignon in exchange for his one-fifth share of Sapelo, which the two would hold jointly until its sale. Six years later (1800), DuBignon purchased the remaining quarter share of Jekyll from the holdings of Grandclos. In the settlement Dumoussay received Blackbeard Island's 1,600 acres in addition to 400 acres at Mackay's Old Fields, the only land he owned on Sapelo itself at the time of his death three months later. Chappedelaine's portion was about 2,000 acres on Sapelo South End, including Hanging Bull. Boisfeillet's share was High Point, Bourbon Field, and Raccoon Bluff, in all about 1,800 acres. The net result was that Dumoussay and

---

Morrow, Ga., cited in Thomas, "Sapelo Company," 46-49, and Keber, *Seas of Gold*, 180. Sapelo Island was then apportioned to Liberty County, McIntosh County being created in December 1793.

Chappedelaine together now held sixty per cent of Sapelo and Blackbeard, and a little over fifty per cent of Sapelo itself.[114]

The end of the Sapelo Company was played out with death as the principal player. Villehuchet had departed for France in the spring of 1792, never to return. He was arrested, and executed by guillotine in June 1794, one day after his trial before the Revolutionary Tribunal. Grandclos Mesle nearly suffered a similar fate. In December 1793, he fled Brittany to London barely ahead of the Revolutionary authorities.

The final act was played out during five days in the late summer of 1794. Chappedelaine continued to argue with his uncle, Boisfeillet, over money. Adding to an increasingly combustible situation was the fact that Chappedelaine and Dumoussay were having trouble with their crops. Some of the island's eighty slaves on the island were stealing wood from the Company's corn barns to use in their own houses. The Company's white workers, some French, were often surly, frequently requiring Company-purchased rum to bribe them to work. Moreover, there was rising discontent between Dumoussay and Chappedelaine.

Dumoussay arrived at Sapelo from Savannah in mid-August. Two weeks later he fell seriously ill from fever, sank rapidly, and died on September 11, a Thursday. That weekend, Chappedelaine reviewed Dumoussay's papers in the house they shared, and realized he had been omitted from the latter's will executed the year before.

---

[114] *Georgia Gazette*, May 15, 1794, June 5, 1794, June 19, 1794, and July 24, 1794; deed of agreement between DuBignon, Chappedelaine, and Dumoussay, June 14, 1794, Deed Book R, 248-50, Chatham County Records; Deed Book CD, 300-01; Glynn County Records, recorded January 11, 1800; Thomas, "Sapelo Company," 48-49.

Chappedelaine thus spent a fretful weekend while preparations were made for Dumoussay's burial. His thoughts undoubtedly focused on the deceptions of Dumoussay, rather than his unexpected death, and the fact that he had been duped by his partner who owed him a considerable amount of money. Dumoussay was buried a day, perhaps two, after his death. The gravesite in the sandy soil above the marsh near the High Point house was obliterated over time, ravaged by tides, storms and erosion, eventually to disappear. A stone marker was later placed at the High Point grave.[115]

Four days after Dumoussay's death, on Monday, September 15, Chappedelaine had a final, fatal, confrontation with his uncle. Embittered by Dumoussay's treachery, Chappedelaine was in no mood for accommodation, for he undoubtedly attributed much of his misfortune to Boisfeillet. Words could not settle an argument with his uncle this time—a bullet would do that. During a heated altercation Boisfeillet shot and killed Chappedelaine, an occurrence announced in the *Georgia Gazette*: "...on Sapelo Island, the 15th instant, was unhappily deprived of existence, by being shot, M. Hyacinthe De Chappedelaine, aged about 40 years—a gentleman who while alive was beloved by his friends, respected by his acquaintances, and esteemed as a worthy member of society by the community at large. Mr. Picot Boisfeillet, of Sapelo, is in the custody of the Sheriff of this county, being charged with shooting the above gentleman."[116]

---

[115] Dumoussay probably died of food poisoning. His grave marker was recovered in the 1970s, and displayed at the University of Georgia Marine Institute. It is now on display at the Sapelo Island Visitors Center. The French burials are discussed later in this section.

[116] *Georgia Gazette*, September 25, 1794. The murder of Chappedelaine likely occurred at the house he was sharing with Dumoussay near Spanish

In a codicil to his will added two days before his death, Chappedelaine stipulated that he be buried at Hanging Bull, part of his land on Sapelo's west side. No evidence of his grave has been found there, and it is more likely that he was buried near Dumoussay at High Point. Boisfeillet was indicted for murder by a McIntosh County grand jury, but the charges were dismissed in early 1797.

As the only remaining partner on the island, Boisfeillet's later activities are murky. Part of the confusion is the provenance of the appellative *Bourbon* for one of Boisfeillet's holdings. It is likely that neither Boisfeillet nor his heirs named the tract "Bourbon" during the period of French ownership. Significantly, the use of the name "Bourbon" does not appear in any antebellum documents or plantation records that have come to light. Indeed, the name does not appear in primary documents until just after the Civil War. It has been suggested that Boisfeillet may have named the tract in respect to his supposed familial connections to the royal Bourbon family of France, but there is no evidence to support that thesis.[117]

Boisfeillet probably never built a house at Bourbon. While that may have been his early intent no evidence suggests that he ever attempted to build there.[118] When he arrived at Sapelo in early 1793, Boisfeillet and his family occupied the Company house at High Point. With his financial troubles, and the continued availability of

---

Fort, but it could have occurred at the High Point house then occupied by Boisfeillet.

[117] Boisfeuillet [sic] Genealogy, Picot B. Floyd Collection, Floyd and Boisfeuillet family papers, Collection 2044, GHS. Picot Floyd (1913-1989) was the son of Savannah architect-historian Marmaduke Hamilton Floyd (1888-1949), and Delores Boisfeuillet Floyd (1887-1966).

[118] Rachel Laura DeVan Perrine, "Bourbon Field: Preliminary Investigations of a Barrier Island Plantation Site," MA Thesis, University of Tennessee at Chattanooga, 2008.

the High Point dwelling, particularly after the deaths of Dumoussay and Chappedelaine, it is difficult to see how Picot would have felt compelled to construct a new dwelling at Bourbon. He thus almost certainly lived at the High Point house until his death in 1800.

Boisfeillet probably planted cotton and provision crops on Sapelo for several years, engaging John Lafong (1759-1819) as his overseer at Bourbon and Raccoon Bluff, the latter continuing to work for Boisfeillet's widow after Picot's death. About 1800, Lafong acquired Patterson Island through marriage, it being a marsh hammock near Teakettle Creek between Sapelo and the mainland; there he developed his own plantation.[119]

Boisfeillet is perhaps the saddest of the French investors. He was debt-ridden, inept as manager of his own affairs, and often petulant toward his colleagues. "He expects to reap without sowing, and believes it is possible to be well off with no work...such a partner, born rich, having never worked, would consume the profits without producing any," was the uncharitable assessment of Boisfeillet by Grandclos Mesle as early as October 1791.[120] The unhappy Boisfeillet died on August 13, 1800 at the age of fifty-six after having "lived out his last years prisoner to the decomposing remains of the Sapelo Company." He was buried the next day; no trace of his grave remains.

Boisfeillet was in such financial straits before his death that he sued the estates of both Dumoussay and Chappedelaine, realizing a

---

[119] *Darien Gazette*, August 30, 1819.
[120] Grandclos Mesle to Dumoussay, October 25, 1791, cited in Keber, *Seas of Gold*, 198. Grandclos Mesle and Dumoussay were unhappy with Boisfeillet, feeling the latter was evading responsibility for paying his share of the Company's expenses.

judgment in 1797 of three thousand dollars when balanced against money owed his late nephew. His will of March 1799 left his Sapelo property to his wife and children; his widow, Marie Anna Larmandie, died less than a year later, in March 1801 at the age of forty. Boisfeillet's one-fifth interest in the Company's holdings was divided into fourths among his children who began selling their father's properties in 1817. One of the Boisfeillet daughters, Servanne, received High Point, and her husband John Montalet administered the family's estate until his death in 1814.

As noted, the "Bourbon" place-name apparently was rarely used in the plantation era, for its appearance in a primary source document has not been found until 1871 in the A.C. McKinley journal.[121] Edward Swarbreck, owner of most of the North End of Sapelo Island, purchased Bourbon in 1817, or soon thereafter, from the Boisfeillet heirs, and may have built structures there for slaves or crop storage. He sold Bourbon to Charles Rogers as part of the latter's 1827 purchase of Chocolate, followed by Thomas Spalding's acquisition in 1843. The degree to which Swarbreck, Rogers and Spalding utilized Bourbon Field is uncertain. Rogers may have leased Bourbon and King Savannah to Thomas King, a planter from the McIntosh County mainland, for cotton cultivation in the 1830s. In her memoir Ella Spalding incorrectly notes that King owned Bourbon. However, King could have leased land there for a time before the tract came into Spalding's possession. If so, King did not long use the tract, for by 1840, he had moved to Bibb County,

---

[121] Buddy Sullivan, ed., *Postbellum Sapelo Island: The Reconstruction Journal of Archibald Carlisle McKinley* (privately published, 2020), 132 and 132n, journal entry of April 29, 1871.

Georgia. King's possible involvement with Bourbon also raises the possibility that King Savannah, a tract of grassland and pine woods contiguous to Bourbon and Raccoon Bluff, is named for him.

The 1859 Coast Survey chart of Sapelo Sound and the later 1868 topographic map, *Doboy Sound and Vicinity,* each note three structures at Bourbon near the creek leading to lower Dumoussay Field. The provenance of these buildings is unknown—they may have been placed by Swarbreck, Rogers or perhaps Randolph Spalding. Their purpose was likely for slave housing and cotton storage. A 1961 Sapelo map showing points of historical interest, possibly prepared for R.J. Reynolds or the Marine Institute, incorrectly notes "Traces of Home of Picot de Boisfeillet" on the upper part of Bourbon near the creek, but shows no other structures.

For the French Sapelo Company, legal complications continued for years. Three of the six partners were dead before the end of 1794, one by beheading, and two others by sickness and murder during a chaotic summer weekend. Dechenaux was executor of the estates of the latter two, but soon after Chappedelaine died, a nephew sued Dechenaux for what Dumoussay owed Chappedelaine. Chappedelaine had only three slaves, but had been led by Dumoussay to believe he had more. Dumoussay's land included Blackbeard, which because of debts, was sold in 1800 at public auction to the U.S. Navy Department. Eighty slaves owned by the French were included in the sale of Sapelo's South End to Thomas Spalding and Edward Swarbreck in 1802. By 1805 there were three co-owners who held over eighty per cent of Sapelo: Spalding, Swarbreck, and John Montalet.

Despite the Company's breakup, Sapelo was not devoid of activity in the period from 1795 until the appearance of Swarbreck and Spalding in 1801-02. Live oak cutting under contract was undertaken on both Sapelo and Blackbeard, and small-scale planting remained active. James Charles Anthony desVergers (d. 1806), a refugee of the Haitian slave revolt, lived on Sapelo in the late 1790s, probably as an overseer for agents of the defunct Company. Another French connection emerged from a Savannah newspaper notice reporting the death of Charles Francis Chevalier on Sapelo in December 1798. While no additional details were given, it may be that Chevalier, like desVergers, was an overseer or workman in the employ of agents of the Company, or perhaps someone employed by the Company who had remained on the island after the breakup.

There was another linkage to the Company after its dissolution. Louis Harrington, brother-in-law of Grandclos Mesle, left France in 1795, and settled in Savannah. In 1797 Harrington purchased the shares of Sapelo and Jekyll held by his brother-in-law and Villehuchet, the Sapelo share including the Chocolate tract. By 1799, he had also acquired the one-fifth Sapelo share held by Chappedelaine. Harrington sold his share of Jekyll to DuBignon in early 1800, and in 1801 sold Chocolate and other Sapelo North End land to Richard Leake and Edward Swarbreck. Harrington continued to live in Savannah until selling his remaining holdings and returning to France in 1810.[122]

---

[122] For desVergers, see the *Columbian Museum and Savannah Advertiser*, July 28, 1797 and June 7, 1806. For Chevalier, see *Early Deaths in Savannah, Georgia, 1763-1803* (Savannah: Georgia Historical Society, 1993). For Louis Harrington's ownership of Sapelo property, see the *Columbian Museum and Savannah Advertiser*, January 11, 1799.

John Montalet: Last of the French Legacy

John Montalet's path to Sapelo Island was as unusual as it was interesting. Montalet (1760-1814), French born as Jean Baptiste Mocquet, Montalet, was a planter on San Domingo (Haiti) who in 1797 migrated to Savannah in the wake of the Haitian slave insurrection.[123] In December 1798, Montalet purchased the Hermitage rice plantation on the Savannah River for $2,785.[124] Utilizing slaves brought from Haiti, Montalet cultivated rice at the Hermitage while settling comfortably into life among Savannah society. His obituary in the *Savannah Republican* in 1814 noted that Montalet had been "brought up amongst the most fashionable circles [and] retained the manners of an accomplished gentleman."

It was his local social interaction that led to Montalet's marriage in October 1802 to Servanne de Boisfeillet. The union was fortuitous for Montalet; Servanne was the daughter of the late Picot de Boisfeillet of Sapelo Island. Unfortunately, Montalet's marriage to Servanne was all too brief: "Tragedy ended this delightful existence," for on June 14, 1805, the Cathedral register recorded the interment "in the burial ground of the City of Savannah, Mrs. Servanne Angelique Charlotte Picot de Boisfeillet, native of France, aged about

---

[123] Kenneth H. Thomas, Jr., "Montalet of Savannah and Sapelo: The Man and the Myth," paper presented at the Georgia Historical Society, Savannah, November 1994; and Savannah Writers Project, Mary Granger, ed., *Savannah River Plantations* (Savannah: Georgia Historical Society, 1947), 429-32.

[124] Deed Book T (1798), 145, App. 14; 189, App. 15, Chatham County Records.

eighteen years, wife of John Berard Mocquet de Montalet, planter of the County of Chatham..."[125]

When her father died in 1800, Servanne Boisfeillet inherited Sapelo High Point. After his marriage to Servanne, Montalet administered High Point, Bourbon and Raccoon Bluff for the Boisfeillet children but he never owned the latter two tracts. In 1803, Montalet mortgaged the Hermitage and ten slaves for $6,000.[126] Also that year he purchased from the Dumoussay estate the 400 acres of Mackay's Old Fields on Sapelo's North End. However, his legal ownership of the tract is unclear since deed records indicate that Montalet had not actually paid for the property at the time of his death in 1814.[127]

After his wife's death, and with Hermitage mortgaged, Montalet relocated to High Point, residing in the house overlooking Sapelo Sound occupied earlier by the Sapelo Company. He made improvements to the residence, adding a piazza with an expansive view of the Sound, and planted crops utilizing slaves brought to the island from Savannah. Montalet grew sea island cotton at the Old Fields, and supposedly possessed about one hundred slaves.[128]

A connection between Sapelo and Cumberland islands involved Montalet and another Frenchmen. Peter Bernardey (1784-1827) spent part of his childhood on Sapelo during the French ownership, later migrating to Cumberland where he planted cotton. In a

---

[125] *Savannah River Plantations*, 430, 431.
[126] Deed Book Y (1803), 4, App. 16, Chatham County Records.
[127] Thomas, "Montalet of Savannah and Sapelo."
[128] Montalet's slave dispositions are from Thomas, "Montalet of Savannah and Sapelo." His ownership of as many as a hundred slaves on Sapelo is probably excessive.

promissory note in December 1810, Montalet agreed to pay Bernardey $400 from his next cotton crop, then a month later promised to pay an additional $100 from his current harvest. Repayment was never made, for in 1816, Bernardey successfully brought suit against Montalet's estate for recovery of the two sums of money.[129]

Montalet never remarried, living on Sapelo until his death in June 1814. Noted the *Savannah Republican*: "Died on the 3rd instant at his plantation on Sapelo, Marquis de Montalet, aged [fifty-four] years. This gentleman was esteemed and respected by his friends and acquaintances…Poor Montalet! May thy soul rest in peace is the prayer of one who loved thee sincerely."[130] Like his French countrymen who preceded him to Sapelo, Montalet died having very little of his own, and was encumbered by debt. He was ten years delinquent on his local property taxes at the time he died, and Chatham County records show that he had a debt of $5,369, which the auction bid for the sale of Hermitage failed to cover. Francis Hopkins, an executor of Montalet's estate, acquired "Montalet's Point" (High Point) shortly after the latter's death, and owned the tract and the house at the time of his own death in 1821.[131]

A footnote to the Montalet story emerged a century later. In 1912, several litigants claiming to be Montalet descendants attempted to sue for land comprising a portion of the town of Nancy, France, in the name of the family of Leopold LeFils. The suit claimed the property was owned by Montalet at the time of the French

---

[129] Wayne-Stites-Anderson Papers, Collection 846, GHS.
[130] *Savannah Republican*, June 11, 1814.
[131] Deed Book 2I (1815), 336, App. 17, Chatham County Records; Thomas, "Montalet of Savannah and Sapelo."

Revolution. This unusual action was filed by, among others, James A. LeFils of Omaha, Nebraska. James LeFils was the son of Armand LeFils (1790-1875), a long-time McIntosh County civic official. The younger LeFils argued that his (supposed) grandfather, Montalet, "acquired Sapelo Island by purchase and established a French colony on the north end of it. Walls of ruined buildings now mark the residence of this famous refuge..." A brother, William W. LeFils of Jefferson County, Alabama, claimed in a separate deposition:

"the lawful son of Armand LeFils, who was a son of Marquis de Montleley [sic]...That affiant was born December 12, 1832 and when about fourteen years of age accompanied his father Armand LeFils to Sapelo Island and on the north end of that island, at what is known as Sapelo High Point, his father pointed out to him the grave of affiant's grand-father, the Marquis de Montleley. That affiant's grand-father lived on said island and was buried near his residence, his being the only grave of a white person buried on the island."

Armand LeFils was clearly not the son of Montalet, but rather that of Bernard Robert LeFils and Elizabeth LeFils, the former a Savannah merchant and factor. The LeFils-Sapelo connection is established by virtue of the elder LeFils being a business associate of Christophe DuBignon and Dumoussay de La Vauve of the Sapelo Company. LeFils had traveled on the same vessel that conveyed the two Frenchmen from Brittany to Savannah in early 1791.[132]

Dumoussay, Chappedelaine, and Boisfeillet were all interred on Sapelo. The grave referenced in the 1912 affidavit could as easily have been that of Dumoussay, marked by a stone tablet at the time, rather than that of Montalet. This story assumes additional mystery

---

[132] Lefils Family Affidavit, Collection 490, Folder 1, GHS; Thomas, "Sapelo Company," 40. In his will Dumoussay left bequests to Bernard LeFils and his family.

when, in an April 1912 deposition, several McIntosh County residents

"who depose and say that they are thoroughly familiar with Sapelo Island and know of their own knowledge that there are two and only two graves of white people on that certain portion of Sapelo Island known as Sapelo high point, or within four miles thereof, and that one of these graves contains the remains of Frances Maria Lois Demossey [sic], and the other grave, now unmarked by a stone, contains the remains of the Marquis de Monteley [sic]—as shown by a certain head stone known to deponents to have been in place at the grave—but which has now disappeared—its location being unknown to deponents—but is supposed by them to have been buried by the great gale of October 2nd 1898, which said storm did great damage to the burying place, so much so that the bones of the said Marquis de Monteley had to be removed quite recently to another place for re-interment."[133]

In his 1914 memoir, Charles Spalding Wylly notes that in the 1830s Charles Rogers placed a marble slab from Montalet's grave over his barn at Chocolate, "and for years there was nothing to mark the lonely grave on High Point as Montalet's save tradition. In the tidal wave of 1898, the sea encroached, tore open the grave, and scattered the bones upon the shore." The Wylly reference is conjectural, for the "scattered bones" could have been those of Dumoussay, or possibly Boisfeillet. Concomitantly, there may be some veracity to Wylly's account. A marble slab from Montalet's grave could have found its way to Chocolate, several miles south of High Point. Embedded in the façade of an outer wall of the tabby barn, which still stands, is a marble block on which is inscribed the

---

[133] Lefils Family Affidavit. The local citizens deposed in 1912 were C.O. Fulton (d. 1911), executor, Charles L. Bass (1853-1919), Sarah S. McKinley (1844-1916), and Alexander Duplin McIntosh (1828-1915).

date of the building's construction, 1831, and Rogers' initials. Could this have come from a Montalet gravestone at High Point?

The location of the graves of Montalet and his three French predecessors is unknown, although Montalet was likely buried near his High Point house. Unless his marker is a part of the Chocolate barn, the question remains as to why no headstone has been found for Montalet, even though one was discovered for Dumoussay. The affidavit's reference to "ruins" is probably to the tabby foundations of a house built at High Point just after the Civil War, not to a structure built or rebuilt on the same site by the Sapelo Company. Neither Patrick Mackay nor the French used tabby, but there is a possibility Montalet did on the counsel of Spalding who was using tabby in his South End structures at the time Montalet came to Sapelo. The tabby remains (still visible) are more likely the foundations of the house built on or near the original house site by postwar North End owner John Griswold. That being the case, a good argument could be made that the tabby came from blocks sawn at Chocolate for Griswold.

Land Use & Landscape: Antebellum Sapelo Island

The outstanding example of an innovative planter employing the ecosystem of the tidewater, with all its various elements, in the implementation of his agrarian pursuits was Thomas Spalding of Sapelo. Spalding was a remarkable man. He possessed the essential qualities to be a successful planter: finely-tuned agricultural sensibilities, procedural discipline, and a thorough understanding of his local environment. Spalding was imbued with an unusually strong sense of *place*, with a concomitant belief in the *permanency* of place, a philosophy that equipped him with the insights that underlay his inquisitive nature and predilection for innovation. His localist perspective enabled him to make the ecology of the tidewater work for him. Spalding fully understood the salutary effects of his local environment—temperate climate, river hydrology, ideal soil conditions for cotton, cane and rice—upon efficient crop methods and production. He was possessed of great capacity for interpreting local weather phenomena, reflected in a sagacious awareness of the cyclical nature of temperature variations, and the effects of soil conditions, wind, water and tides on his planting systems. Spalding usually correctly anticipated the first and last frosts of the season, and make distinctions between rainstorms, northeasters and hurricanes. His propensity for "sensing" relative humidity, the degree of barometric pressure, and other conditions was an important component in the efficacy of his crop management. Spalding was thus the consummate "scientific farmer" and, ipso facto, one of the most efficient plantation owners on the tidewater.

Spalding was born at Frederica, St. Simons Island, on March 25, 1774, the only child of James and Margery McIntosh Spalding. He was descended from the Spaldings of Perthshire, Scotland, who held title to the Barony of Ashantilly, and the McIntosh family (Mohr) of Inverness, Scotland. James Spalding (1734-1794) came to America about 1760, and soon thereafter entered into a partnership with Donald Mackay of Savannah to open trading houses in Georgia and East Florida. Following Mackay's death in 1768, Spalding collaborated with Roger Kelsall, and established a trading post at Frederica, living there in a house, Orange Hall, originally built for James Oglethorpe. In 1772, Spalding married Margery McIntosh (1754-1818), daughter of William McIntosh of St. Andrews Parish. Her grandfather was John Mohr McIntosh, leader of the Highland Scots at New Inverness (Darien) in 1736.[134]

A Loyalist during the Revolution in order to protect his interests, Spalding and his family refugeed to British East Florida where he and Kelsall operated several trading posts.[135] Spalding's properties were confiscated by the state of Georgia near the end of the war, but despite being almost ruined financially Spalding, in July 1783, successfully petitioned the legislature to be removed from the confiscation list of Loyalist properties, and thus retain many of his

---

[134] The Ashantilly estate was originally awarded to Sir Peter Spalding by Robert the Bruce in recognition of the former's exploits at Berwick Castle in 1318. E. Merton Coulter, *Thomas Spalding of Sapelo* (Baton Rouge: Louisiana State University Press, 1940), 1-10, cover Spalding's early life. See also Buddy Sullivan, *Thomas Spalding, Antebellum Planter of Sapelo* (privately published, 2019).

[135] Allen D. Candler, *The Revolutionary Records of the State of Georgia* (Atlanta, 1908) 1:146. For James Spalding's activities during and after the Revolution, see Wilbur Henry Siebert, *Loyalists in East Florida, 1774-1785* (Deland, Fla.: Florida State Historical Society, 1929), 9-10.

pre-war holdings.[136] In 1786, Spalding acquired 800 acres on the south end of St. Simons, which he named Orange Grove (later Retreat), and by 1790 possessed about 5,550 acres, and ninety-four slaves. He was among the first to cultivate sea island cotton after the Revolution. Spalding died in November 1794 at the age of sixty.[137]

Thomas Spalding acquired his formal education in Massachusetts, after which he studied law at Savannah under the tutelage of the prominent jurist Thomas Gibbons, being admitted to the Georgia bar in 1795. Later that year, Spalding married Sarah Leake (1778-1843), the only child of Richard and Jane Martin Leake.[138] A surgeon from Cork, Ireland, Leake (1747-1802) successfully planted cotton at Jekyll Island, for which he had become administrator in 1784, being the son-in-law of the owner, the late Clement Martin. In 1791, Leake sold Jekyll to the Sapelo Company, and later moved to Belleville on the Sapelo River where he leased land from the Troup family before purchasing the tract in 1795. There he cultivated cotton, provision crops and citrus. The Spalding couple resided briefly at Orange Grove where Spalding managed the legal affairs of his late father as well as continuing cotton operations. The father-in-law, Leake, occasionally expressed frustration with Spalding's St. Simons activity, apparently due to the displacement of his daughter some distance from Belleville. In a rather churlish epistle to Spalding in 1797, Leake complained, "It is somewhat astonishing that you can be so blindly partiall [sic] to the spot you are on as to make it a residence when you must experience the want of everything that can make a

---

[136] Candler, *Revolutionary Records of Georgia*, 3:255.
[137] *Georgia Gazette* (Savannah), November 13, 1794.
[138] Ibid., November 12, 1795.

family happy." Leake's petulance was founded on selfish motives—he was weary of commuting by water between Belleville and Orange Grove for visits.[139]

Following a term in the Georgia senate, Thomas and Sarah, in 1800-01, spent a year and a half in England and France during which time Spalding made important London financial connections. In 1803-04, Spalding again served in the state senate then won a disputed election to the U.S. House of Representatives for 1805-06, losing his bid for reelection in 1806. Merton Coulter, Spalding's biographer, notes that Spalding "was never an ambitious man for personal glory. The national political scene, he had now found out, was not more attractive to him because it was bigger than the Georgia scene; in fact, he liked the Georgia scene better, and was never, throughout the rest of his life, to wander very far away from it. He was a broad-minded localist in the most refined Jefferson sense."[140] Spalding again served in the state senate, 1808-10, and 1812-14.

Spalding's acquisition of land on Sapelo Island began with his father-in-law's 1791 sale of Jekyll Island to the French consortium, and Leake's subsequent interaction with several of the French investors. In 1801, while the Spaldings were in England, Leake and Edward Swarbreck began negotiations with Louis Harrington of Savannah for purchase of the latter's land on the South End of Sapelo formerly owned by the French company, and tracts on the North End, including Chocolate. The Chocolate transaction was

---

[139] Richard Leake Account Book, 1785-1801, and Richard Leake to Thomas Spalding, November 28, 1797, both in Spalding Family Papers, Collection 750, series 9, box 2, GHS.
[140] Coulter, *Thomas Spalding*, 31.

completed in 1801. In March 1802, after the Spaldings' return from Europe, Leake died unexpectedly in Savannah of an undisclosed "short but severe illness of five days." He left his estate to his daughter Sarah to be administered by her husband.[141] Thus Spalding acquired a half-interest in Chocolate with Swarbreck.[142]

With Leake's death it was left for Swarbreck and Spalding, as executor of his father-in-law's estate, to complete the negotiations with Harrington for the purchase of about 5,000 acres of upland and marsh on Sapelo's South End. This transaction gave Spalding a half-interest with Swarbreck in the South End before the end of 1802, as well as Chocolate earlier. When combined with a later purchase of additional South End land from Harrington Spalding became owner of a sizeable amount of property. By 1804 he was owner or co-owner of about three-fourths of Sapelo.[143]

---

[141] Family Bible, Spalding Family Papers, box 3, GHS.

[142] Spalding and Swarbreck were previously connected, probably through Spalding's father-in-law, Richard Leake, having exchanged correspondence as early as 1799.

[143] The seventy-five per cent ownership is calculated thusly by Kenneth H. Thomas: Spalding was co-owner with Swarbreck of the South End, one-fifth, and the Chocolate tract, one-fifth; Spalding was probably sole owner of the former DuBignon tract, one-fifth, "which would be sixty per cent of the Sapelo Company's holdings. Since only 400 acres was given to Dumoussay [Mackay's Old Fields], Spalding's theoretical 6,000 acres out of the eighteenth century estimate of 7,800 acres would then be seventy-five per cent." The 1760 Yonge and DeBrahm survey actually listed 7,700 acres of high land on Sapelo, and 220 acres on Little Sapelo Island and adjoining hammocks. Thomas, "The Sapelo Company: Five Frenchmen on the Georgia Coast, 1789-1794," *Proceedings and Papers of the Georgia Association of Historians* 10 (1989): 64, n. 123. See also "Some Memoranda in Relation to Thomas Spalding, late of Sapelo Island, by his son, Charles Spalding," June 1878, Spalding Family Papers, series 2, box 1, item 16, GHS. Professor Coulter makes no mention in his Spalding biography of Leake and Swarbreck's involvement in the purchase of South End.

A loan from British bankers enabled Spalding to finance his South End acquisitions, with additional funds coming from the sale to William Page in 1804 of his Orange Grove house and 300 acres on St. Simons for $10,000.[144] There is no surviving documented confirmation, but Spalding and Swarbreck presumably later swapped their respective half-interests, giving Spalding sole possession of the South End, and Swarbreck ownership of Chocolate. Whether this occurred in the 1804-06 timeframe is unclear. It could be that the agreement between the two occurred later based on the ambitious construction of buildings at Chocolate ca. 1815-20, in which Swarbreck and Spalding apparently collaborated.

Spalding thus began building his antebellum plantation empire, the only period in Sapelo's history in which the island was profitable to its owner. He never owned the entire island. By the time of his death in 1851, Spalding held everything but Raccoon Bluff in the east-central section of Sapelo, nearly 1,000 acres of upland and marsh. Other acquisitions were Black Island near Darien, Sutherland's Bluff on the Sapelo River, and Cambers Island in the Altamaha delta. The 1825 McIntosh County tax digest shows Spalding as the largest local landowner with 7,910 acres of cultivable land, this being before he acquired additional acreage on Sapelo's North End in 1843. He was the second largest slave owner in the county to the Pierce Butler estate, and paid $199 in taxes in 1825,

---

[144] Glynn County deeds, 1804, in Spalding Family Papers, series 1, box 1, GHS. C.S. Wylly, "The Story of Sapelo" (unpub. ms., 1914), states that Spalding received a loan of $100,000 from London bankers at 3½ per cent interest, payable in ten years. William Page later expanded his holdings on the south end of St. Simons, renaming the Spalding tract Retreat.

compared to the Butlers' $257.[145] Spalding brought "slaves, sea island cotton, rice and sugar cane to Sapelo Island, along with considerable organization and energy...and placed great emphasis on the permanence of his empire."[146]

* * *

To know Spalding it is necessary to understand the exceptionalist approach he took in implementing his farming methods. In his era he was often considered different, occasionally even radical, in some aspects of his techniques. His experiments resulted in successful implementation of crop rotation and diversification, and his planting of sugar cane enabled him to be the first Georgian to manufacture sugar commercially.

Concurrent with his sugar making, Spalding established a technological paradigm for the use of tabby in the construction of his mill works. The promulgation of his cane and tabby methods were such that they were emulated by many of his contemporaries. The remains of tabby buildings at Sapelo, and elsewhere in coastal Georgia, are testimony to Spalding's resourcefulness. These ubiquitous monuments to his vision serve as tangible reminders of the influence he had on his times. He delighted in sharing his successes with his contemporaries, but did so only after a suitable period of experimentation to determine that his concepts were sufficiently sustainable within the fabric of local environmental conditions.

---

[145] McIntosh County Tax Digest, 1825, GDAH.
[146] Emory M. Thomas, "The South and the Sea: Some Thoughts on the Southern Maritime Tradition," *Georgia Historical Quarterly* 67 (Summer 1983): 160.

Spalding was a leader in the cultivation of sea island cotton, setting enduring standards for the production of that staple. Spalding pursued an agrarian philosophy predicated not only on the cultivation of his money staples—cotton and cane on Sapelo, and rice in the Altamaha delta—but also on the secondary provision crops by which he sustained his labor force and livestock.

Spalding's motives regarding crop rotation and diversification were synonymous with his fervent regionalism. He wanted to retard the western migration of Georgia farmers by improving agricultural conditions in the east; history has shown, however, that the westward population flow remained unchecked throughout the nineteenth century and farmers who remained in the southeast "seemed determined to live or die on staple crops.[147] Spalding noted, "I will repeat what I say, the more strongly to impress this great agricultural truth upon your minds. That in the skillful alteration of green crops, and grain crops, the whole theory of agriculture rests; and I invite your attention to the examples which confirm it."[148]

An example of Spalding putting his ideas to work was in the cultivation of sugar cane as a secondary staple crop to supplement his cotton. His success in this regard is validated by his reporting earnings of $12,500 from his sugar crop in 1814.[149] The end of the War of 1812 brought non-importation and embargo acts and thus led other local planters to pursue the culture of sugar cane. His

---

[147] King, ed., Georgia Voices, 123.
[148] Thomas Spalding, "Union Agricultural Society," American Farmer VII (1825-26): 186.
[149] Thomas Spalding, "On the Cultivation of Sugar Cane, Erecting of Proper Buildings and Manufacturing of Sugar," Southern Agriculturist II (February 1829): 55.

creativity was not confined to Sapelo. For his planter contemporaries who grew rice in the nearby Altamaha delta, including his son Charles who cultivated the commodity at Cambers Island, Spalding devised in 1835 a system of transporting rice bundles from the fields to the threshing works by building wooden rollers, carts and rail tracks, with planks over the rice canals and ditches "to render great and important benefits, as well to the servant as to the master of the plantation." It was typical Spalding calculation—easing the labors of his bondsmen while simultaneously enhancing operational profitability. Rice was planted in April and harvested beginning in September. Cotton was planted between mid-March and early April while picking began in late August and continued until early December. Cane planting began in mid-October, and was harvested in the fall of the following year from late October into December, after the rice had been harvested and cotton picking was well along.[150] Although Spalding worked diligently to further his sugar endeavors, the true cash crop at Sapelo was sea island cotton.

Because both long staple and short-staple cotton were the most profitable crop commodities for the antebellum tidewater planters, it will be useful to assess the staples from the perspective of the ecological characteristics of the section. Sea island cotton was first introduced into the United States by several coastal Georgia planters, including James Spalding of St. Simons Island, shortly after the American Revolution.

Sea island cotton was introduced into the United States on a systematic basis by several Georgia planters simultaneously soon after the American Revolution although there is some evidence the staple

---

[150] Thomas Spalding, "On the Culture of the Sugar Cane," *Southern Agriculturist* I (1828): 553.

was cultivated sporadically in tidewater Georgia in the years just before the Revolution. The strain of long-staple, or black-seed, cotton developed from seeds sent to Georgia planters from the Bahama islands, and the West Indian island of Anguilla. Thomas Spalding noted that his father, James Spalding, received his first Anguilla seeds in the winter of 1786, and planted them the following spring. Anguilla sea island cotton quickly became the preferred variety among coastal planters in Georgia and South Carolina.

Some accounts have the first sea island cotton being produced earlier: writing in the *Southern Agriculturist* in 1844, Spalding himself noted, "The first bale of Sea-Island cotton that was ever produced in Georgia was grown by Alexander Bissett, Esq., of St. Simons Island, I think in the year 1778. In the winter of 1785 and 1786, I know of three parcels of cotton seed being sent from the Bahamas, to friends in Georgia; Col. Kelsall sent to my father a small box of cotton-seed; the surveyor Genl. of the Bahamas, Col. Tattnall, sent to his son, afterwards Governor Tattnall of Georgia, a parcel of cotton-seed; Alexander Bissett's father, sent a box of cotton-seed to his son in the year 1786; this cotton gave no fruit, but the winter being moderate, and the land new and warm, both my father and Mr. Bissett had seed from the rattoon, and the plant became acclimatized." Nicholas Turnbull, in a November 1799 letter to the *Georgia Gazette*, made no mention of Spalding or Bissett, averring instead that the first sea island cotton was cultivated by John Earle of Skidaway Island in 1767. Turnbull added that he grew black seed cotton at Whitemarsh Island in 1787, and shipped it to England, adding further that "Old

Mr. Patrick M'Kay, on the Island of Sapelo, planted cotton as a crop. These are facts well known..."[151]

Writing to the editors of the *Savannah Georgian* in the spring of 1828, Thomas Spalding provided a detailed account of sea island cotton in Georgia:

"It has been intimated to me that possibly this notification has originated in some one desirous of information and as I am at present the only person alive who recollects distinctly the introduction of the sea island cotton. It is known to many that cotton was cultivated for domestic purposes from Virginia to Georgia, being anterior to the Revolutionary War. Jefferson speaks of it in his *Notes on Virginia*. Bartram speaks of it in his *Travels* as growing in Georgia. And I have understood that twenty-two acres were cultivated by Col. [Philip] Delegal upon a small island [Skidaway] near Savannah before the Revolution; but this was the green seed, or short staple cotton. Just about the commencement of the Revolutionary War, Sir Richard Arkwright had invented the Spinning Jenny, and cotton ginning became a matter of great interest in England. Cotton rose much in price, its various qualities attracted notice, and the world was searched for the finer kinds. The Island of Bourbon was alone found to produce them, and yet the Bourbon cotton greatly resembled in its growth our green seed cotton...The Revolutionary War ended in 1783 [and] England offered to the unhappy settlers of this country who had followed her standard a home in but two of her provinces. To the provincials of the north she offered Nova Scotia. To the provincials of the south she offered the Bahama Islands. Many of the former inhabitants of the Carolinas and of Georgia passed over from Florida to the Bahamas with their slaves, but what could they cultivate? The rocky soil and arid lands of those Islands could not grow sugar-cane. Coffee would grow but produced no fruit. There was one plant that would grow and that bore abundantly, it was cotton. The seed, as I have been informed by respectable gentlemen from the Bahamas, was in the first instance produced from a small island in the West Indies celebrated for its

---

[151] Thomas Spalding, "On the Cotton Gin and the Introduction of Cotton," *Southern Agriculturist* 4 (1844, new series): 106-111; *Georgia Gazette*, November 28, 1799. "The Beginning of Cotton Cultivation in Georgia," *Georgia Historical Quarterly* 1 (March 1917): 39-45.

cotton, called Anguilla. It was therefore long after its introduction into this country called *Anguilla seed.*

"The quality of the Bahama cotton was then considered among the best grown…The winter of '86 brought several parcels of cotton seed from the Bahamas to Georgia. Among them (in distinct remembrance to my mind) was a parcel to the late Governor Tattnall of Georgia; and another parcel at the same time was transmitted by Col. Roger Kelsal, of Exuma (who was among the first if not the very first successful grower of cotton) to my father, Mr. James Spalding, then residing on St. Simons Island, Georgia, who had been connected in business with Col. Kelsal before the Revolution. I have heard that Governor Tattnall, then a young man, gave the seed to Mr. Nichol Turnbull, lately deceased, who cultivated it from that period successfully. I know my father planted his cotton in the spring of 1787 upon the banks of a small rice field on St. Simons Island. The land was rich and warm; the cotton grew large and blossomed, but did not open its fruit. It however rationed, or grew from its root the following year. The difficulty was now over. The cotton adapted itself to the climate and every successive year from 1787 saw the long staple cotton extending itself along the shores of Georgia where an enlightened population, engaged in the cultivation of indigo, readily adopted it"[152]

As confirmed by Spalding, several coastal planters simultaneously experimented with sea island cotton for the first time in 1787, including James Spalding at St. Simons, Richard Leake at Jekyll Island, Francis Levett at Harris Neck, and Nicholas Turnbull and others in the Savannah area. Although his father had been among those who started sea island cotton cultivation on the southeast coast, Spalding affirmed that being the first to grow the staple could not be attributed to one person.[153]

---

[152] Thomas Spalding, in *The Athenian* (Athens, Ga.), June 17, 1828, reprinted from the *Savannah Georgian.* Sea island cotton replaced indigo cultivation in Georgia and South Carolina almost overnight.
[153] Thomas Spalding, "On the Introduction of Sea-Island Cotton into Georgia," *Southern Agriculturist* IV (1831): 133.

Spalding continued the cotton operations begun by his father at Orange Grove plantation (later Retreat) on the south end of St. Simons Island following the death of the latter in 1794. The golden age of sea island cotton was from 1790 to about 1825, when market prices for the staple were at their highest. The crop thrived on the coast from Charleston to northeast Florida, particularly on the islands, but also to about twenty-five miles inland from the sea.

Spalding refined long-staple cotton cultivation, and was the first to adopt the practice of planting in tighter, thicker rows; this experiment proved successful in that the yield per acre was about 350 pounds—a considerable improvement over the 100 pounds or less per acre yielded by earlier methods. Spalding began planting his cotton on Sapelo Island each year about April 1st, and not later than April 15th. His innovative methods matured as the result of continual experimentation, and trial and error: "When Sea Island cotton was first grown, it was planted upon the flat land at five-apart; it was quite too thin, and although the plant grew generally well, the product rarely reflected one hundred lbs. per acre, and at four acres to the hand, gave about four hundred labor..."[154]

The soils of the barrier islands and the immediate coastal mainland were ideal as they were well-drained and nutrient-rich for long staple cotton on pine lands and cleared oak hammocks. Up to about 1840, sea island and short staple cotton were also occasionally cultivated as a rotation crop in the fertile bottomlands of the Altamaha delta. With the adoption of sea island cotton in Georgia in 1786-87 it became apparent that the black-seed staple was a superior variety over that cultivated in the interior. Coastal planters were

---

[154] Thomas Spalding, "On the Cotton Gin and the Introduction of Cotton," *Southern Cultivator* II (1844): 83.

impressed by the plant's adaptability to the tidewater environment, and they began large-scale cotton production. By 1798, sea island cotton had replaced indigo as the tidewater's primary cash crop. Cotton brought top prices on the English market, and South Carolina and Georgia planters realized great profits. In 1828, extra fine sea island cotton was selling at two dollars a pound, the highest price ever obtained for the staple.[155]

Sea island cotton cultivation was limited to the immediate coast, particularly the barrier islands where the plant thrived in the porous sandy soils and saline atmosphere up to about thirty miles inland. Seed was planted in early spring, then hoed frequently until it began to sprout in early July. The crop was harvested and processed from September until early December. The picking of cotton was tedious. A hand rarely averaged more than seventy-five to 100 pounds picked per day, compared to upland fields in which hands picked 200 or more pounds in a day's work. G.G. Johnson notes:

"The preparation of the staple for market was the most tedious part of the growth of sea-island cotton. Before 1820 sea-island cotton was suited primarily only for coarse fabrics. As the demand for the long staple became greater for making fine laces and muslins planters were forced to use more painstaking methods. The gin house, although only a simple barn, had separate rooms for the different processes. Upon being dried, it was taken to the whipper which extracted the sand and imperfect fibers, and then sent to the assorters. From the sorters, the staple went to the gins, and from there to the moting tables. The lint was then packed into round bags of about three hundred pounds each, 1,500 pounds of seed cotton being required for a bale of this size.

"Whitemarsh B. Seabrook of Edisto Island estimated in 1844 that fifty-four laborers were required to prepare the seed cotton for market. On the average plantation it required from fifty to sixty days of labor to cultivate and gin a bale of fine cotton. The routine of labor on a sea-island cotton plantation from planting time until the crops were laid is illustrated by that on John Fripp's

---

[155] Although dated, an especially insightful technical overview of antebellum sea island cotton cultivation is Guion Griffis Johnson, *A Social History of the Sea Islands with Special Reference to St. Helena Island, South Carolina* (Chapel Hill: University of North Carolina Press, 1930), 23-30, 46-73.

Bluff plantation. In 1856 when John E. Fripp of St. Helena Island bought the Chechessee Bluff plantation of about 560 acres he equipped it as follows: a saddle, or sulkey, horse and a pair of carriage horses; four mules; eighty-eight stock cattle; six oxen; a large flat boat and two small ones; four good and three 'indifferent' plows; three mule or horse carts, two ox carts, plow line chains; collars; one small corn mill, a small sugar mill; spades, axes, and hoes."[156]

One of the techniques by which many coastal planters enhanced the potential of their sea island cotton yield was the use of *Spartina* marsh and marsh mud to fertilize their crops. This manuring method was utilized both for its convenience and the accessibility of the resource—another excellent example by which local ecological conditions could be adapted to provide sustainability and profitability for an agricultural enterprise; by the late 1820s the system of manuring with marsh and mud was in widespread use. Saltmarsh mud was within easy reach of the cotton fields on most of the local plantations. The usual method of application began with slaves going out in boats to the nearby marshes in the creeks and rivers, loading them with marsh mud, then returning to the fields and applying it at the rate of about forty ox cart loads to the acre. According to prominent rice grower Robert F.W. Allston of Georgetown District, South Carolina, some planters made a compost of the marsh mud by mixing it with "farm-yard, cow pen and stable litter, salt marsh and even salt, applied to the land in winter at the rate of forty, fifty and seventy cart loads."[157]

The value of employing marsh mud as a fertilizer for sea island cotton cultivation lay in its content of saline and organic matter. Marsh mud has a low lime content, however, thus cotton planters such as Thomas Spalding, John Couper, and others, addressed the lime deficiency by applying crushed

---

[156] Ibid., 29-30, 47, 49.
[157] R.F.W. Allston, "Essay on Sea Coast Crops; read before the Agricultural Association of the Planting States," Charleston, S.C., 1854.

oyster shell over their cotton fields beneath layers of *Spartina* and marsh mud. Spalding disdained the use of chemical fertilizers for his cotton and sugar cane, preferring instead to utilize natural animal manures, marsh mud and *Spartina* on his fields. In 1837, the *Southern Agriculturist* reported that the use of marsh grass was a suitable substitute for the marsh mud as a fertilizer:

"[Marsh] may be gathered in the summer, and put up in heaps, for use in the following spring. Putting in the marsh at so early a period gives it abundant time to rot by the ensuing spring ... the marsh must be put in heaps to rot during the summer, for the field is then occupied with the cotton. With a good scythe ... one fellow will do six times as much at cutting marsh as in digging mud: and when it is considered that six cartloads of marsh will manure a task better than 21 loads of mud, the balance is greatly in favor of marsh ... Some planters object to marsh, and say that it produces 'blue' in cotton; but no one need apprehend this, if the marsh has been put into the land so as to give it sufficient time to rot, before the cotton-plant reaches it."[158]

In 1844, Spalding predicted that difficult times lay ahead for the planters of sea island cotton, warning, "For in spite of a zeal and intelligence brought to act upon the subject without parallel, the crops are yearly diminishing; until to grow sea island Cotton is one of the most profitless pursuits within the limits of the United States." The decline of long-staple cotton is partly attributable to the deaths of planters who carried their secret methods of selecting seed with them to the grave. The Civil War intervened, and by 1867 the sea island cotton seed had so deteriorated that it was then predicted in the agricultural journal *DeBow's Review* that the business would never return to its previous standard. In late 1832, John D. Legare, editor of the *Southern Agriculturist*, toured the Georgia coastal plantations. Legare's comments regarding Sapelo Island provide a

---

[158] *Southern Agriculturist* X (1837): 175; Thomas Spalding, "Brief Notes," *Southern Agriculturist* I (1828): 59.

contemporaneous picture of Spalding's agricultural methods. Legare's report was published in 1833:

"A boat and hands having been kindly sent for us, we proceeded on the 4th of December [1832], from the residence of Dr. Tunno, on Champneys Island to Sapello, a distance of fourteen miles, and which we reached a little after 12 o'clock. The afternoon and evening of the day of our arrival was passed in most agreeable conversation with Mr. Spalding, whom we were glad to find without company. The next morning we rode out to view the southern part of the island, occupied by Mr. Spalding, who owns a large portion of the island, the remainder is owned and occupied by Dr. Rogers whose plantation we had not the time to visit. Mr. Spalding's residence is situated at the extreme south end of the island, in a beautiful grove of live oaks. On passing from among these, the spectator who visits the island for the first time is struck with the peculiar appearance presented him, instead of meeting with a thick growth of trees, such as is common on all sea-islands on our coast, he suddenly finds himself in a prairie, extending to the north almost as far as can be seen. This island is situated at the mouth of the northern branch of the Altamaha river, and is about ten miles long and two and a half miles in its widest part; it contains about ten thousand acres above the flowing of the tide, made up of hummock lands, covered with live oak and pine, to the extent of two or three thousand acres, and at least three thousand acres of prairie lands ... which are considered fertile and are cultivated in cotton and corn. This land appears to be made up of what appears to be a rich vegetable mould, in some places, six feet deep, resting on white sand. In its uncultivated state, it is thickly covered with various grasses and affords fine pasturage...

"In our morning ride, we passed through a considerable portion of this prairie land, and visited the fields of sugar cane and cotton, and the establishment for manufacturing sugar, consisting of mill, boiling and curing-houses, all made of tabby. These are all at a distance of at least three miles from the mansion, with the exception of a small cotton field near the house. The intermediate space is principally prairie lands. On our return, we retired to the library, and as the day was disagreeable, we employed ourselves in obtaining the following particulars from Mr. Spalding, which we noted down at the time.

Thomas Spalding of Sapelo.

"The agricultural products of this island are cotton, sugar, corn, &c. On this island was the first cultivation of cane for the production of sugar within the Atlantic States. Here the growth of cane for that purpose was begun in 1806, and has been continued ever since. The product of sugar could not be taken for the last twenty years above 700 pounds. Mr. Spalding has partly erected, and will have in operation during the next season, a set of works for boiling sugar in vacuum, which will enable him to manufacture [sugar] of a superior quality, as it has been satisfactorily ascertained, that the improvement by this process is very great. Fifty hands are employed per diem, in taking in and manufacturing from two to three acres of cane, according to its qualities; twenty hands are employed in stripping, ten hands in chopping, ten hands with loading of carts, and about ten hands about the mill and boiling house. Having found from long experience that a vertical cattle-mill would not express the juices from the blue cane sufficiently, it was determined to erect a horizontal watermill, excavating for the purpose about five acres of marsh land, eighteen inches below the surface of high water, so as to be able to work with neap-tides a few hours. This mill is connected to the water-wheel by a coupling box, and will be all-sufficient to take off from one hundred to one hundred and fifty acres of cane ...

"In the course of conversation, Mr. Spalding gave us the following account of the culture of sea-island cotton, and his present mode. Having been an eyewitness, although very young, to the first introduction of long-staple cotton into the United States, the changes the cultivation has gone through, are distinctly in remembrance. The cultivation on Sapello does not differ materially from the course that was pursued on St. Simon's. The only novelty in the cultivation has been in making the ridges in prairie or low lands, permanent and unchangeable for a series of years. The cultivation in that description of land is continuous, alternate rows of corn and cotton occupying the field, and the corn succeeding to the cotton alternately each successive year. On the prairie lands, the growth of the cotton is from four to eight feet high — it is lower on the hummock lands, which are quite sandy. The finest quality is produced on the former. Mr. Spalding keeps on this island four hundred and fifty head of cattle, of which ninety are working oxen. These have been regularly herded during the day, and penned at night for the last ten years. The manure thus acquired is all applied to the sugarcane crop. The oxen were formerly used for the sugar-mill and carting, but now are employed in the carts only. The other cattle are kept merely for plantation use. No sheep are now kept on the island. A large flock was brought down and promised well, but were all swept off by the gale of 1824, which overflowed the island, doing considerable damage, from which the land has not even yet recovered. We were shown a large grove of Orange trees, and some Date trees, both in a very unpromising state. The Orange trees had been very much injured by the severe frosts of 1830, '31 and '32, most of them have been killed. On the afternoon of the 6th of

December, we left Sapello for St. Simons Island ..."[159]

It is no exaggeration to say that Spalding was a philosopher argues Professor Coulter. Spalding "had a pattern for living, and the fundamental elements in that pattern were permanence and unity...his great common denominators were localism, regionalism, state rights...he never talked in generalities—he read his philosophy of life into everything he was doing..."[160]

The basic ideation of Spalding's practices was embodied in his conviction that crop diversification was advantageous, even necessary, for tidewater planters. Dependence on cotton alone, he reasoned, could lead to financial ruin. Thus the paradigmatic expression of Spalding's philosophy was found in his adherence to maximizing the growing cycles of his staple crops in tandem with his secondary crops (corn, peas, sweet potatoes), almost always in rotation.

Besides experimenting with sugar cane, Spalding occasionally cultivated various "irregular" crops: indigo, silk, olives, dates, oranges, and native and exotic grasses for livestock forage. The validation of Spalding's theoretical competence was the coast itself: he was convinced the section was one of the most ideally-suited regions of America for agriculture.

Spalding's philosophy, not unlike that of the ancient Greeks, was embodied in his understanding of the linkage between profitability and his environment—that is to say, the benefits to be realized from

---

[159] J.D. Legare, "Account of an Agricultural Excursion into the South of Georgia," *Southern Agriculturist* VI (1833): 138-47.

[160] E. Merton Coulter, *Thomas Spalding of Sapelo*, (Baton Rouge: Louisiana State University Press, 1940), 128-29.

the proper utilization of the local sub-tropical weather, soils, tides, and river hydrology in association with what crops prospered, and those that did not. The fundamental expression of Spalding's ecological intuition, and therefore of his acute awareness of *place*, was elucidated in May 1824 in an address before the Union Agricultural Society. Using his knowledge of the classics, Spalding tendentiously made the parallel of the Georgia coast with the ancient agricultural kingdoms of the Mediterranean and Mesopotamia:

"Gentlemen, we are in the climate of Chaldea and of Egypt, of Greece, of Tyre, and of Carthage. We are in a land where rice, wheat and cane, indigo, cotton and silk, where the olive and the vine not only grow but will find their favorite home if man will only lend his aid…Let us turn with renovated energy, let us turn with renewed exertions, to the repairing of the past, and the improvement of the future, remembering, that when God abandoned man in paradise, to save him from despair, he plucked from Eden's bower one Flower and planted it in his bosom; watered by love divine, it grew, and grows there still. It is Hope…"[161]

Spalding, Sugar & Tabby

The profoundest expression of Thomas Spalding's advocacy of permanence and place lies in his use of *tabby* as a natural building material for his plantation structures. His philosophy of permanence, with a concomitant percipience of his environmental circumstances, is demonstrated through a desire for his buildings to last for more than one generation. Spalding's structures were intended to embrace permanence through *strength* and *solidity*, rather than the provisional

---

[161] "Address of Hon. Thomas Spalding before the Union Agricultural Society, Darien, May 13, 1824," *Darien Gazette*, May 13, 1824.

use of wooden buildings, which tended to decay in the humid coastal climate. This is the intrinsic concept behind Spalding's use of tabby, and is tactile certification of his passion for order and stability. The most observable legacies of Spalding are the remains of tabbies on Sapelo Island and the mainland.

Spalding's greatest hopes for diversification lay in the cultivation and processing of sugar cane. While cotton was the most consistently profitable of Sapelo's market crops, it was his experimentation with cane, in conflation with his refinement of tabby, in which Spalding made his greatest contribution; his adoption of cane as a rotation crop was a catalyst for his use of tabby. It is important to understand that his experiments with cane and tabby were symbiotic—one went hand-in-hand with the other. Spalding's resourcefulness, along with his characteristic analytical approach, organization, and economy of resources, impelled the development of sugar and tabby on parallel tracks and both, not surprisingly, succeeded beyond expectations.

Spalding initially planted Jamaican sugar cane originating in the Pacific islands. Soon thereafter, John McQueen, Jr. of Savannah introduced the faster-growing ribbon variety of cane from Jamaica, so named for its striped stalks. McQueen distributed the cane to his friends, including Spalding, and it quickly replaced the Otaheite variety previously grown on the Georgia coast. In 1829, Spalding described his initial venture with cane at Sapelo as beginning "in the year 1805 [when] I began the cultivation of Sugar Cane with 100 plants. I had long before been impressed with the opinion that it would answer as well in Georgia as in Louisiana, for one of my early friends, the late Mr. John McQueen of Savannah, had spent the winter of '96 and '97 in Louisiana," and had observed how well

Jamaican cane flourished there. Spalding added, quite properly, that he was the first Georgian to plant sugar cane for "sugar as a [commercial] crop."[162]

Coulter rightly refers to Spalding as the "father of the Georgia sugar industry." The progress he made is reflected in his reported earnings: "My sugar works were very costly, though of a very common character, in the year of '14 however, my crop of sugar amounted to $12,500, from the labor of fifty slaves; the next year brought peace with it, and my neighbors, Major Butler, Major Wood, and others, became cultivators of Sugar."[163]

So valuable was Spalding's sugar supply at Sapelo that the blockading British navy had designs on confiscating it late in the War of 1812 but was unable to do so. Soon after, the Milledgeville Georgia Journal reported that Spalding was "the first individual who planted sugar cane in Georgia systematically." The Georgia Republican, also of Milledgeville, noted in April 1815 that the Savannah market was offering "ninety-five hogsheads of Georgia Sugar, made by Thomas Spalding, Esqr. of Sapelo island equal, if not superior in quality to any imported from the West Indies."[164] A week later, the Georgia Journal predicted that "It will not be long before this most valuable article [sugar] will become one of the stable commodities of our state. We shall be no longer dependent on the

---

[162] Spalding, "On the Culture of the Sugar Cane," 553-56; Spalding, "On the Cultivation of Sugar Cane, Erecting of Proper Buildings," 55; Carlyle Sitterson, *Sugar Country: The Cane Sugar Industry in the South, 1753-1950* (Lexington; University of Kentucky Press, 1953), 31-37. John McQueen Jr. (1773-1822) was the son of John McQueen who owned Sapelo Island from 1784-1789.

[163] Spalding, "On the Cultivation of Sugar Cane, Erecting of Proper Buildings," 55.

[164] Georgia Republican (Milledgeville), April 11, 1815.

European colonies in the West Indies for Sugar, rum, and molasses." The article pointed out that cultivation of cane in the southern section of Georgia could potentially be more profitable than that of cotton. "On my plantation, since the War of 1812," Spalding wrote in the Southern Agriculturist, "there never has been one Kettle of juice which has failed making Sugar; and the hurricane year (1824) excepted, of making Sugar of a fine quality."[165]

In 1816, Spalding composed a detailed treatise on sugar production, complete with itemized cost estimates and specifications for his mule-powered tabby sugar works, elaborately entitled *Observations on the Method of Planting and Cultivating the Sugar-Cane of Georgia and South Carolina, Together with the Process of Boiling and Granulating; and a Description of the Fixtures Requisite for Grinding and Boiling; in a Letter from Thomas Spalding, Esq. to Major General Thomas Pinckney, with an Appendix.*[166] This important tract established Spalding as the recognized authority on the cultivation and production of cane and sugar in the southern coastal region.

The peak years for the sugar industry on the Georgia coast are 1828-1832. Spalding had success with sugar production through the 1820s, aided by tariffs placed on raw sugar during the War of 1812. Though the tariff was reduced after the war, prices remained high until the early 1830s when sugar production began a gradual decline. After the War of 1812 the industry expanded due to protection from foreign competition by the high tariffs on imported sugar, improved

---

[165] Spalding, "On the Cultivation of Sugar Cane, Erecting of Proper Buildings," 55.
[166] This rare pamphlet is reprinted in E. Merton Coulter, ed., *Georgia's Disputed Ruins* (Chapel Hill: University of North Carolina Press, 1937), 228-63. It is one of the most instructive of the many tracts authored by Spalding.

domestic markets for sugar and unstable rice and cotton markets. By the late 1820s, some planters felt conditions were good for increased sugar production. A letter in the Southern Agriculturist in 1828 noted that "if all those who could make sugar, would commence and quit the cotton business, those who could not make sugar, would get better prices for their cotton. There is no danger of glutting the Sugar market, for our country has too little Cane land to supply the growing demand, which increases faster than the population."[167] In 1832, import duties were lowered to about sixty per cent of the American market value and this, along with the deflated foreign markets and increases in rice and cotton prices, led to the end of sugar activities on many plantations in the South, including a curtailment on Sapelo. Sugar production declined in the 1830s due, Spalding felt, to the lack of adequate tariff protection. Spalding also believed that the British had sought to manipulate the world sugar market to injure American production. The price of sugar from 1830 to 1840 averaged about six cents a pound.[168]

Spalding introduced sugar manufacturing to Georgia and remained an enthusiastic advocate of its production for almost three decades. His Observations on sugar production are continually instructive:

"As the cane grows, it requires to be worked in the same manner and about as often as cotton; so much so, that for three years last past, my Overseer has given each year eight hoeings to my cane as well as to my cotton. The limits to be put then to the culture of Sugar, does not arise in this country from the difficulty of either

---

[167] Letter to the Editor, *Southern Agriculturist* I (1828): 182.
[168] Thomas Spalding, "Culture of the Sugar Cane (I)," American Agriculturist III (1844): 166.

planting or attending it, but arises from the limited period which we have for manufacturing sugar."[169]

In the same tract, Spalding demonstrated his considerable architectural skills by providing a detailed description of his sugar works built on the southwest side of Sapelo Island on lower Barn Creek. The octagonal tabby sugar mill housed a vertical rolling mill with an adjacent rectangular boiling and curing building. His influence is evident because this style of facility was emulated at the Thicket in McIntosh County and at Elizafield plantation in Glynn County. In 1825, Spalding's cousin, John Houstoun McIntosh, built a tabby sugarhouse in Camden County, an endeavor influenced by Spalding. Of his own sugar works, Spalding noted in Observations:

"The mill house I have erected is forty-one feet in diameter, of tabby, and octagonal in its form ... the danger of fire, the superior durability, and the better appearance of the buildings, should make us prefer either tabby or brick ... the outer walls of this building are sixteen feet high ... Within about seven feet distance from the outer wall, is a circular inner wall, which rises ten feet; and from this wall to the outer one is a strong joint work, which is covered with two-inch Planks for a Tread for the Mules, Horses, or Oxen, that work the Mill ... there are two several doors, at opposite sides of the Mill-House in the lower story; the one for bringing cane to the Mill, and the other for carrying out the expressed cane; and these doors are six feet wide; there is also a door in the upper story with an inclined plane leading to it, to carry up the Mules, Horses, or Oxen that work the Mill.[170]

Spalding's mill was the vertical type: the machinery was elevated from the surface of the ground on a "strong foundation of masonry,

---

[169] Thomas Spalding, *Observations on the Method of Planting and Cultivating the Sugar-Cane of Georgia and South Carolina*, Agricultural Society of South Carolina, Charleston, 1816.
[170] Ibid.

eight feet high, so as to be within two feet of a level with the Horseway." The cane was fed through rollers from the lower level then the juice ran through gutters into receivers in the boiling house where it was clarified by adding lime. Hot sugar-molasses was poured into coolers then taken to be cured. Molasses drained from the cooled mixture left the raw sugar in the barrels, or tierces, of sugar. Proper boiling left raw sugar of good quality if the grains were lightly colored. In those times, refinement to pure white sugar was considered excessively expensive, thus processing generally ended with the raw product.[171]

While cotton was the most consistently profitable of Sapelo's market crops, it was his experimentation with sugar cane, in conflation with his refinement of tabby, in which Spalding made his greatest contribution; his adoption of cane as a rotation crop was a catalyst for his use of tabby. It is important to understand that his experiments with cane and tabby were symbiotic—one went hand-in-hand with the other. Spalding's resourcefulness, along with his characteristic analytical approach, organization, and economy of resources, impelled the development of sugar and tabby on parallel tracks and both, not surprisingly, succeeded beyond expectations.

Spalding's advocacy of permanence and place lies in his use of tabby as a natural building material for his plantation structures. His philosophy of permanence, with a concomitant percipience of his environmental circumstances, is demonstrated through a desire for his buildings to last for more than one generation. Spalding's structures were intended to embrace permanence through *strength*

---

[171] Thomas Spalding, "Letter to the Editor," *Southern Agriculturist* II (February 1829): 100-02.

and *solidity*, rather than the provisional use of wooden buildings, which tended to decay in the humid coastal climate. This is the intrinsic concept behind Spalding's use of tabby, and is tactile certification of his passion for order and stability. The most observable legacies of Spalding are the remains of tabbies on Sapelo Island and the mainland.

The use of tabby on the Georgia coast was the perfect example of its adherents adapting the ecological circumstances of the region to their benefit. The tidewater proliferated in the availability of natural materials used in making tabby, particularly oyster shell from the Indian middens and along the tidal creeks and rivers. Construction was relatively inexpensive and the result usually proved to be quite durable. Tabby remains around McIntosh County are proof of this durability. Some of the best extant examples are the remains of Spalding's sugar mill on Sapelo, the waterfront at Darien, the ruins of William Carnochan's mill works at the Thicket, Baisden's Bluff at Crescent, and at Belleville.

In the 1920s and 1930s much was written on a scholarly level about coastal tabby; one group favored the theory that tabby ruins on Georgia's coast were those of seventeenth century Spanish missions, and another group, which subsequently proved correct, held that the ruins were those of early nineteenth century sugar houses and other plantation structures. An important scholarly treatment of the origins of Georgia tabby, and the procedure by which tabby was made and utilized in antebellum construction was published in 1937 as *Georgia's Disputed Ruins*, edited by Merton Coulter with the main evidentiary essays prepared by architectural historian Marmaduke H. Floyd, and Smithsonian Institution archaeologist James A. Ford.

This important book, the product of scholarly research, proved beyond doubt that the "so-called Spanish mission ruins [at the Thicket] were actually the remains of William Carnochan's sugar mill and rum distillery which operated at the Thicket in the early 1820s...For a time prior to that, a number of misleading statements had been circulated by historians and laymen insisting that such ruins as those at the Thicket, at Spalding's Sapelo sugar mill, and Robert Grant's sugar mill at Elizafield on the Altamaha River, were attributable to the Spanish mission presence. The evidence presented in *Georgia's Disputed Ruins* proved otherwise.

Much of the current understanding of antebellum tabby emerged from the 1930s investigations of Savannah architect Marmaduke Hamilton Floyd (1888-1949). In a seminal essay, "Certain Tabby Ruins on the Georgia Coast," in *Georgia's Disputed Ruins*, Floyd analyzed coastal tabby ruins, including those at Sapelo Island and the nearby Thicket on the mainland. He proved (as he already knew) that Georgia's tabby was that of antebellum plantation structures, not the vestiges of seventeenth century Spanish missions as had been claimed by several scholars.[172]

The writings of Professor Herbert E. Bolton of the University of California, Professor John Tate Lanning of Duke University and Mary Ross alluded in the 1920s and 1930s to the tabby ruins at various points on the Georgia coast as being Spanish mission remains. Of particular note were the ruins at the Thicket which these scholars said were definitely the remains of the large Spanish Tolomato mission. During the early 1930s, the "abandoned oyster-

---

[172] Floyd, "Certain Tabby Ruins," op. cit., 3-189, in *Georgia's Disputed Ruins.*

shell buildings rekindled a romantic spirit among many who eagerly attributed them to seventeenth century Franciscan missionaries... photographs and reconstructions of Georgia's so-called 'Spanish ruins' cropped up in newspapers (including a double-page rotogravure in the *Atlanta Constitution* and a feature story in the *New York Times*), magazines such as *National Geographic,* and even scholarly volumes (especially the influential *The Debatable Land* by Herbert Bolton and Mary Ross)."[173]

The scholars, Floyd and Ford, and the editing of professor Coulter, with the project under the sponsorship of the Savannah chapter of the Georgia Society of the Colonial Dames of America, which was interested in establishing the provenance of the coastal ruins, began serious research into the tabby situation after this plethora of "Spanish" publicity. "Drawing together an impressive array of historical, architectural and archaeological evidence, Coulter and his colleagues correctly concluded in 1937 that the tabby ruins of coastal Georgia resulted from nineteenth century plantation construction. Not a single tabby in Georgia can be attributed to the Spanish period. Coulter's work created a rift in academic circles and generated bold headlines ... The scholarship of Bolton and Ross was particularly targeted and harshly discredited."[174]

The tract which was published to report the findings, *Georgia's Disputed Ruins,* contained the especially enlightening essay relevant to

---

[173] David Hurst Thomas, *St. Catherines: An Island in Time* (Athens: University of Georgia Press, 2010), 7.
[174] Ibid., 8. See a cogent analysis of the controversy in Joseph Floyd, "The Ghosts of Guale: Sugar Houses, Spanish Missions, and the Struggle for Georgia's Colonial Heritage," *Georgia Historical Quarterly* 97 (Winter 2013): 387-410.

tabby sugar houses by Marmaduke Floyd, the largest component of the book. Floyd showed conclusively that the tabby remains at the Thicket were not that of the Tolomato mission. He placed the actual mission site five miles south of the Thicket on the later site of Fort King George. These and other findings dictated that much of coastal Georgia's history literally be rewritten. Floyd noted in his essay, "Certain Tabby Ruins on the Georgia Coast":

"The *National Geographic Magazine* in the issue of February 1934 again spread over the nation the myth that tabby ruins in Georgia were those of Spanish missions. An illustrated article by W. Robert Moore carried a number of statements and photographs referring to tabby ruins as missions ... Moore described the ruins of Spalding's sugar works on Sapelo as follows: 'On the west shore, commanding the approach to the Florida Passage, stand the tabby ruins of the octagonal fort built by the Spaniards in 1680 ... Thomas Spalding built a sugar mill on the foundation, and within recent years the "long tabby" has been converted into a guesthouse.'[175] This statement is obviously based on the 1930 edition of *Our Todays and Yesterdays* [by Brunswick historian Margaret Davis Cate] which maintained that the nineteenth-century planters converted the Spanish mission ruins into sugar houses."[176]

This matter is addressed, and put to rest, by an obscure letter written by Mrs. Kate McKinley Treanor of Athens to I.F. Arnow of St. Marys in 1932. This letter, if it became known to them, must surely have caused no little amount of discomfiture among those who held out for the theory that the tabby ruins were the remains of Spanish missions:

---

[175] W. Robert Moore, "The Golden Isles of Guale," *National Geographic* LXV, 2 (February 1934), 235.
[176] Floyd, "Certain Tabby Ruins," 184-85; also Sullivan, *Sapelo: People and Place*, chapter 5.

"During my childhood and youth," wrote Mrs. Treanor, "I lived on Sapelo Island, in the home of my Uncle by marriage, Thomas Spaulding [sic]. I have the perfectly vivid recollection of my Uncle explaining the uses of the two or three buildings where his grandfather, the first Thomas Spaulding, built of tabby made by his slaves. The octagon was the cane mill; he showed me the tabby walk by which the oxen were taken up to the main story for grinding the cane. The long tabby house which, at that time, he had fitted up as a dwelling had always been known as the 'Sugar house.' If the Spaniards ever had anything to do with these buildings my Uncle did not know it. He was positive the work was all done by his grandfather ... All this is now called the 'San Jose Mission.' Later on I bought this property, lived in the 'Sugar House' for several years and finally sold it to Mr. Coffin...Our early coast planters made their own sugar, and made these buildings for that purpose. There is an old Spanish fort near the north end of Sapelo, but I think the Mission was an afterthought..."[177]

The findings contained in *Georgia's Disputed Ruins* received further validity and substantiation three years later with the publication of Coulter's important work, *Thomas Spalding of Sapelo*. By then, the Spanish "mission myth" had completely been laid to rest.

Spalding composed detailed instructions on the use and application of tabby. His frequent contributions to the *Southern Agriculturist* and other journals eruditely described his use of tabby and the ideation of his architectural concepts regarding construction techniques. There were no natural stone formations on Sapelo Island, and Spalding did not wish to build with wood, which was prone to decay in the sub-tropical coastal environment. Thus he turned to tabby, a material with which he was familiar from his childhood at Frederica. Spalding felt tabby was more permanent and durable than brick. It was "the best and cheapest material that has ever been employed by man, for the erection of permanent

---

[177] Letter contained in Coulter, ed., *Georgia's Disputed Ruins*, 218-19.

or even beautiful buildings, with moderate means."[178] Building with tabby ended with the colonial period, thus it was left to Spalding to resurrect its use. After his utilization of tabby for his plantation buildings and residence on Sapelo, many people on the South Carolina and Georgia tidewater began to adopt his methods. Spalding was surprised that more people in the region did not use tabby, feeling that possibly being due to "the reluctance that is felt by men in adopting anything that is new."[179] He related the specifics of his tabby construction, emphasizing the mixture in equal parts of oyster shells, lime, sand and water placed in plank forms while wet and built up to the desired height. Spalding recommended that tabby work be done between March and July and that roofs should be made flat and covered with tar and sand.[180]

Spalding's experiments with tabby and architecture in general paralleled his agricultural innovations. One conduit for channeling his philosophical energy toward crop diversification lay in sugar cane, and cane led directly to his adoption of tabby. The enthusiasm with which Spalding approached his sugar venture is clearly seen in his Sapelo Island tabby buildings. An 1816 Spalding letter effectively synthesizes this approach:

"Tabby is composed of shells, lime and sand in equal proportions; they are well mixed together upon a floor with water; and then put into boxes the thickness of your walls. The boxes are made of good boards and are kept apart by pins, at every three or four feet, which as soon as the Tabby begins to harden are driven and the boxes saved for another round. This in the summer will be in two or three days. Care must be taken in carrying up your walls, that they be kept straight by a line and perpendicular with a plumbob. As Tabby is very strong the walls need not be any thicker than a brick house.

---

[178] Thomas Spalding, "A Sketch of the Life of General James Oglethorpe," Georgia Historical Society, *Collections* I (1840): 248.
[179] Thomas Spalding, "On the mode of Constructing Tabby Buildings, and the propriety of improving our plantations in a permanent manner," *Southern Agriculturist* III (1830): 617. The reader is referred to the discussion earlier in this chapter relating to Spalding's tabby sugar mill at Sapelo Island.
[180] Ibid., 617-20.

Care must be taken that they are not run up too fast lest heavy rains, high winds, or their own weight, while green, bring them down. When dry they become like a heap of living rock, and grow stronger with the time. They are the cheapest buildings I know of, the easiest in construction, may be made very beautiful and very permanent. They are the buildings of Spain, the boast of Barbary where some of them have stood there for many centuries. All the success is in the making of the boxes carefully, carefully mixing the material and a thorough dry season."[181]

Spalding obtained his lime made by burning oyster shells. When mixed with fresh water, the residual ash from the shells made an ideal adhesive when combined with shell and sand. The materials were readily available in the tidal rivers and creeks around Sapelo or from the island's mounds and middens. In his letter of July 1844 to N.C. Whiting of Connecticut, previously cited, Spalding noted:

"Tabby [is] a mixture of shells, lime and sand in equal proportions by measure and not weight, makes the best and cheapest buildings, where the materials are at hand, I have ever seen; and when rough cast, equals in beauty stone. The drift shells, after the oyster is dead, thrown up along the shores of our rivers, are also used, but the salt should be washed out. In my immediate neighborhood from following my example, there are more tabby buildings than all of Georgia besides. I generally made my people mix the materials one day and put it into boxes the two following, very soft, as the better to amalgamate. 10 Bushels of lime, 10 Bushels of Sand, ten bushels of shells and ten bushels of water make 16 cubic feet of wall. I have made my walls 14 inches thick; below the lower floor 2 feet; for the second story 10 inches—beyond that I would not erect Tabby buildings."[182]

---

[181] Thomas Spalding to unknown recipient, from Sapelo Island, July 30, 1816, Spalding Family Papers, series 1, box 1, GHS.
[182] Thomas Spalding to N.C. Whiting, July 29, 1844, cited in Floyd, "Certain Tabby Ruins on the Georgia Coast," 72-76. Floyd quotes the letter to Whiting in its entirety, and includes reproductions of Spalding's sketches of the planks, spreader pins and wires to describe his method of constructing boxes for pouring wet tabby, and a sketch of the finished walls of a tabby building.

As noted, tabby ruins of especial interest in McIntosh County are those found on the banks of Crum Creek at the Thicket, five miles northeast of Darien. These are the remains of a sugar mill and rum distillery constructed by Scottish-born William Carnochan (1774-1825), a Darien businessman who also had part interest in the Darien Eastern Steam Sawmill. Carnochan came to Georgia from Jamaica with expertise in manufacturing sugar and rum. In February 1817 the Savannah and Darien firm of Carnochan and Mitchell advertised that they had for sale "14 puncheons of 4th proof Georgia Rum, equal in flavor and quality to Jamaica. A constant supply of the above can be had here [Savannah] or at the Distillery, Darien, on very accommodating terms to country merchants and others."[183] It is thus reasonable to assume that 1816 was the year in which the tabby sugar works and rum distillery at the Thicket were completed, and Carnochan began planting cane and making sugar and rum. In March 1816, Spalding referred to the buildings at the Thicket as being "Neatly executed in Tabby."[184] Carnochan's enterprise was short-lived, however. The September 1824 hurricane greatly damaged the operations at the Thicket and the Carnochan mill was never rebuilt.

Spalding and Slavery

Slavery was an institution upon which the antebellum agricultural economy of the rural South depended. For Spalding and his planting contemporaries, slavery was a necessary evil that he personally regarded with exceeding distaste. "His response to such a fixed

---

[183] *Columbian Museum and Savannah Daily Gazette,* February 10, 1817.
[184] Floyd, "Certain Tabby Ruins," 112.

institution in the social and economic order of the time was to moderate it as much as possible."[185] Spalding gave his slaves leeway and freedom, allowing them time to develop personal interests and agrarian pursuits. He disliked slavery, and it showed so much that some planters referred to Sapelo as "Nigger Heaven" because of Spalding's relaxed treatment of his workers.

Sapelo's bondsmen had their own communities built around the areas of cultivation on the island. As the fields were cleared and Spalding's plantation grew, "villages with huts of thatched roofs and walls plastered inside and out had sprung up in favorable spots; these were styled settlements, such as New Barn Creek, Behavior, Hanging Bull, and in each, a head man, inappropriately called a driver, (for he seldom drove) was placed in charge of probably one hundred souls..."[186] The Sapelo plantation books of 1840 to 1851 documenting 400 slaves "show that the birth rate was 60, 70 and 80, while the death rate was 5, 6 and 7."[187]

Spalding acquired his slaves in Charleston and Savannah, and others from the West Indies. He developed his labor force at an early stage of his plantation career, seeking to obtain blacks of equal sexes, and rarely more than fifty at a time. He allowed his slaves to raise their own hogs and poultry, and the more privileged were permitted to have cattle and horses. Spalding had a reputation for keeping his slaves together, unless he had occasion to include slaves in the sale of land. In 1806, he advertised in the *Columbian Museum and Savannah Intelligencer* the sale of Black Island, which included "one hundred

---

[185] Crook and O'Grady, "Spalding's Sugar Works Site," 7.
[186] Charles Spalding Wylly, *These Memories* (Brunswick, Ga., 1916), 12.
[187] Elizabeth Spalding Willingham, "Sapelo Island," unpub. ms., 1973, copy in Buddy Sullivan Papers, Collection 2433, GHS.

seasoned slaves." Since Spalding was still in possession of Black Island in 1824, he presumably did not find a buyer, or he took it off the market. Deed records allude to the transfer of Black Island from Spalding to his son Charles in April 1841, with the slaves as part of the transaction:

"...Said Thomas Spalding in consideration of his paternal offer of the sum of Thirty Thousand Dollars, to him paid by the aforesaid Charles H. Spalding hath bargained and sold a certain tract of land containing One thousand acres known as Black Island, being three hundred acres of Hammock land seven hundred acres of Fresh marsh and Brackish marsh and One Hundred and eleven Negroes now upon the said Island."[188]

A Spalding slave might occasionally run away — "Not many," notes Coulter, "for when a slave had been with him long enough to learn his plantation methods, he had learned enough to want to stay." The Savannah press had this item not long after Spalding acquired the southern half of Sapelo:

"20 Dollars Reward. Ran away from the subscriber, on the island of Sapelo, a Negro Man of the name of Landau, about five feet, nine inches high, stout and well made, pleasing countenance, speaks both French and English, about forty-five years of age. The fellow was the property of the late Francis Dumoussay, and is marked by him in the breast S. 24: he is supposed to be lurking about the city of Savannah or Sapelo Main. — Any person delivering this fellow to Thomas Decheneaux in Savannah, or the subscriber at Sapelo Island, or securing him in any gaol in the State of Georgia, shall receive the above reward. Thomas Spalding."[189]

It is not known if Landau was recovered.

---

[188] Deed Book A (1841), 302-03, RMCG.
[189] *Columbian Museum and Savannah Advertiser*, March 7, 1807.

Spalding probably had a role in the development of agriculture at Creighton Island, west of Sapelo across Mud River. Creighton was purchased from the estate of Patrick Gibson by Spalding's son- in- law, William Cooke in 1838. Spalding also likely influenced the construction of tabby dwellings on the north end of the island for the slave population, particularly at Chocolate. During the antebellum period, Spalding cultivated cotton on a portion of Little Sapelo Island and kept several slaves there to maintain the crop. In 1822, Spalding purchased from William Mein 600 acres and 125 slaves on Hutchinson Island at Savannah.[190] Spalding sold his Chatham County holdings in the early 1840s. Spalding rarely purchased any slaves after this.

Testimony to Spalding's concern for the care of his workers is the fact that he was averse to subjecting his bondmen to the rigors and the poor health conditions associated with the rice tracts. C.S. Wylly relates that Spalding told his son Charles Spalding amid their discussions of the potential profitability of rice cultivation at Cambers Island, "I will never subject any dependent of mine [slaves] to such climatic dangers, nor can I think it right to exact the increased amount of labor that would be necessary." In 1837, Spalding possessed 421 bondsmen, second only to the Butlers in McIntosh County.[191]

"It was Spalding's hope that his slaves might progress through serfdom to a measure of liberty and independence," notes Coulter. "They should be attached to the land and they should not be sold

---

[190] *Savannah Georgian*, August 8, 1822; Coulter, *Thomas Spalding of Sapelo*, 42.
[191] Wylly, "The Story of Sapelo;" McIntosh County Tax Digest, 1837, GDAH.

away from it."[192] Thus, Spalding rarely ever sold a slave—tradition holds that Spalding did not sell any slaves but there is no supporting documentation.

Everything considered, however, it is impossible to characterize slavery at Sapelo, or anywhere else the institution was practiced, in anything but the worst of pejoratives—toilsome, burdensome, onerous, and arduous are at once adjectivally appropriate. "There is no way to romanticize the back-bending labor these workers were forced to perform," notes William McFeely. "Among the many recorded reminiscences of Bilali...nothing tells us what these people who were doing [Sapelo's] labor thought about their work and all of the other aspects of their lives."[193]

Sapelo's bondsmen apparently took a certain amount of pride in being Spalding slaves. Georgia Bryan Conrad wrote in 1901, "On Sapelo I used to know a family of Negroes who worshipped Mahomet. They were tall and well-formed with good features. They conversed with us in English but in talking among themselves they used a foreign tongue that no one else understood. These negroes held themselves aloof from the others as if they were conscious of their own superiority..."[194] The culture of the Geechee descendants of Sapelo slaves was inherited from their island forebears. In the 1930s research of importance was conducted by the Savannah Unit of the Work Projects Administration's Georgia Writers' Project, resulting in the publication of *Drums and Shadows: Survival Studies*

---

[192] Coulter, *Thomas Spalding of Sapelo*, 85.
[193] William S. McFeely, *Sapelo's People: A Long Walk into Freedom* (New York: Norton, 1994), 42-43.
[194] Georgia Bryan Conrad, "Reminiscences of a Southern Woman," *The Southern Workman*, 1901.

among the Georgia Coastal Negroes. A chapter drawn from the oral histories taken from Sapelo's Geechee in 1938-39 reveals a number of traditional beliefs. For example,

"If an owl hoots on top of the house or near the house, it is supposed to be a sign of death. A counteractive is to throw salt on the fire, burn an old shoe, or turn pockets the wrong side out ... It is also considered bad luck to start on a journey and have to turn back ... A frizzled chicken is known as a wise chicken and is used to find lost articles. If something has been buried and its place forgotten, a frizzled chicken can, according to the islanders, find the place and scratch up the lost article."[195]

Muhammad Bilali was Sapelo Island's most famous slave. He was born in Timbo in what is now Guinea in west Africa, probably in the mid-1770s, though it is difficult to ascertain the exact year of his birth. Estimates range from 1760 to 1779, with the later date being more likely. According to a 1931 affidavit by Benjamin L. Goulding, then the custodian of Bilali's diary, Bilali "was about 80" when he died in 1859.[196]

Bilali apparently spent about ten years as a slave in the Bahamas before being brought to Sapelo. There are conflicting accounts as to how he came to Georgia. C. S. Wylly, states that he was purchased in Charleston by Thomas Spalding either in 1802 or 1803. William S. McFeely (1994) asserted that Bilali was encountered by Spalding in

---

[195] Georgia Writers' Project, Savannah Unit, *Drums and Shadows, Survival Studies among the Georgia Coastal Negroes*, (Athens: University of Georgia Press, 1940), 158-72.

[196] B.G. Martin, "Sapelo Island's Arabic Document: The Bilali Diary in Context," *Georgia Historical Quarterly* 78 (1994): 589-601.

the Bahamas, and because of his knowledge of sea island cotton, Spalding brought Bilali and his family to Sapelo.[197]

Among Spalding's views on slavery was that supervision of bondsmen, and plantation operations in general, was more efficient when conducted by black managers and drivers rather than the typical white overseer. After his first several years at Sapelo Spalding never hired a white overseer. In one of his agricultural tracts he noted that he managed his plantations "without the intervention of any white man." Farming operations were supervised either directly by himself or by his black drivers. The most prominent of these was Bilali, Spalding's overseer for much of the antebellum period. An educated Mohammedan, Bilali was the patriarch of the Spalding slaves, and next to Spalding himself, the most powerful man on Sapelo Island.

Bilali's expertise with long-staple cotton in the Bahamas led to his being appointed head driver at Sapelo not long after he came to the island—tantamount to being the plantation overseer in charge of day-to-day farming operations. Because of his responsibilities, Bilali was a privileged slave. Literate, highly-skilled, and possessed of a complete understanding of Spalding's agricultural ideology, Bilali effectively supervised planting, and managed the labor force. Spalding placed complete trust in Bilali, and on the frequent occasions that the former was away from Sapelo, Bilali was left in charge of the island. He was, in essence, a plantation manager in every sense, tasked with far more responsibility than would be found among slaves at other plantations.

---

[197] McFeely, *Sapelo's People*, 36-38.

Bilali had a large family of twelve sons and seven daughters. Phoebe, his wife, may have been born in the West Indies. According to Cornelia Walker Bailey, the great-great-great-granddaughter of Bilali, Phoebe was "from the islands" in the Caribbean. It is likely that some of the couple's children were born in the Bahamas before they came to Sapelo, and possibly all seven daughters. Bilali's Sapelo legacy cannot be over-stated. It extends from the family's arrival on the island to the present day.

When interviewed in 1939 by the Georgia Writers' Project, Katie Brown (1853-1940) of Sapelo, "one of the oldest inhabitants" of the island at the time, and great-granddaughter of Bilali, told of his daughters' names being "Magret, Bentoo, Chaalut, Medina, Yaruba, Fatima, and Hestuh," several of which are distinctly Muslim names. One of the second generation of Bilali descendants was his daughter "Bentoo" (Bintu), Katie Brown's great-aunt, her name evolving to Minto Bell when she married. Minto's gravestone is in Behavior Cemetery, and like her sisters, she migrated from the Bahamas to Sapelo with her parents when she was young.[198]

Bilali and his family "all worshiped Mahomet" according to Lydia Parrish in *Slave Songs of the Georgia Sea Islands* (1942). Katie Brown described in detail her ancestors' disciplined approach to their religion, and their daily prayers to Allah: "Magret an uh daughter Cotto use tuh say dat Bilali and he wife Phoebe pray on duh bead. Dey wuz bery puhticulah bout duh time dey pray and dey bery regluh bout duh hour. Wen duh sun come up, wen it straight obuh head an wen it set, das duh time dey pray. Dey bow tuh duh sun an hab lill

---

[198] Georgia Writers' Project, *Drums and Shadows*, 159-63.

mat tuh kneel on..." Magret, who became Margaret Hillery on her marriage, made rice cakes in observance of Muslim holy days, according to Brown. Rice was an important staple in the slaves' diet on Sapelo, and was grown at Hog Hammock and Raccoon Bluff for much of the nineteenth and twentieth centuries. In a style adopted from their African roots, Margaret's rice cakes were made of moistened grains mortared into a paste with a wooden pestle, then flattened and spiced with sugar and honey.

Wylly states (without attribution) that Spalding assigned to Bilali the defense of Sapelo late in the War of 1812 when British naval forces were raiding plantations on nearby islands. He supposedly obtained a consignment of muskets from the state militia, and had Bilali drill a number of reliable bondsmen to challenge the British should they attempt to land. The British never threatened Sapelo, whether because of the rumors of Spalding's slave defenders or not. Though the story of "slave militia" has never been fully substantiated, it nonetheless has the ring of truth based on an understanding of Spalding's methods, and those of his trusted black overseer. There can be little doubt that because of Bilali's management, coupled with Spalding's unequivocal trust in him, conditions for Sapelo's enslaved people were probably better than at most plantations.

Bilali outlived his owner by several years, being given his papers of manumission upon Spalding's death, as stipulated in the latter's will. In declining health, Bilali moved to Darien where he died in 1859. In Darien, he was befriended by Rev. Francis R. Goulding of the Presbyterian Church to whom Bilali gave his "diary" of thirteen pages for safekeeping. This important record reflects Bilali's devotion to his religious beliefs, and is one of the rarest and most significant of antebellum slave documents because of its uniqueness as an original Arabic manuscript. Goulding's son Benjamin donated the diary to the Georgia State Library in 1930, before it was transferred to the Hargrett Rare Book and Manuscript Library at the University of Georgia in 1992.

St. Simons folklorist Lydia Parrish was one of those showing an early interest in the diary, providing copies to Melville Herskovits, an anthropologist, and linguist Joseph Greenberg in hopes of obtaining an accurate translation. Although only able to read a portion of its Arabic text, Greenberg was the first to analyze the manuscript and assess it as a religious lay document. Over the years other scholars have attempted to produce a translation. Most of the diary appears to be a compilation of religious sentiments and the performance of prayer. The paper on which the diary was written is probably of Italian origin manufactured for the Islamic trade and only available on the African continent. Thus it is possible that Bilali brought the paper with him on a slave ship from west Africa, though slaves were rarely allowed to take personal possessions with them when placed in bondage. Conversely, he may have obtained the paper for his diary in the Bahamas prior to coming to Sapelo. In summary, some mysteries continue, and much remains to be learned about Bilali and his manuscript.

Had more Spalding documents survived they would doubtlessly reflect the views of James Couper whose surviving records are extensive. For example, Spalding's papers would likely reveal that his standards for slave diets exceeded those of most planters. Rations for a Sapelo slave family typically consisted of corn, rice, sweet potatoes, peas, pork, salted fish, and molasses, supplemented by food the slaves grew or otherwise acquired for themselves. Acreage at Sapelo was set aside for growing provision crops for the sustenance of the work force.

Slave diets at Sapelo were supplemented by food fish and shellfish: mullet, croaker, sea trout, crabs, oysters, clams and shrimp were abundant and easily obtainable in the tidal creeks. There were seasonal allocations of clothing for the men and women, outlays of work clothes, shoes, blankets, and sewing cloth supplied from stocks imported from Savannah. Spalding provided his bondsmen with extra clothing and farm implements, as well as cookware, crockery, and other items no longer needed from the main house, standard practice at many island plantations. Most of Spalding's records have been lost making it problematic in ascertaining the details of his management.

Slave quarters at Sapelo varied in style and construction. Duplex tabby dwellings were built at Behavior, South End, Hanging Bull, and Chocolate, reflecting Spalding's tendencies toward permanence and stability. The use of tabby for housing was common on the island plantations where the natural materials were available from Indian mounds and creek banks.

Sapelo's slave settlements were Chocolate, Hanging Bull, New Barn Creek, and Behavior, the latter two being contiguous to the fields at Long Tabby. The *Topographical Reconnaissance of Sapelo Island, Georgia,* prepared by H.S. DuVal for the U.S. Coast Survey in 1857, is useful for determining the sites of antebellum structures on Sapelo. The map delineates several buildings at Long Tabby, labeled "Mr. Spalding's Plantation," including the sugar mill, and what is likely a cotton barn. To the east near a forested oak grove are symbols for a cluster of slave dwellings within, and contiguous to Behavior. Seventeen structures are shown, some enclosed by fences.

Archaeological investigation has uncovered remains of two small (six feet by twelve) tabby slave houses, one at Behavior proper, and the other just north of Behavior at New Barn Creek-Bush Camp Field. The 1857 survey shows a layout of thirteen houses at Behavior over an area of roughly sixty acres, with four additional houses north of the main group at New Barn Creek, three of which are situated parallel to the High Point road. Based on the layout of the dwellings, and assuming full occupancy, there would have been just over 100 slaves in the Behavior settlement.[199] The 1868 Coast Survey topographic map, *Doboy Sound and Vicinity*, shows additional structures at Behavior, indicating construction of houses by returning freedmen.

Behavior was home to the earliest of Spalding's enslaved people. Bilali and his wife Phoebe probably lived at Behavior; they were among the first of Spalding's acquired slaves, as were Carolina and Hannah, who later adopted the surname Underwood. Bilali, Phoebe and their daughters, along with Carolina and Hannah, were likely among the bondsmen Spalding purchased during one of his trips to the Bahamas in 1802-03. The 1870 census showed the Underwoods to both be about ninety-five years old; they died in 1873 in a house fire on Sapelo. Bilali died a freedman in 1859; the year of Phoebe's death is unknown.

---

[199] H.S. DuVal, U.S. Coast Survey, *Topographical Reconnaissance of Sapelo Island, Georgia*, 1857, RG 23 (Records of the U.S. Coast and Geodetic Survey), NARA, cited hereafter as 1857 DuVal survey; Ray Crook, Cornelia Bailey, Norma Harris and Karen Smith, *Sapelo Voices* (Carrollton: State University of West Georgia, 2003), 18-20.

East of Behavior, at a settlement labeled "Hog Hammock" on the 1857 map, were three more structures near the marsh. The map reveals another settlement of a dozen dwellings just northwest of the Spalding house, indicating that about eighty bondsmen lived there working a nearby cotton field, tending livestock at Root Patch and Flora Bottom, and serving as domestic servants at South End House. The DuVal map identifies several larger structures near the mansion, possibly a barn and other outbuildings, and a dock at South End Creek. Taken together, the number of slave dwellings mapped at South End, Behavior, Hanging Bull and Chocolate would have accommodated over 350 bondsmen. The 1860 census enumerated 370 Sapelo bondsmen living in almost 60 dwellings. The reduced total from 1837 reflects the sale of some of Spalding's mainland properties before and after his death. The 1860 count included 252 slaves on Randolph Spalding's Sapelo plantations inherited from his father, and 118 attached to his brother-in-law Michael Kenan's plantation (Hanging Bull).[200]

Thomas Spalding's last years were made lonelier by the loss of his wife Sarah who died in May 1843 at age sixty-five. The couple had endured an inordinate amount of grief during their forty-eight years of marriage through the premature loss of many of their children. "By all accounts", notes Ronald Ridgley, "[Spalding] was a gracious man, fond of his family. It was a family that knew deep sorrow because only five of the sixteen children outlived their parents..."[201]

---

[200] U.S. Census, 1860, McIntosh County, Slave Schedules.
[201] Ronald H. Ridgley, "Thomas Spalding," *Dictionary of Georgia Biography* (Athens: University of Georgia Press, 1986), 913.

Seven children died in childbirth. The first Spalding son, James (1797-1820), barely reached manhood before his life ended. In 1818, the young Spalding won election as McIntosh County state representative. In November 1820, during the legislative session at Milledgeville, he died of influenza. A Spalding daughter, Hester Margery, died in her early twenties in 1824, possibly in childbirth; Margaret died in 1800, aged three weeks; Margery in 1806 at the age of two; Thomas in 1819 at six; Emily Screven in 1824 just before her seventh birthday; and Mary Ann Elizabeth in 1818 just before turning fifteen. The latter death was particularly sad for the Spaldings; they buried Mary Ann at Ashantilly, the first of her family to be interred in the family plot, a small tract that later became St. Andrew Cemetery.

Professor Coulter, in a passage of lapidary elegance, places the child there "to sleep the long sleep beneath the giant old live oaks draped with funereal moss—and there to be followed by other Spaldings until there should grow up a veritable Spalding City of the Dead."[202] The longest lived of the children were Charles Harris Spalding, died in 1887 at the age of seventy-nine; Catherine Spalding Kenan, in 1881 at seventy-one; Elizabeth Sarah Wylly, in 1876 at seventy; and Jane Martin Leake Brailsford, in 1861 at sixty-five. The youngest child, Randolph Spalding, died in 1862 at thirty-nine. Following is an extract from the diary of Michael J. Kenan of Milledgeville (1807-1875) written in 1869 relevant to his observations about the Spalding family of Sapelo Island:

"Family Origins—I intermarried on the 25th March 1832 with Catherine

---

[202] Coulter, *Thomas Spalding of Sapelo*, 285.

Anna Spalding, daughter of the Hon. Thomas Spalding of Sapelo Island, McIntosh County, Georgia. I was of the legal profession, but abandoned it because of deafness and a greater partiality for the life of a planter...I prosecuted my planting interests [on Sapelo Island and in Baldwin County] until the War of Secession came, which swept all means in that line, in common with all other Southern Planters, so far as labor capital attached. Randolph Spalding, the last of my wife's father and mother, married Mary Bass of Columbus, Georgia, 1843, and settled at Chocolate, North End of Sapelo Island. Here Randolph lived until his dwelling was consumed by fire in 1851 or '52. He was a large Sea Island Cotton Planter; and represented McIntosh County, both as Representative &. Senator, for several terms. He was Colonel of Infantry in the Confederate Army...Mr. Spalding, my wife's father, was a resident of Sapelo Island for more than forty years. His greatest agricultural labors were upon Sapelo. Here he cultivated both the sugar cane and Sea Island Cotton and amassed quite a fortune. A great reader of books, his choice and extensive library was his sanctum. Hospitable to the fullest extent of his ample means he ever displayed the welcome of his house alike to friends and strangers. A graceful and fluent writer, he contributed often to the Periodicals of his time, principally upon Agricultural Topics. He wrote a 'Sketch of the Life of Genl. Oglethorpe" [1840] for, and published among the transactions of the Georgia Historical Society...His wife had preceded him in death some seven or eight years. Of this estimable lady it seems mere superflousness to speak: 'Grace was in all her steps—heaven in her eye, in every gesture, dignity and love.' Gifted with a mind superlatively vast and eminently virtuous, she was polished and adorned by all that the innocence of art could infuse, or social position suggest...She was a Christian, a lifelong Christian, whose lamp was ever filled with oil, trimmed and burning, patiently waiting the summons that welcomes her hence..."[203]

Spalding made his will in 1848 with provisions to satisfy debts, and provide for several of his grandchildren. The remainder of his property he left in trust for his namesake grandson, Thomas Spalding, son of Randolph and Mary Spalding. At the time he died Spalding owed $10,000 to the State Bank of Georgia, $5,000 to his friend Edmund Molyneux, British consul at Savannah, and $1,850 on a note guaranteed for his son Charles. At the time the will was

---

[203] Kenan diary, 1836-1871, Michael J. Kenan Papers, Collection 948, GHS.

made there were 250 slaves in Spalding's estate. Twenty families of slaves were to go to his grandson, William Brailsford of Sutherland's Bluff. Additional obligations compelled Spalding to add a codicil: "I am again unfortunate and must sell forty-nine Negroes and three old nurses in order to pay my debts to the State Bank. This will reduce one thousand dollars to five hundred dollars to my daughter Elizabeth Wylly to educate her two oldest sons."[204]

The final act of Spalding's public life was memorable. Attending the state convention at Milledgeville in December 1850, Spalding addressed the gathering arguing for the preservation of the Union during a time of national debate over slavery and states' rights. His convention speech was stirring, and it was evident that he sensed his life was nearing an end. Spalding orated that the occasion was "an appropriate [and] a graceful termination of my long life...from a small people we have become a great nation under our Constitution, and rather than that Constitution shall perish I would wish that myself and every human that has a drop of my blood in his veins should perish. To use the words of Homer: 'Before that dreadful day, may me and mine lay pressed beneath our monumental clay.'"[205]

At nearly seventy-seven, in feeble health, and mentally exhausted by his efforts at the convention, Spalding returned from Milledgeville in wet, chilly weather. He fell ill, and died quietly at Ashantilly on January 4, 1851, being buried beside his wife and mother in the nearby family plot. A local account commented, "If there was nothing in his life to dazzle by its brilliancy, it was one of usefulness

---

[204] McIntosh County Probate Records, Will of Thomas Spalding, Will Book 49, RMCG. The two grandsons in the codicil were Thomas Spalding Wylly (1831-1922) and Alexander C. Wylly (1833-1911).
[205] *Southern Recorder* (Milledgeville), December 17, 1850.

and honor—unblemished by none of the vices into which poor human erring humanity often falls. [He was] exemplary in all the virtues which most adorn the human character."[206] A century later Coulter penned an epitaph that rightfully placed Spalding among the pantheon of outstanding Georgians:

"...'A high-minded man feels no enmity,' Spalding wrote shortly before his death...[His] fundamental good sense, broad patriotism properly integrated with his love of locality and region, his venturesome spirit for economic progress—all were evident to his contemporaries...He had no sense of humor, yet he was fond of paradoxes and was the author of many singular expressions. He abominated music, and he would not tolerate dancing, and card-playing...[but] Spalding's life was not a failure; he did not live in vain. He got much out of his seventy-seven years and he gave more."[207]

---

[206] *Savannah Georgian,* January 17, 1851.
[207] Coulter, *Thomas Spalding of Sapelo,* 304-06.

Roswell King, Jr. & Plantation Management

On the 7th of August 1854, the Rev. Charles Colcock Jones, a Presbyterian clergyman from Maybank plantation, Liberty County, Georgia, reported in a letter to his son:

"We have had much sadness in our little circle since we last wrote you. Our old and kind friend and neighbor Mr. King is *No more!* He was taken violently ill with inflammation of the stomach, and after three days' illness (the last of which he was in a comatose state) he died on the evening of July 1st. You may picture to yourself the distress of his family. Your brother and myself performed the last sad office of friendship, preparing him for his grave. Your Aunt Susan made his shroud. It has created a great vacuum in our little community. I performed his funeral service at Woodville on Sabbath afternoon the 2nd, and he was interred at Midway on Monday the 3rd…"

In an addendum to her husband's letter, Mrs. Mary Jones added:

"…Mr. King came from South Hampton Wednesday night sick; on Saturday his reason departed; that night, at half-past ten o'clock his soul passed from time to eternity! Our poor friend Mrs. King has been almost distracted…His family are all sadly affected…"[208]

Thus concluded the final chapter in the eventful life of Roswell King, Jr., a tidewater Georgia agriculturist to be regarded by future historians as one of the most efficient plantation managers of his time.

King (1796-1854) was the first son of his better-known father, Roswell King, Sr. The younger King, like his forebear, was closely

---

[208] Robert Manson Myers, ed., *The Children of Pride, A True Story of Georgia and the Civil War* (New Haven, Conn.: Yale University Press, 1972), 69-70.

associated with the famous Pierce Butler plantation estates in Georgia, in addition to managing his own plantation interests at his two Liberty County estates, South Hampton and Woodville.

Liberty County and its neighbor to the south, McIntosh, lay astride the middle portion of the Georgia coast, forty and sixty miles, respectively, below Savannah, the principal agricultural market and seaport of the region. The most enduring physical symbol of Liberty County, the single structure that is most evocative of the county's antebellum history, is the old Midway Congregational Church. This simple, New England style white frame edifice built in 1792, is nestled amidst a canopy of old live oaks along US Highway 17 and served as the religious and cultural center of the local planter society scattered along the tidal rivers and creeks of the eastern section of the county.

Puritans immigrating to Georgia from South Carolina established the original congregation of the Midway Church in the early 1750s.[209] By the early nineteenth century, the church was the spiritual center of the region and for most of the 1800s was pastored by Presbyterian clergy. One of the most notable of these was the Rev. Charles Colcock Jones (1804-1863), patriarch of the Liberty County family whose correspondence form the basis of *The Children of Pride,* edited by Robert Manson Myers and published in 1972.[210]

The planter establishment of antebellum Liberty and McIntosh counties was predicated upon the successful pursuit of agriculture which, in turn, was largely made possible through the labors of

---

[209] James Stacy, ed., *History and Published Records of the Midway Congregational Church, Liberty County, Georgia* (1894 and 1903, reprinted, The Reprint Co., Spartanburg, S.C., 1979, 1987).
[210] Myers, ed., *Children of Pride,* prologue, 7-31.

several thousand African slaves. The interior of Midway Church exemplifies a legacy of this time with its upper circular gallery supported by white columns, a section of the sanctuary designed for the seating of the slaves who attended Sunday services with their owners.

After the Revolution Liberty County became an agricultural region typical of the southern tidewater in which planter economies dictated the structure of everything from commerce and business affairs to social life, and the marriages by which lasting mergers between the planter families were consummated. These families lived on their coastal plantations during the late fall and winter months then retreated to the drier uplands during the malarial period from late spring through early fall. Some, including the Jones and King families, had summer homes on Colonel's Island, a marsh island between the mainland and St. Catherines that benefited from the cooling breezes from the nearby ocean. Others, such as Andrew Walthour, one of the wealthiest planters of the section, had secondary residences in the inland sand hill areas away from the immediate coast. In the first two decades of the nineteenth century several of these "resort" communities were established in central and western Liberty County, including Flemington, Walthourville and Jonesville.[211]

---

[211] Jonesville was actually in the uppermost section of neighboring McIntosh County, near Bull Town Swamp and about ten miles south of Midway. Its part-time residents were almost exclusively those with their primary abodes in Liberty. See Stacy, *History and Published Records*, 58-59, and Buddy Sullivan, *Early Days on the Georgia Tidewater*, all editions, 1990-2018, which includes a colonial and antebellum review of Jonesville.

In addition to Midway there were several other settlements in Liberty County. To the east was Sunbury, on the broad tidal Medway River, settled during the colonial period, and which once rivaled Savannah in commercial importance. A few miles south was Riceborough, a small port on the North Newport River serving coasting vessels engaged in the carrying trade for the shipment of agricultural goods. To the northwest, in the interior of the county, was Hinesville that, in 1837, replaced Riceborough as the county seat. Just west of Hinesville was the settlement of Taylor's Creek near the Canoochee River that, in its time, was the educational center of the county.[212]

In 1850, as was the case throughout the tidewater, the wealth of Liberty County was concentrated among only a handful of planters. In the lower section, nearest the coast, there were about one hundred tracts on which agriculture was being practiced to some degree. The 1850 U.S. census reported a white population of 2,002 in Liberty County. The slave population that year was nearly three times that of whites at 5,908. Of the 362 white families enumerated, almost 70 per cent owned slaves, although 41 per cent of these owned less than ten slaves. About 90 per cent of the county's slave owners owned less than 50 bondsmen. Conversely, there were 32 slave owners who possessed more than 50 bondsmen, second only to Chatham (Savannah), among Georgia's counties in 1850.

---

[212] John M. Sheftall, *Sunbury on the Medway: A Selective History of the Town, Inhabitants and Fortifications* (Atlanta: Georgia Department of Natural Resources, 1977); Bird Yarbrough, Paul Yarbrough, eds., *Taylor's Creek, A Story of the Community and Her People* (Taylor's Creek Cemetery Association, 1963), revised edition, edited by Wyman May, 1986.

The 1850 agricultural census for Liberty reveals that there were several plantations in excess of 1,000 acres on which more than one hundred slaves labored. Liberty was typical of the tidewater planter class in which one's wealth was measured in terms of the amount of acreage and numbers of bondsmen one possessed. George W. Walthour was one of the wealthiest planters in the county with 206 slaves and 9,000 acres of which about 6,000 constituted improved (cultivated) acreage; John B. Barnard owned 2,000 acres and 124 slaves; Moses L. Jones possessed 6,987 acres and 110 slaves; Joseph Lane, the second largest slave owner in the county, owned 192 bondsmen and 1,062 acres; Charles C. Jones owned 107 slaves and 3,749 acres on his two crop-producing plantations, Maybank and Montevideo; the Estate of Joseph Jones held 120 slaves; Roswell King, Jr. had 141 slaves working his 3,357 acres on two tracts in lower Liberty, the majority of his bondsmen engaged in labor at South Hampton; and Jacob Waldburg owned 118 slaves and 2,000 acres of improved land on St. Catherines Island. Waldburg's 19,000 acres of upland and marsh at St. Catherines made him the largest landowner in Liberty County in 1850, while William B. Gaulden was second with 9,533 acres. There were three other properties worth noting: the Estate of Louis LeConte containing 3,183 acres and 45 slaves; the Estate of William LeConte, which comprised 1,720 acres and 66 slaves; and an unspecified aggregation of acreage valued at the considerable sum of $36,650 owned by the Estate of John Lambert.

A decade later, the 1860 census revealed that the percentage of families possessing slaves in Liberty County was significantly lower—58 per cent, with 33 families owning more than 50 slaves with seven of these possessing more than 100. The largest owners on the eve of the Civil War were George Walthour with 300 bondsmen, Jacob Waldburg with 255, John B. Barnard with 132, Charlton Hines with 130 and William B. Gaulden with 122.[213]

In 1825, Roswell King, Jr., married Julia Rebecca Maxwell (1808-1892) of Liberty County. Julia Maxwell was a daughter of Colonel Audley Maxwell (1766-1840) and Mary Stevens Maxwell (1772-1850) of Liberty County. The Kings had nine children who attained maturity: Mary Elizabeth King (1827-1871), wife of Dr. Charlton Henry Wells; James Audley Maxwell King (1829-1920); George Frederick King (1831-1914); William Henry King (1833-1865); Roswell King III (1836-1911); Isabel Couper King (1842-1921), wife of Mathews Robert Tunno; Julian Clarence King (1844-1901); Bayard Hand King (1846-1929); and John Butler King (1848-1904).[214]

Julia King, who survived her husband by thirty-eight years, proved to be a strong, supportive and reliable wife to Roswell, Jr., a fact that occasionally emerges from King's journal. Her parents, Audley and Mary Maxwell, had a plantation, Carnichfergus, near Midway. The Maxwells, perhaps reflective of their Scottish heritage, regularly attended the Midway Congregational Church which emphasized the Presbyterian theology. Most of the King children were born in Liberty County. One of the sons, James Audley Maxwell King, known familiarly as "Audley," became a third generation family planter and attained a favorable reputation for his abilities. Mrs. Mary Jones, writing on Christmas Day, 1851, describes Audley as an

---

[213] U.S. Census, Liberty County, Georgia, 1850, 1860 slave and agricultural schedules.
[214] Myers, ed., *Children of Pride*, 1584.

"established planter... [who] fills admirably a useful position in the family, not only governing the plantation but all the little folks at home. His services could not well be dispensed with. To his mother especially he is a most dutiful and affectionate son..." When his father died in 1854, Audley King assumed the responsibility for the family plantations, for many of his mother's affairs and for the younger children of the family.

Six of the King sons served in the Confederate Army and one, William Henry, was killed in action at Sayler's Creek only three days before Lee's surrender at Appomattox. The third Roswell King, "Rossie," a favorite of his mother, was not as successful a planter as his two namesake forebears. After being paroled following the war, Rossie King took up planting near Walthourville and at one of the family's estates, South Hampton. The results were less than notable—"Rossie will not clear expenses at South Hampton," observed Laura Maxwell Buttolph in the fall of 1867. After the death of his wife in 1872, Rossie King sent his six motherless children to be raised by his brother Audley at Woodville on Colonel's Island. He died "in obscurity" in Liberty County in 1911 and was survived by two families—one white, the other black.[215]

In a deed of sale dated July 4, 1826, James Nephew of McIntosh County awarded the 1,950 acres of South Hampton plantation, just south of Riceborough, to his daughter, Catherine Margaret Nephew King (1804-1887) and son-in-law Barrington King, younger brother of Roswell King, Jr. As part of this transaction, King, Jr. and Charles

---

[215] Ibid., 1581, 1585; Malcolm Bell, Jr., *Major Butler's Legacy: Five Generations of a Slaveholding Family* (Athens: University of Georgia Press, 1987), 532.

West, "in consideration of the sum of one dollar," were appointed trustees of the property. The deed describes South Hampton as being "bounded on the west by the Sunbury road, on the north by a line running along the center of the North Canal...to a point where Boyne Creek intersects with the [canal] usually known as old lower flood gate...so as to take in the whole of the old rice fields..." These areas are shown on an 1821 resurvey of South Hampton prepared attendant to the acquisition of the tract by James Nephew and place the tract east of the "Public Road to Sunbury" and "the Road to Darien." Nearby, as part of this antebellum road—long since disused as a thoroughfare—was a public ferry providing passage across the North Newport River. From that point, the road proceeded to the small 1840s settlement of Dorchester, and thence to Sunbury on the Medway River.

King, Jr., acquired ownership of South Hampton, along with a number of slaves, on February 1, 1838 from his brother Barrington at a purchase cost of $17,200, according to Liberty County deed records. Included in this transaction were the 1,950 acres of the plantation, along with all the buildings and various appurtenances including "the Sugar Mill, boilers, coolers, machinery & apparatus, the horse Gins and Corn Mill...also the ox carts & plantation tools & utensils belonging to the plantation whereon I [Barrington King] now reside in the County of Liberty, known as South Hampton, also the Cane Seed on said plantation & Fifty head of Cattle...also the following slaves, twenty-one in number, named George, Eve, Richard, Carpenter Peter, Letty, Sam, Manny, Maria, John, Caroline, Monday, Mary, Amy, Joseph, Cain, Jack, Sarah, Hetty, Junius,

Nickolas, & Brutus, together with the future issue & increase of the females..."[216]

Based on King's notes in his journal, cotton was a heavily cultivated staple crop at South Hampton but, as noted earlier, King also produced considerable amounts of rice and sugar cane there. King grew rice to a larger extent than might be imagined considering that South Hampton was not in the proximity of a delta estuary in the manner of Butler's Island, with the consequent benefit of tideflow irrigation. Rice at South Hampton apparently thrived, however, in swampy bottomland acreage irrigated by brackish waters from Boyne Creek and the nearby North Newport River. The 1821 resurvey of South Hampton, delineates "Canal and Rice Field Dam" bisecting Boyne Creek, a stream that meandered eastward before its merger with the North Newport and identified on later (and present) maps as Payne Creek. Abutting the rice dam were 103 acres of rice fields in three sections, the area utilized by King for his rice crop, and to which he frequently alludes in his journal.

---

[216] Deed Book I (1826), 207-08, Book K (1838), 472, Liberty County Records; also "1821 Resurvey of Thomas Young's South Hampton Plantation," Georgia Surveyor General Department, Georgia Department of Archives and History, Atlanta. James Nephew (1760-1827), who owned rice and cotton lands in McIntosh County, had acquired South Hampton in 1821 from the estate of the late Thomas Young before awarding the tract to his daughter and son-in-law five years later. South Hampton remained in possession of the King family until 1877 in which year Roswell "Rossie" King III, heavily encumbered with debt, mortgaged the plantation to John L. Villalenga of Savannah. In addition to the lien on the property in consideration of loans made to him by Villalenga, Rossie King, for $2,054, deeded South Hampton's livestock, farm equipment and tools, and all of the furnishings in the buildings at South Hampton. Deed Book R, 530, Liberty County Records.

King also cultivated corn, peas and sweet potatoes as provision crops at South Hampton, largely to sustain the 127 slaves (as enumerated in his estate at the time of his death in 1854) engaged in various pursuits at the plantation. Here also were a simple, but comfortable, residence along with various farm outbuildings and quarters for the slaves.

    King's acquisition of South Hampton in 1838 and his intention to devote his full energies to crop production there was the determining factor in his first resignation from the employ of the Butler estate the same year.

King and his family spent the summers and early fall at the family's Colonel's Island retreat, Woodville, a tract of 54 acres at Halfmoon Bluff several miles east of South Hampton and accessible by road, or even more conveniently by way of the North Newport River. King made frequent trips by boat between the two plantations during this time of year to manage his farming affairs at South Hampton, while also supervising his cultivation of crops at Woodville and Yellow Bluff, the latter a tract on the east side of Colonel's Island overlooking the salt marshes and the inland waterway. The family typically spent the late fall and winter months at South Hampton, a time of great activity when the plantation's staple and provision crops were being harvested and processed for market. Throughout the year, after re-engagement as the Butlers' manager in 1841, King made regular monthly trips by stagecoach to see to the operations of the Butler plantations in McIntosh and Glynn counties.

    Colonel's Island was a marsh island connected to the Liberty County mainland by a causeway, with St. Catherines Island and the inland waterway to its east. Originally named Bermuda Island during the colonial period, it purportedly came to be called Colonel's Island during the Revolution due to a number of military officers living there. The Kings' closest friends and neighbors on Colonel's Island were the Rev. and Mrs. Charles Colcock Jones of nearby Maybank, a cotton plantation of 700 acres. "The many, many years of kind intercourse and unbroken friendship we have enjoyed make them all especially near and dear," Mrs. Mary Jones wrote of the Kings in 1858.

Maybank was on the northwest part of the island overlooking Jones Creek and the Medway River. C.C. Jones owned two other Liberty County properties: Montevideo, a rice and cotton tract of 941 acres on the south bank of the North Newport River about a mile and a half southeast of Riceborough, and Arcadia, a tract of 1,996 ½ acres further inland, spreading westward from Midway toward McIntosh Station. The extensive correspondence of the Jones family indicates that their comfortable house at Montevideo, built in 1833 and enlarged in 1856, was always a favorite residence, while another house at Arcadia was less favored. Like Woodville for the Kings, Maybank was the summer residence for the Joneses, being preferred for its cooling summer breezes and healthier climate.

Woodville was at Halfmoon Bluff, south of Maybank. King had oversight of another property on Colonel's Island, this being, as noted, Yellow Bluff on the east side of the island overlooking St. Catherines Sound. Yellow Bluff, a tract of 1,000 acres, had been acquired at public auction in 1829 by Audley Maxwell, father of Julia King. Upon Maxwell's death in 1840, part of this tract was left to Julia, with another portion being awarded to her brother, Joseph E.

Maxwell. In April 1843, Roswell King, Jr. paid Joseph Maxwell $1,500 for the latter's share of Yellow Bluff, in trust for his wife Julia.

The land at Woodville, like that at nearby Yellow Bluff, had been property in the estate of Audley Maxwell bequeathed to Julia King. Julia also inherited 52 slaves from her father, most of these being utilized in agricultural and domestic pursuits at Woodville and Yellow Bluff. King's journal makes a number of references to his cultivation of sea island cotton at both Woodville and Yellow Bluff in the 1840s and 1850s. At some point, apparently while King was still in the employ of the Butlers and before he had purchased South Hampton, King built a house at Woodville for use as a family summer retreat so that his wife might maintain close contact with the numerous members of her family on or near Colonel's Island and the nearby Midway district.

Julia Rebecca King (1863-1952), daughter of James Audley Maxwell King and Catherine Lewis King, and granddaughter of Roswell, Jr., provides several useful descriptions of Woodville written from the perspective of almost a century later. In one of these, from a letter written in November 1930, she compares the Colonel's Island property with the site on which her forebear once lived at Hampton Point, St. Simons Island. "I [was] struck with the resemblance of Hampton Point to Woodville on the Half Moon Bluff on this [Colonel's] island, the summer house of my grandfather, Roswell King, Jr.—only Woodville is far, far more beautiful than Hampton Point, the bluff crowned with beautiful trees, & ocean going boats pass back & forth. Four-masted schooners have gone by there going up North Newport River for lumber—we will show you when you come—people say it looks like a park."

In another letter written two decades later, in August 1950, fourteen years after Julia King had removed to Merritt Island, Florida, she remarked that her grandfather had "built a big, beautiful house—said to have been an unusually fine house—at quite a distance from the river and he named the place 'Woodville' and the place...was known far & wide for its beauty and hospitality—Roses, flowering shrubs & trees—fruit trees of every kind—there were great oaks, gigantic cedars, wide grassy lawns & a greenhouse..."

Julia King's correspondence provides other insights and details regarding the life and times of the families of Colonel's Island—both before, and long after her grandfather's death:

> "We put down five artesian wells at Maxwellton [another Maxwell residence on the island]—everybody wanted an artesian well in those days [1890s]. The one at our 'Bird Refuge' was a six inch well & it had such a strong flow that for years it made a great roaring sound—like distant thunder. At Maxwellton we had five artesian wells & five miles of waterfront...I don't know how many people lived at the two little islands near Half Moon Bluff called the Dunham Hammocks [now Cattle Hammock]. There was a causeway, a corduroy road connecting them to Colonel's Island...Reuben King & Joseph Austin owned the two islands. Reuben King was a younger brother of Roswell King [Sr.] my great-grandfather. Reuben King owned a place called 'Mallow' on the Sapelo River in McIntosh County. His old home there is now called Pine Harbor & is a very popular resort. Reuben King married Abigail Austin, daughter of Joseph Austin whose plantation called 'Melon Bluff' (because of the big melons raised there) is west of Half Moon—if you go westward along the River you will go by Melon Bluff. Reuben King & Joseph Austin sold the two little islands to

Thomas Dunham whose plantation called 'Cedar Point' was north of Colonel's Island on the mainland..."[217]

As the crow flies, South Hampton, King's primary agricultural tract, was only a few miles west of Woodville. Communication between two plantations was usually by water via the North Newport River, utilizing the incoming or outgoing tides by bateau or sailboat. The route by land was longer and circuitous—but nonetheless occasionally used, particularly in times of inclement weather.

King, Jr. twice served the Butler interests in McIntosh and Glynn counties as plantation manager, the first being a tenure from 1819 until October 1838 when he resigned to pursue the development of his own plantation affairs in Liberty County. Less than three years later, consequent upon the death of the Butler's new manager, Thomas Oden, King returned to oversee the Butler interests, serving on this second occasion from 1841 until 1854, when he proffered his second resignation. King died unexpectedly several months later.

Engineering the Tidewater: Rice Cultivation in the Altamaha Delta

On the river plantations a skill perfected by west African farmers was adopted by South Carolina planters in the early eighteenth century, later by those of Georgia, by which tidal ebbs and flows and saltwater/freshwater interaction were utilized to achieve high levels

---

[217] Julia King Papers, Collection 1070, folder 1:7, GHS, contains the remarks of Julia King written in 1930. The other recollections of Miss King quoted, in addition to deeds relating to the disposition of Woodville and Yellow Bluff, are from her papers on deposit at the Midway Museum, Midway, Ga.

of rice productivity. Both Kings, Sr. and Jr., employed the tideflow method at Butler's Island, a practice followed by virtually all of the planters on the river plantations. This process enabled greater acreages to be planted and higher yields per acre.[218] Tideflow cultivation created higher expectations from planters who, incumbent upon the expensive nature of this activity, invested considerable outlays of capital in acquiring the requisite labor force for large-scale production. Prime field slaves were expensive. Additionally, the necessary tools, boats, threshing and pounding mills, outbuildings, slave quarters and other accoutrements arguably made rice cultivation the most expensive of southern agricultural

---

[218] Scholarly treatments of south Atlantic rice production include Mart Stewart, *"What Nature Suffers to Groe": Life, Labor and Landscape on the Georgia Coast, 1680-1920* (Athens: University of Georgia Press, 1996); Julia Floyd Smith, *Slavery and Rice Culture in Lowcountry Georgia, 1750-1860* (Knoxville: University of Tennessee Press, 1985); James M. Clifton, ed., *Life and Labor on Argyle Island: Letters and Documents of a Savannah River Rice Plantation, 1833-1867* (Savannah, Ga.: Beehive Press, 1978); William Dusinberre, *Them Dark Days: Slavery in the American Rice Swamps* (New York: Oxford University Press, 1996); Albert Virgil House, ed., *Planter Management and Capitalism in Antebellum Georgia: The Journal of Hugh Fraser Grant, Ricegrower* (New York: Columbia University Press, 1954); and Gray, *History of Agriculture in the Southern United States to 1860*, op. cit. Useful contemporary accounts of rice cultivation and plantation management are contained in the plantation journals and account books of Roswell King, Jr. in Buddy Sullivan, ed., *"All Under Bank" Roswell King, Jr. and Plantation Management in Tidewater Georgia, 1819-1854* (Midway, Ga.; the Midway Museum, 2013 reprint of 2003 1st edit.); those of the Manigault family in Clifton, ed., *Life and Labor on Argyle Island*; and the plantation journal of Richard James Arnold, rice planter of Bryan County, in Charles Hoffmann and Tess Hoffmann, *North by South: The Two Lives of Richard James Arnold* (Athens: University of Georgia Press, 1988). The most useful primary sources for the Altamaha are in the James Hamilton Couper Plantation Records, 1818-1854, four vols., Southern Historical Collection (SHC), University of North Carolina, Chapel Hill.

enterprises. Frederick Law Olmsted explains the rice process in *A Journey in the Seaboard Slave States* in 1856, at the height of the era:

"The rice-harvest commences early in September. The water having been all drawn off the field the previous ebb tide, the negroes reap the rice with sickles, taking three or four rows of it at a cut. The stubble is left about a foot in height, and the rice is laid across the top of it, so that it will dry rapidly. One or two days afterwards it is tied in small sheaves, and then immediately carried to the barn or stack-yard. This is often some miles distant; yet the whole crop of many plantations is transported to it on the heads of the laborers. This work, at the hottest season of the year, in the midst of the recently-exposed mire of the rice fields, is acknowledged to be exceedingly severe, and must be very hazardous to the health, even of negroes. When there is a canal running in the rear of the plantations, a part of the transportation of the crop is made by scows; and very recently, a low, broad-wheeled cart or truck, which can be drawn by negroes on the embankments, has been introduced, first at the suggestion of a Northerner, to relieve the labor. Threshing commences immediately after harvest, occupying the best of the plantation force for most of the winter. It is done on an earthen floor, in the open air, and the rice is cleaned by carrying it on the heads of the negroes, by a ladder, up on to a platform, twenty feet from the ground, and pouring it slowly down, so that the wind will drive off the chaff, and leave the grain in a heap under the platform. But on most large plantations, threshing machines driven either by horse-power or by steam-power, have been lately adopted, of course, with great economy.

"The usual crop of rice is from thirty to sixty bushels from an acre, but even as high as one hundred bushels is sometimes obtained. Its weight (in the rough) is from forty-one to forty-nine pounds per bushel. The usual price paid for it (in the rough), in Charleston and Savannah, is from eighty cents to one dollar a bushel ... Planters usually employ their factors — merchants residing in Charleston, Savannah or Wilmington, the three rice ports — to sell their crop by sample. The purchasers are merchants, mill-owners, or the agents of foreign rice mills. Rice is used in the rice-district as a constant article of food, never being absent from the breakfast and dinner-table of many families. On the rice plantations, particularly those furnished with a hulling mill, it is given a good deal to the negroes, more especially during the seasons of their harvest labor, and at the holidays."[219]

The cultivation of rice was centered in the fertile bottomlands of freshwater river systems that benefited from an infusion of nutrient-rich soils from the uplands of the Georgia piedmont. Rice cultivation in these areas made effective use of tideflow irrigation amid freshwater marsh systems for the alternating cycles of flooding and draining fields. For example, one of the largest of the rice plantations, that at Butler's Island in the Altamaha River delta, was managed on the basis of the tideflow process of freshwater flow and freshwater marshes, a practice followed by the larger planters on the river plantations of the southeastern coast. The process resulted in greater productivity and higher yields per acre cultivated.

Writing in the *Southern Agriculturist* in 1828, Roswell King, Jr., manager of the Butler's Island rice plantation, noted that "...it is easier to ditch eight hundred cubic feet of marsh, than four hundred feet of rooty river swamp..."—But the cultivation system of river bottomlands was contingent upon the abilities of (prior to 1865) the slave bondsman—"In harvesting a crop of Rice, some acres are heavier, or further off, than others, some hands are quicker, or more able, than others," King commented.[220]

Rice planting began in late March and early April following plowing and other tasks associated with field preparation.

---

[219] Frederick Law Olmsted, *A Journey in the Seaboard Slave States* (New York, 1856), contained in Olmsted, *The Cotton Kingdom* (New York: Alfred A. Knopf, 1953).

[220] Roswell King, Jr., "On the Management of the Butler Estate and the Cultivation of the Sugar Cane," Letter to the Editor, *Southern Agriculturist* (1) December 1828.

Cultivation on the tideflow plantations required staggered plantings so that the various facets of tending the crop could be spaced at different intervals. Fields were laid out as a series of squares of eighteen to twenty-five acres each, penetrated by a grid of drainage ditches to facilitate the flow of water. Embankments separated the squares and provided foot access for workers tending the fields. The largest levees were those along the riverbanks of the tideflow plantations. Tidegates built at intervals in the river levee facilitated the introduction or removal of water from the fields. Proper irrigation required regular ditching by the workforce to prevent the buildup of silt resulting from the flooding and drainage of the rice squares. The grid-like layout of a rice plantation thus represented a complex system of hydraulics, all predicated on the proper balance of a multiplicity of environmental factors, including landscape, soils, marshes, water, tides and, not least, an assortment of weather conditions.

From 1819 to 1861, Butler's Island often had over nine hundred acres per year under cultivation. In aggregate, the island comprised 1,500 acres of Altamaha delta bottomland—acreage that was originally brackish river swamp thick with cypress, gum and maple trees. The preparation of the island for rice planting required inordinate amounts of labor to expedite the difficult work of removing the timber, undergrowth and clearing stumps, followed by the building of embankments around and within the island, and the construction of the heavy, wooden tidegates (or trunks) for the management of the water flow. The soils of the Altamaha delta were extremely fertile, both for the culture of cotton and sugar cane, but most especially so for that of rice.

The seasonal yield of the rice crop usually depended on the techniques employed by the planter, as well as conditions over which the planter often had little or no control—saltwater intrusion, insect infestation, and the vagaries of weather. Efficient management was essential, James H. Couper being the best example. Couper planted his first rice crop at Hopeton-on-the-Altamaha in 1821 with a consequent steady increase in his yields-per-acre into the 1840s. In 1827, Couper's crop produced a yield of about forty-nine bushels per acre on 351½ acres planted. A decade later, Couper was producing about sixty bushels of rice per acre on 684 acres "under bank."[221]

Like rice, the management of long-staple sea island cotton was labor intensive and required considerable investment by the planter. Unlike rice, however, cotton was a dry-culture crop. Excessive moisture in the soil generally caused deterioration of the roots of the cotton plants. Paradoxically, considerable amounts of sea island cotton were grown for a number of years at Butler's Island, the low-lying rice tract, the damp bottomlands of which were often below the level of the river.

The production of the cotton staple required a high degree of fertilization, chiefly a variety of manures. The utilization of tidal salt marsh was frequently the preferred method of infusing nutrients into the soils upon which cotton was cultivated. Thus, as in rice cultivation, many coastal planters effectively utilized the local ecology

---

[221] James Hamilton Couper Plantation Records, 1818-1854, Southern Historical Collection, University of North Carolina, Chapel Hill, in Albert Virgil House, ed., *Planter Management and Capitalism in Antebellum Georgia: The Journal of Hugh Fraser Grant, Ricegrower* (New York: Columbia University Press, 1954).

in respect to producing their cotton, being reliant on natural marsh grass, marsh mud and crushed oyster shell for fertilizing purposes. The routine task work of plantation slaves regularly included carting salt marsh cuttings and mud for spreading in the cotton fields, both on the large island plantations as well as on the mainland tracts.

A typical crop yield at Butler's Island was two hundred pounds of cotton and three barrels of rice to the acre. According to Roswell King, Jr., a neighboring cotton plantation, Hampton on St. Simons Island (a dry, upland property), rarely yielded more than 250 pounds of cotton to the acre—which makes the Butler's Island yield even more impressive considering its dampness. For a time, cotton and rice were planted simultaneously on Butler's Island, as evidenced in the crop reports of the Butler Estate in the 1830s.

Whether the tideflow or the swamp reservoir cultivating techniques were used, prime field hands were each responsible for the maintenance of four to five acres of rice during the season. On many plantations the daily work of slaves was segmented into tasks— each hand was assigned a task, typically eight or nine hours to complete a day's work, or some fraction thereof according to a worker's age, physical ability and health. Tasks were usually assigned by the head driver, a skilled slave appointed by the overseer or plantation owner to supervise the daily work of the field hands. At Butler's Island, Roswell King, Jr., employed the task system of labor, and like most of his contemporaries, he tailored the concept to suit the requirements of his operations. Writing in 1828, King noted that

"the tasks given are calculated to require so much labor. It is as easy to cut three tasks of Rice as it is to bind two, or to bring two home. It is easier to ditch eight hundred cubic feet of marsh, than four hundred feet of rooty river swamp...But the system was almost universally contingent upon the physical capability of a given worker—In harvesting a crop of Rice, some acres are heavier, or further off, than others, some hands quicker or more able than others...Frequently, by Friday night, I have nearly as much Rice in, as if the regular task during the week had been given. There may be fifteen to twenty acres left; say bring it in, [and] the balance of the week is yours..."[222]

The effectiveness of the task system was predicated upon the efficiency of the driver who held the most important position in the plantation slave hierarchy, being second only to the white overseer in terms of authority and responsibility. The driver supervised a number of sub-drivers and managed the day-to-day planting, growing and harvesting processes. King preferred that his drivers hold themselves apart and above the rest of the plantation's work force— "It is a great point in having the principal drivers [be] men that can support their dignity," King notes. "A condescension to familiarity should be prohibited. Young Negroes are put to work early, twelve to fourteen years old...It keeps them out of mischief and by giving them light tasks, thirty to forty rows, they acquire habits of perseverance and industry."[223]

Seasonal rice planting was begun in late March and early April following plowing, and other tasks associated with field preparation. Cultivation on the tideflow plantations required staggered plantings

---

[222] Roswell King, Jr., "On the Management of the Butler Estate and the Cultivation of the Sugar Cane," (Letter to the Editor), *Southern Agriculturist* I (December 1828): 523-30.

[223] King, Jr., "On the Management of the Butler Estate," 524; Albert V. House, "Labor-Management Problems on Georgia Rice Plantations, 1840-1860," *Agricultural History* 28 (October 1954); James Herbert Stone, "Black Leadership in the Old South: The Slave Drivers of the Rice Kingdom," Ph.D. dissertation, Florida State University, 1976.

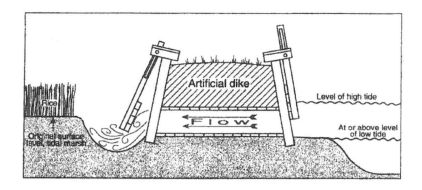

Typical tidegate water-flow arrangement on a low country rice plantation.

so that the various facets of tending the crop could be spaced at different intervals. Fields were laid out as a series of squares of eighteen to twenty-five acres each, penetrated by a grid of drainage ditches to facilitate the flow of water. Levees (embankments) separated the squares and provided foot access for workers tending the fields. The largest levees were those along the riverbanks of the plantation. Heavy wooden tidegates built at intervals in the river levee controlled the introduction and subsequent removal of water from the fields. Proper irrigation required regular ditching to prevent the build-up of silt from flooding and draining the fields. Ditching was considered the most labor-intensive work on a rice plantation. The grid-like layout of the tracts under cultivation in South Carolina and Georgia represented a complex irrigation system based on elemental hydraulics incorporating local environmental conditions — soil, river hydrology and tide.

Butler's Island had 600 to 900 acres under cultivation in rice at any given time almost continuously from 1819 to 1861. The delta island was comprised of about 1,500 acres overall of Altamaha River bottomland, acreage that was originally brackish river swamp, thick with assorted vegetation, including cypress, gum and maple. Making Butler's Island cultivable for rice entailed great amounts of labor involving the difficult and tedious work of removing the timber and heavy vegetative undergrowth, followed by the removal of stumps. The next step entailed building earthen embankments around the island and the construction of trunks (tidegates) to manage the water flow. A network of irrigation ditches for the flooding of the fields was then prepared. The soil of the lower Altamaha basin was quite fertile for rice, and also for cotton and sugar cane. Butler noted that his rice island lay amidst "the best pitch of the tide," meaning that it was ideally situated far enough from the Atlantic to utilize the flow of fresh water from upriver, yet near enough to the sea for the utilization of the tides for flooding and draining his fields.[224]

Proper preparation of the bottomland soil, rich with upcountry clays and nutrients conveyed by the river, was essential prior to rice planting. This process began in the winter with the burning off of the stubble from the previous season followed by the chopping of weeds and the pulverizing and plowing of the fields. King reported to Thomas Butler in Philadelphia in 1830 that, in properly prepared soil, a fragile and immature rice plant "needles through without difficulty." Rice seed was planted by hand with a small hoe after which the fields were flooded—the "sprout flow"—by releasing fresh water on the ebbing tide into the rice squares through the wooden tidegates (fig. 13a). The water was distributed to the interior fields by means of canals, irrigation ditches and quarter drains. The tidegates

---

[224] Roswell King, Jr. to Thomas Butler, Butler Family Papers, HSP.

were connected to the outer rice squares abutting the river levees, while the inner squares were flooded by a main canal connected to the smaller ditches.[225]

The tidegates, heavily anchored in the river mud and embankments by thick pilings, were hinged in such a manner that they could swing open with the pressure of the water against them, away from the bank, when the fields were drained. On the flooding stages, an outer tidegate was opened to allow water coming from upriver to enter on the ebbing tide. An inner gate was opened by the pressure of the water against it. When the desired height of water in the fields was reached the trunk was closed. The trunks required constant maintenance and upkeep, always from the most efficient and experienced hands. Capable trunk-minders were critical components of the workforce of any rice plantation.

When the grain sprouted after several weeks on the initial flooding, water was drained to prevent the delicate sprouts from floating away. The rice shoots were then allowed to grow in the damp soil for about three weeks. By the first of May grass and weeds growing among the shoots had to be regularly hoed, usually by the women of the workforce. The second irrigation, the "point flow," was then applied to cover just the tops of the maturing plants. After a week the water was gradually drained off once again until it covered half the plants. This was the "long flow" and it was allowed to remain on the field until the rice was sturdy enough to stand. More weeding followed then the water was gradually drained completely off the field. After more weeding and hoeing, the "lay-by flow," sometimes

---

[225] J.D. Legare, "Synopsis of the Culture of Rice," *Southern Agriculturist*, 2nd Series, I (February 1841), 80-83.

called the "harvest flow," was allowed to flood the field about the first of July. This flooding lasted seven to eight weeks with periodic draining of stagnant water and inflows of fresh water.

The size of one's crop often depended on the techniques employed by the planter as well as conditions over which the planter had little or no control, including local soil conditions, insect and "rice bird" intrusion on the crop, accidental introduction of salt water through a burst embankment and the vagaries of the weather. James H. Couper planted his first rice crop at Hopeton-on-the-Altamaha in 1821 with a consequent increase in his yields-per acre into the 1840s. In 1827, Couper's crop produced a yield of 17,571 bushels of rice on 351 ½ acres planted—an average of about 49 bushels per acre. Couper's average yield per acre was consistently over 50 bushels per acre during the 1840s; his most productive year, for which records are available, was in 1839 when his yield was 60.4 bushels to the acre. By then Couper was planting rice on 684 acres, almost double the acreage he had under cultivation in the late 1820s.[226]

Yields varied in the tidewater from about 40 bushels to the acre in South Carolina to about 50 in Georgia. The records of Gowrie plantation on Argyle Island in the Savannah River show that Charles and Louis Manigault had yields of 38, 40 and 39.5 bushels per acre on 500 acres planted in the years 1852, 1855 and 1857, respectively. One could argue that this is inconsistent with the established trend on the Georgia coast, but it should be noted that Gowrie was the northernmost Georgia rice plantation before going into South

---

[226] James Hamilton Couper Plantation Papers, 1818-1854, SHC.

Carolina. Crop yields were more in the range of 50 to 55 bushels per acre in the Ogeechee, Altamaha and Satilla river districts further down the coast.[227]

Rice planted in the first week of April was usually ready for harvest by late August or early September. The removal of the lay-by flow of water occurred just before the grain was fully ripe. Shortly after, the fully-matured rice was cut with sharp, curved sickles called rice hooks (or reap-hooks) and laid on the ground atop the stubble. Cutting rice in the wet, muddy fields amid the humidity and heat of late summer required the labor of most of the slave force; it was one of the most laborious aspects of the rice planting cycle. After being allowed to dry, the cut rice stalks were tied into sheaves and transported to the rice yard at the plantation mill by shallow-draft barges, called flats, through the network of canals.[228]

Most of the rice shipped to the Savannah and Charleston markets from the Georgia plantations was in the form of "rough rice," rice that had been threshed, winnowed and cleaned of chaff and straw, but not pounded (polished). On some plantations rice was threshed by beating the stalks with flail sticks on elevated threshing floors. Later, many plantations acquired steam-powered threshing engines to more efficiently expedite the preparation of rice for shipment.[229]

---

[227] Thomas Spalding, "On the Culture, Harvesting and Threshing of Rice, and On the Rust in Cotton," *Southern Agriculturist* VIII (1835); Robert F.W. Allston, "Essay on Sea Coast Crops," *DeBow's Review* 16 (June 1851); James Hamilton Couper Plantation Records, SHC; Louis Manigault, plantation records for Gowrie and East Hermitage plantations on the Savannah River, 1845-1876, Collection 1290, GHS.

[228] Richard J. Arnold, "Directions for Planting Rice," 1842, Arnold-Screven Papers, Series J, SHC.

[229] James Potter Papers and Rice Plantation Journal (Savannah River), 1828-1831, Manuscript Collection 630, GHS.

Threshing and winnowing began in early September, and in the case of rough rice shipments to market were made in stages throughout the fall and early winter. By the mid-nineteenth century, increasing numbers of planters were utilizing newly-developed threshing machinery. In 1851, for example, steam-powered rice threshers, while expensive for even the larger plantations (the machinery could cost from $3,000 to $7,000), had been improved to the point where they could process up to 1,200 bushels per day.[230]

The more prosperous planters often equipped their plantations with a pounding mill to facilitate on the plantation itself the final stage in preparing the crop for market, that of the processing of rough rice to "clean rice" by pounding. Pounding removed the outer shell then polished the rice kernels by a system of steam-powered stone pestles. This equipment was prohibitively expensive, and only the largest plantations had their own pounding mills. Roswell King, Jr. was a proponent of on-site, steam-powered pounding mills, feeling they improved the plantation's efficiency, productivity and profitability. Pounding mills utilized tidal power until the availability of steam engines came to the fore in the 1820s. Meanwhile, until the advent of the wider use of steam-powered machinery, threshing continued to be implemented by the laborious hand-flailing method on threshing floors.

In 1791-92, Jonathan Lucas of South Carolina built the first tidal-powered rice mill, a method that was eventually, until the emergence of steam-powered machinery, employed to facilitate all the several steps of rice processing—grinding, winnowing, pounding, screening

---

[230] R.F.W. Allston, "Rice," *DeBow's Review* I (1846), 340-42; *DeBow's Review* XI (1851), 306.

and polishing. Steam-driven pounding machinery was later introduced and improved technologically, and was in general use by the 1830s although an investment of between $12,000 to $18,000 for these devices made it prohibitively expensive for all but the largest rice planters. Smaller planters were compelled to either pay "tolls" to their wealthier neighbors to process their rice, or shipped their unpounded "rough" rice to the markets in Savannah or Charleston for pounding. Polished rice from the plantations with mills was shipped to market as "clean" rice in wooden barrel (tierces). About 200 bushels of harvested rice yielded one 600-pound tierce of clean rice.[231]

Greatly increased production resulting from the development of steam pounding mills placed unacceptable constraints on the hand threshers to keep pace, and mechanized processes were soon developed for the threshing stage. Consequent upon these technological improvements was the need for increased cooperage to accommodate the increased amount of processed rice. More bondsmen were thus employed in the construction of wooden barrels, or tierces, for the storage of polished rice as it came from the pounding mill.[232] Rice mills, such as the Butler's Island mill, or the mill at Cat Head near Darien, were located near riverbanks to facilitate the loading of tierces of rice on to coasting vessels for shipment to market. Brick was the preferred choice of material in rice mill construction. Large chimneys and sheds containing the steam engine and boiler were connected to the main structure. The

---

[231] Heyward, *Seed from Madagascar*, 41; House, *Planter Management*, 61-62.
[232] "Agricultural Notes," James Hamilton Couper papers, 55, SHC; House, ed., *Planter Management*, 62.

mill was devoted to the various phases of the rice milling process, from threshing to pounding, screening and cleaning and to barreling, loading and storage.[233]

The key process in the milling procedure was the cracking of the outer shell of the rice without damaging the inner core of the grain. This was achieved by machinery which raised and lowered a series of slotted timbers called "pestles" above a mortar filled with rough rice. The pestles pounded the rice from an exacting height with the precise degree of pressure needed to break the outer shell but not harm the inner grain. Mills on the Georgia coast utilized the system of pestles to pound rice until the introduction of Deforest's mill machinery in the mid-1830s. This entailed a much superior and more rapid method of crushing the rice shells between fixed and revolving stone cylinders.[234] Albert V. House makes the observation that the capacity of most of the Georgia pounding mills did not reach that of the South Carolina mills, "with the possible exception of that operated by James Hamilton Couper at Hopeton on the Altamaha."[38] Some of the smaller Georgia coast mills utilized fewer pestles working at slower speeds with tidal power or small steam engines. At Gowrie, the Manigault plantation on the Savannah River, there were "turned out 8 to 10 barrels with each tide" with some 460 barrels pounded during a three-month period in the 1832-33 season.[235]

In 1832, King successfully prevailed upon Thomas Butler to allow him to acquire a steam engine to power the rice threshing mill and

---

[233] House, ed., *Planter Management*, 62.
[234] Ibid., 64.
[235] Slave Record Book (Gowrie plantation), 1833, Manigault Papers, SHC.

pounding machinery at Butler's Island. This mill was built near the overseer's house adjacent to the river landing at Butler's Island and was ready for operation in late 1833. Because the ground at the mill site was subject to periods of wetness, even occasional flooding since it was below the level of the nearby Butler River, King employed the slaves in the emplacement of thick pilings in the soil to provide greater stability for the engine, its housing and brick stack. The operation of the steam pounding mill created increased demands for energy sources. Pine land had been acquired in 1814 by Roswell King, Sr. at Woodville on the south branch of the Altamaha to provide fuel for the sugar boilers at Butler's Island as well as timber for construction purposes.[236] The installation of the pounding mill placed greater demands on the Woodville tract as the primary source for fuel to operate the mill engine. This device typically required up to twelve cords of wood to pound one hundred tierces of rice. Planters had the option of shipping their rough rice to Savannah where it was sold in bushels of 45 to 50 pounds, and then pounded at mills on the Savannah River.[237] Or, as previously noted, they could contract neighboring planters who had their own mills to pound their rice for a fee. Clean rice, shipped to the factors in tierces holding about 600 pounds of rice each, generally brought greater profits to the planter.[238]

---

[236] Roswell King, Jr. to Thomas Butler, Butler Family Papers, HSP.
[237] Manigault Papers, Gowrie plantation books, SHC; Manigault plantation records (Gowrie), GHS.
[238] Roswell King, Jr., to Thomas Butler, December 19, 1833, Butler Family Papers, HSP. The production and marketing of rice, particularly regarding the role of the factorage system once the crop has reached the markets, is most completely covered in House, ed., *Planter Management and Capitalism in Antebellum Georgia*, 38-81.

Wooden tierces were often manufactured at the rice markets as exemplified by an advertisement by the factorage of Robert Habersham & Son in the noting that the firm was seeking "Contracts for one to five hundred thousand Pine Staves suitable for Rice Casks."[239] However, more planters of the antebellum period preferred to ship their crop to market in the form of rough rice since most could not afford pounding machinery, it being more expedient to allow their factors to attend to the details of processing and marketing.

The leading late antebellum rice producers in Georgia were Louis Manigault, James F. Potter, William H. Gibbons, James P. Screven, Ralph E. Elliott, Arthur Heyward, Langdon Cheves, and Francis H. McLeod, all of Chatham County; Richard James Arnold, Thomas Savage Clay and George W. McAllister of Bryan County; Roswell King, George W. Walthour and Charlton Hines of Liberty County; Pierce and John Butler, Phineas M. Nightingale, Jacob Barrett, Robert B. Rhett, Thomas M. Forman, Norman P. Gignilliat, William R. Gignilliat and Robert L. Morris, all of McIntosh County; James Hamilton Couper, Francis P. Corbin, George C. Dent, James M. Troup, Hugh Fraser Grant and T. Pinckney Huger of Glynn County; and Stephen King, George Owens, John Bailey, Duncan L. Clinch and George Lang, of Camden.

---

[239] *Savannah Daily Republican*, July 19, 1860; Charles E. Pearson, "Captain Charles Stevens and the Antebellum Georgia Coasting Trade," *Georgia Historical Quarterly* 75 (Fall 1991): 488.

Cotton & Sugar Cane in the Rice Delta

As in rice production, Georgia's coastal environment—soils, climate, and the proximity of the sea—established the fundamental ecological desirability of planting sea island cotton from the South Carolina barrier islands southward to northeast Florida. The islands, with their exposure to salt air and breezes off the ocean, were particularly conducive to the cultivation of the sea island, black seed, variety of cotton with its silky, delicate strands that brought a much higher price on the markets than the upland-grown, short-staple cotton. Sea island cotton was also grown extensively on the adjoining mainland, in areas with porous soils and good exposure to salt air. Roswell King, Jr. successfully grew the staple at both his Woodville (marsh island) and South Hampton (mainland) plantations in Liberty County.[240]

Like rice, the management of sea island cotton was labor intensive and required considerable investment by the planter. Unlike rice, however, cotton was a dry-culture crop. Excessive moisture in the soil generally caused deterioration of the roots of the cotton plants. Paradoxically, sizeable amounts of sea island cotton were grown for a number of years at Butler's Island, the low-lying rice tract, the damp bottomlands of which were often below the level of the surrounding river delta. In this moist, but very rich, soil, Major Pierce Butler was able to produce sea island cotton as a rotation crop at Butler's Island.

---

[240] Sullivan, ed., "*All Under Bank*," 21-24, relates the plantation operations of Roswell King, Jr. in Liberty County. Specifics of activities and incidents at Butler's Island, Hampton, South Hampton and Woodville plantations are related in selected extracts, with annotation, from King's daily journal in the same volume, 42-120.

The largest cotton tract on the Butler estates was at Hampton, on the north end of St. Simons Island, with additional acreage devoted to the staple at neighboring St. Anne's, a contiguous cotton tract on the south end of Hampton, and on the banked marshland at Experiment on Little St. Simons Island across the Hampton River from the main plantation. At Butler's Island the average allotment of cotton land to one slave was five acres, with the average yield per acre varying between 150 and 250 pounds. A testament to the early interest in cultivating cotton on the rice island is indicated in the "Statement of Cotton Crops for the Year 1823" for Hampton, Experiment and Butler's Island. On April 5, King documented the shipment of 12,938 pounds of cotton from Butler's Island alone "to Liverpool via Savannah" and, on May 9, the shipment of an additional 18,251 pounds—an impressive yield for that year by any measure.[241]

In addition to cotton, Butler also grew sugar cane as a rotation crop at Butler's Island. As noted earlier, Thomas Spalding often visited Major Butler's rice island and was impressed by the farm principles applied there, both from Butler's perspective as a planner and in the initiative of both Kings to efficiently implement those plans. A typical yield at Butler's Island was two hundred pounds of cotton and three barrels of clean rice to the acre. According to King, Jr., Hampton, a dry, upland property, rarely yielded in excess of 250 pounds to the acre, which makes the Butler's Island yields all the more notable. For a time, cotton and rice were cultivated simultaneously at Butler's Island as seen in several crop reports during the 1830s. For example, in 1836, there was shipped from

---

[241] Roswell King plantation notes, Julia King Papers, Midway Museum, Midway, Ga.

Butler's Island to the Charleston factorage of Chisholm & Taylor 1,021,306 pounds of rice cultivated on 609 acres, along with 23 bales of sea island cotton planted on 110 acres.[242]

King, Jr.'s plantation account book for 1844 further documents the shipment of cotton from Butler's Island. For example, King notes on January 3, 1844 that he shipped 35 bales of sea island cotton to the Charleston factorage of Harrison & Latham "on account of J. & P. Butler, pr schooner R[oswell] King." Another entry of the same date reports the shipment of 248 ½ tierces of rice on the same vessel, presumably consigned to the same factor. Not all the Butlers' rice and cotton went to Charleston. King's daybook entries of April 15 and May 3, 1844 note the shipment of five tierces of dirty (rough) rice to nearby Darien, sold to the firm of S.Y. Collins & Company at the price of $331.53.[243] By the late 1840s cotton production on the island had largely ceased due to the increased attention to rice production. With the conversion of cotton lands, in addition to newly prepared river swampland, devoted to rice in the late 1840s, annual rice shipments from Butler's Island were exceeding 2.5 million pounds on the eve of the Civil War.[244]

Cotton production required a high degree of specialized fertilization, chiefly a variety of manures. As in rice production King and his contemporaries effectively utilized the local ecosystem in respect to cotton, relying on natural marsh grass (*Spartina alterniflora*), nutrient-rich marsh mud, and crushed oyster shell for fertilization purposes. The routine task work of tidewater plantation slaves

---

[242] Roswell King, Jr., annual crop reports, Butler Family Papers, HSP.
[243] Roswell King, Jr., "Day Book for Estate of J. & P. Butler in Georgia, 1844," Margaret Davis Cate Collection, Collection 997, GHS.
[244] U.S. Census, McIntosh County, Agricultural Schedules, 1860.

regularly included carting salt marsh cuttings, crushed shell and mud for spreading in the cotton fields, both on the large island plantations as well as the mainland cotton tracts.[245] In his journal, King frequently mentions fertilization of his fields with marsh mud and marsh grass.

Planting of long-staple cotton began in mid-March. On some mainland plantations, planters grew rice and cotton simultaneously, an effort that required considerable attention to the proper management of both crops. King was typical of this approach as he cultivated both staples at South Hampton, in addition to some acreage devoted to short-staple (petit) cotton. During the growing cycle, field hands periodically removed weeds and grasses by hoeing while also "thinning" the cotton plants to prevent their coming into contact with each other. In a report to the Butler family in 1833 King wrote that early thinning entailed "the True principle of cotton planting" and led to earlier development of the pod."[246]

After several hoeings, the cotton pods began to bloom in July, with the first bolls beginning to open by early August. Sea island cotton was particularly vulnerable to sudden weather changes, especially the heavy rains produced by summer thunderstorms. Proper attention thus had to be given to employing small ditches between the ridges of cotton to allow the draining off of excess water.

---

[245] Thomas Spalding, "Brief Notes," *Southern Agriculturist* I (December 1828); King, Jr., "On the Management of the Butler Estate"; King, Jr., "Day Book for Estate of J. & P. Butler, 1844," GHS. A useful account of this process is provided in Guion Griffis Johnson, *A Social History of the Sea Islands with Special Reference to St. Helena Island, South Carolina* (Chapel Hill: University of North Carolina Press, 1930), 55-59.

[246] Roswell King, Jr. to Thomas Butler, September 29, 1833, Butler Family Papers, HSP.

To avoid damaging the sensitive plants, little or no hoeing was done on the crop following the appearance of the pods.

After the bolls began to appear a series of up to a dozen pickings began. The slave force picked cotton according to task, or task-row, and the cotton was gathered and stored at the plantation complex where it was thoroughly dried. The season during which cotton was harvested usually ran in tandem with that of rice although cotton continued to be picked well into the winter, long after all the rice was in. Throughout the late summer and fall the workforce sorted, ginned and moted the cotton. Most coastal planters employed a mechanical roller gin developed by Joseph Eve in the Bahamas in 1785, a year before the first sea island cotton was grown on Georgia. Eve's roller gin removed the seeds from the delicate strands of cotton with less damage to the fibers than the barbed-gin developed several years later by Eli Whitney near Savannah. The Whitney model was specifically designed to process the tougher, more durable upland (short-staple) cotton.[247] The hand-moting of cotton entailed the removal of cracked seeds and yellowed bolls. After ginning, cotton was sorted by quality, following which it was packed in 300-pound bags for shipment to market. Later in the antebellum period some planters baled their cotton for shipment although bagging remained the preferred method for the coastal planters since damage was more liable to occur to cotton pressed or packed into bales. Screw presses

---

[247] Thomas Spalding, "On the Introduction of Sea-Island Cotton into Georgia," *Southern Agriculturist* IV (March 1831); Spalding, "Cotton—Its Introduction and Progress of Its Culture in the United States," *Southern Agriculturist* VIII (January 1835); Gray, *History of Agriculture*, 721-31; Mart A. Stewart, "Land Use and Landscapes: Environment and Social Change in Coastal Georgia, 1680-1880," Ph.D. dissertation, Emory University, 1988, 258-265.

commonly utilized in baling upland grown cotton are rarely mentioned in the surviving records and journals of the tidewater planters.

The most productive period of the sea island cotton industry was from 1790 to about 1825, after which markets for the commodity began to decline resulting in depressed prices for the staple. Cotton production came to require increased investments in capital and labor, and gradually overcame its profitability. Nonetheless, sea island cotton continued to be cultivated in coastal Georgia and the South Carolina lowcountry for the rest of the antebellum period. The Civil War all but ended its production and the industry never recovered to any appreciable degree after the war.

A third staple cultivated by King, Jr., both in Liberty County and at Butler's Island, was that of sugar cane. Cane production was chiefly a rotational crop and was always secondary to rice and cotton. Many coastal planters favored its utility as a means of rotation and diversification, as advocated by one of the South's leading agrarians, Thomas Spalding of Sapelo Island. Spalding introduced the culture of sugar cane, initially based on Jamaican techniques, to coastal Georgia in 1805, by his own account. In 1809 he constructed a tabby sugar cane press and boiling mill on Sapelo for the manufacture of sugar and molasses.[248] Spalding's cane crop of 1814 was valued at $12,500, a circumstance that undoubtedly influenced his neighbor, Major Butler, to engage in cane planting operations of his own. J.H.

---

[248] Thomas Spalding, "On the Cultivation of the Sugar Cane, Erecting of Proper Buildings, and Manufacture of Sugar," *Southern Agriculturist* II (February 1829); Marmaduke Floyd, "Certain Tabby Ruins on the Georgia Coast," in E. Merton Coulter, ed., *Georgia's Disputed Ruins* (Chapel Hill: University of North Carolina Press, 1937), 3-189.

Couper at Hopeton, and others, adopted Spalding's methods of cultivation and manufacture. By 1830 Couper had become the largest sugar producer on the Georgia coast.[249]

Drained rice lands were considered ideal for the cultivation of cane as the crop required a fair amount of water. Thus, cane was often grown on a two-or-three-year rotation in selected rice ditches between December and February after the majority of the work entailed with the harvesting and threshing of the rice crop had been completed. King noted, however, that when cultivating cane "the water in the ditches should be prevented from stagnating or growing so hot as to scald the root of the Cane."[250]

Depending on when the cane seed was planted, harvesting occurred in late October, typically when the first frost set the sap. The stalks of the cane were cut near the ground then were taken to the plantation sugar mill where the processing of grinding the cane and boiling the expressed juice was facilitated during the winter months. Many sugar mills in coastal Georgia were modeled on Spalding's example. Later, Couper improved the milling process and his Hopeton sugar works were considered the most advanced on the southern coast in the early 1830s. These mills utilized animal and water (tide-driven) power to operate their heavy grinding rollers.[251]

---

[249] J.D. Legare, "Account of an Agricultural Excursion Made into the South of Georgia in the Winter of 1832," *Southern Agriculturist* VI (May-November 1833); James H. Couper, "Essay on the Rotation of Crops," *Southern Agriculturist* VI (February 1833). See also James M. Clifton, "Hopeton, Model Plantation of the Antebellum South," *Georgia Historical Quarterly* 66 (Winter 1982): 429-49.

[250] King, Jr., "On the Management of the Butler Estate."

[251] James H. Couper, "Account of, and Directions for Erecting a Sugar Establishment," *Southern Agriculturist* IV (May 1831); J.D. Legare, "Account

King, Jr.'s initial enthusiasm for sugar production was considerably less than that of his father, Roswell King, Sr., who managed the Butler plantations from 1802 to 1819. "My knowledge of the culture of the Sugar Cane is not very extensive," King, Jr. admitted in a lengthy contribution on his farm management techniques to the *Southern Agriculturist* in 1828. "It has been cultivated with us since 1815, and has been found more profitable than Cotton and less precarious than Rice; not so liable to be injured in gales...In 1824, fifty-six acres that were ground, the product was 39 hhds. of Sugar, about 1,200 lbs. net, each. The Cane was much injured by lodging and wreck matter."[252] King's comments in this regard were based on the widespread hurricane damage sustained by the plantations of the lower Georgia coast in September 1824. By 1838, however, King's acceptance of the cultivation of sugar cane as a supplemental staple crop to his rice and cotton had apparently increased, as reflected in his purchase that year of South Hampton plantation in lower Liberty County. The production of sugar and molasses was already a part of the work at South Hampton at the time of King's acquisition of the property. It is a testimony to his keener interest in the staple that he continued and expanded the activity.

Like Spalding, King acknowledged that moist bottomlands were most conducive to the efficient production of cane. He noted, "The best lands for Cane are strong provision land, or river swamp. If possible, the plants should be put in the ground in November, about

---

of an Agricultural Excursion"; Sullivan, *Sapelo: People and Place*, chapters 4, 5; Stewart, *What Nature Suffers to Groe*, 122-26.
[252] King, Jr., "On the Management of the Butler Estate."

three inches deep; they will be safe against frosts. Strong lands will afford such a growth that very little can be done after the 15th of June until September…I have known Cane to lay all winter in a canal and be perfect. About the 1st of November we commence grinding and boiling."[253] Pierce Butler adopted many of the cane planting and grinding techniques developed by Spalding. In 1828, Spalding observed that the senior King had, some years earlier, produced 140,000 pounds of sugar from about 110 acres planted—an impressive feat under any circumstances, but particularly so for the consistently damp soil of Butler's Island. In this respect, one is led to wonder why Butler did not concentrate more of his sugar planting activities at Hampton on St. Simons Island, in ecological conditions almost identical to those of nearby Sapelo Island where Spalding had been so successfully cultivating cane since 1805.[254]

Interestingly, both Kings implemented the cultivation, on Butler's instructions, of copious numbers of sour orange trees along the banked river levees of Butler's Island. They presented an unusual view when approaching the island landing by water from Darien or St. Simons. Butler and other rice planters advocated the planting of small trees or shrubs on the embankments as a means of stabilizing the soil against the erosive effects of the river on flooding or ebbing tides. Note of these orange trees was made in March 1828 by Basil Hall, a Scotsman touring the region: "In coming from Hopeton to Darien, we stopped at Butler's Island, the most valuable plantation on this river. We walked across the island on which there is the

---

[253] Ibid.
[254] Ibid. See also, Spalding, "Brief Notes."

greatest number of oranges, sour oranges that I have ever seen. There are also lemon trees in abundance & sweet orange trees."[255]

Rice, cotton and molasses were conveyed from the plantations and small towns along the inland waterway on small one and two-masted coasting vessels especially built to navigate the shallow estuaries, tidal mudflats and creeks of coastal Georgia and lower South Carolina. Typical of the watermen who engaged in this trade were Charles Stevens and Charles Thomson, "coasting captains" who, among others, regularly called on the plantations of Glynn, McIntosh and Liberty counties to load cargoes of cotton, rice and other agricultural commodities for transport to the larger markets of Savannah, Charleston and Beaufort.[256]

The freighting activity played an important role it in the tidewater agricultural economy. Charles Stevens of St. Simons Island was one of the more enterprising of the coasting captains, operating several vessels for the transport of plantation staples, among them the *Splendid*, the *America* and the *Northern Belle*. Two other prominent vessels during the 1840s and 1850s were the *Science* and the *Cotton Plant*, both enrolled at Savannah by the factorage of Robert Habersham & Son. The vessels were typically single-masted sloops and two-masted fore-and-aft rigged schooners built with shallow drafts to navigate the often shallow inland waterway between the barrier islands and the mainland. The coasting captains were well-versed in the nuances of sailing the local waters, always conscious of

---

[255] Basil Hall, *Travels in North America* (Edinburgh, 1829), III, 212-27.
[256] Pearson, "Captain Charles Stevens," 486-88.

barely-submerged sandbars and the mudflats that extended from the marshes on bends in the creeks and rivers at low tide.

Cotton and rice were shipped to the Charleston and Savannah factors during the fall and winter, with cotton shipments extending into the spring based on the time-consuming stages of the harvest—picking, ginning, moting and packing the cotton into bags or bales. Some plantations had their own vessels to expedite the transport of staples. A case in point is the schooner *Roswell King,* which regularly conveyed cotton and rice from the Butler plantations to the factorages in Charleston. The *Roswell King* is frequently noted in King, Jr.'s plantation journal and account book during the 1840s and 1850s.[257] This vessel would have been engaged purely in accommodating the shipping needs of the Butlers' cotton from Hampton and the clean rice from Butler's Island. King does not mention *Roswell King* in connection with his own planting interests in Liberty County. He does, however, cite the names of several other vessels that often shipped his crops—*Young Eagle* and *Fort George Packet* are examples.

The most prominent factorage in Savannah during the antebellum period was that of Robert Habersham & Son on Bay Street overlooking Factor's Walk and the Savannah River. The Habershams were among the most prominent families of coastal Georgia with a legacy going back to the early years of the colony and the Revolutionary movement in Savannah. Robert Habersham served as the "middle man," or agent, for many planters on the

---

[257] For example, Roswell King, Jr., plantation journal, entry of Feb. 1, 1845, cited in Sullivan, ed., *"All Under Bank,"* 42; King, Jr., "Day Book for Estate of J. & P. Butler, 1844."

Georgia and lower South Carolina coasts. His firm also accommodated the pounding of rice in the rough, and he had several of his own vessels to transport crops from the plantations to Savannah. Additionally, he often advanced funds to planters against the next year's crop, among assorted other financial and marketing services. A good example of the kinds of planter's expenses for a typical crop year, and the corresponding interaction with his factor, is provided in the account book of Hugh Fraser Grant, proprietor of Elizafield rice plantation on the Glynn County side of the Altamaha delta. Grant reimbursed the Habersham firm for a variety of items. For instance, in October 1848, "paid my note to R. Habersham & Son $4,373.10." Examples of these expenses for a two-month period in 1851 include $287.50 to Captain Stevens for two shipments of his rice totaling 5,750 bushels, $225.00 for 300 bushels of corn, $6.25 for a barrel of lime, and $21.00 for "6 cases Claret @ $3 ½." Grant's account book reports with regularity the delivery via Captain Stevens' *Splendid* a variety of goods and household necessities, including muslin, linen, needles and thread, 3,000 "Segars," at $6, food items such as corn, pork, rice flour and coffee, seed rice, and building materials—door sashes, lathes, tools, coal and a variety of implements needed for the daily operation of a rice plantation, including $90.00 disbursed for a "Windfan" and $350.00 "Cash paid for Engine." Offsetting these expenses were the profits gained from a typical rice plantation operation in the Altamaha delta. In the late summer of 1844 Grant notes income in the amount of $500.86 for the sale of 899 bushels of rice; early the next year "4 Bags Sea Island Cotton @ 15" brought him $143.80. The sale of an aggregate of 8,100 bushels of rice in the first half of 1845 netted Grant profits amounting to about $6,300 for the previous harvesting season.[258]

Coasting vessels plied the inland waterway between Georgetown and northeast Florida with calls at the plantations on the barrier islands and the fresh-water rivers, as well as the smaller market hubs of Beaufort, Riceborough, Darien, Brunswick, St. Marys and Fernandina. A typical case in the shipping and factorage process was Captain Stevens. A random review of the *Savannah Daily Georgian* for early 1843 provides a useful glimpse of a typical week of shipping activity with lists of vessels, their owner or masters, and the cargoes carried, along with their origination points. Thus, the sloop *Splendid*, Captain Stevens, from the May River, South Carolina, with 1,300 bushels of rough rice weighing approximately 58,500 pounds, and 22 bales of Sea Island cotton consigned to "P.H. Behn and R. Habersham & Son." As the *Daily Georgian* reported that the market for rice that week was 79 to 90 cents per bushel, Stevens's cargo would have brought as much as $1,170. With the freight charge on rice at five to six cents per bushel at that time, Stevens would have received about $70 for transporting this one cargo.[259] The cotton transported by Stevens on this trip amounted to 7,700 pounds, a cargo worth about $1,155 based on the market of 15 cents per pound. Fees for shipping cotton during this period were about one dollar per bag or bale. Commission costs paid to the factor by the

---

[258] Hugh Fraser Grant, Plantation Account Book, December 1844-May 1845, March-April 1851, cited in House, ed., *Planter Management*, 186-87, 206. See also Dale E. Swan, "The Structure and Profitability of the Antebellum Rice Industry: 1859," Ph.D. dissertation, University of North Carolina, 1972.
[259] *Savannah Daily Georgian*, Jan. 16, 1843; House, ed., *Planter Management*, 66-71, 76-77.

planter typically ran about 2.5 per cent of the gross sale price of the crop. When the cotton is added to the rice shipment, the *Splendid's* cargo would have aggregated to about thirty-three tons—*Splendid* itself was 48 feet in length and displaced 38 ½ tons, unloaded.[260]

In the winter of 1843, the *Daily Georgian* documents a considerable amount shipping activity at Savannah, predicated on the increasing deliveries of shipments of processed rice and cotton from the preceding harvesting season: the schooner *Hamilton*, Captain Peter Thomson, arrived from the Ogeechee River district with 2,300 bushels of rough rice and 31 bales of sea island cotton; sloop *Independence*, from Brunswick, Wilson, master, with 133 bales of sea island cotton; schooner *Albemarle*, from the Ogeechee River, Kain, master, with 2,000 bushels of rough rice; sloop *Eutaw*, Grieve, master, from Sapelo Island with 31 bales of sea island cotton;; sloop *Georgia*, William Worthington, from Manigault's Mill, Savannah River, with clean rice; sloop *Swallow*, Burton, master, from Daufuskie Island with a cargo of lumber; and again, sloop *Splendid*, on the 25th, from Sapelo Island with 102 bales of sea island cotton consigned to several Savannah factors.[261]

Stevens acquired the sloop *America* in 1847. Early in 1852 the *Savannah Georgian* reported the arrival at the Savannah waterfront of the *America* with a cargo of eight bales of sea island cotton and 3,300 bushels of rough rice from Darien consigned to the factorages of Elias Reed and Robert Habersham & Son.[262] Several weeks later, the

---

[260] Charles E. Pearson, "Charles Stevens of St. Simons Island, Coasting Captain," (Baton Rouge, La., 1990), 17, 18.
[261] *Savannah Daily Georgian*, January 16, 1843; February 25, 1843.
[262] *Savannah Georgian*, January 31, 1852.

America was back from Darien with 3,600 bushels of rice from Elizafield plantation, and forty bales of cotton, all consigned to Habersham.[263] The arrival in Savannah of another Stevens vessel, the *Northern Belle*, with a cargo of 124 bales of sea island cotton from Sapelo Island and possibly some neighboring plantations, was reported in 1859.[264] By the mid-1850s much of the coasting trade was being carried on by steam-powered vessels on the inland passage. However, most of the rice shipments were still conveyed by the sailing sloops and schooners due to the inordinate weight of these cargoes, which were usually unsuited for the deeper-draft steamboats.

Surviving account books and financial records of several tidewater rice planters reflect the expenses incumbent upon the planter in the implementation of an efficient operation. An important contribution to an understanding of the accounting side of a rice plantation and the reliance of the planter on his market agent (factor) in Savannah or Charleston is reflected in the account book of Hugh Fraser Grant (noted earlier in this section) in Albert V. House's 1954 study *Planter Management and Capitalism in Antebellum Georgia*. Grant was the proprietor of Elizafield plantation on the Glynn County side of the Altamaha delta opposite Butler's and Champneys islands in McIntosh County. A good example of the kinds of planter's expenses for a typical crop year, and the corresponding interaction with his factor, is provided in Grant's account book, as he reimbursed the Habersham firm for a variety of items. A number of which are cited in the discussion of factors and the freighting trade above.

Grant notes in his plantation account book for the period 1839-

---

[263] Ibid., February 25, 1852.
[264] *Savannah Daily Morning News*, March 17, 1859.

40 that he cleared land on Champneys Island in late 1839. His account book lists the number of slaves being daily utilized for this work. After an entry dated December 5, 1839, there is the notation, "Champneys Island sold to John C. Tunno." This may have given Tunno possession of all of Champneys although part of it was being leased to Jacob Barrett of Charleston for rice cultivation. Fanny Kemble noted that at the end of January 1839, she "rowed with Mr. Butler to another island in the broad waters of the Altamaha called Tunno's Island, to return the visit of a certain Dr. Tunno, the proprietor of the island, named after him."[265] Kemble also mentions Jacob Barrett who, in 1839 rented part of Champneys Island from Hugh Grant for rice production (before Grant's sale to Tunno). Barrett had his rice threshed at the nearby Butler's Island mill: "I was interrupted by a visit from Mr. B[arrett], a neighboring planter, who came to transact some business with Mr. B[utler] about rice which he had sent to our mill to have threshed, and the price to be paid for such threshing."[266]

Grant's plantation account book notes several business transactions involving John Champneys Tunno. For instance, an entry of March 27, 1842 notes Tunno as a "Debtor in a/c [account] with H F G — 9 Barrels of Lime, Settled ..." In 1843, Tunno had on account with Grant "... 1000 boards @ $16 settled, 1000 Shingles @ $3, One Broun Horse 75.00, 4 Mortice locks settled, 268 Bushels of Rice @ 75 Settled $163.50, 1 Keg white lead $12.00, 5 gals paint Oil

---

[265] Kemble, *Journal*, 154.
[266] Ibid., 117. In a footnote to this passage, Kemble journal editor John Scott notes that the first "Mr. B" mentioned here could have been Thomas Bryan, proprietor of nearby Broughton Island, but adds that Bryan (later Forman) typically threshed his rice at his own mill at Broughton.

$1.12, $5.62½."[267] The Champneys Island overseers' house, slave quarters and rice wharf were situated on the eastern side of the island, fronting on Wood Cut, across from western end of Broughton Island, with convenient access to two branches of the Altamaha River.

Slave Conditions at Butler's Island

Reliable overseers of the Altamaha River plantations were a critical element in the efficient management of agricultural operations. The underlying efficiency that was the signature of Butler's Island was largely due to the fact that its management remained in the same family, the two Kings, for almost fifty years. As crucial as proper crop management was to the overall productivity of the estate, it was in the realm of labor management that usually dictated the level of profits from the plantation. King, Jr. wrote in 1828 that when his father assumed the management of Pierce Butler's plantations in 1802, he found the slave force "very disorderly, which is invariably the case when there is a frequent change of managers." As noted, it was incumbent upon the manager, or his overseer, to select competent, and loyal, drivers to directly supervise the labor force and assign duties and tasks for the daily fieldwork and other work on the plantation. "An order from a driver is to be as implicitly obeyed as if it came by myself, nor do I counteract the execution unless directly injurious," King wrote in his 1828 letter to the editor of the Southern Agriculturist. King's observations in this one instance reveal much about the man and his views on slave management:

---

[267] Hugh Fraser Grant Account Book, 1839-43, in House, ed., *Planter Management*, 270-71, op. cit.

"Rules and regulations were established. I may say laws, a few forcible examples made, after a regular trial in which every degree of justice was exhibited, was the first step. But the grand point was to suppress the brutality and licentiousness practiced by the principal men on [the plantation], say the drivers and tradesmen. More punishment is inflicted on every plantation by the men in power, from private pique, than from neglect of duty...The owner or overseer knows that with a given number of hands, such a portion of work is to be done. The driver, to screen favorites, or to apply their time to his own purposes, imposes a heavy task on some...When I pass sentence myself, various modes of punishment are adopted, the lash least of all.—Digging stumps, or clearing away trash about the settlements, in their own time; but the most severe is confinement six months or twelves, or longer. No intercourse is allowed with other plantations. A certain number are allowed to go to town [Darien] on Sundays to dispose of eggs, poultry, coopers' ware, canoes &c. but must be home by 12 o'clock unless by special permit...The lash is unfortunate and too much used; every mode of punishment must be devised in preference to that..."[268]

King's reference to "drivers" requires elaboration. The driver, an intelligent slave, knowledgeable about the plantation and appointed by the overseer from among the slave population, was responsible for carrying out the instructions of the overseer. Drivers were important ingredients in the efficient workings of the plantation. "The overseer generally made use of several drivers. One was designated as the head driver and acted as a sub-overseer, and the other drivers were responsible for the work of a smaller group of from thirty to forty field hands."[269] Butler's Island had a head driver who "assigned the tasks, pronounced punishments, gave permission for the men to leave the island, and performed many other duties in addition to giving out food allotments to the slaves."[270] But there was another

---

[268] Ibid.
[269] Smith, *Slavery and Rice Culture*, 67.
[270] Ibid., 69.

side of Roswell King, Jr., one that was considerably less humane. In her *Journal,* Fanny Kemble Butler notes:

> "I have been interrupted by several visits ... one from a poor creature called Judy, whose sad story and condition affected me most painfully. She told me a miserable story of her former experience on the plantation under Mr. King's overseer-ship. It seems that Jem Valiant (an extremely difficult subject, a mulatto lad, whose valor is sufficiently accounted for now by the influence of the mutinous white blood) was her first-born, the son of Mr. King, who forced her, flogged her severely for having resisted him, and then sent her off, as a further punishment, to Five Pound — a horrible swamp in a remote corner of the estate to which the slaves are sometimes banished for such offenses as are not sufficiently atoned for by the lash."[271]

In 1829, a slave named Sampson was said to have been a bad influence on Balaam and Emanuel, causing the latter to die after punishment was administered by King. Sampson and six other slaves then ran away from Butler's Island. Another slave, Scy, was unusually intelligent, and he and Sampson fostered unrest among the slaves and were a source of constant trouble for King, Jr.[272] There were about fifty shotguns were in the possession of Butler's Island slaves, with Roswell King, Jr.'s approval, for the purpose of hunting game. After the trouble with Scy and Sampson, King gave instructions for the collection of the firearms, but Sampson kept his and hid it. Nonetheless, Scy and Sampson were not successful in their effort to get rid of King, Jr. King used the episode to consolidate his power and domination over the lives of the slaves. King permitted the slaves

---

[271] Frances Anne Kemble, *Journal of a Residence on a Georgian Plantation in 1838-1839,* edited by John A. Scott (New York: Alfred A. Knopf, 1961), 238. All citations to the Kemble journal hereafter are from the 1961 Knopf edition.
[272] Stewart, *"What Nature Suffers to Groe,"* 175-76.

to go to Darien on Saturdays to sell pigs, eggs, produce and other goods. The slaves had a good deal of mobility about the plantation and the immediate region, more than one might be led to believe if one accepts the common, though often misleading, assumptions about slavery along the rice coast. King did try to order the lives and environment of the bondsmen, but he was often frustrated by the irregularities in their behavior.

In tidewater Georgia, Thomas Spalding, Richard James Arnold, Thomas Savage Clay, and John Couper and his son James Hamilton Couper were among a group of planters considered the most humane in the management of their slaves. Each of these owners, and a few others, treated their bondsmen with a greater degree of liberality and benevolence than was usually the case on either the tidewater or the interior plantations. This stands in contrast to slave management at the Butler plantations. It cannot be a coincidence that the crop production and the overall efficiency of the plantations of those who adhered to the philosophies of Spalding, the Coupers, and others, usually surpassed the output and profitability of the farms of their less humane neighbors.

In December 1832, John D. Legare, editor of the *Southern Agriculturist,* visited Hopeton and concluded that James Couper's plantation was one of the most efficiently-managed he had seen during his travels about the South—a determination that could not have been reached without insights into Couper's handling of his workforce. "We hesitate not to say *Hopeton* is decidedly the best plantation we have ever visited," Legare wrote, "and we doubt whether it can be equaled in the Southern States; and when we consider the extent of the crops, the variety of the same, and the number of operatives who have to be directed and managed, it will not be presumptuous to say that it may fairly challenge comparison with any establishment of the United States."[273]

The foregoing regarding Hopeton and James H. Couper should not be taken as an indictment of the management of Butler's Island by the two Kings when compared to that of Hopeton. Irrespective of the attitudes of both Kings regarding slave management, Butler's Island was efficiently-run, and most importantly in Major Butler's view, usually quite profitable. Up to the early 1820s the emphasis of crop production was placed on sea island cotton, both at Hampton and as a rotation crop at Butler's Island. With the gradual decline in cotton profits after 1825, increased attention was given to rice production at the "tide island" with encouraging results. From 1821 through 1833 the average annual rice production at Butler's island was 1,246 tierces. In subsequent years production increased by as much as forty-three per cent, excepting years when the plantation was subjected to hurricanes and other weather-related events, including freshets. By 1835, machinery was in place for more expeditious processing of harvested rice—a steam-powered mill, an animal-powered mill and two tidal mills. As noted earlier, the first steam mill at Butler's Island was built in 1833, with both threshing and pounding machinery installed at a cost of $20,000. When the transition in management was made from King, Sr. to his son in 1819, the valuation of the land, slaves and structures on the Butler plantations was assessed at $288,027. By the 1850s, the value of the slaves alone was estimated to be more than $300,000. Annual

---

[273] Legare, "Account of an Agricultural Excursion," 359-60, 362-63.

returns on the crops at Hampton and Butler's Island ranged from $20,000 to $50,00 per annum, averaged against years when there were net losses, such as in the hurricane years and immediately after, 1804, 1813 and 1824. As previously noted, the losses from the first two hurricanes compelled Pierce Butler to consider selling his Georgia estates.[274]

The proper care and health of the workforce, particularly in its feeding and housing, were essential elements in the management of any tidewater plantation, especially the rice plantations that, as we have seen, represented the most labor-intensive of agricultural operations, under the most difficult environmental conditions. The feeding of slaves on the rice tracts was generally regarded to have been better than that afforded on most upland cotton plantations, but that often depended on the management approach taken by the owner/overseer. King, Jr., like the majority of his contemporaries who understood that reasonable care of the labor force contributed to overall productivity—and profitability—of the operation, did not take these matters lightly. "Slave owners cannot be too particular to whom they intrust [sic] the health (I may say life) and morals of what may justly be termed the sinews of an estate," he noted. "A master, or overseer, should be the kind friend and monitor to the slave, not the oppressor." King's views on managing slaves of different age groups reveal his particular attention to the proper feeding of the younger people. He reported in 1828 that among the Butlers' Georgia holdings "there are two hundred and thirty eight Negroes from

---

[274] Roswell King, Jr. to Thomas Butler, March 25, 1832, April 22, 1832 and February 22, 1833; Roswell King, Sr. to Pierce Butler, July 19, 1819; Pierce M. Butler, Plantation Ledger, 1851-1855, Butler Family Papers, HSP.

fifteen years down, and everyone knows they do not increase in proportion to a large gang, as in a small one, with the same attention. I cannot exemplify in too strong terms the great advantage resulting from preparing the food for Negroes—They will object to it at first, but no people are more easily convinced of anything tending to their comfort than they are."[275]

King reports his satisfaction, though in somewhat unusual terms, with the results of his program of feeding the young slaves of Butler's Island. "During the summer, little Negroes should have an extra mess. I find at Butler's Island, where there are one hundred and fourteen little Negroes, that it costs less than two cents each in giving them a feed of Okra soup, with Pork, or a little Molasses, or Hominy or Small Rice. The great advantage is that there is not a *dirt eater* among them—an incurable propensity produced from a morbid state of the stomach, arising from the want of the proper quantity of wholesome food and at a proper time."[276]

The account books kept by King in the 1840s reveal the feeding of the slaves under his care was probably no better or no worse than the majority of tidewater planters. At Butler's Island rations for a slave family typically consisted of regular provisions of corn, rice, pork, salted fish and molasses. Most plantations devoted a percentage of acreage to the cultivation of provision crops, both for the sustenance of the work force, and for the plantation livestock. Any excess was sent to the markets for sale. Provision crops grown by King included sweet potatoes, corn, and peas. As might be expected, the river plantations provided their work force with rations of rice

---

[275] King, "On the Management of the Butler Estate."
[276] Ibid.

from the local crop, while the local waterways provided an abundance of shellfish.

The swampy, malarial bottomlands of the Altamaha River delta made for a harsh environment with various attendant health concerns. Although slaves were particularly adaptable to conditions in the rice swamps there were, nonetheless, serious health concerns and high mortality rates, more so than on the upland plantations. Even older slaves well-acclimated to local conditions were not immune to disease. "It appears we have few Negroes here [Hampton] that are suitable for the rice swamp," King, Sr. wrote Major Butler in 1813. "We have at least 20 at the rice island which I would like to move if we had suitable highland for them. When you purchase more of course some of them will not be so profitable in a rice swamp and it is necessary we should arrange for land more suitable." At Butler's Island, both Kings reported high incidences of fevers, measles, influenza, cholera, intestinal disorders and whooping cough. During spring freshets, when the river frequently overflowed its banks and contaminated water and food supplies, the incidence of sickness invariably went up. This became especially pronounced in the 1830s when freshets were more prevalent. "This is the sickly season for the Negroes at the rice island. There are 14 to 15 in the hospital, none dangerously ill. I believe it owing to their drinking river water," King, Sr. wrote to Major Butler in the spring of 1815. King, Jr., usually relocated his work force to higher ground during freshets to reduce the possibility of disease. Contaminated river water caused outbreaks of cholera, diarrhea, dysentery, typhoid and hepatitis in the slave force, particularly among infants and young children. The infant mortality rate at Butler's Island was inordinately high compared to drier island plantations. In 1829 King, Jr. noted that "You will perceive that the mortality among infants is very high particularly at #6 at this place [Butler's Island]. The state of the atmosphere is certainly injurious to infants. The proportion of young people at this place is far behind St. Simons."[277]

Slave quarters on rice plantations were a good deal less substantial than the more permanent tabby-walled dwellings often found on the cotton plantations of the barrier islands. Extensive evidence of slave tabbies can still be seen at St. Simons, Sapelo, St. Catherines and Ossabaw islands, all areas of sea island cotton cultivation. The remains of slave houses on the rice plantations, however, are practically non-existent due to the almost universal use of wood. Scattered remnants of brick and tabby brick utilized for chimneys and foundations on the rice plantations are occasionally in evidence in the Altamaha delta, including Butler's Island where Theresa Singleton conducted archaeological investigations in the late 1970s pursuant to doctoral dissertation research. But wood, particularly in the damp, humid conditions of the river tracts, tended to deteriorate rather quickly, therefore little or no evidence remains of these structures. A contemporary description of slave housing at Butler's Island written by the geologist Charles Lyell during a visit to the section in early 1846 provides useful clues:

> "The Negro houses there were neat, and white-washed, all floored with wood, each with an apartment called the hall, two sleeping rooms, and a loft for the children; but it is evident that on these rice farms, where the Negroes associate

---

[277] Roswell King, Sr. to Major Pierce Butler, August 22, 1813 and April 30, 1815; Roswell King, Jr. to Thomas Butler, January 5, 1829, February 15, 1835 and March 8, 1835, Butler Family Papers, HSP.

with scarcely any whites, except the overseer and his family...they must remain far more stationary than where, as in a large part of Georgia,, they are about equal in number to the whites, or even form a minority..."[278]

The slave quarters at Butler's Island collectively comprised four separate "settlements." The dwellings themselves were duplexes of frame construction with brick chimneys. Most of these structures were built of hand-hewn cypress, an abundant supply of which was to be found in the river swamps. Thus the dearth of extensive archaeological evidence, except for scattered remains of brick, of slave living conditions at Butler's Island and the other low-lying rice plantations in the Altamaha delta.[279]

Singleton's investigations of the Butler's Island settlements provided important clues into slave population dynamics, not only for the Butler plantation, but also for those of a typical Georgia rice plantation during the antebellum period. Following are salient extracts from Singleton's findings and conclusions (1980):

"The most obvious modifications [to the slave settlement sites] are U.S. Highway 17, which roughly coincides with the canal east of slave settlement #1 and Interstate 95, which crosses the island in the vicinity of settlement #2. Also, 20th-century buildings from the Huston occupation are present at settlement #1. These are presently used for waterfowl management activities...Because Butler's Island is generally low-lying, grass-covered marshland, sites tended to be located on infrequent high spots, which are presently covered with trees and shrubs, notably hackberry, persimmon and fig. All sites were associated with this tree growth. Additionally, some sites,

---

[278] Charles Lyell, *Second Visit to the United States of North America* (New York, 1849), vol. I.
[279] Theresa Ann Singleton, "The Archaeology of Afro-American Slavery in Coastal Georgia: A Regional Perception of Slave Household and Community Patterns," Ph.D. dissertation, 1980. This study entails an archaeological analysis of the four slave settlements at Butler's Island.

such as the slave settlements, were also indicated in aerial photographs by the detection of antebellum drainage ditches, which surround and separate these from former rice fields. The slave settlements correspond exactly with the area designations I, II, III, and IV on the 1877 U.S.G.S. Map [of Butler's Island]. Historic photographs provide suggestions for the placement of structures designated in slave settlement #1. The steam-powered mill is precisely identified by ruins of the two chimneys which are presently standing. A sketch drawn by Roswell King, Sr., [1813] pinpoints the location of a sawmill and both tidal mills…Previous archaeological assessments made in 1956 were used to locate the slave cemetery. Through waterfowl management dredging activities, a number of coffins were unearthed in the area indicated as the slave cemetery. It was noted that the coffins were made of cypress and that the skeletal material was poorly preserved. Most of the coffins were evidently those of infants, a finding which supports the historical evidence of a high infant mortality rate at Butler's Island. On the basis of information obtained from local informants, the cemetery was identified as a slave burial ground. These informants claim to have had ancestors buried there. The location of a cemetery could not be found in the plantation records, but both Fanny Kemble and Frances Leigh mention a slave burial ground. Unfortunately, neither identified its location…The site located between slave settlements #3 and #4 appears to have been a mill or other industrial site. No structural features are evident, but a nearby impounding pond and the site's layout appear to be similar to that of the excavated tidal mill. More specifically, historic evidence suggests that this was the site of a sugar mill. Roswell King placed the 'sugar works' at Butler's Island halfway between slave settlements #3 and #4 [Roswell King, Sr. to Pierce Butler, April 20, 1816, Butler Family Papers, HSP].

"The investigators were most interested in the slave settlements. Settlement #1, just off U.S. 17, made it more accessible than the other slave sites. Unlike the other slave sites, it is not subjected to management flooding in the fall and winter…The approximate locations of certain structures at settlement #1 are well-documented in historic photographs. However, with the exception of the steam mill ruins, no surface indications of these structures presently exist. Settlement #1 was the administrative nucleus for the plantation and it included the overseer's house, blacksmithing and shoe-making sheds, warehouses, and a meat-curing house. Also, the largest technical nucleus for the island, a tidal mill and steam mill, and the greatest number of slave dwellings, were located there. For the Butler's Island slaves, settlement #1 must also have served as headquarters. The slave hospital, which occasionally served as a chapel and recreational center, was located there [Kemble *Journal*, 131]. Each of the remaining slave villages contained technical equipment for the processing and storage of plantation staples, in addition to slave dwellings.

Settlement #2 contained long-staple cotton processing equipment, and the slaves living there possibly engaged only in the production of cotton. Both settlements #3 and #4 contained rice storage facilities and were equidistant from sugar processing machinery. At Butler's Island these villages tended to isolate the slaves from other centers of the plantation complex. The only time a slave needed to go to the plantation headquarters at settlement #1 was to see the overseer or head driver, to go to the hospital, or for an occasional church or other meeting. Most of their time was spent in the rice fields adjacent to their settlement or at their own quarters. From the planter's perspective, this isolation maintained economic efficiency and social control. But for the slaves, it may have substantially reinforced the very limited contact prevailing between blacks and whites as well as between acculturated blacks and those that were not so well acculturated. Within these isolated villages slaves had the opportunity to retain African folkways. Perhaps this explains why the rice coast has preserved more evidence of African retentions than any other former antebellum crop region within the United States...

"Testing and historic photographs of slave houses at settlement #1 provide evidence of architectural style. All of the slave structures at Butler's Island were evidently duplex dwellings with central chimneys...Frame, brick and tabby constructions were typical of the tidewater. All indications are that the slave dwellings at Butler's Island were of frame construction, evidently made of cypress. Ultimately, the investigations of slave villages at Butler's Island centered on slave settlement #4. This site was evidently the best preserved of the four settlements. Visually apparent above the ground were five chimney falls. The clearing of the chimneys revealed that these were H-shaped hearths, presumably of duplex slave dwellings with central fireplaces. At slave settlement #4, structure one provided evidence of cypress construction. [Found] were a large fragment of hand-hewn cypress, possibly the remains of the floor. Additional fragments were found scattered around the chimney. The vast majority of the artifacts from settlement #4 were of antebellum date. Artifacts found at structure one, settlement #4, included a door hinge, adze, scissors, axe head, padlock, wood fragments, hoe, and rice sickle. Several curve-shaped iron fragments suggestive of pots or kettles were recovered. Two kettle legs were the only diagnostic artifacts of cooking equipment. These were evidently legs to tripodal cauldrons, which often weighed up to 60 pounds when empty. Iron cooking pots were often supplied to the slaves for cooking purposes."[280]

---

[280] Singleton, "The Archaeology of Afro-American Slavery," 103-05, 114-18.

Aside from considerations of labor management, and the care and maintenance of the work force, probably the greatest concern of the rice planter was with fluctuations of weather. Rice planters, out of necessity, were astute weather watchers, constantly sensitive to the nuances of climatic changes. They learned to identify trends through their study of atmospheric conditions, climate patterns from year to year, and the frequent inclination of the river to flood its banks during spring freshets. Much of King's plantation journal consists of his personal observations and commentary on daily weather conditions and patterns. Like most of his planter contemporaries, King was keenly analytical in this regard, for the weather and tidal changes caused by circumstances of weather were critical to any rice grower. Fall and winter northeasters often would create breaks in the levees and embankments with potential damage to the crop from salt water intrusion into the fields. King relates a range of weather patterns in his journal, ranging from droughts in which crops suffered from "want of water," to an over-abundance of rainfall and the consequent damage to fields, levees and tidegates. There are instances in his writings where he seems to exhibit a "sixth sense" on weather phenomena, as exemplified by his journal entry of September 6, 1846 when he reports: "Some thunder this morning & cloudy. Fine & clear at midday, wind East. *There is something peculiar in the atmosphere. Meats become putrid in a short time. 12 hours. Not eatable in 24 hours, unless heavily Salted*" (King's emphasis).[281]

King had been manager for the Butlers for five years when the planters of the section were assailed by the worst recorded hurricane

---

[281] Roswell King Journal, September 6, 1846, cited in Sullivan, ed., "All Under Bank," 53.

to ever strike the region, the storm of September 14-15, 1824. The hurricane caused widespread crop and property loss among the island and river plantations. In a letter to Thomas Butler after the storm, King reported the loss of the entire rice crop at Butler's Island along with damage to the cotton fields, slave quarters, tidegates and other infrastructure at both Butler's Island and Hampton. On the remote auxiliary tract at Experiment on Little St. Simons Island over fifty head of cattle were lost as well as all the crops. In a later letter to Butler, King estimated that losses would amount to about $60,000 with five years required to set all the damage right and recoup the financial deficits.[282]

King's journal covers the years from 1838 until his death in 1854, thus we do not have the details of the 1824 hurricane from his on-the-scene perspective. He does elucidate in some detail, however, on a hurricane in October 1846 that imparted considerable damage by tidal flooding of his crops, both in Liberty County and at Butler's Island. These kinds of observations underscore the critical nature of the need for as much understanding as possible of weather circumstances by the tidewater planters. Throughout the southern tidewater the writings of the planters reflect the minutiae of weather during the antebellum period, and afterwards.

Yellow Fever and the Mosquito Connection

Another environmental consideration with direct parallels to tidewater agriculture in general, and the rice industry in particular, is

---

[282] King, Jr. to Thomas Butler, September 26, 1824, Butler Family Papers, HSP.

that of the prevalence of yellow fever and malaria, and their connectivity with tidal marshes, mud and water attendant to the breeding of mosquitoes. There is ample documentation in support of the thesis that the mosquito, species of the family *Culicidae* and specifically referred to here as within the genera *Anopheles*, has been prevalent in the Altamaha River delta, including the immediate environs of the town of Darien, since at least the early eighteenth century.

The earliest English settlement of the region was in the summer of 1721 when South Carolina Rangers under John Barnwell built Fort King George on the north branch of the Altamaha River, one mile east of the later site of Darien. Barnwell kept a journal in which he frequently alluded to the difficult conditions of building the fort. The local mosquito came in for particular note—for example, on July 13, 1721, while engaged in digging the foundations of the fort, Barnwell reports:

"The men found thick, nasty, water …the men have been in a Mutiny about their work…The Cypruss can't be got out of the Swamp without wading naked up to the waist or sometimes to the neck, which is a Terrible Slavery, and Especially now in the dog days *when Musketos are in their Vigour…*"[283]

In her documented account of the establishment of Fort King George, local historian Bessie Mary Lewis, who utilized Barnwell's Journals as her primary source, noted: "The heat was nigh

---

[283] Journal of Colonel John Barnwell, entry of July 13, 1721, *South Carolina Historical & Genealogical Magazine*, XXVII, October 1926. Present author's italics.

unbearable. The mosquitoes, Satan's army with swords of fire and poison, were in swarms...Small wonder the men mutinied..."[284]

Three years after Oglethorpe and the Trustees founded the Georgia colony in 1733, the town of New Inverness (later Darien) was established by Scottish Highlanders. A contemporary journalist, Edward Kimber of London, visited Darien and the Altamaha River region soon after. Writing of his experiences in the *London Magazine* in 1744, Kimber reported that his party traveled in an "open, fixed-oar'd Boat...and slept and watched by Turns, finding, from being frequently inured to it, no more Incommodity in this method of traveling and *Muskettos*, and other Vermin that, like a Swarm of Locusts, infest the hot months in these Countries..."[285]

Prior to the Civil War, the delta bottomlands of the lower Altamaha basin were cleared, drained, banked and irrigated for cultivation of rice. The developing rice industry was the direct consequence of "engineering the tidewater" and it was built upon the labor of African slaves imported into the Altamaha district. Just how financially lucrative this activity was is demonstrated by over 12 million pounds of clean (hulled) rice being produced annually in the Altamaha delta in the peak decade of the 1850s.

The continual physical modifications of the landscape effected a gradual change in the ecological dynamic of the region. Recent scholarship has determined that flooding of rice fields and the impoundment of water on the fields through the utilization of wooden rice trunks were factors that led to a greater occurrence of

---

[284] Bessie M. Lewis, *Old Fort King George*, (Brunswick, Ga., 1973), 3.
[285] Edward Kimber, *Itinerant Observations in America*, Kevin J. Hayes, ed. (London, 1998), 31.

mosquito infestation with a consequent rise in the incidence of mosquito-borne diseases.

Anopheles was the primary transmitter of malaria in the Altamaha. Plantation records and contemporary newspaper accounts are rife with instances of malaria breakouts in Darien and the surrounding plantations of the Altamaha district. "Mosquitoes travel no more than three or four miles away from their habitat, so human hosts must also live in sufficient density in an area to nurture mosquito-borne diseases. Malaria and yellow fever were, therefore, diseases of plantations and towns rather than of the frontier. By the early nineteenth century much of the low-lying coast had dug itself into plantation districts, and yellow fever threatened towns in the low country…" notes historian Mart Stewart.

Amid the overarching complexity of the Southern plantation system, labor conditions on the low country rice tracts were the most difficult. Slaves had toiled in the wet, marshy rice fields under harsh, demanding conditions since the early 1700s in South Carolina and, after 1750, in Georgia. Captain Basil Hall, an English travel writer who visited the Altamaha district in 1828, observed that the growing of rice was "the most unhealthy work in which the slaves were employed, and that in spite of every care, they sank under it in great numbers. The causes of this dreadful mortality are the constant moisture and heat of the atmosphere, together with the alternating flooding and drying of the fields on which the Negroes are perpetually at work, often ankle deep in mud, with their bare heads exposed to the fierce rays of the sun."

The poor sanitary conditions on rice plantations debilitated the slaves, and reduced their resistance to ward off infections.

Conversely, the slaves were not nearly as affected by mosquito-borne illnesses such as malaria and yellow fever, as were their white owners. This explains the migration of white plantation families from the Altamaha district to the drier uplands of Georgia during the summer and early fall—coincident to the season of greatest mosquito infestation. In the spring of 1903, James Troup Dent of Hofwyl plantation screened the porches and windows of his home on the mosquito-infested banks of the Altamaha and remained there with his family throughout the malaria season. Dent suspected that the heavy prevalence of mosquitoes in the Altamaha caused the transmission of malaria and that by reducing their exposure to the insects he and his family would be protected from the summer diseases. The Dents suffered no ill effects and families throughout the section adopted his screening methods in future years.[286]

In plantation days, and for many years afterwards, the connection was not made between the incidence of disease and the prevalence of mosquitoes in the Altamaha. Instead, a far more radical theory prevailed, as described by Albert Virgil House of Columbia University: "In keeping with the usual custom on the Georgia coast [plantation families] removed to a camp or summer house far enough back from the coast so that the smell of salt water was no longer in the air. This reflected the contemporary belief that some sort of miasma or disease-breeding fog was given off by the marshes after sundown, which spelled fever and possibly death to white men. Modern science has shown that this 'fog' was malaria-bearing

---

[286] Ophelia Troup Dent, Memoirs, unpub. ms., copy on file at Hofwyl-Broadfield Plantation State Historic Site, Brunswick, Ga.

mosquitoes. The black slave population had a large degree of immunity from the bite of the Anopheles species of mosquitoes and could thus remain in the area at all times..." In his plantation account book, Altamaha rice planter Hugh Fraser Grant noted on May 5, 1840, "Left Elizafield for the Summer by paying a visit to the Island [St. Simons] for a few days & then to the Sand Hills."[287]

Malcolm Bell, Jr., biographer of the Pierce Butler family, based much of his research on slave conditions, some of which was concerned with mosquito infestation in the region around Darien. "Working as they did in the natural habitat of the Anopheles mosquito, the rice slave was subject to the dreadful malarial fever but fortunately was able to generate an immunity that helped to withstand the onslaught of that treacherous disease," Bell observed. He continued, "Unfortunately, the immunity that was welcomed by the slaves and their owners had a side effect not recognized until generations later. It is the devastating sickle cell anemia that is believed by scientists to have been generated by that same malarial immunity."[288] Yellow fever epidemics were prevalent in the southeastern coastal areas of the United States for several hundred years after the European settlement of the western hemisphere. Before the discovery of the cause and cure of yellow fever in 1900, coastal towns were always subject to the ravages of the dreaded disease. Little was known about yellow fever in the 1800s other than it had a short incubation phase, was almost always fatal (usually an 80 per cent mortality rate), that it was often associated with coastal

---

[287] House, *Planter Management and Capitalism in Antebellum Georgia*, 10-11.
[288] Malcolm Bell, paper presented at the Seminar for Lowcountry Studies, Savannah, Ga., November 1, 1986.

cities, incoming ships and hot weather, and that it disappeared with the first frost of the year, usually by late October.

Residents of the Altamaha region, like everyone else, assumed yellow fever was caused by the "miasma," a noxious effluvium that supposedly emanated from putrescent matter in the swamps and salt marshes, and thought to float in the night air, especially in the night mists as a fog. Armed with these beliefs, people sat in closed, unventilated rooms during the stifling, humid summer months in their efforts to escape the "miasma", a situation that undoubtedly led to additional health issues. The alternative, as noted, particularly for the planters of the Altamaha basin, was to depart the coastal region during the summer and early fall.

The evidence of mosquito infestation in the Darien region is made compellingly clear in the observations of Dr. James Holmes, Darien's physician before and after the Civil War, who wrote:

"I have been repeatedly asked how it was that people would now live in Darien the year round and enjoy good health. In times gone by it was considered hazardous to health, and life even, to remain here after the twentieth of June or, at the latest, July one…The fever of those days in and around Darien was of a highly contagious, bilious type, which prostrated the patient from the start. With strangers the fever was almost always fatal, particularly during the latter part of August and September. Meanwhile, the acclimated and older residents scrupulously avoided the night air. The Ridge and Baisden's Bluff refugees always left town by the setting of the sun and returned to their business in the morning…Savannah had its yearly malarial fever before the introduction of the dry-culture system of growing rice. Dry culture of the rice fields and lowlands surrounding Darien, however, has never been attempted. Up to 1820 and long after that time, every available acre was planted in rice and fresh clearings were made nearly opposite the town…The great Harrison freshet of 1841 swept away vast quantities of filth from our lowlands and river banks. The town itself was cleansed of the accumulation of a half-century's decay by the war fire. The conclusion is thus irresistible that the health of Darien has progressed in ratio to the number of acres of surrounding lowland cultivated. *For it is the turning up of the soil and exposing the decayed vegetable matter that exhumes the poisonous malaria...*"[289]

Holmes elucidated the opinions, although inaccurate as we now know, regarding the cause of malaria and transmission of malaria and yellow fever *before* the determination was made in 1900 by U.S. Army physician Walter Reed and others that the Anopheles mosquito was determined to be the chief transmitter. However, the important thing to understand here is that Holmes, a trained medical professional of the 1860s and 1870s, was, in his foregoing observations, unknowingly moving toward a conclusion that would correctly identify the source and transmission of the fevers.

There is evidence to support the conclusion that coastal municipalities bordered by wetlands managed for rice cultivation were among the unhealthiest places to live in the United States in the 1800s. Savannah is a case in point with major yellow fever epidemics in 1820, 1854 and 1876. It did not help of course that basic health and sanitation standards were practically non-existent in the urban centers through most of the century. Vessels arriving in coastal seaports carrying yellow fever contagion among their crews often created local epidemics through the transmission of the disease by mosquitoes. The outbreaks of yellow fever in Savannah in 1854 and 1876 resulted in the deaths of over a thousand persons each.

---

[289] James Holmes, "From Dr. Bullie's Notes," *Darien Timber Gazette*, October 19, 1877. Present author's italics.

Of greater salience to the present study is the fact that Savannah's 1854 epidemic spread to Darien, which was, like Savannah, a center for rice cultivation. The 1854 outbreak was Darien's worst experience with yellow fever. It is not clear how many Darien citizens died of the disease since there was no local newspaper at the time, but apparently it was a goodly number. Town doctor Holmes noted, "My notes are full of the deaths from yellow fever in 1854—of many personal friends and daily acquaintances...I might fill pages with the history of that terrible scourge...I will only add the remarkable fact that out of our large colored population, there were but few cases of yellow fever and no deaths..."[290] In another account, written while the fever was raging in Darien, Holmes advised that "none of you return until informed by friends at home *of a frost and settled cool weather...*"[291] Again, Holmes is referring to the understood fact that the incidence and recurrence of tropical diseases in Darien and other tidewater locales subsided with the onset of the cold weather in the fall. Oddly, Holmes and his contemporaries, as tantalizing as it must have been, never made the connection that the first frost also happened to coincide with the end of the mosquito infestation, with its attendant reduction in the incidence of disease.

When the 1876 fever epidemic caused the deaths of 1,066 people in Savannah and another 112 in Brunswick, the federal government established quarantine stations along the Georgia coast for the

---

[290] James Holmes, "Dr. Bullie's Notes, *Darien Timber Gazette*, September 3, 1875. The population of Darien in the decade of the 1850s was about 500 residents, about a third of whom were black.
[291] James Holmes, Letter to the Editor, *Savannah Daily Morning News*, October 17, 1854. Present author's italics.

requisite inspection of vessels approaching local ports from tropical waters, including the Caribbean and South America. One of the most active of these facilities was the South Atlantic Quarantine on federally owned Blackbeard Island, near Darien. It operated from 1880 to 1909, by which time the incidence of yellow fever was almost non-existent in the United States, following the conclusions of Reed and his colleagues connecting the disease and its transmission by mosquito a few years earlier.[292]

Frances Anne Kemble at Butler's Island

Frances Anne Kemble (1809-1893) was a year older than Pierce Mease Butler (1810-1867). She was already an established actress, specializing in Shakespearean soliloquies, when, accompanied by her father, she came to the United States for an American tour, and met Butler in Philadelphia. They married in June 1834 and from the outset, it seemed (and was) an odd match. They were different in many ways — he the carefree, somewhat irresponsible young lion of Philadelphia society; she, the pampered English actress, the toast of London society in her mid-twenties. "Although I feel that I have come to know and understand Fanny Kemble and Pierce Butler, I say

---

[292] See Sullivan, *Early Days on the Georgia Tidewater*, all editions, for details on the operation of the Blackbeard Island federal quarantine station and its connection with yellow fever. There was also a "quarantine ground" on the beach of Queen's Island immediately south of Sapelo Island and near the Wolf Island range beacon. This was utilized in the 1860s and 1870s for the treatment of yellow fever cases from timber ships entering the Doboy Sound harbor. See for example, *Darien Timber Gazette*, September 29, 1876.

again that I cannot fathom how these two opposites came together," Malcolm Bell remarked.[293]

Fanny Kemble was a member of one the leading abolitionist families in England. Her father, Charles Kemble, was passionate in this regard, sentiments adopted by Fanny as she matured. Butler and his brother John were among the largest slave owners in Georgia, a situation that would have been anathema to the Kembles. How could they not have known about the Butlers' ownership of some nine hundred bondsmen in Georgia? John Scott, editor of the reissue of the Kemble *Journal* in 1961, posits that while Fanny loved Pierce Butler from the outset, the marriage may well have been more of financial convenience as Kemble's father was heavily in debt—that being one reason for Fanny's two-year acting tour "in that dreadful America."[294] Although the Butler-Kemble union produced two healthy daughters, the marriage proved to be an unhappy one almost from the start: "The best that the social and cultural circles of the States could offer appeared crude and amusing to brilliant, spoiled, impetuous Fanny Kemble Butler," Burnette Vanstory noted.[295]

Near the end of 1838, Pierce Mease Butler, after consultation with his brother John, deemed it a propitious time to inspect the family's Georgia properties to address legal matters, as well as meet with Thomas Oden, who had recently been engaged as the rice plantation overseer. Oden replaced Roswell King, Jr., who had resigned to pursue plantation interests in Liberty County. Fanny

---

[293] Malcolm Bell, Jr., lecture before the Lower Altamaha Historical Society, Darien, Ga., December 15, 1988.
[294] Kemble, *Journal,* op. cit., Editor's Introduction by John A. Scott, xiv.
[295] Burnette Vanstory, *Georgia's Land of the Golden Isles* (Athens: University of Georgia Press, 1956), 86.

Butler, who had never visited the South, insisted on accompanying her husband on the trip, as well as being the Butlers' two small children, three-year-old Sarah (Sally) and Frances (Fan), who was a year old. The Butler brothers initially insisted that Fanny not accompany her husband to the plantations but they eventually relented—"I am going to Georgia," Fanny wrote in 1838, "prejudiced against slavery, for I am an Englishwoman, in whom the absence of such a prejudice would be disgraceful."[296]

The Butlers departed Philadelphia on December 21, 1838, bound southward, travelling by train, stagecoach and steamboat with stops in Charleston and Savannah. Bell notes that had the Butlers gotten to Charleston a few days before Christmas they could have sailed directly to Butler's Island on the Butler schooner *Roswell King* that had departed for the Altamaha on Christmas Eve. After a brief stop at Savannah for supplies and to make a new boat connection, the Butlers arrived at the Darien wharf on December 30 on the steamboat *Ocmulgee.* Butler loaded his wife, their two daughters, children's nurse and baggage aboard plantation boats manned by Butler slaves for the short trip from Darien, through Generals Cut, to the rice plantation. Upon reaching the landing on the Butler River near the steam mill, Fanny observed the slaves, her husband's "dreadful possessions," crowded about the wharf "jumping, dancing, shouting, laughing and clapping their hands and using the most extravagant and ludicrous gesticulations to express their ecstasy at our arrival."[297] In the days following their arrival, Fanny Butler began her explorations around Butler's Island and the adjoining sections of

---

[296] Kemble, *Journal*, Editor's Introduction, xxiv.
[297] Kemble, *Journal*, 49.

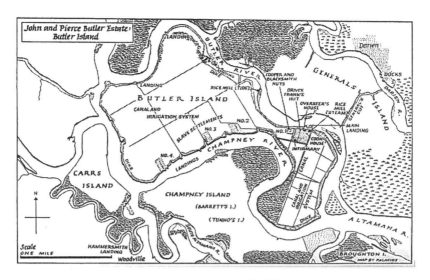

Layout of Butler's Island plantation, ca. 1840. (Alfred A. Knopf, with permission)

the lower Altamaha delta, making observations in the letters that later comprised her *Journal of a Residence on a Georgian Plantation*:

The Rice Mill — "A large building on the banks of the river, within a few yards of the house we occupy. There are three threshing mills; one worked by steam; one by the tide; and one by the horses. It is worked by a steam engine of thirty horsepower and, besides threshing a great part of our own rice, is kept constantly employed by the neighboring planters who send their grain to it in preference to the more distant mill at Savannah." A brick rice mill chimney still stands on Butler's Island beside U.S. Highway 17. The precise year of its construction is uncertain. Roswell King, Jr.'s letters to the Butlers, cited earlier, certify that a steam threshing and pounding mill was built on the site in 1833, thus the existing brick chimney could date from then. A U.S. Coast and Geodetic Survey air photo compilation map of the lower Altamaha delta dated 1933 has "Butler's Rice Mill Chimney 1858" labeled on the map, but that does not necessarily mean the chimney was constructed in that year; then too, the existing chimney may possibly be a stack built later (1858?) to replace that of the original mill. The stack is delineated on the 1869 Coast Survey topographic map, *Altamaha Sound, Georgia*, but unlike the later map, no year is indicated.[298]

The Main Landing — Near the rice mill, and adjacent to the overseer's house where the Butlers lodged, "a pretty schooner, which carries the produce of the estate to Charleston and Savannah, lay alongside the wharf."[299] This was the *Roswell King*, the plantation vessel the Butlers had just missed at Charleston.

Embankments and Dikes — "Pursuing my walk along the river's bank, upon an artificial dike, sufficiently high and broad to protect the field from inundation by the ordinary rising of the tide; for the whole island is below the high water mark..."[300] Tide-gates were raised to allow water into the rice fields. When the tide-gate was down the tide pushed against it and no water could enter.

The Overseer's House — There was no fine plantation home on Butler's Island—the low-lying island's susceptibility to flooding would never have permitted that. Also, the humid, malarial conditions of the area made it impossible for the white overseers to live on the island during the warm months. The better homes were built on the island plantations, in the case of the Butlers, at Hampton. The quarters at Butler's Island was somewhat crude, a far cry from the

---

[298] Ibid., 54-55; U.S. Coast and Geodetic Survey, *Planimetric Air Map of Altamaha River*, Register No. T-5122, 1933, and idem., *Altamaha Sound and Vicinity, Georgia*, Register No. T-1114, 1869, RG 23 (Records of the U.S. Coast and Geodetic Survey), NARA.
[299] Kemble, *Journal*, 49.
[300] Ibid., 55.

standard to which Fanny Butler was accustomed. "Of our three apartments, one is for sitting, eating and living room, and is sixteen feet by fifteen feet. The walls are plastered indeed, but are neither painted nor papered. It is divided from our bedroom by a dingy wooden partition covered all over with hooks, pegs and nails."[301] The house was vandalized by looters during the Civil War, "stripped of all its contents…Windsor chairs, pine tables, featherbeds, the mahogany card table at which [Fanny] penned parts of her fateful journal, all gone."[302] After the war Butler improved and enlarged the dwelling on his return to the plantation with his daughter, Frances. She lived in the house until 1876, the last several years with her new English husband, James W. Leigh, before departing. The house remained on the property until the early part of the twentieth century, and was situated on about the same spot upon which the present Butler's Island house now stands.

Blacksmith's and Cooper's Shops — "I passed the blacksmith's and cooper's shops. At the first, all the common iron implements of husbandry or household use for the estate are made, and at the latter, all the rice barrels necessary for the crop, besides the tubs and buckets for the use of the people and cedar tubs, of noble dimensions and exceedingly neat workmanship, for our own household purposes."[303]

The Slave Settlements — "There are four settlements or villages (or, as the Negroes call them, camps) on the island, consisting of from ten to twenty houses, and to each settlement is annexed a cook's

---

[301] Ibid., 63.
[302] Bell, *Major Butler's Legacy*, 395.
[303] Kemble, *Journal*, 55.

shop with capacious cauldrons, and the oldest wife of the settlement, for officiating priestess. The cabins consist of one room about twelve feet by fifteen, with a couple of closets smaller and closer than the stateroom of a ship, divided off from the main room and each other by rough wooden partitions, in which the inhabitants sleep ... Two families (sometimes eight and ten in number) reside in one of these huts, which are mere wooden frames pinned, as it were, to the earth by a brick chimney outside. A wide ditch runs immediately at the back of these dwellings, which is filled and emptied daily by the tide. Attached to each hovel is a small scrap of ground for a garden, which, however, is for the most part, untended and uncultivated. The 1869 Coast Survey topographic map delineates two parallel rows of dwellings immediately south of the overseer's house and plantation complex—slave Settlement No. 1.

During their stay of six and a half weeks at Butler's Island, Fanny "had such passionate quarrels with her husband about the management of the plantations and handling of the slaves that she 'even suspected herself to be an intolerable nuisance.'"[304] Fanny was depressed both by her surroundings and the conditions she observed. She encouraged the slaves to discuss their grievances with her. Her attitudes regarding slavery form the bedrock of her letters, later *Journal*, composed while at Butler's Island, starting with her arrival at the end of 1838. The last entry is dated April 17, 1839 with the Butlers departing Hampton Point for the north the following day. Half the *Journal* covers the period at Butler's Island (December 30, 1838 to February 16, 1839), and the second half to the period spent

---

[304] Kemble, *Journal*, Editor's Introduction, xxxiii-xxxv.

at St. Simons Island (February 16 to April 17, 1839). The original *Journal*, published in 1863, consisted of thirty-one letters to her friend, Elizabeth Sedgewick of Lenox, Massachusetts. "Little explanation is necessary as to why Fanny kept this *Journal*," noted John Scott. "Writing down her thoughts, keeping a record of her life, came naturally to her...A theoretical understanding of the evils of slavery was but poor preparation for the shock of contact with reality. She experienced agonies of grief. An outlet for her feelings was imperative, and she resorted to the supreme and ultimate consolation in her life, writing."[305] Bell remarked that

"Her immediate hesitance as to the evils of slavery was short lived ... [In] her documentation of the wrongs of slavery I found no reason to doubt the story she told ... The antipathy in Southerners to the *Journal* was prompted by the belief that Fanny moved the British government away from supporting the Confederacy to hasten its downfall. Historians now disregard that, for the *Journal* appeared almost simultaneously with Gettysburg and the sentiment of the English parliament had already begun its move from South to North. And, of course, many Southerners believed she gave a completely false picture of slavery."[306]

As overseer of the rice plantation, Thomas Oden was living in the dwelling near the landing (which he vacated for the Butlers) and was still new to his position in December 1838. Oden was apparently a hard taskmaster, inheriting the same unyielding qualities as the recently-departed Roswell King, Jr. According to Kemble, Oden flogged the slave Harriet, allegedly for complaining to Fanny that women did not have time to keep their children

---

[305] Ibid., xlii.
[306] Bell lecture. For the "false picture of slavery," see Margaret Davis Cate, "Mistakes in Fanny Kemble's Georgia Journal," *Georgia Historical Quarterly* 44 (March 1960): 1-17.

clean on the plantation. Oden also whipped Chloe, reportedly for impudence, action that Butler defended in a bitter confrontation with his wife. Another example of plantation justice noted in the *Journal* involved Scylla, a Hampton slave who gave birth to a mulatto child by Roswell King, Jr. Scylla was flogged on orders of Mrs. King then banished to the remote plantation settlement of Five Pound on Buttermilk Sound. Another slave, Teresa, was flogged by Oden for complaining to Fanny Butler "of her back being broken by hard work and child bearing."[307]

"As to beatings, Fanny Butler soon realized the driver's lash was no mere symbol of authority…old Teresa was flogged for complaining to her distraught 'Missus.' Pierce Butler justified the punishment in an angry confrontation with his wife who reported in her journal. 'I retorted, the manifest injustice of unpaid and enforced labor, the brutal inhumanity of allowing a man to strip and lash a woman, the mother of ten children; to exact from her toil, which was to maintain in luxury idle young, the owners of the plantation.' To the young Englishwoman the lash was the 'hateful implement,' an emblem representing all the evils of slavery."[308]

Fanny Butler interceded on behalf of Psyche and her husband Joe, preventing the family from being separated with part of it being sold to a plantation in Alabama. Psyche was about twenty, possibly a mulatto, and was known on the rice plantation as "Sack," or "Sackey." In the cemetery off the Ridge Road on the outskirts of Darien where many of the former Butler slaves were buried after the Civil War, there is the marked grave of Sackey Davis. Malcolm Bell advances the possibility that this could be the resting place of Psyche, who became one of Kemble's favorites among the Butler's Island bondsmen.[309]

---

[307] Kemble, *Journal*, 99-100, 160-61.
[308] Bell, *Major Butler's Legacy*, 274. Kemble's comments regarding whipping are in Kemble, *Journal*, 161.
[309] Bell, *Major Butler's Legacy*, 587 (n18). Bell adds that the names of Psyche and the other Butler slaves come from two sources, the William Page list of May 4, 1793, and

One of the most moving entries in the *Journal* is Fanny's account of the evening funeral for the slave Shadrach on Butler's Island in early 1839. Shadrach had died of pneumonia after an illness lasting three days. He was tended by Dr. James Holmes, the plantation physician for the Butler estates. Pierce Butler himself sat up with Shadrach on the last night of his life. In a procession illuminated by the light of pinewood torches, Shadrach was buried in a water-filled grave in the plantation's slave cemetery (probably near slave Settlement No. 3. See plantation map this section). Pierce and Fanny Butler attended the funeral with the assembled island slaves. Fanny wept as Shadrach's coffin was lowered into a grave awash with ground water. She noted, "I cannot tell you how profoundly the ceremony, if such it could be called, affected me. There was nothing in the simple and pathetic supplication of the poor black artisan to check or interfere with the solemn influences of the whole scene."[310]

Kemble was particularly affected by the plight of slaves banished as punishment for various infractions to isolated Five Pound on Buttermilk Sound, a desolate place at the west end of Experiment plantation on Little St. Simons Island. One of these was Judy, whose sufferings were described earlier in this chapter. "The dismal loneliness of the place to these poor people," notes Kemble, "who are as dependent as children upon companionship and sympathy, makes this solitary exile a much-dreaded infliction; and this poor creature [Judy] said that, bad as the flogging was, she would sooner have taken that again than the dreadful lonely days and nights she spent on the penal swamp of Five Pound."[311] Experiment grew cotton and rice in

---

the Inventory and Appraisement of the Estate of Captain John Butler, February 13, 1849, both in Butler Family Papers, HSP.

[310] Kemble, *Journal*, 146-47.

[311] Ibid., 238.

rotation on a tract that is now mostly deep *Spartina* marsh. There was some minimal rice cultivation at Five Pound, and because of its remoteness and the notorious purpose for which it was employed by the Kings as a place of penance and punishment for unruly slaves, it was appropriately referred to by Kemble as "the swamp Botany Bay of the plantation."[312]

Communication between Hampton, Experiment, Butler's Island, and Darien was by way of the meandering tidal rivers and creeks of the delta. Major Butler directed his slaves, under the supervision of the driver, "Old Bram," to dig a canal through the salt marsh to extend a tidal creek across from Hampton Point, thus connecting Hampton with the south branch of the Altamaha River. This initiative shortened the water route to Butler's Island.[313] The marsh cut-through, called Bram's Noble Ditch, was a considerable undertaking. "Presumably, a rowboat could leave Hampton Plantation at the beginning of a flood tide and go in a direct route to Butler's Island with favorable tides and river currents the entire distance. By Bram's Noble Ditch, a journey of 4 ¼ miles from St. Simons to Butler's Island, the time is shortened, while the [pre-canal] journey by river is two miles longer. Thus [the canal], still visible but grown up in marsh grass made the communications between Butler's Island and Hampton more feasible." Bram's Noble Ditch, still visible but largely covered by marsh, made communication between the two

---

[312] Ibid., 269; Bell, *Major Butler's Legacy*, 107, 147, 163, 477.
[313] U.S. Coast Survey, *Altamaha Sound and Vicinity, Georgia*, 1869, op. cit., mapped shortly after the Civil War, clearly defines the canal through the marsh of Little St. Simons Island linking the Hampton River with the south branch of the Altamaha River.

plantations more convenient.[314] A similar project, Generals Cut, was also expedited by extending a tidal creek through the Generals Island marsh, and was achieved about the same time, 1808. In this instance Butler directed slaves from the rice plantation to dig a cut through the marsh to link the Butler River with the Darien River to facilitate ease of travel to and from Butler's Island to nearby Darien.

King, Jr. made a brief visit to Butler's Island during the six-week period the Butlers were there in the winter of 1838-39, in relation to his relinquishing the reins of supervision to Oden. Surprisingly, Kemble actually found King to be quite agreeable—at first. "He is a remarkable man, and is much respected for his integrity and honorable dealing by everybody here," she writes. "His activity and energy are wonderful, and the mere fact of his having charge of for nineteen years and personally governing without any assistance whatever, seven hundred people scattered over three large tracts of land...certainly bespeaks efficiency and energy of a very uncommon order."[315] Kemble related a "most interesting conversation" with King regarding slavery and King's attitudes towards slavery:

"You may be sure that I listened with infinite interest to the opinions of a man of uncommon shrewdness and sagacity, who was born in the very bosom of it, and has passed his whole life among slaves. If anyone is competent to judge of its effects, such a man is this one; and this was his verdict: 'I hate slavery with all my heart [said King]. I consider it an absolute curse wherever it exists. It will keep those states where it does exist fifty years behind the others in improvement and prosperity.' Further on the conversation he made this most remarkable observation: 'As for its being an irremediable evil—a thing not to be helped or got rid of—that's all nonsense; for as

---

[314] Frederick C. Marland, review of *Major Butler's Legacy*, Lower Altamaha Historical Society, *Altamaha Echoes* II (1), September 1987.
[315] Kemble, *Journal*, 109.

soon as people become convinced that it is in their interest to get rid of it, they will soon find the means to do so, depend upon it..."[316]

These were remarkable, almost prophetic, words coming from King, a man who, like many of his contemporaries, was totally reliant on the institution of slavery for his livelihood. Nonetheless, the example of the slave Sinda, as related by Kemble, demonstrates the unwavering inflexibility of King in enforcing discipline upon the work force in the severest terms:

> "I was seized hold of by a hideous old Negress named Sinda, who had come to pay me a visit, and of whom Mr. [Butler] told me a strange anecdote. She passed at one time for a prophetess among her fellow slaves on the plantation and had acquired such an ascendancy over them, that having given out... that the world was to come to an end at a certain time, and that not a very remote one, the belief in her assertion took such possession of the people on the estate that they refused to work, and the rice and cotton fields were threatened with an indefinite fallow in consequence of the strike on the part of the cultivators. Mr. K[ing] who was then overseer of the property, perceived the impossibility of arguing, remonstrating, or even flogging this solemn panic out of the minds of the slaves. They were utterly impracticable; so, like a very shrewd man as he was, he acquiesced in their determination not to work; but he expressed to them his belief that Sinda was mistaken, and he warned her that, if at the appointed time, it proved so, she would be severely punished. I do not know if he confided to the slaves what he thought likely to be the result if she was in the right; but poor Sinda was in the wrong. Her day of judgement came indeed, and a severe one it proved, for Mr. K[ing] had her tremendously flogged..."[317]

Kemble's initially favorable sentiments toward King resulting from her interview with him in early 1839 were to be drastically altered in view of her subsequent conversations with several of the

---

[316] Ibid., 111-12.
[317] Ibid., 119.

slave men and women. One bondsman related to Kemble that King forbade churchgoing and did not consider slave marriages binding. "It shocked her still more to discover that Mr. King's features could be traced in several of the young mulatto faces on the Butler estates...Many lurid stories concerning Mr. King and the women slaves, and the cruelty of his punishments, were brought to Fanny."[318]

Despite the documented instances of his severity toward the slaves, and they are fairly extensive both in the accounts of visitors such as Kemble, and in King's own journal, King nonetheless was regarded as a highly competent agriculturist and plantation manager. His own writings demonstrate his awareness of the importance of maintaining the proper health of his slaves. But King also never hesitated to use the whip. His journals are rife with vaguely disguised references to his frequent administration of the lash. King's attitudes toward his chattel bondsmen are demonstrated in another, quite different, sphere. By the time of his marriage to Julia Maxwell in 1825, he had fathered a number of mulatto children by the women of the Butler plantations. This accounts for the negative attitudes of King's wife toward some of the female members of the Butler workforce. Despite the otherwise well-documented admirable qualities of Julia King, "her good qualities were put aside when she ordered the punishment of the slaves Judy and Scylla for bringing her husband's children into a world far more difficult and miserable than her own."[319] Kemble further iterates that "the all-efficient and

---

[318] Margaret Armstrong, *Fanny Kemble, A Passionate Victorian* (New York: Macmillan, 1938), 236-37; Kemble, *Journal*, 201, 238, 310.
[319] Bell, *Major Butler's Legacy*, 532.

all-satisfactory Mr. King" fathered a son, Ben, by the married slave Minda, a child "whose extremely light color and straight, handsome features and striking resemblance to Mr. King had suggested suspicions of a rather unpleasant nature to me."[320]

During her sojourn, Kemble made several visits to Darien where she became acquainted with, and greatly admired, Orallie Troup, daughter of the former Governor, George Michael Troup, and Dr. James Holmes. To Fanny, Holmes was one of the few McIntosh Countians she found to be socially acceptable during her visit. She also visited (apparently unannounced) sixty-one-year old Sarah Leake Spalding, "the old lady mistress," of Ashantilly, and wife of prominent planter Thomas Spalding. Fanny was certainly not enamored with Darien. Her descriptions of the antebellum Georgia tidewater — "the outer bounds of civilized creation, the very end of the world" — included an observation about Darien:

"The abomination of desolation is but a poor type of its forlorn appearance as half buried in sand, its struggling, tumble-down wooden houses peer over the muddy bank of the thick slimy river. The whole town lies in a bed of sand…at every step I took my feet were ankle deep in the soil, and I had cause to rejoice that I was booted for the occasion…The houses seemed scattered about here and there, apparently without any design, and looked, for the most part, either unfinished or ruinous."[321]

Paradoxically perhaps, Fanny reveled in the ecology and natural beauty of the Georgia coast, though the ubiquitous Spanish moss often depressed her "particularly when covering a naked cypress with a 'banner of death' that made it seem 'the most funereal spectacle in

---

[320] Kemble, *Journal*, 201.
[321] Ibid., 115.

all the vegetable kingdom.'"[322] Fanny's eloquent portrayal of this — to her — strange and confusing land is both notable and eloquent:

> "Toward sunset I went on the river to take my rowing lesson. A darling little canoe, which carries two oars and a steersman, and rejoices in the appropriate title of the *Dolphin*, is my especial vessel; and with Jack's help and instructions, I contrived this evening to row upward of half a mile ... A small bank of mud and sand, covered with reedy, coarse grass, divides the river into two arms on this side of the island; the deep channel is on the outside of this bank, and as we rowed home this evening, the tide having fallen, we scraped sand almost the whole way. The whole course of this noble river is full of shoals, banks, mud and sand bars, and the navigation, which is difficult to those who know it well, is utterly baffling to the inexperienced ... the water, again, cloudy and yellow, like pea soup, rolling turbid and thick with alluvium, which it both gathers and deposits as it sweeps along with a swollen, smooth rapidity that almost deceives the eye. Amphibious creatures, alligators, serpents, and wild fowl haunt these yet but half-formed regions, where land and water are of the consistency of hasty pudding ... But then the sky — if no human chisel ever yet cut breath, neither did any human pen ever write light; if it did, mine should spread out before you these unspeakable glories of these Southern heavens, the saffron brightness of morning, the blue intense brilliancy of noon, the golden splendor and the rosy softness of sunset ... Heaven itself does not seem brighter or more beautiful to the imagination than these surpassing pageants of fiery rays, and piled-up beds of orange, golden clouds, with edges too bright to look on, scattered wreaths of faintest rosy bloom, amber streaks and pale green lakes between, and amid sky all mingled blue and rose tints, a spectacle to make one fall over the side of the boat, with one's head broken off with looking adoringly upward."[323]

After six and a half weeks at Butler's Island, Butler moved his family to St. Simons Island so that he could more closely inspect the Hampton plantation. "Six weeks on Butler's Island had put her

---

[322] Bell lecture.
[323] Kemble, *Journal*, 86-87.

[Fanny] through six years' worth of dismaying discoveries and searing emotions," notes Bell. "She now hoped that the other plantation would be a change for the better in further ways." Thus, on February 16, 1839 the Butlers departed by boat for Hampton:

"Our voyage from the rice to the cotton plantation was performed on the *Lily*, which looked like a soldier's baggage wagon and an emigrant transport combined. Our crew consisted of eight men. Forward in the bow were miscellaneous livestock, pots, pans, household furniture, kitchen utensils and an indescribable variety of heterogeneous necessities. Enthroned upon beds, bedding, tables, and other chattels, sat that poor, pretty chattel, Psyche, with her small chattel children, midships sat the two tiny free women [Fanny's little girls, Sally and Fan] and myself, and in the stern Mr. Butler steering…We rowed down the huge stream, the men keeping time and tune to their oars, with extemporaneous chants of adieu to the rice island and its denizens."[324]

Fanny's sojourn at Hampton was somewhat more diverse than that at the more remote rice plantation. Her St. Simons journal has additional passages describing her affinity for the natural landscape, and accounts of social outings with other St. Simons planters, including visits to John and Rebecca (Maxwell) Couper at neighboring Cannon's Point.

The Butlers' union had been less than harmonious almost from the start, due largely to the issue of slavery. Not surprisingly, following the Georgia sojourn of nearly four months, relations between the couple took a decided turn for the worse. Fanny tried vainly to hold the marriage together but, as John A. Scott, in his scholarly editing of the Kemble *Journal* in 1961, observed: "Pierce Butler's love for her [Fanny] had quite vanished; it had been replaced

---

[324] Bell, *Major Butler's Legacy,* 219; Kemble, *Journal,* 194-95.

Habersham Mungin rowing through General Cut. He was born a slave at Butler's Island. Photo ca. 1915. (Used with permission of the Lenox Library, Lenox, Massachusetts).

by an icy, calculating hatred ... Butler imposed unendurable conditions upon her as the price for the continued right to live under the same roof with her children and him."[325] Kemble left Butler in 1845 and returned to England. Butler filed for divorce three years later on grounds that his wife had deserted him; in November 1849, in a case which, by then, had caused a sensation, a Pennsylvania court awarded Butler both the divorce and custody of the two girls. Fanny resumed her acting career, performing before enthusiastic audiences on both sides of the Atlantic.

In the 1850s, Kemble was pressured by her abolitionist friends to publish her *Journal* but she deferred, Scott feels, because she did not want to further aggravate her situation regarding her children — she worried that her former husband would alienate them from her even more and "jeopardize her hopes for eventual reunion with them." By

---

[325] John A. Scott, in *Journal of Negro History*, October 1961.

the Civil War, the situation had changed: "Her children had come of age, and she was able once more to enjoy their company; the estate which had been the scene and the source of her sufferings was no more," Scott noted.[326] The *Journal* was published in London in May 1863 and in New York in July. The English edition appeared after the tide of popular opinion in England had begun to swing in favor of the North. By the time the American edition appeared, Gettysburg had been fought and Lee's Army of Northern Virginia was in retreat. Thus, contrary to the opinions and writings of Southern historians in the years after the war, Kemble's *Journal,* and its anti-slavery message, had nothing to do with turning the British against the South.

The war divided the family. Fanny and Sarah, by then the wife of Dr. Owen Jones Wister and the mother of young Owen Wister, were pro-Union. Frances and her father, in favoring the continuation of slavery, supported the South. After the war, Fanny Kemble alternated her time between England and America, periodically living in Lenox, Massachusetts. She returned to England to stay in 1877, and died in 1893.

Roswell King, Jr., South Hampton & Butler's Island in the 1840s and 1850s

For a considerable period, Roswell King, Jr, served in a dual capacity as manager and overseer for the Butler estates. As previously noted, the overseer was the critical link between the planter and the labor force. On most coastal plantations the overseer had direct supervision of crop management and the slave force. One of the

---

[326] Kemble, *Journal,* Editor's Introduction, xlv-liii.

reasons Hopeton plantation was one of the most efficient in the South was Couper's judicious selection of qualified resident overseers. Three of Hopeton's overseers during the period 1827-1854, Thomas Oden, Baillie Forester and Daniel McDonald, were considered among the most competent on the Georgia coast. King, Jr. certainly fits into this category. King, in fact, like his father before him, may be considered to be in a class of "super-overseer" since his responsibilities as a resident manager exceeded those of the ordinary overseer.

Fanny Kemble points out in her *Journal* that Thomas Oden had fourteen years' service as an overseer for Couper before he came to Butler's Island in 1838 to assume supervision from the recently departed King. King felt that one man was incapable of effectively managing both the Butler properties at Butler's Island and Hampton. However, Thomas Butler, in ceding the ownership of the family's Georgia estates to brothers John Mease Butler and Pierce Mease Butler, Major Butler's grandsons, upon attaining their majority in 1836, expressed complete satisfaction with the capabilities of King. "In justice to Mr. King, Junr, the manager of the estate," Thomas Butler wrote, "I ought to say that a correspondence with him of fourteen years has led me to entertain the highest opinion of his judgment as a planter, and a no less smaller opinion of his integrity..." Butler did not hesitate, however, to elucidate at least one of his manager's faults—"His manner of expressing himself has occasionally been somewhat abrupt," Butler observed, "but he never—I am persuaded, intended to be disrespectful."[327]

---

[327] Thomas Butler, probably to Pierce Mease Butler, April 27, 1836, Wister Family Papers, HSP. The outstanding scholarly treatment of plantation

When King resigned as Butler manager in October 1838, he intended to shift his focus to his newly-acquired South Hampton plantation, about twenty-five miles north of Butler's Island.[52] Less than three years after resigning, however, King was back in the employ of the Butlers, resuming his supervision of Butler's Island and Hampton following Oden's death in January 1841. King's second tenure as Butler manager lasted from 1841 until shortly before his death in 1854. William K. Scarborough, in his investigation of Southern plantation overseers, provides this assessment of King:

> "King once more became associated with the Butler estate. Serving in the capacity of steward, he made periodic trips [from Liberty County] to the Butler holdings, where he assumed responsibility for the books and accounts, rode over the crops with the two overseers, gave out Negro clothing and reported to Captain John Butler during the latter's infrequent visits from Charleston, S.C. During one period of more than a week [April 14-23, 1843], King was 'engaged at Butler's Island making & putting up new Brush Screen & Middling Screw, &c. &c. at the Steam Mill.' King retained his position as general agent for the Butler interests in Georgia until 1854, all the while operating his own planting establishments. He was, without doubt, an extraordinary man."[328]

---

overseers is William K. Scarborough, *The Overseer: Plantation Management in the Old South* (Baton Rouge: Louisiana State University Press, 1966). King is mentioned on pp. 39, and 168-69 in this study. One of the reasons Pierce M. Butler went to Georgia in late 1838, accompanied by his wife, Fanny Kemble Butler, and their two small children, was to meet with James Gowen, appointed to oversee the Hampton cotton plantation, and Thomas Oden, the new overseer at Butler's Island.
[328] Scarborough, *The Overseer*, 168-69.

As noted in his journal, King routinely travelled between his plantations in Liberty County to supervise the Butler operations in McIntosh and Glynn beginning with his second tenure in early 1841. King's journal for the period 1845 through 1854 documents a visitation schedule to the Butler properties of about once a month from Liberty, a routine that remained constant until his second resignation in 1854.[329]

During the second management period, King supervised two overseers, James Gowen at the Hampton cotton plantation, and Alexander Blue, the overseer at the Butler's Island rice plantation. The Butler brothers were absentee owners, but nonetheless were closely attuned to the activities of their plantations. John Butler (b. 1806), however, died in 1847 during military service in the Mexican War, and his younger brother, Pierce M. Butler, assumed oversight of the Georgia properties.

The financial affairs of the two plantations, with the concomitant involvement of King, Jr., were managed by Thomas C. James of Philadelphia, trustee of John Butler's estate and guardian of Pierce M. Butler's finances.[330] The latter Butler, who had had only minimal involvement in the activities of the Georgia properties before the death of his brother, turned most of the business and legal affairs over to James in the early 1850s. On several occasions King chided Butler for his non-involvement in the plantations, and for his frequent lack of response to King's letters and reports. For all intents and purposes then, King was managing virtually every aspect of the

---

[329] King's plantation journal for the 1845-1854 period is transcribed and edited by the present writer. See Sullivan, ed., *"All Under Bank."*
[330] Bell, *Major Butler's Legacy*, 344, 347.

Butler lands. Nonetheless, he often expressed a need "to be sustained by the owners." The properties, King wrote in 1849, were "of that kind that unless judiciously guided, can very readily be shaken to pieces."[331]

By 1847 Butler's Island had expanded in response to increased rice markets. The plantation now had two steam-powered threshing machines to maintain sufficient pace with the pounding mill. Alexander Blue supervised more than 500 slaves at Butler's Island—524 were enumerated in the 1850 McIntosh County population census—with 254 of these classified by King and Blue as prime slaves between the ages of fifteen and forty-five.

During this period Blue reported to King that some of the rice fields were beginning to show signs of wearing out, with a consequent depletion of fertility due to the stress of continual plantings. Despite the liberal use of fertilizers this phenomenon was not uncommon, and provided the rationale for the rotation of crops at many plantations. Reduced soil fertility was clearly a cause for concern at Butler's Island. Blue's response was to employ gangs of slaves to reclaim and develop sections of the rice island not previously cultivated. By 1848, partly as a result of Blue's efforts to plant on fresh soil, production at Butler's Island had exceeded most of the goals established by King. Thus, in noting the seeding of about 1,000 acres in rice, Blue reported in a communication to Pierce M.

---

[331] Roswell King, Jr. to Pierce M. Butler, Sept. 27, 1849, Wister Family Papers, HSP.

Butler that irrigation ditches had been prepared in the newly cleared land and that "Butler's Island may be said to be all under bank."[332]

Increased acreage devoted to cultivation apparently produced the desired results very quickly. In the 1849 crop year Butler's Island had a yield of 1.52 million pounds of rice, the most in the Altamaha district of Glynn and McIntosh counties, and one of the highest aggregates on the southern tidewater that season. The only local plantation approaching those numbers was Hopeton, still under the management of James H. Couper in 1849, then later by Francis P. Corbin.

In January 1849, a detailed inventory and appraisement of the 840 slaves at Hampton and Butler's Island was conducted by the sworn appraisers of the John Butler estate, Roswell King, Jr., Alexander Blue and Alexander Mitchel. The inventory was conducted over several days in consultation with Thomas C. James who was continuing in his role as executor of John Butler and co-trustee of the family's Georgia holdings. Broken down, the listing enumerated 267 male slaves, 253 females, 321 children aged twelve and under, and nineteen slaves of old age, or who had outlived their families. Fifty-five men and forty-five women were listed at age fifty or over, with eighty-five year old Renty being the oldest. Four of the prime male slaves were accorded the highest valuation at $1,000 each, these being drivers Frank, Angus and Morris, and John, a blacksmith. The family receiving the highest aggregate valuation,

---

[332] Alexander Blue to Pierce M. Butler, Oct. 18, 1847, Dec. 3, 1847, and March 2, 1848, Butler Family Papers, HSP; Roswell King, Jr. to Pierce M. Butler, April 28, 1848, Wister Family Papers, HSP.

$4,050, was that of Frank, a field worker, his wife Clarinda, and their eight children. The total value of the 840 bondsmen was assessed to be $281,125, an average of $334.67 per slave.[333]

In August 1853, again with King's direct involvement, Pierce M. Butler finalized the purchase of leased lands on Generals Island, an adjacent rice tract to Butler's Island and immediately opposite Darien on the north branch of the Altamaha River delta. This 700-acre parcel was acquired from the estate of William H. Mongin of Daufuskie Island, South Carolina. Also at this time, Butler purchased town lots in Darien, with adjoining marshland, and a house at the Ridge, s residential settlement three miles northeast of town, for use as a summer refuge during the malarial season. The total cost of these acquisitions was in excess of $36,000.[334]

In March 1854, partly because of declining health, King "closed the Books on the Butler Estate" and for the second time resigned as manager of that family's Georgia plantations. It was King's desire to devote more attention to his Liberty County plantations, both of which were now largely under the day-to-day supervision of his son, Audley King.

---

[333] Roswell King, Jr., plantation journal, January 15-February 1, 1849, in Sullivan, ed., "*All Under Bank,*" 64-65; Captain John Butler Estate, Inventory and Appraisement, Butler Family Papers, HSP, cited in Bell, *Major Butler's Legacy*, 315-16.

[334] Deed Book A, 454-57, McIntosh County Records; Roswell King, Jr., Plantation Journal, May 4, 1853 and June 7, 1853, in Sullivan, ed., "All Under Bank," 87-88. Generals Cut was the dividing boundary between the western and eastern halves of Generals Island, the Butler interests having the western portion and that on the east side of the cut being acquired by Robert B. Rhett of Charleston.

King's journal outlines, often in monotonous detail, the daily work associated with crop production both at South Hampton and at Butler's Island. By 1850 King was placing increasing reliance on Audley. However, the elder King attended to his affairs at South Hampton and Colonel's Island with the same high degree of proficiency that he did for the Butlers. By all accounts King was one of the most productive among many in the planter class in Liberty County, in addition to being one of the most prominent land and slave owners in terms of acreage and numbers of bondsmen.

In filing his local tax return in 1852, King reported ownership of 170 slaves (including those of his wife), valued at $56,100. The highest value of these was placed upon Prophet, age 39, at $1,000; Ben, 41, a carpenter, at $1,000; Paris, 38, a driver, at $1,000; and James, 44, a driver, at $800. King's valuation on his property was stated at $13,000, comprising a total of 3,357 acres of "improved land, hammock land, poor pine land, salt marsh & inland swamp," 120 head of cattle valued at $600, six mules, eight horses, four colts and 30 sheep, valued in the aggregate at $1,055; furniture, plates, books and maps valued at $200, and $4,000 in stock in the Ogeechee Causeway. With some $75,000 in total assets, less about $11,000 in debts, King had a net property worth that year of $63,919—no small amount for that day, by any account.[335]

---

[335] Roswell King, Jr., plantation journal, various entries. King's tax returns for the years cited are contained in Julia King Papers, Midway Museum. The Ogeechee Causeway (Turnpike) refers to the public roadway through the rice fields to the Ogeechee River (King's Bridge) in Bryan County just north of present day Richmond Hill.

The long hours associated with his constant attention to farm management at home, coupled with the monthly trips to the Altamaha to supervise the Butler interests, not surprisingly exacted a toll on King's physical health and stamina. His health was never that good even by his own admission. In his journal one discovers frequent references to his bouts with rheumatism and assorted other ailments. "Have been more biliously indisposed since 1 June than the last 12 summers put together," King noted on August 28, 1853. Indeed, his increasing susceptibility to a variety of physical difficulties was likely the primary consideration in his resignation as the Butlers' manager in the spring of 1854. King's recurring health problems possibly contributed to his sudden severe illness and death in the summer of the same year, apparently of complications relating to the epidemics of dysentery and fever which were affecting much of the slave population of lower Liberty County at that time. King's journal alludes to serious outbreaks of dysentery among his own slaves at South Hampton, Woodville and Yellow Bluff during June 1854, shortly before his death on July 1st.

As would be expected, most of the Kings' social life revolved around frequent interaction with their immediate family, friends and neighbors in the Midway district. Among them the Joneses, Maxwells, Quartermans and Mallards. Much of this activity occurred during the summer and fall when the King family resided at Colonel's Island. King's journal also reflects a regular assemblage of friends, family members and neighboring planters from three counties calling on the family during their winter and spring sojourn at South Hampton on the mainland.

The religious life of the Kings, and of most families in the district, was centered upon the Midway Congregational Church. The pastors of the church during this period, usually reflecting a Presbyterian-oriented training, doctrine and theology, were the Rev. Robert Quarterman (served 1823-1847), the Rev. I.S.K. Axson (co-pastor 1836-1853), and the Rev. T.S. Winn (co-pastor 1848-1855). A granddaughter of Rev. Axson, Ellen Louise Axson, was the first wife of President Woodrow Wilson.

There are references to the Midway church throughout the King journal, which is somewhat of a paradox considering that Roswell King, Jr. himself was not known as an especially religious, much less pious, man, a fact documented among the writings of his closest associates. The journal references may therefore be considered as more symbolic of the importance attached to this church by the majority of people of the region rather than the spirituality of King. King occasionally alludes to his family's attendance at Sunday services at Midway, but one suspects that King's being in church was more a gesture toward preservation of appearance than because of his religiosity. It should also be noted in this context that a number of the slaves of the lower Liberty County plantations attended the Midway church with their owners—the original slave galleries above the church's sanctuary are eloquent testimony to this, and perhaps reflect the admonitions of King's Presbyterian clergyman friend, Rev. Charles Colcock Jones, who advocated the "Religious Instruction" of the slaves at all the coastal plantations. These sentiments are most clearly elucidated in the voluminous Jones family correspondence from 1854 to 1868 contained in *The Children of Pride* (1972) and the magisterial study by Erskine Clark of Jones family slaves and their owners, *Dwelling Place: A Plantation Epic* (2005).

On July 1, 1854, at Woodville, as noted by Mary Jones at the opening of this narrative, the soul of Roswell King, Jr., "passed from time to eternity." King left his sizeable estate to his children, consisting of his land holdings and 127 slaves, "50 head of cattle, 11 oxen, 26 hogs, 5 mules, 1 colt," and assorted wagons, carts, barrows and boats, and his interest in the Ogeechee Turnpike.[336]

King's will was made in 1840, fourteen years before his death, and it had remained unchanged. In the will he left words and instructions to his sons and his executors entailing business advice as well as sounding a somewhat cautionary note:

> "My sons I wish well instructed in the English language and mathematics until the age of seventeen, then apprenticed until the age of twenty-one to a merchant, house carpenter, cabinet maker, machinist, shipwright, millwright, or blacksmith. But should [any] of my sons prefer a more learned and lasting mode of life, either physic, law or gospel, and their means will warrant it, my executors are requested

---

[336] Julia King Papers, Midway Museum; Myers, ed., *The Children of Pride*, 70. The exact cause of King's death is undetermined, although his demise is most likely attributable to his exposure to dysentery and scarlet fever outbreaks among his slaves during the final two months of his life. His journal alludes to scarlet fever outbreaks among some of his family members during the same period. Three days before his death on July 1, 1854, King "was taken violently ill with inflammation of the stomach," reported Mrs. Mary Jones, a family friend and neighbor. Mrs. Jones is describing symptoms consistent with dysentery. She further indicates that King was "comatose" on the final day of his life, attesting to the severity of his violent illness. Food poisoning, not uncommon in the hot weather of summer in that era, and yellow fever are other possibilities for King's demise. However, based on the sketchy information gleaned from surviving accounts, the latter is not likely. There were indeed yellow fever epidemics at Savannah and Darien in 1854, but its course ran from mid-August to mid-October, some weeks prior to King's death.

to admit it. Wishing my sons to become useful members in the community in which they live, I desire that my executors hereinafter named do retain the property consolidated and undivided until the youngest child shall have attained the age of seventeen years."[337]

C.C. Jones was of the opinion that King's will was poorly devised. It is likely that King expected to live beyond his actual fifty-eight years, long enough for most, if not all, of his sons to attain their majority.

"The estate is to be kept together until the youngest child is twenty-one [sic]—a period some fifteen years off!" Jones remarked in a letter two months after King's death. "Will made in 1840; children then all young. The case is altered now, and the will should have been altered; and I understand Mr. King intended to alter it. Business matters of moment should never be left for the morrow!"[338]

While adored by his wife and children and called by them "Nature's Nobleman," King was provided with perhaps a far more telling kind of epitaph and commentary on his life by Jones, who wrote of his late friend and neighbor, "In a spiritual point of view Mr. King's death is a very melancholy one! He died as he lived..."

"Which was to say, hard, and without repentance," concluded, unsympathetically, Butler biographer Malcolm Bell. Perhaps a more appropriate closure may be affixed to the story of Roswell King, Jr., through the words of his then-elderly granddaughter, Julia King, written in 1950, almost a century after King's death. Miss King provides a poignant note of finality, not only to the King family and their years at Woodville, but to the lost plantation culture in

---

[337] Julia King Papers, Midway Museum.
[338] Myers, ed., *The Children of Pride*, 83.

tidewater Georgia: "The approach to [Woodville] was very beautiful—an immensely wide avenue bordered on each side with great glorious red oak trees—all gone—all forgotten, passed away into oblivion—Storms & hurricanes & fires & time have all done their worst! The last time I went to Woodville it was a pathless wilderness."

Butler's Island Before and After the War

Despite the increasing size of rice yields at Butler's Island, Pierce Butler was experiencing financial difficulties. An ineffective, and often disinterested, plantation owner to begin with, Butler "continued to dissipate his income by gambling at cards and by speculating in the stock market. His life remained in turmoil, reaching a crisis in ten-year intervals," notes Malcolm Bell. The year 1856 was disappointing for Butler. His losses were in such a poor state that the management of his affairs was placed with a triumvirate of Henry Fisher, his brother-in-law George Cadwalader, and Thomas C. James, his fellow trustee of John Butler's estate. In addition, Butler's annual payments of $1,500 to his former wife, Fanny Kemble, had fallen in arrears.

America was rushing headlong toward the Civil War, the issue between North and South revolving around slave state and free. Charles Augustus Lafayette Lamar (1824-1865), an advocate of re-opening the slave trade in the United States, financed an illegal slave-smuggling venture on the Georgia coast. Lamar was a wealthy Savannahian and god-child of the Marquis de Lafayette. The importation of slaves into the U.S. had been illegal since 1808. In November 1858, 409 Africans were illegally landed in the dead of night on the inland side of Jekyll Island near the plantation of Lamar's friends, John and Henry DuBignon, from the sailing yacht *Wanderer*, a fast vessel owned by William C. Corrie, Lamar's partner in the smuggling venture. The slaves were quickly dispersed to buyers, and the *Wanderer* cleaned of evidence of the misdeed. But local port authorities, acting on rumors, detained the yacht-slaver, and following an investigation, federal charges were levelled against Lamar, Corrie and others. The case in Savannah federal court was heard in November 1859 by United States Supreme Court Justice James Moore Wayne (1790-1867), a native Savannahian and the son of Richard Wayne, a former agent for Major Pierce Butler in the 1790s. Justice Wayne, appointed to the Supreme Court in 1835, was a Unionist and opposed secession. Despite Wayne's firm charge to a Savannah jury, Lamar and his colleagues were acquitted of an obvious flaunting of federal law, an outcome that received the approval of most Savannahians.[339]

Another notable occurrence in the news of Savannah in an eventful year of 1859 was the auction of many of the Butler slaves from McIntosh and Glynn counties. Pierce Butler had squandered much of the plantations' income through poor management and his dissolute lifestyle. To satisfy his creditors and remain solvent he was forced, in March 1859, to advertise for the auction of half of the estate's 900 slaves. On February 25, 1859, Gabriella Manigault Morris Butler (1808-1871), widow of John Mease Butler, traveled from Charleston to Savannah where she met with two of the trustees appointed to stabilize Pierce M. Butler's tangled financial affairs, George Cadwalader (husband of Frances Mease, sister of Pierce and John Butler), and Thomas C. James. James had arrived in Savannah from Butler's Island where he had coordinated the division of slaves

---

[339] For Lamar, see Myers, ed., *Children of Pride*, 1588. Lamar was shot and killed by a Union captor at Columbus, Georgia in April 1865, a week after Lee's surrender at Appomattox. The most authoritative account of the *Wanderer* incident is Tom Henderson Wells, *The Slave Ship Wanderer* (Athens: University of Georgia Press, 1967), the federal court proceedings being covered on pp. 53-62. For Butler's financial difficulties see Bell, *Major Butler's Legacy*, 319.

between those of the John Butler estate and those of Pierce M. Butler to be sold. Gabriella was there to protect the interests of her grandson, Francis Butler, and to agree to the auction of Butler bondsmen to be conducted by slave dealer Captain Joseph Bryan.

Altamaha planters Thomas M. Forman of Broughton Island, James Hamilton Couper of Hopeton and Thomas Pinckney Huger of Evelyn plantation were appointed by James to appraise and divide the Butler slaves for sale. It was a tedious process: for example, the first two slaves listed were sixty-one-year old Frank, a driver, with no listed value, and his fifty-eight-year old wife Betty, valued at $100. Betty was the mother of Renty, fathered by Roswell King, Jr. The slave with the highest value was thirty-one-year old Hampton, valued at $1,800. The highest valued woman was Catherine, eighteen, at $1,000.[340]

Some 459 Butler slaves were transported by rail and steamboat to Savannah for the auction to be held March 2-3, 1859 at the Ten Broeck racecourse three miles west of Savannah on the Central of Georgia Railroad. "Slave dealer Bryan was enthusiastic over prospects for a successful sale as Butler blacks were known to be well-trained and were believed dependable for a full measure of work. Although [Bryan's] advertisement did not mention the Butler ownership, the fact was well known from news stories appearing with the notices of the sale..."[341]

---

[340] Bell, *Major Butler's Legacy*, 326-27, citing records of the division of Butler slaves in Deed Book 3-S, 247-55, Chatham County Superior Court records, and Deed Book N, 52-71, Glynn County Superior Court records, abbreviated copies in Wister Family Records, HSP. For Frank, Betty and Renty, see Kemble, *Journal*, 176 (note), 249-50.

[341] Bell, *Major Butler's Legacy*, 328; *Savannah Republican*, February 26, 1859; *Savannah Daily Morning News*, February 24, 1859 and February 26, 1850.

During two days, 436 Butler slaves were sold for a total of $300,205. According to the *Savannah Daily Morning News*, the auction brought "an average of a little over $716 a head, a price well in excess of the average value of $572.47 estimated by the appraisers when the slaves were divided between Pierce Butler and his brother's estate...the sale was largely attended by gentlemen from different portions of our state and from South Carolina."[342]

Pierce Butler was present at the Ten Broeck racecourse for both days of the sale. "Sufficient emotion was packed into the racecourse stables without so false a picture of the life of a Butler slave, Malcolm Bell notes. "Had [reporters] seen Shadrach's body laid in a grave half filled with ground water, or seen Judy and Scylla strung up and lashed for birthing the plantation manager's children he could have written without idealizing plantation life..."[343] Though the slaves were classified in family groups they were not always sold together. Those who purchased Butler slaves in the well-advertised auction came from Alabama, South Carolina, and middle Georgia. Ironically, many of the slaves sold at the auction, the largest that ever occurred in coastal Georgia and known to slaves, freedmen and history alike as "The Weeping Time," came back to Butler's Island after the Civil War. Bell, invoking Fanny Kemble, adds an appropriate postscript to this sad event:

"As Fanny Kemble was staying in Philadelphia at the time of the sale, there is no doubt she was well aware of what to her was a tragic event. No one, the slaves excepted, realized the import as she did. She said the sale of his slaves 'caused him [Butler] extreme pain and mortification,' conditions not evident on those days of rain at

---

[342] *Savannah Daily Morning News*, March 4, 1859.
[343] Bell, *Major Butler's Legacy*, 333.

Savannah's Ten Broeck racecourse…she called off any attempts to 'settle' with Pierce Butler on the matter of his past due payments agreed to in the divorce settlement. She believed his financial situation was so improved that it 'promises a comfortable maintenance hence forward to his daughters.' She preferred not to talk of this unfortunate matter, dismissing the subject with 'I knew he had met with domestic calamity.'"[344]

The fall of 1859 saw probably the most productive crop in the history of Butler's Island with a yield of 2.6 million pounds of rice harvested by the remaining 505 slaves.[345] In 1860, Butler visited the family's plantations at Hampton Point and Butler's Island. "The change was quickly evident," Bell notes. "Once-thriving Hampton was all but abandoned, the total work force was reduced by one half … he stayed in the house at Butler's Island where he had been with his family twenty years before."[346] A large amount of rice was shipped from Butler's Island in the fall and winter of 1860-61 but it was clear by then that an era was rushing toward a close. The war divided even more an already divided family:

"Very much pro-Union were Fanny Kemble, Sarah and [her husband] Dr. Wister … Pierce Butler in Philadelphia … left no doubt as to his feelings, or to those of his daughter Frances. The [Sidney George] Fisher diary revealed; 'Butler is eager for secession & has just returned from Georgia, where he says there is no difference of opinion. He said he came here only to buy arms and intends to return

---

[344] Ibid., 340, citing Kemble, *Further Records* (New York, 1891), 326, 366, and Frances Anne Kemble Collection, 79-28423, Library of Congress.
[345] U.S. Census, McIntosh County, Slave and Agricultural Schedules, 1860. The slave auction had been conducted in March 1859. The rice harvest began in August, and was that which was reported in the 1860 agricultural census. The census slave count would likely have been enumerated in the latter half of 1859 or early 1860. The conclusion to be drawn is that virtually all the Butler slaves were employed at the rice plantation, with operations at Hampton virtually suspended.
[346] Bell, *Major Butler's Legacy*, 342.

immediately and join the army. He will take his daughter Fanny with him and has bought a rifle for her, too, for he says even the women in the South are going to fight.'"[347]

Butler made another trip to Georgia just as Southern forces attacked Fort Sumter in April 1861. "The great threat to the Butler empire was the war. Whatever his sentiments, Pierce Butler knew the plantations would become unmanageable in a nation torn by conflict," Bell notes. The plantations, for a fact, did become unmanageable. Butler was under arrest in New York for a short time because of his publicly-espoused pro-Southern sentiments. He was released on condition that he not visit South Carolina "without a passport from the secretary of state. He would have had greater reason to visit Georgia, but as it turned out, chose not to go to either state until the war had ended … He remained close to Philadelphia, holding fast to his desire for a Southern victory while his plantation world disintegrated."[348]

* * *

After the capture and occupation of Savannah by federal forces in December 1864 events of an unusual nature began to occur that would greatly affect the aftermath of the war in coastal Georgia. Major General William T. Sherman's Special Field Order No. 15 of January 16, 1865 set aside as reservations for former slaves the sea islands from Charleston to the St. Johns River, and the abandoned plantation lands from the coast to thirty miles inland. The Order stipulated that no white persons could live in these areas. In effect, the federal government was confiscating all the coastal lands owned by the pre-war planters for the use of the freedmen

---

[347] Ibid., 343.
[348] Ibid., 345, 350-51.

who would have exclusive management of their affairs on the islands subject only to U.S. military authorities.

Food was scarce in the coastal counties in the months following the end of the war in April 1865. The food-producing plantations were largely destroyed, and few farm animals had been left by the invading federal forces. The Bureau of Refugees, Freedmen and Abandoned Lands set up branch offices in the coastal counties as the process of Reconstruction began. These were initially expedited by U.S. Army officers who were later replaced by War Department civilian employees of the Freedmen's Bureau. The Bureau controlled civic affairs in coastal Georgia for five years until Georgia was readmitted to the Union in 1870.

All six coastal counties had majority black populations before the Civil War, and consequently had large numbers of freedmen after the war, along with displaced white people; many of the freedmen remained on the plantations working with their former owners in a loosely-organized system of cropsharing. In McIntosh County, the 1870 census showed that Darien's population comprised 111 whites and 435 blacks, figures substantially different from those of the 1860 census that had Darien with 315 whites and 255 blacks. Many of the white people in 1870 were living at outlying areas such as the Ridge after their homes in town had been burned in 1863. The county population in 1870 was 4,484, with blacks holding a majority of 3,288 to 1,196 whites. The 1860 census listed 4,063 slaves, 54 free blacks, and 1,429 whites in the county. Whites in coastal Georgia had little left but their land after the war ended. No matter their financial status before the war, many were now virtually destitute. There was little money for either blacks or whites. Norman Page Gignilliat reportedly said to his former slaves after the war that nothing had changed—he sent them back to the rice fields saying, "Roll up your sleeves, get back in the fields, make me one hundred bushels of rice, and

I will give you one hundred acres of land." Thus, land served as currency for many planters, at least until economic conditions had stabilized and improved.

The freed slaves aspired to acquire their own land and assert their newly-gained independence. Many obtained property through the barter system or by wills and gifts from their former owners. Others bought land on credit and paid their mortgages from profits gained by working the land. the coastal freedmen thus became independent farmers sooner than many of their contemporaries on other parts of the South. Some left the plantations and "squatted" on land in the pine barrens where they built cabins for their families and scratched out an acre or two for cultivation of crops. In Darien, where the war quickly resulted in the replacement of rice by timber as the primary cash export, blacks found numerous opportunities for employment. By 1870, blacks held sixty-seven of the seventy-six jobs in the labor positions at sawmills at Darien, its environs, and at Doboy Island.[349]

In 1866, Pierce Butler and his daughter Frances, then in her late twenties, came to Butler's Island from Philadelphia to re-establish the rice plantation. Like her mother, Fanny Kemble, Frances Butler kept a record of events, and in 1883 published *Ten Years on a Georgia Plantation Since the War*. Her prose, while lacking the style and polish of that of her mother, nonetheless offers a useful glimpse of race, labor conditions and life in general in the Darien area during Reconstruction. It may be the best contemporary account of post-war life in coastal Georgia. Like their mother and father, the two Butler daughters offer interesting studies in contrast. The first child of the Pierce Butler-Fanny Kemble union, Sarah (1835-1908) was similar to her mother in spirit and

---

[349] U.S. Census, 1860 and 1870, Population Schedules, McIntosh County; Russell Duncan, *Freedom's Shore: Tunis Campbell and the Georgia Freedmen* (Athens: University of Georgia Press, 1986), 56-57.

sentiment, evident from the anti-slavery, pro-Union attitudes she embraced before and during the Civil War. Frances (1838-1910), on the other hand, adopted her father's pro-slavery, pro-South views. She never ceased to believe that blacks fared better as slaves than as free people.

When the Butlers returned many of the freedmen of Butler's Island returned to work for the family, this time as wage-earning employees, as the Butlers resumed rice planting in 1866-67. Frances acquired insight and expertise in the ways of crop management, benefitting from the experience of her workers and her father.[350] "There was another side to the picture, one oft-repeated along the coast. In the past, the master had produced his crop with the aid of discipline enforced by the lash. That, of course, was no longer possible, and it was often a challenging task to get the freedmen to do regular and dependable work."[351] Pierce Butler made the fatal mistake of remaining at Butler's Island during the fetid summer of 1867, and fell ill with malaria in mid-August. His suffering did not last long. Rowed to Darien by young former slave Liverpool Hazzard, Butler was taken to his friend Dr. James Holmes at the Ridge. There the master of Butler's Island expired; "his disease was congestive chills, and his death was sudden and unexpected" several days later.[352] The Butler-Wister family received the news with varying reaction:

"...Sarah Wister's grief, and the visitation to Philadelphia of mother and maid, 'physical & nervous shock.' Sarah became ill, suffered a failure of memory, and became agitated over the inability to be alone...Fanny Kemble had little to say regarding her own feelings on Pierce Butler's death and seemed unaware of any untoward intrusion into the lives of the Wisters. There was nothing in her letters to show she recognized the distress of her daughters....Unlike her sister, Frances Butler was not overwhelmed with grief. Her immediate concern was to protect and to continue what she and her

---

[350] Bell, *Major Butler's Legacy*, op. cit., 394-405.
[351] Dorothy Marshall, *Fanny Kemble* (New York: St. Martin's Press, 1977), 247.
[352] *Savannah Daily News Herald*, August 22, 1867.

father had begun in postwar Georgia. The Butler agents in Savannah had sent distress signals to Philadelphia urging attention to the plantations. With energy and determination mindful of the one for whom she was named, Frances Butler responded by enlisting the aid of her brother-in-law Owen Jones Wister, and together they traveled south to put things in order…"[353]

Frances Butler thus returned from the north in October 1867, accompanied by her brother- in-law, Dr. Owen Wister, with the intention of carrying on operations at Butler's Island. The Savannah agents had not exaggerated. The immediate problem to be addressed was settling accounts with the freedmen against the 1867 first-year rice crop that had failed to produce the anticipated profits. Wister managed to accrue six thousand dollars to pay the workers but Frances realized to her chagrin that many of the hands used their pay to purchase their own land in the environs of Darien and begin farming on their own. The radically-altered political dynamic in Darien fueled by the new-found black voting power contributed to often tendentious labor relations between Frances Butler and her workers. Tunis Campbell arrived on the scene in 1868 to find a town where blacks greatly outnumbered whites, and "very much a 'political and spiritual overlord,' Campbell preached, promised and won voting rights for the black majority." These developments were directly felt at Butler's Island where the freedmen "were given imagined cause to obstruct work and to flaunt their independence."[354] Frances Butler's frustrations were evident:

"The negroes this year and the following seemed to reach the climax of lawless independence, and I never slept without a loaded pistol by my bed. Their whole manner was changed; they took to calling their former owners by their last name with any title before it, constantly spoke of my agent as old R_____, dropped the pleasant term of 'Mistress,' took to calling me 'Miss Fanny,' walked about with guns on their shoulders, worked just as much and when as

---

[353] Bell, *Major Butler's Legacy*, 402-04.
[354] Ibid., 412.

they pleased, and tried speaking to me with their hats on, or not touching them to me when they passed me on the banks.. This last rudeness I never permitted for a moment, and always said sharply, 'Take your hat off instantly,' and was obliged to take a tone with them generally which I had never done before. One or two, who seemed rather more inclined to be insolent than the rest, I dismissed, always saying, 'You are free to leave the place, but not to stay here and behave as you please, for I am free too, and moreover own the place, and so have a right to give my orders on it, and have them obeyed'...[The white planters] entertained the idea of seeing if they could not buy Campbell over, and induce him by heavy bribes to work for us, or rather to use his influence over our negroes to make them work for us. And this proposition was made to me, but I could not consent to such a plan. In the first place it was utterly opposed to my notions of what was right, and my pride revolted from the idea of making any such bargain with a creature like Campbell; besides which I felt sure it was bad policy, that if we bought him one day he would sell us out the next. So I refused to have anything to do with the project."[355] .

In 1869, Frances met a young Anglican clergyman, the vicar of Stoneleigh, James Wentworth Leigh (1838-1923), in New York. They were married in England in 1871. In August 1873 the Leighs moved to Georgia and settled in the overseers' house at Butler's Island. Leigh assumed the management of the plantation, and his buoyant personality soon won over the black workers. He began conducting Episcopalian services for the blacks in late 1873, as well as ministering to them in other supportive ways. Leigh also worked with Rev. Robert Clute and the white Episcopalian congregation at St. Andrew's church. The local Episcopalians were in the midst of planning their new church during this period, and Leigh helped them obtain designs from England. However, it was his missionary work among the former slaves that resulted in achievements of a permanent and lasting nature long after Leigh had left Darien to return to England several years later. His supervision of rice

---

[355] Frances Butler Leigh, *Ten Years on a Georgia Plantation Since the War* (New York: Negro Universities Press, 1969 reprint of original 1883 London edition), 133-38

cultivation at Butler's Island provided him with ample opportunity of laying the foundations for what was to become the black Episcopalian congregation of Darien.

Leigh's most memorable contribution, and the source of his greatest satisfaction, was in establishing a new freedmen's church in Darien. In early 1876, he acquired architectural plans based on a small stone Anglican church near Stoneleigh, the Leigh's family home in England, and used these as the basis for the new black church in Darien. Leigh named the church St. Cyprian's in honor of the martyred African bishop. The freedmen of Butler's Island and Darien did the work themselves, the *Darien Timber Gazette* noting, "the colored Episcopalians are progressing rapidly with their new church. It will be a real neat structure."[356] The church of tabby, brick and lumber from Darien's mills, was completed later that year. St. Cyprian's was consecrated by Bishop John W. Beckwith of Savannah, "a most solemn and interesting ceremony," with one side of the church "filled with white citizens, the other side with coloured citizens."[357] Thirty communicants received Holy Communion, in addition to six vestrymen from St. Andrew's.

Frances Butler Leigh was never able to reconcile to the societal changes wrought by the war; she had a difficult time understanding the evolution of the blacks from subservience to independence, writing in 1868:

"... Notwithstanding our giving the negroes the very best things at cost price, they much preferred going to Darien to spend their money on inferior goods and at greatly increased rates. I suppose, poor people, it was natural they should like to swagger a little, and spend their newly, but certainly not hardly-earned money freely, and it was an immense relief to my pocket and labors to give up shop-keeping. Two or three Northern political agents arrived in Darien, and summoned all the negroes to attend meetings. I in vain reasoned

---

[356] *Darien Timber Gazette,* March 24, 1876.
[357] James Wentworth Leigh, *Other Days* (London, 1921), 158-60; Frances B. Leigh, *Ten Years on a Georgia Plantation,* 246.

with the negroes, and did all in my power to prevent their attending these meetings, not because I cared in the least which way they voted, but because it interfered so terribly with their work. I doubled the watchmen at night and did all I could to prevent strangers from landing on the Island; but one morning found that during the night a notice had been put up on the wharf, calling upon all the people to attend a political meeting on pain of being fined five hundred dollars, or exiled to a foreign land. I knew if the people once broke off, no more work would be done for at least a week; this would have cost me two hundred acres of rice."[358]

A description of Butler's Island during the Reconstruction period is contained in *Ten Years on a Georgia Plantation*. In a letter by James Leigh in 1873, included as an appendix to his wife's memoir, he noted:

"[Butler's was] an island of about 1,600 acres surrounded by a muddy-looking river, called by the romantic-sounding Indian name of the Altamaha ... Our castle is a neat but not gaudy little frame house, with a piazza in front of it. The interior is in accordance with its modest exterior; a small hall, a pantry, and two comfortable bed-rooms on the ground- floor, and two more comfortable bed-rooms over the dining and drawing-rooms. At the rear of the house about twelve yards, is what is called the colony, where are situated the kitchen, servants' sitting-room and bedrooms, the laundry and dairy. Behind the colony is Settlement No. 1 where the coloured people reside. It consists of an avenue of orange trees, on each side of which are rows of wooden houses ... Immediately in front of our garden is the Altamaha river, with the landing-place for the boats, and from which all the water supply is drawn. On the left of us is the overseer's house, a larger and more imposing edifice, although not so comfortable as ours. On the right are the barns and the new threshing mill and engine, which are very nearly finished, and present a magnificent appearance from the river. The old mill, with all the valuable machinery, was burnt down a year ago. The rest of the Island consists of rice-fields, of which about 1,000 acres are under cultivation or cultivable, some marsh land covered with thick bamboo and reeds, in which the wild duck do congregate, and some scrubby brushwood; also Settlements Nos. 2 and 3, an old, rickety, but very large barn, a ruined mill, a ruined sugar-house ..."[359]

---

[358] Frances B. Leigh, *Ten Years on a Georgia Plantation*, 96-97.
[359] Frances B. Leigh, *Ten Years on a Georgia Plantation Since the War* (Savannah, Ga.: Beehive Press edition, 1992), 107-11.

In *Major Butler's Legacy,* Malcolm Bell introduces us to a group of unforgettable African American players during this period of the Butler's Island story. One of course, is Liverpool Hazzard, whom Bell describes as rowing a desperately sick Pierce Butler from the island to Dr. Holmes in August 1867. Liverpool lived in Darien, and in the 1920s and 1930s, became something of a tourist attraction. For a small fee he would sing an old boating chantey as he once did during the dugout races on the river before and after the Civil War when he was a young man. Butler plantation records show that Hazzard was born in 1851. Thus, Liverpool was eighty-seven when he died in 1938, not 110 as his promoters claimed. He enjoyed telling of his recollections of the Butlers, Wisters and Leighs, from his childhood memories of being a slave, and in the years after emancipation talking of slave lore, and songs. Some of Liverpool Hazzard's songs are included in Lydia Parrish's volume, *Slave Songs of the Georgia Sea Islands,* the definitive work on the subject.[360] Other blacks were Aleck and Daphne Alexander, the surname the couple adopted during Reconstruction. They maintained their contacts with the Butler family, particularly Frances Leigh and Sarah Wister. Daphne was the daughter of Minda and Roswell King, Jr. Both Daphne and Aleck appear in Fanny Kemble's *Journal*. The former slave Carolina died in 1866 as a free man at the age of 100, his funeral at Hampton Point attended by Pierce Butler and Frances Butler. Dan Wing was often mentioned in the letters of James and Frances Butler Leigh in the 1870s; he was a mulatto descendant of driver Morris, and said to be a bright young man. The Leighs took Wing to England with them when they departed Butler's Island for good in early 1877; he served as a domestic in the Leigh household. After returning to Georgia, Wing played a role in helping to subdue passions during the unrest in 1899

---

[360] Lydia Parrish, *Slave Songs of the Georgia Sea Islands* (New York, 1942); Bell, *Major Butler's Legacy,* 557.

precipitated by the Henry Delegal case.³⁶¹ (See chapter 11 for the story of this incident and the peripheral involvement therein by the Leigh and Wister families).

By 1876, James and Frances Leigh were beginning to feel they had reached the end of their labors in coastal Georgia. Their second child had been born and died in January 1876. The 1875 rice crop had resulted in a loss of one thousand pounds sterling to the Leighs, largely because of the failures of their Savannah agent. By this time, Georgia markets were being depressed by increased production of Louisiana rice—"James Leigh's hard work had finally brought to harvest fine crops that unfortunately reached markets depressed by a huge production of Louisiana rice."³⁶² In August 1876, a yellow fever epidemic, the worst since that of 1854, broke out in Savannah. Lasting through October, the fever claimed the lives of 1,066 people in Savannah, an event that practically paralyzed the Georgia coast commercially because of the region's dependence on that city, then still the largest in Georgia with a population of thirty thousand. Meanwhile, a decade of physical and mental exertion, and investment, finally exacted its toll on Frances Leigh. The Leighs returned to England in early 1877 and left their rice operation under the management of an overseer. As Frances notes,

"And now I have come to these last three years of my history. In the autumn of 1877, not a year after our return to England, our old friend and agent Major D_____ died, and in many ways his loss was an irreparable one to us, but nothing showed the changed and improved condition of the negroes more than the fact that his death did not in the least unsettle them, and that the work went steadily on just the same. A few years before, a sort of panic would have seized them, and the idea taken possession of them that a new man would not pay them, or would work them too hard, or make new rules, &c. &c., and it would have been months before we got them quieted

---

³⁶¹ Bell, *Major Butler's Legacy*, 549, 553, 564-65.
³⁶² Ibid., 424.

and settled down again…In September of the year 1878 a terrible storm visited the Southern coast. The hurricane swept over the Island just in the middle of the harvest, and quite half the crop was entirely destroyed, and the rest injured. What was saved was only rescued by the most energetic and laborious efforts on the part of the negroes, who did their utmost. Day after day they did almost double their usual task, several times working right through the night, and twice all Sundays; cheerfully and willingly, not as men who were working for wages, but as men whose heart was in their work, and who felt their interests to be the same as their employer's. Later on in the same year my husband returned to the United States and revisited the property, but finding everything working well and satisfactorily, only remained about six weeks…"[363]

The Leighs initially intended to sell the family lands in Georgia, but the poor market for rice in the mid-to-late 1870s made Butler's Island a poor prospect, certainly on the terms that Frances Leigh wanted in order to settle their accumulation of debt. Thus, the decision was made to have an overseer manage the rice plantation under the Leighs' supervision from England; later, it was decided to lease the rice tidelands and remove themselves from direct association with the plantation. It was a bittersweet departure for the Leighs. Fanny Kemble noted that

"I do not think my dear James' liking for a Georgia plantation life so strange as it appears to you. I was fascinated by the wild singular beauty of those sea islands, and the solitary, half-savage freedom of the life on those southern rivers and sounds; and *but for the slavery*, should have enjoyed my existence there extremely. Sarah, when she came back this winter from visiting her sister, after her illness, said the place and the life and the climate were all like an enchanting dream…"[364]

"While his wife and daughter Alice celebrated Christmas 1876 at York

---

[363] Frances B. Leigh, *Ten Years on a Georgia Plantation*, Beehive edition, 154-55.
[364] Frances Anne Kemble to Harriet St. Leger, *Further Records* (New York, 1891).

Farm in Pennsylvania with Fanny Kemble and Sarah, Dr. Wister, and Dan [the Wisters' son] joined them from Butler Place across the road, James Leigh was quite alone on Butler's Island. He ordered a dugout canoe with four oarsmen who sang 'their quaint songs' on a moonlit trip to Hampton. Bundled against the cold, he manned the steering oar from the stern of the boat to arrive at the abandoned plantation just at midnight. On New Year's Day the 'St. Simons people came up to the house to bid me God-speed...'" Several days later, Leigh conducted his farewell service at St. Cyprian's. Bell notes:

"As they neared the time for their departure, Frances Leigh was relieved they had not sold. She held to 'her passionate preference for the place' and to the hope that the venture on the Altamaha might yet prove successful. She knew James Leigh would miss the great satisfaction he found in his agricultural existence and in the fishing, boating, and hunting that had been such a happy part of his life. Most of all, she knew, he would miss his missionary work with the black people. True, she would have preferred to have lived the life Major Butler envisioned when his slaves built the big house at Hampton, or to have enjoyed the luxuries described by Aaron Burr [from Hampton] in his letter to [his daughter] Theodosia. But she, too, had her own luxuries—oranges 'like fruits of paradise with their royal color and delicious fragrance.' And when on a Sunday, James Leigh was doing his missionary work at St. Cyprian's, did she not attend Darien's parish church in the grand manner? A parishioner thought so: 'She would come over to church in Darien in great state in a log canoe rowed by negro men. Those men would wear red shirts and sailor caps one winter, the next perhaps blue shirts…They would walk ahead of her to the church—two of them would go in taking a foot warmer and a rug, which they would place in her pew, then she would come in with Alice, the governess and the ward. After church the men would be lined up on both sides of the steps, till she came out, quite like royalty.'"[365]

---

[365] Bell, *Major Butler's Legacy*, 426. The description quoted by Bell of Frances Leigh attending church at St. Cyprian's is extracted from Thomas Hilton's memoirs. For the full quote see Buddy Sullivan, ed., *High Water on the Bar: An Operational Perspective of a Tidewater Timber Port, with the Memoir of Thomas Hilton* (Darien, Ga.: Darien Downtown Development Authority, 2009), 67-68.

Rice cultivation at Butler's and the other Altamaha islands was barely profitable some years, yet successful in others, thus the work continued. Butler's Island was supervised for the Leighs in the late 1870s and early 1880s by James Maxwell Couper (1837-1918), son of James Hamilton and Caroline Wylly Couper, formerly of Hopeton and Altama. Though still a Butler family property, the island was left largely untenanted during much of the later 1880s and 1890s. A portion of Butler's Island was leased for cultivation during some of this period, one of the lessees being local planter Thomas Hart Gignilliat. In April 1901, Frances Leigh leased Butler's to William H. Strain for an annual rental of $125, with Mrs. Emma Strain given an option to buy the island for $10,000 "This was the same land Major Butler, in 1818, offered [to sell] for $506,000, although that amount did include 582 slaves at $450 each, giving an asking price of $244,100 for the plantation alone." A deed of December 4, 1905 between William H. Strain and Emma E. Strain, executrix of the late Adam Strain (d. 1897) involved the transfer of

"All that tract of land known as Champneys Island lying in the Altamaha River being bounded east by the Altamaha River, west by the south branch of the Altamaha River, north and northeast and northwest by the South Middle branch of the Altamaha River, containing 937 acres, more or less. Also all of the following personal property situated on Butler's Island, surrounded by the waters of the Altamaha River, to wit; One Saw Mill, one 32/54 J.I. Case thrasher, one 14/18 Steam Straw Press, one Barnard & Lee's rice clipper, 21 carts and wagons, 22 sets of harnesses, 22 plows, three ditch harrows, three McCormick mowers, three Hoozies Rice Drills, two cultivators."[366]

A year later there occurred the formal sale of Butler's Island to the Strain family; for the first time in 120 years, the island was no longer among the

---

[366] Deed Book H, 52-54 (1901), RMCG; Deed Book H (1905), 531, RMCG. Bell, *Major Butler's Legacy*, 460.

Butler family's holdings:

"Kingdom of Great Britain.
County of Warwick.

"This indenture, made December 28, 1906 between Mrs. Frances Butler Leigh, of the County of Hertford, England, party of the first part, and Mrs. Emma E. Strain, Executrix of the will of Adam Strain, deceased, of the County of McIntosh and State of Georgia, United States of America, party of the second part. Witnesseth that for the sum of $10,000 Mrs. Leigh has granted, bargained, sold and conveyed unto the party of the second part all that certain tract of land known as Butler's Island, containing 1,600 acres, more or less, and bounded on the north and east by the Middle North Branch of the Altamaha River, on the south and west by the Middle South Branch of the Altamaha River ... together with all houses, out-houses, stables, yards, gardens, easements and privileges ..."[367]

William H. Strain and his younger brother Robert A. Strain had leased Butler's Island together before William H. Strain exercised an option to purchase the tract in 1906; he acquired Generals Island in 1907. The Strains were the sons of Adam and Emma Strain of Darien. At the time of the transactions with the Leighs, W.H. Strain was the senior member of the firm of Adam Strain's Sons. Completing the series of transactions by which the Butlers divested themselves of their Georgia properties was a January 7, 1907 deed

"between Frances B. Leigh of Hertford, England, Sarah B. Wister of Philadelphia, Pennsylvania, et al. of the first part, and John D. Clarke, Robert Manson and Robert A. Strain, each of Darien, of the second part, [whereby] for the sum of $1,500, the parties of the first part have granted, bargained, sold and conveyed that tract of land known as General's Island, lying immediately opposite the town of Darien, and bounded on the south by a river known as the Middle River, being a branch of the Altamaha, on the southeast by General's Cut, on the north by Darien River, being a branch of the Altamaha which runs by and between the town of Darien and the said General's Island, and west and southwest by Butler's River, being a branch of

---

[367] Deed Book I (1906), 121-22, RMCG.

Butler's Island and bridge, looking south, circa 1928.

the Altamaha River, containing about 800 acres, more or less, of which 300 acres are rice lands and the balance uncleared land. The parties of the first part jointly and severally covenant that Pierce Butler, late a resident of McIntosh County, Georgia, died intestate and that his sole heirs at law at the present time are his two daughters, Mrs. Frances B. Leigh and Mrs. Sarah B. Wister, parties of the first part ..."[368]

"The $1,500 received was but a small fraction of the $36,000 paid for the same land in 1853 by Pierce Butler and the estate of his brother John," notes Bell of the sale of Generals Island by the two sisters. For two or three years, the Strains and Mansons attempted to profit from rice on some of the former Butler lands, but with very little success, for by 1910, the south Atlantic rice industry was little more than a memory.

Frances Anne Kemble died peacefully at the Leighs' home near London on January 15, 1893—with "not a groan, not a struggle, her spirit must have flown straight up to God." Her literary legacy and her Shakespearean talents, both in America and England, would live on for generations. She had made eighteen crossings of the Atlantic between England and America between

---

[368] Deed Book I (1907), 160, RMCG.

1834 and 1877, the last being early in the latter year when she accompanied James and Frances Leigh, and their young daughter Alice, on their move to England. In 1890, less than three years before her death, James T. Dent of Hofwyl plantation, near Butler's Island and a friend of the Leighs, visited Kemble in London. Dent later related comments Kemble made to him, which he viewed as a "softening of her views" on slavery: "I suppose the South will never forgive me for what I wrote about slavery. I was a *young and passionate woman*. I have *bitterly regretted* many things that I wrote in that book. I do not mean that my attitude on slavery has changed. That is the same. But when I think of the awful results of the war to those who were dear to me, I have much to be sorry for." James Troup Dent (1848-1913) was the son of George C. and Ophelia Troup Dent of Hofwyl plantation (chapter 6). In 1880, Dent married Mariam Gratz Cohen, an energetic woman who helped bring Hofwyl and Broadfield back into Dent family ownership after they had been foreclosed on after the Civil War. The Dents lived in the overseer's house built by his parents in 1851. Their daughter, Miss Ophelia Dent (1886-1973), the last of the Troup-Dent family to live at Hofwyl, made the tract available to the state of Georgia for educational purposes upon her death. To another visitor in 1890, Georgia Page King Wilder, whose family had owned Retreat plantation at St. Simons Island, Kemble is said to have remarked, "I wonder why my husband *had not strangled me—I was a fanatic!*"[369]

    Henry James, the great American novelist and friend and admirer of Fanny Kemble wrote an essay in her memory, noting that her plantation *Journal* was the finest of her writing—"strong, insistent, one-sided...the most valuable

---

[369] Eleanor Brianzoni to Frances Cobbe, in Frances Anne Kemble Letters to Various People, Folger Shakespeare Library, Washington, D.C., cited in Bell, *Major Butler's Legacy*, 449; copies of letters written by James T. Dent, July 29, 1912, and Georgia Wilder, August 28, 1912, in Margaret Davis Cate Collection, Collection 997, GHS, published in Caroline Couper Lovell, *The Golden Isles of Georgia* (Boston, 1932), 209-13.

account…of strong emotion…of impressions begotten of that old Southern life which we are too apt to see today as through a haze of Indian summer."[370]

In 1908, Sarah Butler Wister died at Butler Place in Philadelphia where she had been born seventy-three years earlier. "She was remembered in her last years riding sidesaddle, 'dressed entirely in dove gray with a gray bowler hat,' or at home, 'tall, slender and old…Hampton plantation, which had not sold, was left to her son Dan [Owen Wister].'"[371] Two years later, her sister Frances died in England at age seventy-two, her life no doubt shortened by the stresses and turmoil of civil war, Reconstruction and attempting to resurrect the rice plantation thirty years earlier. "The plantation people remembered Frances Leigh. When news of her death reach Darien, the Mann School of St. Cyprian's was draped in black and kept that way 'for forty-two days & People came from all around for days & weeks to see it.'"[372] At the time of Leigh's death, her husband, James W. Leigh, had become the Very Reverend Honorable Dean Leigh of the cathedral of Hereford. He died in 1923 at the age of eighty-five.

The fifth, and last, generation of the Butler family to hold title to the Butler lands in McIntosh and Glynn counties was that of Owen Wister (1860-1938) who was born into the abolitionist branch of the family as the son of Dr. Owen Jones Wister and Sarah Butler Wister. As a lad of seven he had accompanied his mother on a visit to her sister Frances Butler and her father, Pierce M. Butler, at the Altamaha lands in 1867. Young Wister, known as Dan to the family, was an accomplished scholar and musician who received his schooling in Europe and at Harvard. He had a close relationship with his

---

[370] Henry James, *Essays in London and Elsewhere*, (New York, 1893), 107, cited in Bell, *Major Butler's Legacy*, 449.
[371] Fanny Kemble Wister, *That I May Tell You* (Wayne, Pa., 1979), 171-75, 205, cited in Bell, *Major Butler's Legacy*, 470.
[372] James W. Leigh, *Other Days*, 220, cited in Bell, *Major Butler's Legacy*, 471.

grandmother, Fanny Kemble, both being writers and skilled musicians. In 1898, Wister married Mary Channing, his second cousin once removed, and the couple spent considerable time in Charleston, a locale both Wisters came to greatly appreciate. It was in Charleston during the winter of 1902 that Wister completed his first novel, and best-known work, *The Virginian*, and it was Charleston that provided the setting for his second novel, *Lady Baltimore*, a story that elicited criticism when it was published in 1906 because of its handling of the slavery issue. The controversy stemmed from Wister's sympathetic treatment of Charleston aristocracy during the slavery era, and in his "sweeping indictment of the Northern people...[who] you made your swine devils, and your angels practically all Southerners," as expressed in a letter to Wister from his friend Theodore Roosevelt, who was President at the time.[373] In his introduction to *Lady Baltimore*, after its serialization in the *Saturday Evening Post*, Wister noted, "Certain passages have been interpreted most surprisingly to signify a feeling against the colored race, that is by no means mine. My only wish regarding these people, to whom we owe an immeasurable responsibility, is to see the best that is in them prevail."[374] Better known, and better received, was Wister's historical novel, *The Virginian*, which achieved considerable journalistic success and popularity among a wide reading audience in both the United States and Europe. In its review, the *New York* Times commented "Owen Wister has come pretty near to writing the American novel." The last connection to the Georgia lands of the Butler family was that of Dan Wister who had inherited his mother's Hampton Point tract. In 1920 he sold Major Butler's old 3,880-acre cotton plantation to

---

[373] Owen Wister, *Roosevelt: The Story of a Friendship* (New York, 1930), pages 247-65, relating the differences that arose between Wister and Roosevelt because of *Lady Baltimore*.
[374] Owen Wister, *Lady Baltimore* (New York, 1925 reissue of 1906 edition), ix.

a St. Simons development company for $45,000; the company defaulted on their loan, and in 1923 Wister resold Hampton to John A. Metcalf for $25,000. Wister died in July 1938 at the age of seventy-eight.

Colonel Tillinghast L. Huston (1867-1938) was part owner of the New York Yankees when Babe Ruth was making baseball history. In 1927, the year Ruth hit a record sixty home runs, Huston acquired Butler's Island at a sheriff's sale. The same year, he began construction of the three-story residence on about the same plot that the plantation overseer's house had stood. Huston developed Butler's Island into an efficient dairy operation, processing and shipping milk in the eastern U.S., and followed with a successful truck farming operation featuring iceberg lettuce, celery and flowers that were marketed nationwide. Huston upgraded and modernized the dikes and canals of the former rice fields, a project that benefitted from his engineering background. It is propitious that at the time Huston was initiating his agricultural activities at Butler's and Champneys islands, the 1929 *Soil Survey of McIntosh County* provided topographical information about the Altamaha delta and a map:

"Altamaha clay is the first bottom soil along the Altamaha River, much of which was used in the past for rice production. Recently, efforts have been made to utilize some of the land for the production of truck crops, fruits and bulbs. Recently a substation of the Georgia Coastal Plain Experiment Station has been established on this soil on Butler Island, and intensive cropping of truck crops has been started on Butler and Champney Islands. The work so far has been experimental, but indications are that these islands can be used profitably for some of the crops mentioned. The original tree growth was similar to that on the river swamp, but the old rice fields support no tree growth, only a tall growth of fresh-water rushes, reeds and grasses. This is one of the strongest soils and perhaps, inherently, the most fertile soil in McIntosh County. The results of fertilizer tests being conducted by the Georgia Coastal Plain Experiment Station on Butler Island should have a marked influence on the kinds and amounts of fertilizer used in the county hereafter. A fertilizer plot demonstration was started in the spring of 1929 on corn planted on

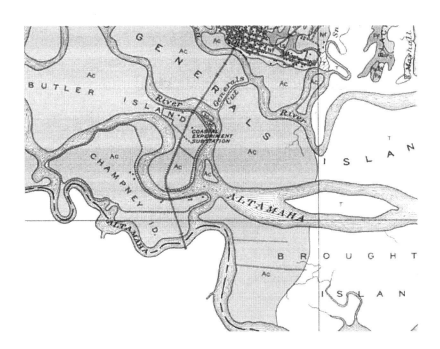

Detail from the 1929 soil survey map delineating Butler's Island area.

Eulonia fine sandy loam soil in the southwestern part of the county. The experiment station on Butler Island is also conducting fertilizer tests on Altamaha clay soils as is an experimental truck farm on Champney Island."[375]

Rotogravure sections of the *Atlanta Constitution* in 1925, 1929 and 1936 were published in flood years, and depicted the effects of river flooding at Butler's Island. In her "Low Country Diary" column in November 1973, historian Bessie Lewis noted, "These photographs [in the three rotogravure sections] must seem unbelievable to newcomers in our area — but are very real to those of us who were here during those great freshets. Those were the years of the constant heavy rains in the interior which swelled the rivers to overflowing, broke the levees on the Altamaha, and caused untold damage and suffering to those who lived in the immediate area." The photographs in

---

[375] G.L. Fuller, B.H. Hendrickson and J.W. Moon, *Soil Survey of McIntosh County, Georgia*, Series 1929, No. 6, Bureau of Chemistry and Soils, U.S. Department of Agriculture, 1932.

a spring, 1936 issue of the *Constitution* effectively support the preceding statements by Lewis, as they depict Butler's Island submerged, with water completely covering the lettuce fields and Huston's citrus orchards. The Guernsey cows normally kept in the dairy barn alongside the Atlantic Coastal Highway had been moved to higher ground for safety; Huston himself is pictured by photographer Kenneth Rogers sitting in a bateau near the screened porch of his house over what was left of his submerged garden. Despite the calamity of the flood, Huston is shown waving cheerfully at the photographer.[376]

Huston died at Butler's Island in March 1938 at the age of seventy-one. The island continued to be operated as a profitable truck farm after Huston's death. The peak years for the farm came immediately following World War II from 1945 to the early 1950s. In 1953, some 25,000 crates of Great Lakes variety iceberg lettuce were shipped from Butler's Island. Beans, cauliflower and cabbage were also marketed on a large scale. In August 1949, Butler's and Champney islands were sold from the Huston estate to Richard J. Reynolds, Jr. of Winston-Salem, North Carolina and Sapelo Island for $42,500. In the early 1950s, the buildings along U.S. 17 on Butler's Island included the dairy barn, then used as a vegetable packing building, three additional barns, equipment sheds and garage, and a seven-room house and servants building near the main house. The Butler's Island manager during the 1940s and early 1950s was Herbert H. Bryan. Bryan and his family resided in the Huston house and were actively involved in the business and social life of McIntosh County. Truck farming on Butler's Island ended in 1954 when Reynolds sold the island to the state of Georgia. Butler's became a waterfowl refuge and is now the headquarters of the Altamaha Waterfowl Management Area,

---

[376] *Atlanta Constitution Sunday magazine*, April 26, 1936.

administered by the Georgia Department of Natural Resources.[377]

Now Butler's Island is quiet, comfortably so, and almost as ecologically wild and untamed as the day so many generations earlier that Major Butler acquired his "tide island" for rice cultivation. The ghosts are still there, however, for those who believe, and the brooding old brick rice mill stack still stands in silent repose and survey to the ghosts. The ghosts are indeed present, testimony to the enslaved people who labored here, and the island's renewal and revival after the dogs of civil war and beyond, followed by assessment and reassessment in the waning years of the twentieth and early twenty-first centuries. The author's mentor and friend, the estimable late Malcolm Bell, provides a fitting and most appropriate epitaph to the story of Butler's Island:

"Following a series of foreclosure sales, the island enjoyed a brief period of agricultural rejuvenation after being acquired at a sheriff's sale in 1927 by Col. Tillinghast L. Huston, an owner of the world's champion New York Yankees in the days of George Herman "Babe" Ruth. Colonel Huston brought in a

---

[377] Records of the Game Management Section, Region 7, Wildlife Resources Division, GDNR. A fictionalized account of the final years of private ownership of Butler's Island is told in a voluminous 1,672-page, two-volume novel, *Hurry Sundown* (New York: Doubleday, 1964) by Bert and Katya Gilden. It is a story of greed, racial bigotry and idealism set in the immediate aftermath of World War II on Butler's Island, in Darien, and parts of McIntosh County. The fictional truck crop operation on Butler's Island gives insights on ditching, dynamite and mechanized farming set against a backdrop of the farm manager, a local native, attempting to acquire contiguous bottomland that vaguely appears to be on River Road west of Darien, possibly on the Potosi and Ceylon tracts. This tedious story has a tragic ending and often portrays Darien and some of its citizens in a negative light, creating some local resentment when the book was published in 1964. The Gildens camouflaged local place-names—Butler's Island is "Sunset Hill," the Altamaha River is the "Ocachee," Darien is "Arcady", Valona is "Fallona" and McIntosh County is "Colfax County"—but made little attempt to disguise certain real-life people such as A.S. Poppell and his son Tom H. Poppell, sheriffs during the period of the book, and superior court judge Mel Price, substituting different names for them, and others. The book and subsequent 1967 motion picture directed by Otto Preminger drew mostly poor reviews.

fine herd of dairy cattle and installed electric milking equipment. The old rice fields were revitalized for the planting of iceberg lettuce, celery, canna lilies, and gladioli, a venture that may well have succeeded had the imaginative Colonel Huston lived to direct his enterprise through the difficult years of the depression. In the late 1940s Richard Reynolds of the North Carolina tobacco family purchased Butler's Island and gave it a halfhearted try in the manner of Colonel Huston. The island today is a wildlife refuge owned and managed by the state of Georgia. From the Butler days, the rice, the cotton, sugar cane, oranges, and those who labored in the fields are gone. Huston's and Reynolds's dairy cattle, lettuce, celery and acres of flowers are gone too. Unchanged are the turgid branches of the Altamaha in which the island rests—still very much the 'mud sponge' Fanny Kemble Butler encountered in 1839. U.S. Highway 17 is built upon the roadbed of the long-abandoned Georgia Coast and Piedmont Railroad. It crosses the old plantation, as does Interstate Highway 95. The rice field banks and the tall towerlike chimney of one of the Butler rice mills are the most prominent relics of the past, but scattered over the island are other ruins, most of which are covered by deepening layers of silt or enveloped in a dense overgrowth of plantlife. For a time during the hot summer months of 1978 and 1979, a group of young people from the University of Florida worked on the island in an archaeological search for the several slave settlements and other plantation structures that existed when the Butlers were in prominence. The search was a project headed by a young woman, Theresa Singleton, who was to use her report of findings as a doctoral dissertation at the university. The young archaeologists found Butler's Island a true test, for Altamaha freshets and years of neglect of the restraining rice field banks in the early part of the century had caused silt-laden sites to be reduced to vague outlines and piles of rubble where chimneys had collapsed and crumbled. Singleton, who is a descendent of free blacks in Charleston, and her fellow students developed an appreciative understanding of her African forebears. It was a turnabout—a Butler's Island workforce of whites and one Oriental supervised by a black, and a black woman at that."[378]

* * *

The study of African American culture and folkways in coastal Georgia, *Drums and Shadows: Survival Studies among the Georgia Coastal Negroes*, published in 1940, tells the story of Jane Lewis of Darien,

---

[378] Bell, *Major Butler's Legacy*, 478-79.

more familiarly known as "Aunty Jane, and born a slave before the Civil War." Along with Liverpool Hazzard, discussed earlier, of the same generation, Jane Lewis represents a timeless bridge between McIntosh County's plantation past and more modern times. According to Jane, she was born about 1823, which if true would have made her about 115 years of age when she was interviewed by Mary Granger of the Georgia Writers' Project, Savannah Unit, in 1938. Most of the Darien interviews were conducted at homes in the Mentionville section in the environs of Cathead Creek and Old River Road, traditionally Darien's black community since antebellum times. *Drums and Shadows* begins its Darien segment by noting that

"The Negroes of the Darien section are proud of their Darien ancestry. When the younger people migrate to larger communities, it is a common thing to hear them say proudly, 'My people come from Darien.' One of the most typical settlements is opposite the Todd Grant Negro school. A few houses are clustered about the knoll facing the school building, and more dilapidated board shacks are scattered over the little hill. At the top is Aunty Jane Lewis' cabin, surrounded by small sheds and fences patches of ground where chickens and a goat are kept from wandering too far...Aunty Jane claims she is one hundred and fifteen years old, and to see the small bent woman with the deeply-lined black skin and filmy eyes is to believe her claim. Her voice is high-pitched, with the thin timbre of extreme age, but she still moves with sudden agile gestures. We interrupted the old woman's reminiscences about plantation days to question her about funeral customs. 'We didn alluz hab too much time fuh big fewnul in dem days cuz deah wuz wuk tuh to be done an ef yuh ain do yuh wuk, yuh git whipped. Lots uh time dey jis dig a hole in duh groun an put duh body in it, but wenebuh we kin, we hab a settin-up...dey sho did hab regluh feastes in dem days [for the mourners]. But tuhday, at mos settin-ups, yuh don git nuttin but coffee an bread. Den dey would cook a regluh meal and dey wud kill a chicken in front uh duh doe, wring he neck an cook um fuh duh feas. Den wen we all finish, we take wut victuals lef an put it in a dish by duh chimley an das fuh duh sperrit tuh hab a las good meal. We cubbuh up duh dish an deah's many a time Ise heah duh sperrit lif um. We ain preach duh suhmon wen we bury um but we waits a wile so's all duh relations kin come."

In the 1930s, Henry and Clara Ford of Dearborn, Michigan spent their winters at their property at Ways Station (later Richmond Hill) about forty miles north of Darien. The Fords met Jane Lewis on one of their visits to McIntosh County and saw that she was in such need they took it upon themselves in 1939 to build her a new house adjacent to the wooden shack on River Road in which she had been living. They also provided food and medical care for Jane, including weekly visits by a nurse, until she died. Another member of the Darien Geechee community who was interviewed by the Savannah Unit was Wallace Quarterman. When asked his age, Quarterman responded, "Ise bawn July 14, 1844. Now figguh dat out fuh yufsef, missus. Ise bawn at Sout Hampton, Libuty County, an I belong tuh Roswell King, but he done die long bout sometime in duh fifties an Ise sole fuh debt tuh Colonel Fred Waring on Skidaway Ilun…" Also interviewed were William Rogers, then aged seventy-two, Priscilla McCollough, "bawn tree yeahs fo freedom in Sumtuh, Sout Calina," and Lawrence Baker, born circa 1860.

Ten miles west of Darien, on the edge of Buffalo Swamp at the end of a sandy road two miles south of Cox, is Possum Point. Reposing there was a small black settlement "set back from the roadway [with] occasional small dwelling places, with boards turned dun-colored from age and exposure. Neatly tended vegetable and flower gardens stretch out to the front and sides of the houses. The owners can be found industriously working in the gardens, sitting on the porches, or gathered in little groups along the road." Possum

Point is at the headwaters of Lewis Creek; the *Drums and Shadows* account described the "leisurely fishing, with long bamboo poles," by the people of the community. Among those interviewed at Possum Point were seventy-three-year old Rachel Anderson, and her husband Alec Anderson, born "three years before freedom." Like Jane Lewis, the Andersons described funeral customs:

"We asked if they had ever heard that a frizzled chicken could dig up conjure for a victim and they both nodded in affirmation. 'Chickin can sho dig up conjuh. Alluz hab heah uh dat,' they echoed. 'Use tuh alluz beat duh drum at fewnals. Right attuh duh pusson die, dey beat um tuh tell udduhs bout duh fewnal. Dey beat a long beat. Den dey stop. Den dey beat annuduh long beat. Ebrybody know dat dis mean somebody die....Wen dey fix the cawpse, dey put pennies in duh eyes and dey put salt on duh stomach tuh keep it frum purgin. Ebrybody put duh hands on um tuh say good-bye. On duh way tuh duh grabe dey beat duh drum as dey is machin long. Wen duh body is put in duh grabe, ebrybody shout roun duh grabe in a suckle, singin an prayin. Each one trow a handful uh dut in duh grabe..."

Hopeton: Model Plantation of the Antebellum South

Hopeton, a plantation managed and half-owned by James H. Couper, was the premier rice and sugar tract in the Altamaha delta, situated on the south bank of the Altamaha River in Glynn County, and the furthest upriver of the delta plantations. In 1805, John Couper of Cannon's Point, St. Simons Island, and his partner, James Hamilton of Philadelphia, began purchasing Altamaha properties from David Deas and Arthur Middleton. Included in the acquisitions by Couper and Hamilton was the 4,500-acre Altamaha tract known as Hopeton, secured from the estate of their Charleston backer, William Hopeton, who had originally acquired the tract as a Crown grant in 1763.

Carr's Island, on the McIntosh County side of the river across from Hopeton, was an extension of Hopeton plantation, later being cultivated in rice and cotton by James H. Couper. Carr's was separated from Butler's and Wright's islands on the north by the south branch of the Altamaha, and bounded on the south by Hammersmith Creek, across which lay Hopeton and later the adjoining Altama tract. Carr's was originally a 1761 Crown grant to Captain Mark Carr, one of Oglethorpe's officers at Frederica during the war with Spain. A January 1, 1827 deed conveyed from John Couper to James Hamilton and James H. Couper

"2,000 acres in Glynn County on the Altamaha River, known as Hopeton Plantation formerly the property of Nathaniel Russell of Charleston, S.C. and by him deeded March 7, 1816 to the grantor John Couper; 500 acres on the same river in Glynn Co., being Tract No. 2 of tract originally granted David Deas; and 250 acres known as Carr's Island on said river, in McIntosh County, granted Mark Carr and confiscated as property of the late Basil Couper, dec'd and deeded to grantor Feb. 6, 1819."[379]

---

[379] Deed Book H (1827), 74, Glynn County records.

Wright's Island, another McIntosh County rice tract, was to the immediate east of Carr's Island and separated from the latter by a small creek. Wright's comprised 847 acres, and was abutted on its north side by Cambers Island, separated from it by a shallow tidal stream known as Minnow Creek. Hopeton was immediately to the south of Wright's. Cambers, Wright's, and Carr's islands, like the rest of the delta, were dense Altamaha swampland before portions were improved for the cultivation of rice in the early 1800s. Wright's, a 1761 Crown grant to colonial governor James Wright, was owned by Thomas Spalding during part of the antebellum period.[380] Spalding held Wright's and adjoining Cambers, both being cultivated in rice by his son, Charles Harris Spalding.

Woodville, also known as the Hammersmith tract, was on the Glynn County side of the river, being part of the original 1763 grant to David Deas of South Carolina. Woodville became one of Major Pierce Butler's properties and was situated between Hopeton and Elizafield. There was a river landing at Woodville called Butler's Landing, later Hammersmith Landing, as it was on Hammersmith Creek. Across the creek from the landing was Carr's Island. Boats from Darien and the other rice islands made connections with the Glynn County mainland at Butler's Landing during the antebellum period. In her *Journal*, Fanny Kemble described Woodville:

"I have been walking to another cluster of Negro huts, known as Number Two on Butler's Island, and here we took a boat and rowed across the broad brimming Altamaha to a place called Woodville, on a part of the estate named Hammersmith. This settlement is on the mainland, and consists apparently of a house (to which the overseer retires when the poisonous malaria of the rice plantation compels him to withdraw from it), and a few deplorably miserable hovels, which appeared to be chiefly occupied by the most decrepit and infirm samples of humanity it was ever my melancholy lot to behold. The air of this pine barren is salubrious compared with that of the

---

[380] Deed Book 10 (1939), 515, RMCG.

rice islands, and here some of the oldest slaves who will not die yet, and cannot work anymore, are sent, as it were, out of the way."[381]

In 1840, the Butler estate sold Woodville and the Hammersmith tract to the James Hamilton estate and it became part of Hopeton. James H. Couper bought the eastern half of Hopeton, including the Hammersmith tract, from the Hamilton estate, and this became Couper's Altama plantation. The following is extracted from an article by the author appearing in the *Darien News* in 1992 summarizing the Altamaha rice district:

"Evidence of antebellum plantation activity is abundant throughout the Altamaha delta. On Broughton Island, at the point where the largest of two plantation canals bisect the river, are the brick ruins of the rice mill at the site of the slave settlement. Rotting timbers in the mud at low tide are the remains of the loading wharves at Broughton plantation. The Butler's Island rice mill chimney, built by slave labor, is the most visible symbol of the tidewater rice industry in antebellum McIntosh County. A casual walk through the remote slave settlements (Nos. 2, 3 and 4) on Butler's usually yields bits of old glass and ceramic associated with the plantation era. On the back side of Potosi Island, across Cathead Creek from Darien, the tabby ruins of Jacob Wood's plantation house, built ca. 1806, remain. Potosi's sugar mill ruins still stand, facing Darien River just east of the present I-95 highway bridge. Rotting dock pilings can still be seen at the east end of Cambers Island where the Spaldings, and later, Phineas Miller Nightingale, cultivated rice and housed slaves. The rice canals, dikes and embankments can still be seen throughout the delta. At Elizafield, the tabby remains of Robert Grant's octagonal sugar mill and rectangular boiling house, built ca. 1816 and modeled on the Spalding plan, are situated where Six Mile Creek once gave convenient access to the river. At the sugar mill site Six Mile Creek no longer exists, its flow having been diverted by the construction of the Brunswick-Altamaha Canal through Elizafield and Evelyn plantations in the late 1830s."[382]

---

[381] Kemble, *Journal*, op. cit., 126.
[382] See Marmaduke Floyd, "Certain Tabby Ruins on the Georgia Coast," in E. Merton Coulter, ed., *Georgia's Disputed Ruins* (Chapel Hill: University of North Carolina Press, 1937), 133-41. In the same volume, see James A. Ford, "An Archaeological Report on the Elizafield Ruins," 193-225, for an analysis of Grant's tabby sugar mill ruins, mistakenly thought to be remains of a Spanish mission complex.

James Hamilton Couper (1794-1866) was the son of John Couper (1759-1850) and Rebecca Maxwell Couper (1775-1845), and grew up at his parents' St. Simons cotton plantation, Cannon's Point. In 1818, four years after he graduated with honors from Yale College, James H. Couper was appointed by his father and Hamilton to manage Hopeton plantation. Couper came to own one-half interest in Hopeton with the James Hamilton estate until 1841 when he sold his share to pay off debts. On Christmas Day 1827, in a lavish wedding at Cannon's Point, Couper married Caroline Georgia Wylly (1811-1897), daughter of Alexander Campbell Wylly and Margaret Armstrong Wylly of the neighboring St. Simons plantation, The Village. For over twenty-five years, James and Caroline Couper lived in a three-story, tabby-wood frame plantation house at Hopeton built by Couper from a converted sugar house.

Couper was an erudite man of books, letters and great scientific intellect. He was also one of the most proficient and insightful planters in the southeastern United States as he brought a unique approach to the skills of administering a plantation coupled with thoughtful and effective management of the enslaved people of Hopeton. Like his friend Thomas Spalding, James H. Couper "brought a scientific approach to his planting and was careful and considerate in the employment of his slaves as his father had been before him."[383] In 1833, John D. Legare of the *Southern Agriculturist*, the most influential farm journal of the period, observed of his visit to the plantation:

"We hesitate not to say Hopeton is decidedly the best regulated plantation we ever visited, and we doubt whether it can be equaled (certainly not surpassed) in the Southern States. Whilst here, we visited the nursery and

---

[383] Bell, *Major Butler's Legacy*, op. cit., 515.

hospital, the negro quarters, the cotton-house, and the other offices, together with a number of the rice fields. All the crops had been harvested except the cane, and we had the pleasure of seeing all the operations connected with this valuable crop to the final preparation for market."[384]

Hopeton exemplified a degree of versatility rare among Southern plantations. Whereas most large and small plantations concentrated on producing one, or perhaps two, staple crops, Couper simultaneously cultivated three major staples with excellent results—cotton, rice and sugar cane. An extensive amount of documentation from Hopeton survives; Couper's detailed records show Hopeton to be a well-managed and highly-efficient operation from the standpoints of crop production, slave management and profitability.

In 1818 Hopeton had 544 acres under cultivation; by 1841 the total had increased to 957 acres; and by 1857, 1,025 acres. The original slave force in 1806 was 637, decreasing to about 500 by the mid-1840s. Sea island and short staple cotton were the primary staple crops planted at Hopeton until 1825 when a decline in prices resulted in a depression in the cotton market. Couper's plantation records, on deposit in the Southern Historical Collection at Chapel Hill, North Carolina, show that Hopeton produced 147,543 pounds of seed cotton in 1818, or 147 ½ bales; the peak year was 1819 with 261,383 pounds from 566 acres planted. In the late 1820s, Couper cultivated cotton, rice and sugar cane in near-equal proportions.

As with all tidewater planters, weather played a role in Couper's agrarian calculations. In 1819, Couper reported that "in the Spring, the Cotton is very generally destroyed by Frost. On the 14th Octr. a sharp white frost

---

[384] John D. Legare, "Account of an Agricultural Excursion Made into the South of Georgia," *Southern Agriculturist* VI (1833).

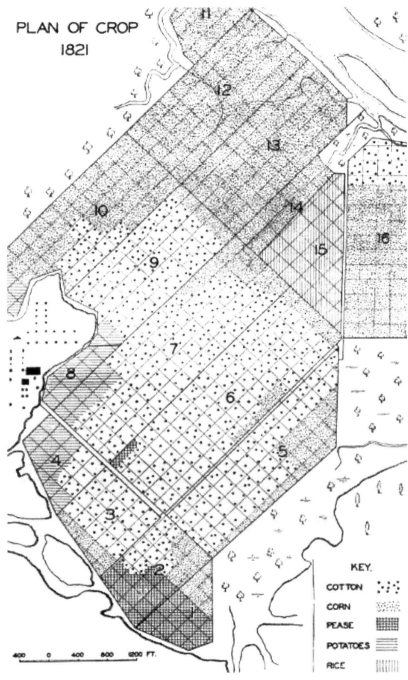

Couper's crop plan for the 1821 growing season at Hopeton.

destroyed about 70 acres of cotton at Hopeton." In 1826, he noted: "This is the only Cotton crop since 1818 which has not been cut off by spring freshets, early fall frosts, or gales of wind." A year later, Couper reported, "A very high fresh wind which occurred about the end of May nearly destroyed the Cotton in Carrs Is."[385]

Sugar was the plantation's most profitable money staple from 1825-33 during which time Couper constructed one of the most elaborate sugar mills in the South. In 1828, with Couper convinced that sugar would continue to be profitable, he planted 48½ acres in cane with a yield of 5,411 pounds of sugar and 650 gallons of molasses. The next year, he had just over 200 acres planted in cane with gradual increases until 1833.

Many sugar mills in coastal Georgia were modeled on Spalding's example. Later, Couper improved the milling process and his Hopeton sugar works were considered the most advanced on the southern coast in the early 1830s. These mills utilized animal and water (tide-driven) power to operate their heavy grinding rollers.[386]

By 1834 Couper had shifted his focus to rice as U.S. tariff policies had begun to undercut the production of domestic sugar. Couper planted his first rice crop at Hopeton-on-the-Altamaha in 1821 with a consequent increase in his yields-per acre into the 1840s. In 1827, Couper's crop produced a yield of 17,571 bushels of rice on 351 ½ acres planted—an average of about 49 bushels per acre. Couper's

---

[385] James Hamilton Couper Plantation Records, 1818-1854, SHC. This indicates Couper was initially utilizing Carr's Island for cotton cultivation, then later for rice.
[386] James H. Couper, "Account of, and Directions for Erecting a Sugar Establishment," *Southern Agriculturist* IV (May 1831); J.D. Legare, "Account of an Agricultural Excursion."

average yield per acre was consistently over 50 bushels per acre during the 1840s; his most productive year, for which records are available, was in 1839 when his yield was 60.4 bushels to the acre. By then Couper was planting rice on 684 acres, almost double the acreage he had under cultivation in the late 1820s.[387]

Couper's initial rice crop at Hopeton in 1821 was thirty-one acres under bank, with an increase to 338 acres by 1826. In 1829 Couper had a nearly equal distribution in planted acreage for the three staples—246 acres in cotton, 202 in sugar cane and 234 in rice. After 1834 rice was the primary staple crop produced at Hopeton.

For the fourteen-year period 1827-1840 the average rice yield per acre at Hopeton was 53.3 bushels. The maximum yield occurred in 1839 with 60.4 bushels per acre. Some individual fields occasionally produced as many as 85 bushels per acre, according to Couper's records. By 1841, some 714 acres were being planted in rice. In a letter of March 6, 1857 Couper wrote to his co-manager Francis P. Corbin that he intended to plant 810 acres in rice that year at Hopeton, a total exceeded only by Butler's Island in the Altamaha district. The 810 acres of rice was from an aggregate of 1,025 acres under cultivation; the only other staple still produced by then at Hopeton was sugar cane, a mere 25 acres. The remaining acreage was devoted to provision crops.[388]

One of the most interesting features about Hopeton, attributable

---

[387] James Hamilton Couper Plantation Papers, 1818-1854, SHC.
[388] Much of the foregoing is based on the analysis of crop production at Hopeton by James M. Clifton, "Hopeton: Model Plantation of the Antebellum South," *Georgia Historical Quarterly* 66 (Winter 1982): 429-49. Clifton utilized the extensive James H. Couper plantation records in the Southern Historical Collection at Chapel Hill, North Carolina, and the F.P. Corbin Papers at Duke University.

to Couper's engineering expertise, was the main irrigation canal of three miles in length, it being about fifteen feet in width and four-and-a-half feet in depth, that coursed from the Altamaha River past the plantation complex at which were located the rice and sugar mills, the cotton gin, and the Hopeton main house, thence to the fields of cultivation, before finally looping back to the river. Large floodgates of seventy-five feet in length with four pairs of gates at the canal entrance controlled the flow of fresh water from the river; a floodgate of thirty-five feet with two tidegates was at the other end of the canal. Couper also installed a portable railroad with moveable wooden rails, a unique device among Southern plantations, to facilitate the transfer of cane and rice from the fields to the main canal, then on to the mill complex.[389]

James H. Couper and Thomas Spalding of Sapelo Island were regarded as the most scientific and innovative planters in tidewater Georgia. They were similar in their agrarian sophistication. For example, both were in accord in their views on slave management. In 1846, Sir Charles Lyell described Couper as a benevolent slave owner and "discerned at Hopeton an hereditary regard and attachment between master and slave."[390] Frederika Bremer described Couper in 1849 as "a disciplinarian, with great practical tact, and also some benevolence in the treatment of Negroes."[391] And Amelia Murray, lady-in-waiting to Queen Victoria, visited Hopeton in 1855 and was so impressed by Couper's skill in slave management, she "became so committed to a defense of slavery that she horrified British public

---

[389] Legare, "Account of an Agricultural Excursion," 362-65.
[390] Lyell, *Second Visit to the United States,* op. cit. 261-63. For Spalding's views on slavery, see chapter 5.
[391] Frederika Bremer, *The Homes of the New World* (New York, 1853), 2:489.

opinion and was dismissed from office."[392]

One of the reasons Hopeton plantation was one of the most efficient in the South was Couper's judicious selection of qualified resident overseers. Three of Hopeton's overseers during the period 1827-1854, Thomas Oden, Baillie Forester and Daniel McDonald, were considered among the most competent on the Georgia coast. In 1849, Daniel McDonald (1811-1893) left the employ of Couper when he purchased from William J. McIntosh Fair Hope plantation on the Sapelo River in McIntosh County, where he transitioned from efficient overseer to equally efficient and prosperous plantation owner.

John Couper sustained serious financial losses at Cannon's Point resulting from the 1824 hurricane and the loss of his cotton crop to caterpillar infestation a year later. To satisfy the accumulation of debt resulting from these losses, Couper was compelled in 1827 to sell his half-interest in Hopeton to his former partner, James Hamilton. In turn, Hamilton sold one-half interest in Hopeton and 381 slaves to James H. Couper for $137,000 to be paid over a period of fifteen years at 6 per cent interest. J.H. Couper was to receive half the plantation profits and $2,000 per year as manager. In 1841, Couper mortgaged his half interest in Hopeton back to the James Hamilton estate to free himself of debt. From 1841 to 1854 Couper continued to manage Hopeton for a salary of $5,000 a year ($6,000 a year the last two years) but no longer benefiting from half the profits of the plantation. In 1852, Francis Porteus Corbin (1801-1876) of Philadelphia and Paris, France, husband of Agnes Rebecca Hamilton Corbin (1801-1894), daughter of James Hamilton and heiress to Hopeton plantation, assumed the administrator's role for

---

[392] Clifton, "Hopeton: Model Plantation," 441.

Hopeton; by then, most of the Hamilton properties had been willed to the Corbins' son, Richard W. Corbin (1839-1922), and his sisters, Isabella (1835-1894) and Elizabeth (1837-1906). After James Hamilton died in 1829, Couper negotiated with Hamilton's Corbin heirs for the purchase of the southeastern portion of Hopeton, the Hammersmith tract, including Woodville. Although he shared management of Hopeton with Francis Corbin from 1852 until the Civil War began nine years later, Couper began to look toward retirement, thus he and his wife Caroline Wylly Couper built a new residence near Hammersmith Landing, naming it Altama. Completed in 1857, it was a beautiful property accentuated by live oaks, palms and a view of the ricelands toward Darien. Altama was two stories and built of stucco-covered tabby, with a portico over the front entrance.

With Hopeton's administrative oversight assumed by Francis Corbin from 1852, and with his own role now that of an on-site manager, Couper devoted more attention to planting rice at Altama. Weakened by malaria and debt, Couper had considered selling Altama in 1851 soon after the death of his father, John Couper. He wrote, "Disgusted with the constantly recurring sickness if a rice plantation and warned by my age to withdraw in time and labors and exhaustion, I have determined to sell Altama Plantation, and have advertised it in the Charleston and Savannah papers. If I sell I shall bring the Altama gang to St. Simons and divide them between Hamilton and Cannon's Point. I shall avoid the dangerous and laborious expense of my present summer trips up the river. I may make a smaller amount of saleable crops but I shall gain in the health of the Negroes, and in the reduced plantation expenses." He failed to sell Altama and cultivated there and at the two St. Simons plantations. The 1860 census listed Couper with an estate valued at $176,000, and personal property amounting to $131,000, including 210 slaves.[393]

Couper was against both secession and the South's being in the Civil War. All five of his sons served the Confederate cause. Two of them died of fever in Virginia, Hamilton in 1861, and John the following year. Broken spiritually and financially, and unable to accept the loss of two of his sons in a conflict he was against from the beginning, Couper suffered a stroke in 1863 and died in 1866, living "to see the entire work of his lifetime in ruins." He and many members of the Couper-Wylly families are buried in Christ Church Cemetery, St. Simons Island. James M. Clifton notes in an insightful essay about Couper: "Hopeton was truly a model plantation of the antebellum South. Probably no other plantation saw a comparable degree of production in three major staples. Nor was any other plantation perhaps as renowned for its benevolent and humane slave treatment practices. Hopeton's proprietor, James Hamilton Couper, was one of the most skilled and scientific farmers of his day. His gracious and courtly manner of living at Hopeton became the envy of planters near and afar..."

In 1870, the Couper heirs mortgaged Altama to the Corbins. A

---

[393] James Hamilton Couper Plantation Records (1818-1854), SHC; Hopeton Plantation Account Book, No. 185, SHC; John Couper Collection (1775-1963), Hargrett Research and Manuscript Library, University of Georgia, Athens; Couper-Fraser Family Papers, Collection 265, GHS; Memories of Charles Spalding Wylly, Mackay-Stiles Papers, SHC; "List of Slaves Belonging to James Hamilton and John Couper," January 1806, and correspondence from James H. Couper to Francis P. Corbin, both in Francis Porteus Corbin Papers, Duke University, Durham, North Carolina; John Solomon Otto, *Cannon's Point Plantation, 1794-1860* (London: Academic Press, 1984), 27, 29.

group of Shakers from Ohio held the Hopeton-Altama tract from 1898 to 1902 with hopes of recruiting new followers in the area and attempting to revive the old plantation for cattle raising and rice cultivation. Although the Shakers produced a rice crop valued at $10,000 in 1899, their overall efforts were unsuccessful and they returned to Ohio. From 1902 to 1914 the tract was owned by two Ohio investors. In 1914, Hopeton-Altama was acquired by William Du Pont of Wilmington, Delaware as a winter home and hunting preserve. He renamed the entire tract Altama. Du Pont trained race horses and built a new house at Altama, based on the original 1857 Couper house. Cator Woolford of Atlanta, a friend and mentor of Alfred W. Jones, Sr. of Sea Island, bought Altama in 1933. Woolford expanded the main house and added a swimming pool before his death in 1944. A year later, in 1945, Jones purchased the property and developed it as a family retreat, hunting preserve for guests and as a tree farm. Jones also donated an adjoining tract of land to the Boys Estate, a training facility and refuge for homeless boys. The 6,000 acres of upland and marsh on the Altamaha that is Altama expanded as a protected resource and a scientifically-grown-and-harvested tree farm through the 1980s behind the energetic conservation initiatives of Jones and, after his death in 1982, the Sea Island Company. The Company sold Altama in 2010 to a private equity firm which planned to develop the tract with private homes and timbering operations. Economic conditions precluded the venture and, in 2015, with financial assistance from The Nature Conservancy, the 3,986-acre tract and main house were acquired by the Georgia Department of Natural Resources for conservation, public education and game management purposes.

Canal Building in Coastal Georgia

Following the examples set in the north in the 1820s and 1830s, coastal Georgia planters and businessmen realized that similar construction projects on the southern tidewater could potentially provide significant economic improvements to their region. Thus evolved two simultaneous canal building initiatives with the ultimate objective of linking the three major fresh-water rivers of the Georgia coast, the Savannah, Ogeechee and Altamaha.

Much of the inland cotton in the 1820s was being rafted down the Oconee, Ocmulgee and Altamaha rivers to Darien, the only port near the mouth of the Altamaha. However, Darien had a poor harbor, often being barely navigable at low tide from the sea entrance to Doboy Sound. Savannah investors, seeking to siphon off some of Darien's lucrative cotton trade, saw the possibility of linking Savannah with the Ogeechee and Altamaha rivers with a canal linking the two rivers with the Savannah River.

In December 1824, the Georgia legislature granted a charter to Ebenezer Jenkes to build a canal between the Savannah and Ogeechee. A year later, Jenkes received an additional permit to extend the canal to the Altamaha River.[394] Jenkes owned a toll road that ran through a portion of Effingham County en route to Savannah, the road entering Bryan County where it turned at present-day Blitchton, then crossed Black Creek on its way southward to Eden, the Bryan County seat. The bridge over the

---

[394] *Acts of the General Assembly of the State of Georgia, Incorporating the Savannah, Ogeechee and Altamaha Canal Company* (Washington, D.C., 1838).

Ogeechee River linking the upper corner of Bryan with Effingham was a toll bridge also operated by Jenkes in the 1820s. It was shown on maps as "Jenkes Bridge" as early as 1818.[395]

Jenkes sold stock in his canal to prominent Savannahians while the local press enthusiastically endorsed the project—"Let is no longer slumber in apathy, let us leave off talking and go to digging," said one newspaper in early 1826.[396] Canal supporters predicted the waterway from the Ogeechee River to Savannah would increase the city's cotton trade to 100,000 bales annually, provide an additional conduit for timber exports from the pine forests of southeast Georgia and ultimately make Savannah the leading port in the South.[397]

By 1827, however, Jenkes had failed to raise the necessary capital to keep the canal effort moving forward, thus a group of Savannah citizens formed the Savannah, Ogeechee and Altamaha Canal Company to raise funds, sell stock and engage a design engineer. While Jenkes remained involved in the project as a contractor, the new charter required him to assign all his rights to the new company.

Meanwhile, in 1826, the Georgia legislature incorporated the Brunswick Canal Company, with eight Glynn County promotors, James Gould, Thomas B. King, Daniel Blue, Stephen C. King, John Burnett, Jr., John Hardee, William B. Davis and Henry DuBignon, with the intent to build a canal to link the Altamaha River to the Turtle River, thus providing access to the Brunswick harbor.[398]

---

[395] Daniel Strurges, "A Map of the State of Georgia," Savannah, Ga., 1818; also William G. Bonner, comp., "Map of the State of Georgia," Milledgeville, Ga., 1847.
[396] *The Georgian* (Savannah), March 13, 1826.
[397] Mark R. Finlay, "The Savannah and Ogeechee Canal," *Canal History and Technology Proceedings* 14 (March 1995), 10.
[398] *Acts of the General Assembly of the State of Georgia* (1826), 55.

However, the promotors accomplished little in the four-year limit of the charter; in 1830, the state issued a new charter to William B. Davis and Urbanus Dart, both of Brunswick. About the same time the state began issuing permits for state-owned slaves to be used in public improvement projects, and between 1831 and 1834, Davis and Dart utilized state-owned slaves to improve the navigation at the Altamaha end, at Six Mile Creek, of the proposed canal.

As a result of the canal activity on the Savannah, Ogeechee and Altamaha rivers, the commercial rivalry intensified between Savannah, Darien and Brunswick. All three aspired to be the state's leading seaport, although clearly Savannah was in the preeminent position with the construction of the Central of Georgia Railroad from the state's interior to the city in the mid-1830s. Development of a railroad also began to enter the construction proposals among the Brunswick backers, with some preferring a rail link to the Altamaha rather than a canal. Brunswick was endowed with one of the finest natural deep-water harbors on the southern coast—a Navy Department survey later determined it to be best harbor south of Norfolk, Virginia—but the developing town had the drawback of not having a fresh-water river coming from the interior, an asset that had made Darien and Savannah prominent cotton ports.[399]

In 1833, three Glynn County commissioners, John G. Polhill, Hugh Lawson and Moses Fort, extolled the virtues of Brunswick's natural harbor and its healthful setting and favored construction of

---

[399] For the cotton economy of antebellum Darien, see Buddy Sullivan, *Early Days on the Georgia Tidewater*, all editions, 1990-2020; and Sullivan, *Darien, Georgia: A History of the Town & Its Environs* (privately published, 2020).

an "avenue to the Altamaha."[400] The contiguous Glynn County rice tracts of Elizafield and Evelyn plantations, owned and managed by Hugh Fraser Grant and his brother Charles, fronted on the Altamaha in the area where the proposed canal or railroad would link with the river. In supporting the railroad concept from Brunswick to the Altamaha, they recommended uniting it with either

"Railroad Creek, or with the river itself, or with Six Mile Creek; the latter think the most eligible as this creek is wide and deep enough for up-country boats and enters the river in a deep bight, which makes it very convenient for boats to enter. In either route the distance [from the south bank of the Altamaha to the start of a canal or railroad] will be rather over half a mile, and may be either excavated to the fine bluff [at Elizafield plantation] by a canal and basin, or the road be extended through the swamp, which are rice fields in cultivation. Before it enters the ocean, the Altamaha divides itself into four branches; on the southern branch, which from examination and information we found to be the deepest and best for navigating boats, the rail-road will end."[401]

A year after this report was made, Thomas Butler King of Retreat plantation, St. Simons Island, one of the 1826 promoters, assumed charge of the project and returned its direction to that of a canal rather than a railroad. In 1834, a new charter was issued by the state, with King, his brother Stephen C. King, and William W. Hazzard replacing Davis and Dart as incorporators. Soon thereafter, King, at his own personal expense, arranged for a Boston civil engineer, Loammi Baldwin, to survey and plan a canal route, as well as provide canal specifications and costs. Baldwin proposed a canal that would run twelve miles in a north-south direction from Six Mile Creek

---

[400] *Acts* (1832), 253; "Report on the Brunswick Canal and Railroad," House Document 122, 24th Congress, 2nd Session, 1836, 13-21.
[401] Ibid., 16.

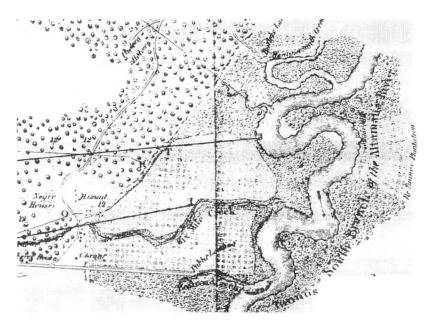

The portion of the Baldwin survey map that delineates the canal's convergence on Six Mile Creek, which then enters the south branch of Altamaha River (right). At left are "Negro Houses" and the house of "H. Grant," these being on Hugh F. Grant's Elizafield rice plantation.

at the South Altamaha River to Academy Creek, which enters the Brunswick harbor. It was to be fifty-four feet wide at the surface and carry a six-foot depth with locks and spillways predicated upon the tides at either end.[402]

A topographic map (above) accompanying Baldwin's 1836 survey for the canal provides useful insights not only into the Brunswick-Altamaha Canal, but also particulars of the rice tracts at the upper end of the canal. The canal's northern terminus was its opening into

---

[402] "Report on the Brunswick Canal and Railroad, Glynn County, Georgia, with an Appendix Containing the Charter and Commissioners, Report by Loammi Baldwin, Esq., Civil Engineer," Boston, 1837; "Brunswick-Altamaha Canal Study," Brunswick-Glynn County Joint Planning Commission, August 1981, 13-26; Edward M. Steel, "Flush Times in Brunswick, Georgia in the 1830s," *Georgia Historical Quarterly* 39 (September 1955): 231-38.

Six Mile Creek, a tidal tributary of the south branch of the Altamaha that flows through the rice fields and meets the river just east of the present I-95 highway bridge. Six Mile Creek was the natural boundary between the two Grant family plantations, Elizafield on the west side of the creek, and Evelyn on the east. Directly across the river from the mouth of Six Mile Creek were the rice fields of Tunno's (Champneys) Island. Some of the features shown on the survey map are the houses of Hugh F. Grant at Elizafield and Charles Grant at neighboring Evelyn. "Negro houses" are delineated near H.F. Grant's dwelling. Across the river is shown "Dr. Tunno's plantation" with a sugar mill on Tunno's waterfront, reflective of the great interest at the time of the local planters in supplementing their rice crops with sugar production. The map also identifies Hugh Grant's sugar mill on the high ground at Six Mile Creek, the tabby remains of which are still in evidence near the marsh. The grid of rice fields is meticulously drawn for Elizafield, Evelyn and Tunno's Island. Further west, near Hopeton plantation, are shown Hammersmith Creek and "Butler's Landing."

Up the coast, meanwhile, work was underway on the Savannah-Ogeechee Canal. In 1826, Henry McAlpin conveyed to the canal company a right-of-way for the canal through part of his Hermitage plantation, just west of present downtown Savannah.[403] Digging work progressed from Savannah, but at the end of 1829 there were complaints of the "want of competent engineers," and concerns over the "ignorance and miscalculations and failures of the contractor and

---

[403] Savannah Writers Project, Mary Granger, ed., *Savannah River Plantations* (Savannah: Georgia Historical Society, 1947), 438.

above all, the difficulty in procuring proper laborers."[404] Much of the work was done by slaves leased from the Savannah River plantations, with the highest number of laborers acquired in March 1828 when 577 workers were employed at digging the canal and building its brick locks. Some of the workers were Irish laborers.[405]

For over four years the workers "cut timber, cleared paths, built embankments and constructed brick locks in the heat, humidity, and disease environment of the Georgia low country."[406] By the end of 1830, work was completed on the Savannah-Ogeechee Canal at a total cost of $175,000. The canal linked the Savannah and Ogeechee rivers, covering a distance of 16.5 miles with a depth of five feet. The canal had six locks which were about eighteen feet wide and 102 feet in length. Four were lift locks with two being tidal locks. The first cargo to be transported through the canal was a barge load of timber and bricks destined for the Vale Royal plantation of Joseph Stiles on lock two near the junction with the Savannah River.[407] The canal in this section traversed the lower end of Musgrove Creek between Vale Royal and the western side of Savannah. One account notes that "even in this streamlined age it is not difficult to picture mules trudging lazily along the winding treadway of the canal drawing in their wake the awkward flat-boats piled with the raw products of the highland country."[408]

After crossing just over sixteen miles of Chatham County from Savannah, the canal connected with the Ogeechee River at Dillon's

---

[404] Savannah *Georgian*, December 4, 1829.
[405] Finlay, "The Savannah and Ogeechee Canal," 12, 14.
[406] Ibid., 14.
[407] Savannah *Georgian*, December 23, 1830.
[408] Savannah Writers Project, *Savannah River Plantations*, 466.

Bridge, a point slightly above the confluence of the Canoochee River with the Ogeechee, and just west of the present Interstate Highway 95 bridge over the Ogeechee. At the Fort Argyle landing on the Bryan County side of the river just upstream from the canal's entrance, agricultural commodities from local farms and timber from the interior departed for Savannah via the canal.

Despite a promising start, the canal encountered problems in the first years after its completion, ranging from mounting debts for maintenance due to broken embankments, and the loss of important customers. Additionally, the company's head of its board of directors, Alexander Telfair, resigned. Because of these issues, the company abandoned its plans to extend the canal southward from the Ogeechee to the Altamaha. In 1833, the Central of Georgia Railroad and Banking Company of Savannah was formed to reach inland agricultural markets. Construction on the railroad began on Savannah's west side in late 1836 about the same times as the Savannah, Ogeechee and Altamaha Canal Company declared bankruptcy.[409] The state of Georgia sold its interest in the canal to William W. Gordon of Savannah, president of the Central Railroad, for $10,000, and the Savannah *Georgian*, once a solid backer of the project, admitted the canal had made no profit, "nor from present appearances is it likely that any benefit will be derived from it."[410]

To the south, in Glynn County, work finally began on the Brunswick-Altamaha Canal following the approval of the Baldwin

---

[409] Savannah *Georgian*, November 3, 1836, November 10, 1836; Thomas Gamble, *A History of the City Government of Savannah from 1790 to 1901* (Savannah: City Council, 1900), 169-71.
[410] Finlay, "The Savannah and Ogeechee Canal," 18, citing the Savannah *Georgian*, December 7, 1836.

survey and specifications, and financial investment by several Boston supporters. Actual work on the canal began in December 1836 under the supervision of Edward Hammond. One of the early problems faced by Hammond was securing a reliable work force.[411] Five hundred Irish workers from Boston were brought south to expedite the initial work, but after three months of labor starting in January 1837, the company dismissed them because of local complaints—"the whole country is kept in alarm by their drunken riots and vagrant habits."[412] Thomas B. King recommended the leasing of slaves from the local rice plantations, and about four hundred were brought in to replace the departed Irish workers.

Soon thereafter, F. & A. Pratt, former contractors on the New York and Erie Canal, was brought on to expedite the remainder of the work; in January 1838 the firm advertised for the hiring of 1,000 blacks, with $15 a month to be paid for "steady prime men" and $13 for "able women." Each hired slave received 3½ pounds of pork or bacon and ten quarters of seed per week, with housing provided in "comfortable shanties."[413] During 1838, about 1,000 slaves labored on digging the Brunswick-Altamaha Canal, but the contractors determined that the work was too difficult for them—all but two hundred slaves were dismissed and two hundred Irish workers were hired as replacements. Though the slaves and the Irish both worked on the canal they were purposely kept from working together by the contractors. During her sojourn at the nearby plantation of her husband, Pierce M. Butler, at Butler's Island, Frances Anne Kemble

---

[411] "Brunswick-Altamaha Canal Study," op. cit., 21.
[412] Brunswick *Advocate*, June 15, 1837.
[413] Ibid., January 18, 1838, June 14, 1838.

observed that "The Irish hate the Negroes even more than the Americans do, and there would be no bound to their murderous animosity if they were brought in contact with them on the same portion of the works of the Brunswick Canal."[414] Though pains were taken to keep the whites and the blacks apart, nothing could prevent the unruly Irish from fighting among themselves and, as in 1837, two opposing groups got out of control and the militia had to be called in to restore order.

By the spring of 1838, five miles of canal had been dug and work began on the locks, to be built of lightwood pine timber placed on pilings. By June 1839, work had been completed on the first seven miles of the canal from its southern, Brunswick, end, and three miles were complete from Six Mile Creek on the Altamaha River end.

Then disaster struck the canal company, precipitated by a financial panic in October 1839 that primarily affected the southern cotton states and the suspension of all specie payments by the Bank of the United States of Pennsylvania. Work on the canal was ended a month later, with almost ten miles completed at a cost of about $500,000.[415]

The project remained in abeyance for over a decade before being resumed in 1851, continuing to June 1854. In late 1852 it was reported that only about 30,000 square yards of excavation remained to complete the full twelve miles of the canal, with a lock at each end under construction. On this phase of the work about five hundred black laborers were leased from the plantations. For example on May

---

[414] Frances Anne Kemble, *Journal of a Residence on a Georgian Plantation in 1838-39* (New York: Knopf, 1961 edition), 124.
[415] "Annual Report of the President and Directors of the City of Brunswick, Georgia" (New York, 1853), 6.

9, 1854 and again on May 13, nine and eleven slaves from Hugh F. Grant's Elizafield plantation were hired to work on the canal at its juncture with Six Mile Creek.[416]

The canal opened on June 1, 1854 to the appropriate public celebration with boats and flats departing the lower lock and proceeding north to the Altamaha lock. By then, the original intent of the canal was somewhat ambiguous as the majority of cotton from the interior coming to the coast for shipment was going into Savannah by rail. Darien's once-lucrative cotton trade had largely ended by 1842, and the canal's completion came too late to benefit Brunswick in the export cotton.

As with the Savannah-Ogeechee canal, the Brunswick-Altamaha Canal encountered maintenance difficulties soon after opening. By 1860, the canal was abandoned. After the Civil War several attempts were made to revive the use of the canal to benefit Brunswick's growing importance as a naval stores processing center. However, an 1866 re-incorporation of the Brunswick & Altamaha Canal Company failed to produce the funding for needed repairs and improvements. Further evidence that the canal had become obsolete was that in 1888-89 a U.S. Army Corps of Engineers survey of the Altamaha River failed to mention the south channel of the river and the canal in its recommended improvements.[417]

A final effort in 1891 was also unsuccessful after promotors made application to the state legislature to operate and maintain the canal

---

[416] Albert V. House, ed., *Planter Management and Capitalism in Antebellum Georgia: The Journal of Hugh Fraser Grant, Ricegrower* (New York: Columbia University Press, 1954), 289.
[417] O.M. Carter, "Survey of the Altamaha River," House Document 283, 51st Congress, 2nd Session (1891), 1-16.

"for transportation of vessels, boats, barges, and other water-crafts, timber, lumber, and other products and things, and for that purpose to construct such locks, dams, booms, and other contrivances as may be necessary..."[418]

By then hardly used, and under the control of John E. DuBignon, the Brunswick-Altamaha Canal was sold to Glynn County in September 1918.[419]

The Savannah-Ogeechee Canal was a far more successful venture than the Brunswick-Altamaha Canal. In the 1840s and 1850s, the Savannah-backed canal was extensively utilized to move timber from the Ogeechee River to the saw mills in Savannah, particularly the Vale Royal mill at the Savannah end of the canal. In 1847, Benjamin Stiles sold 275 acres of the Vale Royal rice plantation at the mouth of the canal to William B. Giles of North Carolina. Giles built at Vale Royal one of the largest saw mills in the United States, with the capacity to produce eight million board feet of lumber per year.[420] In 1850, the Savannah Patent Brick Plant was established along the upper end of the canal, with plans to produce up to 12 million bricks per year; in 1853, the brick company built a basin along the canal. Fur evidence of the growing use of the canal in the antebellum era is the increased shipment of rice via the canal to the Savannah market from the Ogeechee plantations on both the Chatham County and Bryan County sides of the river. Some 12,350 bushels of rice were

---

[418] *Acts* (1890-91), I, 474.
[419] Glynn County deed records (1918), Book 3-J, 265-66.
[420] Savannah Writers Project, *Savannah River Plantations*, op. cit., 469.

transported by barge through the canal in the early 1850s.[421]

According to the manuscript slave census of 1850 for Chatham County, the slave ownership of Savannah businesses served by the Savannah-Ogeechee Canal in 1849 were Upper Steam Rice Mill (65), Savannah Steam Rice Mill (11), Central Rail Road (123), Robert Lachlison, iron founder (14), James Lachlison, iron founder (2), Savannah Brick Company (25), James L. Rossignol, brick industry (4), Bradley & Giles, lumber, saw mill (65), and John B. Bacon, lumber and saw mill (8).[422]

In 1860, the canal's board of directors investigated the possibility of establishing a link between the canal and the recently-opened Savannah, Albany & Gulf Railroad, a line that ran from Savannah through Chatham County and crossed the Ogeechee River to Bryan County a short distance downstream from King's Ferry and close to the canal's juncture with the river. This initiative was interrupted by the onset of the Civil War. In December 1864 the canal was the scene of several skirmishes between Union and Confederate units during Sherman's operations to invest Savannah. One of the engagements resulted in the burning of Dillon's bridge near the canal's Ogeechee lock. The Confederates also opened up some of the embankments along the canal's route, "turning fields into neck-deep marshes in efforts to delay their enemy. Union soldiers were victorious, however, and soon used canal boats to float supplies to

---

[421] *Savannah Daily Morning News*, May 8, 1853; Savannah *Georgian*, April 13, 1850; Account Ledger, Savannah and Ogeechee Canal Company, Central of Georgia Railway Papers, Collection 1362RR-20, GHS.

[422] U.S. 7th Census (1850), Georgia, Chatham County, slave and agricultural schedules.

fellow soldiers."[423]

By 1866, damages to the canal incurred late in the war had been repaired and the canal was back in use to move timber from the Ogeechee to the Savannah mills. The directors made surveys for a proposed extension to the nearby Canoochee River to establish a route across the middle part of Bryan County to gain access to timber tracts theretofore untapped.[424] The canal's use apparently continued to be extensive into the 1880s. One report noted that "a large amount of timber, rice and wood passes through [the canal] every year, adding very materially to the commerce of the city and returning handsome dividends to the stockholders. It is estimated that over $150,000 of traffic passed through it to the city last year."[425]

The Savannah yellow fever epidemic of late summer and the early fall of 1876, in which over 1,000 persons perished, had an eventual impact on the Savannah-Ogeechee Canal. Savannah city officials suspected that the canal, with its stagnant water and poor drainage, might be linked to the spread of disease, and ordered that new culverts be constructed. Local physicians made pronouncements in 1888 and 1893 to the effect that the canal should be abandoned entirely, feeling it was a prime source of cholera and fever. A local newspaper opined that the canal should be regularly flushed with

---

[423] Finlay, "The Savannah-Ogeechee Canal," citing reports in *The War of the Rebellion: Official Records of the Union and Confederate Armies*, Series I, v. 54 (Washington, D.C., 1893).
[424] Savannah and Ogeechee Canal Company, Minute Book 3, January 1871 and January 1873, Central of Georgia Railway Papers, GHS.
[425] *Savannah Morning News*, August 8, 1883.

fresh water to prevent contamination.[426]

The canal was clearly coming to the end of its usefulness and profitability. Drought and low water occasionally caused a suspension of operations, and debts began to accumulate with the need for repairs to locks and embankments. The reduction of timber resources by 1890 led to diminishing business, as much of the marketable timber contiguous to the Ogeechee and Canoochee rivers, most of which was earmarked for the Savannah mills, had been depleted by the late 1880s.

In 1870, the Central of Georgia Railroad and Banking Company purchased the Giles Company's lumber yards and, in the 1880s, gradually converted the site at the canal's Savannah River terminus to wharfage and warehousing for its subsidiary operation, the Ocean Steamship Company. Also built at the site were a grain elevator and cotton-press to accommodate the upland cotton arriving at Savannah by rail. In 1891, the Ocean Steamship Company removed the canal's No. 1 Lock, nearest the Savannah River, raised bridges and extended the canal basin to create docking facilities for its cargo vessels—"more than fifty years after the Central Railroad first challenged the canal company for cargoes, the railroad's victory was final."[427]

With the canal in great disrepair, the waterway was turned over to

---

[426] James J. Waring, *The Epidemic at Savannah, 1876, Its Causes, The Measures of Prevention* (Savannah, Ga.: Morning News Co., 1879); Savannah Drainage Commission, Minute Book, 1877-1885, Collection 5600-DC10, GHS; *Savannah Morning News*, September 9, 1888 and January 17, 1893.

[427] Finlay, "The Savannah-Ogeechee Canal," 24, citing *Savannah Morning News*, May 26, 1880, April 14, 1885, March 20, 1888, April 9, 1891; Minute Book of the Ocean Steamship Company, March 1885, Central of Georgia Railway Papers, GHS; *56th Annual Report of the President and Directors of the Central Railroad and Banking Company of Georgia, 1891* (Savannah, Ga.: Nichols, 1891), 21.

the City of Savannah by the Central Railroad in 1914 as part of a local drainage project. In 1936, the U.S. Army Corps of Engineers described the canal as a "non-functioning drainage ditch," a far cry from one hundred years earlier when the Savannah-Ogeechee Canal had been a far more important "ditch."

A Rice Planter on Bryan Neck: Richard James Arnold

The nineteenth century rice plantations on the Ogeechee River in lower Bryan County, though statistically lesser producers of the staple than those on the Savannah and Altamaha rivers, were nonetheless consistently productive. The history of the Bryan Neck tracts and, more significantly, the story of the families who occupied them for several generations, is both interesting and intriguing, and provide an important component amid the overall fabric of the Georgia low country's agricultural, economic and social history.

Mary Elliott Butler (1748-1789), born in Charles Town, was the only child of William and Elizabeth Butler. William Butler (1715-1761) was granted Ogeechee River lands on Bryan Neck, including the tract called Sterling Hill, part of which later became part of Tranquilla plantation. Butler was a distant cousin of Major Pierce Butler of South Carolina who, after the Revolution, acquired Georgia plantation lands in the Altamaha River district.[428]

In 1767, Mary Butler married Thomas Savage (1738-1786), an Englishman who acquired rice lands on the Ogeechee through his marriage to Mary. One of these tracts was Silk Hope fronting on the Ogeechee within the present Richmond Hill city limits east of US Highway 17. Savage was a Charles Town merchant of some importance, but devoted increasing energies to the production of rice

---

[428] Much of the following paper is extracted from Buddy Sullivan, *From Beautiful Zion to Red Bird Creek: A History of Bryan County, Georgia* (Pembroke, Ga., 2000), chapters 6 and 7.

in Georgia. He later acquired the Sterling Bluff tract downriver from Silk Hope.

Savage was supportive of the cause of American independence and was interned by the British in St. Augustine in 1780. After the war, Savage spent his winters at Silk Hope, endeavoring to rebuild his fortune. He had plans to build a permanent residence at Sterling Bluff just before his death in 1786.[429] Savage's will, probated in 1786, left his properties to his wife, Mary, specifically Point plantation upriver from Silk Hope, Sterling Bluff, Silk Hope and Genesis Point (later the site of Fort McAllister), tracts near old Fort Argyle up the Ogeechee and Thoroughgood, a 5,000-acre tract of pine land on the Canoochee River where Savage cut saw timber for commercial purposes after the Revolution. Mary Butler Savage died of malarial fever at Silk Hope at the age of forty-one in July 1789.[430]

The daughter of Thomas and Mary Savage, Mary Ann Savage (1770-1844), married Joseph Clay, Jr. (1764-1811) in 1789. Clay was a graduate of Princeton, studied law in Williamsburg, Virginia, and returned to his native Savannah to practice law and become a distinguished jurist. In 1803, Clay did an unusual thing—he converted from the Episcopalian faith to the Baptist faith and became a Baptist minister, being ordained as such in 1804. To staid, stiff Savannah society, this development caused a sensational stir. A typical reaction was that of Savannah merchant and rice factor Robert Mackay:

---

[429] Clay Family Papers, Collection 125, folders 1-3, GHS.
[430] Ibid.

"...Mr. Clay made his debut yesterday as a Babtist [sic] preacher & I must confess I was never more mortified or disappointed.—His Pray'r was undoubtedly a very excellent one, but delivered in the full perfection of Methodistical Cant—even this however did not drown the musick of his voice, with all the beauty of eloquence & persuasion I have often admired in it at the Bar...I think Mr. Toblers application of the opinion of Festus is not amiss—it may be *learning–something* at all events has made him *Mad*—"[431]

Joseph and Mary Ann Savage Clay had four children: Mary Clay (1790-1867), who married William Rufus Grat, a prominent Boston businessman who was linked to the Clay family through its annual summer sojourns in New England; Anne Clay (1796-1842, who never married; Thomas Savage Clay (1801-1849), to be discussed following, and Eliza Caroline Clay (1805-1895), who also never married. Eliza was born in Bryan County at Tranquilla plantation.[432]

In 1821, the widowed Mary Savage Clay returned to Bryan County and with her son, Thomas Savage Clay, purchased Dublin, an Ogeechee River rice tract of 487 acres, from Mary Maxwell McIntosh, whereupon the name of the tract was changed to Richmond. In 1823, a bond for the adjoining Cherry Hill tract, recorded its eastward boundary as being that of "Thomas S. Clay, called Richmond, lately called Dublin."[433]

---

[431] Robert Mackay to Eliza Mackay, September 19, 1803, in Walter Charlton Hartridge, ed., *The Letters of Robert Mackay to His Wife* (Athens: University of Georgia Press, 1949), 32-33; Mabel Freeman Lafar, "The Baptist Church of Savannah, Georgia: History, Records and Register," manuscript collection, GHS.

[432] Robert Manson Myers, ed., *The Children of Pride, A True Story of Georgia and the Civil War* (New Haven: Yale University Press, 1972), 1491.

[433] Bryan County deed records, Superior Court, Pembroke, Ga., Book D. The definitive source for the Clay family of Bryan County is Carolyn Clay Swiggart, *Shades of Gray: The Clay and McAllister Families of Bryan County, Georgia* (Darien, Ct., 1999).

Earlier, in 1817, Mary Maxwell McIntosh had sold the Cherry Hill tract to Raymond P. Demere, Mary E. Demere and Frances Ann Demere for $13,310. The property reverted to Mary McIntosh through foreclosure, before its subsequent purchase by Samuel M. Bond for $4,500. Bond, in turn, sold Cherry Hill to Richard James Arnold, to be discussed following, in 1824 for $9,500.[434]

In the 1820s, Clay and his mother, Mary Savage Clay, built the two-story plantation house at Richmond that was ultimately to be burned by invading Union forces in December 1864 amidst Sherman's operations against Fort McAllister and Savannah.

On May 17, 1836, Thomas Savage Clay married Matilda Willis McAllister (1818-1869), daughter of George Washington McAllister (1781-1850), proprietor of the neighboring Strathy Hall plantation.

Strathy Hall was originally a colonial grant to James Mackay, who died in 1785 and left the tract to his granddaughter Barbara, the wife of William Clark of Bryan Neck, and other grandchildren by Roger Kelsall and James Maxwell. Mackay's descendants apparently chose not to pursue rice production at Strathy Hall and, in May 1817, William Gaston, Jr., administrator of the Mackay estate, was authorized to sell the tract's 1,420 acres to George W. McAllister.

McAllister was a member of an old, established Pennsylvania family, migrating to Savannah in 1800 at the age of nineteen with other members of his family. From the 1820s to the outbreak of the Civil War, McAllister and his son-in-law, Thomas S. Clay of nearby Richmond plantation, along with another neighbor, Richard J,

---

[434] Bryan County deed records, Book D.

Thomas Savage Clay

Arnold, were the leading producers of rice in Bryan County as well as the largest slave owners.

Clay was known as a liberal and humane slave owner, and earned the respect and recognition of his planter peers, both for his agricultural acumen and his social consciousness. Rev. John Winn, a Presbyterian clergyman who pastored the church on Bryan Neck in the 1840s, noted of Clay:

"...Thomas S. Clay used to be called one of 'Nature's Noblemen.' He was indeed an elegant gentleman: tall, dignified, handsome, refined, polite and most engaging. Though his father Judge Clay was a Baptist, the children became Presbyterian, rather siding with the religious creed of their mother who died a member of Bryan Neck church; her ashes lie there to this day. Thomas S. Clay became a leading elder of the church, though at the time of his ordination he candidly avowed a leaning to the Baptist views. He was a slaveholder by inheritance. Through the six years we were his neighbor, his slaveholdings amounted to over two hundred people...A large slaveholder to be sure he was, but the greatest slave to slaves. He was a slaveholder not from covetousness, but from conscience. He was wont to call them his "People,' not slaves. At the event of his death (which was very sudden) one of his servants said they had not lost a master, but a father. Controlled not so much by mercenary as merciful motives, he untiringly nursed them in sickness, and toiled for their religious instruction. Dr. C.C. Jones has recorded of this Clay family that they were 'the originator of the efforts made for the religious improvement of the servants of the household, which have been attended with such satisfactory results.'"[435]

The 1850 U.S. agricultural census noted that the Clay family held 155 slaves dispersed among their several Bryan Neck farm tracts, chiefly Richmond, Tranquilla and Tivoli. By 1860, when Richmond and the other tracts were managed by T.S. Clay's sister, Eliza Caroline Clay, the number of bondsmen had increased to 230, second only to the McAllisters of Strathy Hall. By the late 1830s, to establish an unbroken link between Richmond and Tranquilla, Clay had acquired additional properties, Piercefield, Frugality Hall and Ricedale. He also held the Point, an Ogeechee River rice tract immediately east of the King's Ferry causeway (present U.S. 17), the Tivoli cotton tract on the tidal Medway River on the south side of the Neck, and Thoroughgood, the pineland tract mentioned earlier in the interior of Bryan County on the Canoochee River.

Clay eventually came to possess some 7,700 acres of land by the time of his death in 1849. Surviving plantation accounts in the Clay Family Papers indicate that Richmond, with its large-scale rice

---

[435] Rev. John Winn, "Thomas Savage Clay,", *Christian Observer*, September 8, 1880, in Clay Family Papers, Collection 125, folder 2, GHS.

production, was by far the most profitable of the Clay tracts. Tranquilla and Tivoli were devoted primarily to the production of cotton, while the other lands were utilized chiefly for the cultivation of provision crops—corn, sweet potatoes, pease—to sustain the slave force and the plantation livestock.

In 1836, Clay shipped to his Savannah factor, Robert Habersham & Son, twenty-four bales of sea island cotton, 1,288 bushels of corn, and 7,202 bushels of rice. This degree of production remained fairly constant for the remainder of the antebellum period when Eliza Clay managed the plantations following her brother's death. Tax returns on the estate of Thomas Clay just before the Civil War provide further detail on the extent of the family's properties. In 1861, Tivoli was listed as comprising 458 acres of pine land and twenty acres of salt marsh; Piercefield had "400 acres 2nd quality oak & hickory land, valued at $1 per acre," and 438 acres of pine land; Ricedale, on Sterling Creek, had "40 acres of 2nd quality Tide Swamp," at $50 per acre, and 204 acres of oak and hickory land; Frugality Hall comprised 600 acres; Richmond had 187 acres of "1st quality Tide Swamp valued at $100 per acre," and 300 acres of oak and hickory land; Tranquilla had 400 acres of inland swamp, 450 acres of hickory land and 1,650 acres of pine land; Thoroughgood comprised 2,500 acres; and the Point tract contained 125 acres of "2nd quality Tide Swamp."[436]

The largest number of slaves on the Clay properties was, not surprisingly, at Richmond where the intensity of rice production

---

[436] Bryan County tax digest, 1861, GDAH; Clay Family Papers, GHS; U.S. 7th and 8th census, Bryan County, slave and agricultural schedules; Swiggart, *Shades of Gray*, op. cit.

required the greatest amount of labor; the next largest was on the other side of Bryan Neck at Tivoli where much of the Clay cotton was cultivated. In the 1840s and 1850s the Richmond bondsmen were housed in twenty duplex frame dwellings near the plantation house. When Henry Ford acquired the property in 1925, the brick remains of foundations and chimneys of these structures were still in evidence. Thomas Clay also constructed a brick, steam-powered threshing and pounding mill to process his rice crop before shipment to his factor. As of 2020, the tall brick chimney of the rice mill was still standing near the former Ford house at Richmond. There was also a stable, corn crib (where the bondsmen received allotments of food, clothing and other supplies, rice and cotton barn, and other out buildings. A tidal irrigation canal separated Richmond from Cherry Hill, the rice tract of Richard Arnold abutting the west side of Richmond. Clay and Arnold were close friends and neighbors until the two had a falling out over disputed property lines in 1848.

Thomas S. Clay, in the prime of life, died unexpectedly on October 24, 1849 at the age of forty-eight. Rev. Charles C. Jones of Maybank plantation, Liberty County, lamented the loss of his friend:

"My friend was the most intimate & beloved, out of the circle of immediate relations, which I had in the world…The grave hath received him, God hath taken him, and I am left alone…All our pleasant correspondence has ceased, we can see each other no more, we can take no more delightful walks…I think of him at Tivoli, at Richmond, but he is not in the house, nor on the walks, nor in the fields. We must think of all his excellences, we must think of all his love, and of our loss, and we must weep. Tears must come to our relief…He is universally lamented…"[437]

---

[437] Rev. C.C. Jones to Matilda McAllister Clay, November 6, 1849, in Clay Family Papers, Collection 125, folder 2, GHS.

Clay's widow, Matilda McAllister Clay, was a semi-invalid, thus much of the rearing of their children and management of the plantation devolved upon Clay's younger sister, Eliza Caroline, who lived with the family at Richmond. The five surviving children were Joseph Clay (1838-1914), Thomas Carolin Clay (1841-1897), Anne Clay (1845-1921), Emma Josephine Clay (1847-1928) and Robert Habersham Clay (1849-1924).

Several miles downriver from Richmond was Strathy Hall, the plantation of George W. McAllister. By 1830, McAllister possessed 134 slaves, a number that increased to 194 in 1850, the year of his death. The 1850 agricultural census reported that Strathy Hall's production was 620,000 pounds of rice, 1,500 bushels of corn and 500 bushels of sweet potatoes. Strathy Hall had a tide-powered rice rice mill, the brick ruins of which are still in evidence on the Ogeechee today in the Mill Hill section of the Strathy Hall subdivision.

McAllister's family has a prominent place in the social and economic history of coastal Georgia. His father, Archibald McAllister, was the brother of Matthew McAllister (1758-1823), whose son (George's first cousin) was Matthew Hall McAllister (1800-1865) of Savannah. The latter practiced law in Savannah, was mayor of the city, U.S. District Attorney and a state senator before moving to San Francisco where he became the first U.S. circuit judge of the new state of California. He was the father of Ward McAllister (1827-1895), who was well-known in social circles when he applied the name "Four Hundred" to the elite of New York City society.[438]

G.W. McAllister's second marriage, to Mary Bowman (1792-

---

[438] Cleveland Amory, *Who Killed Society?* (New York, 1960), 118.

1825), produced five children, including Matilda Willis McAllister, wife of Thomas S. Clay, and Joseph Longworth McAllister (1820-1864). Joseph McAllister was born at Strathy Hall, attended Amherst College, practiced law briefly in Savannah, then managed his father's plantation throughout the decade of the 1850s. George McAllister died suddenly on March 18, 1850 after being thrown from a horse, and was buried at the Bryan Neck Presbyterian Church cemetery (now known as Burnt Church Cemetery). Joseph McAllister inherited the family lands at Strathy Hall and Genesis Point. He proved to be an efficient rice planter and was ultimately the largest slave owner in Bryan County with 276 bondsmen on the eve of the Civil War. As captain of the Hardwicke Mounted Rifles which was consolidate in January 1864 as Company H of the 7th Georgia Cavalry, part of J.E.B. Stuart's cavalry corps, McAllister was killed in his first battle at the Confederate victory at Trevilian Station near Louisa Courthouse, Virginia, in June 1864. "He was an upright, useful citizen, charitable to the poor and kind to all, a sagacious and dashing soldier, and a true patriot," noted his obituary. He was buried in the Louisa Courthouse cemetery. Joseph McAllister never married.

The most enduring symbol of Strathy Hall is the two-story frame plantation house built by G.W. McAllister on the Ogeechee River about 1838. Robert Habersham Clay owned the house from 1878 until his death in 1924, enlarging the house by adding a wing and making other improvements. Unlike other plantation structures on the Ogeechee, Strathy Hall was spared destruction during the Union campaign on Bryan Neck, resulting in the capture of McAllister. The house was possibly spared due to the probable knowledge of Union officers that the McAllisters were part of a prominent Northern family. The residences at nearby White Hall and Myrtle Grove, owned by Rhode Island planter-businessman Richard J. Arnold, were also likely spared for the same reason. Strathy Hall was restored by Henry Ford in the 1930s, and remains a private residence at the time of this writing in 2020.

In May 1823, Louisa Caroline Gindrat (1804-1871) married Richard James Arnold (1796-1873), son of a wealthy, established business family of Providence, Rhode Island. Louisa Gindrat was born at Whitehall plantation in lower Bryan County on the Ogeechee River just west of the site of the colonial town of Hardwicke. She was a contemporary of children growing up at other plantations on Bryan Neck, including Thomas Savage Clay (born in 1801).

Through his marriage to Louisa Gindrat Richard J. Arnold acquired the considerable holdings of his wife's Bryan County dowry, including White Hall plantation and its 1,300 acres of rice and cotton land, and sixty-eight slaves. White Hall was somewhat less than profitable in the 1820s with an 1823 crop yield of only ninety barrels of rice and six bags of good cotton. In addition, some of the Gindrat lands, including Mulberry Hill upriver between the Point and Silk Hope tracts, was heavily mortgaged.[439]

---

[439] Richard J. Arnold to Samuel G. Arnold, December 12, 1823, Welcome Arnold Papers, John Carte Brown Library, Providence, Rhode Island, cited in Charles Hoffmann and Tess Hoffmann, *North by South, The Two Lives of Richard James Arnold* (Athens: University of Georgia Press, 1988). This meticulously researched work is the most authoritative account of Arnold's plantation activities in Georgia. It is also the most detailed treatment of any Bryan County plantation currently available.

It was about this same time that Arnold decided to invest his considerable Rhode Island family inheritance into the Georgia plantation of his new wife—a decision that caused no small amount of consternation among his New England relatives, for not only would Arnold become a substantial slave owner, but his presence in Bryan County would require his presence there half the year. Rhode Island was not as abolitionist as neighboring Massachusetts. The profitability of the slave trade, and the later investment by Rhode Island merchants in textile mills based on the slave-based economy of the South, made the abolition slower to develop in that state.[440]

Thus began a pattern by which Richard and Louisa Arnold, for nearly four decades, spent their fall and winter months at White Hall and the spring and summer in Providence and Newport. Doubtless Arnold consulted with young Thomas S. Clay, and Clay's uncle, William Savage of nearby Silk Hope plantation, both of whom advised Arnold to purchase the Cherry Hill tract upriver from White Hall between Richmond and Silk Hope. Another newcomer to the Ogeechee at this time was G.W. McAllister whose Strathy Hall plantation lay between White Hall and Richmond. The Clays, Savages and McAllisters had become a close-knit Bryan Neck society and the Arnolds soon found themselves agreeably and comfortably situated within the group.

In early 1824, Arnold purchased an additional 600 acres of "Prime land opposite White Hall" for $3,500. This acquisition became known as the Myrtle Grove tract, and was then represented as an extension of White Hall plantation. According to Arnold's will

---

[440] Slavery was not abolished in Rhode Island until 1842.

dated January 10, 1846, a document affirmed the addition of 1,200 acres to the original 1,300 acres of White Hall between 1823 and 1845.[441]

A warranty deed dated June 1, 1861 by which Arnold transferred White Hall to his son, Thomas Clay Arnold, stated that White Hall consisted of several tracts of land, "bounded and containing as follows: on the North by Strathy Hall Plantation owned by Estate of McCalister [sic]; on the South and Southeast by lands of John M. Middleton; and on the East and Northeast by the Great Ogeechee River."[442] The long, looping tract of rice bottom lands which forms the Seven Mile bend of the Ogeechee is delineated as "Arnold's Point" on antebellum maps. Most of this large tract was under cultivation in rice and was a patchwork of canals, irrigation ditches, embankments and tidegates supporting the operations of White Hall plantation, and the neighboring tract of John M. Middleton.

The Myrtle Grove tract was conveyed, and made separate from White Hall, in June 1871 from Arnold to his granddaughter Louisa (Luly) Arnold Appleton, wife of George Lyman Appleton, being described as lying "parallel with White Hall South Avenue to a fence which divides it from White Hall proper to Hardwicke Road, thence along said road to Pinkey House, the property of George P. Screven, until it makes to the Ogeechee River..."[443] Myrtle Grove passed out of Arnold-Appleton ownership in 1909 when it was acquired by William W. Gordon, then being purchased in 1920 by Mrs. Allethaire Ludlow Elkins, later Rotan. Allethaire Rotan changed the

---

[441] Bryan County Probate Court records, Will Book 1 (1846), 28.
[442] Bryan County deed records, Book I, 72-74.
[443] Bryan County deed records, Book J, 193.

name of Myrtle Grove to Folly Farms, which originally had been part of the neighboring Pinkey House tract dating to the colonial land grant period. In 1949, Myrtle Grove-Folly Farms became the property of Walter W. Meeks, among other parcels constituting lands formerly known as the Maxwell tract, the Pinkey House tract, the Triangle tract and the Kinsale tract.[444]

In December 1824, Arnold invested the remainder of his Rhode Island inheritance, $30,000, into the purchase of the Cherry Hill rice tract several miles upriver from White Hall and adjacent to the Clay family's Richmond plantation. He paid $9,500 for the land and buildings at Cherry Hill, and twice that sum for the sixty-three slaves who were there producing rice.[445] This acquisition solidified Arnold's long-range plan to diversify his crop production: White Hall had the best land for the cultivation of cotton, while Cherry Hill was more suited to tideflow rice cultivation.

The Arnold family retained ownership of Cherry Hill for more than half a century. In 1874, the tract went by inheritance to another of Arnold's sons, William Eliot Arnold, then went out of the family by foreclosure in 1877. It was eventually acquired in April 1925 by Henry Ford during his consolidation of much of the land on Bryan Neck.

For four decades, Richard James Arnold was to demonstrate business and management skills and acumen which were to make him of the largest and most productive of antebellum planters in tidewater Georgia. By 1860, he was the leading rice producer in

---

[444] Bryan County deed records, Book W, 250-52; Book DD, 238-39; Book 3-C, 402-04.
[445] Bryan County deed records, Book D (1817, 1823, 1824).

Bryan County, as well as the county's wealthiest and most prominent citizen, even though he resided in the county only about half the year.

A stickler for detail, Arnold kept accounts of many of his Georgia activities. Portions of his plantation journal for the years 1847-49 have survived, and provide valuable insights into the management of an Ogeechee River rice plantation.[446] By the middle 1840s, Arnold had become the third largest planter in Bryan County behind his neighbors Thomas S. Clay and G.W. McAllister. His slaveholdings, which numbered 131 at the time of his acquisition of White Hall and Cherry Hill in 1823 and 1824, respectively, increased to 186 in 1850, and then to a high of 195 on the eve of the Civil War. His total land holdings in Bryan County, including additional Ogeechee River tracts and interior lands on the Canoochee River, amounted to about 11,000 acres.[447]

Arnold's biographers, Charles and Tess Hoffmann, describe Arnold in the prime of life in terms that reflect why this unique man easily qualifies as one of the most interesting and important personages in Bryan County history:

"In 1847 the Arnolds appeared to enjoy the best of both possible worlds, wintering in Georgia and summering in Rhode Island, respected in both communities. By this time, Arnold's image of himself as a southern planter concerned with the efficient economics

---

[446] Hoffmann and Hoffmann, *North by South*, op. cit., use Arnold's agricultural journal as the basis for their book. Extracts with accompanying annotation are also contained in Sullivan, *From Beautiful Zion to Red Bird Creek*, op. cit., chapter 7.

[447] U.S. 7th and 8th Census, Bryan County, 1850 and 1860, slave and agricultural schedules. Tables reviewing Bryan County's leading land and slave holders, plus crop production, are contained in Sullivan, *From Beautiful Zion to Red Bird Creek*, 141, 142.

Richard James Arnold.

of the plantation system had enlarged to include Christian paternalism—he was a kind, good master who had by chance of marriage 'inherited' his slaves, and was deeply concerned for their social and moral welfare. From that point of view all aspects of the system, including slavery itself, were part of God's design to Christianize and civilize the slaves. Thus [Frederick Law] Olmsted, accepting Arnold's self-image, could describe him in 1853 as a 'religious man' without calculating the moral cost of his owning slaves."[448]

Thus, perhaps the most balanced picture that emerges of the Arnold plantations on Bryan Neck comes from the writings of, paradoxically, a northerner on a tour of southern plantations to gather impressions and make observations of slavery and agricultural matters. In January 1853, Frederick Law Olmsted arrived at White

---

[448] Hoffmann and Hoffmann, *North by South*, 13.

Hall for a first-hand observation of Arnold's methods. Arnold is identified only as "Mr. X" in Olmsted's work, A *Journey in the Seaboard Slave States* (1856), in which he describes, after observing only one working day's activity, Arnold's plantation as "a model of what slavery should be in America—a benevolent, patriarchal and civilizing institution."[449]

A crucial business connection for Arnold was his factor, the firm of Robert Habersham & Son in Savannah. The Habersham firm specialized in in advancing monies to coastal planters with good credit against an upcoming crop, and the marketing, with commensurate fees, of plantation commodities from low country planters in Georgia and South Carolina. The Habershams provided multiple services to the Arnold family, including those of banker, accountant, trustee, crop agent, business advisor and friend. Typical of their interaction were those in the spring of 1848. In April of that year Arnold shipped from Cherry Hill and White Hall to Habersham the final 1,500 bushels of clean rice from the previous year's crop on the coasting freighter *Cotton Plant*, and then prepared for their annual trip to Rhode Island for the summer season. On April 21, 1848 Habersham & Son expedited the payment of a bill for $153.47 for shoes and $362.40 for blankets and other supplies distributed to the slaves the previous winter. The same day, Arnold received from

---

[449] Frederick Law Olmsted, *A Journey in the Seaboard Slave States* (New York, 1856), contained in Olmsted, *The Cotton Kingdom* (New York, Knopf, 1953). Olmsted (1822-1903) is best known for designing New York's Central Park and parks in other major cities, including Chicago, Boston and Washington.

Habersham $300.00 cash "on a/c" much of which was spent on family expenses and gifts on the trip to the North.[450]

"Richard Arnold was by no means the stereotype of the southern planter sitting on the piazza drinking mint juleps served by liveried house servants," note the Hoffmanns. "He was deeply involved in the detailed planning and day-to-day operation of his business."[451] The Arnolds were also quite engaged with the other planter families of Bryan Neck. There was frequent association with their close friends and neighbors, the Clays of Richmond and the McAllisters of Strathy Hall. In the winter of 1847-48, relations cooled somewhat between Arnold and Thomas Clay resulting from a boundary dispute over rice land and the Clay canal between Richmond and Cherry Hill. A year later Clay was dead. Louisa Arnold had grown up with the Clay and McAllister children, so there were natural bonds between the families.

Other Arnold friends on Bryan Neck were Charles H. Starr (b. 1800) and his wife Sarah J. Starr (b. 1808). Starr was a cotton planter and proprietor of Silver Stream plantation on the lower Tivoli River several miles down the Neck from the Arnolds. Another associate was Raymond P. Demere (b. 1792), as reflected in Arnold's journal entry for January 28, 1847 which noted, "…Ginned 175 lbs mouted [moted] 175 lbs & Sorted 500 lbs—White Hall Cotton our family dined at Mr Demere's this day in Co with Mr & Mrs Starr."[452] Other neighbors were William Patterson and Dr. Thomas Charlton,

---

[450] Richard J. Arnold Plantation Account Book, vol. 8, citing April 15, 21 and 28, 1848, Richard J. Arnold Papers, Rhode Island Historical Society.
[451] Hoffmann and Hoffmann, *North by South*, 36.
[452] Richard J. Arnold Plantation Journal, Arnold-Screven Papers, Southern Historical Collection (SHC), University of North Carolina, Chapel Hill.

Charles W. Rogers and his family of Kilkenny plantation about nine miles down Bryan Neck from White Hall, and Savannah friends such as the Habershams, George Noble Jones and his wife Mary Nuttall Jones of Wormsloe plantation on the Isle of Hope.

The crop reports from the U.S. agricultural censuses for 1850 and 1860 (the first detailed reports available) attest to the growth of Arnold's farm operations. In the 1850 census, reflecting the 1849 crop year, Arnold's plantations produced 630,000 pounds of rice, the most by any local planter. Behind Arnold was George W. McAllister with 420,000 pounds, followed by Thomas S. Clay and Eliza C. Clay with 366,000 pounds, and John P. Hines with 160,000. A decade later, the 1860 reports reveal greater disparity between the Bryan Neck planters. Arnold's plantations produced 665,000 pounds of rice in the 1859 crop year, double the production of the next highest total, that of John M. Middleton with 332,000 pounds. Arnold also produced 300 bales of cotton that year, by far the highest total for Bryan County.

Richard and Louisa Arnold had seven surviving children: Eliza Harriet (1825-1906), who married William Brenton Greene in 1846; Louisa Gindrat (1828-1905) who married Samuel Greene Arnold, Jr., her first cousin, in 1848; Richard James, Jr. (1834-1899) who married Mary Clarke in 1860; Thomas Clay (1836-1875) who married Elizabeth Screven in 1870; William Eliot (1838-1883) who married Helen Foreman in 1871; Mary Cornelia (1841-1928) who married William Talbott in 1861; and Susan Allen (1843- ?) who married John M. Johnson in 1872. During the Civil War Arnold remained in Rhode Island and entrusted the Bryan County operations to his son, Thomas Clay Arnold. After the war, and throughout most of the

Reconstruction period, Thomas Arnold managed the family's rice operations at Cherry Hill with considerable success (see ff.). He died at White Hall in December 1875 and was buried in Savannah's Laurel Grove Cemetery.

* * *

Arnold continued to add to his land holdings, which enabled him to expand his planting activities to newer properties beyond White Hall and Cherry Hill. In 1844, he acquired one-half interest in Silk Hope, the tract adjacent to (west) and upriver from Cherry Hill, on the Ogeechee within the present city of Richmond Hill. Silk Hope, as discussed earlier, was the former plantation of William Savage who died in 1838. Arnold got his half of Silk Hope from John Pray Hines (1821-1864), a young Bryan Neck planter who had become a friend of Arnold and his family. Hines was the son of Lewis Hines (1795-1840), who had acquired Silk Hope in 1839 from the Savage estate.[453]

Arnold's plantation journal reveals that he was producing rice at Silk Hope in January 1847, the earliest available entry for the journal. He had actually begun expanding his interests beyond Cherry Hill as early as 1835 with the purchase of one-half interest in the Sans Souci tract, it being largely pine land and therefore unsuitable for rice cultivation. In addition to half interests in Silk Hope and Sans Souci, Arnold acquired other upper Ogeechee properties, including Sedgefield and one-half interest in Mulberry Hill in 1849, both within the present town limits of Richmond Hill.

---

[453] Myers, ed., *Children of Pride*, op. cit., 1550. John P. Hines was killed while serving in the Confederate forces near Richmond, Virginia, in the spring of 1864.

A deed of February 18, 1857 conveyed all of the acreage of Sans Souci and Mulberry Hill from John P. Hines to Arnold, and describes Mulberry Hill as being partly bounded on the north by the Point tract (estate of Thomas S. Clay), east by the half of Mulberry Hill already owned by Arnold, south by the Bryan Neck road, and west by the causeway through the rice fields to King's Ferry bridge on the Ogeechee river. Mulberry Hill immediately west (upriver) of, and adjoining the Silk Hope rice fields, and contiguous to that portion of Sedgefield with a small amount of rice tideland frontage, had been briefly owned by Abraham Gindrat, the father of Arnold's wife Louisa. Arnold's first one-half interest in Mulberry Hill was rented land in late 1847 before his outright acquisition of the tract in the purchases in 1849 and 1857. His journal entry of December 3, 1847 notes: "This day agreed with J. Bailey to plant his part of Mulbery [sic] Hill—I am to have it for two years, to clean up the square nearest the River that has not been planted and put whatever ditches I may think proper in it and a new trunk. The clearing to be rent for two years use of the Plantation." In order to obtain the rice fields of Sedgefield from Edward E. Pynchon of Liberty County in 1848, Arnold also had to purchase two tracts of pine land of 1,200 acres. Sedgefield's rice frontage comprised 240 acres, the section that most interested Arnold. "Had a long talk with Mr Pynchon about buying his place & I think it probable tomorrow we may close a bargain," he noted in his journal on February 28, 1848. Three days later he noted, "Spent one hour with Mr Pynchon & agreed to take Sedgefield Jany 1 1849 & to pay $8000 provided he does not trade with William Way tomorrow." Included in this transaction were "all

Tideflow rice cultivation on the Ogeechee River, ca. 1860.

the timbre [sic], Trunks & fencing, laths & posts in the place," related to the cultivation of rice.[454]

On February 17, 1857, Arnold notes in his plantation account book the payment of $11,000 to John Pray Hines for properties being "the whole of Orange Grove Plantation and one half each of the Mulbery [sic] and Sans Souci Plantations."[455] These acquisitions completed Arnold's accumulation of lower Bryan County land and gave him title to an almost contiguous tract of rice tidelands from Cherry Hill upriver to the King's Ferry causeway, excepting the half

---

[454] Richard J. Arnold Plantation Journal, entries of December 3, 1847, February 28, 1848 and March 9, 1848, Arnold-Screven Papers, SHC; Bryan County deed records, Book H, 344; Richard J. Arnold Account Book, vol. 8, February 17 and July 3, 1857, Arnold Papers, op. cit.

[455] Richard J. Arnold Account Book, vol. 8, February 17, 1857, Arnold Papers. Orange Grove was a smaller Ogeechee rice tract immediately west of Mulberry Hill and the King's Ferry causeway.

of Silk Hope he did not own. He deeded all of these tracts to his son, Thomas Clay Arnold, in May 1861.[456] The 1860 Bryan County census shows Arnold with real estate holdings valued at $70,000 and a personal estate valued at $103,000, figures that easily made him the wealthiest man in the county.[457]

With his growing property acquisitions, Arnold began to encounter occasional problems with his neighbors over boundary delineations and surveys. One of these disagreements was with G.W. McAllister whose Strathy Hall plantation bounded Arnold's White Hall tract on its west (upriver) side. Another involved William J. Way whose rice frontage on the river comprised the half of Silk Hope not owned by Arnold. The west half of Silk Hope, abutting Arnold's Mulberry Hill and Sedgefield tracts was owned by Way, while the east half was owned by Arnold, abutting the west side of his Cherry Hill plantation. Each of the halves of Silk Hope comprised about 700 acres, including rice tideland and forested upland. Way acquired his portion from Edward E. Pynchon in April 1844 for $12,000. Arnold, about the same time, purchased his half of Silk Hope from John P. Hines whose father, Lewis Hines, had acquired the whole tract from the William Savage estate.[458]

---

[456] Arnold-Screven Papers, SHC; Bryan County deed records, Book H.
[457] Based on inflation, $70,000 in 1860 converts to $2.1 million in 2020; $103,000 converts to $3.2 million from 1860 to 2020.
[458] William J. Way was born in 1810 in Liberty County. His name is associated with the settlement, Way's Station, that a century later became Richmond Hill during the Henry Ford era. Way was allied by marriage to the Hines family of Bryan and Liberty counties. As noted, Lewis Hines and his son, John Pray Hines, had farming operations in and around Cross Roads, the original name of the settlement that became Way's Station, later Richmond Hill. In addition to half of Silk Hope where he cultivated rice, Way had a cotton tract at White Oak plantation, with the city limits of present Richmond Hill. The 1860 federal agricultural census for Bryan

In early 1863 William Way sold his 750 acres at Silk Hope to Thomas C. Arnold, thus giving the Arnolds possession of the entire tract. Arnold's difficulties with Way arose over conflicting surveys of the boundaries between their respective halves of Silk Hope.

The most serious disagreement was that between Arnold and his close friend Thomas Savage Clay. During his negotiations with Edward Pynchon in the winter of 1847-48 for the purchase of rice lands, Arnold had a dispute with Clay over one of the boundaries of the proposed acquisition that ran along the old Clay canal. Arnold's biographers, Charles and Tess Hoffmann, refer to Arnold as "a very litigious man" and noted that the boundary problem was a "sore point" between Arnold and Clay. Arnold's sister, Eliza Harriet Allen, referred to the incident as "a family difficulty." Death ended the "difficulty" as Clay died suddenly in October 1849.[459]

County revealed that Way had a personal estate valued at $30,000 with ownership of sixty-two slaves and 350 acres of improved land on which he produced 59,000 pounds of rice in the 1859 crop year. In late 1856 construction on the new Savannah, Albany & Gulf Railroad passed from Chatham County across the Ogeechee River into Bryan County just downstream from King's Ferry, with the tracks laid out along the middle of Silk Hope plantation, on the line separating the halves owned by Way and Richard Arnold within the present Richmond Hill town limits. A depot was designated at this point, to be called Way's Station, or in the usual railroad parlance of the era, "Way's No. 1 ½" being the second scheduled stop for trains outbound from Savannah. During 1857 work continued on the railroad through Liberty and McIntosh counties; by the spring of 1858, James P. Screven, president of the Savannah, Albany & Gulf, reported to his stockholders that on August 1, 1857 the road had been completed to Doctortown on the Altamaha River, some fifty miles southwest of Savannah. See Annual Reports, S.A. & G. R.R. Papers, GHS.
[459] Bryan County deed records, Book F, 252; Hoffmann and Hoffmann, *North by South*, 36-37, 116.

* * *

In order to achieve diversification of his crop output, Arnold began cultivating sugar cane in the early 1840s with an end toward the milling and manufacture of cane by-products, chiefly syrup and molasses. Prior to starting his sugar operation, Arnold had constructed a steam-powered rice mill at Cherry Hill to facilitate the hulling and polishing of his rice. Two letters from his brother-in-law, Zechariah Allen of Providence, in December 1843 provide instructions to Arnold for the installation and operation of the steam engine and other equipment to run the "eleven pestle" rice mill. In February 1847, Arnold began building a brick sugar works to process the juice of his cane into syrup and molasses, a process that had been introduced to the Georgia coastal planters before the War of 1812.[460]

Arnolds journal entry for February 27, 1847 reports, succinctly, "Carpenters workg on Sugar Mill," and the same entry again on March 2, followed by considerably more detail on a busy following day highlighted by the arrival of building materials aboard a coasting schooner: "Two Black Masons commence workg on foundations for Sugar Mill & I am to pay $2.25 pr m [month] find them with provisions & tinder to mix Mortar & curing Brick & if I think the care worth 25 cts more pr m I am to give it, but not otherwise—To day the Cotton plant arrived at C Hill with 12000 Brick for me. Carpenters all at work on Sugar House."[461]

---

[460] See the chapter about Thomas Spalding and his sugar works at Sapelo Island earlier in this book. Arnold was almost certainly familiar with Spalding's methods in cane cultivation and processing techniques through his reading of the farm journals of the antebellum period, periodicals such as *The Southern Agriculturist, The Southern Cultivator,* and *DeBow's Review.*
[461] Richard J. Arnold Plantation Journal, Arnold-Screven Papers, SHC.

For all his enthusiasm, however, Arnold's sugar venture was not overly successful, apparently due to defective machinery purchased from the Savannah firm of Robert Lachlison, which specialized in the manufacture of machinery for rice and sugar works for the planters of tidewater Georgia and South Carolina.[462] The result was that, not surprisingly from what we have already seen, Arnold sued Lachlison for these difficulties, as documented in Arnold's journal:

March 22, 1847—"Lackleson [sic] came to C[herry] Hill today to arrange for Sugar Mill."
January 18, 1848—"Arkwright came out to see Sugar Mill & returned Same day & Says he will guarantee that he can fix the Mill to run well as it is now geared. I consented he should try. Lackleson agreeing to take the risk."
February 3, 1848—"Mill broke down @ 3 oclock have barreled off the last 3 days 13 Bbls Syrup should have been done in one day."
February 5, 1848—"at C Hill broke down the Sugar Mill being the third time this week four cogs broke this day."
February 9, 1848—"Carpenters came to C Hill by order of Lackleson to fix Mill."
February 11, 1848—"Lacklesons two Black Carpenters & my three working on Sugar Mill."

Finally, after more than a year of trouble with his mill equipment, Arnold had had enough with Robert Lachlison's firm, as attested by a final reference to the problem in his plantation journal on April 13, 1849: "This day C H Starr J F Maxwell & Charles H Harden

---

[462] This is the same Lachlison family that, with their relatives, the Hiltons, operated saw mills in McIntosh County, about forty miles south of the Ogeechee, before and after the Civil War. The Hilton interests, then known as the Hilton-Dodge Lumber Company, established a saw mill operation in Bryan County, at Belfast on the Medway River, in the early 1900s. See numerous references in Buddy Sullivan, *Early Days on the Georgia Tidewater*, all editions, 1990-2020; and Sullivan, *Darien, Georgia: A History of the Town & Its Environs* (privately published, 2020).

took Mr Fergusons deposition in my case with Lackleson & J F Maxwell is to carry it to Savh & hand it to the Clerk."[463]

An important individual in the day-to-day operations of Arnold's plantations was Amos Morel, a slave born about 1820. Morel was Arnold's head driver in the 1850s and 1860s, it being the highest position a plantation slave could attain. Frederick Law Olmsted, during his brief visit to Arnold's plantations in early 1853, observed that Morel "was a fine-looking fellow…on Sunday he had passed us, well dressed, well mounted, and as he raised his hat to salute us, there was nothing in his manner of appearance, except his colour, to distinguish him from a gentleman of good breeding and fortune."[464] While this description is probably somewhat idealized, Olmsted, as we have seen, considered Arnold to be an "enlightened" slave owner, which created a favorable impression of Arnold's reliance on Morel's considerable abilities and intelligence.[465] By the early 1850s, Morel had been given a great deal of responsibility by Arnold, particularly during the latter's lengthy absences on his spring and summer sojourns to the north. During those periods Morel was responsible only to the plantation overseer. Olmsted, through his interviews with Arnold, noted that Amos Morel's duties

> "were those of a steward, or intendant. He carried, by a strap at the waist, a very large number of keys, and had charge of all the stores and provisions, tools and materials of the plantations, as well as of all their produce before it was shipped to market. He weighed and

---

[463] Richard J. Arnold plantation journal, Arnold-Screven Papers, SHC. Charles W. Ferguson was Arnold's overseer.
[464] Olmsted, *Journey in the Seaboard Slave States*, op. cit.
[465] Charles Hoffmann and Tess Hoffmann, "The Limits of Paternalism: Driver-Master Relations on a Bryan County Plantation," *Georgia Historical Quarterly* 67 (Fall 1983), 322-23.

measured out all the rations of the slaves and the cattle, superintended the mechanics, and made and repaired, as was necessary, all the machinery, including the steam-engine."[466]

Morel had the advantage of having had something of an education through his being the son of one of the favored house servants. Morel learned the rudiments of reading and writing (though such was illegal for bondsmen in Georgia and other Southern states) during the resident tutoring of the Arnold children at White Hall during the winter months. In the late 1830s and the 1840s Morel learned the trade of blacksmithing and machinery repair during the period Arnold was having his rice mill built at Cherry Hill. Arnold apparently invested $500 in the training of Morel as an "engineer" (machinist) in Savannah, where he was hired out for his abilities with the proceeds of his work in town going into the plantation accounts. Arnold returned Morel to Bryan County in 1846 because his skills in operating and repairing the engines of rice mills and cotton gins were needed on the Ogeechee plantations. In allowing Morel to spend several years in Savannah, essentially on his own and as his "own man," Arnold had firmly cemented Morel's loyalty to the family, a factor that would be increasingly important over the next two decades.

By 1850, Morel had come to have as much authority over the running of the plantations as Arnold's overseer, Charles W. Ferguson. Arnold, in fact, skillfully utilized Morel as a check against the occasional excesses and indulgences of Ferguson as exemplified in the letters and reports written by Morel to his owner during the

---

[466] Olmsted, *Journey in the Seaboard Slave States.*

six months of the year when Arnold was in Rhode Island. The following communication in the summer of 1852 is typical:

"Dear Master—Please to remember me to Mistress and all the family. I am sorry to inform you that I have had to break William of his driver ship and have given him his hoe, since you have left William has got in debt to the other drivers 3 days and gets along very badly with his work on account of having too many favorites in the field. I have put Big Peter in his place to drive and would be glad to hear from you if you approve of what I have done. The Carpenters are getting along very badly with their work, they have not got the flat house done as yet. I am satisfied that it would be to your interest to get some white person to take charge of the work, as there is a great deal to be done, and I am fearful that the mill will not be repaired in time enough to receive the rice. I think I am safe in saying that your crop will yield you more this year than it has ever done, it is thought to be good for 60 bu[shels per acre]. Your obedient servant, Amos Morel.[467]

Morel remained loyal to Arnold during the war and Reconstruction. In recognition, Arnold deeded an acre of land near White Hall to Morel and two other former slaves in 1869 so the freedmen could build a church. In February 1871, Morel, using money earned working as a mechanic for the Arnolds, purchased from the estate of Joseph and Caroline Stiles property known as Brisbane's plantation, a tract across the Bryan Neck road from Cherry Hill. Morel later purchased 122 acres at White Oak plantation on the west side of the Savannah-Darien Stage Road. Both tracts are within the present Richmond Hill city limits. He sold off pieces of his Brisbane (familiarly known locally as "Brisbon") land

---

[467] Amos Morel to R.J. Arnold, June 20, 1852, and Morel to Arnold, June 22, 1852, Richard James Arnold Papers, Rhode Island Historical Society, Providence; Charles W. Ferguson to R.J. Arnold, July 16, 1852, Arnold-Screven Papers, SHC. Also see Hoffmann and Hoffmann, "The Limits of Paternalism: Driver-Master Relations," op. cit.

during the 1870s and 1880s and deeded some of it to his wife, Lucretia Morel, and his son-in-law and daughter, Andrew and Sharlot Mattox.[468]

It is important to understand that rice cultivation in the low country of South Carolina and Georgia did not end with the war and emancipation, Bryan County being a good case in point. During Kilpatrick's cavalry raid on Bryan Neck in December 1864, much of the Ogeechee plantation infrastructure had been damaged or destroyed. Richard Arnold's holdings at White Hall were more or less intact, but others on Bryan Neck had suffered greatly. The embankments, canals, diches and tidegates had either deteriorated or been damaged, and barns and rice mills were either gone or in poor states of repair.

With the restoration of coastal lands to their pre-war owners following the revocation of Sherman's Field Order 15, implemented in January 1865 during his occupation of Savannah in which the islands and mainland thirty miles inland from the sea from Charleston to Florida were to be awarded to the freed slaves, local rice cultivation resumed sporadically in 1866. Though the system of free slave labor was gone, pre-war Bryan Neck planters such as Arnold, John M. Middleton, Eliza Caroline Clay, and others, were able to begin planting rice crops through the paying of wages to their laborers. It was clear, however, that the defeat of the South and its subsequent military occupation during the years of Reconstruction had drastically altered the perceptions of the former slaves. Thomas Clay Arnold noted:

---

[468] Bryan County deed records, Book J, 151, 154-56; Hoffmann and Hoffmann, *North by South*, 269; Myers, ed., *Children of Pride*, op. cit., 1690.

"I have hired a stranger who is staying at White Hall to hoe around the house and take the straw out of the house and clean it up, but there is no telling whether he will do so or not. No reliance can be placed on the negroes. Col. Sickles [of the local Freedmen's Bureau] told him that he would be held responsible for everything on the place...when we drove up to Cherry Hill no one came out. The Col. Called William & Charles and when they came out they stood by the carriage but neither spoke to me. Col. Sickles told them that the lands had been returned to its owner and if they would not contract for wages or if I did not want them they must leave the place again...we then went to the settlement and Col. Sickles addressed thirty to forty of them telling them that I would be their best friend & advising them to contract, but Batteast spoke up on behalf of the whole plantation and said that they had made up their minds never to work for me again...The Col. left them in great disgust & he says if I can only get enough white labor to start my plantation, that before a month is passed, the negroes will come back to me and beg to be taken back. Not one of them young or old came up to speak to me."[469]

Despite these difficulties, common to most of the former slave-driven rice and cotton plantations of Georgia and South Carolina, the aging Richard Arnold on behalf of his sons in Georgia, invested what remaining capital he possessed in paid labor to get the plantations running again. In February and March 1866, with spring planting imminent, Arnold purchased rice seed for $3,000 and hired sixteen freedmen for the planting, paying them $85.50.[470]

Bryan County was the only district in either South Carolina or Georgia to actually report an increase in rice production in the first federal agricultural census after the war. The local crop in the 1869

---

[469] Thomas C. Arnold to Richard J. Arnold, November 7, 1865, Arnold Papers, op. cit. See the discussion of similar circumstances encountered by Frances Butler Leigh at Butler's Island in McIntosh County, discussed in an earlier chapter of this book.
[470] Richard J. Arnold, Ledger, v. 11, "Expenses Planting, 1866," 528, in Arnold Papers.

reporting year was 2.85 million pounds, almost double the aggregate for the county reported ten years earlier.[471] Almost half the local crop was produced by Thomas Arnold at Cherry Hill and White Hall. He reported 1.073 million pounds of rice produced in 1869, which was likely the highest single-year yield ever recorded for a Bryan County plantation, before or after the war. Arnold was followed by John M. Middleton's crop of 576,000 pounds at Arnold's Point on the Seven Mile Bend, William McGuffin with 300,000 pounds, and Robert Habersham Clay and his sister Eliza Caroline Clay with 215,000 pounds at Richmond. These crops were produced through the hired labor of freedmen whose contracts had been arranged with the planters by the Freemen's Bureau. Rice continued to be an important agricultural staple in Bryan County into the 1880s before a general decline in yields made production no longer profitable, a similar trend in all of the coastal rice-producing counties.

Louisa Gindrat Arnold died in Newport on October 15, 1871; Richard James Arnold died on Providence on March 12, 1873. In the division of the estate, Thomas C. Arnold received White Hall and William Eliot Arnold got Cherry Hill where, in 1874, he built a substantial residence. Due to the mismanagement of Cherry Hill, however, William Arnold accrued heavy debt, resulting in the plantation being sold at public auction to Paul T. Haskell in 1877. Thomas Arnold died in December 1875 and White Hall was purchased at public auction by George L. Appleton, husband of Richard Arnold's granddaughter, Louisa Caroline ("Luly").[472]

---

[471] U.S. 9th Census, Georgia, Bryan County, 1870, agricultural schedules.
[472] Bryan County deed records, Book K, 316, 339.

An epitaph of sorts for three generations of Arnolds in lower Bryan County—who literally had lived in two worlds, North and South—is fittingly provided by Charles and Tess Hoffmann:

"The breaking up of the estate that Arnold had put together over a span of fifty years was completed...[but] the Arnolds did not entirely lose their connection with the land, for Luly Arnold Appleton had returned to her beloved White Hall. But White Hall had been the paradise of her youth. It was no longer a viable rice plantation, and George Appleton turned the Arnold plantation lands into a hunting and fishing preserve for himself and his friends. The negroes no longer labored in the fields. Where Captain Bailey's schooner *Cotton Plant* unloaded bricks to build Richard Arnold's sugar house, and Captain Thompson's sloop *Science* loaded 2,200 bushels of rough rice to be delivered to Habersham and Company in Savannah thirty years earlier, the steam yacht *Gem* could be docked by its owner, George Appleton, for the Arnolds had rebuilt the wharf after the war...On March 28, 1914 the [White Hall] house was deteriorating; the piazza had collapsed, and parts of the house were unsafe to enter. The moss hung heavily from the live oaks: It was all most quiet and peaceful, that last full day in the life of the neglected and decaying old manse. By the next evening White Hall was in flames. The house and two outbuildings burned to the ground beyond repair. Two white adults, strangers to the Arnold family but friends of the Clays, and two black children were the only witnesses to the fire. The white woman wrote that it was better to go in a 'burst of glory rather than slowly and pitifully decay.' But what the two black children felt or said or what message the old manse had for them is unrecorded."[473]

---

[473] Hoffmann and Hoffmann, *North by South*, 270-71. The letter briefly quoted was written March 29, 1914 by Edith Case Skeele, who lived at nearby Myrtle Grove, to Mary Arnold, daughter of Thomas C. Arnold, and is contained among the surviving papers of the Arnold family. George Appleton willed White Hall to Elizabeth Screven Arnold, widow of Thomas Arnold, a commission carried out by his daughter Mary Appleton. Elizabeth Arnold and her daughter, Mary Arnold Nash, sold the White Hall property to Henry Ford in 1925.

Slaves and Religion in Low Country Georgia

Religion and spiritual expression were important to the bondsmen of the Georgia coastal plantations, as it was throughout the agricultural South. Spirituality through its expression in religion and religious practices, symbolized a connection between the slaves' African spiritual heritage with their acquired Christianity in the western hemisphere. The religious music of the slaves, often embodied through their chants and spirituals handed through the generations, was the direct expression of their sorrowful plight and suffering. Black ministers provided the gospel to black congregations in churches established in Charleston and Savannah after the American Revolution. The mission of the ministers often extended to the remote plantations along the coast. They exercised great influence over the slave populations and were, in some cases, given considerable latitude by the white plantation owners. In the rural areas of coastal Georgia it was not uncommon for bondsmen to accompany their masters to Sunday services, worshiping in separate pews. The Darien Presbyterian Church, the Midway Congregational Church and the Bryan Neck Presbyterian Church are examples of this practice in the antebellum period.

At Darien's Presbyterian church, blacks and whites regularly worshiped together before the Civil War. Rev. Francis R. Goulding pastored the church from 1856 until the congregation dispersed in early 1862. In early 1858, Goulding reported, "members are thirty-five whites and fifteen colored, in all fifty," in the church membership.[474] The church apparently experienced growth over the next several years, particularly in the number of slaves attending services as Goulding reported membership as being 120 at the time of its closing because of the war. Half the total, sixty-one, were identified as being black.[475] A "List of Members Reported to Presbytery, April 1857" was compiled by Alexander Mitchel, clerk of session for the Darien church, possibly at the request of Presbytery Moderator Robert Quarterman Mallard at the meeting of Presbytery in Waynesville March 26, 1857. The list included the names of bondsmen, many of whom had the surnames of their owners. Included were slaves owned by such McIntosh County planters and businessmen as Delegal, King, Young, Hopkins, Trezevant, Wylly, Townsend, Robson, Pease, Anderson and McDonald.[476]

Joseph Williams was a free black who worked with Darien's white Presbyterians in the 1850s. He brought a number of local slaves into the church membership, and served as an itinerant preacher at the plantations. "Williams' evangelical work exemplifies the expertise and valuable role of the black preacher in the control of slaves," notes Julia Floyd Smith who researched the religious aspects of slave culture in the antebellum period. "The slaves Sandy, Abram, Sarah and Edmund 'upon profession and examination, together with the recommendation of Joseph Williams, under whose teaching they had sat for the past year,' were received into the church in 1856. On

---

[474] Minutes of Session, Darien Presbyterian Church, Jan. 4, 1858, v. 1 (1821-1869).
[475] Ibid., May 14, 1861.
[476] Ibid., undated. A list of slaves and free blacks entered on the rolls of the church during 1857 and early 1858 is Appendix C in Buddy Sullivan and William G. Haynes, Jr., *History of the First Presbyterian Church of Darien, 1736-1986* (Darien, Ga.: First Presbyterian Church, 1986), 62-63.

another occasion the Presbyterian Session met at Harris Neck where Goulding baptized and extended membership to twenty slaves, one of whom, Lucy, had been expelled because of her 'cold and backsliding state.'" In 1857, the Presbyterian church began a mission branch at Ebenezer between Darien and Sapelo Bridge to minister to the black people of that section of McIntosh County. This effort was also led by Joseph Williams. "Only twice is Ebenezer Church mentioned in the sessional records," notes Presbyterian historian John G. Legare, "and from these minutes we conclude that the Darien church organized the Ebenezer church for the benefit of the colored people of the vicinity. It seems to have had no white members."[477]

There was a revealing item from the Presbyterian sessional record in 1838 relating to the salvation of a black woman, to wit: "Nothing has occurred since the meeting of Session April last to require the members to be called together until now—a state of lamentable supineness has universally prevailed within our bounds—today we have been aroused from our slumbers by the cry of one penitent sinner anxiously seeking the Salvation of her soul." The sessional minutes in 1858 reveal that "the case of Eliza, a servant of Mrs. Jane K. Young of Harris Neck was taken up—It seems she had united with the church there some ten years since, but for six years past had been living in the neglect of Christian duty & in the indulgence of sinful habits—for which she expresses deep sorrow and penitence and for

---

[477] Minutes of Session, Darien Presbyterian Church, Jan. 10, 1857 and December 20, 1857; John G. Legare, "Historical Sketch of Darien Presbyterian Church," 1899, copy in Buddy Sullivan Papers, GHS; Julia Floyd Smith, *Slavery and Rice Culture in Lowcountry Georgia, 1750-1860* (Knoxville: University of Tennessee Press, 1985), 156-57.

the future promises, with God's help, conformity to the laws of the Gospel. We have therefore deemed it best to restore her to the privileges of the church."[478]

It seems clear from the foregoing accounts that antebellum white churches of the coastal region, were generally very rigid in their insistence on conformance to the proper codes of spirituality of the time, and were not inclined to overlook "neglect of Christian duty." The ruling bodies of churches often governed with an unsympathetic and dispassionate approach to affairs in cases such as those of Eliza and Lucy above. "Whites and blacks alike were placed on probation or even excommunicated from the church for misconduct, such as 'back-biting,' excessive drinking, fighting, swearing or immorality."[479]

As noted by Frederick Law Olmsted in observations made during a tour of the South, religion provided the bedrock of "the southern planter's rationalization of slavery as a social institution, whatever the economic reasons."[480] The significance and the meaning attached to this seemingly innocuous statement has been examined, dissected, expounded upon and argued over by American sociologists and religious historians for generations since. In point of fact, many (if not most) of the planters of the South Carolina and Georgia rice-planting districts encouraged their slaves to embrace the Christian faith and consciously adhere to its values.

One of the great paradoxes of this era is seen in Rev. Dr. Charles Colcock Jones (1803-1863) of Maybank plantation, Liberty County.

---

[478] Minutes of Session, Darien Presbyterian Church, Jan. 13, 1838 and May 15, 1856.
[479] Smith, *Slavery and Rice Culture*, 157.
[480] Charles Hoffmann and Tess Hoffmann, *North by South, The Two Worlds of Richard James Arnold* (Athens: University of Georgia Press, 1988), 49.

In 1850, Jones was simultaneously a greatly-respected, practicing Presbyterian clergyman and the possessor of 107 slaves. His position typified the attitudes of many slave-owning Southerners of the time. For antebellum adherents of the Christian faith and its virtues, the conflicting inner struggles evinced through conflating their religion with the bondage of large numbers of their fellow human beings within their midst was not inconsiderable. The ambiguity entailed by the master-slave-Christian doctrine overlap was rarely, if ever, satisfactorily resolved in the conscientiousness of the white plantation classes in the antebellum period, and for a considerable time afterwards.

Clearly, in all good conscience as evoked through his many writings on the subject, Jones strongly advocated the "Religious Instruction of the Negroes" by the tidewater planter class as an essential ingredient in providing for the well-being of the bondsmen, as well as being instrumental in fostering the moral loyalty of the slaves to their masters.[481]

The social order of the plantation and the constantly reinforced concept of slave-to-master subservience was an important element in the Christian training of the bondsmen. The church was the primary vehicle for its implementation. The idea that the slave should be blindly subservient to the plantation master was the foundation for the religious instruction of the bondsmen, a "reflection of the cosmic order of the universe."[482] The oft-repeated theme preached to the

---

[481] Charles C. Jones, *The Religious Instruction of the Negroes in the United States* (Savannah, Ga., 1842), GHS; Charles C. Jones, "The Religious Instruction of the Negroes: A Sermon Delivered Before Associations of Planters in Liberty and McIntosh Counties," Princeton, N.J., 1832, 6-17.

[482] Hoffmann and Hoffmann, *North by South*, 49.

slaves was that absolute obedience to the master was tantamount to obedience by the Christian to God, as all men are God's servants.

In the early 1830s several northern McIntosh County planters were active in a new movement to bring religious instruction to the enslaved people of the local plantations. In his important tract, *The Religious Instruction of the Negroes*, C.C. Jones observed:

"In the winter of 1830 and the spring of 1831, two Associations of planters were formed in Georgia for the special object of affording religious instruction to the Negroes, by their own efforts and by missionaries employed for the purpose. The first was formed by the Rev. Joseph Clay Stiles in McIntosh county, embracing the neighborhood of Harris' Neck, which continued in operation for some time, until by the withdrawment of Mr. Stiles' labors from the neighborhood and the loss of some of the inhabitants by death and removals it ceased. The second was formed in Liberty county by the Midway Congregational church, and the Baptist church under their respective pastors, the Rev. Robert Quarterman and the Rev. Samuel Spry Law."

In March 1831, twenty-nine planters from Liberty County and several from the South Newport River region of McIntosh gathered in Riceborough, the county seat of Liberty, for the organization of "The Liberty County Association for Religious Instruction of the Negroes." In his sermon before the gathering Jones noted, "We are bound to give the Negroes the Gospel. Should we continue to neglect them, our neglect might not only shut their souls out of heaven, but our own. The great object for which we would communicate religious instruction to them slaves is that their souls may be saved. To this all other objects should be subordinate." In the 1830s and 1840s Jones accomplished considerable missionary work among the slaves in the tidewater region.

Jones was known as the "Apostle of the Blacks" for his advocacy of the promulgation of Christianity among the plantation slaves. Jones, Goulding, John Winn, and other antebellum white Presbyterian clergymen, found themselves enmeshed in a crisis of conscience, a moral dilemma, over the issue. The ambivalence so obviously manifested over slavery and religion by Jones and his contemporaries may have been at least partially assuaged by their retention of ownership of their slaves—for obvious reasons of economy, but in some cases, particularly in that of Jones, to devote their spiritual energy toward the religious instruction of not only their own slaves, but those of their neighbors as well. Jones encouraged local slave owners, such as his close friend, Thomas Savage Clay of Bryan County, his uncle, William Maxwell of Liberty County, and others, to strive for the well-being and comfort of their bondsmen. This approach was embraced by the majority of coastal slave owners: "It was in their own enlightened self-interest to improve the moral and social condition of their slaves."[483]

Clay embraced the theories and concepts of Jones, and made an important statement regarding the religious development of slaves when he published a layman's viewpoint for the Georgia Presbytery in 1833 in which he expressed his belief that religious instruction would provide a stabilizing factor in the lives and discipline of the slaves, "doing more for the good order and the quiet of the country than any civil or military patrol we have ever had." Slavery was sanctioned by God, Clay wrote, and "obedience by the slave was to a master who was God's temporal representative on earth."[484]

---

[483] Ibid. See also Robert Manson Myers, ed., *The Children of Pride* (New Haven: Yale University Press, 1972), 1621.
[484] Thomas S. Clay, "Detail of a Plan for the Moral Improvement of Negroes on Plantations," presented before the Georgia Presbytery (1833), 7, 10.

Land Use & Landscape: Harris Neck

The first Harris Neck land claimants petitioned for their tracts in the late 1740s. One of the earliest grantees at Harris Neck was Stephen Dickinson who claimed 200 acres on the lower end of the Neck in 1757. However, evidence points to Dickinson possessing a generally recognized claim, if not title, to land in this area before 1750, as grants to the first two major landholders in that year identify those tracts as being located on "Dickerson's Neck" near "Sappola Sound." In the granting process, years could pass between the time a person entered his initial petition and the time he actually received title to the land. Harris Neck was known as Dickinson's Neck until shortly after 1770.

One of the early grantees at the upper end of Dickinson's Neck was Daniel Demetre (d.1758), who in the early 1750s, acquired sections of land there totaling more than 1,200 acres. The Colonial Records of the State of Georgia identify Demetre as a public servant who had been in the colony since its inception. Demetre was a mariner, being coxswain of the scout boat in the service of Frederica. Demetre also filed claims for acreage on Creighton Island. In 1750, Demetre was granted 500 acres on Dickenson's Neck, the Bethany tract, which was inherited by his stepson, William Thomas Harris in 1758. Demetre was subsequently awarded an additional 250 acres that were added to Bethany making it a 750-acre tract by 1758. In 1750, John Rutledge was granted fifty acres near Bethany, a tract applied for and received by Ann Harris in the name of her son, William Thomas Harris, the same year.[485]

---

[485] "Meeting of the President and Assistants in Council for the Colony of Georgia," November 29, 1749," in Allen D. Candler, ed., *Colonial Records of the State of Georgia* (Atlanta: 1906), 6:298-99; Pat Bryant, comp., *English Crown Grants in St. Andrew Parish, 1755-1775* (Atlanta: Surveyor General

William Harris (ca. 1718-1737) came to Savannah from England in 1734 or 1735. A young clerk, Harris married Ann Cassell (ca. 1719-1758) in Savannah in 1736 or 1737. Harris died of unknown causes in Savannah in 1737. The young couple had a son, William Thomas Harris (1738-1786), born after his father's death. While still living in Savannah with her mother, Anna Cassells Coles Salter and her third husband, Thomas Salter, Harris' widow Ann was awarded a town lot in Frederica by James Oglethorpe in December 1742. She moved there with her son, William Thomas Harris, and her widowed mother, Anna Salter. In April 1752, Ann Harris married Daniel Demetre, also of Frederica. Ann Harris Demetre was apparently quite resourceful, easily the most enterprising woman at Frederica, as she ran a store in the town, and with her husband Daniel Demetre, operated a freight boat between Savannah and St. Simons, and engaged in the timber business for construction at Frederica. In 1753, after the death of Ann's mother, the Demetres removed to Savannah. Daniel and Ann Harris Demetre both died in 1758.

On December 8, 1752, Ann Demetre petitioned for a grant of 500 acres at the upper end of Dickenson's Neck "adjoining land of Daniel Demetre" in the name of her son, William Thomas Harris, still a minor at the time, since women were not allowed to petition for land in their name. A grant of 350 acres was awarded the same month, a tract that went to William Thomas Harris upon the deaths of his mother and step-father in 1758. He acquired an additional 200 acres in his own right in 1758. At the time of his death in 1758, Daniel Demetre had acquired about 1,200 acres on Dickinson's Neck, including the Bethany tract. His stepson, William T. Harris, inherited the 750-acre Bethany tract from Demetre in 1758. Ann Demetre's will, dated

---

Department, GDAH, 1972), 23; Bessie Mary Lewis Papers, Collection 2138, GHS.

February 20, 1755, noted that Bethany had become a joint property of she and Daniel Demetre, and "was to go to the longest lived of us" then to William Thomas Harris. Demetre's will, dated July 12, 1758, identified William Thomas Harris's residence as Bethany, although it is unclear whether the latter's mother and stepfather ever lived at Bethany themselves. When William T. Harris took residence at Bethany as a young man in ca. 1757 or 1758 (possibly earlier) he may have been the first permanent white resident of Harris Neck. In 1758, several slaves lived and worked at Bethany, which may then have been used primarily as livestock range. The inter-relationship of the Harris and Demetre families is clarified in the following extract from Colonial Records documenting an estate settlement of January 5, 1759, an agreement between James Habersham and Francis Harris (brother of the deceased first William Harris), both of Savannah, and William Thomas Harris, "planter of Bethany Plantation, Parish of Saint Andrew." The agreement stated:

"James Habersham and Francis Harris, executors of the will of Daniel Demetre, Marriner, deceased, who intermarried with Ann Harris, Widow, since deceased, who was the widow of William Harris and daughter of [William] Cassell and Anna Cassell, afterwards Anna Salter, also deceased,' agree to convey specified property to William Thomas Harris in satisfaction of the latter's demands against Demetre's estate. In his will, dated July 12, 1758, Demetre bequeathed to William Thomas Harris a 750-acre plantation called Bethany, 'on Dickinson's Neck in the district of Sapala and Newport' with all appurtenances, livestock, and plantation tools and the following slaves: Nicholas, Hagar, Tony, Prince, Belinda, Dinah, James and Silvia, and their issue. By virtue of the will, dated December 19, 1753, of his now-deceased grandmother, Anna Salter, William Thomas Harris lays claim to the aforementioned slaves and their issue and the profit that has accrued by their labor, sundry household goods, and two young valuable Negro men slaves whom Demetre was obliged to buy for Harris in accordance with Anna Salter's will. To prevent suits against Demetre's estate, Habersham and Francis Harris pay William Thomas Harris 20 pounds lawful money of Great Britain and sell to Harris for 10 shillings lawful money of Great Britain ten Negro slaves and the household goods, furniture, and plate at Bethany

Plantation."[486]

William Thomas Harris (1737-1786) married Mary Landree (1738-1817), had several children, and cultivated crops at Bethany until shortly after the Revolution, in which he had served the continental cause as an officer; after the war, Harris was the first speaker of the Georgia general assembly. He died at Bethany in 1786 at the age of forty-eight. William and Mary Harris had three sons, William Thomas Harris, Jr. (1759-1818), James Harris (1760-1804), and John Harris, Sr. (ca. 1770-1839), all who later lived on family lands at Harris Neck.[487]

Following is a summary of the most relevant colonial grants in the South Newport River-Harris Neck region:

Button Gwinnett, 10,000 acres on the east side of the White Chimney River, 1767; Donald Mackintosh, 200 acres on the present site of South Newport near the headwaters of the South Newport River; Sir Patrick Houstoun's Marengo plantation, near the South Newport River west of Harris Neck; Edward Baker's Lebanon plantation, 100 acres west of Harris Neck on the South Newport River, 1773; John Williams, 500 acres on the Bruro River east of Sutherland's Bluff and south of present-day Shellman Bluff, 1771; Henry Calwell, 500 acres on the lower end of Dickenson's Neck, 1753; William Thomas Harris, 350 acres on upper end of Dickenson's Neck, 1752 (with his mother, Ann Harris, as guardian); David Delegal, 300 acres on Dickinson's Neck, fronting on the Julianton River, 1771; John Todd, Sr. and John Todd, Jr., lands west of the upper end of Dickenson's Neck on the South Newport River (Todd's Bluff), 1754; John McDonald, Belvedere Island west of the upper end of Harris Neck on the South Newport River, 1758 (tract subsequently acquired by James Gignilliat); James Gignilliat, Contentment

---

[486] "Marriage Settlement of Ann Harris & Daniel Demetrie," Conveyance Book I (1751-1761), 40-41, GDAH; "Will of Ann Harris Demetrie: Declaration of Uses," Bonds, Bills of Sale. Deeds of Gifts, Powers of Attorney, Book I, 1755-1762, 199-203, GDAH; Bryant, comp., *English Crown Grants in St. Andrew Parish.*
[487] See Isabel Thorpe Mealing, comp., Charles Thorpe of Georgia *and His Descendants, The Harris Family* (Darien, Ga., privately printed, 1993), 107-153, for deeds, wills and other genealogical material on the colonial Harris family.

Bluff near present-day Shellman Bluff.[488]

The earliest determined reference to "Harris Neck" supplanting the name of Dickinson's Neck, appears in the Savannah Georgia Gazette of October 11, 1775. The pre-Revolutionary plantation activities that began along the South Newport River were largely the cultivation of indigo and small quantities of rice. Livestock activities were actively pursued by most of the early settlers. The system of open ranges eliminated the need for extensive fencing, but there is evidence that some enclosure did occur. In 1775, two Harris Neck landowners, David and Philip Delegal, advertised in the Georgia Gazette referenced above that since "evil disposed persons" were engaged in poaching cattle and hogs, and in illegal timber cutting on the Neck, they had found it necessary to post their "inclosures" against trespassers.[489] Several plantations, including Bethany and the Delegals' Delta plantation, were active on Harris Neck in the years before and after the Revolution before the introduction of sea island cotton led to wider plantation development in the 1790s. There is evidence of dwellings for owners, overseers, and slaves, along with the usual assortment of mill houses, barns, poultry sheds, kitchens and wash houses, all needed for the operation of even the smaller plantations.

Francis Levett & Julianton Plantation

The land encompassing the lower half of Harris Neck was originally awarded as Crown grants to Roderick McIntosh and Henry Calwell. About 1754, Calwell was granted 500 acres on the southernmost end of the Neck, a claim not registered until 1763 after Calwell had died.

---

[488] Extracted from Bryant, comp., *English Crown Grants in St. Andrew Parish*.
[489] Georgia Gazette, October 11, 1775.

Calwell's tract was bounded on the north by a 500-acre grant issued to Roderick McIntosh.

Based on post-Revolutionary Loyalist documents Francis Levett, Sr. apparently owned property in Georgia, presumably at Harris Neck, prior to his establishment in British East Florida in 1769. It is known that Levett, Sr. was in London in 1767. On May 8, 1767, Levett, Sr. was granted 10,000 acres on the east side of the St. Johns River, land which became his Julianton plantation in East Florida. This tract, near the present-day town of Mandarin, Florida, was bounded on one side by a 1,250-acre grant claimed by Alexander Creighton.[490] In 1778 Creighton acquired Demetre's Island, later Creighton Island, in St. Andrew Parish.

Removing to East Florida in 1769, Francis Levett, Sr. served on the British Council from 1771-73, also being appointed an assistant judge, possibly because of familial ties with his brother-in-law, the governor of East Florida, Patrick Tonyn. Levett died in late 1774 or early 1775 following his resignation from the British Council amid allegations of fraudulent practices relating to landlord rents and the sale of slaves; he is not listed in subsequent East Florida records.

London-born Francis Levett, Jr. (1753-1802) assumed the management of his father's plantation at the age of twenty-one and was appointed one of nineteen members of the East Florida House of Assembly in March 1781 and served a period as a provost marshal.[491] While in East Florida, Levett married Charlotte Box, daughter of a Loyalist Savannah attorney. She had inherited her

---

[490] Mary B. Graff, *Mandarin on the St. Johns* (Gainesville: University of Florida Press, 1963), 10.
[491] Wilbur Henry Siebert, *Loyalists in East Florida, 1774 to 1785* (Deland, FL: Florida State Historical Society, 1929), v. 2, 228.

father's considerable Florida property, making her independently wealthy. Most British citizens, including some 13,000 Loyalist refugees who migrated from South Carolina and Georgia during the Revolution, left East Florida for the Bahamas, Jamaica, or England from 1783-85 during the transition of the province back to Spanish authority as stipulated in the Treaty of Paris.

In 1785, Levett abandoned the St. John's River plantation and left St. Augustine for the Bahamas with 100 slaves, house frames, household silver and other belongings, briefly attempting to produce cotton there while making Loyalist claims on his late father's estate.[492] It would appear that sometime in 1786 Levett and his family established themselves at Julianton on the lower end of Harris Neck in Liberty County (McIntosh not becoming a separate county from Liberty until December 1793). It is unclear whether this was newly-purchased land by Levett, possibly on counsel from his late father's friend, Henry Laurens, or whether it had been obtained by his father before the Revolution, and retained through Levett's Loyalist claims on his father's estate. If the latter was the case, it was fortunate for Levett that he was able to retain the Harris Neck land.

In 1787 Francis Levett, Jr. and his family thus established themselves on the lower end of Harris Neck, Liberty County, Georgia (McIntosh after 1793), on the plantation he called Julianton, after his mother, Juliana Levett, who had been with him in East Florida. "Julianton" has been spelled several ways over the years of its existence. *Julianton* is the name given by Francis Levett, a spelling supported by Levett himself in his will and the fact that it was also the name of his father's Florida

---

[492] Ibid., 228-37.

plantation. Another nineteenth century spelling, incorrect, is Julington. The spelling which appears on many maps, also incorrect, is Julienton. The latter spelling is noted on the 1859 U.S. Coast Survey chart for Sapelo Sound and subsequent editions of the chart until the early twentieth century.

One of the earliest documented instances regarding Francis Levett, Jr.'s activities in Georgia occurred in a Savannah newspaper in the summer of 1790. Levett is listed as being among those "Defaulters in the several Districts within the County of Chatham who have made no return to the Taxable Property for the Year of our Lord 1790."[493] Two years later, the Grand Jury Presentments for Liberty County makes reference to Levett and Julianton in a development noted earlier in this chapter regarding the Harris Neck road:

"We recommend on a petition from a number of inhabitants praying that a road be cut from the south point of Harris Neck [Julianton], through Eagle's Neck, up to South Newport river, intersecting the main road near South Newport bridge, and that John Bradford, David Delegal, Francis Levett, William Thomas Harris and William Myddleton be appointed commissioners for the same."[494]

Several years later Levett found himself in the midst of a debate waged through the Savannah press as to which Georgia planters introduced sea island cotton to the region. In the fall of 1799, an anonymous "Inhabitant of Chatham County" averred in a letter to the *Columbian Museum and Savannah Advertiser*:

---

[493] *Georgia Gazette*, August 20, 1790.
[494] Ibid., August 30, 1792. Harris Neck and the South Newport River district were a part of Liberty County until December 1793 when the Georgia legislature created McIntosh County from Liberty.

"[Sea island cotton] gave the [early planters] at once a supply of that article from their own territory, and completely foiled the making of indigo in the United States; but thanks to our climate, tho' the planters were compelled to turn their attention to something else, they recollected that cotton could be cultivated on lands that produced indigo, and included their thoughts to that article, and to this most were encouraged by a crop of black seed cotton from seed procured for Major Barnard on Wilmington Island which was raised on the Island of Skidaway, 10,000 lbs. of which crop was shipped to England in the spring of 1791 by Messrs. Johnston and Robertson on account of Francis Levett, Esq. which established the character of Georgia sea island cotton; being the first shipment of any consequence; and to him [Levett] the state is indebted for having it entered as an article of commerce in the British prices current."[495]

Several weeks later, another Chatham County planter, Nicholas Turnbull, made a rather scathing retort with a letter to the *Georgia Gazette*. Turnbull took issue with Levett receiving so much of the credit for the early effort to grow cotton on the Georgia coast. He said, among other things, that John Earle planted sea island cotton on Skidaway Island in 1767, and that he, Turnbull, successfully grew cotton on Whitemarsh Island in 1787 with a shipment to England the same year. Turnbull noted:

"I conceive Mr. Levett is not entitled to any merit, as previous to that time the quantity was made in this state and shipped by the Savannah merchants, and the character firmly established; besides, I do not suppose the trouble was great to Mr. Levett, or cost him anything, and which any one could have done as well as himself...The state is not the least indebted to Mr. Levett for the author's supposed extraordinary shipments or establishment of the staple; I believe the work was completed before Mr. Levett came to the state."[496]

---

[495] *Columbian Museum and Savannah Advertiser*, October 15, 1799..
[496] *Georgia Gazette*, November 28, 1799.

Nicholas Turnbull (1756-1824) is an interesting character in the antebellum tidewater Georgia story. Born at Smyrna in the Levant, he was the son of Andrew Turnbull who founded the colony of New Smyrna on the East Florida coast in 1768. Andrew Turnbull recruited Greeks, Italians and other Mediterranean peoples to establish the colony in Florida. With imported slaves, these colonists grew indigo, sugar cane and other staples in fields cleared from the swamps. The New Smyrna colony was not a success, lasting less than ten years. It failed primarily because of lack of adequate food supplies, a heavy rate of attrition caused by disease spread by swarming mosquitoes and lack of cooperation between the New Smyrna officials and the colonial authorities at St. Augustine. By 1777, the colony had practically ceased to exist.[497] After the Revolution Nicholas Turnbull moved from Florida to Savannah where he became a planter at Skidaway and Whitemarsh islands. As early as 1787 Turnbull planted forty acres of sea island cotton on Whitemarsh Island in Chatham County.[498] By 1792, Turnbull had acquired the Deptford Hill plantation on the Savannah River below the city. Black-seed cotton, according to the Savannah newspaper articles of 1799, was being cultivated on the Chatham islands of Skidaway, Wilmington and Whitemarsh in the late 1780s and early 1790s, about the same time that Francis Levett grew his first cotton at Julianton plantation—as did other Georgia planters, i.e. Richard Leake on Jekyll Island and James Spalding on St. Simons. In an 1828 article on the history of sea island cotton in Georgia, Thomas

---

[497] Carita Doggett Corse, *Dr. Andrew Turnbull and the New Smyrna Colony of Florida*, (Jacksonville, Fla.: Drew Press, 1919).
[498] Savannah Writers Project, *Savannah River Plantations*, Mary Granger, ed., (Savannah, Ga.: Georgia Historical Society, 1947), 33.

Spalding alludes to Turnbull and early cotton cultivation at Skidaway Island in Chatham County. In a letter to Whitemarsh B. Seabrook of Edisto Island, South Carolina in 1844, Spalding disputes Levett's claim to be the first to grow sea island cotton in Georgia.

Levett was certainly among the first to cultivate sea island cotton in the Georgia-South Carolina lowcountry. Julianton plantation was, from all accounts, one of the most efficient on the coast, and Levett was a large slave owner. Levett's own correspondence indicates that he grew cotton at Julianton as early as 1787. Siebert notes that Levett "received some Pernambuco cottonseed, which he cultivated with a success, he declared in 1789, beyond his 'most sanguine expectations.' It has been said that he was probably the first to grow the sea island cotton in the South."[499] It is well documented that others also cultivated sea island cotton in 1786-87, including James Spalding and Richard Leake. Lewis Cecil Gray composed an account of the controversy over the claims to being the first in *History of Agriculture in the Southern United States*, noting:

> "Various accounts attribute the beginnings of the sea-island cotton industry to the year 1786-87, but there has been considerable controversy as to what persons deserve the credit. Levett, a Tory rice planter in Georgia, fled to the Bahamas, but returned to Georgia. In 1786 he received from Patrick Walsh, a seed collector then travelling in South America, three large bags of cotton seed from Pernambuco. Apparently, the value of the gift was not appreciated, for Levett, finding need for the sacks in gathering provisions, shook the seeds out on the dunghill. They sprouted, and in the spring a multitude of plants covered the place. These he transplanted the next year and continued their cultivation subsequently. This claim was also set forth in a letter written by Walsh in 1805 to John Couper of St. Simons Island. William W. Parrott, a merchant of Massachusetts, obtained the story in 1807 from Levett's widow. Levett's claim, at least that he was the first to grow the crop on a large scale for

---

[499] Siebert, *Loyalists in East Florida*, 328.

export i.e. the 1791 shipment of 10,000 pounds to England from the crop raised on Skidaway Island was further supported by the writer who signed himself 'an Inhabitant of Chatham county'. Levett's claim was vigorously disputed by Thomas Spalding who claimed that "in the winter of '86 several persons on the Georgia coast, including Alexander Bisset, Governor Tattnall and Mr. James Spalding, received parcels of cotton seed from friends in the Bahamas. This seed had been sent thither by the Board of Trade from Anguilla as a means of aiding Loyalist refugees. Spalding asserted that Levett did not receive the Pernambuco seed until 1794 or 1795, and that although the Pernambuco cotton bore well and was easily separated from the seed, it was inferior to the Bahama variety and was soon displaced by the latter. Spalding's account has been accepted by many writers; but in addition to its conflict with the Levett claim there are other conflicting claims made by Richard Leake and by Nicholas Turnbull. These conflicting statements appear to suggest that in the same year a number of persons on the Georgia coast received samples of sea-island cotton from the Bahamas and that this circumstance was connected with the settlement of Georgia and South Carolina Loyalist refugees in those islands. There was also a connection between the starting of the new industry and earlier experiments in the New Smyrna colony."[500]

A 1796 survey map by John McKinnon contains revealing details about Julianton plantation. The survey delineates "Julianton River," salt marsh on the west side of the plantation, salt marsh on the east, "David Delegal's Land" to the north (Delta plantation), extensive cotton fields, and provision crops astride the marsh on both sides of the plantation; also, a number of buildings on the lower end of the plantation, including a main house, several outbuildings, and a long single row of slave dwellings. The survey noted that the "Plantation called Julianton, situate on Harris Neck in McIntosh County, State

---

[500] Lewis Cecil Gray, *History of Agriculture in the Southern United States to 1860* (Washington, D.C.: Carnegie Institution, 1933), 730-31. Spalding's comments, Thomas Spalding to Whitemarsh B. Seabrook, January 20, 1844, *Southern Agriculturist*, new series IV, 107.

McKinnon sketch of Francis Levett's Julianton plantation, 1796.

of Georgia [contains] thirteen hundred and sixty-acres, exclusive of marsh."[501]

McKinnon also rendered a drawing of the plantation to supplement his survey.[502] The house is shown in detail, appearing to be an impressive two-story frame structure with dormer windows on an upper third level. Based on archaeological investigations by Larry Babits of Armstrong State College from 1983-85, the Julianton house was in reality not nearly as large as it appears to be depicted by McKinnon. It was about sixteen feet by thirty-six feet, with two stories. McKinnon depicts a tidal slough running near the house flowing to its convergence with the main river. Also shown are several dependencies near the main house, including a barn, a dock, and a row of twenty-three slave dwellings east of the Levett house.

The painting A *Slave Wedding*, rendered in the late eighteenth century might well represent a scene from Julianton plantation. The colors are similar to those used by McKinnon in his sketch of the plantation house and dwellings. The Julianton sketch depicts the layout of the buildings much as they are represented in A *Slave*

---

[501] Survey of March 25, 1796 by John McKinnon, Surveyor, Chatham County, Superior Court Records, Chatham County, Savannah.
[502] John McKinnon, "A South View of Julianton Plantation in Georgia, the Property of Francis Levett, Esq.," 1796.

Wedding. The main house and the slave houses shown in the background of *A Slave Wedding* are identical to those shown in McKinnon's drawing. It is thus possible that McKinnon rendered the wedding scene based on his observations while surveying Julianton for Levett, for the buildings are arranged in the same manner in both the drawing and in the wedding painting depicting the slave dancers. Babits is convinced McKinnon did this painting, which artistically dates to the late eighteenth century.[503] There were about 200 slaves on Julianton plantation in 1796—a sizeable aggregation by any standard.

The 1859 U.S. Coast Survey chart of Sapelo Sound (fig. 20) delineates Julianton, and depicts buildings and a row of slave dwellings aligned almost exactly as those shown in the McKinnon sketch of more than a half century earlier. William Bennett, Levett's grandson who came from England to assume management of the plantation in the mid-1840s, may have added some of the buildings shown on the 1859 chart. Foundation remains show the buildings to have been about sixteen by twenty feet in size. Levett's dock is not shown on the 1859 map, although a few traces of it, or a subsequent dock built on the same site, may be seen at low tide in the Julianton River. Archaeological field work uncovered buttons of all types on the grounds from the late eighteenth and early nineteenth centuries, including coat buttons and those from knee breeches. Foundations of some type of tabby were found on the site, including in the area of the slave dwellings. Levett might have employed some tabby in his

---

[503] Conversation by the author with Larry Babits, Savannah, Ga., June 14, 1994.

buildings as he would have been familiar with its use during his years in East Florida.

Two notices in the *Columbian Museum* allude to Levett in 1802, the year of his death:

"NOTICE—All persons to whom the estate of Francis Levett, Esq., late of Julianton, is indebted are requested to furnish their accounts, or statement of their demands, duly attested...." and, "Twenty Dollars Reward—Will be paid apprehending a young negro man named Damon, the property of the estate of Francis Levett, Esq., dec.—he is about 22 years of age, 5 feet 1 to 3 inches, rather yellow cast, round face, speaks low and thick, downcast look, had on a pair of white negro cloth trousers, red shirt and blue jacket. The above reward will be paid by the Executors for lodging him in gaol or delivering him at Julianton, in M'Intosh county, and all reasonable expenses paid."[504]

The circumstances of Levett's death on September 13, 1802 at an early age, forty-eight, are not known, although it was by some unfortunate illness, according to his obituary in the *Columbian Museum and Savannah Advertiser*, which noted: "Died, after a lingering illness, on the 13th instant, at Julianton, McIntosh County, Francis Levett, Esq. This gentleman, after the peace in 1783, removed from East Florida to this state, pursued the culture of cotton. His family is now in England. His remains were interred by his express directions at Julianton." Levett's grave is one of two at Julianton, the other being that of his son, John Levett, who died in 1808 at the age of twenty-one. There was likely a slave burial ground at Julianton, as was typical for most of the coastal plantations, but no marked graves remain.

---

[504] *Columbian Museum and Savannah Advertiser*, December 7, 1802 and April 15, 1803.

In December 1809, Levett's widow, Charlotte Levett, married William Stephens of Savannah. Stephens (1752-1819) was the grandson and namesake of the first president of the Georgia colony under the Trustees. Stephens was a federal judge in Savannah for the last sixteen years of his life. In *The Letters of Robert Mackay to His Wife* there is an intriguing snippet from a letter by Robert Mackay dated January 27, 1810: "Judge Stephens & Mrs. Levett are actually married—cursed fools—I have no other Georgia news."[505] Unfortunately, this odd remark goes unexplained by both Mackay, and the editor of his letters, Walter C. Hartridge.

After Levett's death, management of Julianton fell largely upon his widow with likely involvement from her second husband. Two children of Francis and Charlotte Levett had connections to the plantation, albeit peripherally. John Levett was born in 1787, possibly at Julianton soon after his parents arrived there from East Florida. Apparently the younger Levett was sent to England for his education for he died of unknown causes at Julianton in October 1808 within months of his return from London. In 1819, William Stephens died at the age of sixty-seven, leaving Charlotte Levett Stephens a widow for the second time. The same year, Charlotte Stephens, Christina Levett (widow of John Levett), and Rev. Thomas Bennett and his wife Charlotte Julia (Levett) Bennett, equally divided Julianton's 195 slaves. The daughter of Francis and Charlotte Levett, Charlotte Julia, was born in 1783. She married Thomas Bennett (d. 1824) in England. The last of the Bennett's six children was William Holtham Bennett, born in January 1825 after his father's death.

---

[505] Walter C. Hartridge, ed., *The Letters of Robert Mackay to His Wife* (Athens: University of Georgia Press, 1949), 205.

William H. Bennett came to Georgia from England in 1846 to manage Julianton for his family; he divided his residence between Julianton and Savannah where he married Jane S. McDonald in 1853. The 1860 Chatham County census lists Bennett's occupation as "Overseer", his age as twenty-five, and his place of birth as Kent, England. In 1858, a son, William, Jr., was born to the Bennetts in Savannah. Bennett remained in Savannah during the Civil War and was affiliated in various capacities with the British consulate in that city. He was the Acting British Consul at Savannah in 1868-69, with records on file of several instances of his intercession on behalf of British shipping interests.[506]

The 1837 McIntosh County tax digest lists Charlotte Stephens as being taxed on ninety slaves and 1,150 acres of land at Julianton plantation. The 1840 census lists Charlotte Stephens in the 22nd G.M. District of McIntosh County, although her primary home was in England at this later period in her life. Charlotte Levett Stephens died in November 1841 at the age of seventy-five. She is buried at Canterbury Cathedral. The 1850 census reveals that William H. Bennett held eighty-five slaves working 800 acres of "improved" land at Julianton. The 1859 Coast Survey chart, *Sapelo Sound, Georgia* shows Julianton plantation on the lower end of Harris Neck as being under full cultivation in cotton and farm staples. A number of dwellings and outbuildings are also indicated on the chart at the site of Julianton.

In 1866, W.H. Bennett sold Julianton plantation to Edward W. Delegal of neighboring Delta plantation to Julianton's north, giving Delegal possession of a sizeable amount of acreage comprising the lower half of Harris Neck. Julianton's sale marked the end of nearly a century of ownership of that tract

---

[506] Papers of the British Consulate in Savannah, Keith Read Collection, Collection 648, GHS.

by Francis Levett and his descendants. The deed of sale was dated July 5, 1866 in Chatham County, being

"Between William H. Bennett of Chatham County and Edward W. Delegal of McIntosh County. Witnesseth that the said William H. Bennett, for the sum of two thousand dollars… hath granted, sold and conveyed unto the said Edward W. Delegal those two tracts or parcels of land lying and being on Harris Neck and Eagle Neck in McIntosh County, [the first] known as Julianton plantation bounded on the north by lands of said Delegal and on the east, west and south by the eastern branch of Sapelo river [Julianton River], containing 1,160 acres more or less, originally granted to Francis Levett; the other tract on Eagle Neck bounded north by Mrs. Harris' Belvedere Plantation and east, west and south by lands of William J. King and the estate of Jonathan Thomas."[507]

An 1894 indenture documents the Delegal family's connection with the Julianton and Delta tracts. This agreement was between

"Edward H. Delegal of the first part and Thomas W. Delegal as trustee of Eleanor M. Delegal, wife of the said Edward H. Delegal…said Edward Delegal in consideration of the natural love and affection he has for his wife and his children does hereby grant and convey to Thomas W. Delegal, trustee all of a certain interest in a tract known as Julington plantation containing 1,500 acres bounded on its North by Delta plantation, on the East, South and West by eastern branch of Sapelo River. Also a certain interest in that plantation known as the Delta plantation containing 1,000 acres, bounded on the North by lands of John W. Muller, South by Julington plantation, on the East and West by salt marsh and eastern branch of Sapelo River."[508]

An 1899 indenture recorded the sale by the Delegal family, for "seven thousand dollars cash", of the Julian-ton tract of 1,355 acres to Irvin Davis of McIntosh County. Five years later, Julianton was sold from the Estate of Irvin Davis to Georgianna Davis, widow of Irvin Davis, and Young Davis "as the highest and best bidder" at public auction for $6,500. In 1908, the tract was

---

[507] Deed Book C (1866, re-recorded 1886), 615-16, RMCG.
[508] Deed Book F (1894), 234-35, RMCG.

sold by the Davis family to L.R Youmans of Emanuel County, Georgia.[509] Irvin Davis, and his heirs, including his widow, Georgianna Davis, had also acquired the "Muller Place" tract just north and east of Delta in the early 1890s, that being the former William J. King plantation later held by his son-in-law, John Muller. A "Plat of Julienton Plantation Surveyed for E.M. Thorpe, Esq., Located in Harris Neck, McIntosh County, Ga." surveyed in March 1917 by Ravenel Gignilliat, Civil Engineer, of Savannah, reported an aggregate of 3,345 acres within the boundaries of Julianton, 1,295 acres of that figure being high land. The survey plat delineates Julianton on the southern end of Harris Neck with the Julianton River flowing south and west of the tract and Little Mud River on the east. On the southeast tip of Julianton's marshes, the survey delineated scattered ballast deposits abutting the Julianton River. This was a 250-acre tract amid the marsh, separated from the Julianton upland by Shell Creek and "The Swash" as indicated on Gignilliat's survey.[510] This area was formerly owned by the Hilton and Dodge Lumber Company and was used by that firm as a loading ground for ships taking on lumber in Sapelo Sound in the 1890s. On May 26, 1917, L.R Youmans sold the Julianton tract to Elisha M. Thorpe of McIntosh County.

Upper Harris Neck Plantations

North of Julianton was Delta plantation, a 1771 Crown grant to David Delegal (ca. 1745-1790) who lived and planted there with his wife Abigail (Green) Delegal before and after the Revolution. A son, Edward Delegal (1787-1823), was born at Harris Neck, and managed Delta until his death at the age of thirty-six in 1823. In 1809, Edward Delegal married his first cousin,

---

[509] Deed Book G (1899), 432; Book H (1904), 474; Book I (1908), 509, RMCG.
[510] Deed Book O (1917), 319-21; Plat Cabinet A (1917), slide 119, RMCG.

Jane Delegal (1777-1857), she being the daughter of Philip and Sarah Delegal. Philip Delegal (d. 1781), brother of David Delegal, planted cotton at Skidaway Island and at other Savannah-area properties before and after the Revolution. Three sons, Edward Wentworth Delegal (1811-1876), Thomas Philip Delegal (1814-1879) and Henry H. Delegal (1816-1863), were born to Edward and Jane Delegal at Delta plantation.

The McIntosh County tax digest of 1825, two years after the death of Edward Delegal, shows Thomas E. Delegal, possibly a brother of Jane Delegal who was managing the estate after the death of Edward, being taxed on fifty slaves and 800 acres of upland at Delta plantation. The 1850 McIntosh County census lists Edward W. Delegal, then age thirty-nine, and his mother, Jane Delegal, age seventy-two, as residents of Delta. The agricultural census that year shows Delegal in possession of sixty-five slaves working 700 acres of improved land at Delta. The Delegal holdings at Harris Neck had expanded by the Civil War. The 1862 county tax digest shows a return by E.W. Delegal on thirty-three slaves and 2,070 acres of property on which he produced twenty bales of cotton and 800 bushels of corn according to the 1860 agricultural census. In 1866, as noted, Delegal acquired Julianton plantation, contiguous to Delta, and giving him ownership of most of the southern half of Harris Neck. Delegal married later in life. His wife Julia Delegal Palmer (1841-1938) was thirty years his junior and remarried twice after Delegal's death in 1876. Julia Delegal Palmer died in Miami, Florida in 1938 at the age of ninety-seven. The Delegals had three daughters, Julia Delegal Quarterman (1861-1918), Katherine Delegal King (1866-1959), and Isabelle Delegal Franks (1872-1960).

North of Delta were the Harris Neck lands of John Harris, William J. King, and Thomas K. Gould, and abutting those was the Thomas family's Peru plantation. The King property adjacent to Delta, later known as the Muller tract, became the Spring Cove tract of Elisha M. Thorpe in 1917. A 1936 indenture records the acquisition of Delta by Isabelle Delegal Franks of Miami. Delta at this time was comprised of 660 acres of upland and was bounded "on the north by Spring Cove Plantation, on the east by Barber's Island River, on the south by Julienton [sic] Plantation, and on the west by the Julienton River; and also known as the Delegal Plantation."[511] This sale of Delta plantation was made by Julia F.D. Palmer, also of Miami, Florida, and a Delegal descendant. Soon thereafter, Delta was acquired by the Thorpe brothers, E.M. Thorpe and Charles Courtney Thorpe, Jr., with the latter devising his share of the holding to his brother. With the acquisition of Delta, Julianton and the Muller-Spring Cove tract, E.M. Thorpe consolidated his substantial amount of land holdings on Harris Neck.

* * *

By 1792 activities in the Harris Neck region merited the construction of a road from Julianton plantation on the south end of the Neck, through Eagle Neck, and along the South Newport River westward to a junction with the Stage Road at South Newport Bridge. Francis Levett joined William Thomas Harris, Jr., David Delegal, John Bradford, and William Myddleton (Middleton) as commissioners of the new road, a conveyor still in use. Charles Thorpe of Sunbury oversaw the road's construction.[512] From 1800 to 1820, cattle raising was an important activity in the area, so much so, that the state legislature approved an "Act for Better Regulating the Fences on Harris Neck."[513] Timbering took place at Harris Neck and its environs in the post-Revolutionary period; live oak was cut for sale to shipbuilders, a frequent

---

[511] Deed Book 7 (1936), 272, RMCG.
[512] Ibid., August 30, 1792; Mealing, *Charles Thorpe of Georgia*, 8.
[513] *Columbian Museum and Savannah Advertiser*, December 21, 1809.

practice on the southeast coast, particularly on the sea islands such as Ossabaw, Sapelo, St. Simons and Cumberland. Although it is unclear to what degree this activity was pursued at Harris Neck, it is known that in 1811 William Thomas Harris, Jr. advertised prime oak and cedar for sale with "a convenient landing for loading same."[514] Vessels transporting cotton on the inland waterway from Darien to Savannah often called at intermediate points to take on additional cargoes of agricultural staples as well as to deliver manufactured goods to the local plantations. Vessels transited the South Newport River from its juncture with Sapelo Sound upriver to the South Newport settlement about twelve miles distant, making stops along the way to load cotton from Harris Neck and nearby plantations.[515] Access to Harris Neck via the South Newport was as practicable as the new road that had been constructed in the 1790s.

By 1820 a sufficient number of white children resided in the South Newport River-Harris Neck region to require a school. Records of the McIntosh County Academy indicate a branch of that institution being established that year at Harris Neck. Classes possibly met in a church or a private home rather than an actual school building.[516] Presbyterian and Baptist congregations were active at Harris Neck from 1820 to 1861. One document notes:

"It being represented by letter & other information to be depended on to this Session that a Religious excitement & revival had commenced on Harris Neck within the jurisdiction of this church & a request made by our members in that quarter that our Pastor should visit them & administer the Sacrament of Our Lord's Supper among them, it was determined to set apart

---

[514] Ibid., October 17, 1811.
[515] Ibid., February 9, 1820.
[516] Virginia Steele Wood, ed., *McIntosh County Academy, Minutes of the Commissioners, 1820-1875 and Account Book of Students* (privately printed, 1973), 3.

the next Sabbath for that purpose, and that this Session meet on the Saturday previous at Harris Neck at 10 o'clock A.M. in order to receive & examine such applicants as might be anxious of coming forward."[517]

Harris Neck residents who "came forward" to join the branch Presbyterian congregation in that section included Jonathan Thomas, Augustus Myddleton, Robert Houstoun, Mrs. Frances L. Baker, Miss Emily Myddleton, Mrs. Mary Ann Houstoun, Miss Eliza Harper, John Forbes, Daniel Young, William Todd, William Dunham and John Calder. Harris Neck planter Edward B. Baker was elected as an elder of the Darien Presbyterian Church in 1830. The Baptist congregation at Harris Neck was admitted to the Sunbury Baptist Association in November 1824. The church was organized by the Rev. Charles O. Screven. In 1831, the Baptist church was moved seven miles west to South Newport where it became South Newport Baptist Church. Trustees of the church that year were Charles J. W. Thorpe, Thomas K. Gould, William J. Cannon, George Rentz, Gideon B. Dean and Henry J. White.

As noted earlier, William Thomas Harris, an early grantee of land on the upper end of the Neck, farmed at Bethany plantation, with interaction with his Harris Neck neighbors, David and Philip Delegal, at Delta plantation to the south. Harris held about 1,100 acres when he died in 1786. His will, devised in 1785 a year before his death, stated that it was his intent that his "real estate be divided equally between my three sons William Thomas, John, and James Harris, each of the younger sons to enjoy the same at the age of 21 years…and bequeath to my beloved wife Mary Harris, my sons William Thomas Harris, my daughters, Ann, Mary, Jane and Sabra [and] my sons John & James, my personal estate after an

---

[517] Minutes of Session, Darien Presbyterian Church, May 12, 1824, v. 1 (1821-1869).

appraisement of the whole it may be made into equal lots, divided to each equal share, to them and their heirs forever..." As noted earlier, William Thomas Harris and his wife, Mary (Landree) Harris, had three sons, two of whom lived and planted at Harris Neck. These were William Thomas Harris, Jr. (1759-1818) and John Harris, Sr. (ca. 1770-1839). However, their brother, James Harris, is the only Harris listed in the 1820 census. The census is apparently in error (not unusual for those times) and "James" was likely John Harris, Jr. as James Harris's death occurred on January 7, 1804. A newspaper legal notice of January 6, 1818 notes that John Harris, probably John, Jr., of McIntosh County applied for administration of the estate of John Neason, which suggests that John, Jr. was living at Harris Neck at that time.[518]

William T. Harris, Jr.'s wife was Mary Margaret Harper Harris (ca. 1772-1866). Their three children were John Harris, Jr. (1790-1847), Jane Elizabeth Harris (1801-1864) and Bright Baker Harris (1808-1875). Evidence points to John Harris, Sr., John Jr.'s uncle, being married to his sister-in-law, Mary Margaret, sometime after the death of his brother in 1818. Meanwhile, the connections among the Harris, Baker, Thomas and Thorpe families began after the Revolution and were often convoluted. Jane Harris, sister of William T. Harris, Jr. and John Harris, Sr., married Bright Baker (b. ca. 1760). Their daughter, Mary Jane Baker, who died in 1816, likely in

---

[518] "Land Grants to William Thomas Harris, the First," in Allen D. Candler, comp., unpublished Colonial Records of the State of Georgia, 27:361, GDAH; Grant Book A, 646, in idem., 380; Will of William Thomas Harris, Sr., August 15, 1785, Liberty County Probate Records, Hinesville, Georgia; McIntosh County Tax Digest, 1825, 1837, GDAH; U.S. Census, McIntosh County, 1820, 1830, 1840; Mealing, *Charles Thorpe of Georgia*, 187.

childbirth, was the first wife of Jonathan Thomas. The daughter of William Thomas, Jr. and Mary Harper Harris, Jane Elizabeth Harris, married Charles J.W. Thorpe. The only Harris in McIntosh County listed with taxable property in the 1825 county digest was John Harris, probably Jr., with twenty-six slaves and 330 acres of improved land inherited from his late father; the 1837 digest lists John Harris, Sr. with thirty-two slaves and 500 acres, and his nephew John Jr. with twenty-two slaves and 350 acres, suggesting that John, Sr. was by then married to the widow of his brother, who had inherited part of her first husband's estate. Both John Sr. and Jr. are listed in the 1830 census. In the 1840 census only one Harris is listed, presumably John Harris, Jr. as John Harris, Sr. died in July 1839, with Margaret M. Harris and William J. King serving as administrators of his estate.[519]

A Savannah newspaper notice in June 1818 listed Benjamin Baker and William Dunham as administrators of the William T. Harris, Jr. estate. The 1837 tax records show John Harris, Sr., brother of the late William Thomas Harris, Jr., and his nephew, John Harris, Jr., living and planting at Harris Neck. John Harris, Sr. died in 1839 at the age of about sixty-nine, with Margaret M. Harris and William J. King administrators of his estate. Harris, Sr. was a fairly substantial planter on the upper end of the Neck. The antebellum Harris family lands were south of, and not within, the present Wildlife Refuge with an eastern boundary on the Barbour Island

---

[519] *Savannah Daily Georgian*, February 27, 1841. John Harris, Jr. died in 1847 at Harris Neck. His second wife, Jane M. Thorpe Harris, age 46, is listed in the population and agricultural census of 1850, presumably with her late husband's land and slaves. In 1854, her son, James M. Harris (1822-1861) requested dismission of guardianship of Jane Harris's younger children. *Savannah Daily Georgian*, October 15, 1854.

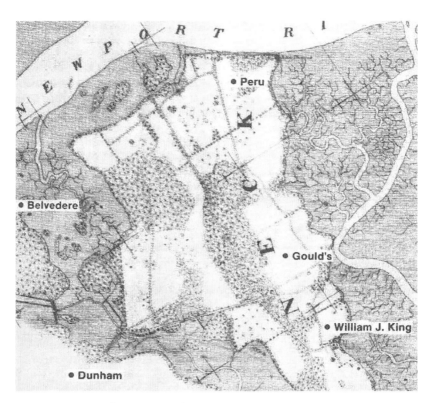

Upper Harris Neck, 1850s, with Peru and adjoining plantations.

River marshes and contiguous to the plantations of William J. King and Jonathan Thomas. In 1837, as noted, both John Harris, Sr. and his nephew, John, Jr., held slaves and acreage on the Neck.[520] In 1850, Jane M. Thorpe Harris, widow of John Harris, Jr., is listed in the agricultural census, presumably with her late husband's holdings. Meanwhile, Margaret Harper Harris, widow of William T. Harris, Jr., and possibly by then the widow of John Harris, Sr., held fifty-nine slaves, and 1,500 improved and unimproved acres. By 1860, Margaret Harris reported ownership of sixty-six slaves and 300 acres of improved land on which were produced nine bales of cotton and

---

[520] *Savannah Daily Republican*, June 22, 1818; McIntosh County Tax Digest, 1825, 1837, GDAH.

550 bushels of corn.[521] These numbers concur with those of two years later when the "John Harris, Sr. estate" was taxed on seventy-three slaves and 1,910 acres of improved and unimproved land.[522] The reference to "estate" in the 1862 digest supports the likelihood of Margaret Harris being the widow of John Harris, Sr. in her second marriage.

East of the Harris lands and south of Peru was the Gould tract on the Barbour River, Bahama plantation, amid which is the present Gould's Cemetery and Gould's Landing. The 1825 tax digest lists William Gould and Richard W. Gould as living at Harris Neck, presumably at Bahama, while the 1837 digest shows Thomas K. Gould there, but not the other two Goulds. Thomas Gould appears to be the most successful of his family to farm at Bahama plantation. South of Bahama was the plantation of William John King. He acquired his Harris Neck acreage at an early age as he is listed as an officer in the McIntosh County militia in 1812 and, with Jonathan Thomas, was executor in 1825 of the estate of Thomas Delegal of nearby Delta. King (see ff.) eventually turned over his plantation to his son, William J. King, Jr. and son-in-law, John Muller.

The only two surviving tax digests for antebellum McIntosh County, 1825 and 1837, and a wartime digest from 1862, provide clues to land use patterns on the upper end of Harris Neck. Twentieth century maps identify the landing on the Barbour Island River in the southeast corner of the present-day Wildlife Refuge as "Gould's Landing." Also identified is a nearby burial ground, "Gould Cemetery." Gould Cemetery is post-Civil War, as no

---

[521] U.S. Census, McIntosh County, Georgia, Slave and Agricultural Schedules, 1850, 1860.
[522] McIntosh County Tax Digest, 1862, GDAH.

identifiable graves in the lot relate to members of the Gould family. It was used by the Harris Neck freedmen and their descendants. A short distance southwest of the cemetery and landing is an older graveyard used by whites, and known locally as the William J. King Cemetery. This antebellum burial ground has long since been obliterated by agricultural and other disturbances, particularly government construction of an airfield on that section of Harris Neck in the 1930s.

A revealing, although biased, glimpse of contemporary antebellum plantation life and conditions emerges from an account of Peru plantation, on the upper end of Harris Neck, by Edward Jonathan Thomas (1840-1929), grandson of the plantation's proprietor, Jonathan Thomas (d. ca. 1849). This memoir, written in 1912, recalled the younger Thomas's early life at Harris Neck in the 1840s and 1850s. Several extracts from this document are worth noting:

"I was born at Savannah, Georgia, March 25, 1840, but a few years after we moved to the old homestead in McIntosh County, some forty miles from this city. My first recollection was of this plantation. It was called 'Peru' on account of its fertility—the legend of Pizarro's gold find being not yet forgotten—situated on South Newport River, a bold and wide salt water stream emptying into Black-Beard [Sapelo] Sound. My grandfather lived at one end of this plantation of three thousand acres, and my father lived at the other...Grandfather Jonathan Thomas died a few years later, leaving his many plantations—Peru, Belvedere, Baker, and Stark, comprising some fifteen thousand acres and about one hundred and twenty five slaves. His remains are buried by a large oak in our private burying ground on the banks of South Newport River.

"There was on the plantation a trusted and intelligent slave called the Driver, who was directly in charge of all field work, Sea-Island cotton, corn, peas, sweet potatoes, sugar cane, melons, and all garden stuff...The slaves were housed in two-room lumber cabins. There was a chimney to each house, and they were allowed a garden. No work was permitted on Sunday, and the slaves attended church services.

They could raise as many chickens as they pleased, and they had boats and went anywhere fishing so long as they came home by daybreak to begin work. They were given two blankets, a suit of wool clothing, and a pair of shoes each winter. They were given a suit of cotton clothing in the summer but no shoes since they went barefooted during the hot months. The older slave men were allowed to keep guns given them by my father. Many had horses and cows which ran in a large free pasture. The pasture extended over thousands of acres of salt marsh. The horses were reared there and therefore were known as 'marsh tackies...' The young Negro men, getting tired of cultivating the fields, would at times run away; that is, they would leave their cabins and seek shelter in the neighboring woods or some isolated hammock which so abundantly are found about plantations on that seaboard."[523]

Peru plantation was shaped as an inverted "L" encompassing the upper part of the present Harris Neck Wildlife Refuge along the South Newport River, then taking in the land on the east side of the Neck along tributaries of the Barbour Island River southward almost to Gould's Landing. Belvedere plantation was west of Peru on the South Newport, separated from Harris Neck by a creek and marsh. The Baker tract was about two miles west of Harris Neck between Lebanon and Belvedere, with the Stark tract east of Baker. Another mainland plantation in the area, and related to the story of Peru, was Marengo, being southwest of Peru and owned by the Houstoun family, which had other acreage in the section. Some of the Houstoun lands were added to Thomas's holdings after his marriage to Mary Ann Houstoun in 1827. Peru included portions of earlier Harris-Demetre lands on the South Newport River as a result of intermarriages between the Harris and Baker families, and between

---

[523] Edward J. Thomas, *Memoirs of a Southerner* (Savannah, Ga.: privately printed, 1923).

the Baker and Thomas families (see ff.). The antebellum Harris lands on the upper end of the Neck were south and east of Peru, fronting on the Barbour Island River and its marshes, and not within the present wildlife refuge. The Harris family tracts adjoined the Thomas and William J. King holdings. Much of the Harris family's original acreage on the Neck had earlier devolved to new owners through marriages.

For about three decades Jonathan Thomas, who died about 1849, held over 10,000 acres of upland and marsh along the South Newport River. Thomas acquired his earliest holdings though his marriage to Mary Jane Baker, who died about 1816, possibly in childbirth when her son John Abbott Thomas was born. The Baker lands included the section of upper Harris Neck that became Peru, the Baker tract west of Harris Neck near Marengo and Mosquito, and the large Stark tract south of the Harris Neck road that extended almost to South Newport. Listed as a justice of the McIntosh County inferior court in 1816, Thomas acquired additional lands later, including the Belvedere and Mosquito tracts (see the material on Belvedere following, and on Mosquito, Stark and Baker.

Belvedere Island was one of the properties acquired by James Gignilliat, Sr. upon his arrival in McIntosh County from South Carolina after the Revolution (see Gignilliat coverage earlier). In 1794, Belvedere was inherited by James Gignilliat, Jr. His daughter, Sarah Catherine Gignilliat (1799-1873), married Edward Perry Postell (1797-1835) of Savannah. In 1806, Postell's father, James Postell (1766-1826) had acquired a 250-acre rice tract on the northern end of Onslow Island on the Savannah River. In 1822, the *Savannah Georgian* reported the marriage "at Col. [James] Postell's in Abbeville, on the 17th ult., Edward Postell, Esq. of Coosawhatchie, to Miss Sarah

Gignilliat, of M'Intosh county, Ga."[524]

Before the marriage of Edward and Sarah Gignilliat Postell, the Gignilliat family apparently had intentions of selling Belvedere. In 1820, a public notice advertised for sale "That well known Cotton Plantation called 'Belvedere' on the South Newport river in McIntosh county." The notice indicated that Belvedere was a 1,500-acre tract of oak, hickory and low swamp land, sixty acres of the latter being under cultivation, a "sufficient proportion of pine barren attached" which produced an excellent quality of cotton. Pine land was considered an attractive quality for a coastal plantation for it afforded good cattle range and was conducive to good health for its residents. According to the notice, Belvedere was admirably suited for a force of from twenty to fifty slaves.[525] The 1825 tax digest lists Postell with forty-eight slaves and 1,400 acres at Belvedere plantation. In the late 1820s Postell apparently encountered financial stresses, as evidenced in the following notice in the *Savannah Georgian*:

"McIntosh Superior Court, April Term, 1830. On petition of Andrew Low, James Taylor and John Low, merchants under the firm of Low, Taylor & Co. stating that Edward P. Postell, by his certain promissory note in writing, bearing date on the first day of January, 1827, promised on the first day of January next from the date thereof, to pay to Messrs. Bulloch & Dunwoody, the sum of $1,211 and that for securing the payment of said sum of money the said Edward P. Postell by his certain deed of mortgage dated 26th day of February 1827, had mortgaged to said Bulloch & Dunwoody all that tract or parcel of land situate, lying and being on the waters of the South New Port River, McIntosh County, called Belvidere [sic], containing fourteen hundred acres, more or less, bounded on the east by lands belonging to Jonathan Thomas, south by lands belonging to said Thomas and W.T. and T. [Thomas] King and on the west by lands of the estate of Wm. Myddleton..."[526]

---

[524] *Savannah Georgian*, September 3, 1822.
[525] *Darien Gazette*, November 4, 1820.
[526] *Savannah Georgian*, April 24, 1830.

Postell's father died in 1826 and his Onslow Island rice lands passed into a trusteeship held by his widow, Jane Eliza Postell of Savannah and her son, Edward P. Postell. The sale of the Onslow tract may have enabled Edward Postell to meet some, if not all, of his financial obligations. In early 1832 E.P. Postell advertised for sale 120 acres of "prime tide swamp" on Onslow Island; a year later, Postell sold the Savannah River holdings to Thomas F. Potter.[527] In the fall of 1835, Postell died at Belvedere in the prime of his life, from what cause we do not know, his obituary simply noting, "Died at his residence in McIntosh County on the night of the 7th inst. Edward P. Postell, in the 38th year of his age."[528] Postell's estate is listed in the 1837 tax digest as comprising forty-four slaves and 1,350 acres at Belvedere.[529]

The same year, the acreage and slaves were advertised for sale, and were purchased by Jonathan Thomas of nearby Peru plantation.[530]

The large Marengo tract in northern St. Andrew Parish south of the South Newport River was a Crown grant to Sir Patrick Houstoun (1698-1762), an officer of the Georgia colony and a man of considerable wealth and land holdings. Houstoun also had a claim to a 1,000-acre grant on Cathead Creek near Darien, and land in other parishes. Sir Patrick had five sons, all of whom became well-known and established in the colony, as did his son-in-law George McIntosh of Rice Hope plantation in St. Andrew Parish.[531] Marengo was located about a mile south of the South Newport River, below Lebanon plantation. and about halfway along the road connecting South Newport and Harris Neck. The chain of title to Marengo is murky after 1762. The tract

---

[527] Granger, ed., *Savannah River Plantations*, 214.
[528] *Savannah Georgian*, October 19, 1835.
[529] McIntosh County Tax Digest, 1837, GDAH.
[530] *Savannah Georgian*, February 4, 1837.
[531] Edith Duncan Johnston, *The Houstouns of Georgia* (Athens: University of Georgia Press, 1950).

could have gone to the next Sir Patrick Houstoun who died in 1785 at the age of forty-three. What seems more likely is that Marengo was inherited by another of the five sons, Dr. James Houstoun, who died in 1793. The second Sir Patrick Houstoun left no heir.

James Edmund Houstoun (1778-1819), son of Dr. James Houstoun, married Mary Ann Williamson (1786-1860) in 1806. Their children were Eliza V. Houstoun (1810-1836), Mary Williamson Houstoun (1815-1871), John W. Houstoun (1817-1861), and James E. Houstoun, Jr. (1819-1852). Eliza Houstoun was the first wife of Charles H. Spalding. She died in 1836, two years after their marriage. James E. Houstoun, Sr. died at Marengo plantation September 15, 1819. His obituary described him as "possessing fine talents, great energy of mind and unshaken integrity — he represented Chatham County and McIntosh County in the Legislature ... he filled several honorary offices, civil and military, and justly acquired the confidence of the state and of all who knew him."[532]

In 1827, Mary Ann Williamson Houstoun of Marengo plantation, widow of James Edmund Houstoun, married Jonathan Thomas of Peru plantation. Thomas was also a widower, his first wife, Mary Jane Baker Thomas, dying prior to 1820. Mary Ann Houstoun Thomas, who had been left her late husband's lands at Marengo and other nearby tracts, merged her considerable acreage with the holdings of Jonathan Thomas. The 1850 census shows the Houstoun children still living at Harris Neck, excepting the deceased Eliza Houstoun Spalding. Mary Ann Houstoun Thomas, age sixty-four, and by then the widow of Jonathan Thomas, was in a household with her daughter Mary W. Houstoun, age thirty-four and son, John W. Houston, age thirty-

---

[532] *Savannah Georgian*, September 21, 1819.

three, presumably at Marengo, while her other son, James E. Houston, Jr., was listed as the only occupant of another household, likely at Mosquito.[533] James E. Houstoun, Jr. planted cotton and provision crops at Mosquito near Marengo, and was the victim in a brutal murder at the hands of several of his slaves. On the evening of June 14, 1852, Houstoun "left his residence alone in a small canoe to visit an island near Harris Neck upon which he had negroes at work . . . the negroes returned, reporting that their master had not arrived on the island." An investigation revealed that Houstoun had been murdered in his sleep on a marsh hammock east of Harris Neck, Wahoo Island, and buried there by the twelve slaves involved in the plot. The murderers were convicted in McIntosh County court and five were hanged.[534]

The antebellum conveyances of land and slaves in the Harris Neck section are often convoluted, confused and jumbled due to the loss of most of McIntosh County's pre-Civil War public records in courthouse fires. Examples of the fluidity of these transactions are revealed in the records of the Thomas and Houstoun families contained among the Mary Williamson Houstoun Papers on deposit at the Georgia Historical Society.[535] Extracts from these documents relevant to the activities of the two families in the Harris Neck area aid in developing chains of title to the properties under discussion here. A deed dated January 7, 1802 between Richard Leake of Belleville plantation, McIntosh County, and James E. Houstoun of Chatham County conveyed a plantation of 700 acres on Bruro Neck, "Known by the name of Leake land," from Leake to Houstoun for $300. It is unclear as to the precise location of this land, but it was likely the tract later known as Priester, a section of upper

---

[533] U.S. Census, McIntosh County, 1850, Population Schedules.
[534] *Savannah Georgian,* July 21, 1852.
[535] Mary Williamson Houstoun Papers, Collection 398, GHS.

Bruro Neck bounded on the north by the Julianton River. The tract adjoins Marengo, being separated from it by salt marsh and Woodruff Creek. It appears the land was either an annex of, or otherwise connected with, Marengo. The 700 acres of "Leake land" probably acquired the Priester designation sometime after 1885.

A bill of sale of March 7, 1827, just before her marriage to Jonathan Thomas, documents the sale (or proposed sale) by Mary Ann W. Houstoun of thirteen slaves, "to wit, Tena, William, Caroline, Joseph, Alexander, Rose, Maria, Juno, Barrack, Hannah, Tom, Grace and Tenah, with the future issue and increase of the female slaves," and 1,300 acres at Marengo to Crawford Davidson of Chatham County for $3,100.[536] This transaction was apparently not consummated since the property remained in the possession of the Houstoun-Thomas family as validated by a deed conveyance of Marengo from Mary Ann Thomas to Jonathan Thomas four years later in 1831.[537] A deed of September 2, 1828 certifies the conveyance at a sheriff's sale of the 488-acre Mosquito tract just west of Belvedere Island on the South Newport River "bounded east by land of E.P. Postell, south by land of the Estate of Bright Baker, west by the land of Mrs. Myddleton and north by salt marsh" to Jonathan Thomas, the highest bidder. This acquisition evolved from the previous owners of Mosquito, William and Mary Myddleton, the tract previously being among the holdings of Bright Baker who, parenthetically, was the father-in-law of Jonathan Thomas from his first marriage. Bright Baker also held lands immediately south of Mosquito between Marengo and the Baker tract, including the Stark

---

[536] Ibid.
[537] *Savannah Georgian*, July 6, 1831.

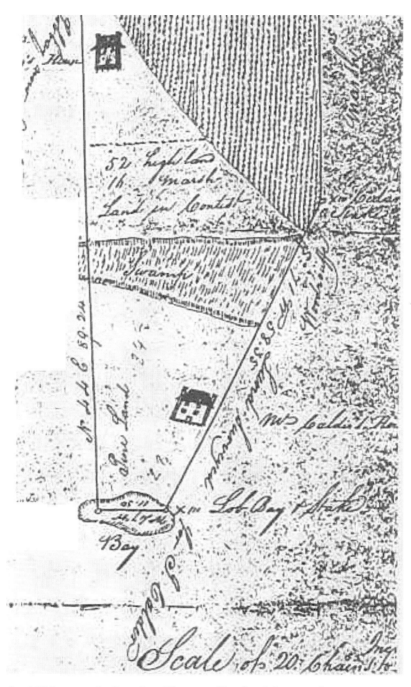

An 1829 survey for Jonathan Thomas of land at Marengo plantation. The area at the top of the plat to the right of the structure is salt marsh.

tract, all properties that devolved upon Jonathan Thomas upon the death of Baker.

A subsequent indenture, dated December 31, 1836, conveyed from Thomas in trust to his wife, Mary Ann Thomas, Mosquito and "400 acres of pine barren land adjoining Marengo, originally part of the Stark tract." Soon thereafter, Thomas placed in trust for his wife "the tract of land known by the name of Maringo [sic] and also eight negroes and their issue and increase." The 1827 sale of slaves by Mary Ann Houstoun cited above was apparently never finalized as they are referred to again in an indenture of April 13, 1839 in which Thomas conveyed to John W. Houstoun, son of James E. and Mary Ann Houstoun, Marengo and twenty-nine slaves. The same document records the bequest by Mary Ann Thomas to her daughter, Mary Williamson Houstoun, the slaves William, Caroline, Joseph, Alexander, Rose, Lucy, Affy, Titus and Betsy, "and that the following Negro Slaves be equally divided between my sons John W. Houstoun and James E. Houstoun, viz: old Maria, Barrack, Juno, Hannah, Maria, Tom, Grace, Tena, Isaac, Phoebe, Cyrus, Bob, Little Maria and Little Barrack."[538]

In 1837, Thomas purchased the 1,350 acres and forty-four slaves of Belvedere from the estate of Edward P. Postell.[539] In 1845 Mary Ann Thomas willed her slaves to her three children, Mary, John and James Houstoun and also "for Mary W. Houstoun and John W. Houstoun Marengo Plantation with Calders Tract, Mosquitoe Tract and 400 acres Pine Land Mr. Thomas gave me, Furniture and everything in my house, one fourth of my cattle and sheep to J.E.

---

[538] Mary Williamson Houstoun Papers, GHS.
[539] *Savannah Georgian*, February 4, 1837.

Houstoun." A later will of February 1, 1847, witnessed by John A. Thomas and William J. King, gave her children eighty-seven slaves valued at $29,650.[540] Extract of a letter of July 29, 1850 from James E. Houstoun, Jr. to his brother, John W. Houstoun, posted from South Newport: "I am perfectly willing that you should take Hector at $500 on condition of his not being brought back to this part of the country...Everything is going on as usual these days since we had the only rain that has been of any service to the crops for two months past. The early corn is entirely lost. About a fourth of a crop of cotton will be made."[541] James Houstoun, Jr. was likely planting all, or a portion, of his cotton at Mosquito and Wahoo Island by 1850. The murder of Houstoun in the summer of 1852 by his slaves probably occurred at Wahoo, a marsh hammock on the Wahoo River, a tidal tributary of the lower South Newport River, and three miles across the marsh from the east side of Harris Neck. Although owned at the time by Harris Neck planter William J. King, Wahoo was either being leased by Houstoun for cotton cultivation, or Houstoun was an overseer in King's employ supervising the islands King owned east of Harris Neck. The following information about Harris Neck, Wahoo and the Houstoun incident was recorded years later by Maude Thorpe, wife of Harris Neck landowner E.M. Thorpe:

"As given [me] by Joe Sallins: His mother was Sarah; his father was Jack Sallins, a house servant. He knew Mr. William J. King & wife Martha who owned a big house on the Spring Cove tract [bought by E.M. Thorpe in 1917]. Jack's grandmother, Teena, was house servant for Mrs. Martha King. Mr. King owned Barbours Island, Oldnors and Wahoo. A gunboat fired on the house [in the Civil War] from the "New Cut." Mr. King had six-oar boats. The overseers carried the hands to farm on the islands. All hands, except two men, were women. Jim Houston [sic], who farmed Wahoo, was killed by the

---

[540] Mary Williamson Houstoun Papers, GHS.
[541] Ibid.

slaves at Houston Creek, and buried in the creek. He was a nice looking man, but was bad. His people did not love him. Julia Tice was little and was the only one who was not hanged. The Harris's owned Belvedere, Statesfield, Johnsfield, Dunham and Dillon. Mrs. Margaret M. Harris was loved by her slaves..."[542]

Across from Wahoo on the upper end of the Neck between Peru (north) and King's plantation (south), was the Bahama plantation of Thomas K. Gould. Now known as Gould's Landing, this site would have been the likely departure point by boat for James. E. Houstoun and others managing the farm operations at Barbour, Oldnor and Wahoo islands. Bahama plantation prospered in the 1830s and 1840s. The 1837 tax digest shows Thomas K. Gould with twenty-one slaves and 268 upland acres at Bahama; the 1840 census listed Gould as possessing twenty-seven slaves. The 1850 census has the "estate of Thomas K. Gould" with twenty-three slaves. Nineteenth century artifacts recovered at the site, such as English-manufactured refined earthenwares, attest to activity associated with the Gould house at Gould's Landing overlooking the marshes toward Wahoo and Barbour islands. Other evidence of antebellum activity is established by faunal material, including fragments of cattle and pig bones, and domestic artifacts which indicate the possible presence of Gould's plantation kitchen near the present cemetery site. Indian activity has also been investigated on the north end of Harris Neck, from Gould's Landing northward to Thomas Landing on the South Newport River. Upper Harris Neck, from all indications, was a

---

[542] Extracted from the private papers of E.M. Thorpe, courtesy of Isabel Thorpe Mealing, Darien, Ga., 1992.

settlement in the Espogache-Tupiqui kingdom.[543]

Resuming the story of Marengo and Peru, Mary Williamson Houstoun Thomas's new will in December 1853 contained the same provisions regarding Marengo and her slaves as her wills of 1845 and 1847, but does not mention Mosquito, which by that time had apparently been conveyed to Mary Ann's son, James E. Houstoun, Jr., since it is known that he had been planting cotton there at the time of his death the year before in 1852.[544] In the mid-to-late 1850s, Mary Ann Thomas, or her heirs, sold Marengo and Mosquito to Charles A. Stebbins. This transaction presumably occurred before Mary Ann's death in 1860; it was certainly after the death of her husband, Jonathan Thomas. The exact year of Thomas' death remains a mystery. He clearly died prior to 1850 as he is not listed in the federal census of that year. His wife Mary Ann Thomas is listed with two of her adult children as members of one household, presumably at Marengo. In the household at Peru in 1850 are John Abbott Thomas (1816-1859), son of the late Jonathan and Mary Jane (Baker) Thomas, his wife Malvina (Huguenin) Thomas (1816-1890) and their five children, all aged ten years or under. The 1850 agricultural census does not list Jonathan Thomas with slave or land holdings, but does list Mary Ann Thomas with 114 slaves and 200 acres of improved land, and John A. Thomas with 104 slaves and 800 acres. Mary Ann's bondsmen presumably included slaves willed her by her husband and those attached to Marengo. Jonathan Thomas probably died ca. 1849, by then having turned over the management and holdings of Peru plantation to his son and his wife. Jonathan Thomas is not listed in the 1850 McIntosh census.

---

[543] "Archaeological Investigations at 9McI41, Harris Neck National Wildlife Refuge," Chad O. Braley, Principal Investigator, for U.S. Fish and Wildlife Service (Athens, 1986), 70, 98, 140.
[544] Mary Williamson Houstoun Papers, GHS.

Mary Ann Thomas died in Savannah in 1854 several years after the death of her husband Jonathan Thomas and either before or shortly after her death, Marengo plantation was sold to Charles Austin Stebbins (1806-1877). Stebbins was born in Massachusetts and moved to the South as a young man, establishing residence in Savannah, and later in Riceborough in lower Liberty County where he operated a general store. About 1860, perhaps earlier, Stebbins acquired the 1,350-acre Marengo plantation, not far from Riceborough. He and his family apparently did not establish residence at Marengo until during or after the Civil War, as they are not listed in the 1860 McIntosh County census. However, he clearly acquired Marengo before the war as he planted there in the 1860s, and had an overseer, William Bryan Nelson (1814-1899). During the war, C.A. Stebbins operated a salt works at Marengo near the tidal headwaters of Carter's Creek which flowed through the upper end of the plantation. Nelson, the overseer, and his family moved to north McIntosh County from North Carolina prior to 1850 as the census of 1850 lists William B. Nelson and his wife Nancy as residents of the 22nd G.M. District. Nelson lived at Marengo in the war years, and obtained lease rights from Stebbins to process turpentine in Marengo's pine lands. One of Nelson's daughters, Wilhelmina, married a Stebbins son, Charles A. Stebbins, Jr. (1838-1914).

The 1870 census lists both Stebbins, Sr. and Stebbins, Jr. as McIntosh residents, presumably living at Marengo plantation. Stebbins died in 1877 and is buried in the Nelson cemetery at Marengo, off Young Man's Road.[545]

---

[545] Young Man's Road was a later conveyor in the area, connecting the Shellman road with the Harris Neck road. There was a sandy road in the antebellum period, and for a time thereafter, that ran from Sutherland's Bluff to South Newport, traversing Marengo. This road is still in use but

The Stebbins family came to play important roles in the economic, business and legal affairs of McIntosh County for the remainder of the nineteenth and throughout the twentieth century. In addition to his daughter's marriage to C.A. Stebbins, Jr., two other of William B. Nelson's daughters wedded men of prominence in the county, these being Robert A. Young, Sr. and William Britt. An 1870 deed conveyed Marengo from Charles A. Stebbins, Sr. to one of his sons, John S. Stebbins, for $1,800, the tract being described as that "formerly belonging to J.E. and Mary Houstoun, known as Marengo plantation containing 1,350 acres, and bounded as described in plat and titles conveyed from Jonathan Thomas and John W. Houstoun and Mary Ann Houstoun."[546] Another of Charles A. Stebbins' sons was King Benjamin Stebbins (1848-1892), who married Theodosia Baker Stebbins (1857-1939), she being a granddaughter of Charles J.W. Thorpe. When she died in 1939 at South Newport, she had never remarried and had outlived her husband by forty-seven years. Both are buried in the Baker Cemetery on the South Newport River. The son of King and Theodosia Stebbins was Charles C. Stebbins, Sr. (1885-1976) who became prominent in the civic and business affairs of Darien.

* * *

Another Harris family property was the Dunham tract on lower Eagle Neck just west of Harris Neck. It was part of a grant apparently acquired by William Thomas Harris before the Revolution. It may have evolved as a Dunham tract for a time through two marriages

---

now ends at the Young Man's Road at the old Marengo tract. Traces of the antebellum road can still be seen.
[546] Deed Book B (1870, re-recorded 1877), 151, RMCG.

between the Harris and Dunham families. One connection is seen through an 1824 legal notice stating that William Dunham and Charles J.W. Thorpe, son-in-law of William T. Harris, Jr. (died 1818), had been appointed administrators of the estate of Elizabeth Harris, she possibly being the widow of James Harris, brother of William T. Harris, Jr. and John Harris.[547] William Dunham is listed as a McIntosh County resident in the 1820 census. Dunham, which then included the Springfield tract, was west of the upper end of Harris Neck, the two tracts separated by marsh and a tidal creek. William Dunham was accepted for membership in the Harris Neck branch of the Darien Presbyterian Church in 1825.[548] The same year, he was taxed on ownership of fifteen slaves and 317 acres, evidence that Dunham was producing cotton and provision crops at Dunham.[549] Dunham and Springfield were on lower Eagle Neck between the Harris Neck road and the upper Julianton River. Springfield abutted Dunham to its south and west. Dunham is referenced as a family tract in the 1865 will of Margaret M. Harris (see ff.). The loss of deed records prior to 1873 due to courthouse fires makes specific, and accurate, chains of title difficult to determine for many of the antebellum tracts. While listed in the 1825 tax digest with slaves and land, Dunham is not recorded as a county resident in either the census of 1830 or 1840, thus he may have farmed the tract for only several years. The original Harris family possession of Dunham before the Revolution and its later use by William Dunham may be validated by two marriages: that of John

---

[547] *Darien Gazette*, February 6, 1824; Mealing, *Charles Thorpe of Georgia*, 8, 77, 187.
[548] Sessional records, Darien Presbyterian Church, v. 1, 1821-1869.
[549] McIntosh County Tax Digest, 1825, GDAH.

Harris, Jr. to Sarah Dunham of Liberty County in 1814 (she died a year later), and, in 1834, that of cousins Ann Harris (1815-1854) daughter of John Harris, Jr. and Sarah Dunham Harris, to Thomas J. Dunham (1810-1885) of Liberty County, son of Rev. Jacob H. Dunham, brother of Sarah Dunham Harris, and Mary Baisden Dunham. William Dunham (1786-1856), born and died in Liberty, and planted for several years at Dunham near Harris Neck, was married to Ann Todd Dunham (b. ca. 1795).[550] Another Dunham, James Harris Dunham (1819-1885) was born in Liberty County, possibly as the son of William and Ann Todd Dunham, and named for the brother of William T. Harris and John Harris, Sr. Coincidentally, Thomas J. Dunham and his wife Ann lived at Dunham plantation in Liberty County and—again coincidentally—it being adjacent to Springfield plantation in Liberty.[551] Thomas Dunham's plantation was near Sunbury west of Colonel's Island. Thomas Dunham and Ann Harris Dunham are buried in Sunbury Cemetery.[552]

In 1855, 600 acres on the South Newport River were sold from the estate of James V.L. Corker of the 22nd G.M. District, McIntosh County, to Thomas J. Dunham of Liberty County. The 1850 census lists the widow of J.V.L. Corker, Anne J. Corker and her son, James A.M. Corker in the 22nd G.M.D. The 600-acre tract, Log Island, west of South Newport settlement, was acquired by Corker in 1840 from Samuel King, and was near the

---

[550] Robert Manson Myers, ed., *The Children of Pride: A True Story of Georgia and the Civil War* (New Haven, CT: Yale University Press, 1972), 1509-10.
[551] Springfield was one of the more common plantation names in the Georgia-South Carolina low country.
[552] Myers, ed., *Children of Pride*, 1509; Liberty County Tax Digest, 1851.

headwaters of South Newport River.[553] One of the children of Charles Thorpe and his wife Anne Jurdine Thorpe was Anne Jurdine Thorpe (1794-1871), wife of James V.L. Corker.[554]

James and Anne Corker also had a daughter, Margaret (1829-1871) who married George Dunham (b. 1825). George Dunham was probably related to the Dunhams already discussed; he and his wife are listed in the 1850 census as residents of Darien. From this discussion, it is clear that the genealogical connections between the Harris, Dunham, Thorpe and Corker families of Liberty and McIntosh counties are extensive and often quite convoluted.

In 1875, the Dunham tract was included as one of the Harris family parcels in the estate of Bright Baker Harris, son of William T. Harris, Jr. and Margaret M. Harris. In 1881, Donald R. McIntosh (1844-1929) acquired Dunham from his father, Lachlan McIntosh (of Donald, 1799-1886) of South Newport. A 1927 timber lease provides further validation of the William T. Harris, Sr. connection to the tract by noting that Dunham was bounded north by the Harris Neck road, south and east by the Julianton River, and west by Springfield, containing approximately 600 acres, being granted by King George II of England to Harris. The lease noted that Dunham was

"bounded on the north by the Harris Neck public road and a creek, south and east by Julienton, or Sapeloe, River, and west by lands of Morison [Springfield] and lands of Travis and Travis, said Tract being known as the old Dunham plantation. Said tract of land herein described being the same granted by King George II of England to Harris, and later on 16th May 1881

---

[553] U.S. Census, McIntosh County, Population Schedules, 1840, 1850; Agricultural Schedules, 1850.
[554] Mealing, *Charles Thorpe of Georgia*, 5-9.

conveyed by Lachlan McIntosh to D.R. McIntosh and in said deed and grant described as containing 350 acres, but by later survey and measurement shown to contain approximately 600 acres."[555]

Across the Julianton River from Springfield is the Priester tract. Priester is bounded on the north and east by marshes and the Julianton River, and to the west by the marshes of Woodruff Creek, the latter named for Joseph Woodruff, whose son-in-law was Ferdinand O'Neal, both being late eighteenth century land owners in the section. Priester is defined by a high bluff overlooking the Julianton River and Springfield. At one time it may have been a part of Marengo plantation, which was to its west. It is not clear how Priester got its name. However, a clue, and hence its possible tie to Marengo, comes in local cemetery records. The death of Emma Stebbins Priester in childbirth is recorded in 1887.[556] She was born in 1866, probably at Marengo plantation as the daughter of Charles A. Stebbins, Jr. and Wilhelmina Stebbins. The 1870 census shows that family as residents of the 22nd G.M.D. However, no Priester surname is listed in the census of 1870 or 1880, nor is any Priester cited in the deed records. However, McIntosh County marriage records indicate that Emma Stebbins married John N. Priester in February 1886. She died a year and a half later. It seems reasonable to assume, based on the available evidence, that John Priester and his new wife, Emma Stebbins from nearby Marengo, settled on the tract sometime during 1886.

The Priester tract was among the later holdings of E.M. Thorpe and the Georgia Land and Livestock Company in the 1920s. In the 1930s, a section of Priester was acquired by J.H. Hawthorne of McIntosh County. The rest of

---

[555] Deed Book 1 (1927), 172, RMCG.
[556] Gladstone, et al., eds., *Cemeteries of McIntosh County*, 241. Emma Priester and her infant are buried in the Stebbins family plot, St. Andrew Cemetery, Darien. The husband of Emma Priester, John N. Priester, may have been listed in the lost 1890 census.

Priester was largely apportioned to the Union Camp Corporation's 1,724-acre holdings in that section known as the Miller No. 1 tract. Tract No. 1 of the Miller No. 1 tract encompassed Priester lands and entailed "All that certain tract or parcel of land containing 546 acres of upland and 33.5 acres of marshland and being generally bounded on the North by the low water mark of the Julienton River and by marsh hereinafter conveyed, on the East by lands now or formerly of J.H. Hawthorne, on the south by the centerline of Hawthorne Road, and on the West by the eastern right of way line of [Old] Shellman Road."[557] On the other side of Woodruff Creek and its marshes, west of Priester and east of Marengo, was a tract of highland described as "containing 169.6 acres bounded on the northeast and southeast by marshlands, on the south by the northern right of way line of [Old] Shellman Road and on the northwest by the eastern right of way line of Young Man's Road and by lands of the Nelson Family [Marengo] Cemetery." This was Union Camp's Tract No. 2 of the Miller No. 1 tract.

* * *

An 1853 deed, concluded after the death of Jonathan Thomas, gives a picture of the inter-relationships of the planters on the upper end of Harris Neck. Three of these, Thomas, John Harris, Sr., and William J. King, as we have seen, had substantial land holdings at Harris Neck and its environs, many of the properties being contiguous to each other. There were connections by marriage between the Thomas, Baker and Harris families dating from the late eighteenth century. For example, as noted earlier, Bright Baker married Jane Harris, daughter of William Thomas Harris, Sr. and

---

[557] Deed Book 67 (1974), 443, RMCG.

Mary Harris.[558] Baker was the father-in-law of Jonathan Thomas whose first wife was Mary Jane Baker. The deed relates the conveyance of Belvedere plantation from the Thomas holdings to those of Margaret Harris:

"This Indenture made the 12th day of December 1853 between William J. King, Executor of the will of Jonathan Thomas, deceased of the first part, and Margaret M. Harris, Administratrix upon the estate of John Harris, Senior, deceased, of the second part. Whereas by a decree rendered in the spring term 1852 of the McIntosh Superior Court it was ordered that the party of the first part should be authorized and empowered to sell and dispose of certain lands forming part of the Estate of Jonathan Thomas and whereas Margaret M. Harris hath become the purchaser of the land as hereinafter described for a full and adequate consideration and price, now therefore William J. King, as acting trustee, hath conveyed unto Margaret M. Harris all that certain tract of land containing 1,200 acres bounded on the north by South Newport River, east by the lands of the estate of Jonathan Thomas [Peru], south by lands of W.J. King, estate of Bennett, and the estate of Jonathan Thomas, and west by lands of Mrs. M.A. Thomas [Mosquito], reserving only the spot of land used as a burying ground..."[559]

* * *

Edward J. Thomas's recollections of antebellum life at Peru plantation included details on structures and people at Harris Neck. For example: "Negro slave cabins" about a mile from one of the "big houses." Church—"Several miles away in some shady grove used by blacks and whites together." Cotton gin—"Great big cotton house." Big house—Two dwellings for the Thomas family, one on the upper and the other on the lower section of the plantation. Family

---

[558] Lucy C. Peel, ed., *Historical Collections of the Joseph Habersham Chapter of the Daughters of the American Revolution* (Atlanta, 1902), 2:329.
[559] Deed Book A (1853, re-recorded 1874), 275-76, RMCG.

cemetery—Near the South Newport River. Buried there is Jonathan Thomas. No trace of this cemetery remains, it likely being disturbed, perhaps eradicated, by land-clearing equipment during the Harris Neck airfield construction. Nearby—"Old lady, Aunt Peggy Harris' plantation," and "Mrs. Anderson, a neighbor." "Aunt Peggy" is Margaret Ann Harris, widow of John Harris, Sr. Ann Susan King Anderson, daughter of William John and Martha C. King of Harris Neck, was the widow of Dr. William J. Anderson (d. 1841). She subsequently married John Muller in 1861. The 1850 census lists Margaret Harris as head of household in the 22nd G.M. District. Her age is given as eighty-three. Also in her household was her son, Bright Baker Harris, age forty-three. The 1860 census lists Margaret Harris as being seventy-nine years of age and Bright B. Harris as age fifty-two. Age and name-spelling discrepancies are common in census data for the antebellum period; the 1860 ages given for the Harrises are more plausible. Edward Thomas recalled: "To make my story complete, I must tell of an old lady, Aunt Peggy Harris, as everybody called her, who owned a plantation and some twenty-five or thirty slaves, all being raised by her during a long life, from a few negro women inherited in her youth. She did not keep her plantation in very good discipline, and hence father, her nearest neighbor, did not like to have his Negroes companionable with hers."[560]

A partial list of the Peru slaves in the late 1850s included Mama Chaney (the Thomas children's nurse), Mama Martha, (head servant), Fanny (servant to Martha Thomas), Phillis (cook), Mamma Peggy (housekeeper), Ann (seamstress), Lizzie (seamstress), Little

---

[560] Thomas, *Memoirs of a Southerner*.

Lucie (maid), Zelieau (maid), Nancy (washerwoman), Old Lucy (keeper of the chickens), Nellie, Daniel Butler, Daddy Phil (coachman), Joe (servant to Edward J. Thomas), Daddy John (driver), William (hostler), Bony (fisherman, husband of Mama Peggy), and Henry (gardener, husband of Nancy).

In the 1850 agricultural census, John A. Thomas reported holdings of 800 acres of "improved" land and 2,200 acres of "unimproved" land at Harris Neck and its environs. He cultivated cotton and provision crops, and raised cattle. Other long-established families in the section are present, including Delegal, Todd, King, Baker, Harris, Thorpe and Caldwell. Life in the South Newport River-Harris Neck area in the 1850s reflected similar economic and social patterns as that of the previous two decades. The younger generations were assuming management of the plantations, and census records attest to a large slave population in the Harris Neck area. No Thomas is shown residing in McIntosh County in the 1860 census, but Peru plantation reported production of twenty bales of cotton and 600 bushels of corn on 600 acres of improved land with seventy-six slaves. In comparison, William Cooke produced fifty-two bales of cotton and 1,200 bushels of corn on 800 acres with ninety-six slaves on Bruro Neck and Creighton Island; William J. King produced forty-five bales of cotton and 1,200 bushels of corn with sixty-seven slaves on 310 acres at Harris Neck; Daniel McDonald reported sixty bales of cotton and 1,500 bushels of corn with sixty-three slaves on 600 acres at Fair Hope; Margaret Ann Harris had nine bales of cotton and 550 bushels of corn with sixty-six slaves on 300 acres; and Edward W. Delegal had twenty bales of cotton and 800 bushels of corn with thirty-five slaves on 1,400 acres at Delta plantation. By far the largest cotton producer based on the 1860 census was Randolph Spalding of Sapelo Island with 200 bales.[561] Two years later, the 1862 wartime tax digest reflects changing conditions in the status of the plantations. The estate of John A. Thomas held 4,000 acres and forty-five slaves; Margaret Harris had 1,910 acres and seventy-three slaves; E.W. Delegal had 2,070 acres and thirty-three slaves; John Muller (William J. King's son-in-law and overseer of his plantation) had 1,475 acres and forty-four slaves; and Charles C. Thorpe had 494 acres (Lebanon plantation) and sixteen slaves.[562]

Near the end of the antebellum period during which Edward Thomas was attending the University of Georgia, his father, John Abbott Thomas, died at Walthourville, Liberty County: "Father died in the year 1859 in his forty-third year; was buried beside my grandfather in the old graveyard on South Newport River. He was not a church man; a man of good deeds, rather than of faith, and goodness and sympathy beamed from him as naturally as light from the glowworm."[563] Rev. Charles C. Jones of Maybank plantation on nearby Colonel's Island, was not as charitable in his assessment of Thomas. In November 1859, Jones noted, "What an unexpected and afflicting death is that of Mr. John A. Thomas! Buried on Monday. About forty-five. Leaves a wife and six or seven fine children. What warnings we have had in this [section]. My son, touch not, taste not, handle not. Another awful warning of the use of spirituous liquors.

---

[561] U.S. Census, McIntosh County, 1860, Agricultural Schedules. The Thomas family had a second home in Walthourville, Liberty County, and resided there in 1860.
[562] McIntosh County Tax Digest, 1862, GDAH.
[563] Thomas, *Memoirs of a Southerner*.

A man of many excellent traits of character. What a melancholy end!"[564]

The Thomas family was not in residence at Peru at the time of Thomas's death. He and his wife, Malvina H. Thomas, a native of Charleston, had a home in Walthourville, where one or more of their children attended school. Thomas died there, apparently quite suddenly. His widow remained at Walthourville, later moving to Savannah where she died in 1890, being buried at Bonaventure Cemetery. Her husband's remains were moved from the family plot at Peru and reburied by her side. Edward Thomas completed degree requirements at Athens in the summer of 1860 amid a backdrop of change:

"On my route home, at most every station, a liberty pole was erected from which flags of various designs were hung, always expressing something defiant of the Yankee. Father's death made it necessary for me to take charge of our plantation, and this, with the unsettled condition of our country, made me forget my individual interest. The first of January 1861, I assumed charge, and with the assistance of our old driver, 'Daddy John,' prepared to plant the usual crops. Our family lived in Walthourville, Liberty County, twenty miles away, in order that the younger members of the family might have school privileges. I kept bachelor's quarters on the plantation…[Later] Federal gunboats could be seen out in the sound, and the neighboring planters became uneasy."

Thomas served in the Confederate army; after the conflict, he was compelled to settle the disorganized affairs of the family's holdings, a circumstance not uncommon among planter families during the post-war turmoil. In 1862, Thomas married Alice Gertrude

---

[564] Charles C. Jones to Charles C. Jones, Jr., November 6, 1859 and November 10, 1859, in Myers, ed., *Children of Pride*, 531, 1701.

Walthour (1843-1927), daughter of prominent Liberty County planter George Washington Walthour (1799-1859). Thomas settled in Savannah after the war where he was a railroad agent, supervisor of Chatham County, and engineer of the Savannah streetcar system. When he died in 1929, he was the oldest living alumnus of the University of Georgia.[565]

* * *

William John King (1790-1861) was a planter with substantial acreage at Harris Neck. His son-in-law, John Muller (b. 1833), acquired many of the properties through his marriage into the family ca. 1861. King's wife was Martha Cooper King (1795-1860). There is early evidence of King's activities in McIntosh County: in 1818 he and Thomas King applied for administration of the estate of Solomon Harper.[566] In October 1823, a public notice reported the application of William J. and Thomas King for leave to sell the estate of Solomon Harper. In early 1825, a notice reported that "Jonathan Thomas and William J. King, Executors of Thomas Delegal, dec'd., give notice to debtors and creditors."[567] William J. King is listed in every census from 1820 to 1860. His son was William John King, Jr. (1823-1885). The 1850 census includes in the King household his wife, daughters Ann (King) Anderson and Mary E. King, and son, William King, Jr., who was noted as "plantation manager." The 1860 census identifies a household comprised of King, age sixty-nine, Martha King, sixty-five, and daughter, Ann (King) Anderson, age forty. In 1862, the estate of William J. King included forty-four slaves and 1,475 acres.[568] The 1870 census lists no Kings in the Harris Neck area but does show a household comprising John Muller, age

---

[565] Thomas, *Memoirs of a Southerner,* Myers, ed., *Children of Pride,* 1700-01.
[566] *Columbian Museum and Savannah Daily Gazette,* May 4, 1818.
[567] *Darien Gazette,* March 1825.
[568] McIntosh County Tax Digest, 1862, GDAH.

thirty-seven of Switzerland, and his wife, Ann Susan (King) (Anderson) Muller, age forty-five. Susan Muller is listed in the 1880 census as being sixty-one years old and in a household with her seventeen-year-old grandson, Edward LeGriel; oddly, John Muller is not listed in the 1880 census but is known to be alive in the 1890s and early 1900s based on land transactions made by him in the Harris Neck section during that period.[569]

An antebellum deed reflects the survey of a 640-acre tract on the South Newport River for Samuel King in 1833, a tract bounded by lands of William McDonald, Lachlan McIntosh (of Donald, b. 1799) and Hugh Ross. Samuel King is listed in the censuses of 1830 and 1840 as being a resident of the 22nd G.M. District, but does not turn up thereafter. He was possibly a relation of William J. King, as was Thomas King, who also had land holdings in the region. Thomas King moved to Bibb County ca 1840 or 1841.[570] Before his relocation to middle Georgia he may also have leased cotton land at Bourbon Field, Sapelo Island.[571]

The King plantation and homeplace was contiguous to the south end of Peru as validated in the memoir of Edward Thomas. Of Ann King Anderson Muller, Thomas noted, "One of our neighbors, Mrs. Anderson, had a son about my age, a nervous and eccentric chap, and a very interesting daughter. I frequently rode or drove to their home, and was always welcome. They were

---

[569] U.S. Census, McIntosh County, 1820 through 1880. John Muller (b. 1833) would have been about seventy a few years into the twentieth century. Census data in antebellum America was often confusing and inaccurate. The author encountered numerous contradictions in census records for names, ages and relationships for residents while researching the antebellum and postbellum history of McIntosh County.
[570] Not to be confused with Thomas Edward King (1829-1863), son of Barrington and Catherine Nephew King of McIntosh and Liberty counties. Myers, ed., *Children of Pride*, 1585.
[571] Sullivan, *Sapelo, People and Place on a Georgia Sea Island*, op. cit., 140.

distant relatives."[572] Following her first husband's death in 1841, Ann Susan Anderson lived with her parents and continued to after her marriage to the family's overseer, John Muller, in 1861. William John King, Jr. became a co-partner of Edward J. Delegal (1815-1892) in the Liberty County firm of King & Delegal, salt-boilers at Half Moon Bluff on the North Newport River.[573] King, Jr. enlisted in the 29th Regiment, Georgia Cavalry, in December 1863 and lived in Liberty County after the Civil War.

According to the records of the Darien Presbyterian Church, William J. King, Sr. was an elder in that church in the late 1850s. These records aid in knowing some of the activities of the King family of Harris Neck in the 1850s and early 1860s. For example, the church records report a meeting of session in March 1838, with Rev. N.A. Pratt and elders Henry Atwood and E.S. Rees in attendance, when approval was made for the dismission of Mrs. Julia King, wife of Roswell King, Jr., "from this church to unite herself to the church in Midway of Liberty County. Also Mrs. Susan M. Anderson, late Miss King, having removed to Macon, applied to be dismissed."[574] The records also note that Ann Susan Anderson had married Dr. William J. Anderson in 1838. He died three years later. An entry in the summer of 1858 shows that the Session convened at Harris Neck with Rev. F.R. Goulding and elder William J. King in attendance. The minutes state:

"Mary, a servant of Mrs. W.J. King, & Lydia, a servant of Mrs. Susan Anderson, being charged with irregularity of life, appeared before Session, made confession of all that was charged against them, but professing a sincere penitence for the same, were suspended from church privileges, indefinitely, until their lives gave proof of their penitence. In the case of Lydia there were some decidedly ameliorating circumstances. They were both earnestly

---

[572] Thomas, *Memoirs of a Southerner*.
[573] Myers, ed., *Children of Pride*, 1062, 1072-73.
[574] Minutes of Session, Darien Presbyterian Church, March 17, 1838, v. 1 (1821-1869).

exhorted to cleave to the Lord with greater circumspection than before. The Sacrament of the Lord's Supper was administered to about fifteen whites & about 25 blacks."[575]

A Presbyterian meeting in early 1861 notes that "Session met at the home of Mr. Wm. J. King, who was confined to his bed by sickness." A note at the bottom of the page of the original record notes: "Wm. King died 8 days afterwards" on February 4, 1861.[576] A final mention of the King family occurred in the spring of 1876 when it was noted that "Mrs. Susan A. Muller was received into the membership of the church by certificate from Midway Congregational Church."[577]

In the 1840s and 1850s, William J. King owned outright, or shared interests in, property that included a portion of Springfield plantation west of Harris Neck, and the nearby islands of Barbour, Oldnor and Wahoo. The topography delineated in the 1859 Coast Survey chart of Sapelo Sound shows that Barbour and Wahoo islands were under cultivation, probably in cotton but possibly in provision crops as well. There is documentation of land transactions relating to the King family in the Harris Neck region during the antebellum period and after. An October 1818 survey for King is among the county records "for 100 acres "on head branch of South Newport River."[578] An 1838 deed links King and the Durant family, which was also engaged in agricultural activities in the 22nd District. This deed, dated May 1, 1838, was the instrument by which Francis Durant

"Planter, for and in consideration of the natural love and affection which I have and do bear unto my beloved son, Joseph C.S. Durant and of ten dollars to me in hand paid by William J. King as Trustee have granted unto the said

---

[575] Ibid., August 29, 1858.
[576] Ibid., January 27, 1861.
[577] Ibid., April 2, 1876, v. 3 (1876-1912).
[578] Land Plat No. 89 (1818), Plat Records, RMCG.

William J. King ... the following property to wit: a negro boy named Ned, and a negro girl named Kate, both slaves. Also, the plantation and improvements on Eagle Neck containing 56 acres, adjoining Springfield, and formerly occupied by Mr. Abernathy, but now occupied and owned by me, the said Francis Durant..."[579]

Another deed, dated January 15, 1853, establishes a connection between King and the Thomas and Houstoun families:

"[This indenture] between Mary A. Thomas, Mary W. Houstoun and Johnson W. Houstoun of Chatham County, and William J. King of McIntosh County. Witnesseth that for the sum of $600, the parties of the first part confirm unto the said William J. King all that plantation on the waters of South Newport River and on both sides of the road leading to Harris Neck, now belonging to heirs of James E. Houstoun late of McIntosh County, deceased, and which were in possession of said James at the time of his death, purchased by the said Mary A. Thomas from George Rentz and conveyed by him to the said Mary A. Thomas on February 8, 1847."[580]

The inference of the deed is that this unnamed tract sold to King by the Houstouns is Mosquito, land that had been in possession of the Thomas and Houstoun families since 1828 (see earlier discussion). It fronted the South Newport River immediately west of Belvedere and extended to the Harris Neck road. James E. Houstoun was farming Mosquito at the time of his death in 1852. George Rentz (1792-1851) is listed in the 1820 and 1830 McIntosh County censuses as living in the Harris Neck area. Rentz was a Trustee of the South Newport Baptist Church when it relocated from Harris Neck seven miles west to South Newport in 1831. He would have been in the Harris Neck area at the time Jonathan Thomas acquired Mosquito in 1828. Rentz and his family removed to Houston County, Georgia before 1840, which makes his owning Mosquito in the 1830s even more problematic. Nor is

---

[579] Deed Book A (1838, re-recorded 1873), RMCG.
[580] Deed Book E (1853, re-recorded 1893), 567, RMCG.

there a record extant of Jonathan or Mary Ann Thomas selling Mosquito to Rentz, or buying it back in 1847. The land in the deed just cited is likely another tract nearby, probably the Rentz tract itself bought by Mary Ann Thomas then awarded to her son, James Houstoun. Additionally, for the selling price of only $600 it could not have been a very large piece of land, likely 100 acres or less, and Mosquito was much larger than that.

King had a part-interest in Springfield, an 840-acre tract across the marsh west of Harris Neck. Springfield was a combination of smaller tracts originally granted to John Houstoun (200 acres), John Barnaby (100 acres), Josiah McLean (200 acres), William McIntosh (100 acres), Robert Houstoun (forty acres), and John Law (200 acres). It was bounded on the north by Harris Neck Road, east by Dunham and Harris Neck Creek, and south by Julianton River. North of Springfield was Belvedere. An 1809 advertisement likely refers to Springfield: "Alexander Currie and Joseph Miller, Admrs. of estate of John Currie, advertise for sale 380 acres of land on Eagle Neck in McIntosh County, Georgia, with neat dwelling house and other buildings, situated on high bluff with a bold creek in front, &c. and a fine spring of water within 100 yards of the house. About 50 acres cleared and under fence."[581] This suggests Springfield. Its "high bluff" on the upper Julianton River is a prominent part of Eagle Neck. Additional records attest to the sale to John Muller by Edward D. Thomson of Liberty County his one-third interest in Springfield, and Barbour, Oldnor and Wahoo islands. This indenture of August 11, 1876 nots that

"Edward D. Thomson has conveyed unto John Muller his undivided one third interest in the islands known as Barbour's, Wahoo, Oldnor's, or Norse, islands, bounded as follows: Barbour's and adjacent marsh lands by Barbour's Island river, Sapelo Sound and creek, Wahoo Island by South Newport river

---

[581] *Columbian Museum & Savannah Advertiser*, May 22, 1809.

and by South Newport Sound and creek, Oldnor's, or Norse, Island by Sapelo Sound and creek, also his undivided one third interest in the following tracts of land on the main in McIntosh County, the Baker, or Home tract, containing 350 acres bounded east by creeks and lands of the Estate of Harris, north by lands of the Estate of Harris, south by lands of the Estate of E.W Delegal; also the Gould tract bounded east by Swain's river [Barbour Island River], north by lands of the Estate of Thomas, south and west by lands of the Estate of Harris containing 130 acres; also the Lowe [Law], Springfield and other tracts on Eagle Neck containing 1,200 acres, bounded east by the Dunham tract and creek, south by a creek, west by lands of the Estate of Thomas, and north by lands of the Estate of Thomas and the places Belvedere and Bennett... the said one third interest of the said Edward D. Thomson in the Estate and under the last Will and Testament of William J. King, late of McIntosh County, and deceased."[582]

In 1890, Muller sold to Elijah P. Butts of McIntosh County Barbour, Oldnor and Wahoo islands, plus 100 acres at Springfield. In 1891, Butts sold the three islands to Robert S. Morison of Chicago. The islands subsequently went, in 1914, to George A. Morison who held them until 1936. A deed recorded February 29, 1892 in Jacksonville, Florida documented the sale to Muller the interests of his wife's grandson, Edward C. LeGriel, in Springfield and other tracts around Harris Neck. LeGriel affirmed to Muller "all the right, title and interest I have under the Will of William J. King, Sr., and as an heir at law of Mrs. Ann S. Muller, formerly Mrs. Ann S. Anderson, my grandmother." The chain of title for Springfield takes another turn in 1911. An indenture in August of that year confirmed the transfer of Springfield from Mrs. E.C. Hewett to Charles C. Stebbins, it being a tract "bounded north by lands of McIntosh, east by a creek and river, south by lands bargained to Sallins and others, and containing 410 acres and being all of the lands purchased by [Hewett] from John Muller by deed dated May 22, 1907. Meanwhile, an 1892 deed certified the sale to Muller the interests of

---

[582] Deed Book C (1876), 290-91, RMCG.

his wife's grandson, Edward C. LeGriel, in Springfield and other tracts. The chain of title for Springfield takes another turn in 1911 as an indenture that year confirmed the transfer of Springfield from Mrs. E.C. Hewett to Charles C. Stebbins, the tract then described as "containing 410 acres and being all of the lands purchased by E.C. Hewett from John Muller by deed dated May 22, 1907." In 1904, Muller sold the 765 acres of the King-Muller family tract at Harris Neck to Georgiana Davis, et al., the deed citing the land as the "Muller Home Place" of 362 acres of high land and 403 acres of marsh bounded east by the Barbour Island river marshes, west and south by Delta plantation, and north and northwest by the former plantation lands of Thomas and Harris. The sale included the two-story frame dwelling house, "15 head of cattle, a buggy, wagon and skiff, and certain household furnishings." A survey plat accompanying the deed shows the house near the marsh on the east, with the road and forested woodland to the west.[583] Georgiana Davis (1855-1911) of the northwestern part of McIntosh County was likely completing a transaction with her children begun by her late husband, Irvin Davis (1853-1904). In 1904, Muller sold the "Muller Place" tract (former King plantation) to Irvin Davis and his wife Georgiana Davis.[584]

Eagle Neck Tracts: Lebanon & Baker

Charles Thorpe (b. 1760) lived at Sunbury, Liberty County, after the Revolution, and was later active in the South Newport River area. In 1789, Thorpe

---

[583] Deed Book H (1904), 400-02, RMCG.
[584] Ibid. See also other records, mortgage records, plat books, 1890-1914, RMCG.

married Anne Jurdine, daughter of Leonard and Elizabeth Jurdine of Liberty County. In 1792, their son, Charles Joseph Washington Thorpe (1792-1874), was born at Sunbury. In 1815, C.J.W. Thorpe, who had by then established himself in north McIntosh County, married Jane Elizabeth Harris (1801-1864), daughter of William Thomas Harris, Jr. and Mary (Harper) Thomas of Harris Neck. The Thorpes lived at Rice Hope plantation near present Eulonia where he was probably an overseer. The eldest son of C.J.W. and Jane Harris Thorpe was Charles Courtney Thorpe (1816-1901). Other children included William Thomas Thorpe (1819-1882), Samuel Randolph J. Thorpe (1825-1890), and John Harris Thorpe (1826-1895). Before the Civil War, C.J.W. and his son, Charles C. Thorpe lived at Lebanon plantation. Charles C. Thorpe married first, Margaret S. Williams, and second, Harriet Elizabeth McDonald. These two generations of the Thorpe family are buried in the Baker Cemetery on the South Newport River west of Lebanon plantation.

Lebanon was on the South Newport River at the upper end of Eagle Neck about halfway between Harris Neck and South Newport. This section was a Crown grant to Edward Baker in May 1773. Lebanon was developed on a peninsula, bounded on its north by marsh and the river, on its west side by Baker's Creek, south and east by Marengo, and east by marsh. The next two tracts east were Mosquito and Belvedere. The Thorpes grew cotton at Lebanon and had a house overlooking the marsh and nearby river. Across the South Newport was Liberty County and Colonel's Island. A partial description of Lebanon:

"This indenture made the 20th day of July, 1891 between Charles C. Thorpe and Edwin W. Thorpe, Charles C. Thorpe, Jr., Mary C. Thorpe, David G. Thorpe, Elisha M. Thorpe, Daniel L. Thorpe, Julie E. Thorpe and Sarah J. Thorpe. The said Charles C. Thorpe, for and in consideration of the natural love and affection of his children grants and conveys unto [his children] all that tract of land consisting of two or more small tracts of land located on

Eagles Neck and known as Lebanon Homeplace of the said Charles C. Thorpe, bounded on the north by South Newport River, and on the South and East by lands of C.O. Fulton [Marengo tract], and on the West by lands of Mrs. A.I. Pease, containing 445 acres, more or less."[585]

West of Lebanon and Baker's Creek was Stark, a large tract originally among the Baker holdings and acquired by Jonathan Thomas through his marriage ca. 1814 to his first wife, Mary Jane Baker. Stark's north end fronted the South Newport River and extended as far west as the junction of the Harris Neck and Shellman-South Newport Road, about a mile east of the South Newport settlement. James J. Garrison surveyed Stark in 1841 for Thomas and determined that the tract comprised 3,015 acres and extended from the South Newport River south about four miles to Minton Swamp.[586] Only a small portion of Stark was cultivated by Thomas, likely for provision crops. After the death of Thomas ca. 1849, Stark was sold off in smaller tracts, sections being acquired by the Thorpes. After 1870, Stark was sold in lots, one example coming in 1881 when William Thomas Thorpe purchased from H.H. Thomas of Savannah Lot No. 2 of 326 acres fronting on the South Newport River less than two miles east of South Newport. W.T. Thorpe (b. 1822), the son of Charles J.W. Thorpe, was a younger brother of Charles C. Thorpe. A June 1889 transaction shows that part of Stark was still in possession of the Thomas family as 350 acres, "The estate of Jonathan Thomas," was leased by Thomas' daughter-in-law, Malvina H. Thomas, and granddaughter, Mattie Thomas, to Edwin W. Thorpe for turpentining.[587] About two miles east of South Newport was Limerick, the home of Samuel R.J. Thorpe, another brother of Charles Courtney Thorpe. According to a

---

[585] Deed Book E (1891), 368-69, RMCG.
[586] Plat Book 1, page 421, folio 843, survey dated October 28, 1841, RMCG.
[587] Deed Book C (1881), 159, Book D (1889), 469, RMCG.

1904 deed, Limerick comprised 225 acres fronting the South Newport River.

Across Baker's Creek and west of Lebanon overlooking the marshes is the Baker-Thorpe Cemetery, identified on some later maps as "Lebanon Cemetery." Nearly all the graves are post-Civil War, and most are from the early 1900s. The earliest tombstone identified in the Baker-Thorpe plot is that of Benjamin Bright Baker, Jr. who died in 1855. Also buried there are Charles J.W. Thorpe and his wife Jane Elizabeth Harris Thorpe, William T. Thorpe, Charles C. Thorpe, Samuel Thorpe, John H. Thorpe, Richard S. Baker, and King Stebbins, as well as their families. Baker-Thorpe Cemetery is probably on land that was once part of the Baker-Thomas family's Stark tract. The 1841 Garrison plat referred to above delineates Stark as extending to the west side of Baker's Creek, which would include the land where the cemetery was started in 1855. The land may have been bequeathed by Jonathan Thomas for family use, or sold by his estate after his death ca. 1849.

South and east of Lebanon, near Marengo and Mosquito, were more of the Baker family lands, a smaller farm tract that came into the Thomas holdings about 1820. As noted earlier, the Bakers also had holdings on upper Harris Neck, land that became Jonathan Thomas's Peru plantation upon his marriage to Mary Jane Baker who died ca. 1816.[588] A December 1876 indenture between Edward J. Thomas and Edwin W. Thorpe records the sale by Thomas of a portion of Baker plantation "bounded as follows: North by the Mosquito Tract, South by Carter's Creek, East by Lot No. 7 and West by C.C. Thorpe."[589] This indicates the Baker tract adjoined both Lebanon and Mosquito. Carter's Creek, a small tidal stream extending westward from Julianton River, lay just south of the Harris Neck public road. A later deed

---

[588] Gladstone, et al. eds., *Cemeteries of McIntosh County, Georgia*, 216. See discussion of the Thomas-Baker connection earlier in this chapter.
[589] Deed Book E (1876, recorded 1892), 336-37, RMCG.

involving the children of Charles C. Thorpe provides additional context into the land that encompassed Lebanon. The May 1917 indenture between brothers Edwin W. Thorpe of Florida and Elisha M. Thorpe of McIntosh County, et al., provided that the former "in consideration of the love and affection he bears his brothers and sisters does grant, give and convey to his brothers and sisters all his right, title and interest in all that parcel of land known as Lebanon or 'The Home Place' containing 604 acres bounded north by the South Newport River, on the east by a tract of land known as Mosquito, on the south by Carter's Creek, and a tract of land known as Marengo, and on the west by said South Newport River and Baker's Creek."[590]

In the 1850 census, Charles J.W. Thorpe is listed as fifty-seven years old and his wife Jane Harris Thorpe as forty-nine. This correlates with their respective birthdates of 1792 and 1801. However, the 1860 census lists Thorpe as being of seventy-nine years, obviously an error; as he would have been only sixty-seven at the time. Thorpe died in 1874 at the age of eighty-two. The 1860 census shows C.J.W. Thorpe as the postmaster of an unnamed post office, probably South Newport. At one time, Thorpe's son, Charles C. Thorpe, owned both Lebanon and Mosquito. On the former, he had two cotton gins, both destroyed by raiding federal forces in the Civil War. During the war, Charles C. Thorpe manufactured salt at Lebanon, the kind of operation that encouraged several Union raids in the South Newport River area. According to Isabel Thorpe Mealing, granddaughter of C.C. Thorpe, one of these raids resulted in the burning of the Lebanon house. After the war, the home was rebuilt on the same site, and it survived into the twentieth century. In 1914, one of C.C. Thorpe's sons, David G. Thorpe, compiled a

---

[590] Deed Book O (1917), 262-63, RMCG.

list of family-owned property lost in the Union raid: "List of Houses, Barns, Gin & supplys [sic] burnt by Union forces at Lebanon 5 miles east of South Newport, Ga. in year 1865. Property of Charles C. Thorpe. 1 dwelling house, 8 rooms; 1 kitchen & dining room, 1 meat & sugar house, 1 2-story barn, 3 tenant houses, 1 gin house, 1 cotton gin, 10,000 pounds of cotton, 1,000 bushels of rice, 200 bushels of peas, 500 bushels of corn, 1 ½ miles fence rails, 1 dairy house, 800 pounds ham &. Bacon."[591]

Charles C. and Harriet McDonald Thorpe's sons were Edwin White Thorpe (1867-1928), Charles Courtney Thorpe, Jr. (1869-1937), David G. Thorpe (1875-1961), and Elisha McDonald Thorpe (1878-1966), all born at Lebanon. In the early twentieth century, Courtney Thorpe, Jr. became a prominent Savannah banker, businessman and civic leader. He was president of the Savannah Bank and Trust Company, and owned a large amount of land. His brother Elisha Thorpe, as we have seen earlier in this chapter, became a prominent businessman and the largest landowner in McIntosh County in the early twentieth century. After the Civil War Lebanon was divided among family members with the tract primarily utilized for livestock and naval stores operations.[592]

Concomitant to this discussion is the Baker family of north McIntosh County, already mentioned several times in this chapter. Edward Bright Baker (b. 1792) was a planter on the Baker family's land west of Harris Neck. He apparently was a son of Bright Baker of the Harris Neck section, and probably a grandson of Edward Baker who had been granted Lebanon and contiguous lands ca. 1773. Bright Baker and his brother, Benjamin Baker, grew up on family lands in the Harris Neck section before the Revolution. As noted

---

[591] Thorpe family private papers, courtesy of Isabel Thorpe Mealing, Darien, Ga., 1992.
[592] *Savannah Morning News,* December 10, 1937 (obituary of Charles Courtney Thorpe, Jr.); Mealing, *Charles Thorpe of Georgia,* 21-23, 155-60.

earlier, Bright Baker married Jane Harris, sister of William Thomas Harris, Jr. and John Harris, and was the father-in-law of Jonathan Thomas of Peru plantation; he was a McIntosh County grand juror in 1806 and held considerable land in northern McIntosh County. Edward B. Baker and Mary Jane Baker were likely the children of Bright and Jane Harris Baker. Bright Baker is not in the 1820 census, apparently being deceased by then. As the son of Bright Baker, Edward Baker would be the brother-in-law of Jonathan Thomas who married Mary Jane Baker about 1814, and in so doing acquired Baker land on the north end of Harris Neck that became Peru plantation. Mary Jane Baker died ca. 1816, likely in childbirth.

In December 1820, Edward Bright Baker married Frances Leonard Jurdine (b. ca. 1805). Baker was an elder in the Darien Presbyterian Church in the 1830s and is listed in the McIntosh County census from 1820 through 1850. The first son of Edward B. and Frances Baker was Benjamin Bright Baker (1824-1855). A second son, John St. Leonard Baker (1829-1861), married Mary Georgia Dunham (1836-1904), daughter of George C. Dunham (1798-1881). John S. Baker was a Darien druggist and, like his older brother, died young—succumbing to yellow fever in Darien on August 26, 1861. The 1837 tax digest shows Edward Baker as owning twenty-six slaves and 645 upland acres. The 1850 census lists him as age fifty-eight and his wife Frances as age forty. Also in this household was Benjamin Bright Baker, then aged twenty-five, and John, twenty-one. They probably lived on the Baker family tract west of Harris Neck, near Lebanon. Parts of the Baker lands west of Peru, as noted earlier, were at one time among the Jonathan Thomas holdings through his first wife, Mary Jane Baker. While the familial relationship between Edward B. Baker and Mary Jane Baker has not been established with certitude, the possibility is very good that they were brother and sister. If so, it could have been that each were left separate tracts by their father Bright Baker—Mary Jane's on the land that became Peru plantation and Edward on the Baker lands west of Harris Neck. In the 1850s, Edward and Frances Baker left McIntosh County as they are listed in the 1860 Duval County, Florida, census.[593]

Reconstruction and Postbellum Harris Neck

The chaos of the war's aftermath was largely that of economic upheaval. Damage to fields, and farm infrastructure in the absence of labor, was irreparable in Reconstruction conditions. Cotton crops could not be cultivated without labor. As Thomas noted, neither labor nor capital for repairs and wages could be easily obtained by the financially-strapped planters. The wartime changes are emphasized in McIntosh County population figures for 1870, reflecting a decline in total population of about one thousand persons since 1845. A description of the county's resources in 1870 refers to rice as the basic agricultural crop, and lumber mills as the only manufacturing interests.[594] In 1870 very few blacks owned land, a situation that would soon change. The census contains a telling phrase: opposite a list of enumerated houses appear the words "homes of the Thomas Place partly unoccupied." In 1878 only thirty per cent of the county's tillable land was cleared and ninety-five per cent of the farm laborers were black.[595] The following document from the public records of McIntosh County contextualizes post-war Harris Neck and the events, often controversial, associated with the section over the ensuing 150 years:

---

[593] U.S. Census, 1820, 1850, McIntosh County; McIntosh County Tax Digest, 1837, GDAH; Myers, ed., *Children of Pride*, 1459.
[594] U.S. 9th Census, 1870, Georgia, McIntosh County, Population and Agricultural Schedules.
[595] U.S. 10th Census, 1880, McIntosh County, Agricultural Schedules.

Last Will and Testament of Margaret Ann Harris, 1865

"This is to certify that I, Margaret Ann Harris, of my own free will bequeath and convey to Robert Delegal, formerly my slave, now a freedman on St. Catherines Island, Liberty County, namely, Harris Neck, Dunham, Belvedere and Dillon Tracts on condition that the aforesaid Robert Delegal provide all that shall be necessary to make me and my son, namely Bright Harris, comfortable while we live. I have tried white men and they have cheated me, abused and driven off all my people. I now choose Robert who I have raised to take care of me and my son, and agree by this my last Will and Testament that all rights and titles vested in me to the aforesaid four tracts of land are on the above condition vested in the aforesaid Robert Delegal I hereby appoint as my Executors T.G. Campbell, general superintendent of St. Catherines & Ausabaw [sic] Islands, Georgia, & T.G. Campbell, Jun. I also convey all rights and title to buildings, tenements & houses to the aforesaid Robert Delegal. September 2, 1865."[596]

The Margaret Harris will was witnessed at St. Catherines Island by Tunis G. Campbell, Hamilton Delegal and Samuel Graham. Margaret died at Harris Neck in early 1866. Her historic document emerged from the origins of land acquisition by the emancipated black people of McIntosh and Liberty counties as the Civil War ended amidst the imposition of martial law on the Georgia coast by military authorities at Hilton Head. The sea islands from Charleston to the St. Johns River, and the abandoned rice plantations up the rivers for thirty miles were to be a reservation for the freed blacks, whereby they would manage their own affairs and be entitled to forty acres of land, based on W.T. Sherman's Field Order No. 15, issued in Savannah in early 1865. Later that year, General Rufus Saxton at

---

[596] Deed Book B (1865, re-recorded 1875), 76, RMCG. Bright B. Harris (1808-1875) was mentally infirm ("idiotic") according to the 1860 census. Margaret M. Harris was in her early to mid-90s when she died. Tunis Campbell, a New Jersey African American, was the Freedmen's Bureau agent for the coastal area.

Hilton Head appointed Campbell, an African American agent for the Freedmen's Bureau, to supervise and resettle freedmen on "certain of the sea islands of Georgia, including St. Catherines, Ossabaw and other islands."

In March 1866 Sherman's directive was rescinded by the U.S. military authorities, on order of President Andrew Johnson, and the islands were restored to their pre-war owners. By late 1866 Campbell was no longer associated with the Freedmen's Bureau but remained on St. Catherines where his family taught school. He made trips to neighboring Sapelo Island to advise the freed slaves in their new-found self-determination. Two speculators had leased part of Sapelo from the Spalding family to grow cotton by paying wages to the resident freedmen. They took advantage of the freedmen, cheating them of their earnings. In late 1866, Davis Tillson, Freedmen's Bureau agent for coastal Georgia who had advocated restoration of the islands to their pre-war owners, issued an order that Campbell, "having been found guilty of dishonest practices and there being good reason to believe that he is advising the freed people on Sapelo Island to pursue a course unjust to their employers," be thenceforth forbidden to visit Sapelo Island "on pain of arrest." Campbell was subsequently evicted from St. Catherines as well.

This document notwithstanding, McIntosh County probate records indicate that when she died in late 1865 or early 1866 Margaret Harris's estate devolved not to Robert Delegal, but to her son Bright Baker Harris. Nine years later, in 1875, Bright Harris died, the last of the long Harris line to live at Harris Neck. His estate was administered by William J. Wallace until September 1876.[597] Margaret Harris's properties were advertised at an administrator's sale in October 1875

"at the Court House door...the following property, to wit: Harris plantation on Harris Neck, containing 300 acres more or less, with one two story house and out houses, bounded on the north by lands of the estate of W.J. King and Thomas, east by salt marsh, south by land of the estate of W.J. King, and west Thomas. One tract of land on Eagle Neck [Dunham], containing 250 acres more or less, with dwelling house, bounded on the north by lands of the estate of Thomas [Baker tract], east by a creek, south by North Sapelo Creek [Julianton River] and west by the lands of the estate of W. J. King, and one other tract containing 1,200 acres, more or less, known as [Belvedere] on Eagle Neck, bounded north by South Newport River, east by lands of the estate of Thomas [Peru], south by lands of the estate of King and Thomas, west by lands originally estate of Thomas [Mosquito]. Terms of sale cash. Purchaser paying for titles. W. J. Wallace Adm'r on the estate of Bright Baker Harris."[598]

On October 5, 1875, the 250-acre Dunham tract was sold to Lachlan McIntosh for $350. The next day a deed was recorded for the sale of the 350-acre Harris tract from the Bright B. Harris Estate to Margaret Bresnan of Chatham County for $350, the property described as "bounded on the east by Gould's River [Barbour Island River], South by lands of the estate of W.J. King, West by estate of Thomas, and North by Thomas and King."[599] On October 15, the Belvedere Island tract of 1,200 acres was sold to Charles O. Fulton for $410.[600]

---

[597] Probate Book 1 (1876), 135, 177, RMCG.
[598] *Darien Timber Gazette*, August 20, 1875.
[599] Deed Book A (1875) 536-38, RMCG.
[600] Deed Book B (1875), 39, RMCG. See the article in the *Darien News*, August 9, 2012 for an analysis of the complexities involving the disposition of the Margaret Harris tracts in the aftermath of the war.

Confusion prevailed as much on the northern McIntosh plantations during Reconstruction as it did around Darien. Edward J. Thomas recalled,

"I had not as yet, since the slaves were free, visited our old plantation home, Peru, in McIntosh County, but I had heard that a goodly number of our old slaves had returned and, without leave or license, simply considered it their privilege to come home, after they were scattered by Sherman's raid. They had taken up their abode in what cabins were left standing and had begun to cultivate the land."[601]

The chaos of the war's aftermath was largely that of economic upheaval. Damage to fields, and farm infrastructure in the absence of labor, was irreparable in Reconstruction conditions. Cotton crops could not be cultivated without labor. As Thomas noted, neither labor nor capital for repairs and wages could be easily obtained by the financially-strapped planters. The wartime changes are emphasized in McIntosh County population figures for 1870, reflecting a decline in total population of about one thousand persons since 1845. A description of the county's resources in 1870 refers to rice as the basic agricultural crop, and lumber mills as the only manufacturing interests.[602] In 1870 very few blacks owned land, a situation that would soon change. The census contains a telling phrase: opposite a list of enumerated houses appear the words "homes of the Thomas Place partly unoccupied." In 1878 only thirty per cent of the county's tillable land was cleared and ninety-five per cent of the farm laborers were black.[603]

While most of the county's farm laborers were African American in the Reconstruction period, an exception at Harris Neck was John Muller, a thirty-seven year old Swiss native who in 1870 was working

---

[601] Thomas, *Memoirs of a Southerner*, op. cit.
[602] U.S. 9th Census, 1870, Georgia, McIntosh County, Population and Agricultural Schedules.
[603] U.S. 10th Census, 1880, McIntosh County, Agricultural Schedules.

the farm operation of his late father-in-law, William J. King, south of Gould's Landing. A community of black private land owners began to evolve at Harris Neck. From 1870 to 1880 the heirs of John A. Thomas owning portions of the former Peru plantation subdivided the land into small tracts which they sold to individuals, many of whom were their former bondsmen. An example of such a sale occurred in 1878 when Eliza H. and John W. Magill sold land comprising Lots 4 and 6 of the former Peru plantation to Frank Proctor. One of the earliest recorded transactions occurred in 1875 and involved Delegal land, not Thomas land, being William Delegal's transfer of property to Jack Sallins.[604] A burial ground for the freedmen and their descendants was established near Gould's Landing, the earliest marked graves being those of Mark Baisden and Kate Rice in 1882. In 1875, McIntosh County established a black school at Harris Neck, the location of which remains unclear. Dunham's store served the community, as did a later store operated by Edward W. Lowe (1855-1927), which may have been located on land later designated as Harris Neck Airfield Tract 150. Lowe is buried in the Gould Cemetery. In 1891, postal service was initiated at Harris Neck at Bahama near Gould's Landing. In 1896, the post office was renamed Lacey. Its location changed in 1908 and service was discontinued in 1914. In 1896, Philadelphia archaeologist Clarence B. Moore conducted field research on the upper end of Harris Neck. In his findings, published in 1897, Moore noted that

---

[604] U.S. Civil Action File No. 56, Harris Neck Airfield Tract List, No. 137. Presumably, land sales at Harris Neck were concluded earlier than 1875. The loss of McIntosh County deed records in the 1873 courthouse fire included records of property transfers made between 1865 and 1873.

the Bahama post office at Harris Neck had "lately been given the name Lacey."[605]

Establishment of the First African Baptist Church at Harris Neck occurred between 1875 and 1880. The surnames of white landowners frequently appear among the names of blacks acquiring Harris Neck land and in other areas of McIntosh County during the 1870s and 80s. The size of the rural community at Harris Neck varied over the years. By 1940, some 171 separate tracts of privately-owned land existed within the boundaries of the present-day Harris Neck Wildlife Refuge. Most of the tracts were small, with some amounting to less than one acre. Some individuals possessed enough property to permit fairly extensive farming activities. Limited quantities of corn, potatoes, oats, sugar cane and some livestock, primarily for home consumption or local marketing, represented the extent of the agricultural activity reported in the 1880 census. Cotton was grown in McIntosh County after the Civil War but in gradually decreasing amounts in the 1870s. However, unlike most of the rest of the South, private land ownership by blacks constituted the rule rather than the exception in coastal Georgia, particularly in Liberty and McIntosh counties. The numbers of black land owners in McIntosh steadily increased and by 1910, eighty-seven percent of the black farm operators in the county owned their land.[606] In 1900 the county population was 6,537, of which 5,081 were black.

There was one aberration amidst the development of African American settlement patterns at Harris Neck during the postbellum period. In the 1880s, a growing number of affluent Northerners had

---

[605] Civil Action File 56, Tract List, 150; Clarence B. Moore, *Certain Aboriginal Mounds on the Georgia Coast* (Philadelphia, 1897), 73.
[606] U.S. 13th Census, 1910, McIntosh County, Agricultural Schedules.

begun to discover the sea islands of South Carolina and Georgia, and their desirability as winter retreats. The islands offered privacy and seclusion amid a temperate climate, and the natural beauty of their ecosystems. Pierre Lorillard (1833-1901), a wealthy tobacco magnate from New York City, was a charter member of the Jekyll Island Club when it was formed in 1886. Lorillard complemented his tobacco fortune by being a Newport, R.I. yachtsman and a prominent racehorse breeder.[607] Possibly in connection with his club membership, Lorillard, while on a yachting cruise along the southern coast, discovered a site that captivated him with its beauty and privacy, the upper end of Harris Neck on the South Newport River.

In 1889, Lorillard purchased river frontage at Harris Neck and developed a retreat: "Mr. Pierre Lorillard of New York has purchased a 30-acre oak grove on the Peru plantation, the old homestead of Major John Thomas...Twenty hands are at work beautifying the plat, where Mr. L. will at an early day erect cottages for himself and guests and stables for his racers."[608] Several weeks later, Editor Grubb of the local weekly again reported on the Lorillard initiative: "The great tobacco man is setting up a sequestered spot for himself near South Newport river. He is building a club house with stables and all other comforts for a hunter's lodge. Mr. L. will have all the hunting and fishing he wants, or any of his friends."[609]

Two women with whom Lorillard associated, Eleanor Van Brunt Clapp (1862-1937) and Miss Lily Allien, also acquired Harris Neck land near the river during the period. According to deed records the

---

[607] William Barton McCash and June Hall McCash, *The Jekyll Island Club, Southern Haven for America's Millionaires* (Athens: University of Georgia Press, 1989), 5, 10.
[608] *Darien Timber Gazette*, January 4, 1890.
[609] Ibid., February 15, 1890.

first of the group to conclude a property transaction was the companion of Lorillard, Lily Allien, later Lily A. Livingston, of New York. A deed of December 28, 1889 recorded the conveyance from Malvina H. Thomas to Allien of twenty-eight acres on the South Newport River on the former Peru plantation. A second deed in February 1890 was concluded by which Malvina Thomas conveyed seven acres to Eleanor Van Brunt Clapp, also of New York.[610] In early March 1890, the *Darien Timber Gazette* noted that "Saturday's *Savannah Morning News* says the schooner *Charmer* arrived yesterday from New York, with a general cargo of merchandise. She had on deck a new steam launch, 60 feet long, named *Lillian*, for Pierre Lorillard, at Harris Neck. The launch is intended as a tender for Mr. Lorillard's steam yacht *Reva*. The launch is one of the newest and most improved vessels of its kind afloat and a complete description of it was recently published in the *Scientific American*. The launch was afloat in the river yesterday."[611]

Two weeks later, March 22, 1890, the *Timber Gazette* noted; "Mr. Pierre Lorillard of New York is erecting a $10,000 mansion at Harris Neck. The building will be completed in about a month. McIntosh County welcomes Mr. L. and all of his kind." The homes constructed on the north end of Harris Neck by Mrs. Clapp, and Lorillard with Miss Allien (Livingston) reflected the lifestyles of the wealthy northerners of the period. The Lorillard-Livingston house was particularly lavish, complete with outdoor fountains and pools. In large measure, these homes represented aberrations in the land-use patterns associated with Harris Neck, for in no sense were they related to the

---

[610] Deed Book D (1889), 543; Book D (1890), 583, RMCG. The first transaction, although in the name of Lily Allien, was presumably on behalf of Pierre Lorillard.
[611] *Darien Timber Gazette,* March 8, 1890.

agricultural life identified with the area. "During their existence the homes acquired considerable local significance, both as landmarks and as oddities. They clearly reflected the trend of the establishment of resort hideaways by wealthy Northerners which affected the sea islands of coastal Georgia during the 1880-1940 period."[612] The Clapp house was destroyed by fire not long after it was built,[613] then later rebuilt, and the Livingston house was dismantled upon the acquisition of the upper end of Harris Neck by the U.S. Fish and Wildlife Service in 1962 (chapter 17). The houses overlooking the South Newport River near Thomas Landing on property now within the Wildlife Refuge have disappeared and few traces remain. There still exists, however, a pool and remains of some of the landscape structures associated with the Lorillard-Livingston house. As for Lorillard himself, his impact on Harris Neck was brief as he died a little over a decade after acquiring his land. Eleanor Clapp continued to live at Harris Neck until her death in 1937.

By 1940, there were 171 separate tracts of privately-owned property within what is now the wildlife refuge. Most of the tracts were small, many of one acre or less, but some individuals possessed sufficient acreage to permit small commercial farming operations for corn, potatoes, oats and sugar cane. Almost no cotton was cultivated in the Harris Neck vicinity or elsewhere in McIntosh County after ca. 1875. Unlike most of the South, private land acquisition by blacks constituted the rule rather than the exception in coastal Georgia.

---

[612] "Archaeology and History of Harris Neck National Wildlife Refuge, McIntosh County, Georgia," Cultural Resource Management, Inc., Interagency Archaeological Services, Atlanta, for U.S. Fish and Wildlife Service, 1979, 75-78. For the broader picture of the Georgia sea islands, see Buddy Sullivan, *The First Conservationists? Northern Money and Lowcountry Georgia, 1866-1930* (Charleston, SC: CreateSpace, 2016).
[613] *Darien Gazette*, November 10, 1894.

Harris Neck, Sapelo Island and lower Liberty County are good examples of this trend. The Geechee residents of Harris Neck constructed homes and outbuildings and supported themselves with small farms and home gardens, yard or pasture livestock, lumbering, turpentine production, and commercial seafood activity, chiefly oyster harvesting. An oyster collecting shed occupied a lot at Harris Neck Tract 154 on the South Newport River in the 1930s and 1940s. The Shell Bluff Canning Company acquired Tract No. 34 in 1906 for oyster processing and marketing. As the decades passed the numbers of black land owners steadily increased. By 1910, eighty-seven per cent of black farm owners in the county owned their land. In 1900, the county population was 6,537, of which 5,081 was black.[614]

A chapter of *Drums and Shadows: Survival Studies among the Georgia Coastal Negroes* is devoted to Harris Neck and its Geechee people, consisting of oral history interviews conducted in the late 1930s. Harris Neck at this time was much like many small settlements along the Georgia coast during this era—remote, isolated, and often far from the centers of population and transportation:

"Turning off from the Coastal Highway, a tree-shaded dirt road leads to Harris Neck, a remote little settlement connected to the mainland by a causeway and located about forty-eight miles south of Savannah. Narrow, rutted roads curve and turn unexpectedly through the densely-wooded area. Set singly or in little clusters of two or three and sometimes hidden by the trees and foliage are the houses of the inhabitants. There is a peaceful atmosphere about the entire island; life flows along in a smoothly gliding stream; the people

---

[614] U.S. Civil Action File No. 56, Tract List; U.S. Census, McIntosh County, Population Schedules, 1900.

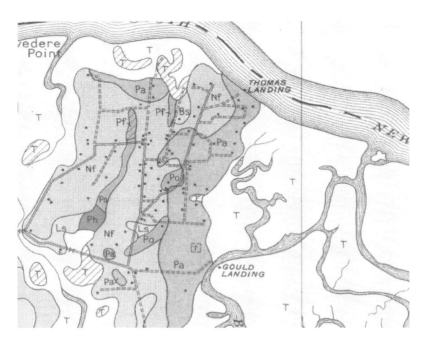

Upper portion of Harris Neck from the soil survey map of 1929 delineating structures, roads and waterways.

seem satisfied for the most part with a simple, uneventful scheme of existence. The first house we stopped at was that of Ed Thorpe, a familiar and well-liked character in the section.[615] A small, neatly-inscribed placard near the gate bore the owner's name. The attractive house was set well back from the road in a large grove of oak trees. A whitewashed fence protected the property. The old man told us he had lived in this particular house for twenty-five years...We discussed Africans and Ed Thorpe remembered that his grandmother had come from Africa. 'She cum frum Africa and uh name was Patience Spaulding,' he began. 'Muh gran say deah wuz lots uh cunjuh in Africa. She tell me dat deah wuz witches wut rode folks. Dey could take off deah skins an hang um up and go out as cats. Wen dey cum back duh nex mawnin, dey would put on duh skins...Folks say duh road to Maringo[616] is hanted. I use tuh lib at Maringo some time back, but I nebuh did see no spirits. Once I tink I see one. Wen I git closuh, it tun out tuh be a big dog.' On this same subject, Isaac

---

[615] Edward Thorpe, Sr. (1864-1940), buried in the Gould Cemetery at Harris Neck.
[616] The former Marengo plantation just west of Harris Neck.

Basden[617] commented, 'Yas'm I hab heah bout duh hanted road tuh Maringo on duh Young Man Road. Lots uh folks say deah is spirits roun deah. Wen yuh try to pass duh fawk in duh road, dub spirits stop yuh sometime an wohn let yuh by...' There were precautions that might be taken in such circumstances according to Liza Basden:[618] 'Mos of duh folks carry sumpm fuh pruhtection. These keep othuh folks frum wukin cunjuh on em. They's made of haiah, an nails, an graveyahd dut, sometimes from pieces of cloth an string...'"[619]

The U.S. Department of Agriculture's 1929 soil map of McIntosh County delineated a well-defined pattern of sandy roads, and numerous dwellings and other structures throughout the section of Harris Neck now encompassed by the wildlife refuge.[620]

Oyster harvesting was an important livelihood for many of the Geechee residents of Harris Neck in the first several decades of the twentieth century. There were productive beds for inter-tidal oysters on the rivers and creeks associated with the three marsh hammocks east of Harris Neck, Barbour, Oldnor and Wahoo. The tidal streams associated with these islands were a source of oysters, including Barbour Island River from Sapelo Sound to Gould's Landing, Wahoo River near Wahoo Island, and Todd River, s small stream penetrating the marshes between Barbour and Oldnor islands. In 1904, Edward S. Ripley of Chicago, Illinois sold the three islands to Robert S. Morison of Massachusetts. The islands then devolved to

---

[617] Isaac Baisden (1877-1954), buried in Gould Cemetery.
[618] Possibly Annie Elizabeth Baisden (1867-1940), buried in Gould Cemetery.
[619] Georgia Writers' Project, Savannah Unit, *Drums and Shadows: Survival Studies among the Georgia Coastal Negroes* (Athens: University of Georgia Press, 1940), 120-32.
[620] *Soil Survey of McIntosh County, Georgia* (Series 1929), U.S. Department of Agriculture, Bureau of Chemistry and Soils, Washington, DC, 1932.

George A. Morison of Milwaukee, Wisconsin, either a son or brother of Robert Morison. In the 1920s Augustus Oemler of Savannah and St. Catherines Island had oyster operations at Harris Neck that provided employment for the locals. George Augustus Oemler (1857-1927) was the leading oyster fisherman in Georgia in the early 1900s with canneries at Wilmington and Wassaw islands in Chatham County and on Back Creek on lower St. Catherines Island. Oemler's wife, Frieda Rauers Oemler (1879-1961) was the daughter of Jacob Rauers, owner of St. Catherines in the late nineteenth and early twentieth centuries. The Oemlers had a house near their cannery on the south end of St. Catherines. In 1928, after Oemler's death, Frieda Oemler leased oyster rights at St. Catherines and its marshes to the Maggione Company of Savannah.

In June 1926, George A. Morison sold Oemler two acres of marsh on the Barbour Island River opposite Gould's Landing to construct an oyster cannery and docks.[621] A year and a half later, in January 1928, Frieda Oemler (widow of Augustus, who died in 1927) sold the two-acre tract to G. Phillip Maggione and Joseph O. Maggione of Savannah, "with improvements in which was conducted by Augustus Oemler an oyster canning factory known as the Oemler Oyster Cannery, together with machinery, tools and equipment, including pipes, shucking houses, tongs, steam cars, boilers, cans and oyster shells, boats, barges, bateaux and one motor-boat equipped with one 30-horse power engine, and four oyster bateaux located on St. Catherines Island."[622]

---

[621] Deed Book Y (1926), 109, "Map of a Proposed Factory Site for Capt. Augustus Oemler on Barbours Island in McIntosh County," RMCG.
[622] Deed Book 1 (1928), 254-58, RMCG.

In 1933, the L.P. Maggione Company acquired eight acres at Gould's Landing from Charles Courtney Thorpe, Jr. of Savannah for oyster processing, this tract being on the opposite side of the Barbour Island River from the Oemler cannery acquired earlier by the Maggiones; in 1936, Joseph O. Maggione sub-leased to Irvin Davis (1893-1962) of McIntosh County the cannery at Gould's Landing "and the right of planting or farming for oysters on any cultivated lands covered by this lease being the islands Barbour, Oldnor and Wahoo, being situated within a large body of marsh lands bounded north by Swains River and South Newport River, south by Sapelo Sound and west by Barbour Island River."[623] In 1936, G.A. Morison sold Barbour, Oldnor and Wahoo islands to E.M. Thorpe and James M. DeFoor.[624]

Barbour and Oldnor were later acquired by John C. Hull. The concrete bridge spanning Barbour Island River linking Gould's Landing to the two-acre tract in the marsh known as Pirates Point, which included only a small patch of vegetation, was not built during the oystering era of the Oemlers and Maggiones as some believe. The bridge was built later by the then-property owner, Dr. John C. Hull. Supervisor of the work was Francis L. Pipkin, with materials supplied by the Capital Concrete Company. In 1958, Hull, a Northerner, acquired 5,000 acres of upland and marsh comprising Barbour and Oldnor islands.[625] His intention was to develop the islands, plans that included the construction of the bridge across the Barbour Island River at Gould's Landing, and a causeway from that point

---

[623] Lease Book B (1936), 146, RMCG.
[624] Deed Book 7 (1936), 153, 261, RMCG.
[625] Deed Book 33 (1958), 20, RMCG.

through the marsh to Barbour Island. Hull began work in 1958 and the bridge was eventually completed. However, the causeway part of the project abruptly ended in 1962 when Hull was accidentally killed during construction work at the site. Ownership of the small Pirates Point tract devolved to Hull's widow, Mabel A. Hull, eventually being acquired as a protected site by The Nature Conservancy. The bridge over Barbour Island River to the hammock was dismantled in 1990; nothing remains of the oyster cannery once on the site.

In 1936, Elisha Thorpe, brother of Courtney Thorpe who also held acreage on Harris Neck, moved his family to the King-Muller house at the Spring Cove tract in the middle section of the Neck. Between them the Thorpe brothers at one time held the majority of acreage at Harris Neck, including land within the present wildlife refuge. In 1937, Eleanor Clapp died, having lived at Harris Neck for nearly half a century. In 1939, the Coastal Electric Membership Corporation ran the first electric power lines to Harris Neck, with power being installed at the Thorpe home at Spring Cove, the Maggione oyster house at Gould's Landing, and the CAA beacon.

Upheaval for the Harris Neck Geechee community, though unforeseen at the time, began in the mid-1930s when the Civil Aeronautics Authority, or its 1934-38 counterpart, the Bureau of Air Commerce, built Intermediate Airfield No. 8 on the upper end of Harris Neck under a renewable lease with E.M. Thorpe. This small, lighted intermediate landing field served the Jacksonville-Richmond air route and was intended primarily for emergency use. The airfield, with runway dimensions of 2,600 feet (east-west) and 2,550 feet (north-south) provided no services and minimal support facilities.[626] The airfield appears on the 1938 state highway map of McIntosh County. The airfield was within the present wildlife refuge a short distance northwest of Gould's Landing. With good approaches from every direction it was a logical site for an emergency field. After the Japanese attack on Pearl Harbor, government regulations concerning existing airfields began to appear. Harris Neck airfield was closed to the public on January 15, 1942.[627] The advantages of the field made it ideal for air flight training, although it was somewhat vulnerable to attack. On July 6, 1942, the U.S. government filed condemnation proceedings for the 1,200 acres of largely African American land for the construction of facilities and development of a training facility. The appropriate court issued its first taking declarations in January 1943.[628] The demolition of structures began at once, and "in a matter of months the community at Harris Neck which stretched almost two hundred years into the past, ceased to exist as a physical entity."[629] The residents were given what was deemed "fair market value" for their land but it was usually below what the properties were actually worth. Of greater consequence was the abrupt disruption of life as it had been known because of the dismantling of homes and the relocation of the people off the Neck to the adjacent mainland. Although the major part of base construction did not begin until

---

[626] "Civil Aeronautics Bulletin," September 1, 1939, 16.
[627] *Civil Aeronautics Journal*, March 15, 1942, Emergency Regulation 60-5951, 80.
[628] Civil Action File No. 56.
[629] "Archaeology and History of Harris Neck National Wildlife Refuge, McIntosh County, Georgia," Cultural Resource Management, Inc., Interagency Archaeological Services, Atlanta, for U.S. Fish and Wildlife Service, 1979.

August 1943, the Army Air Force had improved the CAA runway and added another runway by the end of 1942, with several support buildings. By the end of 1944, the War Department had constructed an assortment of permanent and pre-fabricated buildings. An additional runway and maintenance bays were built. The paved runways, now overgrown with weeds and underbrush, are still in place at the Harris Neck Wildlife Refuge. The buildings constructed were for barracks, warehouses, machine and repair shops, ammunition storage, latrine, and a non-commissioned officers club. The Livingston house at Thomas Landing served as the officer's club.[630]

Following are extracts from an article which provide a picture of life at the airfield:

"Given the fallibility of human memory, the encroachments of time and decay, and the remoteness of the place, it is not surprising few people along the Georgia coast recall the Army airfield at Harris Neck. On December 7, 1941, a detachment of air guardsmen from Hunter Field [Savannah] took over the runway at Harris Neck built in the 1930s. For several years various Army squadrons used Harris Neck for maintenance and aerial gunnery training. There was a runway, a few support buildings, and an ill-ventilated post theater. In the fall of 1943, Harris Neck became a permanent auxiliary base of Dale Mabry Field, Tallahassee, Florida. In February 1944 the P-40 replaced the Aircobra for training purposes. Eleven pre-fabricated buildings and a hangar shed were started in March 1944, and the concrete ramp on the South Newport River was enlarged. An Officers Club was opened. In May 1944 there was a building boom. Pre-fab barracks for 125 men were erected. So too was an NCO Club, a supply building, a new latrine, maintenance and machine shops and pre-fab warehouses. The base historian observed that July

---

[630] U.S. Air Force Archives, Maxwell Air Force Base, Montgomery, Alabama, Records of Harris Neck Army Airfield, Microfilm Reel B2269, Frames 1424, 1436.

[1944] was a very hot and routine month: 'A new floating raft with diving board has been anchored in the South Newport River about 30 yards from the floating dock where the two 42-foot crash boats are tied up. This has provided everyone with the opportunity to escape the torrid heat. At the present time there are many buildings on the field. The military personnel number 129 officers and 575 enlisted men.' In August 1944 Brigadier General Blackburn, commanding general of the III Fighter Command, spent a day inspecting the base. Local people attended an 'open house' and played softball games with teams from the base. Two USO Camp Shows and 'G.I. Movies' were shown along with three different motion pictures at the Post Theatre. Attendance was unusually large. Because of the isolated location of the field a shuttle bus operated on Route 131 to Highway 17. Harris Neck reached its zenith in September 1944 when 32 P-40s and five BT-13 planes were in use. September was an eminently routine month. Two exhaust fans were installed in the Post Theatre and, 'as a result the regular patrons were much more comfortable.' The [local] Women's Club continued their weekly meetings at the Officers Club [Livingston house]. The Club sponsored two events" a dance and a wiener roast. October was a month of cataclysmic change at Harris Neck...Personnel were near peak levels: 130 officers, 400 enlisted. But by the end of November, there were only 16 officers and 57 enlisted. The Orientation program was discontinued. But war summaries from UPI were put on bulletin boards and *Time, Life* and *Reader's Digest* were in the Day Room of the enlisted barracks. On October 18th the pilots evacuated all planes, and base personnel went over to Waycross by truck, bus and private car in advance of a hurricane that struck the coast two days later. Trees were blown down, roads blocked; the crash boat landing was damaged by the high tides and heavy winds. November marked the final decline of the base. Only a handful of officers and men were left. Harris Neck was deactivated in December 1944. All supplies, equipment, files and publications were shipped to Warner Robins and Dale Mabry Field. By December 31st, [almost] three years after the field was opened, the base was completely cleared and policed. Everyone was gone."[631]

---

[631] Charles Rippin, "Harris Neck Army Airfield," *Coastal Quarterly* (Savannah), Fall 1977.

On October 25, 1946, the U.S. War Assets Administration assumed accountability for 2,687 acres at Harris Neck, a routine postwar procedure for confiscated lands previously privately held. In an equally common action, the former air base land passed into the possession of McIntosh County. The structures and facilities at the air base were dismantled through official or unofficial salvage operations, or sold as surplus. An exception was the Livingston house at Thomas Landing, which was not dismantled until re-acquisition of the tract by the federal government.

In the summer of 1949, it was reported that several unoccupied airfield buildings at Harris Neck, including the Livingston house, had been looted and equipment and furnishings stolen, the losses estimated at $22,000. Reports noted that the Livingston house had been "stripped of windows and doors and the electrical and plumbing equipment from the powerhouse removed. The hospital building has been wrecked from end to end. The boiler house was stripped of pipes and heating fixtures, and steam radiators were removed from the main buildings."[632]

In March 1948, Tom H. Poppell (1921-1979) was elected sheriff of McIntosh County, succeeding his father, Adam Strain Poppell (1875-1950) who held the position from 1920 to 1948. Tom Poppell was sheriff for thirty-one years, never losing an election. The *McIntosh County News* reported that Poppell had made one arrest with others anticipated, while the county commissioners assumed direct management of the Harris Neck property. Amid the mismanagement and rising political tensions, publisher Paul Varner believed that "the

---

[632] *McIntosh County News*, July 14, July 28, 1949.

airfield should be closed and a guard placed at the gate until the affair is entirely settled. We also think the Commissioners should develop the property along sound business lines as will be of greatest benefit to the public at large."[633] The issue remained in abeyance until 1951 when Poppell requested that the county commissioners lease him the Livingston house so that it could be operated as an exclusive club. The lease was awarded and the club did business until 1958. When Poppell died of leukemia in 1979, one account noted in summarizing his career:

"Harris Neck was being systematically stripped of anything of value. Furniture and equipment disappeared, as did houses and other buildings constructed by the military. Although several local people reported what was going on, the Federal government was in no rush to check into things. After several years of bureaucratic foot-dragging, the feds finally took action. They informed McIntosh County that its lease of the property to Poppell was illegal because the Federal government had never approved it. Three members of the County Commission, in the late 1950s, revoked Poppell's lease. The two other commissioners, both staunch Poppell supporters, were subsequently charged with fraudulently disposing of some of the Harris Neck valuables. The men were never tried because the charges against them were dropped by the sheriff's close political ally, Judge Mel Price. Because of McIntosh County's mismanagement of Harris Neck, the Federal government reclaimed it and, in 1962, turned it over to the U.S. Fish and Wildlife Service to manage as a game refuge."[634]

After the years of alleged abuses and illegal activities by officials and private citizens, the Federal Aviation Administration reasserted its title to the airfield in 1961. In 1962, the government reclaimed the tract and designated it the Harris Neck National Wildlife Refuge

---

[633] Ibid., July 14, 1949.
[634] *Atlanta Constitution*, August 16, 1979.

under the administration of the U.S. Department of the Interior, Fish and Wildlife Service. Pursuant to development of the refuge, the Livingston house on the South Newport River was sold in 1963 for $310 to Harry Wedincamp of Townsend for salvage, and the air hangar was sold as salvage to Irvin Davis for $50. Removal of virtually all structural evidence of the airbase, excepting the asphalt runways, was expedited. Several brick structures remain and continue to be utilized by the Refuge.

In 1979, Edgar Timmons, Jr., Hercules Anderson, Chris McIntosh, Ted Clark and others at Harris Neck began an effort to assert Timmons' claim to restoration of family land within the refuge. Timmons, et al. subsequently filed an unsuccessful federal lawsuit in 1980 for reclamation of lands. In 1982, the U.S. 11th Circuit Court of Appeals in Atlanta denied the Timmons appeal. Mike Wallace and the CBS program *60 Minutes* visited the Refuge and interviewed area residents in late 1982; the program aired in February 1983. After that, the issue lay dormant and unresolved for over twenty years until 2006 when the Harris Neck Land Trust LLC was formed to assist the descendants of the former Harris Neck land owners to reclaim their land. In 2012, a Briefing Document opposing "Congressional action sought by the Harris Neck Land Trust LLC to obtain lands within the Harris Neck National Wildlife Refuge" was submitted to Representative Jack Kingston by the Friends of the Savannah Coastal Wildlife Refuges, Blue Goose Alliance, Coastal Georgia Audubon Society, Georgia Ornithological Society, Ogeechee Audubon Society, and the Coastal Group of Georgia Sierra Club. In 2013, a meeting was held with FWS staff, attorneys from the Regional Solicitor's Office, attorneys from

Holland and Knight, and Representative Kingston to discuss the Land Trust's request to build permanent residences on the Refuge and to explore development options. In June 2014, Secretary of the Interior Sally Jewell visited Harris Neck National Wildlife Refuge to announce the change of the wood stork's status from endangered to threatened. Jewell and FWS staff met with HNLT representatives. Never during the process of re-designation in the early 1960s was consideration given, either by federal, state or local entities, to return lands to their pre-war African American owners. Ongoing disputes amid the land ownership controversy, concurrent with debate over land reclamation and fair compensation have ensued for forty years, at one point going all the way to the United States Congress. As of 2018, the federal government had shown no inclination to abandon the wildlife refuge, or return any land to the descendants of the traditional Geechee people of Harris Neck.

Postbellum Sapelo Island

The long walk home—literally an exodus to freedom—for many of the formerly enslaved people of Sapelo Island occurred during and after William T. Sherman's march through central Georgia in late 1864. Carrying everything they owned on their backs, Sapelo's people began walking in the wake of Sherman's army, southeast toward the coast over 150 miles from the Milledgeville area where they had been transferred by the Spalding and Kenan families. Many of the freed slaves got to Fort McAllister or Savannah, and eventually made their way home to the island.

Sherman's January 12, 1865 issuance of Field Order No. 15 from his headquarters in occupied Savannah awarded the coastal islands from Charleston to the St. Johns River to the emancipated slaves, a decree that received Congressional sanction in March 1865 whereby "every male citizen whether refugee or freedman…there shall be assigned not more than forty acres of such land."[635]

Pursuant to Sherman's Field Order, Congress approved the new land reservation in March 1865 and General Rufus Saxton was put in charge by Sherman to resettle the freedmen on land tracts of up to forty acres and provide them with titles of ownership. Gen. Oliver O. Howard was charged by President Lincoln to head up a new agency, the Bureau of Refugees, Freedmen, and Abandoned Lands. Howard appointed Saxton to continue his work of establishing the freed

---

[635] Buddy Sullivan, *Sapelo: People and Place on a Georgia Sea Island* (Athens: University of Georgia Press, 2017), chapter 6. For Field Order 15, see William S. McFeely, *Sapelo's People, A Long Walk into Freedom* (New York: W.W. Norton, 1994), 86, 131-32.

blacks on the islands. Saxton, headquartered at Hilton Head, proceeded to confiscate the privately-owned sea islands—Sapelo (Thomas Spalding), St. Catherines (Jacob Waldburg, and the others— and followed by appointing Tunis G. Campbell, an African American agent for the Freedmen's Bureau, "to certain of the sea islands of Georgia, including St. Catherines, Ossabaw and [Sapelo]." Soon thereafter Campbell began overseeing the resettlement of freed slaves on the three islands.

The provisions of the field order enabled the Freedmen's Bureau to begin the redistribution of land in the spring of 1865. In May the Bureau divided 390 acres on Sapelo's South End among the freedmen, land that Thomas Spalding had bequeathed to his namesake grandson, the eighteen-year old son of Randolph and Mary Bass Spalding; the land distribution was measured in plots of from fifteen to forty acres. Fergus Wilson was one of the former Sapelo bondsmen who was an early beneficiary of the military directive. Wilson selected forty acres at Hanging Bull, land he had worked as a teenaged slave before the war. Also at Hanging Bull were descendants of Minto, Margaret, and Hester, three of Muhammad Bilali's daughters. They included Hester's son, Bilally Smith and his wife Hagar, and Minto's four sons, Liberty, Bilally, Fortune and Abram. All had been Kenan plantation slaves. Freedmen's Bureau records show that John Williams was also awarded land at Hanging Bull, and that Jack Hillery received twenty acres on "R. Spaulding [sic] P'n, South End." Other freedmen were given plots all over the island. By June 16, 1865, Campbell was able to report that he had settled

317 former slaves at St. Catherines, and 312 at Sapelo.[636] Some of Sapelo's people who had remained on the island during the war were already working their own farm plots in response to Sherman's directive. In the summer of 1865, Freedmen's Bureau agent William F. Eaton reported that of the 352 freedmen on Sapelo, 130 were self-sustaining by farming on their grants of land, 100 were "nearly" self-sustaining, and 122 new arrivals to the island were in need of assistance. The freedmen were gradually adjusting to their first taste of freedom and self-sufficiency. Following is the report by Eaton pertaining to Sapelo Island, and covering the period through September 30, 1865:

"Thomas Spaulding [sic], Sapelo Id., South End, [Gained] By U.S. Forces, [How Held] Abandoned. Acres cultivated 60, acres woodland 500, acres cleared 1740, total acres 2240. Buildings: 2 dwellings, 22 Miserable Cabins. [Remarks] 130 Freedmen self sustaining on Spaulding's Place. They have raised good crops of corn & cotton.

"Michael Kennen [sic], Sapelo Id. Middle. [Gained] By U.S. Forces. [How Held] Abandoned. Acres cultivated 100, acres woodland 800, acres cleared 1760, total acres 2560. [Remarks] 100 Freedmen, mostly self sustaining.

"Randolph Spaulding, Sapelo Id. North End. [Gained] By U.S. Forces. [How Held] Abandoned. Acres cultivated 75, acres woodland 600, acres cleared 5220, total acres 5820. [Remarks] 122 Freedmen, mostly self sustaining.

"Samuel Street, Sapelo Id., North End. [Gained] By U.S. Forces. [How Held] Abandoned. Acres woodland 400, acres cleared 500, total acres 900.

"Randolph Spaulding, Little Sapelo Id. Acres cleared 100, total acres 100.

"Remarks — There are several other islands which have been abandoned, and yet no one lives upon them, neither have any of the Freedmen located on them. I do not consider them under my care, as I have no instructions touching them. They are Hurds, Mungens [Generals], Nightingales [Cambers], Morris [Potosi], Butlers, Bartletts [Champneys], Broutons'

---

[636] "Report of A.P. Ketchum," Microcopy 798, Rolls 36, 38, RG 105 (Records of the Bureau of Refugees, Freedmen, and Abandoned Lands), NARA, cited hereafter as BRFAL; McFeely, *Sapelo's People*, 82-92, 130-31.

[Broughton], Bird, Jointer and Colonels' Islands."[637]

The land redistribution initiative was not to last, however. With the formal end of the war in May 1865 white owners of the islands demanded their land returned, holding legal titles to the islands, and refusing to recognize the blacks' claims to equity.[638] The owners appealed to state and federal officials, including President Andrew Johnson. Johnson agreed, and issued an Amnesty Proclamation in late May 1865, with updated provisions throughout the summer that stipulated that Confederate pardons include the return of abandoned and redistributed lands. In March 1866 Sherman's directive was rescinded by U.S. military authorities, enabling the restoration of the sea islands to their pre-war owners.[639] Saxton protested these developments and Johnson replaced him with Davis Tillson.

At Sapelo and St. Catherines, armed blacks refused to allow the white owners back on to their land, and "threatened the white agents who tried to regain the lands for former masters."[640] Allen G. Bass

---

[637] National Archives, RG 105, BRFAL, E-1002, "Unregistered Letters, 1867-1868," Monthly Report of William F. Eaton, Agent, for the month ending September 30,1865. Eaton's 1865 report was filed with documents of 1867-68. He has a similar report dated August 31,1865 filed in RG 105, M-869, Roll 33, "Capt. A.P. Ketchum's Records and Abandoned Land Reports, August 1865-December 1868," BRFAL, NARA.

[638] Robert L. Humphries, ed., Introduction by Russell Duncan, *The Journal of Archibald C. McKinley* (Athens: University of Georgia Press, 1991), xxv-xxvi.

[639] "Report of Abandoned and Confiscated Lands for the Month Ending August 31, 1865," Records of South Carolina [including Georgia], July 1865-December 1866, Microcopy 869, Roll 33, 1-2, RG 105, BRFAL, NARA.

[640] Humphries, ed., *McKinley Journal*, Duncan Introduction, xxvi.

Randolph Spalding (1822-1862).

was Freedmen's Bureau agent for McIntosh County, as well as being Thomas Spalding's nephew, and the brother of the widowed Mary Bass Spalding, wife of Randolph Spalding who held title to much of the land on Sapelo. Bass had been overseer at Sapelo in the first year of the Civil War. One Spalding family member later recalled, "They sent a representative to the Island [Bass] to take possession for the owners. But, give it up? No, indeed! When ordered to leave, the negroes declared the land was theirs, and in turn ordered Mr. Bass to leave, threatening to kill him if he did not go."[641] The issue was resolved at Sapelo and the other islands with Tillson sending in troops to disperse the black militiamen. Tillson restored Sapelo and the other islands to their owners and went further by requiring the freedmen to sign contracts for the use of the lands for agriculture—

---

[641] Recollections of Ella Barrow Spalding, letter to Charles Spalding Wylly, August 1914, copy in Buddy Sullivan Papers, Collection 2433, GHS.

tantamount to giving the white owners a degree of control over their former bondsmen once again.[642]

The population distribution of slaves and freedmen before and after the war was fairly consistent. The 1860 census listed 370 bondsmen on Sapelo Island. The 352 freedmen in 1865 were enumerated in sections that corresponded to the pre-war settlements: 130 in twenty-four dwellings at South End (Thomas Spalding II), 100 at Kenan Place (Michael J. Kenan), and 122 at Chocolate and Bourbon (Randolph Spalding Estate). Before, during and immediately after the war there were settlements at South End, including Shell Hammock, New Barn Creek (Bush Camp Field), Behavior, Hog Hammock, Drink Water and Riverside; Kenan, (sometimes referred to as Middle Place in the documents), including Hanging Bull and Lumber Landing; and North End, including Chocolate, Bourbon, and later, Moses Hammock, Belle Marsh and Raccoon Bluff.

Some details from Eaton's September 1865 report to the Freedmen's Bureau are revealing in that they demonstrate the increasing self-sufficiency of Sapelo's former bondsmen. The report documented sixty acres under cultivation on the South End, with "2 dwellings, 22 Miserable Cabins, 130 Freedmen self-sustaining on Spalding's Place. They have raised good crops of corn & cotton." On the former Kenan plantation 100 acres were under cultivation, with another 75 acres being planted on Randolph Spalding's North End, primarily at Chocolate and Bourbon. The report noted that of the

---

[642] See Buddy Sullivan, ed., *Postbellum Sapelo Island, The Reconstruction Journal of Archibald Carlisle McKinley* (privately published 2020), entries of September 9 and 15, 1869, in reference to Allen G. Bass.

900 acres of Samuel Street (Raccoon Bluff), 500 acres were cleared, but none were under cultivation, and that 100 acres of Randolph Spalding high land on Little Sapelo Island were cleared.[643] By December, Eaton reported that most of the freedmen were self-reliant having "raised enough produce to supply themselves almost wholly."

When Sapelo was restored to its pre-war owners by the federal government, a large number of the "settlers" elected to relocate to the mainland. Unprincipled opportunists began to make their appearance about this time, often with unpleasant results for the freedmen. In early 1866, two white speculators, S.D. Dickson and his partner, a man named McBride, leased Sapelo Island's South End from the Randolph Spalding estate for $2,500 a year. Dickson offered Sapelo's freed people liberal terms (two-thirds of the crop) to return to the cotton fields, but most were justifiably reluctant to work for whites. Those who did sign contracts were grossly short-changed to the point of abuse as Dickson and McBride reneged on the original agreement, and "the speculators did not fulfill the generous terms they had originally offered."

When Dickson and McBride opened a "company store" on Sapelo whereby the freedmen could obtain supplies and tools on credit, additional fraud and speculation occurred, to the detriment of the freedmen. Dickson and McBride continued to take advantage of the freedmen, cheating them of many of their earnings from their cotton crops. Toby Maxwell was a freedman who contracted to sell

---

[643] "Monthly Report of William F. Eaton, Agent, for the Month Ending September 30, 1865," Unregistered Letters, 1867-1868, E-1002, RG 105, BRFAL, NARA.

his cotton to the speculators' store. He reported that Dickson and McBride "stole everything the col[ored] men made & that this stealing and outrage was done by the direction of Genl [Davis] Tillson." The freedmen eventually asserted their independence, refusing further contract labor in the fields. "McBride and Dickson fade from the record...the [Freedmen's Bureau] could not persuade black farmers to work for the two."[644]

Meanwhile, Tunis Campbell displayed a propensity for exceeding the limits of his authority; by the end of 1866, he was no longer associated with the Freedmen's Bureau. He remained at St. Catherines, and continued to make regular trips to neighboring Sapelo to counsel the former bondsmen in their new-found self-determination. In late 1866, Davis Tillson, Freedmen's Bureau agent for coastal Georgia who had advocated restoration of the Georgia islands to their pre-war owners, issued an order that "the Rev'd Tunis G. Campbell, late agent of this Bureau, having been found guilty of dishonest practices [allegedly granting, or opposing contracts, and selling timber to steamboats]...and there being good reason to believe that he is advising the freed people on Sapelo Island to pursue a course unjust to their employers, and injurious to themselves, is hereby forbidden to visit Sapelo Island on pain of being arrested."[645] Campbell was evicted from St. Catherines, following which he leased Belleville plantation in McIntosh County.

---

[644] Russell Duncan, *Freedom's Shore, Tunis Campbell and the Georgia Freedmen* (Athens: University of Georgia Press, 1986), 33-34; McFeely, *Sapelo's People*, 135-39. Dickson and McBride are not listed in the 1870 McIntosh County census.

[645] Davis Tillson to O.O. Howard, September 22, 1866, Registers and Letters, Microcopy 752, Roll 37, p. 1065, RG 105, BRFAL, NARA.

During this period there were efforts to provide education for the Sapelo freedmen. In June 1865, Campbell reported that sixty children were being taught at a school on the island.[646] Some were descendants of Muhammad Bilali, Sapelo's first educated black. Among the first students was Liberty Bell, Bilali's adult grandson. In 1866, Campbell notified the American Missionary Association of the need for additional schools at Sapelo. Largely supported by New England churches, this organization laid a foundation for educating freed children in the South. In 1868, the Freedmen's Bureau appointed a thirty-two-year old black Savannah schoolteacher, Hettie Sabattie, to organize classes in Darien. Correspondence between Miss Sabattie and her supervisor reveals that a school for black children was in session on the South End of Sapelo in the winter of 1869 under the aegis of the Missionary Association.[647] Called the Sun Shine School, it is unclear if this was the same school earlier established by Campbell. A year later the teacher at the Sun Shine School, Anthony Wilson, reported that he had twenty-three students, and some were paying tuition. Four students were white, the children of Thomas and Jane Herow.[648]

The 1870 census listed sixty students among the 334 people, black and white, living on Sapelo Island; only four of the male heads of household among the island's fifty-nine families were shown as being "literate." Families with schoolchildren included those of

---

[646] T.G. Campbell to A.P. Ketchum, June 20 and June 30, 1865, "St. Catherines Island," Freedmen's Bureau Records, Collection 5915, GHS.
[647] Whittington B. Johnson, "A Black Teacher and Her School in Reconstruction Darien," *Georgia Historical Quarterly* 75 (Spring 1991): 90-105.
[648] Anthony Wilson report to American Missionary Association, January 1870, cited in McFeely, *Sapelo's People*, 103.

Fortune and Phoebe Bell, Abram and Nancy Bell, and Sampson and Sally Hogg. There were several adult freedmen taking classes as well, thirty-seven-year old Peter Maxwell, and twenty-six-year old James Walker, both farmers, and forty-eight-year old John Lemon. There was possibly a one-room school at Raccoon Bluff as early as 1875 in response to the gradual transition of Geechee residents into the new community. Whether there were one or two schools in the 1870s, educational progress continued to be made. By 1878 there were 139 Sapelo children being schooled, four of them white. By the early 1880s, the children of Sapelo's first blacks to be educated in the 1860s were themselves in school, for example Margaret and Thomas Bell, the children of Scipio Bell who, as a teenager, had studied on the island just after the war.

The foregoing demonstrates that during the Reconstruction and postbellum periods, 1865-1900, important and substantive changes in the dynamics of settlement, land acquisition, and education were being made in relation to the Sapelo freedmen. Of greatest significance was the beginning, and continued steady growth, of black land ownership on the island. Few other places in tidewater Georgia during the period saw such a pronounced evolution of land acquisition and community development than that which occurred at Sapelo.

These sharply defined patterns of property ownership and settlement on Sapelo occurred partly in response to successive cycles of economic and cultural adaptation. Concomitant with the development of their localized, often collectivistic, subsistence agriculture, the solidification of religious, social and family-centric activities in tandem with the island's isolation enabled Sapelo's saltwater Geechee to achieve an unusually high sense of community cohesiveness. Later in the period there developed additional avenues of livelihood extraneous to farming for Sapelo's people. For example, in the late nineteenth and early twentieth centuries, work in the local timber industry, cattle-raising and seafood harvesting supplemented (but did not supplant) agriculture.

Until Reconstruction, land ownership on Sapelo Island had been associated with only three families. From 1870 on, however, black property acquisition and community development in various sections of the island was impelled both by the desire for self-sufficiency by the freedmen, and the necessity by pre-war land owners—primarily Spaldings and Streets—to divest themselves of their Sapelo land to alleviate financial pressures. Freed blacks, individually and in groups, built homes, farmed, and established settlements through purchases of small tracts of acreage amid the former Spalding plantations, and the Street family's Raccoon Bluff tract. In 1870, there were 130 African American families on Sapelo, many of them farming 502 cleared acres at the South End, Chocolate, and Bourbon. Seventy-three bales of cotton were marketed from Sapelo in the 1869 harvesting season. The residential distribution of families in 1870 was largely at Behavior, Hog Hammock, South End, Hanging Bull and Chocolate. In the century after the Civil War, Sapelo's population, mostly African American freedmen and their descendants, fluctuated between 250 to a high of over 500 in the early twentieth century. Many were engaged in lumbering, agriculture, and commercial fishing, and resided in several island settlements, the largest of which were Raccoon Bluff on the North End, and Hog Hammock on the South End.[649]

There evolved on Sapelo a patchwork of settlements. At times there were as many as fifteen Geechee communities on the island, some with as few as two or three families. In addition to Hog Hammock and Raccoon Bluff, there were Behavior-Bush Camp Field (New Barn Creek), Riverside, Shell Hammock, Lumber Landing, Belle Marsh, Bourbon, Drink Water, Hanging Bull, Jacks Hammock, Marys Hammock, Moses Hammock, King Savannah, and Chocolate.[650] Population patterns after 1865 may be deduced by tracking federal census and local records. In 1873, church records indicate there were 141 members of the First African Baptist Church at Hanging Bull. By 1904, there were 196 members of the same church that had moved to Raccoon Bluff. The same year, there were seventy-four congregants of the St. Luke's African Baptist Church at Hog Hammock. This would suggest a Geechee population on Sapelo of over 400 residents around the turn of the century, mostly at

---

[649] U.S. Census, 1870, McIntosh County, Population and Agricultural Schedules; *Savannah Morning News*, September 2, 1870. A genealogical resource for families of the Sapelo freedmen, and their descendants is Mae Ruth Green, "Sapelo Island Families: Studies of Forty-four Families," unpublished, compiled 1981-84, Real Estate Division, GDNR.

[650] There is the possibility of an additional island settlement. In its Sapelo Island chapter, *Drums and Shadows* mentions a praise house at "Silver Bluff" in the 1930s (p. 169), and displays a photograph by Muriel and Malcolm Bell (Plate XVIII) depicting a simple wood-frame structure with a brass bell at the entrance. The location of "Silver Bluff" has not been ascertained, and no mention of the site has been found in any of the primary or secondary Sapelo literature. Georgia Writers' Project, *Drums and Shadows: Survival Studies among the Georgia Coastal Negroes* (Athens: University of Georgia Press, 1940). Cornelia Bailey relates that there were three praise houses on Sapelo: at Hog Hammock, Shell Hammock, and Lumber Landing. Author's conversations with the late Cornelia Walker Bailey, 2012, 2014.

Raccoon Bluff and Hog Hammock.[651]

The abuse of the freedmen by speculators and other outsiders in the first three years of Reconstruction had mostly ended when the Spalding heirs returned to reclaim Sapelo's South End.

The most prominent land acquisitions by the Sapelo freedmen occurred on the North End in the 1870s and 1880s. Starting in 1871, several North End tracts were sold by their white owners to those who had been in bondage only a decade earlier. In November 1885, Amos Sawyer sold a fifty-acre parcel on the west side of the island south of Chocolate to Joseph Jones, whose descendants were the Walker family. This became the Belle Marsh settlement. Sawyer sold two other tracts that year, one to Caesar Sams near Kenan Field, and the other to James Green north of Raccoon Bluff. The latter tract reverted back to Sawyer in 1890.[652]

In the early Reconstruction period, Raccoon Bluff (Street Place) was in the ownership of the heirs of George Street, including an undivided half-interest in the tract held by Samuel Street. In 1871, Hugh M. Street of Prentiss County, Mississippi sold the family's consolidated holdings of almost one thousand acres at Raccoon Bluff to a partnership of freedmen called William Hillery and Company.[653] This tract was the first large aggregation of black-owned property on Sapelo Island.

---

[651] Ray Crook, Cornelia Bailey, Norma Harris, and Karen Smith, eds., *Sapelo Voices: Historical Anthropology and the Oral Traditions of Gullah-Geechee Communities on Sapelo Island, Georgia* (Carrollton: State University of West Georgia, 2003), 25-26.
[652] National Register of Historic Places application document for Hog Hammock and Behavior Cemetery, Kenneth H. Thomas, principal investigator, Historic Preservation Division, GDNR, 1996, 11.
[653] Mortgage Book A (1871), 11-12, RMCG.

The investors' intent was to establish organized farming operations as Raccoon Bluff had convenient access for the shipment of agricultural commodities via Blackbeard Creek. Hillery, a former Sapelo slave, formed the company with two other freedmen, John Grovner and Bilally Bell, with whom he bought the land jointly for $2,000, with a $500 down payment and a loan repayment arrangement for the balance. The three partners of the Hillery Company retained 111 acres each for themselves, and divided 666 acres of the tract into twenty lots of thirty-three acres each. The Raccoon Bluff lots were all elongated and narrow, most leading from the interior near the road down to Blackbeard Creek.[654]

A settlement developed at the Bluff, gradually becoming the largest Geechee community on Sapelo. Some of the earliest settlers were Sampson Hogg and his family, who moved from Hog Hammock, along with the Baileys, Walkers, Halls and Grovners and, soon after, the Bells, Spauldings, Greens and Lemons.[655] The 1880 census indicated the rapid growth of the Hillery Company's venture. By then, sixteen freedmen owned property at Raccoon Bluff, while another twenty-two were leasing farming land. The rental properties were likely based on payments that accrued toward the purchase of the land from the Company. After reviewing surviving documents, William McFeely noted that he "could find no record of the long-term successful marketing of money crops [at Raccoon Bluff]. It was if Sapelo, having expelled the money-makers, wouldn't allow what the rest of America thought of as the right kind of entrepreneurship

---

[654] Resurvey of Raccoon Bluff tract by Paul Wilder, Real Estate Division, GDNR, 2000.
[655] Crook, et al., *Sapelo Voices*, 24; McFeely, *Sapelo's People*, 141-42.

to take hold on its sacred sand. As her people somehow understand, you do with her only what she has to offer—her oysters, her trees for lumbering. And her demands for respect..."[656]

Across the island at Hanging Bull, Abram and Bilally Bell, sons of Minto Bell and grandsons of Muhammad Bilali, organized the First African Baptist Church in May 1866. The church had 141 congregants by 1873. Possibly due to the increasing size of the church, the Second African Baptist Church was organized in 1884, and established at Hog Hammock. Damage from the 1898 hurricane compelled the relocation to Raccoon Bluff of the F.A.B. Church, and the remaining Hanging Bull population, largely completed by 1900. The new church at Raccoon Bluff was constructed in 1899.

Sapelo South End was the most productive antebellum plantation on the island with crops grown at Long Tabby, Root Patch, New Orleans and. Slave settlements attached to these areas were at New Barn Creek (Bush Camp Field), Behavior, Hog Hammock, and near the Spalding house. The largest settlement was Behavior-New Barn Creek, two contiguous tracts east of Long Tabby in proximity to the largest agricultural field on the island (present air strip). Behavior was abandoned as a settlement by the late 1870s due to the growth of Hog Hammock and Raccoon Bluff. In the mid-1880s, Behavior became the island cemetery with the earliest marked burials on the four-acre plot dated 1889 and 1890.

Considering the size of the Behavior settlement, archaeological investigation might identify the tract or a tract nearby as an

---

[656] McFeely, *Sapelo's People*, 143.

antebellum slave burial ground. There was a slave cemetery not far from Behavior, at New Orleans, just southeast of Hog Hammock; it is likely this was the primary burial ground prior to the Civil War, but as of 2016, archaeological investigation has not discovered the location of the New Orleans cemetery. There was also possibly a slave cemetery at Hanging Bull.[657] Another Geechee settlement, not precisely located but thought to be in the southwest part of Sapelo, was Drink Water. This unusual name originates with a sea captain, Rotheus Drinkwater who was peripherally associated with Sapelo in the antebellum period. In a 1964 interview, Charles Hall, Sr. (1874-1967) said that Drink Water was in the South End-Kenan Field area where Liberty Bell and Sam Grovner lived after the Civil War.[658] Liberty Bell is listed in the McIntosh County censuses of 1870 and 1880, and is thought to have lived near the white Spalding-McKinley residential section, thus possibly placing the Drink Water settlement somewhere in an area between Hanging Bill and Long Tabby-Riverside.

To offset financial encumbrances, Thomas Spalding II began selling pieces of his South End land to his brother and sister, and members of the island's black community. McIntosh County deed records indicate the first sales of Spalding land to the freedmen as being May 10, 1878 in Hog Hammock, and September 19 of the same year for land in Shell Hammock, near the present Marine Institute. There were black residences and a praise house at Shell Hammock until the settlement was acquired by R.J. Reynolds about

---

[657] Author's conversation with Cornelia Walker Bailey, July 15, 2014; also, archaeological field reports, Historic Preservation Division, GDNR.
[658] Capt. Rotheus Drinkwater was the son-in-law of James Shearwood, navy timber contractor of Sapelo and Blackbeard islands.

1960 as part of his land exchanges with the island's residents.[659] Enslaved people lived at Hog Hammock before the Civil War after which freedmen further developed the community there. Hall noted that Hog Hammock was named for his paternal grandfather, Sampson, who lived there as a slave, and who adopted the surname Hogg. Sampson was ostensibly in charge of keeping hogs and other livestock for the Spalding plantation. Later, the family surname evolved from Hogg to Hall.[660]

* * *

A significant development was the sale in 1866 of 6,900 acres on the North End for $56,000 by Mary Bass Spalding to John N.A. Griswold of New York City and Newport, Rhode Island. Griswold (1821-1909) also purchased the Couper plantation at Cannon's Point on St. Simons Island. Although rarely visiting Sapelo during his brief ownership, Griswold built a house at High Point, possibly utilizing as his foundations tabby brought from Chocolate.[661] In 1873, Griswold sold the North End to one of his creditors, James E. Cassin of New York for $65,000. This transaction also deeded to Cassin the Duplin River marsh hammocks on the west side of Sapelo immediately north of Little Sapelo Island. These small islands were considered a part of the North end tract. The instrument of their sale from Griswold to Cassin "conveyed and confirmed" to the latter "all those three small islands or Hammocks attached to Little Sapelo

---

[659] Deed Book B (1878), 221-23, RMCG; Crook, et al., *Sapelo Voices*, 34-36; National Register application document, 16.
[660] Crook, et al., *Sapelo Voices*, 24-25; McFeely, *Sapelo's People*, 83-84; National Register application document, 24.
[661] It could be argued that the tabby foundation ruins at High Point are from the Montalet house, enlarged ca. 1809 from an earlier house.

Island called respectively 'Jacks Hammock,' 'Marys Hammock' and 'Pumpkin Hammock' formerly part and parcel of the Plantation of the late Randolph Spalding on the North end of Sapelo Island."[662] Cassin lost the North End in an 1879 foreclosure to Henry P. Townsend of New York who soon thereafter sold the tract to Amos Sawyer.

During the restoration of lands to their pre-war owners, Charles H. Spalding, uncle of Thomas Spalding II (1847-1885), successfully negotiated for the return of the South End that had been willed to his nephew by the latter's grandfather.[663] This order came on December 6, 1867, shortly before the younger Spalding attained his legal majority of age twenty-one. In early 1868 Spalding, the eldest son of Randolph and Mary Spalding, took possession of the reclaimed South End, and moved to the island to live. His brother, Thomas Bourke Spalding (1851-1884), received title to Little Sapelo Island from his mother. In 1874, Bourke Spalding married Ella Barrow (1849-1929), daughter of David C. Barrow, Sr., and a cousin of the McKinleys of Baldwin County. The two brothers and their sister, Sarah (Sallie), eventually settled on different tracts on the South End, Thomas near South End Creek, Bourke at Marsh Landing, and Sallie at Riverside-Long Tabby.

In 1866, Sallie Spalding (1844-1916) married Archibald C. McKinley (1842-1917) of Milledgeville. In 1871 McKinley's sister,

---

[662] Ibid.
[663] Spalding Family Papers, Collection 750, series 5, box 1, GHS. Thomas Spalding's son, Randolph Spalding, held the South End in trust for his minor son, Thomas. Randolph died in 1862 following which his brother, Charles Spalding, held the South End in trust for Thomas until the latter reached his majority in 1868.

Thomas Spalding II (1847-1885).

Sarah Barrow McKinley (1847-1897), married Thomas Spalding. Thomas initially restored his grandfather's sugar house at Long Tabby as a residence before moving in 1877 to his new house built at South End Creek near the abandoned mansion. After the death of her husband, Sarah McKinley Spalding, who later married William C. Wylly, continued to live in that residence until her death in 1897. Bourke and Ella Spalding lived at Riverside-York Landing near the Long Tabby on Barn Creek, from 1874 to circa 1880, at which time they bought, with David C. Barrow, the Marsh Landing tract from Thomas Spalding, and built a home there overlooking the Duplin River. T.B. Spalding's Riverside property was subsequently acquired by David C. Barrow.

Also at Riverside was a friend of the Spaldings and McKinleys, William Nightingale, who acquired the Long Tabby after Thomas

Spalding moved to South End in 1877. The Long Tabby tract was later acquired by the Treanor family, related to the Spaldings by marriage. A.C. and Sallie McKinley built a home overlooking Barn Creek a short distance south of the Long Tabby. This aggregation of inter-related families in the southwest section of Sapelo became known as the "Barn Creek Colony."[664]

Further north at Kenan Field was Spalding Kenan (1836-1907), son of Michael and Catherine Spalding Kenan. Kenan came to Sapelo in 1871, purchasing his parents' tract a year later. A doctor and surgeon, Kenan moved to Darien about 1880 where he practiced medicine and served several terms as mayor. Also at the Duplin River house in the early 1870s were the caretakers, Louis and Elizabeth Bass Livingston of Columbus, Georgia, and their son, Charles Louis Livingston. Elizabeth Livingston was the sister of Mary Bass Spalding, widow of Randolph. The Livingston's daughter, Evelyn Elizabeth Livingston (1836-1894), married Spalding Kenan. The Kenans and the Livingstons frequently interacted with their relatives at Barn Creek.[665]

The 1870 census listed only a few white residents on Sapelo Island, including Thomas and Bourke Spalding, their sister and brother-in-law, the McKinleys, and their mother, Mary Bass Spalding (1823-1898), her brother Allen G. Bass (1814-1884) and his son, Charles L. Bass (1853-1919). The census listed Thomas Spalding as holding Sapelo land valued at $33,000. Other whites on the island were James Thompson, a farmer leasing Spalding land, and his wife;

---

[664] Recollections of Ella Barrow Spalding.
[665] Sullivan, ed., *Postbellum Sapelo Island,* op. cit., goes into considerable detail on the Spalding, McKinley, Kenan and Livingston families, and their interaction on Sapelo Island in the 1870s and 1880s.

and George W. Kinsbury who lived in the Thompson household. Also on the South End were Thomas Herow, a ship's carpenter, John Smith, a bar pilot, and James C. Clarke and Montgomery Styles, the Sapelo lighthouse keepers who were living in government provided housing on the lighthouse island.[666]

In January 1874, Thomas Spalding, T. Bourke Spalding and A.C. McKinley borrowed $5,000 from Francis Upson of Oglethorpe County, an associate of Bourke Spalding's future father-in-law, David C. Barrow. "To secure more effectually the foregoing joint and several single bond, and payment thereof," Thomas Spalding mortgaged to Francis Upson "the South end of Sapelo Island containing seven thousand acres (more or less), bounded north by lands of Mrs. Catherine Kenan and on all other sides by the sea and Doboy Sound and its creek called 'Barn Creek.'" On the same date, T. Bourke Spalding mortgaged to Upson Little Sapelo as additional security until such time that the Spaldings and McKinley repaid the note, including principle and interest at 12 ½ per cent per annum. The mortgages on all of this property, South end and Little Sapelo, were cancelled in 1878 on the signature of David C. Barrow. An indenture in January 1878 between Mary Bass Spalding, Thomas Spalding and A.C. and Sarah Spalding McKinley, as one party, and Thomas Bourke Spalding of the other part, validated the latter's regaining title to Little Sapelo after he mortgaged the island in 1874.

Also on Sapelo Island during this period were the lighthouse keepers and their families. The lighthouse tract and its occupants have an interesting history. The circular brick fourth-order lighthouse

---

[666] U.S. Census, 1870, McIntosh County, Population Schedules.

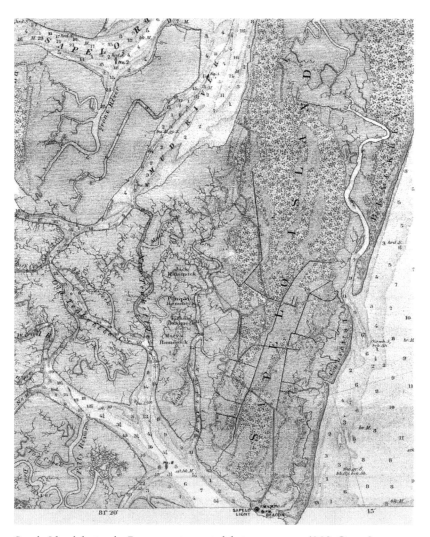

Sapelo Island during the Reconstruction period, being a portion of U.S. Coast Survey Chart No. 156, "From Savannah to Sapelo Island, Georgia," issued in 1876.

built in 1819-20, was inactive in the Civil War, being used as an observation tower by Union naval personnel scouting for Confederate blockade runners. In 1868 the light was reactivated by the Lighthouse Service in response to increasing amounts of shipping frequenting Doboy Sound. The lighthouse tract was originally a small island separated from Sapelo itself by marsh and South End Creek.

Sapelo Island light, photograph taken following the reactivation of the station following the Civil War. The keeper's dwelling at lower right was lost in the 1898 hurricane.

The 1868 U.S. Coast Survey topographic map *Doboy Sound and Vicinity* has an interesting feature: a straight-line plank walk, or causeway, is shown paralleling the creek through the marsh linking the South End with the lighthouse island; no trace of this causeway remains.[667]

In January 1873, a native Irishman, James Cromley, was appointed keeper of the light at an annual salary of $600, becoming the first of three generations of his family to serve in that capacity at Sapelo. The senior Cromley served as head keeper until his death on the last day of 1889, with his son William serving from 1890 to 1900, followed by James (Jimmy) Cromley, Jr. who was appointed keeper in 1900. Robert H. Cromley became assistant keeper in 1912, and later served as the last keeper of the light up to its 1933 deactivation. In the summer of 1875, Tom Spalding sold to Catherine Cromley, acting on behalf of her husband James, the "Lighthouse island, or most of it" a transaction that also included the James Dean family and portions of the hammocks east of the lighthouse. According to this deed,

"Thomas Spalding of the first part and Catherine Cromley of the second part, Witnesseth that said Thomas Spalding, for the sum of two hundred dollars does sell and convey to Catherine Cromley a certain lot of land bounded as follows, viz. — on the North and Northeast by the water of what is known as Dean's Creek, East by the same stream and lands of Frank Dean and one acre in width around the house known as the Arthur Bailey house — South by the waters of Doboy Sound — West by waters of Light House Creek and lands around the house known as the Elijah Clark house. North and Northwest by Light House Creek, the line continuing thence up said creek to the point where at high water said Light House Creek joins Dean's Creek. The said lot of land being an island and on which Sapelo Light house is situated. Said Thomas Spalding by this deed conveys no interest in or title to any lands attached or belonging to

---

[667] *Annual Report of the Lighthouse Board*, 1868, No. 294, RG 26 (Records of the U.S. Coast Guard), NARA; U.S. Coast Survey, *Doboy Sound and Vicinity, Georgia*, 1868, RG 23 (Records of the U.S. Coast and Geodetic Survey), NARA.

said Sapelo Light house."[668]

In a related transaction the month before, June 22, 1875, Spalding sold four acres on Dean Creek to Frank Dean for $100. The tract was in Frank Dean's name — he was only nine years old at the time — with the transaction being signed by his father, James Dean. **The** land entailed "a certain Hammock of land lying on the south point of Sapelo Island, containing four acres ... said Hammock known as 'Dean's Hammock,' and bounded on the South by Doboy Sound, East by Dean's Creek, North by marsh lands of Thomas Spalding and on the north west by lands of said Thomas Spalding, commencing at a point one hundred yards from the said Dean's Hammock." The deed was signed by Thomas Spalding in the presence of James Dean.[669]

A.C. McKinley and His Journal

Archibald Carlisle McKinley was born in 1842. His father, William McKinley (1809-1878) of Lexington, Georgia, married Patience Barrow (1817-1847) of Baldwin County in 1836. They had five children. Patience McKinley died in 1847. William McKinley then married Lucy Anne Andrews Sims (1815-1882), a widow, and they moved to Baldwin County in 1850 when Archibald was eight years old. William farmed and practiced law in Milledgeville, later acquiring property across the Oconee River from Milledgeville. In 1858 he built a brick home there, described as a Gothic-style cottage, which still stands, and owned until her death by Ann McKinley King, grandniece of A.C. McKinley.

---

[668] Deed Book A (1875), 498-99, RMCG.
[669] Deed Book C (1886, re-recorded from 1875), 485-86, RMCG.

According to the federal agricultural census of 1860, William McKinley was in possession of 66 slaves and 1,350 acres of land. Three years later, McKinley had increased his holdings to 75 slaves valued at $75,000 and 5,800 acres of land. This was clearly a prominent family with tangible wealth, further amplified by the fact that McKinley's brother-in-law, David C. Barrow of Oglethorpe County near Athens (Archibald's maternal uncle), owned 400 slaves and 2,670 acres in 1860 and served in Georgia's secession convention of 1861.[670]

Among his various abilities, William McKinley was also an archaeologist: he investigated Native American mounds on Sapelo Island and published his findings in the proceedings of the Smithsonian Institution.[671]

The early section of McKinley's journal, prior to his move to Sapelo Island, reflects details of his planting activities at Walnut Level. He hired black workers to plant his cotton and rented land to others on a sharecropping basis. The federal agricultural census of 1870 notes that McKinley's lands produced 9,340 pounds of cotton in 1869, which sold for 28 cents per pound netting a profit of about $2,600. Professor Russell Duncan notes in his introduction to the 1991 edition of McKinley's journal,

"Obviously, cotton growing was still a highly profitable enterprise for large landholders after the Civil War. [McKinley's] journal helps to dispel the myth that the Civil War left planters destitute. Certainly, they lost investment in their chattel slaves, and crop production was disrupted. Yet the members of the upper class still held land as well as political and social power. McKinley was one of the Baldwin County commissioners who decided on bankruptcy cases, sold property, and ran the county's affairs…The antebellum elite

---

[670] Russell Duncan, Introduction, in Humphries, ed., *McKinley Journal*, op. cit., xxxlv-xxxv.
[671] A review of William McKinley's archaeological investigations on Sapelo Island in the early 1870s, with quoted material from his reports, is contained in Buddy Sullivan, *Sapelo: People and Place on a Georgia Sea Island* (Athens: University of Georgia Press, 2017), 36-45.

retained their economic, social and political power after the war no matter how much they protested to the contrary. Because their laborers were now hired workers who could bargain, stand up to their employers, leave if conditions became intolerable, and not bow and scrape as they were required to during slavery, white southerners wailed that their fortunes, position, and lifestyles were ruined…"[672]

Sometime in September or October of 1869, in the midst of his cotton harvest at Walnut Level, McKinley made the decision to move from Baldwin County to Sapelo Island to join his wife's brothers, Thomas Spalding and Thomas Bourke Spalding, in an agricultural partnership. Thomas Spalding, whose legacy was the South End of Sapelo left him by his namesake grandfather, had intentions of reviving the antebellum cotton operations of his forebears, and solicited the assistance of his brother, Thomas Bourke, and his brother-in-law, Archibald (Archie), to aid in the endeavor.

Upon moving to McIntosh County, McKinley and Sallie initially resided in a rented home at the Ridge, a residential settlement about three miles north of Darien, utilizing some of the furnishings from their Milledgeville home. In the antebellum era, the Ridge was a favored summer community for Darien's business and commercial class where the cooling breezes off nearby Doboy Sound provided relief from the humid and malarial rice fields that surrounded Darien on three sides. During the war, the Ridge was a refuge for a number of Darien residents, both before and after the town was vandalized and burned by Union forces in June 1863.[673]

From 1870 to 1872, Tom Spalding, aided in his efforts by Archie McKinley, produced cotton on Sapelo on lands leased to the island's freedmen, and in separate lease arrangements with John N. Griswold of

---

[672] Duncan, in *McKinley Journal*, xxxvi.
[673] A detailed account of the burning of Darien in contained in Sullivan, *Early Days on the Georgia Tidewater*, op. cit., all editions, but most completely in the 2018 revised edition, 415-31.

Rhode Island who had purchased the North End from Tom's mother, Mary Bass Spalding. In December 1870, the McKinleys moved from the Ridge to Sapelo where they rented a house at High Point from Griswold. On the North End, McKinley rented land from Griswold for $500 a year, planting cotton and sub-leasing the land to the freedmen who paid the rent in shares equal to the cotton harvest. McKinley and the Spaldings grew cotton and leased or sub-leased cotton fields to freedmen at Bourbon Field, Moses Hammock and Raccoon Bluff, and expanded cultivation to small tracts on the South End, including Little Sapelo Island.

According to his journal, in mid-January 1872, Archie and Sallie McKinley, purchased from Tom Spalding one hundred acres on Barn Creek at Long Tabby (Riverside), and moved into the former overseer's house there, a dwelling they improved and added to over the ensuing three-plus decades. During this period, McKinley sold his Walnut Level farm in Baldwin County and rented out his house in Milledgeville.[674]

Meanwhile, Bourke Spalding, independently initially, engaged in the cattle business on the island. McKinley's journal indicates that on July 11, 1871, Bourke Spalding had constructed pens and fences to accommodate ninety-nine head of cattle on the South End, his object being to sell fresh beef to the captains and crews of the numerous timber ships that then frequented the Doboy Sound harbor to discharge ballast and take on cargoes of raw timber brought out from Darien, as well as processed lumber from the saw mills at Darien and Doboy Island.

McKinley's journal reflects the difficulties of attempting to make the cultivation of cotton the profitable enterprise it had it been prior to Emancipation. Thus it was that in late 1872, Tom Spalding and Archie

---

[674] McKinley journal, January 20, 25, 30, 1872.

McKinley abandoned their cotton venture and formed a partnership with Bourke Spalding to expand the latter's beef business, which by that time was proving to be lucrative. They purchased cattle, pastured them on the South End, and slaughtered and sold the beef to timber ships in Doboy Sound, as well as to some vessels off the North End in Sapelo Sound. Most of the cattle were purchased from agents in Savannah and Florida at prices of from $12 to $60 a head, according to McKinley's Journal.

The beef venture by the Spalding brothers and McKinley soon attracted competition from other entrepreneurs in Darien and at Doboy. Apparently, however, they maintained a considerable advantage over their local rivals, no doubt due to the proximity of the main anchorage in Doboy Sound to the South End of Sapelo where most of their cattle herd was available for butchering. In the summer of 1874 the partners purchased a small steamboat to facilitate the transfer of beef from the island to the shipping in the harbor; soon thereafter they initiated passenger service from Doboy Island to Darien to supplement their income from beef sales. All of these activities are documented by McKinley in his journal, including a day-by-day account of the frustrating, and occasionally harrowing, trip of McKinley and his brother Guy navigating the newly-acquired steamboat down the coast from North Carolina to Savannah. In late 1875 and early 1876, the Spaldings and McKinley began selling their beef directly to butchers on Doboy Island, who then delivered the beef to the ships in port, considerably easing the logistical difficulty of delivery to the vessels by the partners.[675]

Russell Duncan at times paints a largely unsympathetic portrait of McKinley and his white contemporaries on Sapelo Island, and in McIntosh County. In his introductory essay in the 1991 edition of the journal, Duncan

---

[675] McKinley journal, December 16, 1875 and January 25, 1876.

perhaps overindulges in a biased portrayal of whites as harboring post-war resentments, and having difficulty in accepting the realities of Emancipation and the radically altered (legal) dynamics of black-to-white interaction. One passage by Duncan suffices to illustrate this perspective:

"The McKinley and Spalding cotton enterprise depended upon black labor tenantry contracts. In March 1871, blacks signed sharecropping contracts—settlement to be due at harvest time. Freedman Caesar Sams paid his rent in cash, $50 in 1872, and by so doing, gained more control over his labor than those who signed for shares…Labor and management did not always get along. In various entries, McKinley writes about labor disputes: 'trouble with our plowhands'; 'My hands, with one exception, took holiday to-day'; and 'All but two of our negroes quit yesterday.' These disputes indicate what freedom meant to blacks. Unlike slaves, freed people had the right to complain and expect redress of their working conditions or they would quit. Even on Sapelo there were other employers who needed labor and would hire it away if given the opportunity; this gave blacks some bargaining power… By standing up for their rights, Sapelo blacks forced whites to treat them with a little respect, with a little equality. That McKinley and other whites had difficulty accepting this fact is clear in McKinley's entry: 'the negroes have been annoying me very much, trying to get the money due them.' That he named his stallion 'Ku Klux' certainly has relevance here. And the frequency with which servants and cooks left McKinley's employ suggests his domestics were poorly treated. That McKinley fired others is an indication that they had refused to play by his rules. There is a kind if freedom in the ability to get fired that blacks did not know during slavery. The old master-slave relationship on Sapelo had been overturned and replaced by employer-employee maneuverings. The freed people were becoming free people."[676]

Duncan offers a more balanced assessment in the concluding remarks to his essay, noting, "[The journal] serves as one more piece of evidence concerning the resilience of the human spirit in a world turned upside down. Blacks and whites searched for the meanings of Reconstruction—what did freedom mean, how much liberty is there, do I still have a right to the land?...McKinley has helped us define the struggles and independence in one

---

[676] Duncan, Introduction, in *McKinley Journal*, xlii-xliii.

localized part of Georgia. His journal helps pose questions and answers about Reconstruction Georgia."[677]

McKinley began recording entries into his daily journal in June 1869, several months before he and his wife Sarah (Sallie) made the decision to move from Baldwin County to Sapelo Island. While his journal begins with activities in and around Milledgeville before the move to the coast, the bulk of McKinley's document details the years he and Sallie lived on Sapelo during the Reconstruction period.

While most of the journal consists of routine, rather mundane, entries relating to weather, illnesses and hunting trips, there is much that is useful to those interested in the postbellum history of Sapelo and coastal Georgia. For example, McKinley provides validation that the waterways played a role of paramount importance in the lives of those who lived at Sapelo and the neighboring islands in the postbellum period. Waterway travel was necessary to get anywhere, and it was never easy. One reads of McKinley rowing an open boat from Sapelo to Darien or the Ridge and back in one day as he employs the flooding, then ebbing, tide to speed his progress. Doboy Sound was quite active. Across the Sound from Sapelo, the Hilton Lumber Company had a sawmill at Doboy Island; the small island was a stop on the inland waterway steamboat route for vessels using the inside passage between Savannah and Florida. McKinley and the Spaldings, while considered "gentlemen farmers," were nonetheless quite entrepreneurial. McKinley reports a degree of profitability from the McKinley-Spalding cotton enterprise from 1870 through 1872, after which the venture is gradually phased out and the men devote their energies to maintaining beef cattle. The Spalding brothers and McKinley made frequent visits to the ships in the harbor,

---

[677] Ibid., xliv.

forming friendships with the masters of the schooners and barks making trips from Europe to Darien for lumber. Colorful descriptions fill McKinley's journal of shipwrecks and storms at sea, of castaways resorting to cannibalism to survive, of fishing and hunting expeditions to the nearby islands.

Despite the occasional tranquil aspects of their island life it was more often a life of back-breaking labor, and hard work amidst the ever-present threat of injury or illness with no medical attention nearby. We read in the journal of frequent attendance at funerals by the young Spaldings. People died from illness and accidents considered minor by modern medical standards. The life expectancy in those times was, by nature, quite low.

McKinley kept his journal for eight years, until the spring of 1877. He then suspended making entries (no reason given) upon his removing to Milledgeville where he and Sallie helped manage the affairs of his ailing father. William McKinley died in May 1878 at the age of sixty-nine after which, in late 1880, the McKinleys returned to their home on Barn Creek on Sapelo where they lived the remainder of their lives. Sarah Spalding died in 1916 and is buried in the Spalding family plot at St. Andrews Cemetery near Darien. Aged and infirm, McKinley moved to Milledgeville after Sallie's death where he was cared for by his half-brother Guy. Archie McKinley died there in 1917 at the age of seventy-five, and was buried in the McKinley family plot in Milledgeville's Memory Hill Cemetery.

The provenance of McKinley's journal is interesting. McKinley left specific instructions for the disposition of his journal—his entry of February 14, 1876 notes that the journal was, upon his death, to go to his wife Sallie first, and to his brother Guy second. Guy McKinley's son, Archibald Carlisle, was the father of Ann McKinley King (1927-2004), grandniece of Archie McKinley. In 1969, the daughters of Archie McKinley's niece, Kate McKinley Taylor Treanor (1864-1946), Honoria Sapelo Treanor (1894-1985) and Helen

Treanor (1891-1972), both of Athens, discovered the journal in the drawer of a piece of furniture owned by their mother that had been moved from Sapelo Island to Athens in the early 1900s. The family assumed the journal was in the drawer of the furniture piece because it had once been in the Sapelo house of Archie and Sallie McKinley, a piece subsequently acquired by Kate Treanor following McKinley's death in 1917. After photo-copying by the University of Georgia Libraries, the Treanor sisters sent the journal to Ann McKinley King of Milledgeville who possessed it until her death in 2004. The journal remains in the possession of the family at the time of the publishing of the present volume in 2020.[678]

A few excerpts that follow convey the essence of the Spalding family's life on Sapelo in the Reconstruction period:

1869. *September 20.* I left Milledgeville at 4 o'clock on my way to Sapelo.

21. Arrived at Savannah at 5½ o'clock a.m. after a very pleasant ride all night on the Central R. Rd. Met Tom & Bourke in Savannah & left with them on the steam boat *Nick King* at 10 o'clock for Sapelo. Went outside where the sea was rather rough, making a good many passengers sick. Arrived at the North end of Sapelo about 4 o'clock, where we left the boat and went to Mr. M.J. Kenan's place.

28. Went fishing this morning to Moses Hammock — had pretty fair luck, but lost one rudder hook & split a hole in the bottom of our boat.

29. Wednesday. We all went to the Beach. Surf very rough with N.E. wind. Afterwards went to the South End to see Baba & to see the live oak grove there which is truly grand.[679]

October 6. This morning we all went over to Raccoon Bluff on the ocean side of the island but owing to bad weather we had poor luck fishing. Having had to paddle our canoe against wind & tide and to walk a good deal, we got back home after dark well tired. On our return we found Mr. A.C. Wylly and

---

[678] Sullivan, ed., *Postbellum Sapelo Island, The Reconstruction Journal of Archibald Carlisle McKinley*, op. cit., is a new edition of the 1991 published version of McKinley's journal, with a new introduction providing better-informed context of Sapelo in the years after the Civil War, and more extensive annotation identifying people, places and events.

[679] "Baba," nickname for Betsy Beagle (1796-1890), former Spalding slave and nursemaid to two generations of Spalding children.

I found a letter from Sallie, written a week ago.[680]

8. We all left Sapelo Island at 8.48 o'clock this morning in a sail boat for Darien. We had a fine breeze for our purposes, sailing across Doboy Sound in just twelve minutes. We all waited in Darien for the *Nick King,* the boat bound for Savannah which came along at 11 o'clock.

1870. *November 3.* Sallie, Bourke & I rode up to the extreme north end of Sapelo to look at the house which Mr. [John] Griswold offers to rent me. Very much pleased with it. This view is truly magnificent overlooking Sapelo Sound. While there the steamer *Eliza Hancox* passed with Mrs. Spalding & Tom aboard returning from Savannah.

1871. *March 22.* We got today from Creighton Island a boatload of sugar cane which Col. [Charles] Spalding gave us for seed.

November 6. Went with Bourke to Bourbon, McCloy [Dumoussay Field] & Drisden Point [Raccoon Bluff] to get the amount of land planted there. The rent on these fields amounts to 3213 lbs of seed cotton.

November 25. Hauled 1284 lbs. cotton from Moses Hammock—this making 6444 lbs rent cotton received thus far from the North end.

1872. *January 5.* Bourke & I went to Darien in the sailboat—got becalmed and didn't get there for seven hours. Brought Mr. R.L. Morris, who was drunk, as far as Myhall Mill on our way back.[681]

February 12. Started splitting rails to make a calf-pen in Oakdale. Caesar Sams paid his last year's rent (fifty dollars) for Jack's Hammock today.

February 26. At work again on our pasture fence. We dug 135 post holes, that putting us within 70 feet of New Orleans creek. Hauled 30 posts.

March 1. We started for the Ridge shortly after day-light. We had a pleasant sail but on our way back a wind & rain squall struck us off

---

[680] Alexander Campbell Wylly (1833-1911) was the son of Alexander William Wylly and Elizabeth Spalding Wylly. Wylly's brother Thomas Spalding Wylly (1831-1922), lived on nearby Creighton Island for several years after the Civil War; another brother, Charles Spalding Wylly, wrote the early history of Sapelo Island in 1914. A.C. Wylly was a surveyor and mapped parts of Sapelo Island in the 1890s.

[681] R.L. Morris, Richard L. Morris (1818-1885), Darien rice planter at Cathead Creek. "Myhall Mill," a sawmill on Mayhall Island on the Darien River, three miles east of Darien.

Heard's Island and we stopped there all night with Capt. Aiken.[682]

March 5. Rode up to Moses Hammock this morning to get a bag of shot left there. Sampson Hillery, an old Negro man aged 96 years, died to-day.

March 13. Spalding Kenan came back & went to Doboy to take the *Lizzie Baker*. I have been busy building a fence across Hog Hammock marsh where I killed two rattle-snakes.

March 21. We hauled two loads of lumber from the house to the new fence. Bourke & Charlie [Bass] have gone to Doboy to meet Tom who is expected on the *Lizzie Baker*. Yesterday we put six of our hogs on Little Sapelo.

1873. *May 16.* This evening we all three went to Doboy to try to raise a loan to enable us to carry on the cattle business, but were unsuccessful.

June 8. Last night old Carolina's house caught fire & came very near burning the old negros (himself & wife) up as neither one could walk. The house burnt down, though they were saved, being burnt very serious however.[683]

December 19. We at last got our flat afloat & off for Darien alongside the tug. Driving and flatting the cattle to the Island has been altogether the most exhausting & tiresome work I ever did in my life.

1874. *June 30.* I took beef to High Point. Hear to-day that the steamer *Clyde* was capsized & wrecked in Sapelo Sound by the heavy blow on the 27th inst.[684]

August 15. On getting up this morning I saw out on the quarantine ground a full-rigged ship which I afterward heard was a ship bound from Havana to New Brunswick & put in here last night

---

[682] "Capt. Aiken," Isaac Means Aiken (1830-1907), native South Carolinian, and proprietor of the Hird Island sawmill near the Ridge.
[683] Carolina Underwood (ca. 1780-1873) and his wife Hannah, both former Spalding slaves, lived at New Barn Creek, near Behavior. They both died soon after the fire.
[684] On June 27, 1874, the *Clyde* was struck by a sudden squall while crossing the exposed waters of the Sound between St. Catherines and Sapelo islands. Despite the capsizing of the vessel, the crew and passengers were saved with no loss of life.

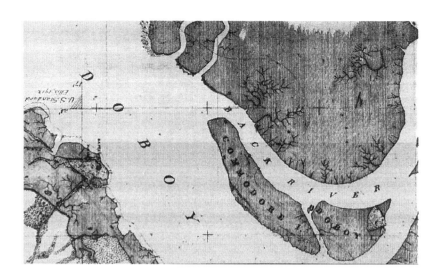

Lower Doboy Sound in the 1870s, looking north to south from bottom to top.

in distress with yellow fever aboard. Capt. & first mate dead and others sick.[685]

1875. *April 30.* Old T.G. Campbell, a notorious negro, was again indicted for false imprisonment to-day. When the Sheriff attempted to carry him to jail, he was prevented from doing so by a mob of furious negroes who fired into the posse. Several on both sides were shot, but none seriously. Altogether however there is an ugly state of affairs in this County.[686]

1877. *February 10.* Find our steamer sunk half-way to her smokestack at high water. I sold my interest in her tonight to Bourke Spalding for 15 dry cows payable 1st January 1879.

February 12. Wind blowing tremendously high. Bourke carried the beef on shortened sail. After getting to Doboy though, it was blowing

---

[685] The ship *William Wilcox* bound in ballast from Havana to Boston entered Doboy Sound on August 15, 1874 with yellow fever aboard, and was immediately confined to quarantine off Queen's Island near the Sound's entrance. The Port Physician, Dr. J.B.L. Baker, treated the sick; the vessel, with its surviving crew, resumed its voyage several weeks later.

[686] Tunis G. Campbell (1812-1891) was a New Jersey-born African American, former Freedmen's Bureau agent and state senator from McIntosh County during Reconstruction. His political dynasty from 1868 to 1876 was supported by a large black coalition in Darien. He was indicted for corruption and sentenced to a year in the state penitentiary, being released in January 1877.

too hard for him to beat back. A tug towed him to the Lighthouse and he rowed up South End Creek.

April 1. Sister Sarah's 30th birthday. All hands rode down to the South end this afternoon to look at her new home in the Grove.[687]

* * *

The postbellum activities of the Spalding and McKinley families at Sapelo Island are documented in Spalding family manuscripts on deposit at the Georgia Historical Society.[688] A selection from the collection provides a useful glimpse of Sapelo's history in the final decades of the nineteenth century and the first decade of the twentieth. A letter dated January 16, 1879 to Thomas Bourke Spalding from his father-in-law, David C. Barrow, Sr., who had invested in land acquisition with Spalding on the South End of Sapelo, including the Marsh Landing acreage:

"Yours of the 8th inst. came to hand day before yesterday. Also tonight two from Ella, informing us she would be here in a week or so. But I answer your letter now, with the hope it may reach you before Ella leaves home.[689] Of course I will do all I can to get two hands for you as you wish. I have heard of two who wish to go to Sapelo, and who at last account were unemployed … Of course Gilson[690] is mean, and only meanness could be expected from him.

---

[687] Sarah McKinley Spalding, wife of Thomas Spalding II. The Spalding's new house was near the abandoned Spalding mansion.
[688] Spalding Family Papers, Collection 750, series 4, box 1, series 5, box 1, GHS.
[689] Ella Patience (Barrow) Spalding, wife of T. Bourke Spalding, daughter of David C. Barrow and his first wife, Sarah Pope Barrow.
[690] Joseph P. Gilson (1824-1913) owned most of the upland of Doboy Island and its contiguous marshes. Gilson had an agreement with the Hiltons, Thomas and Joseph, and James Lachlison Foster for ownership of several acres on the island for the operation of their saw mill and mercantile store. He obviously was somewhat controversial, judging from David Barrow's comments here on litigation involving Gilson and Commodore Island near Doboy.

From what I have heard of his connection with the reporting of Foster for smuggling on Commodore Point, I judge a good many of those on Doboy and elsewhere, who were interested in Commodore Point, are not friendly to him. It seems to me you might go to some of the other mills, and for a small sum, buy refuse sawed stuff at one trip to run the Sapelo a month. I am sure I saw enough refuse stuff lying around Myhall Mill when we went there for boards to run the Sapelo for two months.

"I do trust you will not let the fencing of the marsh fall through if it can possibly be avoided. Of course any arrangement you may think advisable to make with Wm. Wylly touching the fence will be satisfactory to me. But I suggest to you, that as he is only a tenant and not owner, no arrangement with him can be permanent. Therefore, it might be wise to have him either put the fence across from the corner of Behaviour [sic] to the Steamboat (Old) Dock himself or have acknowledge of your ownership of the part you put there in case you have any of it to build. I think it advisable not to take any steps at this time to sell new ground or any other part of the land we purchased from Tom Spalding …Tell Ham Wylly I received his letter relating to the artichokes, and will send them to him. I notice they are to be consigned to Gilson. Are the Wyllys in connection with him in any way?"

Bourke Spalding's account book[691] reflects the day-to-day minutiae and records of beef sales and other activities of the enterprise he started in 1871 to stock cattle on Sapelo Island, and in which his brother Thomas Spalding, and his brother-in-law, Archie McKinley became partners. They slaughtered and sold fresh beef to the shipping that frequented Doboy Sound. The ledger covers the years 1878 through 1883 and lists individuals, the names of ships, amounts of money due or collected, and the dates of transactions. Inside the ledger is a faded white business card: "I will deliver three times a week from steamer Ogeechee, Fresh Beef, Fresh Pork, Live Pigs, Sweet Potatoes, Cabbages, Turnips, &c. &c. Steamer Ogeechee

---

[691] Spalding Family Papers, series 5, box 1, GHS.

will make three trips a week to Darien. Captains taking Beef from the boat will be carried at Half Price. Bourke Spalding."

The ledger contains a record of accounts denoting produce and meat and other items purchased from Spalding by several individuals prominent in the postbellum Sapelo story, including William C. Wylly, A.C. McKinley, William Brailsford, William Nightingale, David Barrow, Thomas Spalding, and Amos Sawyer, among others. There are detailed lists of the amounts of beef slaughtered from 1881-83, and itemized charges for freight shipments and passengers transported on the Spaldings' steamboat *Sapelo,* and later the steamer *Ogeechee* from 1880 to 1883. A typical entry denotes a consignment of freight for McKinley in 1881 that included "monkey wrench, 1 gal. Rum, 2 bottles Gin," and for Tom Spalding in 1883, "1 ham, 2 lbs. tobacco, soda crackers (Polly), shells for gun, shaft mended. Strain bill, $5.64, oil …" The last section of the account book was devoted to a breakdown of the sale of beef and other items to individual ships frequenting Doboy and Sapelo sounds. From 1878-80, sales of beef were made to the bark *Harvest Home,* bark *Ocean,* bark *Friedrich,* bark *Orion,* steam tug *Leon,* brig *Energie,* and bark *Roska,* among others. Notably, the Spalding documents reveal a letter to Tom Spalding, dated December 24, 1884, from the "Office of U.S. Local Inspectors of Steam-Vessels" in Savannah. Bourke Spalding had died unexpectedly only two months before. Tom Spalding was applying for a pilot's license to operate the *Ogeechee,* previously run by his recently deceased brother:

"Thomas Spalding, Doboy, Ga. "Yours of 23d inst. in hand & noted — we herewith enclose your license for yourself as Special Pilot on 'Ogeechee.' We do not find the record of your last license mentioned by you, so send us a certificate from your Health Officer at Brunswick for visual examination. We permit you to take the 'Ogeechee' to Union Island Mill for repairs. But notify us as soon as ready for inspection, before running again."

Only a month after this was written, Tom Spalding himself was dead, the victim of a tragic railroad accident. The untimely deaths of the two brothers, Bourke and Tom Spalding, so close together, and both through unusual circumstances, merit a closer look.

"TERRIBLE ACCIDENT. Killing of Captain Bourke Spalding of Sapelo Island. — Just before going to press this morning the terrible news of the accidental death of Captain Bourke Spalding of Sapelo reaches us. While out hunting yesterday his gun accidentally went off while he was crossing a log, the contents entering his head, doubtless killing him instantly. The body was found alongside of the log yesterday afternoon, search being made for him, for it was ascertained that he was out later than usual ..."[692]

Darien rice grower John G. Legare notes in his journal entry of September 6, 1884, "Capt. Bourke Spalding accidentally shot and killed himself yesterday while hunting by himself. He was buried this evening in St. Andrew Cemetery by lamp light." The thirty-three-year old Spalding was "universally esteemed by the people of McIntosh county, and he will be sadly missed by his family and a host of friends throughout this section," reported the Darien Timber Gazette. After the death of her husband, Ella Barrow Spalding and their only child, five-year old Randolph (a second child, Clara Lucy, born on Sapelo in 1881, died at the age of six months) left Marsh Landing to live in Athens with her father, David Barrow, Sr. In 1891,

---

[692] *Darien Timber Gazette*, September 6, 1884.

Ella and Randolph returned to Marsh Landing with her father and stepmother, living there until 1897. Years later, Randolph Spalding (1879-1954) of Savannah donated Spalding family memorabilia to the Georgia Historical Society, including the family Bible, and the only known portrait of Thomas Spalding, his great-grandfather. He never married, and was the last of the line of Georgia Spaldings descended from James Spalding.[693]

The death of Tom Spalding at the age of thirty-seven was even more unusual in its circumstances. Spalding died January 27, 1885 in Macon, Georgia as he was en route from Atlanta to Sapelo Island, via Milledgeville and Savannah. The following account appeared the next day in a Macon newspaper:

"A HORRIBLE FATE. The Tragic End of Mr. Thomas Spalding of McIntosh County. — 'There is a dead man at the city hall.'

"The above words passed from mouth to mouth at an early hour yesterday morning and soon attracted a large crowd to the point indicated. Stretched upon some scattered hay in the ante room at the city barracks, surrounded by a curious throng, was the pale and ghastly corpse of a young white man. His clothing was plain, but substantial, and his appearance generally was indicative of no ordinary station in life. As he lay outstretched his form weltered in blood, and his neck and shoulder revealed a sickening spectacle. The sight was nothing more nor nothing less than a body almost completely decapitated, and the right shoulder and arm crushed out of all shape. The crowd was busy attempting to discover who the unfortunate was, and the particulars of his horrible fate. It was soon learned that the dead man had been killed by a locomotive and that the accident had occurred only a few hours previously ...

"The night watchman at the barracks was sought and said; 'I know only that he was brought here about 4 o'clock this morning on

---

[693] For Randolph Spalding II, see Spalding Family Papers, series 6, box 1, GHS. The J.G. Legare quote is from Buddy Sullivan, ed., *The Darien Journal of John Girardeau Legare, Ricegrower* (Athens: University of Georgia Press, 2010), 35.

a dray and was accompanied by two officers. There is Mr. McAfee, perhaps he can tell you more.' The gentleman referred to was seated before the stove in the office, and in response to our inquiries, said: 'I was the engineer that ran the locomotive over his body. — the accident occurred this morning about 1:30 o'clock nearly opposite the gate of the Central yards [in Macon]. I had carried the engine and tender nearly to the river bridge, and having switched on to the main track, was backing the locomotive toward the shops. When near the rock warehouse, I noticed that the rear trucks of the tender jumped, and the thought immediately occurred to me that we had run over something. My fireman thought as I did, and was of the opinion that it was a piece of wood. When the engine had gone twelve or fifteen feet further, far enough in fact for the rays of the headlight to stream upon the track, I noticed the body of a man lying crosswise, his head just inside the rails. We went back to him to see what was the matter. When I got there I saw that his head had nearly been cut off and his right shoulder badly crushed. I felt the pulse, and as I did he gave his last gasp. I left the engine and sought a policeman, who had the body removed.

"Dr. Walker testified, after a medical examination, that the 'deceased came to his death by a wound in the neck.' The [coroner's] jury [found] that the deceased came to his death by engine No. 54 of train No. 12 passing over his body. Whether a case of suicide or not, the jury is unable to decide. When the inquest had been concluded, the body was given to Dr. C.H. Hall at his request. He said to the reporter: 'I know the young man well. He is my wife's first cousin. He was a splendid young man and of exceptional habits. He was the son of Randolph Spalding of McIntosh county, and grandson of Col. Thomas Spalding. He was named for him. His father died in the Confederate service in Savannah, at whose death he inherited 9,000 acres of land on Sapelo Island. It was to see about the sale of this land to a Northern syndicate that he left home about a week ago. He was in [Macon] last Friday and dined with Dr. Owen Kenan, a first cousin. He told him at the depot Friday night that he was going to Milledgeville, thence to Athens, and on to Atlanta, to consult with Mr. Samuel Goode, the real estate broker. He has a wife living — no children. His brother, Bourke Spalding, was killed two months ago by the accidental discharge of a gun, while hunting. His home is on Sapelo Island, but he is frequently in Darien. He owned, with his family, the steamer for which he held the pilot's commission, using it in carrying produce between Darien and Sapelo. He was thirty-seven years of age, and married a daughter of Captain McKinley, of

Baldwin County.'

"Later in the day our reporter learned that Mr. Spalding came down from Atlanta on Monday night in company with Messrs. Howell Glenn and Howell Erwin. The trio left the train coming in at 11:45 and went over to Brown's Hotel, where they registered. While standing in the rotunda of the hotel talking, Mr. Spalding suddenly remembered that he had left his hand satchel in the car. His companions told him there was no use to go and look for it, as the train had gone. But he evidently thought he would be able to get to the train, as he left the hotel and went in the direction of the old Rock mill. It is probable that Mr. Spalding thought the train would be taken to the coal shoot for coal before leaving for Savannah. That was the last seen of him. The most probable theory is that while on the track he was knocked down by the tender and run over. He was always known to be a temperate man and a gentleman of established good character."[694]

At the time of their respective deaths in 1884 and 1885, Thomas Spalding and his younger brother Bourke had been engaged in discussions with potential investors and developers for a potential sale or lease of the family's lands on Sapelo Island's South End. As seen in the above account it was on just such a mission to Atlanta and Macon that Tom Spalding was engaged at the time of his death. No records survive to attest to the specifics of potential transactions, but presumably the sale of all, or part, of South End Sapelo would have been for developmental purposes, including a hotel resort and other amenities in proximity to the beach near the remnant of the Spalding plantation house. With Tom Spalding's death further discussions in this regard ended for several years before being revived in the 1890s by Spalding's widow, Sarah (McKinley) Spalding and her second husband William C. Wylly.

A first-hand picture of life on Sapelo in the postbellum period is

---

[694] *Macon Telegraph & Messenger,* January 28, 1885.

provided in a letter by Ella Patience Barrow Spalding to Charles Spalding Wylly in August 1914, in response to Wylly's request for information on that period of Sapelo's history. Wylly, a Thomas Spalding grandson, was preparing a history of the island for new owner Howard E. Coffin:

"Your letter asking me to write of Sapelo as I knew it has been received. I wish my pen were adequate to the task. I wish I could transcribe from mind to paper the story of the life which made the years, years of interest as well as happiness. My first acquaintance with the dear and beautiful place was in 1870. In the spring of that year I went for a visit to my cousin, Mr. A.C. McKinley, who had married Miss Sarah Spalding. They were living then with her mother, Mrs. Randolph Spalding, widow of Col. Randolph Spalding, on the Ridge, near Darien. During my visit we went on a maroon to Sapelo, a very delightful experience for a girl from the up-country, and a most delightful and attractive introduction to the island. Mr. Alex C. Wylly and Thomas Spalding were living at the Kenan place and were our hosts.

"On the North End – Mr. Randolph Spalding's plantation, comprising all the land except Raccoon Bluff from Sapelo High Point to the Kenan line – was sold to a Mr. Griswold of Rhode Island who hoped to make untold dollars raising sea island cotton, but his hopes failed of realization and he, in turn, sold to Mr. Cassin. Finally, the place was bought by Mr. Amos Sawyer, who held it till it was purchased by Mr. Coffin. The Spaldings decided to return to the island to live. Their home had been destroyed, but Mr. Griswold during his tenure had built a very comfortable cottage at High Point and which [he] let to them until a house of their own could be built.

"In January 1871, Thomas Spalding was married to Miss Sarah McKinley, sister of Mr. A.C. McKinley, and all the family moved to the [Griswold] house and lived there until the winter of 1871-72, in the meantime, making the Long Tabby into a most comfortable dwelling. I visited my cousin, Mrs. Thomas Spalding, in 1873 and became quite well acquainted with island life and found it greatly to my liking. In November 1874, I was married to Thomas Bourke Spalding, Col. Randolph Spalding's youngest son. We lived about as far on the [north] side of the Long Tabby as the McKinleys lived on the [south]. At that time, and for years to come, the three families lived almost in sight of each other on the shores of Barn Creek, a beautiful salt water tributary to Duplin River. The house was built before my marriage on a small tract of land my husband bought from his brother. Nothing remains now but the land. And the view! One could sit on the piazza and there in front ran the creek, beyond for miles the ever-beautiful marsh, over there lay Little Sapelo, and beyond the marsh was Doboy Sound, ever changing, ever beautiful. Across it, one could see Doboy Island, Cane Creek, and then, 'afar the dim coast line, a long low reach of palm and pine.' It was very lovely, most of the time calm and peaceful, and oh, how dear! Will any people ever live there on that island who will love it as did those three families who had homes and happiness on Barn Creek's shores?

"At that time Doboy was a great shipping port for yellow pine. I have seen ships lying in Doboy Sound four deep at the wharves. At Doboy, at Cane Creek, and in Back River, there were moored as many as half a hundred at one time — not coastwise schooners, but big, square-riggers of every nationality from across the seas. The industry was a great feeder to Darien, the timber was cut in the interior and rafted down the Altamaha to Darien; there it was measured and sold, thence to Doboy and loaded on ships for export. There was a big sawmill on Doboy and one on Cane Creek where the logs were 'squared' before loading. My husband, seeing the opportunity, bought cattle to raise beef for the shipping. At first he was alone in the enterprise but later his brother and brother-in-law desired to join him, forming a company. They bought a little steamboat for delivering the beef and to carry the captains to Darien for business or pleasure. But the forests were cut away, the bar filled up and the end had come for Doboy.

"Time ran on and our Barn Creek Colony was broken up. Thomas Spalding moved to the South End, the McKinleys returned to Milledgeville in 1877 to be with his father, and we built at Marsh Landing in 1878. My son Randolph was born at Riverside, our Barn Creek home, in 1879; his sister in 1881 — the only children of the family name. The Long Tabby changed hands several times. Mr. William Nightingale bought the place and lived there for a year or two, but gave it up, and afterward, Mr. William Wylly rented it and made it his home. His sister lived with him. Mrs. Kate Treanor, a niece of Mrs. Thomas Spalding [II] and of Mr. [Archie] McKinley, who had lived much on the island, bought and made the Long Tabby her home for several years.

"All our friends loved Sapelo. The most exciting adventure upon which we sallied forth was to watch the Cromleys catch rattle snakes. This horribly fascinating pursuit was followed only in winter, when the snakes were torpid and lay in their dens. They come out on bright sunny days to bask. Whoever saw one sent forthwith to let the Cromleys, who lived at the Light House, know where the den was, and who came with a good stout string tied in a slip noose in the end, and, of all things in which to put a dead beast, a peaceful fishing basket strapped on the back. When the den was reached, Mr. Snake was gently prodded with the staff until roused enough to grow angry so that he would venture out to see who dared. When he put his head out, he put it through a slip noose lying ready. A quick turn of the wrist, a jerk, and there he was captured. My, how angry he would be! That eye, how it glared! Move where you would, it followed, full of evil, full of hate. After capture they were drawn up by the noose to a convenient height on some neighboring tree, and executed by having the head cut off just back of the murderous jaws, after being carefully skinned. They were careful the snake should not bite himself, for they extracted and sold the oil from the bodies as a liniment for rheumatism, getting a good price per ounce. They also cured the skins, mounting some, selling others for belts. Horrid to read of, isn't it? But most exciting to witness, furnishing many thrills to the minute, and gratifying to know there was one snake the less.

"We grew older presently, and gave up our rides and hunts, taking to more sedate pursuits, but found life none the less happy. But the end of our happiness was drawing to a close. Mrs. Thomas Spalding and I left the Island. My son and I in the fall of 1884, Mrs. Spalding in the spring of 1885. None of us were left on the island but my mother-in-law and the McKinleys, until 1891. That year, my father and mother went with my son and myself to live at Marsh Landing. Mrs. Thomas Spalding, now Mrs. William Wylly, returned to the South End shortly after. We left the island in 1897, not to return except for brief visits. In 1911 my place was sold to C.O. Fulton of Darien, and after Mrs. Wylly's death, the South End passed into the hands of parties in Macon..."[695]

The hurricane and "tidal wave" of October 2, 1898 struck the lower and middle Georgia coast a direct blow, and severely impacted Sapelo, the worst such storm to affect the area since 1824. The hurricane made landfall at high tide on a full moon, and put much of the island under water for several hours. Some Sapelo people took refuge in the lighthouse where the water rose up the tower over fifteen feet from the base. The hurricane caused great damage to the coastal islands and the waterfront areas of the mainland. A first-hand account of its effects on Sapelo was provided by A.C. McKinley who with his wife Sallie rode out the hurricane in their home at Riverside-Barn Creek. The following is the text of a letter from McKinley to his nephew William McKinley Cobb[696] of Athens:

---

[695] Spalding Family Papers, Collection 750, Series 7, Box 1, GHS; Buddy Sullivan Papers, Collection 2433, GHS; Charles S. Wylly, "The Story of Sapelo," unpublished, 1914.
[696] William McKinley Cobb (1866-1941) of Athens was a nephew of A.C. and Sarah Spalding McKinley. Thomas R.R. Cobb (1868-1898) was the younger brother of William M. Cobb, being named for his famous uncle, Thomas Reade Rootes Cobb (1823-1862), Georgia attorney, defender of

"Inverness, Ga.
Nov. 4th, 1898

"Dear Willie

"Your kind letter of Oct. 13th recd. & I would have replied sooner, but we have been exceedingly busy trying to patch up the damage done by the terrible hurricane and tidal wave of Oct. 2d. For four weary hours we stood (your Aunt & myself) waist deep in the water. The waves coming across the island—direct from the ocean, covered the tops of our windows. In the house the water was nearly 3 feet deep—in the yard nearly 6 feet on a level. The waves in our yard were fully 12 feet high. Your Aunt S. was sick in bed with fever, but when her bed began to float, she had to get up & stand waist deep in water for hours. We lost most of our possessions—either outright or from damage by salt water. All of our furniture is dropping to pieces, and my bibles—my own, my father's and my grandfather's with all the family records for three generations, were ruined, as the bibles were under water for hours. I hope however that I can copy the family records.

"We are distressed over the sad news of your brother Tom. Your father writes very hopelessly about his condition. It is the saddest case I ever knew. Your Aunt Sallie thanks you for your kind & sympathetic message. We shall always be glad to hear from you. Are you still in the Interior Department? Let me know when you change your address. Your Aunt Sallie joins me in much love to you.
Yr. Aff. Uncle
A.C. McKinley"[697]

"This envelope was under water. Since writing the foregoing, I see by the Charleston paper that poor Tom is dead. You all have our sincerest sympathy."[698]

In 1889, four years after the accidental death of her husband, Sarah McKinley Spalding married William C. Wylly (1842-1923) a Darien rice planter, and first cousin of her late husband. For several

---

slavery and Confederate brigade commander who died in battle at Fredericksburg, Va.

[697] A.C. McKinley to William M. Cobb, November 4, 1898. Another first-hand account of the hurricane, in more detail, was written on November 9th by McKinley's wife, Sallie, to her sister-in-law Ella Barrow Spalding. The complete letter is in Sullivan, ed., *Postbellum Sapelo Island*, 308-13.

[698] The cause of death of the younger T.R.R. Cobb at the age of thirty is not known. He had visited Sapelo Island in recent years, and wrote the article about Sapelo cited several paragraphs earlier.

years, the Wyllys lived in a house built near the ruined South End mansion by Thomas Spalding II. In 1890, Sarah Wylly put up Sapelo South End as collateral on a loan of $10,000 from the Scottish American Mortgage Company Ltd. of Edinburgh, Scotland. She died in 1897, leaving the South End to her husband, and before the repayment of the debt. As administrator of his wife's estate, William Wylly was unable to satisfy the debt, and in 1900, Scottish American foreclosed on the South End. In August 1900, Scottish American Mortgage gained undivided ownership of the South End at a McIntosh County sheriff's sale, a transaction consummated for $5,000. The deed described the tract as being 5,000 acres "more or less, being the southern portion of Sapelo Island, with Cabretta Island, which is a small island containing about 500 acres, and separated from the body of Sapelo Island by a marsh and tide water creek."[699] Scottish American's acquisition did not include the seventy-five acres of the Shell Hammock community. In June 1910, the South End was sold for $10,000 by Scottish American to the Georgia Loan and Trust Company of Macon, acting on behalf of the Sapelo Island Company, a consortium headed by T.H. Boone of Macon. An agreement was reached by which the Sapelo Island Company would make annual payments of $1,000 at six per cent interest until the debt was satisfied.[700] In early 1911, the Sapelo Island Company proceeded with development of the South End as a hunting preserve, and began refurbishing the Spalding house to livability. The mansion was a veritable ruin by that time—period

---

[699] Deed Book G (1900), 484-85, 519-20, RMCG. The 5,000 acres included contiguous marsh.
[700] Deed Book K (1910), 172-73, RMCG.

photographs show the structure without a roof, and only the exterior tabby walls standing among thick underbrush. The Macon group restored the central block, added a new roof with dormer windows for upstairs bedrooms, and made other improvements pursuant to utilization of the house as a hunting lodge.

When Ella Spalding sold the 1,030 acres of the Marsh Landing tract to Charles O. Fulton of Darien for $10,000 in January 1911, the only remaining Spalding family members still living on Sapelo were the McKinleys. Sallie Spalding McKinley, the last of her family's blood line on the island, was island postmaster, her husband Archie being assistant. A post office designated "Inverness, Ga." was opened on Sapelo in 1891 to serve island residents after the closing of the postal facility at Doboy Island. Inverness was so named as there was a "Sapelo, Ga." post office designated in 1887 at Sapelo Bridge (later Eulonia) in McIntosh County. In 1914, the island post office was re-designated "Sapeloe, Ga."[701]

An era was rushing to a conclusion. After more than a century, the Spalding presence on Sapelo, three generations, was near an end. Charles S. Wylly noted in 1914 that only twice in the previous thirty years had he visited Sapelo, the scene of pleasant adolescence memories:

"My memory has been mostly of men whose names are buried in the oblivion of time. On the visit previous to the last, crumbling walls, threatening soon to pass into dust, were all that met the eye. Since then thirty-odd years have gone, and this century has entered its teens — years of love, of hope, of discouragement, of despondency; and now, in May 1914, I have found the noble house restored; every wall rebuilt, white and spotless,

---

[701] Site Files, 1887-1914, RG 28 (U.S. Postal Service Records), NARA. Inverness was a town in the Scottish highlands from whence the Scots came to Georgia in 1736 to found Darien, originally named New Inverness.

and framed in a garniture of green. Solid and reassuring it stands, to claim a new immunity from time and to bid a new defiance to sea and wind, greeting the eastern sun as it rises in its sumptuous splendor and bidding farewell as it sinks in its glories of color to a bed of solemn repose."[702]

A footnote to the Spalding story comes from the elegant prose of William McFeely: "The poverty that had set in after the Civil War did not lose its hold on the island's people, black or white. The impecunious McKinleys—she a stooped, white-haired old lady, he a long-white-bearded Confederate veteran—died in 1916 and 1917, fifty years after the birth and death of their only child. There were no more white Spaldings on the island. The land, as property, had been restored to their family, but it had not produced prosperity for them or for any of the white possessors to which they sold it."[703]

Geechee Settlements: Raccoon Bluff & Hog Hammock

Since its establishment in 1871 with the purchase of almost one thousand acres by the freedmen of the William Hillery Company, the Geechee community at Raccoon Bluff had grown, partly through the migration of families from Hanging Bull and other sections of Sapelo's North End. Sapelo lore tells the story of the new First African Baptist Church at Raccoon Bluff being constructed of lumber gathered from the marsh that had been swept to Sapelo from nearby Blackbeard Island by the 1898 hurricane. This story has merit since part of the South Atlantic Quarantine Station consisting of several wood-frame structures was on the south end of Blackbeard, directly across the marsh from Raccoon Bluff.

---

[702] Charles S. Wylly, "The Story of Sapelo," unpub. ms., 1914.
[703] McFeely, *Sapelo's People*, op. cit., 143.

By 1910, the island communities of Raccoon Bluff, Hog Hammock, Shell Hammock, Lumber Landing and Belle Marsh were well-established. The largest was Raccoon Bluff where the census that year enumerated 194 persons residing in forty-three households. The 1910 census enumerated 163 persons in thirty-three homes at Hog Hammock, with fifty-two people in twelve households at Shell Hammock. Five households with forty-one people were at Lumber Landing, and three more households were at Belle Marsh (Walker and Jones families). There were single Geechee families at Chocolate and King Savannah. Sapelo had an African American population of 539 persons in 109 households in 1910, the peak population for blacks on the island, partly attributable to the timber trade in Sapelo Sound.

The loading of lumber from Darien's sawmills on ships at both ends of Sapelo provided employment for many of Sapelo's Geechee residents. Until the mid-1880s timber loading was mostly in Doboy Sound. From 1889 to 1914 there were loading grounds in Sapelo Sound off Sapelo Island's North End. Local African Americans were employed as stevedores, cutters and sawmill operators in an industry that made Darien the leading exporter of pine timber on the southeast coast. There was a black settlement on the north end of Creighton Island in the 1890s and early 1900s housing the Sapelo Sound timber loaders. The 1900 census counted over one hundred persons, almost all African American, living at Creighton, a time when timber operations peaked for the Darien sawmills. It is likely that some of Sapelo Island's people employed in this activity lived there seasonally, October through March, to discharge ballast and load timber ships at loading facilities on the Front River.

A few of the residents of Raccoon Bluff earned money in tasks at the Blackbeard quarantine, For example, Sophie Bell was employed as a laundress for Blackbeard Island in 1896, and members of the settlement often went by boat to the station to sell eggs, vegetables and chickens. Raccoon Bluff was an active agricultural community, both commercial and subsistence, with cotton, rice, and corn the most prominent crops cultivated at the turn of the century. The 1910 census listed occupations among Raccoon Bluff residents as being those of farmer, farm laborer, sawmill laborer, longshoreman (timber stevedore), timber cutter, sawmill teamster, sawmill fireman, and oysterman. Family surnames then enumerated included Bailey, Bell, Carter, Gardner, Green, Grovner, Hall, Handy, Hillery, Jackson, Johnson, Lotson, Lemon, Maxwell, Mills, Moore, Parker, Roberts, Spaulding, Smith, and Walker.

On the west side of Sapelo, the Kenan family never sold land to the freedmen after the Civil War. However, one community within the Kenan tract did continue until the 1890s, the former slave settlement at Hanging Bull where there were dwellings built in the plantation period. Not long after his purchase of much of the North End in 1881, Amos Sawyer sold parcels of land to several African Americans. One of these transactions was a sixty-acre tract at Lumber Landing, which abutted the north section of Kenan field near the Duplin River, sold in November 1881 to Caesar Sams (1844-1907). Over the ensuing three decades a settlement developed there with a later sawmill and timber dock near the community. From a population of forty-one in 1910, Lumber Landing declined to only a few families by the late 1920s. The 1930 census counted only two households—Mattie Sams and Janie Sams. Most of the Lumber

Nero Jones of Belle Marsh, image by Malcolm and Muriel Bell, ca. 1938. Courtesy of Malcolm Bell III.

Landing tract remained in the Sams family until R.J. Reynolds acquired it in 1956. Many of Sapelo Island's residents engaged in commercial timber and fishing from the mid-1880s through the first three decades of the 1900s, and upper Kenan Field was a focal point. The sawmill and the oyster beds in the nearby Duplin River provided seasonal income during the winter. William C. Wylly operated an oyster cannery at Kenan Field on the Duplin River in the 1890s and early 1900s, providing employment for the island's Geechee.

There were other pockets of Geechee residents scattered about Sapelo. Several black families lived at Bourbon Field as sharecroppers in the 1880s and 1890s during the Sawyer era of North End ownership. These included Liberty Handy with his three sons Manson, Abraham and Edward, and two daughters, Carrie and Lilla, and the families of James Green and Billy Rankin. These were probably the last fulltime residents to ever live on the Bourbon tract.

The 1910 census listed one African American family at Chocolate, possibly descendants of slaves who had worked the plantation there. On a canoe transit of the inland waterway in early 1875, Nathaniel Bishop briefly stopped at Sapelo Island and spent one night with a black family at Chocolate. It may be that Jacob Green, aged sixty-two, who lived on the site with his wife Elisa in 1910, was descended from that family. Green continued to live at Chocolate during the Coffin ownership; he farmed, and likely worked for Coffin as a caretaker for the tract on which Coffin had restored the tabby barn, and a former slave dwelling for use as a hunting lodge. The 1929 soil map notes two structures at Chocolate, one likely being the hunting lodge and the other possibly the Green residence in a restored slave dwelling.[704]

Hog Hammock's configuration, with identification of those who owned its land, was outlined for the first time in 1891 by McIntosh County surveyor Alexander C. Wylly. His detailed plat of the

---

[704] G.L. Fuller, B.H. Hendrickson and J.W. Moon, *Soil Survey of McIntosh County, Georgia*, Series 1929, No. 6, Bureau of Chemistry and Soils, U.S. Department of Agriculture, 1932.

settlement delineated acreage and ownership, and was apportioned to a general survey of Sapelo South End. Wylly made a second South End survey in 1897, mapping lands owned by the widows of Thomas Spalding and Thomas B. Spalding.

Although there are a few similarities, the 1891 Hog Hammock plat is in contrast to the layout and property boundaries of the present community. Wylly defined a series of elongated ten-acre strips of property running west to east on the east side of the road through Hog Hammock. The lots were long and narrow, extending toward the marsh and a tidal creek separating the community from the land of Sarah McKinley Spalding Wylly and Cabretta Island. A group of smaller lots of from two to five acres were on the west side of the road. The sandy road of 1891 followed much the same route as the main road through Hog Hammock does today. The ten-acre lot owners, from north to south, were James Walker, Davis Gilbert, Glasco Campbell, A. Sams, D. Sams, March Carter (two lots), B. Wilson (two lots), Charles Jones, Pero Dixon (two lots), Peter Maxwell (two lots), Shurrey Dunham, Stephen Wylly (two lots), Jack Lemon, Phoebe Bell and Sam Gerry, Rachel Underwood, and Tom Bailey. On the lower end of the grid were the lands of March Wilson (born a slave on Sapelo), with two lots totaling twenty-five acres, and Glasco Bailey with a six-acre lot. The smaller lot owners on the west side of the road were James Lemon (born a Sapelo slave, and saw Union Army service late in the war), B. Smith, S. Wilson, Jack Underwood, and Coffee (Cuffy) Wilson.

On the southern end of Hog Hammock the Wylly plat delineated a tract of twenty-one acres owned by the Johnson family without identifying specific individuals. To Hog Hammock's north was an

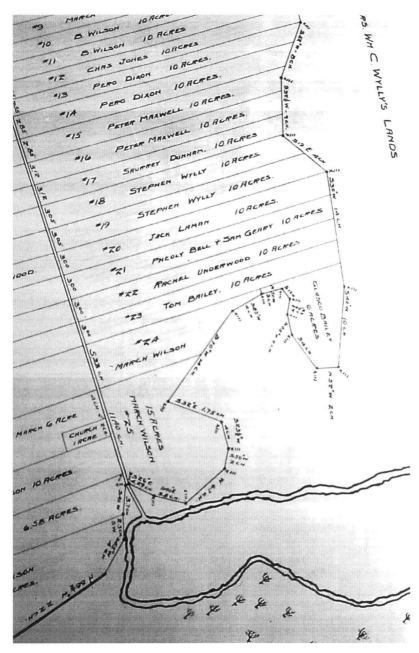

Survey of Hog Hammock by A.C. Wylly, 1891.

irrigation canal possibly associated with rice then being grown in the community, and "Dr. S. Kenan's Land";[705] to the west were the lands of Ella B. Spalding; the community was bordered to its east and south by marsh and the lands of Sarah McKinley Spalding Wylly.[706]

There were several public buildings at Hog Hammock during this period, and shortly after, including a school, one or two stores, and structures for the Masons and the Eastern Star. Later, about 1929, a lodge hall was built for the two organizations, and for other community meetings and events. The Lodge, more usually called the Farmers Alliance hall, had meeting rooms on the second floor, while the local chapter of the Colored Farmers Alliance and Cooperative Union was said to have met on the lower floor. A mainland chapter of the national organization (formed in 1888} began in Darien in 1892, thus it is possible that a branch of the Alliance for black farmers was formed shortly after at Sapelo, either at Hog Hammock or Raccoon Bluff.[707] In 1884, the Second African Baptist Church, later renamed St. Luke's Baptist Church, was established from the First African Baptist Church at Hanging Bull. The new church was built on the March Wilson property, but was identified on the 1891 survey as having its own lot. In 1904, St. Luke's had seventy-four congregants.

---

[705] The 1,500 acre Kenan Field tract to the north and west of Hog Hammock. "S. Kenan" is Spalding Kenan, son of Michael J. and Catherine Spalding Kenan.
[706] Survey Plat, Sapelo Island, "The South End," by Alexander C. Wylly, June 1891, Surveyor General's Department, GDAH.
[707] National Register of Historic Places application document for Hog Hammock and Behavior Cemetery, Kenneth H. Thomas, principal investigator, Historic Preservation Division, GDNR, 1996, 25-26.

Excepting Raccoon Bluff, Hog Hammock was the most populous settlement on Sapelo Island in the late nineteenth and early twentieth centuries. The 1910 census showed that Hog Hammock, including adjacent Johnson Hammock, had 163 residents in thirty-three households, being comprised of a diversity of Geechee families: Bailey, Bell, Carter, Dixon, Durham, Gerry (Gary), Underwood, Wilson, Wylly, Gilbert, Jones, Lemon, Maxwell, Sams, Johnson, Hillery, Lewis and Jackson. Occupations listed for Hog Hammock residents were farmer, oyster harvester, and timber longshoreman.

Behavior Cemetery

Behavior was originally a slave settlement. By the mid-1870s, the freedmen there had begun relocating to other developing communities on the island. Later, a section of Behavior became an African American cemetery, and it continues to be used today as the final resting place for Sapelo's Geechee people. Behavior replaced an earlier slave cemetery at New Orleans, just southeast of Hog Hammock; there were possibly additional cemeteries at the Hanging Bull and Chocolate settlements, although no evidence of these has been found to date. New Orleans cemetery, near the banks of New Orleans Creek, was the burial ground for many of Sapelo's slaves, possibly including Bilali, the patriarch of Sapelo, and his wife Phoebe. Bilali died in 1859, apparently in Darien, while the year of Phoebe's death is unknown. According to Sapelo historian the late Cornelia Walker Bailey (1945-2017), a lifelong Sapelo resident, New Orleans remained an active cemetery even after Behavior became the primary island burial ground in the 1880s. Bailey notes that though partly decimated by the 1898 hurricane, New Orleans may have been used for interments as late as 1918. No remains of this cemetery have been found to date.

An early source for how Behavior got its unusual name came from David C. Barrow, Jr. (1852-1929) of Athens, related by marriage to the Spalding family, and later president of the University of Georgia. Barrow noted, "This place [Behavior] received its name from being a quarter where the most orderly and well-behaved people lived to themselves as slaves."[708]

The Behavior gravesites are not arranged in ordered patterns, but rather are informally scattered about amid the live oaks and palmetto. It is difficult to determine the exact number of interments in Behavior Cemetery as early gravesites likely dating from the 1870s and early 1880s that had wooden markers have since vanished. The three earliest surviving markers all date from 1889, being those of Hilary Carr (1857-1889), Isabella Robinson (1858-1889), and Hannah Watkins (1847-1889). The next two oldest graves are perhaps the most interesting in Behavior. Betsy Beagle (1796-1890) was a household servant for Thomas and Sarah Spalding, and was a nurse to two generations of Spalding children; when she died in 1890 at the age of ninety-four she had outlived her former owners by nearly half a century.

Minto Bell's longevity was even more remarkable. This daughter of Muhammad Bilali was born ca. 1790 in the Bahamas, came to Sapelo with her parents, and was at least one hundred years old when she died August 25, 1890. Minto was recognized as the

---

[708] Ibid., 22-23.

matriarch of Sapelo's people when she became a free woman. She lived with her sons and their families—Liberty, Billali, Abram, and Fortune—on the land at Hanging Bull on which she had once been enslaved.

Traditional Gullah-Geechee beliefs held that burial grounds be placed well away from settled areas. Both New Orleans and Behavior conform to this pattern. The physical body is buried at death, but the spirit of the deceased remains active, often lingering to taunt or tease the living. The spirits therefore must not be disturbed. To appease them, personal possessions were often placed on and around the graves.[709] In the early 1880s, David Barrow, Jr. wrote of Behavior:

"I visited [the] graveyard and was never more curiously affected between amused and serious thoughts...The place is in a grove of large live oaks whose wide spread branches, knarled and knotted, all hung with the natural drapery furnished by the moss, shades the place, giving it a somberness...The epitaphs are written on ordinary headboards and driven in the ground...Old mother Harriet had her epitaph both of the headboard and on the tree...Caesar Sams procured the services of the distinguished artist 'M.W.' to do this honor to his 'Mother in Grace'...Anyone who has seen a signboard with hand painting down the road has seen a very near approach to the Sapelo memorial structures...[The] families have done what they could to perpetuate the memory and properly honor their departed friends, and those plain boards cost greater effort, and therefore I have no doubt greater honor to the simple negroes who lie under the live oaks of Sapelo than do the marble which beautify our city cemeteries..."[710]

In a 1934 *National Geographic* article about the Georgia islands, W. Robert Moore wrote of Behavior, "Short posts are planted at either end of the grave, and upon the mounds of earth are placed cups and

---

[709] Author's conversations with Cornelia Walker Bailey of Sapelo Island.
[710] National Register application document, 23.

dishes, oil lamps, and alarm clocks...the oil lamps are to furnish light through the unknown paths, the alarms are to sound on Judgment Day, and the dishes...are for the personal use of their former owner."[711]

A more contemporary observation comes from Cornelia Bailey: "This is our cemetery here...If you can't afford a headstone, the marker...will be your favorite thing that you like on the grave. So years later, if I come up here, I can find, 'This is where you are buried at because this is where I put your favorite cup at.' So it's used as a marker..."

There is a distinct aura about Behavior that transcends solemnity. It is the most hallowed and sacred ground on Sapelo Island. A connection is inescapable here among, and between, all those who share their communal and eternal rest that is very unlike that of burial grounds elsewhere. It is no wonder that the people of Sapelo hold these grounds in such reverence in a way perhaps best expressed by the words of Cuffy Wilson in 1939: "*Wen yuh hab a fewnul yuh hab tuh ax leab tuh entuh duh cimiterry gate. Duh spirit ain gonuh let yuh in lessn yuh ax leab ub it.*"[712]

Geechee Life at Raccoon Bluff & Hog Hammock, 1920s

The 1920 federal census listed 294 black residents in sixty-one households on Sapelo, out of an island population of 299. There were only two households, headed by Jaives Hart and William Hart,

---

[711] Ibid., 24
[712] Georgia Writers' Project, Savannah Unit, *Drums and Shadows: Survival Studies among the Georgia Coastal Negroes* (Athens: University of Georgia Press, 1940), 165.

with five white residents on greater Sapelo that year. Additionally, there were two Cromley families at the lighthouse, and Robert Raiford who farmed and lived alone on Little Sapelo.

Among the residents at Hog Hammock that year were families with the surnames of Walker, Gilbert, Campbell, Sams, Hall, Carter, Bell, Jones, Dixon, Bailey, Maxwell, Underwood, Williams, Lemon, and Dunlaw. At Shell Hammock on the South End were families named Dixon, Sams, Hillery, Olane and Bell, while Andrew and Phoebe Sherman lived at Lumber Landing, and Joseph and Annie Jones were at Belle Marsh.[713] According to the recollections of A.W. Jones, Sr., there were "several hundred" black residents living on privately-owned lands on Sapelo Island in the 1920s, the majority of whom were at the Raccoon Bluff and Hog Hammock, settlements. The 1930 census showed a population increase to 345 African Americans in seventy-five households, with fifty-two whites in twelve households. Most of the black residents continued to be divided between Raccoon Bluff and Hog Hammock but the census also listed several households at Shell Hammock and Belle Marsh. The majority of whites in the 1920s and early 1930s were employees of Howard Coffin.

The decades of the 1920s and 1930s were probably the peak of the Raccoon Bluff community from the standpoint of population and development. Since the late 1890s it had always been the most populous of the Geechee settlements on Sapelo, and the remoteness of the community, not only from the mainland, but also from most of Sapelo, enabled Raccoon Bluff to develop its own unique identity.

---

[713] Crook, et al., *Sapelo Voices*, op. cit., 28-29.

In 1927, a two-story wooden building was constructed near the First African Baptist Church at Raccoon Bluff to house the Rosenwald school. These privately-funded schools, at one time numbering almost five thousand across the United States, were built primarily for the education of African Americans in the early 20th century. They were particularly needed in the South because of the under-funding of public education for African-American children. Julius Rosenwald, part owner of Sears, Roebuck, began the Rosenwald Fund to provide seed money for the schools. The school at Raccoon Bluff was dismantled with the removal of residents to the South End in the 1950s, with only a portion of the brick chimney left remaining. Another Rosenwald school was established at Hog Hammock in an annex building of the St. Luke Church.

There was at least one general store in the community in this period, that being operated by Joseph Walker from his residence as early as 1910, and continuing to be maintained by his widow, Alice. The 1929 McIntosh County soil map delineated twenty-three houses at Raccoon Bluff, among various other structures, including the store, the F.A.B. Church, and the Rosenwald school.[714] The residential dwellings were one-story, wood-frame structures, and there is likelihood there were additional houses than those delineated on the soil map.

Through the oral histories conducted by Cornelia Bailey and Norma Harris in 1992, and transcribed in *Sapelo Voices*, it has been possible to identify the owners of many of Raccoon Bluff's dwellings in this period. Dan and Rosa Parker were on the west side of the

---

[714] *Soil Survey of McIntosh County, Georgia*, Series 1929.

community near the F.A.B. Church, as was Shad Hall. Several Green families were clustered in the center of Raccoon Bluff, including Moses Green and William Green, as were Luke Walker, and Joseph and Alice Walker. The homes of James and Ida Green, and James Green, Sr., were east of the church near the bluff on Blackbeard Creek. North and east of the church were the households of Alice Smith, Mac Bell, James and Hattie Spaulding, Charles Spaulding, William Spaulding, with James Bell and Sam Grovner further to the north. Several of these families lived at Drism Point, a section of Raccoon Bluff on its north end often referred to by Allen Green and other island Geechee.[715] Southeast of the church were the houses of Sam Roberts, and Lucy Roberts near the marsh. On the lower end of Raccoon Bluff, south of the church, were Peter Roberts and the households of Gibb Lemons, and Tom and Lula Lemons.

Other families in the community in the 1920s included those of Carter, Handy, Politz, Bryant, Rhodes, Truth, and Braun. *Sapelo Voices* notes that there were possibly some residents of Raccoon Bluff not counted in the 1920 census. These may have been some who were included in the 1910 census but who had moved away. It is also important to note that some of the census data in both 1920 and 1930 identified some families only by heads of household or by ownership of houses or property. Some families apparently departed Raccoon Bluff during the 1920s decade, as a number of residents in the 1920 census are not shown in that of 1930, including Braun, Politz, Bryant, Rhodes, and Truth.

---

[715] U.S. Census, 1930, McIntosh County, Population Schedules; Allen Green, conversations with the author, 1993, 1994; Crook, et al., *Sapelo Voices*, 32-33.

Katie Brown, Sapelo Island, late 1930s. Photograph by Malcolm and Muriel Bell. Courtesy of Malcolm Bell, III.

Concomitantly, it is almost impossible to definitively match the census data and information from the oral histories with the dwellings as delineated on the 1929 soil map. While useful in establishing the general pattern and layout of structures in Raccoon Bluff, the map probably indicates only a representation of the houses rather than an actual number.

Agriculture was an important economic mainstay for many in Raccoon Bluff during this period, both for subsistence and for income. This had been a well-established pattern since the settlement had been founded in the early 1870s. Topographic conditions were conducive to crop cultivation as sizeable portions of Raccoon Bluff, and nearby King Savannah, were comprised of especially good soils for crops. Additionally, part of the Drism Point section of the Bluff was a low wetland subject to fresh water inundation from natural sources, and therefore useful for cultivating rice as was often carried out by the Bell and Spaulding families that lived there. The information about rice corroborates that Raccoon Bluff was conducive to planting that staple, first practiced by the French in 1791-92.

Allen Green, and his wife Annie Mae Walker Green, were born at Raccoon Bluff in 1907 and 1912, respectively, and lived in the settlement up to the time of the Reynolds land swaps in the late 1950s, with the subsequent relocation of residents to Hog Hammock. When providing their oral histories to Cornelia Bailey in 1992, the Greens painted a picture of a quiet, peaceful community, unique from the rest of Sapelo Island: "When you get to Raccoon Bluff you find more oak trees, and palmetto," they said. "There's more oak trees there. In Hog Hammock there's more pine trees...The soil is different...the soil is blacker, a heavier soil. And there's more lighter soil in Raccoon Bluff, and better soil."[716] According to the Greens the houses at Raccoon Bluff were built "up high and close together, cause there was so many people living there." The houses

---

[716] Crook, et al., *Sapelo Voices*, 85-86; Allen Green, conversations with the author, 1993, 1994.

Shad Hall, Sapelo Island, late 1930s. Photograph by Malcolm and Muriel Bell. Courtesy of Malcolm Bell, III.

had outdoor privies, and wells for their water supply, most furnished with hand pumps. Allen Green noted, "They dig a deep hole...and they put a barrel in there. Some people have a top over it, and some had it open...After that they'd get this hand pump...In our yard we had a lot of fruit trees, apple trees. My mother had a lot of apple trees, and a grape arbor...and a banana tree." The Greens noted that rice and corn were the chief crops grown in the 1920s and 1930s. "We shell the corn...we had a mill, then we ground the corn, and you get three things out of that corn when you grind it. You get grits, and you get the meal, and the husk. 'Bout all we have left [the husks] for the hogs."

A contemporary picture of 1930s Geechee life on Sapelo was provided by "outsiders" as part of the research for the Depression-era Federal Writers Project volume, *Drums and Shadows: Survival Studies among the Georgia Coastal Negroes*. A chapter in this compilation of oral histories is devoted to Sapelo as part of the survey of coastal African American settlements conducted by the Georgia Writers' Project. The effort was coordinated by Mary Granger of Savannah, and aided by Savannah photographer-historians Malcolm Bell, Jr. and his wife Muriel Barrow Bell.

During their visit to the island in 1939, the Bells photographed local Geechee residents in several communities to produce a remarkable set of black-and-white images that forever froze in time the African American faces of Depression-era Sapelo. Project director Granger conducted interviews with Sapelo's people, including Katie Brown (1853-1940), great-granddaughter of black overseer Muhammad Bilali, Julia Grovener (1857-1938), Katie Grovener, George Smith, Shad Hall of Hog Hammock (formerly of Raccoon Bluff), Nero Jones of Belle Marsh, and Cuffy Wilson and Phoebe Gilbert (1891-1947), both of Shell Hammock. In addition to images of Brown, Hall, Wilson and Jones, there are photos in *Drums and Shadows* of Sapelo's John Bryant (1881-1965) at Raccoon Bluff, and Eddie Hall (1908-1977) and his ox cart on one of Sapelo's sandy roads. One passage of

Eddie Hall and his ox cart, Sapelo Island, ca. 1938. Photograph by Malcolm and Muriel Bell. Courtesy of Malcolm Bell, III.

this study places the island, and its people, in a cultural context only one or two generations removed from slavery:

"Small Negro settlements are scattered at the north end of Sapelo and are reached by winding roads cut through the tropical woodlands and brush. The Negroes are descendants of the slaves of the plantation era. Many lead an easy, carefree, life which consists chiefly of fishing, crabbing and cultivating a small patch of garden, while others engage in regular employment at the sawmill or in the company offices. Living an isolated island existence, they have preserved many customs and beliefs of their ancestors, as well as the dialect of the older coastal Negro. An oxcart jogging along a tree shaded road is a familiar sight and, with the guidance of a Negro boy named Julius, we discovered instances of crude wooden implements in common usage. The many Negroes interviewed gave a graphic picture of survival elements that have persisted since the days when slave ships brought their ancestors to the new country"[717]

Among the occupations listed for Sapelo's Geechee in the 1930 census were farmer, housekeeper, maid, and cook. The census data matched several occupations with the people who held them, including Alex Johnson (laundry foreman), Ascilba Kittrell (porter), Grant Johnson (truck driver), Emmett Johnson (carpenter), Joseph Bill (fisherman), Alice Walker (general store owner), Katie Campbell (Raccoon Bluff teacher), and Berdis Palmer (Shell Hammock teacher). The occupations indicate that many residents were employed by Coffin on the South End at the oyster cannery, the boat yard and marine railway, and in construction projects for shell roads.

The 1930 census identified thirty-seven residential dwellings at Hog Hammock and adjoining Johnson Hammock, findings that are

---

[717] Georgia Writers' Project, Savannah Unit, *Drums and Shadows: Survival Studies among the Georgia Coastal Negroes* (Athens: University of Georgia Press, 1940), 158-59. Katie Brown and Bilali are also covered in chapter 4 of the present study. The cover and interior photographs of Eddie Hall guiding his ox cart (p. 494) down a sandy Sapelo road in both the 1940 and the 1986 editions of *Drums and Shadows* are incorrectly captioned as being that of Julius Bailey (1911-1950). Author's conversation with Cornelia Walker Bailey, July 15, 2014; also, "Cornelia Bailey and Julius Bailey, Jr. say this is Eddie Hall," email communication from Malcolm Bell III, June 22, 2014.

consistent with the 1929 soil map. Most of Hog Hammock's population at this time was concentrated in the middle and northern portions of the community, largely being comprised of families such as Hall, Hillery, Bailey, Wilson, and Williams. Several Johnson families comprised the majority of residents on the south end of Hog Hammock, and included Bennie and Theresa Johnson, Emmett and Emma Johnson, and John and Maggie Mills.

The soil map delineated the St. Luke Baptist Church, and the school north of Johnson Hammock, and the Farmers Alliance building a little further north. Specific households included those of Richard and Eliza Bailey, Cuffy and Hannah Wilson, Katie Underwood, March and Bella Maxwell, Aaron and Sarah Wilson, Gardner and Clara Hillery, March and Nancy Bailey, and Edward Camel, among others. One white resident lived at Hog Hammock in 1930, the retired lighthouse keeper, Jimmy Cromley, who operated a general store in the settlement.[718]

Samuel Hillery, born at Hog Hammock in 1914, recalls that growing up, the community had "the church [and] a little prayer house. But I ain't never remember going to the prayer house…St. Luke, that's the first church I was going to school at. You didn't have no school house [until later] then they had a little school coming from the road by Jimmy's [Cromley] house…" Hillery recalled three public buildings in Hog Hammock in the 1930s: the school, St. Luke's Church, and the Farmers Alliance Hall. He placed the construction of the latter about 1929 or 1930, with the structure containing a social hall, and meeting rooms on the second level for

---

[718] Crook, et al., *Sapelo Voices*, 35.

the Farmers Alliance, Eastern Star, and Masonic Lodge. Hillery emphasized that Sapelo's communities were largely self-sustaining. "You didn't have to buy all them rice and grits you have to buy now. You beat your own rice and grind your own corn. Most everybody always had they own corn mill. Had they own mortar to beat they own r rice…You could do all that, [and also] fishing and hunting. No reason for no fish…I used to plant most anything, corn, rice, potatoes, peas, beans, greens, turnips, cabbage…" Several Hog Hammock residents planted sugar cane, and pressed it to make syrup. Hillery and his family always had an abundance of hogs and chickens, the feeding of which came from kitchen scraps, and residue from crops.

Rosa Jones Mills, born at Hog Hammock in 1914, recalled that a horse or a cow was used to plow for corn planting, adding that livestock were an essential component in the well-being of the community. "Cows, and horses, and the hogs, you had to feed them corn shucks and rice straw. You don't throw nothin' like that away," Mills recollected. "You had corn, and then you had scrap potatoes and stuff to feed the hogs with. And in the summer you go in the marsh and cut the marsh grass, and you give that to the hog, and he eat that, and you have to keep the trough full of water…"[719]

In addition to subsistence crops grown at home there was an abundance of food away from the settlements. For the men, hunting was an integral part of community life with rabbit, raccoon, opossum, deer, and wild turkey being taken in the woods; on the marsh fringe mink and otter were plentiful. Sam Hillery and others

---

[719] Crook, et al., *Sapelo Voices*, oral histories, 124-179.

made their own cast nets to gather shrimp and fish—mullet, trout, bass—in the tidal creeks around Sapelo. "Try and catch catfish, too. Catfish just ties up your net." Cast netting was often facilitated from skiffs known in the coastal region as bateaux. "Well, most of 'em bateaux. We call 'em a bateaux you know."

Life was quite purposeful in Sapelo's Geechee communities. People were resourceful; they worked hard, little time was wasted, and everything was grown, hand-made, or manufactured incorporating value and utility. These traits extended to the children. "Plenty of children in Hog Hammock then," Hillery recalled. My dad got a little trash, better rake 'em…in them days children will rake you the whole yard if you got a bag for it, the trash too. You give about fifty cents. That was big pay…"

In 1930 there were eleven families at Shell Hammock on the South End, including Lee and Bell Sams, Anthony Sams, Peggy Dixon, Herman and Anna Hillery, Gibb and Dianna Hillery, Dan and Nettie Dixon, Phoebe Gilbert, Dan and Rosa Parker, Ascilba and Belle Kittrell, Randolph and Gracie Lewis, and Rayfield and Isabelle Hillery. A short distance north, at Oakdale, was the family of Robert and Mary Olane. There was also a praise house at Shell Hammock.[720]

By the late 1920s, most of Sapelo Island's population was concentrated in the three settlements at Raccoon Bluff, Hog Hammock, and Shell Hammock, the number of families at Lumber Landing having declined to only two. The 1930 census showed that Mattie Sams, and three daughters, Jessie, May, and Marie, lived on

---

[720] Cornelia Walker Bailey, conversations with the author, 2012, 2013.

the north end of Lumber Landing on the High Point road nearest the marsh, while Janie Sams lived on the other side of the road with her two sisters, May and Daisy. An earlier resident, Phoebe Sams Sherman, moved to Hog Hammock before the 1930 census was taken.

Another family, that of Georgia Jones, widow of Charlie Jones, and her six sons and four daughters, also relocated to Hog Hammock just before 1930, The Jones family had lived in the old Kenan house, although the condition of the dwelling was probably poor, it having been built well before the Civil War. There were two families at Belle Marsh in 1930: Nero and Nancy Jones occupied a house with their children Freddie and Anna, and Hicks and Hettie Walker resided in a second home with their son Gibb. The two homes at Belle Marsh were located between Moses Hammock and the High Point road, both being delineated on the 1929 soil map.[721]

---

[721] Ibid. See also Crook, et al., *Sapelo Voices*, 31.

Racial Unrest in Darien & McIntosh County

Darien and McIntosh County endured serious social unrest in the summer of 1899, problems that were symptomatic of an era of similar difficulties across the South during the onset of the Jim Crow era. Racial tension in Darien evolving from an incident in August 1899 created bitter feelings that took years to overcome. A black man, Henry Delegal, was accused of the rape of a young white woman, Matilda Ann Hope, in northern McIntosh County. Some authorities have noted that the white woman was not of "the best character" and that even many whites in the community thought that the charges against Delegal had been trumped up. It is not known for certain if Delegal was the father of the child the Hope woman bore in July 1899.

McIntosh County sheriff Thomas B. Blount made plans to transfer Delegal to Savannah for safekeeping, but many local blacks interpreted this as a pretext for turning Delegal over to a white lynch mob. Numerous blacks, many of them armed, converged on the county jail in Darien and prevented several attempts by Blount to remove Delegal. Among those jailed in the disturbance were several former slaves, or descendants of slaves from Butler's Island: Renty Young, Simon Devereaux, Andrew Young, John and Richard Coffee, Marshall Dowsey, and William and Jack Cooper.[722] The incident received coverage in newspapers throughout Georgia, most of it detrimental to Delegal when Matilda Hope charged Delegal with rape eight months after the alleged assault.

---

[722] *Darien Gazette*, Aug. 26, 1899; *Savannah Morning News*, Aug. 24-27, 1899; John G. Legare journal, in Sullivan, ed., *Darien Journal*, 58-59; Malcolm Bell, Jr., *Major Butler's Legacy* (Athens: University of Georgia Press, 1987), 456.

"Delegal is of the big, black type, with slouching gait and an altogether disreputable appearance, which however may have been enhanced by his stay in jail and the probable fear he has for his life," reported one Savannah account. Two weeks later, the same paper noted "there were many in Darien who would like to see the negro legally executed just for the wholesome effect it would have. Fortunately for justice and the negro, those so inclined, if there really are any, were not able to have their wish realized." The article further added that it was "commonly stated" by the white people of Darien that they thought Delegal was innocent of the rape charge.[723] "The sheriff's attempt to move Delegal galvanized blacks throughout the county," notes W.F. Brundage. "Among the blacks who gathered to protect the jail were rural farmers from nearby Sapelo Island, day laborers, sawmill workers, and domestic servants. The combination of McIntosh County's large black population (about eighty per cent), much of which enjoyed considerable economic independence, articulate leadership and deeply rooted community ties, created an atmosphere conducive to a collective challenge to [white] mob violence."[724]

The African American "insurrectionists" maintained a close watch on events at the local jail and each time the sheriff attempted to move Delegal hundreds of blacks gathered, summoned to the scene by the ringing of the bell of the nearby First African Baptist Church. McIntosh County's large black populace was determined to

---

[723] *Savannah Morning News*, August 24, September 9, 1899; Bell, *Major Butler's Legacy*, 627 (n5).
[724] W. Fitzhugh Brundage, "The Darien Insurrection of 1899: Black Protest during the Nadir of Race Relations," *Georgia Historical Quarterly* 74 (Summer 1990): 234-53. This paper is the outstanding scholarly account of the Darien incident.

protect Delegal. This reaction was, as Brundage notes, "the predictable and understandable expression of the heritage and attitudes of blacks in McIntosh County."[725] Local authorities then decided to arrest some of the organizers of the protest, including Delegal's sons and wife. An incident at the Delegal home resulted in the death of temporary deputy Joseph E. Townsend, a white man, from a shotgun blast fired by one of the Delegal sons. Surprisingly, no white uprising followed. The militia commander induced the sheriff's posse to remain calm and to refrain from violence. The Delegal men then surrendered and were moved to the Darien jail. At the request of Darien mayor Spalding Kenan, militia troops from Savannah were dispatched by rail to Darien by Governor Allen D. Candler to maintain order. Colonel Alexander R. Lawton, commander of the militia unit, is credited with preventing additional bloodshed as he kept in check the local posse bent on avenging Townsend. Townsend (1856-1899), under contract to the Florida Central & Peninsular Railroad in 1885, had secured acquisition of rights of way through western McIntosh County for the building of the line through the section, completed in 1893. William R. Townsend, Jr. was among those who searched for and arrested those accused of killing his brother.

The black leaders of Darien, including clergy, the chairman of the local Republican Party, the Port Collector, and the editor of the local black newspaper, the *Darien Spectator*, prevailed upon the leaders of the riot to turn themselves in and order was gradually restored. The black leaders included Baptist ministers E.M. Brawley, Paul R. Mifflin, and J.P Davis, black Presbyterian minister J.D. Taylor, Rev. G.W. Butler of the

---

[725] Ibid., 241.

African Methodist Episcopal church. Rev. F.M. Mann of St. Cyprian's Episcopal church, Charles R. Jackson, postmaster of Darien, John C. Lawton, federal collector of customs for Darien, S.W. McIver, chairman of the local Republican Party, Dan Wing, a respected citizen of Darien, and James L. Grant, editor of the *Darien Spectator*. Rev. F.M. Mann was the rector of St. Cyprian's Episcopal Church in the 1880s and 1890s. His wife, Mary Mann, was the daughter of Aleck and Daphne Alexander, former Butler slaves. Mary founded the Mann School for black children in the late 1880s, an initiative supported by James and Frances Butler Leigh from England. Several hundred dollars to help fund the school was raised from a benefit play by Frances Leigh and her daughter Alice. Mary Mann's sister, Dora Jeannette, was her assistant at the Mann School. Rev. and Mrs. Mann had longstanding ties with the Leighs and Sarah Butler Wister. At the time of the Darien unrest Rev. Mann telegraphed Sarah Wister for assistance, and the Wisters, Shaws and several other families provided funds for the legal defense of Henry Delegal and the "rioters."[726] Mann followed up his telegram with a letter to Sarah Wister in relation to the Darien trouble:

"Dear Madam—I sent per telegraph that the Superior Court is in special session trying the colored people charged with the killing of Mr. Thownsend [sic] and those for riot. The Colored People that belonged to you who are charged with being implicated in this riot are as follows: Renty Young, the son of Isaac Young, Simon Devereaux, Jr., the son of old Simon Devereaux, Andrew Young, the grandson of old Captain Caesar Young, John & Richard Coffee, the sons of Nero Coffee, Marshall Dowsey, the son of old Amos Dowsey, William and Jack Cooper, the grandsons of old Tony Maxwell, Kitt Alexander & old Carter Williamson. The whole affair grew out of excitement. No one was killed or even injured in the riot, no one's property destroyed or molested. I consulted Dan Wing & others, and what these people need now is money to help pay their lawyer to defend them in court. The White People

---

[726] Bell, *Major Butler's Legacy*, 451, 452, 456, 559-60.

do not seem to be anxious to injure the Colored People."[727]

After calm had been restored, twenty-four of the alleged insurrectionists were convicted of rioting and received fines from Judge Paul E. Seabrook ranging from two hundred and fifty to one thousand dollars, and prison terms of twelve months hard labor. Later, following their trial in Effingham County, John and Edward Delegal, charged with the murder of Joseph Townsend, were given life sentences. A Chatham County jury acquitted Henry Delegal of the rape charge which had precipitated the turmoil.[728] From Philadelphia, Sarah Wister raised money to pay the legal defense of Delegal and those accused of rioting. In March 1900 she composed a typewritten letter and sent it to those who had contributed to the defense fund:

"Henry Delegal was tried in Savannah for his alleged offense, and promptly acquitted. His wife and sons were tried in Effingham County for murder, she was acquitted, the sons were found guilty, but recommended to mercy, and sentenced to imprisonment for life. More than half the Negroes arrested for riot were discharged, the rest fined or confined to imprisonment for a year. Their counsel, Judge Twiggs of Savannah, moved for a new trial on some technical irregularity. It was granted to one of the Delegal sons, but refused to the other, and to the rioters. Judge Twiggs appealed to the Supreme Court of Georgia which in January, reversed the sentence of the other Delegal, and ordered a new trial to take place in May..."[729]

In summarizing this unhappy state of affairs, Brundage noted that

"the conclusion of the Darien 'insurrection' left little doubt that whites could suppress organized black protest [and] stiff penalties meted out to the 'rioters' in McIntosh County were cruel reminders of the transparent racial bias of Georgia's courts. But the 'insurrection' also exposed several distinctive

---

[727] F.M. Mann to Sarah Butler Wister August 31, 1899, Wister Family Papers, HSP.
[728] Minute Book E (1896-1905), 174-97, 227-28, McIntosh County Superior Court, RMCG.
[729] Sarah Wister, letter to benefactor, March 20, 1900, Wister Family Papers, HSP.

characteristics of race relations in the region. Both the restrained response of the local whites and the Savannah militia commander to the black protesters and their willingness to work with local black leaders to quell tensions typified the meticulously maintained tone and conventions of race relations in the region. In addition, the organization and militancy of coastal blacks also served as a warning to whites that blacks would not let mob violence pass without protest."[730]

Not surprisingly, John G. Legare, a Darien rice grower, took a traditionalist Southern view of the events in reporting the racial unrest of August 1899 in his journal (see ff.). He expressed outrage at the murder of Townsend, echoing the sentiments of most of Darien's white populace, and felt the overall tone of the incident had stained the reputation of his town. He left little doubt as to where the responsibility lay for the trouble, as well as who should be blamed for the unfortunate developments.[731]

However, the Darien protest demonstrates that shows of unity, and even force, by local blacks could intimidate whites and help curb the tendency during that period of whites lynching blacks with impunity. The action by the McIntosh County black community was spontaneous, and without leadership and organization, but was effective because of its unity, which was largely invisible to local white authorities at the time. "Local black leaders did not provoke, lead or control the 'Insurrection.' They only played a role in ending the confrontation and in regaining the trust of local whites," Brundage concluded.[732] Since Reconstruction, Georgia coastal blacks had

---

[730] Brundage, "The Darien Insurrection of 1899," 247-48.
[731] Buddy Sullivan, *The Darien Journal of John Girardeau Legare, Ricegrower* (Athens: University of Georgia Press, 2010).
[732] W. Fitzhugh Brundage, "Black Response to White Violence, 1880-1930," lectures at the Georgia Historical Society, Savannah, and Lower Altamaha Historical Society, Darien, May 1992.

gained their strength through numbers as well as their collective sense of unity and purpose. The freedmen of the rice and cotton plantations were in the majority in the coastal counties. Legare and his neighbors failed to understand that in McIntosh County, economic opportunities for African Americans in the timber industry, beginning immediately after the Civil War, along with the permanent political power base established by Tunis Campbell in the late 1860s, had laid the foundation for collective challenge and confrontation when they felt threatened. Henry Delegal was much more than a lone accused rapist. He was symbolic of the mounting frustrations collectively felt by the local black citizenry.

Legare is representative of the white Civil War generation that guided Darien economic and civic matters in the postbellum era. Like many of his contemporaries he committed his thoughts to paper, largely for his own introspection rather than with public distribution in mind. Like his local colleague, Richard Grubb, extracts from Legare's daily journal provide an interesting first-hand glimpse of life in 1890s Darien. Following are his observations, though biased, on the 1899 racial troubles, in addition to other notes relating to his production of rice in the Altamaha delta:

December 31, 1895. During this year I managed Butler's Island for Mrs. Leigh, and planted General's Island on my own account. I came out just about even, perhaps a little behind.
September 10, 1896. The Champneys Island mill was burnt by a spark from the Engine at 4:30 o'clock this evening. I had 2,900 bushels of rice in the building, of which we saved 1,300 bushels in good condition, and 500 bushels too poor to ship.
September 29, 1896. We had a terrible storm today. It came up suddenly and unexpectedly. Champneys Island — 17 out of 25 buildings were blown down. General's Island — all my sheds were blown down, and about 50 sacks of my rice dumped in the river. Butler's Island — dwelling badly injured, the

feedbarn torn down and two negro houses. Crop badly damaged. Darien — the streets are impassable because of fallen trees. St. Cyprians Church (Episcopal) and the negro Methodist church are blown down. The white Methodist church is badly twisted, the Presbyterian church is blown out of plumb. Mansfield's store is wrecked, the Knights of Pythias Hall above Mansfield's is ruined. In the surrounding county the turpentine industry is ruined, so many of its pine trees are blown down...

August 9, 1897. The Bell Telephone Co. completed their long distance telephone line to Darien today, and it was opened for business.

October 5, 1898. We had a terrible storm last Sunday the 2nd inst. accompanied by a tidal wave of immense proportions. There were 32 persons drowned on Champneys Island....Five of our mules were found in a swamp on Elizafield in Glynn Co. and I had to go and get them...I find it impossible to get hands. The lumber people are paying common laborers from $1.20 to $2.50 a day & rations, and the negroes will not therefore work for me for 75 cents a day and so, not much has been accomplished so far."

Thursday, July 6th, 1899. Fire in town. The following buildings were burned. The Faries house occupied by Mr. William Hunter, and the beautiful Presbyterian Church building. Several other buildings caught but were put out...The furniture and doors & sashes of the Church were saved in a damaged condition. The Church cost $4,100.00 and was insured for $2,000.00. We are going to try to rebuild at once. This is a heavy blow to us as a congregation.

Wednesday, August 23rd, 1899. The negroes prevented the Sheriff from taking Henry Delegal to Savannah this morning for safekeeping. Delegal is charged with the rape of a white woman named Matilda Hope. The negroes believed that he was being taken from jail to be lynched. Thereupon the Governor ordered about 200 troops from Savannah, who arrived here at 7 p.m. and took him off with them. There is great excitement and trouble is feared, as the negroes are quite violent in their talk. It is hoped that it will end in talk.

Friday, August 25. There is a great commotion in the community. Messrs. O. Hopkins and Jos. E. Townsend were sent out about 16 miles last night to arrest the sons of Henry Delegal and in making the attempt the negroes shot Mr. Townsend in the abdomen, from which wound he died soon after. Mr. Hopkins was shot in the shoulder, his being only a slight wound. There is intense excitement in Darien, and a lynching for tonight is probable. The authorities have arrested & jailed so far 35 negroes, both men and women...

Wednesday, August 30. The Superior Court met in extra session today, to try the participants in the late race troubles, and I am elected Foreman of the Grand Jury.

Friday, September 1st. The Grand Jury...found true bills against 39 negroes for Rioting, and three negroes for murder, and no bills against 22 darkies for lack of evidence.

Saturday, September 2. I shipped today by Tug *Maggie* Capt. Judkins, 1,680 bushels of rough rice to Savannah.

Thursday, September 7th. The extra session of the Superior Court adjourned today. There were about 21 Rioters convicted and fined, the fines aggregating $10,500.00. Henry Delegal charged with rape, the cause of the whole trouble, was tried and a mistrial had. The Judge had previously granted a change of venue in the case of the State vs. John Edward and Mirander Delegal — murder — he today granted a change of venue to Henry also. All the prisoners will be tried in Effingham County next week.

September 16. We hear today from Effingham County that Henry Delegal has been acquitted of the charge of rape, and John Delegal charged with murder has been sentenced to the penitentiary for life. Edward & Mirander Delegal ere tried for murder of Jos. E. Townsend. Edward was sent to the penitentiary for life and Mirander was acquitted. Shipped today by Capt. Judkins one Lighter full, 2,340 bushels white rice by my weights.

Monday, Sept. 18th. Edward & Mirander Delegal were tried in Effingham Co. last Saturday, for murder of Jos. E. Townsend. Edward was sent to the Penitentiary for life, and Mirander was acquitted. Shipped today by Capt. Judkins one Lighter full, 2340 bushels white rice by my weights.

H.E. Coffin and R.J. Reynolds at Sapelo & After

As the twentieth century's second decade began Sapelo Island entered a distinctly new phase in its history and culture, followed by a brief period in the 1920s when the island actually realized a degree of managed development with profits as a goal.

Howard Coffin and Sapelo were in many ways evocative of an earlier era when his predecessor, Thomas Spalding, built an island empire with energy, skill and vision. When comparing the two men who left their mark on the island a century apart there can be very little ambiguity, for Coffin surely was to early twentieth century Sapelo almost exactly what Spalding was to the early nineteenth. There were genuine commonalities of purpose, intent, and philosophy between the two visionaries, and they were both men of principle, intellect and wisdom.

Mindful of the obvious technological progression from one century to the next, the distillation of the similarities between Coffin and Spalding is most clearly defined in their shared sense of *place* and *permanence* when it came to Sapelo Island.

Howard Earle Coffin was born in West Milton, Ohio, on September 6, 1873. Upon entering the University of Michigan in 1893, he studied engineering where he developed the skills to build a single-cycle, gasoline-fueled internal combustion engine. In 1898-99 he built his first automobile—by hand. Coffin was first employed by Ransom Olds in Detroit as chief engineer in the development of the popular Oldsmobile.

In 1907, Coffin and two friends, Roy D. Chapin and Fred Bezner, also Olds employees, went out on their own and formed their own company. Their firm became the Hudson Motor Car Company in 1909 with Chapin as president, Coffin as chief engineer, designer, and vice president, and Bezner as vice president in charge of purchasing. By the end of 1910, the Hudson Company was experiencing rapid growth, and was worth $5 million. Coffin made much of his fortune by developing standardized materials and parts for automobile assembly. He and another of his Detroit colleagues, Henry Ford, played pivotal roles in early motor car design.[733]

To promote their automotive development and outreach the three partners became proponents of auto racing. It was this interest that first brought Coffin to coastal Georgia. He attended the American Grand Prix road races in Savannah in 1910, after which he was invited to join a fishing trip at a fish camp on nearby Skidaway Island. The visit captured Coffin's fancy and "Georgia's dreamy coastline ever thereafter would be in his blood."[734]

Coffin's enthusiasm for racing led him again to Savannah in 1911 for the Vanderbilt Cup Race. It was on this visit that he learned through Savannah mayor George Tiedeman, and real estate broker Wayne Cunningham that Sapelo Island might be available for purchase. Coffin visited the island later that year as a guest of the Macon hunting club, explored Sapelo's beaches, marshes and

---

[733] Burnette Vanstory, *Howard Earle Coffin* (Sea Island, Ga., 1969), 7; Maxwell Taylor Courson, "Howard Earle Coffin, King of the Georgia Coast," *Georgia Historical Quarterly* 83 (1999): 321-24.
[734] Harold Martin, *This Happy Isle: The Story of Sea Island and the Cloister* (Sea Island, Ga., 1977), 7.

uplands, and met some of the island's residents. There were only a few white people then living on Sapelo, including the aging McKinleys, Archie and Sallie, and her cousin Charles Bass at Barn Creek, two families at Riverside, and two Cromley families at the lighthouse.

Coffin was intrigued by Sapelo's fascinating history, its natural beauty, and the easy-going lifestyle that enabled him to feel blissfully detached from his hectic life in Detroit. Coffin was hooked. With Cunningham as his agent, and David C. Barrow, Jr. as his attorney, Coffin began negotiations with the various owners of the island; by early 1912 he had successfully concluded the transactions by which he acquired the island that would become the unrelenting passion of the remainder of his life.[735]

For just under $150,000, Coffin acquired approximately 20,000 acres of Sapelo's upland and surrounding marshes from the Macon group, and five families that collectively owned most of the island's acreage. The breakdown and consolidation of Coffin's acquisitions were: 5,000 acres on the South End, including Cabretta Island, from the Scottish American Mortgage Company, as lien holder for the Sapelo Island Company; 7,000 upland North End acres, including Chocolate, Bourbon and High Point, from the Amos Sawyer family; 1,030 upland acres of the Marsh Landing tract from the C.O. Fulton estate; and 1,400 upland acres from the Kenan family.

Two smaller tracts on Barn Creek were not initially purchased. These were held by the Treanor family (eighty acres at Long Tabby), and the McKinleys (100 acres on Barn Creek nearby). Coffin added

---

[735] "Sapelo Sold to Westerner," *Savannah Morning News*, June 13, 1912; *Darien Gazette*, June 15, 1912.

these tracts to his holdings just after the First World War. The McKinleys were by then deceased—Sarah McKinley died in 1916, and is buried at Darien's St. Andrews Cemetery, and A.C. McKinley died a year later, being interred in Milledgeville's City Cemetery. Coffin's arrangement with these residents when he bought Sapelo was the right of first refusal on their property upon their death or moving from the island. In this manner Coffin acquired the last of the remaining Spalding family land on Sapelo.

In 1920, Coffin bought Little Sapelo Island's 200 acres of upland, and non-cultivable high-phase tidal marsh from Elizabeth Sherman Souther.[736] Coffin did not attempt to purchase African American land in the several communities on Sapelo, the most prominent being Raccoon Bluff, Hog Hammock, Shell Hammock, Lumber Landing and Belle Marsh. However, Coffin did purchase several small unoccupied lots at Raccoon Bluff in 1913 and 1914 shortly after he purchased most of the island. This was possibly to facilitate his access to Blackbeard Island, the south end of which was across the marsh from Raccoon Bluff.

Attuned to the island's history, Coffin returned Sapelo's name to its old English spelling, *Sapeloe,* soon after his acquisition. For man and island it was an ideal match as Sapelo became the perfect conduit for Coffin's creative instincts. "The rehabilitation of Sapelo satisfied the urge to construct and develop that was a leading force in Coffin's nature, while the peace, privacy and serenity of the island brought relaxation and escape from the pressures of the outside

---

[736] Deed Book K (1912), 172-75, 205-06, 234-35, 310-12, 312-14, Deed Book Q (1920), 533, Deed Book 6 (1934), 16, RMCG. Specifics and property demarcations of the multiple transactions are outlined in Buddy Sullivan, *Early Days on the Georgia Tidewater,* all editions, 1990-2018.

world. He was the perfect host and delighted in sharing the pleasures of Sapelo with friends and family."[737]

Coffin and his wife Matilda (Teddie) began regular visits to Sapelo from their Grosse Pointe, Michigan home. For several years they lived in the old Spalding house that had been partially refurbished by the Macon sportsmen group in 1911. It was in 1914-15 that the Coffins had the outdoor pool built at the front entrance while making other modifications and improvements.

Much of Coffin's time from 1915 through 1918 was dictated by pressing national events. He was appointed to the Navy Consulting Board by President Woodrow Wilson, and during the U.S. involvement in the First World War, 1917-18, Coffin provided consultation to the War and Navy departments in the military applications of gasoline-powered engines for vehicles and aircraft. He served on the Council of National Defense, an unofficial wartime cabinet, and headed the Aircraft Production Board. After the war, Coffin helped organize National Air Transport, and encouraged investment in the fledgling aviation business; he served for two years as chairman of the board of the entity that would eventually become the largest privately-owned airline in the world, United Air Lines.

Howard Coffin's years at Sapelo Island had important and enduring effects on coastal Georgia. He was rather a late arrival in the cavalcade of wealthy Northerners who since the early 1880s had accrued substantial amounts of coastal property, particularly on the sea islands. Coffin continued a discrete trend of the private acquisition of coastal lands that would be held among several

---

[737] Vanstory, *Howard Earle Coffin*, 19.

South End Landing, Sapelo island, early 1920s.

prominent families, or groups of families, for three generations until the 1960s and 1970s when many of the properties came under state or federal management and protection.

Coffin fit the mold perfectly; he expanded his national vision that was initially grounded in his contributions to the Detroit automotive industry directly to Sapelo, then to coastal Georgia, and beyond. By the time his efforts at Sapelo reached their apogee in 1930, it had become obvious there was an intensely intellectual underpinning behind Coffin's purpose and sagacity.

It is no coincidence that his initiatives on Sapelo almost exactly mirrored those of Spalding a century earlier. Coffin was every bit the dreamer Spalding had been, both for Sapelo and for his adopted state of Georgia. Sapelo—and certainly Sea Island later—represented the formulation of Coffin's own instrumentality, the tangible aspects congenial to his own interests. His energy, inquisitiveness, and innovation manifested by his accomplishments in Georgia, and the residual concepts of his vision endured long after his death.

Coffin devoted increasing attention to Sapelo after 1918. He was the first island owner after emancipation to develop Sapelo in concert with the provision of economic opportunities for the island's black residents; for the first time the large Geechee population found sustained employment available on the island itself. The 1920s saw substantive improvements made to Sapelo—at times, Coffin's initiatives seemed to be endless. Like Spalding, Coffin was simultaneously innovator, experimenter, scientist, and amateur architect; he literally brought Sapelo into the twentieth century.

He needed a mind as keen as his, with energy and resourcefulness to match, to help him realize his ambitions. Thus it was that in 1923, Coffin brought his young cousin, Alfred W. (Bill) Jones (1902-1982) to Sapelo to serve as island manager, and to supervise a surfeit of new projects. It was Jones, like a modern-day Bilali, who implemented the day-to-day details of fulfilling Coffin's plans.

Immediately upon arriving Jones began overseeing the building of a network of shell roads, and clearing long-fallow agricultural fields to resurrect large-scale agriculture. He put his engineering skills to good use. Irrigation ditches were blasted out with dynamite to replace Spalding's canals from a century earlier. With characteristic energy, Jones hired Sapelo's black residents to cut the pine timber growing on the former cotton fields of the North End, and used other local residents to operate the Duplin River sawmill; he supervised the building of a barn, stables, and other farm structures on the South End near the main house.

The 1929 McIntosh County soil map is instructive, for it attests to Sapelo's growth during the twenties by delineating a network of sand and shell roads, irrigation canals, boat docks, and new residential and agricultural structures on the South End. In 1930, Coffin and Jones were employing over 200 persons on Sapelo. Never in anyone's memory had the island been so busy, energetic, and full of promise for all who lived and worked there:

"It was, as Jones remembers, truly a time of wine and roses, those few years before the crash. Everyone was rich, and enjoying their riches. Coffin, from his investments in automobile stocks, airplane stock, and Detroit real estate, had an income of roughly $800,000 a year. He was spending a quarter of a million dollars a year on Sapelo. Jones soon found himself becoming more and more deeply involved with the management of the plantation. The island needed roads, and he laid out new ones and bossed their construction, curving them around the fine old trees, which he was careful to preserve…All around him things were happening, people were busy clearing the fields and horseback trails, planting pastures for beef and dairy herds, bridging creeks and digging artesian wells…"[738]

By the early 1930s, Sapelo had a beef cattle herd of some 1,000 head, crossed with pure Aberdeen Angus bulls. Coffin and Jones developed over 3,000 acres of open savannas for sustaining the herd, seeded primarily with carpet and Bermuda grasses, and lespedeza to enable year-around grazing. There were artesian wells scattered about the island to keep the cattle watered, thirty-six in all, drilled at depths of from 300 to 700 feet.

Another effort was Coffin's drainage of Sapelo's low-lying areas to reduce mosquito infestation. His installation of iron tide gates in a diking system is still in evidence today. Manmade fresh-water ponds were built, one on the North End in 1927, now the Reynolds Duck Pond, to provide habitat for ducks and other waterfowl.

To expand his timber operations, Coffin acquired 700 acres of pine land on the mainland, a transaction facilitated by local attorney Paul Varner, Coffin's land agent. Varner had also supervised the dynamiting of drainage ditches for Coffin on Sapelo. Coffin's purchase of Little Sapelo Island opened further possibilities. The

---

[738] Martin, *This Happy Isle*, 14, 17.

Little Sapelo Island, caretaker's house and landing, 1920s.

island was utilized as a hunting preserve, which included chachalaca birds imported in 1923 from Guatemala. A frame dwelling was built on Little Sapelo to house the caretaker; three artesian wells were drilled, and the tract was developed for the breeding of game birds. This acquisition included the small marsh islands along the Duplin north of Little Sapelo: Mary, Fishing, Pumpkin, and Jack hammocks.

The greenhouse, designed and built in 1925 just east of the Coffin mansion by the William H. Lutton Company of New Jersey, exemplified Coffin's enthusiasm for architecture. A botanist oversaw the diverse array of plants brought in and three full-time gardeners were employed.

To maintain his flotilla of twenty-seven boats and barges, Coffin constructed a marine railway on South End Creek. Three boats were built on Sapelo during Jones's tenure as plantation manager, and much of his time was spent coordinating boat operations and repairs. Nearby was the South End farm complex, wooden structures later replaced in 1936-37 by R.J. Reynolds with the more permanent structures that became the Marine Institute in the 1950s. Coffin had adjacent structures to house machine and carpentry shops, with a boat house on the creek. A power generating plant was built overlooking South End Creek, later upgraded with new equipment by Reynolds in 1935. Jones supervised road building, including the digging of culverts to drain low-lying land for road beds, and hauling in tons of oyster shell to surface the roads.[739]

In 1921-22, a two-story Spanish-style administration building was constructed for Sapeloe Plantation between the main house and the South End farm complex. It included offices for Coffin and the island superintendent, a general office, refrigerator room, kitchen, dining room, and, on the second floor, a central lounge, sun room and eight bedrooms, with an open terrace extending across the front of the second floor elevation.

The same year, Coffin restored the Long Tabby sugar house. Rebuilt on two floors, Long Tabby was designed as a guest house, and featured a lounge with two fireplaces, living room, dining room, butler's pantry and kitchen, all on the ground floor, with seven bedrooms and two baths on the second floor. In front of Long Tabby, overlooking the Barn Creek marshes and Little Sapelo, Coffin installed an in-ground swimming pool for the enjoyment of guests.

Seafood processing had been a part of Sapelo Island's economy since 1900 when William C. Wylly briefly operated an oyster cannery on the Duplin River. Later, Coffin and Jones revived seafood operations when they developed a cannery on the upper branch of Barn Creek, a section of that stream that came to be known as Factory Creek. Oysters were harvested from the nearby creeks in the fall and winter with production shifting to shrimp in the summer

---

[739] Coffin Papers, Sea Island Company archives, Sea Island, Ga.

Yacht at Marsh Landing, lower Duplin River, 1920s.

and fall. Managed for a time by Paul Varner, the cannery provided steady employment for the island's Geechee population; by 1922, the cannery was marketing "Sapeloe Plantation Shrimp" and "Sapeloe Plantation Oysters," with labels featuring a picture of South End House. The rusting remains of the cannery's boilers near the creek are testimony to this activity.

Coffin was particularly enthusiastic about his cannery. The venture fulfilled an important purpose in providing Sapelo's black women with steady employment in the factory, and the men with work harvesting the oysters in the nearby creeks. Years later, Bill Jones recalled an amusing anecdote regarding some of the women who worked at the factory: Jones "could never understand why the black oyster shuckers and shrimp peelers would take off their aprons and go next door to the commissary to buy a ten-cent can of Portuguese sardines for lunch." The seafood venture also enabled Coffin to experiment with oyster seeding in the waters around Sapelo, partly in response to scientific surveys relating to production.[740]

---

[740] Paul S. Galtsoff and R.H. Luce, *Oyster Investigations in Georgia* (Washington, D.C.: U.S. Department of Commerce, Bureau of Fisheries, 1930); Martin, *This Happy Isle*, 22.

Coffin started another canning operation at Darien, and purchased all the marsh lands with their oyster beds around Altamaha Sound between Sapelo and Little St. Simons islands. The acquisition included over 35,000 acres of marsh, and small tracts of upland on Wolf and Egg islands. Coffin employed persons with the requisite expertise to implement his scientific oyster farming project; seed oysters were planted at carefully chosen depths, and overcrowded beds were broken up where the oysters were too small at maturity to warrant harvesting. The effort was largely successful, and within several years the beds on the lower end of McIntosh County's coast were exceedingly productive. However, Coffin eventually terminated the effort due to the encroachment of poachers who constantly raided his oyster lands.

Coffin's interest in natural habitats led to his involvement in the protection of federally-owned Blackbeard Island. When the South Atlantic Quarantine at Blackbeard was deactivated in 1910, the island was largely untended. Coffin wanted Blackbeard to be off limits to hunters to enable government-sponsored biological wildlife research to be conducted there. He became something of a self-appointed caretaker for the island, and for ten years spent $20,000 of his own money to pay for security watchmen to protect Blackbeard from game poachers. Sapelo's game lands were similarly protected.

In 1927, Coffin contracted Luders Marine Construction of Stamford, Connecticut to build a 124-foot power yacht, *Zapala*, a vessel grossing 159 tons with a white-painted wood hull, teak and cedar decks, three double and two single staterooms, and a dining salon finished in walnut. A freshwater system supplied 1,500 gallons of water in copper tanks; the vessel had a permanent crew of seven.

Howard E. Coffin, Sapelo island, 1920s.

The yacht replaced Coffin's earlier pleasure craft, the *Miramar* houseboat. The white frame house at the head of the Marsh Landing causeway, built years earlier by Bourke Spalding, was restored for the use of *Zapala's* captain, engineer and other personnel.

The Marsh Landing dock was suitably expanded to accommodate the *Zapala*, and other vessels arriving at Sapelo Island. In early 1928, Niles F. Schuh, who had succeeded Jones as Coffin's Sapeloe Plantation manager, made application to the U.S. Army Corps of Engineers, Savannah District, for the construction of the new Marsh Landing facility, to be built of cypress decking upon metal-capped palmetto pilings, with a frame of creosoted timber. A dock house was built at the end of the pier on the Duplin River, and included an enclosed waiting room, a storage room and a telephone connected to the Coffin mansion.[741]

Howard and Teddie Coffin implemented plans in 1918 to begin a complete restoration of the mansion pursuant to their intention to make Sapelo Island their permanent home. Photographs from 1920 depict the mansion completely gutted except for the original exterior tabby walls. Detroit architect Albert Kahn prepared several designs for the rebuilding for Coffin's approval. The construction work was overseen by Arthur Wilson, a Swedish contractor who simultaneously supervised the restoration of the north end residence on nearby St. Catherines Island in which Coffin had a financial interest with Clement M. Keys and James C. Willson. The rebuilt South End House was to be "a palatial estate built on the tabby foundations and walls of Thomas Spalding's original house…The new main house was completed in 1925 with its lavish living room, library, indoor swimming pool, huge upstairs ballroom and nautical recreation room and lounge in the downstairs basement…"[742]

Coffin involved himself personally in the reconstruction of the Sapelo house. Utilizing Sallie Spalding's 1858 sketch as a guide, Kahn and Coffin effectively recreated the antebellum exterior as it originally appeared a century earlier. Sapelo's owner immersed himself into every aspect of the reconstruction. Harold Martin, based on his extensive interviews with Bill Jones, Sr., noted that "Coffin would come down to Sapelo from Detroit periodically, arriving

---

[741] Niles H. Schuh to Corps of Engineers, Savannah District, January 17, 1928, Coffin Papers, Sea Island Company archives.
[742] Martin, *This Happy Isle*, 16.

The Coffin house as completed, rear view, ca. 1927.

unexpectedly, to look into every detail of what the house builder, Arthur Wilson, had done during his absence. Frequently, he would order what had been built torn down and done over again. As a result, the house was built and rebuilt about three times before Coffin was finally satisfied…Scribbling on the back of an envelope, Coffin would lay out a work schedule for the next two or three months, and Jones and Wilson would have to take it from there…"[743]

Jones recalled that it was a house "centered around a high-ceilinged living room, heavily beamed in the Spanish manner, where Coffin loved to entertain with a lavish hand…Off this room, with its massive stone fireplace, lay the indoor swimming pool where Coffin would take his morning cold-water plunge; the dining room with its

---

[743] Ibid., 21.

Sapelo South End, ca. 1925. Main house is at center, Coffin's water garden is at lower left, Nanny Goat Beach at top.

long refectory table...a billiard room and a library. Off the living room were two master bedrooms, and upstairs was a ballroom, which could also be used as a movie theater. Downstairs, in a vast, stone-floored, rough-beamed basement, was one of Coffin's favorite rooms."[744]

W. Robert Moore, writing in the *National Geographic* magazine in February 1934, noted, "Nowhere else have I seen such a delightful setting for a great house as that on Sapeloe. In the midst of a cathedral-like bower of oaks, stands the majestic colonial house..."[745]

---

[744] Martin, *This Happy Isle*, 16.
[745] W. Robert Moore, "The Golden Isles of Guale," *National Geographic Magazine* LXV (February 1934): 242. Moore's piece featured Coffin, Sapelo and Sea Island; *The Cloister Bells*, special publication of the Sea Island Company, 1930, featured a photogravure spread on the Sapelo house. Sea Island Company archives.

Many prominent people visited Sapelo from 1924 to 1934. Two presidents, Calvin Coolidge and Herbert Hoover, came to the island as did the aviator, Charles A. Lindbergh. President Coolidge, and the First Lady, Grace, were guests of the Coffins as the highlight of a promotional campaign conducted by Coffin's friend Charles Redden for the newly-opened Cloister resort at Sea Island. Coolidge's visit occurred in late December 1928 near the end of his administration.

The President's party arrived in Brunswick by special train from Washington, D.C. on December 26th, being met there by Mr. and Mrs. Coffin, after which they were conveyed to Sapelo aboard the *Zapala*. The first morning after his arrival Coolidge, an avid sportsman, availed himself of the island's hunting opportunities. Jones escorted Coolidge to Little Sapelo where the president bagged three pheasants and two wild turkeys in the first of several hunts during his vacation.[21]

On Saturday, December 29, the President and First Lady were entertained with a "rodeo" at Nanny Goat Beach staged by Sapelo's African American residents. The event featured horseback races, and terrapin races on the hard beach sand. In 1981 Ronester Johnson of Hog Hammock recalled the events of that interesting day: "We had the horse race on the beach and we had the ox cart race. We had the turtle race...He [Coolidge] was standing on the beach waving with an eleven-gallon hat on. Eleven gallon—largest eleven-gallon hat I ever seen....We killed a deer that morning...He [Coolidge] was in the ox cart. He shoot a deer...He set up in the wagon. He got a gun across his lap."[746]

---

[746] *Atlanta Constitution*, December 31, 1928. A section of photographs accompanying the article was captioned "President and Mrs. Coolidge Enjoy

President Coolidge and Howard Coffin at Sapelo, late 1928.

Also during their Sapelo sojourn the Coolidges enjoyed a trip aboard the *Zapala* to the newly-opened Cloister at nearby Sea Island Beach. There, Coolidge planted a ceremonial live oak sapling that came to be known as the "Constitution Oak." The Coolidges also visited the lodge at Cabin Bluff, Coffin's 60,000-acre hunting preserve in Camden County.

During the Sapelo visit oil portraits of Calvin and Grace Coolidge were rendered by the English artist Frank O. Salisbury (1874-1962) who had accompanied the presidential party from Washington. Salisbury was renowned on both sides of the Atlantic for his work. During his career he rendered portraits of Sir Winston Churchill,

---

Georgia Vacation," and depicted scenes of the rodeo, and the president viewing the proceedings wearing his "eleven-gallon" hat.

Andrew Carnegie, Franklin D. Roosevelt, Earl Mountbatten, Richard Burton, and the British general, Sir Bernard Montgomery, in addition to Coolidge.

The President and First Lady sat for their portraits in the library annex on the main floor of the Coffin mansion.

"I painted Mr. Coolidge in a light suit," Salisbury later wrote. "We tried a robe and black suit, but he looked like a parson. He had a great sense of dry humor. I was never able to fathom his silence, whether his mind was solving some abstruse problem or whether it was a mere blank. There were five of us who sat down to meals every day, but he seldom joined in the conversation....After dinner he would sit in the drawing room for coffee, and on one or two occasions entered into lengthy conversations with Mr. Coffin concerning conditions in the motor industry..."[747]

After the Coolidges returned to Washington Salisbury remained at Sapelo to paint portraits of Howard and Matilda Coffin. The finished paintings were displayed facing each other on the north and south walls of the mansion's great room.

The Lindbergh visit six weeks later occurred with considerably less fanfare than that of Coolidge. Almost two years after his historic solo transatlantic flight from New York to Paris in 1927, Lindbergh was flying mail for Pan American between New York, Cuba, and Mexico. On February 12, 1929, the wedding engagement was announced between Lindbergh and Anne Spencer Morrow, daughter of the U.S. ambassador to Mexico, Dwight Morrow. Three days later Lindbergh, en route from Miami to Washington, landed on Sapelo Island where he had a pre-arranged meeting with Coffin and Clement Keys, the

---

[747] Frank O. Salisbury, *Portrait and Pageant: Kings, Presidents and People* (London, 1944), 91-96.

chief officers of the Transcontinental Aviation Corporation for which Lindbergh was a consultant.

The aviator landed his single-engine Curtiss biplane in a cleared cow pasture on the lower end of Flora Bottom, a short distance from the mansion. After meeting with Coffin and Keys, followed by lunch, Lindbergh flew off Sapelo at 1:48 p.m. after a visit of two-and-a-half hours.[748]

Other Sapelo visitors included Coffin's three Detroit friends, Henry Ford, who had established a winter residence near Savannah at Ways Station (later Richmond Hill), H.N. Torrey of Ossabaw Island, and banker and automotive executive Eugene W. Lewis; also, Edsel Ford of Dearborn, Michigan, golfer Bobby Jones of Atlanta, Cason and Fuller Callaway, textile executives from LaGrange, Georgia, Ivan Allen, Sr., and Coca-Cola owner Asa G. Candler, both of Atlanta, Clare Booth Brokaw (later Luce of the Time magazine fortune), boxing great Gene Tunney, *Atlanta Constitution* editor Clark Howell, and Walter F. George, U.S. Senator from Georgia. Tobacco heir Richard J. Reynolds, Jr. of Winston-Salem, North Carolina visited Sapelo in 1932 and 1933. The author Ben Ames Williams visited Sapelo during this period, writing portions of his novel *Great Oaks* while on the island. Published in 1930, the book is a

---

[748] *Brunswick News*, February 15, 1929. Another aviator associated with Coffin was Paul R. Redfern, a local pilot who, under the sponsorship of Coffin and Paul Varner, undertook to become the first to fly solo from the United States to Rio de Janeiro, Brazil, a distance 4,600 miles. Taking off in the *Port of Brunswick* amid great fanfare from Sea Island Beach on August 25, 1927, the bold venture turned into tragedy as Redfern was never heard from again. His plane was last observed flying over a town on the coast of Venezuela. It was theorized that Redfern's plane crashed in the jungles of Dutch Guiana.

fictionalized account of Sapelo's history, based partly on the 1914 Sapelo history prepared for Coffin by Charles Spalding Wylly.

As Coolidge had ended his administration with a visit to Sapelo, so did his successor, Herbert Hoover who, with his wife Lou Henry Hoover, was the guest of Coffin in late 1932. It was an unhappy time for Coffin; he had lost his beloved wife Matilda who had died of heart failure the previous February, and he was suffering serious financial losses as a result of the Depression. Hoover had been defeated in an electoral landslide by Franklin D. Roosevelt in the 1932 election, thus his brief one-day visit to Sapelo was a far more somber occasion than the 1928 presidential visit. The Hoovers' signatures in the Coffin house Guest Register were entered on Christmas Day, 1932.[749]

* * *

There continued to be pockets of white settlement on Sapelo's South End from 1920 to 1935. In 1930, there were fifty-two whites living in twelve households on the island. These included members of the Cromley family at the lighthouse, contractors and workmen associated with Coffin's restoration of Long Tabby and the main house, and the Hackels at Riverside. Emanuel Hackel managed the commissary at the oyster and shrimp cannery on Factory Creek, while his wife, Annie, was the Sapelo postmaster in the 1920s. The post office at this time was in the commissary.

The 1930 census noted one white person living at Raccoon Bluff, Katie Campbell, the teacher at the Rosenwald school. The majority

---

[749] Coffin Guest Register, Sapeloe Island, 1917-1934, Sea Island Company archives.

of the occupations identified in the census for both the white and black people of the island were connected with the operations of Coffin's Sapeloe Plantation. Some of these included dragline operator, foreman for road building, machinist, dairyman, stock farm manager, laundress, carpenter, herdsman, gardener, and fisherman. At the South End mansion were a cook, steward, nurse and four maids.

A number of structures associated with these activities were outlined on the 1929 soil map, including the restored Long Tabby and its accompanying swimming pool, the Factory Creek commissary and cannery, the Coffin mansion, the South End farm complex, and residential structures in the Geechee communities. The 1930 census reflected this period as being the peak of Coffin's activities on the island. With the onset of the Depression the white population declined.

In 1933, the federal government deactivated the lighthouse in response to the almost complete of shipping utilizing Doboy Sound and Darien by that time. In a Revocable License issued in May 1933 to lightkeeper Robert H. Cromley, the keeper and his family were given the option of retaining occupancy of the lighthouse reservation for five years: "Whereas, the Sapelo Lighthouse Reservation, containing one hundred and ninety-five acres with two dwellings, out-buildings and Sapelo Lighthouse located thereon under the control of the Secretary of Commerce, will no longer be required exclusively for lighthouse purposes after June 1, 1933." In 1934, the 100-foot steel tower was dismantled and transported to South Fox Island in Lake Michigan. The two keepers' dwellings were also removed; nothing remains at the site of the 1905 tower now except the five concrete foundation pads. After 113 years, lighthouse activity had come to an end on Sapelo Island, and the abandoned brick tower built in 1820 stood alone, a silent sentinel keeping watch over Doboy Sound.[750]

The automobile had precipitated a transportation revolution in America by the mid-1920s; the Atlantic Coastal Highway (U.S. 17) was the conveyor for an increasing flow of travelers through coastal Georgia, primarily northerners en route to the warmer climate of south Florida. Coffin envisioned that the Georgia coastal islands could attract many of these travelers. St. Simons was a potential resort destination, particularly after the construction in 1924 of the causeway and bridges to the island from Brunswick, a project designed and built by local native and engineer Fernando J. Torras.

In 1925, Coffin began purchasing former plantation properties on St. Simons, including the Retreat tract where he laid out the Sea Island Golf Club, followed by his acquisition the following year of a five-mile strip of beach and marsh known locally as Glynn Isle (formerly Long Island), which he renamed Sea Island Beach. There, Coffin immediately laid plans to develop the Sea Island Company, and build a resort hotel. After paving roads and laying lines for electricity, water and telephones to Sea Island, Coffin and Bill Jones engaged prominent Palm Beach architect Addison Mizner to design the new Cloister Hotel, which opened in the fall of 1928. Coffin hoped to attract wealthy northerners to the Cloister as a winter alternative to the developing south Florida resorts.

---

[750] Revocable License dated May 4, 1933, issued to R.H. Cromley from the U.S. Lighthouse Service, Site File, Georgia, No. 12, 2nd site, RG 26, NARA; *Darien Gazette,* May 26, 1933. See the 1932 R.H. Cromley image on page 6.

The Cloister was an instant success. To facilitate access to Sea Island, Coffin and Jones started a bus line from Jacksonville and Savannah to Brunswick. Another contribution to the coastal Georgia economy by Coffin was his support of a growing industry by which south Georgia pine trees were industrially converted to pulpwood and paper products. Coffin's association with George Mead of the Mead Paper Company played a role in the successful effort by Mead and Scott Paper Company to form the Brunswick Pulp and Paper Company in 1936. This venture (now Georgia-Pacific) evolved into one of the largest pulp-paper manufacturers in the world.

Meanwhile, Coffin and Jones brought in skilled people to manage Sea Island and the Cloister, most notably Jones' lifelong friend, James D. Compton of Dayton, Ohio. Also on board were Irving A. Harned, Charles F. Redden, T. Miesse Baumgardner, and legal experts Paul Varner and Judge C.M. Tyson. Early support for the venture was provided by Eugene W. Lewis of Detroit, who invested in the Sea Island Company, Cator Woolford, who bought Altama Plantation in Glynn County (later selling it to Bill Jones), and J.W. McSwiney of the Mead Corporation.

The end of the decade of the 1920s was a prosperous time for Sapelo, and for much of coastal Georgia. Economic rehabilitation was well underway, and numerous employment opportunities for the area's poorer and middle classes had been created. A renewed economic and social stability had been achieved in several of the smaller communities between Savannah, Brunswick, and Jacksonville, largely on the strength of investments and ideas from men like Coffin, Henry Ford, and Bill Jones.

There were troubling times looming, however, triggered by the October 1929 market crash. By late 1930, the financial burden began to tell on Coffin and Jones, particularly in regard to Sea Island. Coffin was encumbered by debt, having been compelled to borrow large sums of money to fund the Cloister. Sea Island's fiscal liability was magnified by the huge outlays of cash that had been drawn to build Sapelo Island's new infrastructure during the 1920s.

Jones recalled that in his first five years at Sapelo "whatever he needed in the way of workmen, materials or money, all he had to do was ask. When the bills came in, he would sit down and dash off a note to Coffin's Realty Investment Company in Detroit, from which, in that booming time, all blessings flowed. Whatever he might ask for, $10,000, $20,000, $50,000, back a check would come, no questions asked." The Sea Island and Sapelo bills mounted but then, no one saw the crash coming. When the market imploded, leading to the Great Depression, it was the worst calamity that could have happened, and at the worst possible time for Coffin.

Irrespective of these developments, Coffin was still optimistic in the fall of 1930 when he gave an important address to the Georgia Bar Association at Sea Island. He urged the development of more statewide transportation, and the promotion of Georgia as an attractive place to live and do business:

"We have a bit of philanthropy, and a good deal of business tied up together in this project [Sea Island]," Coffin noted. "As a matter of experience, I have had a part in the past in starting at least two semi-philanthropic projects, both of which have paid better than almost anything else I ever went into...In any big project of this kind there is bound to be a lean period, when everything is going out, and very little coming in...It is the people doing things that we want here. It is these people doing things that Georgia needs…to the end that we may all take an even greater pride in Georgia as the finest [place] in the whole world in which to live, to work, and to play."[751]

As the Depression worsened in the early 1930s, Sea Island struggled to survive. Coffin turned over the financial management of Sea Island to Jones, and the operation of the Cloister to Compton. For legal purposes, Coffin signed over all his assets to Jones in March 1932. Jones and his wife, Katherine Talbott Jones ("Kit"), reduced their own salary to $500 a month, using Kit's own money to pay for groceries at their Sea Island home.[752] Jones was determined to persevere, but cash was immediately needed to redeem outstanding bonds which would keep Sea Island and the Cloister solvent.

The solution was as obvious as it was painful: Coffin's beloved Sapelo would have to be the sacrificial lamb on the altar of financial expediency, an endgame to breathe desperately-needed money into Sea Island. Compton's publicity personnel began cranking out promotional literature about Sapelo in an effort to attract potential buyers.[753] To Jones' vast relief, Richard W. Courts, an Atlanta broker with wide connections in national financial circles, provided the necessary salvation: "Twenty-eight year old Richard J. Reynolds, Jr., tired of wandering the world on his own freighter and beset by family sorrows, was looking for a quiet hideaway. At the invitation of Dick Courts, he was brought down to Sapelo to see the place…Not long

---

[751] Howard E. Coffin, "Georgia's Future and Some of Her Undeveloped Resources. An Address Before the Annual Meeting of the Georgia Bar Association, The Cloister Hotel, Sea Island Beach, Ga.," 1930, Sea Island Company archives.
[752] Martin, *This Happy Isle*, 64-65.
[753] "Sapeloe Island, The Queen of the Golden Isles," promotional booklet, 1933, Sea Island Company archives.

after, he agreed to pay Bill Jones $700,000 for Sapelo with another $50,000 added if the yacht *Zapala* was thrown in..."[754]

Knowing Coffin and Jones were in financial straits Reynolds lowballed his offer for the island and mansion. "Sapelo was Coffin's passion and his home. The $50,000 offered for the yacht was a fraction of its commissioning cost. But very few people had as much money as Dick Reynolds...Eventually Jones helped Coffin realize he had little choice; for the Sea Island resort to survive, Sapelo must be sold. Coffin begged Dick to keep the deal secret for a year so that publicity surrounding the transfer would not adversely affect Sea Island's development. Dick agreed. Soon Dick had his seafront residence and one of the world's greatest yachts, obtained at a fire-sale price, perhaps ten per cent of their real value."[755]

The instrument by which Sapelo was sold by Jones (for Coffin) to Reynolds was dated April 14, 1934. The sale did not include the areas of Sapelo that Coffin did not own: the settlements of Raccoon Bluff, Hog Hammock, Belle Marsh, Shell Hammock and Lumber Landing, Behavior Cemetery and the lighthouse tract.[756]

The complexity of the financial arrangements notwithstanding, the disposal of Sapelo, along with the sale of Detroit Realty bonds, enabled the Sea Island Company to regain its corporate footing and

---

[754] Martin, *This Happy Isle*, 67.
[755] Patrick Reynolds and Tom Shachtman, *The Gilded Leaf: Triumph, Tragedy and Tobacco, Three Generations of the R.J. Reynolds Family and Fortune* (Boston: Little, Brown, 1989), 188-89.
[756] Deed Book 6 (1934), 43-47, Deed Book 18 (1949), 135-39, RMCG. The latter document pertains to the mainland Meridian Landing tract, the point of boat access to and from Sapelo Island.

ride out the Depression. The company gradually acquired solvency, and by 1941 was turning solid profits.

There is a melancholy footnote to the twenty-two year Coffin experience with Sapelo. Coffin was a lonely man in 1937 when he entered into a disastrous second marriage in New York, to Gladys Baker, a free-lance journalist much younger than Coffin. Unhappy and despondent, Coffin returned to Georgia after only a few months, and lived for a time with Bill and Kit Jones at Sea Island. On November 21, 1937, while the Joneses were returning from a trip to New York making arrangements for Coffin's quiet divorce from his second wife, they got the tragic news from Jim Compton that Coffin was dead. "Seeing no way out of his troubles, he had taken his own life with a rifle…"[757] Coffin was buried beside Matilda at St. Simons' Christ Church Cemetery where their plots have been carefully maintained by the Jones family and Sea Island over the years.

Even inclusive of Spalding, no period of Sapelo ownership had seen more dynamism, improvement, and overall benefit to the population of the island than that of Howard Coffin. The significance of his productive impact on Darien, Brunswick, St. Simons, and Sea Island also cannot be overstated. Coffin's ideas, energy, and money helped lift Glynn and McIntosh counties out of their economic lethargy in the 1920s and early 1930s, possibly creating momentum that made the difficulties of the Depression less oppressive than in other areas. Clark Howell, publisher of the *Atlanta*

---

[757] Martin, *This Happy Isle*, 70-71.

Constitution, perceptively noted that Coffin "was in some respects a greater Georgian than many of us native sons, for he had the vision to discern and develop what our state possessed when we were perhaps less observant, less audacious, and less willing to gamble on our judgement. His dynamic influence, his creative mind and understanding spirit will be found here so long as a single child remains to play, or a weary soul to seek refreshment."[758] Howell made these remarks in 1939 on the occasion of the dedication of the Howard E. Coffin Recreational Center in Brunswick. Later, there was another tribute to Coffin's memory. On January 21, 1944 the World War II Liberty ship SS *Howard E. Coffin* was launched at the Brunswick shipyard, christened by Katherine "Kit" Jones and Dorothy Torras as they broke the traditional bottle of champagne across the vessel's bow. The *Coffin* was the twenty-fourth of ninety-nine Liberty ships built at Brunswick.

Coffin left other legacies to Sapelo. One that is often overlooked is his awareness of the importance of historical documentation and its preservation. Many of Sapelo's records, building plans, and other documents are preserved in the Sea Island archives. A large collection of photographs, many taken by Coffin himself, depicts Sapelo's people and places between 1912 and 1934, and have contributed immensely to the historiography of the coast. This collection, in possession of the Jones family, offers rare glimpses of African American life on Sapelo in the early twentieth century as well as recording the progress of Coffin's projects.

---

[758] Ibid., 71.

* * *

Excepting the present African American community, Sapelo Island's last era of private ownership was that of R.J. Reynolds, Jr., the high-flying, free-spirited heir to a North Carolina cigarette fortune. Reynolds brought to Sapelo modernization, mechanics, and science—in addition to four different wives—during a thirty-year span that, in many aspects was a contrast both in outlook and lifestyle from his Sapelo predecessors, Thomas Spalding and H.E. Coffin. Unlike them, Reynolds never made Sapelo his full-time home, but regularly visited the island for stays of varying length, often simply to escape the vicissitudes of his personal and professional life on the mainland.

Richard Joshua "Dick" Reynolds, Jr. (1906-1964) of Winston-Salem, North Carolina was the son of that city's founder of the Reynolds Tobacco Company, and like Spalding, was twenty-eight years old when he bought Sapelo in 1934. His epitaph might easily be written to describe a life unfulfilled. It was certainly a life of paradoxes. Reynolds was wealthy, witty, ambitious, highly intelligent, philanthropic, an icon of his times in industrial and financial America. His business and political acumen, partly built on the legacy of his father's tobacco fortune, made him one of the nation's best known figures by the middle of the twentieth century. Yet he was simultaneously a tragically flawed figure. He had a disastrous personal life that was filled with turbulence, broken relationships, alcoholism and infidelity, and he died at the relatively young age of 58 under what some have described as questionable circumstances.

As a young man Reynolds became a key player on the national scene in business, politics and philanthropy. In 1940 he salvaged a failing Delta Airlines with the purchase of a large block of stock that gave the fledgling airline financial stability. The same year Reynolds' energetic fund-raising efforts in North Carolina helped secure Franklin D. Roosevelt's unprecedented third presidential term, for which Reynolds was rewarded by being appointed treasurer of the Democratic National Committee. In 1941 he was elected mayor of Winston-Salem with a ninety per cent plurality. Yet for all these achievements he remained unsettled both in his personal and public life; he was as restless as he was successful.

Reynolds was a licensed pilot, often travelled the country by air, and was a leader in the U.S. aviation industry. But his real love was the sea. He was a world-class yachtsman, read extensively on maritime history and the marine sciences, and was a decorated naval officer in the Pacific War. Reynolds got much use of Coffin's former yacht, *Zapala*, part of his Sapelo purchase package. For several years, Reynolds and his first wife made annual voyages to the Mediterranean and the French Riviera in the *Zapala*, as well as to Bermuda, and along the Atlantic coast.

Pursuant to these nautical interests, and not long after acquiring Sapelo, Reynolds had a workboat designed to fulfil specific logistical requirements. Ronester Johnson of Hog Hammock recalled that Coffin initiated boatbuilding on the South End in the early 1920s, work continued by Reynolds at the boat yard and marine railway on South End Creek. Johnson noted that his father, Emmett Johnson, Sr., was a skilled boat carpenter: "He built on the *Kit Jones,* [which] was built right here on Sapelo—every bit, except for the keel—the pine wasn't long enough. It was built of yellow pine. And all the ribs were cut from oak. And there was no nails, all pegs..."[759]

The *Kit Jones*, a 61-foot workboat designed to transport freight and passengers, was propelled by a 100-horsepower Atlas diesel engine. Reynolds named the boat for Katherine T. Jones, wife of his Sea Island friend, Alfred W. Jones, Sr. The *Kit* was designed to towboat specifications in 1938 by the New York firm of Sparkman & Stephens, Inc., on contract to Reynolds. Utilizing Sapelo oak and pine, Norwegian boat-builder Hulga Spar was engaged to construct the vessel at the South End boatyard. The *Kit Jones* was a solid, durable craft, and was utilized for passenger, mail, and supply delivery from the mainland to Sapelo. When Reynolds later acquired a new ferry, the *Janet*, he awarded the *Kit* to the University of Georgia Marine Institute for use as a research vessel. Later, the *Kit* was utilized in a similar capacity by the Skidaway Institute of Oceanography.

In many respects, Reynolds proved as energetic as Coffin, continuing the agricultural and timbering operations initiated by his predecessor. From 1935-37, Reynolds rebuilt the quadrangle farm complex on the South End, constructing office and apartment buildings, and a two-story masonry barn with a red clay-tiled roof. These new structures replaced Coffin's earlier frame buildings on the same site. Reynolds also commissioned a German sculptor, Fritz Zimmer, to render the Turkey Fountain statuary in the quadrangle courtyard.

---

[759] *Coastlines Georgia*, Coastal Resources Division, GDNR, 1981.

Reynolds was employing 180 workers in 1935, most working in various road, artesian well, and building projects supervised by his island manager, Girard Bullen. Cattle-grazing was expanded, and dairy facilities were developed in the new barn to process milk for sale to mainland outlets. Reynolds employed a number of Sapelo's Geechee residents in the dairy, as domestics at the main house, as boat operators, and at the Duplin River sawmill.

As Reynolds was completing his purchase of the island in 1934, the National Park Service conducted a feasibility study to make Sapelo a national seashore. The report viewed the proposal unfavorably, concluding that public access and federal acquisition of the island were probably insurmountable hurdles. "Access seems inadequate for this project," the study noted, adding that automobile access could be achieved by building a causeway and bridges from the mainland to Creighton Island, then to the west side of Sapelo, "But the cost of such work over the seven-mile stretch of marsh and open water seems prohibitive...The beach area [of Sapelo] does not have sufficient elevation or width for permanent or intensive use...If the problems of providing access, and the cost of acquisition come within the realm of reason, this area should be considered of unusual merit for its scenic beauty and historic interest rather than for its value as a bathing beach for intensive public use." The report noted that Sapelo's new owner was unlikely to be willing to sell to the government, and if he did, the cost of acquisition would be at minimum $1.33 million.

Reynolds met his first wife, Elizabeth Dillard (1909-1961) in the summer of 1932 at Reynolda, the family estate in Winston-Salem; after a short engagement they were married in Winston on New

Year's Day 1933. Nicknamed "Blitz" by Reynolds for her assertive, often fiery, personality, she bore Reynolds four sons: Josh (1933), John (1936), Zach (1938) and Will (1940).

America entered the Second World War in late 1941; in June 1942 Reynolds resigned as mayor of Winston-Salem, and met with FDR to submit his resignation as DNC treasurer, following which he began U.S. Navy training in navigation and aviation. Reynolds served with distinction during the war years, attaining the rank of Lieutenant Commander. In the fall of 1944 he sailed from San Diego to the war front in the south Pacific theater, serving as navigation officer aboard the escort carrier *Makin Island* (CVE 93). Reynolds earned his campaign ribbons, including a Bronze Star, by guiding the carrier through several kamikaze attacks by Japanese warplanes in high-intensity operations in the Philippines at Leyte Gulf and Lingayen, and later at Iwo Jima and Okinawa.

While its owner was half a world away in the Pacific War, the global conflict also had its effects on Sapelo Island. Two Coast Guard submarine watch stations were maintained, one at High Point, and the other at the abandoned lighthouse tract. German U-boats prowling the U.S. east coast often attacked American cargo ships and tankers in 1942 and 1943 (two tankers were sunk off St. Simons Island), and the coastal watch stations played an important role as spotters for the submarines that occasionally surfaced in nearshore waters to charge batteries and seek supplies.

Reynolds and Blitz divorced in 1946; in August of the same year he married his second wife, movie starlet Marianne O'Brien (1918-1985). Reynolds had met O'Brien in the fall of 1944 just before his departure for the Philippines from San Diego on the *Makin Island.*

Elizabeth and Dick Reynolds with sons, John (l) and Josh, 1937.

His marriage with Blitz had grown stale, even tumultuous, and the red-headed movie starlet was like a breath of fresh air for the returning war hero. Their short marriage produced two sons, Patrick and Michael.

As in his first marriage, Reynolds and Marianne often entertained lavishly during their trips to Sapelo, both at the main house, and aboard the *Zapala*. Being quite wealthy, Reynolds was often excessively extravagant in his entertaining. But occasionally "...the eating, drinking, and partying wore thin...To get away from the guests, Dick and Marianne fled to a tree house near Cabretta beach, a two-mile stretch of long-dead trees and driftwood. Blackbeard was rumored to have buried his treasure there, Dick told Marianne as they cuddled in the tree house and cooked chili, away from the intruders they'd invited to their paradise..."[760]

The main house was undergoing gradual modernization during this period. In 1936, Reynolds hired Atlanta architect Philip T. Shutze (1890-1982), a Georgia Tech graduate, to design and oversee the modification of the house, and update it to suit his preferences.[761] Shutze contracted the Italian-born Atlanta bird artist Athos Menaboni (1896-1990), accompanied by his wife Sara, to paint murals of tropical birds and flora on the walls in the swimming pool area and solarium, and the pirate murals in the downstairs game room; in 1939, Menaboni coordinated the re-design of the upstairs ballroom in a motif that appropriately reflected its new name, the Circus Room.

Under contract to Reynolds, R.N. White, Jr. conducted a survey of Sapelo Island in 1940, the result of which was a detailed map updating the location of all the island's structures. White consolidated data from aerial photographs and U.S. Geological Survey topographic maps to compile an accurate cartographic picture of Sapelo that delineated structures, including houses, roads, bridges, fences, culverts, docks, artesian wells, power lines, cultivated fields, abandoned fields, and pastures. Cleared fields were shown south of Long Tabby where Reynolds, in 1934, had laid out a grass airstrip and built a metal hangar for his private plane, and at Flora Bottom and Root Patch northwest of the mansion. The Geechee

---

[760] Reynolds and Shachtman, *Gilded Leaf*, op. cit., 235.
[761] Shutze's plans for the modernization are on deposit at Georgia Tech. Another Georgia Tech architectural graduate, Augustus E. Constantine, designed the South End farm complex built by Reynolds from 1935-37.

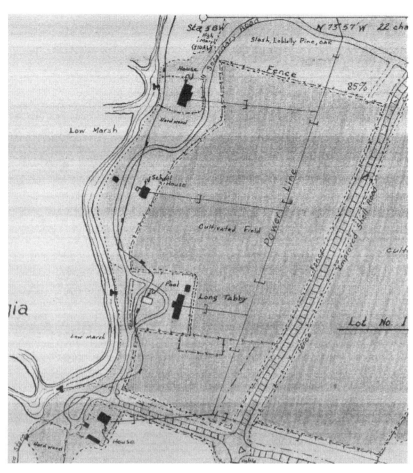

Detail of 1940 R.N. White survey delineating Long Tabby and Barn Creek.

communities were shown, as were natural features, including pine and hardwood forests, grasslands, high and low marshes, ponds and beaches. The White map also noted the location of the portable Sears houses built by Reynolds, one at Chocolate overlooking Mud River, and others on the South End. These structures were transported to Sapelo in parts and assembled on-site.[762]

---

[762] R.N. White, Jr., Survey of Sapelo Island, Surveyor General's Office, GDAH, Morrow, 1940.

Reynolds upgraded Coffin's power generating plant near the mansion. He named his small electric company Atlas Utilities, and it generated electric power for the South End, with lines eventually extended to Hog Hammock in the late 1950s. The first power lines from the mainland were run to Sapelo by the Georgia Power Company in the early 1960s. Atlas Utilities also managed the island's telephone service, named the Sapelo Island Telephone Company until its acquisition by Darien Telephone in 1972. At that time the Sapelo Island exchange had forty-five extensions on the South End; the only telephone at Hog Hammock was a pay station at the home of Herman Hillery whose job it was to answer the phone and hand-deliver messages to residents. This rather primitive system of communication improved when Darien Telephone installed lines in the community in the 1970s.

Primary access across Doboy Sound from Sapelo to the mainland landing at Meridian dock continued to be by water, first with the *Kit Jones*, then in 1960 by a new ferry, the *Janet*, by which Reynolds established regular ferry service between the island and mainland. Hog Hammock cousins Fred Johnson and Benny Johnson were captains of the *Janet*, which was replaced in 1978 by the new Department of Natural Resources state-run ferry, *Sapelo Queen*.

In 1949, so that he might write off some of the great expense associated with maintaining Sapelo, Reynolds embarked on a business enterprise that briefly opened the island to the public. The Sapelo Plantation Inn provided visitors with a unique—and expensive—opportunity to experience the hospitality of Sapelo's owner in a variety of ways. Guests could enjoy movies in the dairy barn's second-floor theater; they could browse the shops on the quadrangle courtyard, savor the amenities of the main house and nearby Azalea Cottage; and sunbathe on Nanny Goat Beach a short distance away. An article appearing in the summer of 1949 by Atlanta journalist Andrew Sparks extolled the virtues of Reynolds' venture:

"One of Georgia's most fabulous spots, Sapelo Island, was recently opened to paying guests...Sapelo is still a private paradise, owned by Richard J. Reynolds of Winston-Salem, N.C., but now its mansion has been turned into the sort of exclusive guest house where luxury-affording visitors can find wilderness seclusion in the midst of every comfort. There are also handsome [quadrangle] apartments; about 40 guests can be accommodated...The island is accessible only by plane and boat...from Darien to Meridian, a white shell road turns off from the pavement and winds through the marsh down an avenue of stunted cedars to the Sapelo dock...At the dock we were met by Ted Peterson, manager...We boarded a work boat, the *Kit Jones,* and cruised through wide tidal waters into Doughboy [sic] Sound where one has an expansive view of the Atlantic between the abandoned lighthouse on Sapelo and the tip of Wolf Island. On the horizon was a string of tiny rock islands built up where English sailing ships dropped ballast on their trips to the New World. The *Kit Jones* turned into Teakettle River, part of the inland waterway, then into Duplin River to the Island dock..."[763]

Reynolds' son, Patrick Cleveland, born to Dick and Marianne in 1948, described the venture in somewhat more acerbic terms in his book about the Reynolds family, *The Gilded Leaf*: "While the paying guests were about, a bathing-suited Marianne would emerge to dip in the outdoor pool or just to take in the sun. Her movie-star figure made the male guests gawk; they'd talk with her and she with them....benevolence and anger: alcoholics often veer back and forth

---

[763] *Atlanta Journal-Constitution Sunday Magazine,* July 17, 1949.

between these, embracing extremes as the tides of inebriation and sobriety come and go. In 1949, Dick didn't stay on the wagon long. How could he have guests staying in his South End mansion without having a polite drink with them? He loved being a good host..."[764]

In 1949-50, Reynolds entered discussions with local and state officials over a proposal to construct a causeway linking the mainland with Sapelo and Blackbeard islands. Seeking increased profitability, Reynolds wanted to provide automotive access—quick and convenient—for guests visiting the Sapelo Plantation Inn. Meanwhile, the state of Georgia was exploring the idea of acquiring Blackbeard from the U.S. Department of the Interior, and developing a state-managed beach resort similar to that envisioned for Jekyll Island, which the state had acquired several years earlier. Engineering studies were conducted, the results of which determined that a causeway was not financially feasible based on a projected a $3 million price tag, an exorbitant amount of money in 1950. The federal government was also unwilling to cede Blackbeard to the state.

The Plantation Inn venture ultimately proved unsuccessful—there simply were not enough high-paying guests to suit the proprietor—and Reynolds closed the facility in 1951. Two years later Reynolds granted the dairy barn and other buildings around the quadrangle to the University of Georgia for a marine biological research station.

During this period, Reynolds operated a summer camp for underprivileged boys under the direction of his friend, Richard Orme Flinn, Jr., pastor of the Carrollton, Georgia Presbyterian Church. From 1948-52, the Long Tabby guest house and its swimming pool

---

[764] Reynolds and Shachtman, *Gilded Leaf*, 241-42.

were utilized for the boys camp, and several bunk houses and a dining hall were built close by. There evolved additional projects during this period: having long been interested in forest management, and its applications both scientific and economic, Reynolds revived Sapelo's timber operations in 1954. North End timber, much of it destined for Cuba and Haiti, was processed at the Duplin River sawmill on the upper end of Kenan Field,

Reynolds developed lasting ties with several members of the Darien community including his attorney and agent, Paul Varner, and county sheriff Tom Poppell. The local Durant family was also closely associated with Reynolds and Sapelo. Tom Durant (1909-1961) was Reynolds' secretary and manager of the Plantation Inn during its three years of operation, also serving as island manager during the 1950s. Durant was discharged by Reynolds in 1960, allegedly for disloyalty—Reynolds thought Durant was feeding information about his finances and declining health to his third wife, Muriel Reynolds, near the end of the marriage. Reynolds then appointed Durant's brother, Frank E. Durant (1899-1983), as island manager; he served in that capacity through the 1960s. Charles Durant was employed on Sapelo by the University of Georgia in the post-Reynolds era, and played a role in the growth of the Marine Institute.

Dick Reynolds divorced Marianne O'Brien Reynolds in 1952, and later that year married two-time divorcee Muriel Greenough (1915-1980) of New York City, and a native of Calgary, Alberta. The marriage vows were spoken on the front lawn of the Sapelo mansion, and thus began arguably the stormiest of Reynolds' four marriages.

In the late 1950s, Reynolds' health declined, exacerbated by years of excessive drinking. A heavy smoker, he also began to experience increasingly frequent bouts of emphysema. "Sapelo, an island of fantasy for Dick Reynolds, now became Sapelo, air-conditioned prison. In the latter part of 1958, Dick was confined mostly to the air-conditioned patio [solarium] and bedroom, separated from the moist atmosphere of the indoor pool by a glass wall."[765]

Reynolds' relations with Muriel grew increasingly contentious. Muriel was supposedly frequently given to odd behavior on the main house premises: "She was outspoken to the point of rudeness not only to Dick and the servants, but also to the occasional guests. Dick suspected that she was paying or had coerced some of the employees to spy on him..."[766] Doctors from Atlanta, Savannah, and Winston-Salem attending to Reynolds on Sapelo noted that his declining health typically improved during the periods when Muriel was away from the island.

Matters reached a head, and divorce proceedings began in May 1960. Muriel's lawyers "tried to get the trial shifted away from Darien, arguing that because Reynolds was McIntosh County's most prominent citizen, his wife could not get a fair trial there...Dick had financed Sheriff Tom Poppell's [1960] re-election campaign and paid for an American Legion building in Darien, a gymnasium for the black high school, and a community swimming pool. The local judge, offended, ruled that Dick could get a fair trial in Darien..." Thus it came as no surprise that after a two-week trial a local jury awarded Reynolds the settlement he desired.

---

[765] Ibid., 265.
[766] Ibid., 266.

Less than a year later, in April 1961, the 55-year old Reynolds began his fourth marriage, this being to Annemarie Schmidt (b. 1929) of Germany. Meanwhile, Muriel won an appeal of the 1960 divorce, partly because Reynolds did not testify in person at the first trial. A second trial was held in Darien in May 1962 in what amounted to a media circus. Reynolds gave testimony (taking oxygen every few minutes while doing so), defending himself against Muriel's charges of his alcoholism and mental abuse.[767] This time, the local jury ruled even more favorably for Reynolds' than it had at the first trial, "stating that he did not have to pay a cent of alimony to Muriel...It was a complete victory for Dick..."[768]

Despite the favorable court outcomes, Reynolds felt besieged by Muriel after the divorce as her lawyers promised continuous appeals and press coverage. Dick decided he had had enough of America, and after meeting with his four oldest sons at Sapelo in late spring 1962, he and Annemarie departed for Europe to take up permanent residence in Switzerland.

There is a story that just before departing Sapelo for the last time, the ailing Reynolds took Fred and Cracker Johnson, and other trusted blacks from Hog Hammock, with him to retrieve bags of gold he had hidden in various parts of the island over the years. He assured the Johnsons they would be taken care of in the event of his death, and that Ledyard Staples, his accountant and business manager, would keep the main house open for visitors so that the island's blacks could have continued employment. A few days later

---

[767] *Darien News*, May 10-17, 1962.
[768] Reynolds and Shachtman, *Gilded Leaf*, 284.

Reynolds left Sapelo for the last time "with his treasure, his oxygen bottles, his fourth wife...and his memories."[769]

His health continued to deteriorate, and he died suddenly in Lucerne on December 14, 1964, at the age of fifty-eight.[770] Two days later Annemarie gave birth to Reynolds' seventh child, his first daughter, Irene Sabine Reynolds. In the following weeks, Reynolds' family in America, including his sons, were stunned to discover they had been disinherited, and that Reynolds had left everything, including Sapelo, to Annemarie.

Elizabeth "Blitz" Reynolds died of colon cancer in 1961 at the age of fifty-two. In the late 1960s, two other ex-wives, Marianne and Muriel, became close and often met to discuss their belief that Annemarie had not only convinced Reynolds to change his will but also caused Reynolds' death. There were legal claims to over $50 million of Reynolds' estate, and to Sapelo (Marianne claimed Reynolds left her the island with a deed written on a paper napkin during their engagement). Numerous suits and appeals by the two ex-wives, and other family members, were to no avail, and none of the suspicions over Reynolds' death, the legitimacy of his will, or the settlement of his estate were ever legally resolved. Muriel Reynolds and Marianne Reynolds died in 1980 and 1985, respectively.

Ledyard Staples continued to have oversight of Sapelo for the Reynolds estate in the 1960s and 1970s during the period when the island was transitioning to state ownership. He played a major role in the business and financial management of Reynolds' Sapelo Island

---

[769] Ibid., 286.
[770] The cause of death was apparently excessive pure oxygen on Reynolds' brain.

Research Foundation. In 1969, Annemarie Reynolds, as executor of her husband's estate, facilitated the first of two transactions by which Sapelo Island was sold to the state of Georgia.

Undoubtedly the greatest legacy left by R.J. Reynolds to Sapelo Island was the creation of the Sapelo Island Research Foundation and enabling the University of Georgia to establish a permanent marine research laboratory on the island. The seeds for the Marine Institute were planted in the summer of 1948 when two University of Georgia biology professors, Eugene P. Odum and Donald C. Scott, and a young Georgia Game and Fish biologist, James Jenkins, visited Sapelo in hopes of spotting the chachalaca bird introduced to the island from Central America by Howard Coffin. While at Sapelo, Odum, Scott, and Jenkins enjoyed an unscheduled visit with Reynolds who was enthusiastic about the natural history of the coast, though his primary interests lay in agriculture and forestry. Reynolds had also been expanding his interests in animal husbandry with his Sapelo dairy cattle operations. During their visit Odum and Scott broached the subject to Reynolds about the potential utility of Sapelo as the site of a marine research laboratory. Reynolds was not enthusiastic initially.[771]

Four years later, by which time his Plantation Inn had closed, Reynolds was more receptive; in 1952, he invited University of Georgia president O.C. Aderhold, Gene Odum, and other UGA scientists to Sapelo to discuss establishing a foundation for biological and agricultural research. Odum once again saw the opportunity to

---

[771] Betty Jean Craige, *Eugene Odum, Ecosystem Ecologist & Environmentalist* (Athens: University of Georgia Press, 2001), 54-58.

conduct applied ecological research using Sapelo Island as a remote campus from Athens. Interested in pursuing research related to the Georgia salt marshes, Odum, with Scott's support, made a proposal to Reynolds for the University to use Sapelo as a biological station. Field investigations in marsh ecology, and other disciplines related to marine biology would be conducted in tandem with research in forestry and agriculture to satisfy Reynolds' interests.

Reynolds was enthusiastic. He finalized a contract with Aderhold and George H. Boyd, dean of the Graduate School at UGA, in the summer of 1953 to establish the University of Georgia Marine Biological Laboratory. Reynolds agreed to provide the scientists the South End marshes to conduct field research, and the buildings on the quadrangle of the former dairy complex, including barn, shops and apartments. By late August 1953, using an initial grant of $25,000, Odum had in place the first resident director of the Marine Laboratory, Robert A. Ragotzkie, a hydrologist who had recently earned his Ph.D.

Ragotzkie began converting the dairy barn into a laboratory, and added resident research staff. In early 1954, Theodore J. Starr, a microbiologist, became the first recruited scientist; he pursued studies at Sapelo until the fall of 1955. In September 1954, Lawrence R. Pomeroy, an invertebrate zoologist, arrived at the laboratory, followed in June 1955 by John M. Teal, an ecosystem ecologist who had pursued energy flow studies as a graduate student. Ragotzkie, Pomeroy and Teal worked together on Sapelo as full-time scientists for four years; they resided in the quadrangle apartments, worked in the marshes and uplands of Sapelo, and consolidated their investigations at the barn laboratory. They utilized the *Kit Jones* to transport supplies and equipment from the mainland.

The work of these early researchers laid the foundation for the scientific achievements for the next fifty years at Sapelo. Teal departed for Nova Scotia in 1959, and after that the Woods Hole Oceanographic Institute; the legacy of his Sapelo research has been perpetuated by two enduring studies that evolved from his experiences on the island—*Portrait of an Island* and *Life and Death of a Salt Marsh*, both co-written with his wife, Mildred Teal. Ragotzkie and Pomeroy left in 1960 for the University of Wisconsin and the Athens main campus, respectively.

George H. Lauff was the second director of the laboratory, from 1960-62, with Vernon J. Henry serving as director from 1964-70. The laboratory's official name was changed to the University of Georgia Marine Institute (UGAMI) in 1959, with Boyd serving as administrative head from Athens. The name of Reynolds' foundation was changed the same year, from the Sapelo Island Agricultural and Forestry Foundation to the Sapelo Island Research Foundation (SIRF), with annual funding allocated to support research programs at the Marine Institute.

Although Odum conducted research on Sapelo in its early years, he had no administrative role in the facility. Nonetheless, the findings emanating from the Marine Institute in its first two decades influenced his evolving philosophy of ecology and environmentalism:

Three sections of Sapelo Island were purchased from the Reynolds estate with public funds at different times. Each of the funding sources placed stipulations on the utilization of the relevant properties. It is fortunate that when Reynolds died in 1964, he was married to the only one of his four wives that had an interest in science and the general conservation of Sapelo. It is possible, perhaps likely, that any one of the three previous wives, or their heirs, would have sold the island to private entities, potentially opening the way to commercial and residential development reflecting that of other areas of the southeast coast in the previous decade.

As a widow hoping to extend her late husband's legacy to Sapelo and coastal Georgia, Annemarie Schmidt Reynolds remained involved with the island through the 1970s, particularly with the Sapelo Island Research Foundation (SIRF). In 1969 Mrs. Reynolds made it possible for the state of Georgia to purchase the North End tract of about 8,200 acres (the upper two-thirds of Sapelo), the result of which was the creation of the R.J. Reynolds Wildlife Refuge, later re-designated R.J. Reynolds Wildlife Management Area.

The state acquisition was facilitated through the Georgia Game and Fish Commission, and achieved through Pittman-Robertson Federal Aid funds, seventy-five per cent, and state funds, twenty-five per cent.[772] The Sapelo Island Research Foundation retained sole control and oversight of the lower third of the island from 1969 through 1976, including the Marine Institute campus, main house, and Marsh Landing. Since the Reynolds Wildlife Refuge was a federal aid initiative based mostly on funds derived from sportsmen, the primary use of the North End was to provide wildlife enhancement programs and public hunting opportunities. Much of the active wildlife management (continuing to the present day)

---

[772] The Game and Fish Commission was re-designated as the Georgia Department of Natural Resources—GDNR—in 1973. The Game and Fish Division of GDNR became the Wildlife Resources Division in 1992.

involved game species, particularly white tailed deer. Beginning in 1970, the Game and Fish Division of the Department of Natural Resources began wildlife and forest management activities on the Refuge, programs designed to improve habitat diversity, and increase populations of game, and nongame wildlife. Surveys, inventories and research tasks were conducted to develop professional habitat management. Game and Fish also implemented seasonal public hunting, a popular outreach program that continued to develop, particularly with GDNR's construction of a hunt camp at Moses Hammock.

State acquisition of the remaining portion of Sapelo, and consequently nearly the entirety of the island's 10,900 upland acres, was completed with two purchases from the Research Foundation in 1976. The first, the Sapelo Island Natural Area, was acquired with funds from the Land and Water Conservation Fund matched with fifty per cent state funds. This area south of Hog Hammock, and east of the East Perimeter road was designated for public recreation, education, and scientific research. "Natural area" was somewhat of a misnomer, as that part of Sapelo had been impacted by human activity for over 150 years.

Of greater significance was the state's acquisition in late 1976 of 5,905 acres of upland and marsh on the western and southern sections of Sapelo (nearly a third of the island), designated the Sapelo Island National Estuarine Sanctuary (SINES). The tract entailed about 4,000 acres of marsh in the Duplin River estuary, and almost 2,000 acres of upland south of the Reynolds WMA, including the SIRF's land comprising the Marine Institute leased to the University System of Georgia's Board of Regents. This addition gave the state oversight for all of Sapelo excepting the Hog Hammock community's 427 acres, several small disputed tracts at Raccoon Bluff, and two hundred acres of upland and marsh at the lighthouse.[773]

About 250 African Americans lived on Sapelo Island in the early 1950s, mostly at Raccoon Bluff and Hog Hammock. The 1954 U.S. Geological Survey topographic map of Sapelo delineated about forty structures in Hog Hammock, mostly dwellings.

In 1963, the Geechee population was down to 211 residents living almost exclusively at Hog Hammock. Roughly half that number comprised those who had relocated to Hog Hammock from Raccoon Bluff through a series of land exchanges instigated by R.J. Reynolds. There was continued population decline as residents moved to the mainland, and by the early 1970s there were only about 150 Geechee still on Sapelo. By 1990, Hog Hammock's population had fallen still further, to about seventy people.

The story is a depressing one in almost every particular. Reynolds wished to acquire the lands contained within Sapelo's black communities, particularly those on the North End. In 1950, his attorneys initiated land exchanges to consolidate the island's Geechee into one community at Hog Hammock. The largest community to be consolidated was Raccoon Bluff, but Reynolds also wanted the land at Belle Marsh, Lumber Landing and Shell Hammock, plus some scattered private plots in other parts of Sapelo. Reynolds facilitated this with the intention of transforming

---

[773] Board of Regents of the University System of Georgia and the Georgia Department of Natural Resources, "A Proposal to Establish a National Estuarine Sanctuary in the State of Georgia," State Office of Planning and Budget, Atlanta, January 10, 1975.

everything north of Hog Hammock into a limited-access wildlife and hunting preserve.

It was a gradual process: Belle Marsh was closed in 1950, Lumber Landing in 1956, Shell Hammock in 1960, and by 1964 Raccoon Bluff had been vacated. Understandably, most of Sapelo's people were not enamored of the arrangement. As an inducement Reynolds ran a line from his South End generator plant to provide electricity to Hog Hammock; water lines were installed, several houses built, and a schoolteacher was hired to instruct the community's children. Reynolds also provided a few jobs for residents. "Since nearly all the residents now worked for him, [Reynolds] sometimes held court like a feudal lord, adjusting disputes, meting out small punishments."[774]

Another of Reynolds' motives for consolidation was control. He wanted as much of Sapelo's acreage under his imprimatur as possible, and the way to achieve that was direct acquisition of the Geechee land at Raccoon Bluff and Shell Hammock. During the 1950s he purchased some lots, and pressured residents for the exchange of other properties for land at Hog Hammock. Virtually all of Raccoon Bluff had been bought or exchanged by the time Reynolds' died, though he failed to obtain clear title to some tracts. By then, the families had relocated to Hog Hammock, and rebuilt their homes.

Raccoon Bluff, dating to the 1870s, had been Sapelo's largest community for years. Reynolds changed everything. The loss of traditional lands was simultaneously traumatic, transformative, and permanent, evolving with little or no negotiation. By mid-1964, the

---

[774] Reynolds and Shachtman, *Gilded Leaf*, 193.

community was completely vacated, with many houses dismantled and moved, leaving Hog Hammock as Sapelo's only Geechee settlement. At the time he died Reynolds possessed virtually all the land on Sapelo outside of Hog Hammock, excepting small tracts at Raccoon Bluff; the upper two-thirds of the island had been depopulated to facilitate Reynolds' hunting preserve.

Many of Sapelo's people were unhappy and dispirited with what amounted to the forced waiver of their land. Most moved against their wishes, though there were a few incentives: more homes added to the electric power service, a school, and a modern new sanctuary for Raccoon Bluff's First African Baptist congregation. After the church acquired land in Hog Hammock in 1963 services continued to be held at Raccoon Bluff until completion of the new sanctuary in 1968.

Island lore relates that Eddie Hall and Allen Green were the last Raccoon Bluff residents to relocate to Hog Hammock. Green (1907-1998), who became known for the craftsmanship of his sweet-grass baskets, was born at Raccoon Bluff and, except for several years as a young man, had lived there his whole life. For a time Green refused to leave his homeplace but was eventually forced to do so.[775]

The story of Green and his unhappy removal from a lifelong home perfectly symbolizes the persistent struggle of Sapelo's Geechee community to preserve its identity. It has endured the travails of private, then state, management of the island, with increasing acquisition of Hog Hammock land by outsiders in the 1990s and

---

[775] Author's conversations with Allen Green, 1993, 1994; William S. McFeely, *Sapelo's People: A Long Walk into Freedom* (New York, W.W. Norton, 1994), 142.

2000s. The consolidation completed in the early 1960s was followed by Hog Hammock's seemingly-continuous rear-guard war of attrition to stave off development, land sales and exchanges, and the growing encroachment of non-traditional property owners.

Sapelo's people, some with ancestral island roots reaching to the late 1700s, came to realize both in a physical, and a psychological sense that they were gradually losing that sense of *place* that had existed for them for generations. The cultural integrity of Hog Hammock, and that of the lost island communities, was in peril of being severely diluted. Lifelong resident Cornelia Bailey (1945-2017), descendant of Bilali, black overseer of Thomas Spalding, is one who refuses to concede an inch of her precious, hard-won land: "We don't need a sign that says Hog Hammock *WAS* here," she says. "We want a sign that says Hog Hammock *IS* here."

Pulitzer Prize historian William S. McFeely put it best in the evocative and poignant story of his sojourn on Sapelo in the early 1990s learning the lifeways and traditions of the island's people: "The story of these long twentieth century years, years within the memory of Sapelo's people, is not the story I came back to the island to tell. I came not to interrogate, but to visit. I was there not to master the intricate, delicate negotiations attendant to the community's painful efforts to survive, but, instead, to grasp its domestic tranquilities. The pain of loneliness, of uncertainty, of old age, lies beneath its quiet, of course. There are, after all, only sixty-seven people left in Hog Hammock. But what strikes you over and over again is the duration of their story, of their endurance."[776]

---

[776] McFeely, *Sapelo's People*, 151.

With the end of the Reynolds era, and the Marine Institute providing only minimal employment in the 1970s, many Hog Hammock residents relocated to the mainland, a trend particularly prevalent among the younger people seeking jobs. Community assistance in the form of small grants ($25,000 annually in the 1970s) came from the Sapelo Island Research Foundation. The SIRF aid was far from adequate, and some community residents were near destitute during this period. "Fred and Cracker Johnson, and their wives, who had cared for Dick in his time on the island—and especially when he was sick—discovered to their horror that the destruction of Dick Reynolds' records in 1964 had made it next to impossible to prove they had been employed by Dick and therefore ought to be receiving Social Security payments for the years they spent working for him."[777]

State acquisition of Sapelo in 1969 and 1976 placed new, unanticipated, pressures on the island's future preservation. The Reynolds house provided some employment for residents, being managed in the 1980s and early 1990s by the Marine Institute as a conference facility for scientific and educational groups. However, the house urgently needed repairs and modernization. The mansion was showing visible signs of wear by the time President Jimmy Carter and his family utilized it during an Easter visit to Sapelo in April 1979. Unfortunately, the necessary funding to undertake improvements was not forthcoming from the Board of Regents, and the historic structure continued to deteriorate.

---

[777] Reynolds and Shachtman, *Gilded Leaf*, 313.

During the mid-1980s there was a proposal by the state to convert the South End into a convention center, with utilization of the main house, and construction of additional lodging and meeting facilities. The plan was to make Sapelo more attractive to tourists, thus generating funds for repairs to the island's infrastructure. Conversely, such an initiative would clearly jeopardize or disrupt Sapelo's delicate ecological balance, the coherence of ongoing scientific research and, not least of all, the Geechee community. The outcry and opposition to the proposal from coastal environmentalists was swift and vehement, and GDNR shelved the plan in 1986. Repairs to the mansion were finally implemented when GDNR assumed management of the house in 1993; the facility continued to be operated by the state as a public lodge.

GDNR's gradual expansion of Sapelo Island's public access and educational opportunities provided employment for Hog Hammock residents as ferry boat operators, tour guides, mechanics, and maintenance workers, while the Marine Institute also continued to provide jobs. Most significantly, however, the entrepreneurial spirit of some Hog Hammock residents began to manifest itself. Several overnight lodging facilities were started; a store or two opened to serve island residents and visitors, and locals began offering guided tours of the South End with the emphasis on Geechee culture and history.

Church offerings were accumulated and saved, and a match by the SIRF enabled the purchase of a small motor vessel for the community—the *Miss St. Luke*—with experienced watermen such as Tracy Walker and George Walker operating the boat to provide services, most importantly as a means of emergency medical transport to the mainland. In 1996, Hog Hammock's 427 acres, and Behavior Cemetery were placed on the National Register of Historic Places.

The physical nature of the community at the turn of the twenty-first century showed it still to be bounded by marsh on the east and southeast, the "Autobahn" to the west, and a northern boundary that was originally an irrigation canal and embankment that separated the 1969 South End division of the island from the North End. There were about fifty houses scattered in an irregular pattern through the community. Among these were several historic structures, including the St. Luke's Baptist Church (ca. 1924), the Farmer's Alliance Lodge Hall (ca. 1929), First African Baptist Church (1968), and the former Rosenwald school now attached to St. Luke's.

The frame homes are largely simple, vernacular-style structures, one-story and most with gabled roofs and front porches. In his survey of Hog Hammock preparatory to listing on the National Register, Thomas indicated that some of the community's dwellings were built in the 1920-1940 period, while others date from the post-World War II era. Other houses in the vernacular style were built from 1955-65 in response to the arrival of residents from other settlements.

Greater access to Sapelo after 1980 resulted in increasing exposure of its natural and cultural uniqueness, with a consequent rise in public awareness and interest in the island. Not surprisingly, this trend initiated a growing appeal and reach for property ownership by "outsiders." Hog Hammock, being essentially the only developable private tract on Sapelo due to state ownership of the island, was logically the focus of property acquisition. In the 1980s and 1990s, pieces of Hog Hammock property were gradually sold off by the non-resident heirs of traditional Sapelo land owners. By 2000, the hold on their community by traditional Geechee was becoming tenuous as the movement for land acquisition gained momentum. Part-time and seasonal homes were being constructed, some quite elaborate by Sapelo standards, and mostly by non-traditional (white) residents, accompanied by concern and resentment by traditional residents of which only about seventy remained by 2010.

"If you're going to keep the culture, it's a black culture," said Charles Hall, former president of the Sapelo Island Cultural and Revitalization Society, a preservation organization started by descendants. "It's a black language. So every time you dilute it, you're getting away from it." Cornelia Bailey, slave descendant and Geechee historian of Sapelo, was even more pointed: "On the verge of sounding racist — which I have been accused of, which I don't give a hoot — I would rather my community be all black. I would rather have my community what it was in the '50s. Am I in your mainland community trying to buy your land?" she asked. "Why are you trying to buy mine? Can you sleep in two beds at once? I tell them, 'My land is for my children, my grandchildren and even for the unborn.'"[778]

In an attempt to allay the growing trend toward gentrification, and to protect the integrity of Sapelo's culture, the state established the Sapelo Island Heritage Authority to control, and theoretically protect, 180 acres within Hog Hammock.[779] The construction of expensive homes by non-traditional residents naturally led to greatly-elevated property taxes for all in Hog Hammock. This especially impacted the community's traditional residents, adding additional

---

[778] *New York Times,* May 4, 2008.
[779] 2010 Georgia Code, § 12-3-441 Title 12, Conservation and Natural Resources, Part 7, Sapelo Island Heritage Authority.

threats to the sustainability of Sapelo's traditional culture. After McIntosh County's property revaluation in 2012 many Hog Hammock home owners saw their assessments increased 500 to 800 per cent. For Sapelo's traditional residents the tax increases from the high valuations meant the potential extinction of their community.

This unfortunate situation captured national attention in 2012 and 2013, with coverage from the *New York Times* and CNN, among other media. Bailey publicly expressed her shock at seeing the taxes on her property rise from $256 to almost $2,000 in one year. "People are calling and offering sympathy and saying, 'I wish they couldn't do that to you all,' " she said. "We need legal help. We need money to pay legal help. We need good ideas and suggestions. If we don't get these taxes down to a decent level, we don't have a chance in hell to bring back young people to the island."[780] Local tax assessors and judicial officials were inundated with appeals contesting the land appraisals; in 2014, McIntosh County provided a modicum of relief by implementing a thirty per cent reduction for Hog Hammock property assessments under appeal for 2012 and 2013 taxes. Most saw it as only a temporary reprieve.[781]

---

[780] *Charleston Post and Courier*, November 27, 2013.

[781] In late 2015, fifty-seven residents and property owners of Hog Hammock filed a federal lawsuit that contended that discrimination and neglect by state and local authorities had created an erosion of the cultural integrity of state-owned Sapelo Island's African American community. The suit alleged that traditional Geechee residents pay exorbitant property taxes because their community has evolved into a vacation community with luxurious homes built by outsiders, and that traditional residents receive "no services whatsoever" from the state or McIntosh County. In June 2016 a federal district court judge ruled that the state of Georgia is "not immune" from lawsuits filed against it for discrimination. *Atlanta Journal Constitution*, December 9, 2015; *Georgia Times-Union* (Jacksonville), June 18, 2016.

Land Use & Landscape: Ossabaw Island

The Colonial Records of Georgia contain a substantial amount of documentation reflecting the rather convoluted legal course involving the dispensation of several of the coastal islands during the 1750s. In 1747, Indian interpreter Mary Musgrove and her husband, Anglican reverend Thomas Bosomworth, influenced Malatchi, chief of the Creek nation, to dispense a letter of conveyance to the couple of the islands of Ossabaw, St. Catherines and Sapelo. Bosomworth encouraged his wife to claim the three islands from the British crown as compensation for her services as an interpreter and intermediary to Oglethorpe and other authorities in the early years of the Georgia colony.

A circuitous series of legal maneuverings ensued by which the British colonial office disputed the claims of the Bosomworths, and in 1759 the courts dismissed the case. A settlement was reached by which the crown held Ossabaw and Sapelo with St. Catherines being conveyed to Thomas and Mary Musgrove Bosomworth. The colonial council also awarded Mary £2,100 sterling as further reward for her services, these monies to come from the public sale of Ossabaw and Sapelo.

In May 1760, the two islands were purchased at auction by land speculator Grey Elliott, a member of the colonial council and surveyor of the colony. Elliott bought Ossabaw for £1,325 sterling in a transaction formalized through a royal grant dated October 31, 1760. Ossabaw was described as "all that island...lying and being on the seacoast in the Parish of St. Philip in our Province of Georgia, containing seven thousand six hundred acres [upland] and bounded on the South by the Ocean, Northward by the River Great Ogeechee, and Westward by the marshes, creeks and branches leading through St. Catherines Sound through a Southern branch of said River Great Ogeechee."[782] Survey plats of both Ossabaw and Sapelo were prepared by Henry Yonge and William G. DeBrahm in 1760.

Elliott quickly divested himself of his properties, conveying Ossabaw to Henry Bourquin, and Sapelo to Patrick Mackay. Bourquin soon thereafter sold Ossabaw to his son-in-law John Morel, Sr. in two separate transactions, the last in 1763. Morel was a Savannah merchant who had acquired considerable acreage on the upper Georgia coast during this period. After his first wife died, Morel married Mary Bryan, daughter of Jonathan Bryan, a transplanted South Carolina planter, owner of Georgia lands.

Live oak timber operations, by which oak from Georgia's barrier islands was cut and sold to northern shipbuilders, were conducted on Ossabaw before and after the American Revolution. For example, in 1770 John Morel advertised that "on proper notice [I] will engage to cut any quantity of Live Oak and Cedar ship timbers, of any shape or size required, and will deliver the same at proper landings on Ossabaw. On Ossabaw apply to Mr. Daniel Giroud in the absence of John Morel."[783]

Morel continued to promote the availability of live oak timber on Ossabaw in 1774; the same year saw Daniel Giroud cited as the

---

[782] Allen D. Candler, ed., *The Colonial Records of the State of Georgia* (Atlanta, 1904-16), 8: 86, 323. See also Pat Bryant, comp., English Crown Grants for Islands in Georgia, 1755-1775 (Atlanta: Georgia Surveyor General Department, 1972).
[783] *Georgia Gazette* (Savannah), April 18, 1770.

builder of a 200-ton brig at the Beaulieu shipyard on the mainland south of Savannah. Morel had an estate at Beaulieu, often the scene of colonial shipbuilding activities. Earlier, the *Elizabeth*, with a keel of eighty-four feet, was built on Ossabaw by John Wand. Ossabaw's extensive live oak forests, like those of the other islands, were to be in considerable demand for timber by northern shipbuilders well into the nineteenth century.

Morel's death in 1776 resulted in the ownership of Ossabaw Island being split among his sons. By 1817 the island had been divided into three separate plantation properties among the sons and grandsons of Morel, Sr. The North End went to Bryan Morel, Middle Place to Peter Henry Morel, and the South End to John Morel, Jr. South End was later subdivided to create the Buckhead tract. North End Place on the upper end of Ossabaw near present-day Torrey Landing was where John Morel, Sr. presumably had the original plantation house on the island. Middle Place is immediately south of North End on the west side of Ossabaw. Buckhead is south of Middle Place, on the south side of Buckhead Creek while South End is in the southwestern section of Ossabaw with the primary landing on Newell Creek, a tidal stream on the island's marsh side that empties into the Bear River, part of the intracoastal waterway.

John Morel, Jr. (1759-1802) was heavily invested with his father's Beaulieu plantation on the Chatham County mainland until 1785 when he removed to Tweedside, a Savannah River rice plantation awarded his family after the Revolution by the Commissioners of confiscated Estates (of Loyalist lands). Additionally, Morel was managing agricultural operations in the cultivation of indigo, tobacco and sea island cotton at Ossabaw South End where he kept a portion of his slaves. It is possible that Morel shifted groups of his slaves back and forth between his Savannah River rice operations and Ossabaw.[784] In 1796 and 1797 Morel advertised several hundred bushels of seed rice for sale, which is illustrative of the increasing profitability of his Savannah River operations at Tweedside and Argyle Island.[785]

In 1797, Morel advertised his tract on Argyle Island for sale. As these were some of the best rice lands on the Savannah River, Morel's decision seems to have been based more on the fact that some coastal planters were shifting their agricultural energies into the production of sea island cotton by the start of the nineteenth century. Morel's shifting focus to his Ossabaw operations and cotton production is exemplified by a notice in the Savannah newspapers in 1799: "WANTED: An overseer to take charge of a plantation on the Island of Ossabaw, on which is worked from forty to fifty hands—he must understand the culture of Cotton and management of Negroes, with a wife that understands the taking care of a Dairy..."[786] With the decline in rice production created by the shifting of labor to sea island cotton cultivation by some planters, the markets for rice realized a substantial increase. This precipitated another revision in the direction of Morel's farming strategy in which he saw the advantages of cultivating both staple crops more evenly—diversification enabled greater potential for agricultural profitability.

---

[784] Mary Granger, ed., *Savannah River Plantations* (Savannah: Georgia Historical Society, 1947), 216-17.
[785] *Columbian Museum and Savannah Advertiser*, May 3, 1796 and March 21, 1797.
[786] Ibid., January 11, 1799.

In his will dated July 21, 1802, Morel recommended the sale of Pembroke, an inland plantation, adding that his "money shall be laid out in the further purchase of Negroes for the Improvement and Cultivation of my lands on Ossabaw and Savannah River estates, and should my Executor think it advisable to purchase any real estate or Plantation of River Swamp in a Proper Pitch of the Tide near my plantation or adjoining Tweedside on Savannah River."[787] Morel, Jr. died in 1802 and decreed that his plantation lands and 115 slaves be equally divided among his four children. These were Thomas Morel, John Morel, Henry Morel and Anne Morel Rutherford. Thomas Morel assumed the management of Tweedside, later constructing a rice pounding mill that considerably augmented that plantation's operational profitability.[788]

Ossabaw's North End tract was inherited by Bryan Morel (1769-1812) from his father, John Morel, Sr., after which it devolved to the former's son, Bryan McQueen Morel (1803-1875) who was still a minor at the time of his father's death. It was during the first two decades of the nineteenth century that Ossabaw's live oak timber realized its greatest demand by the northern shipyards for the construction of warships for the Navy and for merchant vessels. This is evidenced by Bryan Morel's advertising, possibly for lease, a portion of his Ossabaw land, it being "adapted to the cultivation of cotton, indigo or corn—for quantity or quality of live oak timbers in its woods...and excellent and extensive range for stock of all

---

[787] Will Book D, 31, App. 118, in records of the Court of Ordinary, Chatham County, Savannah, cited in Granger, ed., *Savannah River Plantations*, 218.
[788] *Columbian Museum and Savannah Daily Gazette,* March 27, 1817.

kinds."[789] Bryan M. Morel had operations in the cultivation of cotton and provision crops at North End Place in the 1840s and 1850s. Testimony to this activity are the remains of several tabby slave dwellings just west of the present Clubhouse, and in proximity to the Morel plantation house and cotton fields.

In 1886, after 125 years of Morel family ownership, the North End was sold to James M. Waterbury of New York City. A survey plat made by William Hughes, Jr. of Liberty County at the time of the sale to Waterbury showed North End Place to be comprised of 2,155 acres of upland and "second lowland," and 2,445 acres of marsh, giving the tract an aggregate of 4,600 acres. The plat delineated a landing near the present Torrey Landing, and a notation at the intersection of South End Road leading to the three tabby slave houses that "mansion stood here."[790] This was at or very near the present Clubhouse site. The wording of the survey notation indicates that the Morel house was no longer standing in 1886. Evidence suggests that there were two dwellings on the site, both of which apparently had burned sometime prior to the 1886 acquisition of North End Place by Waterbury.

Ossabaw's Middle Place tract was inherited by Peter Henry Morel (1757-1812) who in turn sold the property in 1806 to David Johnston who also owned half of nearby St. Catherines Island at the time. Johnston subsequently sold Middle Place to Patrick Houstoun, his brother James Johnston Jr.'s brother-in-law. James Johnston Jr. was the father-in-law of George J. Kollock who, as we shall see, came

---

[789] *Columbian Museum and Savannah Daily Advertiser,* May 7, 1797.
[790] William Hughes, Jr., 1886 Resurvey of Bryan Morel Plantation, Map Book 1, 188, Chatham County Superior Court records.

to acquire the South End in 1852. Patrick Houstoun died in 1839, upon which Middle Place went to his daughter Georgia Ann Moodie Houstoun (1805-1880) following her marriage to Alexander McDonald of McIntosh County, Georgia.[791]

Alexander McDonald had extensive plantation operations at Middle Place in the 1840s and 1850s, cultivating sea island cotton as his money staple with a work force of sixty-nine slaves. The McDonalds apparently had their primary residence in Glynn County, but there was an overseer's dwelling at Middle Place which would indicate that McDonald spent part of his time at Ossabaw seeing to his farming activities. The remains of tabby slave dwellings stand as silent witness to the plantation heyday of Middle Place. A local surveyor, William Hughes, described Middle Place on a plat prepared in April 1855:

> "The above plan is a delineation of the most valuable cotton plantation on the seacoast of Georgia situate in Chatham County on Ossabaw Island. I consider it second to none. The site is also well adapted to the culture of corn, sugar cane, rye oats, potatoes, peas, etc. This plantation is not only desirable for its prosperity of soil, but for the healthiness of its atmosphere, the convenience of fishing and hunting, and...transportation. Mr. Alexander McDonald is the proprietor of these lands and long may he enjoy pleasure and prosperity but mindful of that eternal home..."[792]

---

[791] National Register of Historic Places application for Ossabaw Island, Kenneth H. Thomas, Jr., principal investigator for Georgia Department of Natural Resources, Historic Preservation Division, 1995 (hereafter cited as National Register application).
[792] Ossabaw Island Collection and Torrey Family Papers, Manuscript Collection 1326, Georgia Historical Society (GHS), Savannah.

The McDonalds later relocated to Rome, Georgia, where they lived the remainder of their lives. They left Middle Place to their daughter, Georgia H. McDonald Harper (1846-1905) who sold the tract in 1898 to her son, Donald Harper. Chatham County deed records indicate that Middle Place comprised 2,316 acres but it is unclear if the acreage represented an aggregate of high ground and marsh, or solely cultivable upland, the latter scenario being more likely.

John Morel, Jr., as we have seen, inherited the South End of Ossabaw in the division of his father's estate. In 1809, seven years after the death of Morel, the tract was subdivided into two properties, South End and Buckhead, the latter going to Morel's only daughter, Mary Ann Morel Rutherford (1786-1826).

Buckhead was the scene of some agricultural activity, though apparently not as extensive as that conducted on Ossabaw's three larger plantations, North End Place, Middle Place and South End. In 1828, Nathanael Greene Rutherford, husband of the late Mary Ann Morel, had a dozen slaves "employed in the cultivation of Little Buckhead Hammock." The Rutherfords' only child, Mary Rutherford Simmons, lived in Hancock County. After her death in 1858, ownership of Buckhead devolved to her children, the tract subsequently coming into the ownership of Charles S. Cary, a grandson of Mary R. Simmons. Cary was the last of the Morel family descendants to own land on Ossabaw; in 1916 he sold the approximately 4,000 acres of Buckhead's upland and marsh to Henry D. Weed of Savannah.

South End was foreclosed on in 1828 by the Bank of the State of Georgia, and the tract was held by several owners before being acquired by George Jones Kollock (1810-1894) of Savannah, he having connections by marriage to the McDonalds, owners of neighboring Middle Place. Kollock cultivated cotton and provision crops at South End until the Civil War disrupted his activities.

Kollock married Priscilla Augusta Johnston in 1836. She died in childbirth later the same year, following which Kollock married Susan Marion Johnston in 1840. Kollock practiced law in Savannah from 1832 to 1836. He then moved to Retreat plantation at Coffee Bluff on the Forest River, a tidal tributary of the Little Ogeechee River south of Savannah. In addition to Retreat and Ossabaw South End, Kollock owned a third plantation, Rosedew, on Rose Dhu Island on the Little Ogeechee between Coffee Bluff and Ossabaw Sound. Kollock acquired Retreat in 1837, it being a 309-acre tract that his infant daughter by his first marriage had inherited from her aunt, Priscilla Houstoun.[793]

Kollock employed an overseer and nineteen slaves to cultivate cotton at Coffee Bluff. He acquired Rose Dhu Island, with its Rosedew plantation of 550 acres, in 1838. This was a tract that, like Retreat, had originally been granted to Sir Patrick Houstoun before the Revolution. Kollock subsequently sold the Coffee Bluff and Rose Dhu tracts in 1848; by 1849 he had relocated his slave force to South End Ossabaw to cultivate cotton and corn.[794]

There is correspondence that relates to precisely when Kollock initiated his planting operations at South End. Writing from Savannah to his wife on January 24, 1849, Kollock noted that two

---

[793] Kollock Papers, Manuscript Collection 470, GHS.
[794] George J. Kollock Plantation Books, 1849-1861, MS Series 3 (Ossabaw Island, Georgia), Southern Historical Collection (SHC), University of North Carolina, Chapel Hill.

trips had been made "down to Ossabaw to take my Overseer & his family and some of the negroes to the south end. And some of the negroes are down now with the flat carrying mules, etc. I think of sending all the mules & some more of the negroes down by the flat...and then I will be able to take the corn & the rest of the things on one load in the Sloop..."[795] After 1850, Kollock and his family lived at their Woodlands plantation in Clarkesville, Habersham County, Georgia.

Because of the great number of surviving records, Kollock's activities on the South End during the antebellum period are the most fully documented of any of the Ossabaw Island plantations. The Kollock plantation and account books that report the minutiae of the various operations of the 1850s on the South End reflect the kind of detail that is typical of sea island cotton plantations on the south Atlantic coast. For example, Kollock's farm records, most of which are deposited in the Southern Historical Collection at Chapel Hill, North Carolina, contain insightful information relating to plantation operations in general, birth and death records of slaves, sick lists, acquisition of food and farm supplies, clothing for the slave force, and household equipment acquired and how utilized. The account books confirm that Kollock began planting at Ossabaw in 1849, three years before he actually finalized his purchase of the tract.[796]

As Kollock was an absentee owner, the South End account books were maintained by his overseer, J.W. Gilliam, beginning July 12,

---

[795] Kollock Papers, GHS.
[796] Kollock Plantation Books, SHC.

1849. Curiously, the journal entry for the next day, July 13th, appears in a different handwriting and remarks that Gilliam was in the custody of the Savannah police on unspecified charges. The plantation records detail the work carried out by the bondsmen at South End, as well as that by contract workers. These tasks included the planting and maintenance of the cotton crop followed by post-harvest ginning and moting, and the cultivation of provision crops, such as corn, peas and sweet potatoes. Other entries relate to the cutting of timber, clearing brush, and listing, ditching, plowing, grubbing, planting and hoeing the crop fields. The Kollock journals list the names of the bondsmen working the South End plantation, their morbidity and mortality, and the seasonal distribution of tools, clothing, shoes and blankets.[797]

In 1850, Kollock estimated the value of his cotton crop at six thousand dollars based on a yield of 20,000 pounds of "clean" cotton harvested, ginned and baled. He also reported the construction of a cotton gin at South End to process his crop. Considerable acreage in corn was planted, both as a subsistence crop for the work force and livestock, and as a secondary cash crop, but corn did not bring as high a return proportionally as cotton, the primary staple. As additional subsistence crops for the work force, the Kollock plantation cultivated sugar cane, rice, peas, and sweet potatoes. In 1850, Kollock reported possession of seventy-two slaves. Ten years later, the slave census shows Kollock owned seventy-one bondsmen

---

[797] Ibid.

living in twelve houses at South End.[798]

Additional correspondence in the Kollock papers relate to his interaction with two Portsmouth, Virginia shipbuilders, William R. Page and E.F. Campbell, in 1857. Their firm contracted ship construction for the government and other entities. Letters between Kollock, the Portsmouth yard and the Navy Department indicate Navy inquiries about the potential cutting of between 50,000 and 200,000 cubic feet of live oak timber on Ossabaw.[799]

In 1863, in the midst of the Civil War, Kollock noted that the ironclad ram *Savannah*, built at Savannah by the Henry F. Willink shipyard, was constructed of oak from Ossabaw Island. The vessel served in the harbor defense of Savannah until it was destroyed by the Confederates in December 1864 to prevent its capture as W.T. Sherman's armies approached Savannah at the end of the March to the Sea. Henry Willink was a prominent Savannah shipbuilder with business connections to Kollock and other local civic leaders. He maintained his building yard and a marine railway on the south shore of Hutchinson Island opposite the city of Savannah, building coasting vessels and ocean-going cargo ships.[800] Willink was also a contractor for the Confederate States Navy. An account by his daughter noted that "at the opening of the Civil War, H.F. Willink's ship-yard at the eastern edge of Savannah was the largest and best equipped yard in Savannah."[801] In addition to the *Savannah*, the

---

[798] 7th U.S. Census, Agricultural Schedules, Georgia, Chatham County, 1850; 7th and 8th U.S. Census, Slave Schedules, Georgia, Chatham County, 1850, 1860. See also Kollock Papers, GHS.
[799] Kollock Papers, GHS.
[800] *Savannah Daily Morning News*, September 1, 1859.
[801] Willink Papers, Manuscript Collection 872, GHS.

Willink yard built the ironclad *Milledgeville* and the gunboat *Macon* for the Confederate Navy.

Kollock continued his plantation operations on Ossabaw Island until the spring of 1862 when the Union naval blockade of the coast made all such activities on the Georgia islands prohibitive.

In the early 1870s the 2,500 upland acres of South End was sold to the Habersham family of Savannah. In 1883, William Neyle Habersham (1817-1899) and his siblings sold the tract to Archibald Rogers of New York City, Habersham's nephew by marriage. Rogers (1852-1928), a northern industrialist noted for his railroad construction, divested himself of the South End in 1895 to Carolin C. Maxwell of Bryan County and Savannah who in turn immediately sold the tract to William L. Nevin, an agent for the Wannamaker family of Philadelphia.

* * *

A notable naval action occurred in waters contiguous to Ossabaw during the Civil War, this being the celebrated, and surprising, Confederate capture of the USS *Water Witch*, a 378-ton sidewheel gunboat mounting four guns, and manned by eighty officers and men commanded by Lieutenant Austin Pendergrast. On the night of June 2-3, 1864, the *Water Witch* was on blockade patrol in Ossabaw Sound, having anchored at the mouth of the Ogeechee River a half-mile north of the entrance to Bradley Creek on Ossabaw Island, and a mile and a half southeast of Raccoon Key. Lieutenant Thomas Postell Pelot, CSN, formerly of the U.S. Navy and now executive officer of the ironclad-floating battery CSS *Georgia*, was ordered to take a hand-picked force on a boat expedition to surprise and capture the *Water Witch*. Pelot had assembled fifteen officers and 117 men in seven boats and had arrived at Beaulieu battery on the lower end of Vernon River by way of Skidaway Narrows the night before. The Confederate contingent there learned that the *Water Witch* was cruising in St. Catherines Sound off the south end of Ossabaw. The *Water Witch* returned to the Ogeechee the next night, anchoring, as noted, for the evening in the mouth of the river.

At 2 a.m. on the 3rd, a dark and rainy night, the Confederate force arrived at the Union vessel's anchorage. Moses Dallas was a black pilot from Savannah who led Pelot's boats through the stormy darkness to the anchorage of the Water Witch. The boats closed in, the Confederates boarded, and after a sharp and bloody pistol and cutlass fight, captured the vessel. During the melee, both Pelot and Dallas were killed on the deck of the *Water Witch*. The captured gunboat was taken up the Vernon River to the protection of the Beaulieu battery, then later was moved to White Bluff where it remained for the remainder of the war.[802]

In early 1865, Tunis G. Campbell (1812-1891), a New Jersey-born African American and friend of abolitionist Frederick Douglass, was appointed superintendent of several of the Georgia sea islands by General Rufus Saxton, head of the federal government's Bureau of Refugees, Freedmen and Abandoned Lands. Campbell was placed in charge of Ossabaw, St. Catherines and Sapelo islands with

---

[802] *Official Records of the Union and Confederate Navies in the War of the Rebellion*, v. 15 (Washington, D.C., 1903), 501-02. These records are contained in *The USS Water Witch*, Georgia Historical Society, 1974.

instructions to organize self-government and educational programs for the freed bondsmen of the coast.[803]

In July 1865, the Freedmen's Bureau was reporting that numbers of the freed slaves of Ossabaw were cultivating crops on the island. Soon after, some blacks began leaving Ossabaw upon the restoration of the coastal islands to their pre-war owners.[804] Campbell reported to the Bureau at the end of 1865 that there were seventy-eight freedmen on Ossabaw Island, 369 on St. Catherines and 352 on Sapelo.

In the spring of 1866, Campbell petitioned the American Missionary Association for teachers and the establishment of two schools for the children of freedmen on Ossabaw. He sought similar arrangements for St. Catherines and Sapelo. Campbell's efforts were successful and school programs were set up for children as well as adult freedmen on all three islands. In March 1867, an act of Congress formally restored the sea islands to their pre-war owners. In the wake of accusations of corruption and "having been found guilty of dishonest practices," Campbell was evicted from St. Catherines Island by the federal government in early 1867; he subsequently set up a powerful political machine on the mainland at Darien in McIntosh County.

The pattern of African American settlement on Ossabaw after the Civil War differs somewhat from that of the other large sea islands of South Carolina and Georgia. Unlike at Sapelo, Cumberland, St. Catherines and Hilton Head, the freedmen never became

---

[803] Russell Duncan, *Freedom's Shore: Tunis Campbell and the Georgia Freedmen* (Athens: University of Georgia Press, 1986), 18-29.
[804] *Savannah Daily Herald,* November 11, 1865.

landowners during the Reconstruction and postbellum eras. Nonetheless, the Ossabaw freedmen were planting cotton on George J. Kollock's South End tract in the spring of 1866, a pattern that was repeated in other parts of the island for several years.

The 1880 U.S. Census counted 160 people living in forty dwellings on Ossabaw Island. An African American church was established on Ossabaw in 1878 with the congregation organizing under the name Hinder Me Not Baptist Church, with sixty-eight members and Rev. B.O. Butler as minister. Several years later, Brother Thomas Bonds was pastor of the church, which had sixty-one members in 1885.[805] The congregation of Hinder Me Not later relocated to the Chatham County mainland community of Pin Point south of Savannah. There it split into two congregations, one moving to the Montgomery community.[806] Traditional lore asserts that some of Ossabaw's Geechee people relocated to Pin Point as early as the 1880s, although deed records indicate that it was in 1896 that Ossabaw's freedmen purchased land at Pin Point from Savannah judge Henry McAlpin. A year later, a small tract at Pin Point was purchased on which to build a sanctuary for the Sweetfield of Eden Church. Pin Point and Montgomery were near sites such as Vernon

---

[805] National Register application, 65-66. Some accounts and church records identify Thomas Bonds as the founder of Hinder Me Not church.
[806] Pin Point is on the Burnside River east of Skidaway Island in unincorporated Chatham County. Montgomery is nearby, further east. Pin Point remains one of the traditional African American communities of the greater Savannah area. The community is best known as being the birthplace of U.S. Supreme Court Justice Clarence Thomas (b. 1948). The Pin Point Heritage Museum interprets the history and culture of the Geechee community, and is in the former Varn and Sons Oyster Cannery that years earlier had employed many Pin Point residents.

View, Coffee Bluff and Rose Dhu Island, areas owned and cultivated by several of Ossabaw's pre-Revolutionary and antebellum planters—Morels, Houstouns, Johnstons and Kollocks.

African Americans remaining on Ossabaw until the end of the nineteenth century maintained ties with family and friends who moved to the mainland, as well as other freedmen of that section of Chatham County, circumstances at least partly attributable to the movement of bondsmen between Ossabaw and the mainland plantations of their owners during the antebellum period. The archaeologist Clarence B. Moore noted the presence of several African American families living at Middle Place during his investigation of Native American burial mounds in that section of Ossabaw in the fall of 1896.

A hurricane in 1881 and two others in the decade of the 1890s that were damaging to agriculture likely contributed to the migration of Ossabaw's Geechee to the mainland. In August 1893 a particularly devastating hurricane stuck the upper Georgia and lower South Carolina coasts, causing great loss of life and heavy property damage, especially on the sea islands from Ossabaw northward to Beaufort, South Carolina. Another hurricane in 1898 further discouraged Ossabaw's few remaining African American residents.

By the turn of the twentieth century, Ossabaw was almost devoid of residents. By then the Geechee had completed their movement to the mainland, an occurrence that unfortunately resulted in the gradual loss of knowledge in later generations as to the locations of traditional historic sites, including church, cemetery and dwellings.[807]

---

[807] National Register application, 66, notes the death of Thomas Sams, a 38-year old African American, who was murdered on Ossabaw in 1890, and

When the U.S. Census was taken on Ossabaw in June 1900 only six persons were living on the island—four whites, and two single black males, both farm workers.

In 1886, as previously noted, the Morel family descendants sold Ossabaw's North End Place to James M. Waterbury (c. 1852-1931), a prominent businessman from New York City. He was a founder of the New York Yacht Club, an avid huntsman and outdoor enthusiast, and his sons were international polo players. In his obituary, Waterbury was described as "a leading sportsman" and Westchester County, where he had a country estate, was "a gathering spot for lovers of riding, hunting and polo."[808]

Waterbury and his family apparently spent little time at Ossabaw. In June 1895 North End Place and the South End were conveyed by Carolin C. Maxwell to William L. Nevin in trust for John Wannamaker of Philadelphia. North End and South End had each been conveyed to Maxwell for a period of less than a month by Waterbury and Archibald Rogers, respectively, before their immediate conveyance to the Wannamaker interests. Rogers of New York had held South End for twelve years as a hunting site but details of his use of the tract during that time, if any, are murky. Middle Place was added to the Wannamaker holdings in 1903, giving that family ownership of all of Ossabaw except for the Buckhead tract.[809]

---

reported in the *Savannah Morning News*. This unfortunate occurrence may have encouraged some to leave the island for the mainland.

[808] *New York Times*, July 13 and July 30, 1931, cited in National Register application, 58.

[809] National Register application, 58. The deed for North End Place was conveyed directly to Wannamaker in 1902.

John Wannamaker (1838-1922) was a Philadelphia merchant, and religious, civic and political leader. In 1861 he founded the well-known Wannamaker department store chain. A new Wannamaker store, known as the "Grand Depot" when it opened in 1875 in a refurbished railroad depot in the heart of Philadelphia, was one of the largest department stores in the United States in the late nineteenth century. In 1910, the Wannamaker Building, a twelve-story granite structure built on the same site, was opened and dedicated by President William Howard Taft. Wannamaker served in the Benjamin Harrison administration as U.S. Postmaster General from 1889-93. By the time of his death in 1922 the John Wannamaker Company was one of the most recognizable and prominent corporate names in America,

There is conflicting information regarding the provenance of the Clubhouse on the North End. Eleanor Torrey West once noted that the Wannamaker family built the Clubhouse in the late 1890s near the head of the later Torrey Landing causeway, further noting that the family dismantled a clubhouse building used in the Philadelphia Centennial International Exhibition in 1876, and had it transported to Ossabaw where it was rebuilt as a family lodge. Subsequent research undertaken during the structure's restoration in 1999 makes a more valid argument that the Clubhouse was a pre-fabricated structure built in the late 1880s by North End owner James M. Waterbury for use as a hunting lodge. The initials "J.M.W." are stamped on many of the wooden framing pieces. Whatever its origin, there is evidence that the Clubhouse is on the site of two former Morel dwellings that burned and their sites indicated on the 1886 plat discussed earlier in this paper. "A chimney covering a window suggests that this house was placed against an existing chimney."[810]

In 1906, the son of John Wannamaker, Thomas Wannamaker, sold an aggregate of 9,416 acres of upland on Ossabaw comprising North End, Middle Place and South End, to John H. Carr. In May 1907 all three tracts were acquired by Henry Davis Weed of Savannah through his intermediary, John Carr. The fourth Ossabaw tract, Buckhead, was bought by Weed in March 1916, thus consolidating all the divisions of the island under one owner for the first time since John Morel Sr.'s death in 1776.

Henry D. Weed (1872-1960), a Harvard graduate, owned and managed a successful Savannah wholesale and retail hardware company, and served on the Savannah Board of Trade. In 1916, Weed affirmed that there were dwellings and cultivated fields on all four of Ossabaw's tracts, each with a resident overseer. Despite Ossabaw being ideally suited for his hunting and other recreational interests, Weed was apparently acquiring clear title to each of the tracts for future sale to other buyers. Confirmation of this emerged when, almost immediately after he gained title to Buckhead, he sold the entire island of "24,000 acres" on March 22, 1916 to a consortium of buyers from the Strachan Shipping Company, George F. Armstrong, George P. Walker, Frank D.M. Strachan, Harry G. Strachan and Robert W. Groves.

---

[810] Ibid., 59. The Ossabaw Clubhouse is now maintained by the Ossabaw Island Foundation for educational retreats, symposia and meetings as part of its education and outreach programs, and provides accommodations for groups of up to twenty-two people. A nearby structure, the Boarding House, built in 1918 during the Strachan period of island ownership, has also been restored, and can accommodate eight people.

From 1916 to 1924, Ossabaw was owned by these individuals under different corporate names. They had their primary residences and business in Savannah and Brunswick and maintained Ossabaw primarily for hunting and fishing by the owners, their families and their guests: "According to Mr. J.J. Hinely, the son of the Superintendent for Mr. Armstrong, the island was used for hunting. Mr. Armstrong kept a kennel of hunting dogs at the North End, and the Superintendent and his family lived in what is called the Boarding House [built ca. 1918] today."[811]

Ossabaw's modern history began in 1924 when the island was purchased for $150,000 by Dr. Henry Norton Torrey and his wife Nell Ford Torrey of Detroit, Michigan. The Torreys had purchased a seasonal home, Greenwich, on the Wilmington River near Savannah in 1917. The house burned in early 1923 by accident.[812] Rather than rebuild Greenwich, the family sought other property for their winter residence. Ossabaw fit their needs perfectly with its isolation, history and natural beauty.[813]

H.N. Torrey (1880-1945) was an industrial surgeon with Harper Hospital in Detroit while Nell Torrey was the daughter of John B.

---

[811] Ibid., 68.

[812] *Savannah Morning News*, January 28, 1923.

[813] In an interview in 2001, Sandy Torrey West tells the story that Ossabaw was actually purchased on a whim by her mother, Nell, while her father was away. Mrs. Torrey "never dreamed her offer of $150,000 would be accepted" by the partners of the Strachan Company. Mrs. West also noted that she hated the island, "with all its marsh and boggy swamps" when she first went there as an eleven-year-old child in 1924. But as time and events would prove Sandy Torrey West became the most ardent advocate for the preservation of Ossabaw the island has ever known. *Savannah Morning News*, January 4, 2001.

Ford, founder of the Pittsburgh Plate Glass Company and the Wyandotte Chemical Company in Michigan.

From 1924 until late 1925 the Torreys built their 20,000-square foot Ossabaw residence, a beautiful tile-roofed Spanish revival home on the island's North End overlooking Ossabaw Sound, and designed by Savannah architect Henrik Wallin. Set in a natural landscape of live oaks, palms, and spectacular gardens impressively laid out by both Mrs. Torrey and the prominent landscape architect Ellen Biddle Shipman, the new main house featured stuccoed exterior walls, terra-cotta ornamentation, red-tile roofs, and iron balconies and window grills.[814] The house was designed in such a way that each room had a connection to the kitchen to enable family and guests to easily ring for service from the staff. The Torrey family spent their first winter season in the house starting in January 1926.

The Torreys had a yacht and acquired a small tract for a mainland dock at Vernon View on Burnside Island south of Savannah. The main Ossabaw dock, Torrey Landing, was at the North End near the residence, and featured a picturesque causeway lined with palms. The Torreys brought a Packard automobile to the island, along with a chauffeur; a tutor often accompanied the family from Michigan to work with their children during the seasonal sojourns. The Torreys also built a tennis court and a miniature golf course near the main house, and a beach house at Bradley Beach on the ocean side of the island.

---

[814] Loraine M. Cooney, comp., *Garden History of Georgia*, 1733-1933 (Atlanta: Peachtree Garden Club, 1933), 349-53.

For a time, H.N. Torrey continued the farming operations that were ongoing at Middle Place, Buckhead and South End when he bought Ossabaw. These activities on the former plantation tracts probably began during the Henry Weed ownership of the island, and continued during the brief Strachan ownership period. In the mid-1920s there were several supervisors overseeing the farming activities—John Harrison at Middle Place, a Mr. Hope at Buckhead and Sam Cooler at South End.

Shortly after acquiring Ossabaw Torrey researched the records in the Georgia Historical Society pursuant to writing an informal monograph about the island's early history, *The Story of Ossabaw* (1926). In the introduction, he relates his family's early impressions of the uniqueness of their island:

> "Ossabaw's highlands are heavily wooded, with live oak, virgin pine and palmetto predominating and the vegetation is semi-tropical and very luxuriant. The soil is exceedingly fertile and is especially adapted to the raising of cotton and sugar cane; in fact, these Islands before the Civil War were celebrated for the fine quality of long staple cotton grown upon them. The salt marshes of Ossabaw are many miles in extent and have a peculiar beauty and fascination to all lovers of the Georgia coast. Traversing these marshes and extending into the highlands are many salt rivers and creeks which afford splendid fishing. The beach on the ocean is fifteen miles long, nearly half a mile wide at low tide and with its hard, white surface rivals the speedway at Daytona. The primitive and original atmosphere of Ossabaw has always been maintained, and the property today retains its natural beauty and charm. The woods still abound in game of nearly every kind and description…When we bought the island in 1924, the deer were estimated to number five thousand, the wild cattle about two thousand and the wild boar at least ten thousand. The cattle and the boar have all descended from domestic stock which has been wild for

generations. Owing to tick infection in the cattle, we decided to eradicate them, but as the animals were very wild and dangerous, and their range so extensive, it proved a most difficult problem. However, one year's work by Texas cowboys completed the task. The wild boar proved a different proposition, and in spite of the most strenuous endeavors, we have only managed to keep down the natural increase. They range in size from small pigs to boars three hundred pounds in weight, which with their long, sharp tusks, great strength and ability, make savage foes when at bay. Ossabaw, with its white egret and heron rookeries, its thousands of ducks, snipe, quail, pheasants and wild turkeys, is a veritable bird Paradise. Also it is renowned for its sea food—oysters, clams, fish, diamond-backed terrapin and sea turtles. These turtles attain an enormous size: their shells, in some cases are five feet in diameter. One of the great summer sports is hunting turtle eggs on the beach at moonlight..."[815]

Prominent visitors came to Ossabaw in the 1920s and 1930s, among them the Torreys' coastal neighbors, Howard and Matilda Coffin of Sapelo Island, also of Detroit. Henry and Clara Ford of Detroit occasionally visited the Torreys during the Fords' winter trips to Ways Station on the Bryan County mainland. The first recorded visit to Ossabaw by the Fords was February 24, 1926 in the first months of main house occupancy by the Torreys.[816] Other visitors were R.J. Reynolds, Jr., who bought Sapelo from Coffin in 1934, the actress Lily Pons, Mills B. Lane of Savannah, and Alvan Mccauley who founded the Packard Motor Company.

---

[815] H.N. Torrey, *The Story of Ossabaw*, privately printed, 1926, from the Introduction.
[816] Main House Guest Register, v. 1, 1926-1988, Ossabaw Island Collection, GHS.

Dr. Torrey died in 1945. His widow, Nell Ford Torrey, visited Ossabaw only infrequently thereafter until her death in 1959. Their son, William Ford Torrey, lived on the island and oversaw timbering and pine tree planting operations, and a sawmill operated on the island in the late 1950s and early 1960s. The younger Torrey died in 1956. The Torreys' daughter, Eleanor Torrey (b. 1913), married John Shallcross in 1935, later divorced, then was wedded to sculptor Clifford B. West, Jr. in a marriage ceremony held on Ossabaw in March 1952. Roger Parker, the longtime caretaker and assistant to Mrs. West, came to Ossabaw following his uncle who arrived in 1951. The Caretaker's House, where the Parker family lived for many years, was built in 1955.

In 1961, Eleanor "Sandy" Torrey West and Clifford West established the Ossabaw Foundation for the preservation and educational enhancement of the island. In implementing the goals of the Foundation, the Wests coordinated four ongoing programs in the 1960s and 1970s—the Ossabaw Island Project, the Genesis Project, the Professional Research Program, and the Public Use and Education Program.

The highly-successful Ossabaw Island Project was an interdisciplinary program through which qualified participants were invited to the island from the U.S. and abroad to pursue their research and creativity in the arts, humanities, and sciences while benefiting from the isolation and solitude of Ossabaw. During the eight months a year the Project operated the Wests lived in the Clubhouse while the resident scholars resided in the main house.

The Genesis Project was begun in 1970 and was active until 1982. In it, Sandy West provided Ossabaw as a platform for people of all skills and talents to come to the island to undertake independent projects and initiatives, usually associated with ecological, botanical, zoological and archaeological investigations. Genesis participants lived in rustic quarters they built themselves at Middle Place on the west side of the island. There were few amenities and participants cultivated their own food; some of the wood-frame structures still remain overlooking the marshes at Middle Place.

The Public Use and Education Program has been continued to the present day in an innovative and energetic format coordinated by the Ossabaw Foundation. This initiative grew out of the Wests' desire for people to experience and appreciate the natural environment of Ossabaw Island. Out of this program came a camping site for limited stays, both for researchers and the public, and day trip programs for qualified groups coming to the island for environmental and cultural education. The main house continues to be used on a limited basis for meetings and symposia. In 1999, the Clubhouse was substantially restored by the Foundation with the support of grants, and was made available to qualified groups to conduct educational meetings, symposia, and field trips on Ossabaw the year around.

In 1978, through a combination of purchase with public funds and a donation by the Torrey and West families, largely coordinated by the efforts of Sandy Torrey West who wished to see her island preserved from overuse or development, the State of Georgia acquired Ossabaw for $8 million. Ossabaw became a state Heritage Preserve to be used solely for "natural, scientific and cultural study, research and education and environmentally sound preservation of the island's ecosystem." The state built a hunting facility at South

End-Newell Creek to complement the camping facility built in 1971 at South Beach for the use of educational groups.

Mrs. West retained a 24-acre life estate on the North End, including the main house. Sandy West continued to live in the Ossabaw home built by her parents until 2016, when her age and declining health compelled her to move to the Savannah mainland to live the remainder of her life. At the time of this writing in 2020, she was still living at the age of 107. Until very recently Sandy West continued to be a strong advocate both for Ossabaw and the Georgia coast, and she played a key role in the reinvigoration of the Ossabaw Foundation in 1994. At that time, Leopold Adler II of Savannah, whose wife, Emma Morel Adler, is directly descended from Ossabaw's first colonial owner, became the Foundation's president.

Henry Ford and the Great Ogeechee

If there were no river, there would have been no Henry Ford in Richmond Hill almost a century ago. For Ford, the Great Ogeechee was the attraction, the impelling force which lured him in 1925 to an impoverished backwater then known as Ways Station.

The dark meandering waters of the Ogeechee, in so many ways a river of mystery, beckoned Ford long before there was a Richmond Hill. The Ogeechee has always had that kind of effect on people—that regal stream whose tannic currents emanate from the rolling piedmont of the Georgia upcountry, before seeking their merger with the ebb and flow of the tides in its lower reaches. The "River" has held an allure for generations of coastal Georgians, particularly for those in the immediate environs of Bryan Neck.

Ford's love affair with the River may be said to have begun rather inauspiciously. Perhaps the genesis lay in a casual conversation between friends far from the Ogeechee, on the shores of the Gulf of Mexico at Fort Myers in southwest Florida. These friends constituted a remarkable consolidation of energy and intellect—there was Ford, of course, an established "captain" of American industry; there was also Harvey Firestone, who wished to develop a viable domestic rubber market in America; the renowned inventor, Thomas A. Edison, was there, as was the famed naturalist and botanist, John Burroughs.

It has been said, though not completely substantiated, that it was Burroughs who first brought the Ogeechee to Ford's attention. One fairly credible story has it that Ford and Burroughs were touring part of the U.S. east coast on a boat excursion. When reaching this area

Burroughs is said to have pointed down the Ogeechee and commented to Ford, "This is good bird watching country."

Whatever the case, Ford did not forget the natural beauty of the River and, not inconsequentially, the river's dynamic economic potential, particularly in light of the impoverished state of many of the families he saw along the malarial, mosquito-infested lower Ogeechee on Bryan Neck.

There is another factor to be considered in Ford's subsequent involvement with Georgia, the Ogeechee River and the little hamlet of Ways Station. In 1923, Ford and his wife Clara, while on a trip south, visited the town of Rome in northeast Georgia where they toured the Berry School. The Fords were impressed with this unusual school founded in 1902 by Martha Berry where the poor, semi-literate young men of north Georgia were taught vocational skills, with an emphasis on agricultural training. So moved by these initiatives, Ford (as he had done for similar institutions in New England and Michigan) donated several million dollars to the Berry School. These Ford educational endowments would soon be applied in similar fashion to the people of lower Bryan County, the tangible evidences of which continue to be an integral part of the present Richmond Hill community.

But for Ford, Firestone and Edison the idea was the melding of the American automotive industry with its relevant scientific applications, and just how the Ogeechee River basin might be implemented as the formulaic catalyst for such an initiative. From the outset, Ford's vision was to integrate science, agriculture and industry into a viable enterprise that would be of benefit not only to Ford's commercial vision, but also in a myriad of ways to the people of Bryan Neck. Ford and Firestone, the industrial giants of the Model-T Ford and the rubber tire industry, were irked that Great Britain had for years maintained an almost exclusive monopoly on the world rubber market. Surely, it would be far more commercially desirable to bring a portion of that market to the United States.

Could rubber trees be cultivated on the banks of the Ogeechee? This was the original concept, the dynamic behind the arrival of Henry Ford at the village that came to be Richmond Hill. Ford, Firestone and Edison, with the necessary botanical input from John Burroughs, had established the Edison Research Institute in Fort Myers specifically for experiments in rubber cultivation.

The emergence of Ford on the Ogeechee River starting in 1925 was the direct result of the inconclusive aspects of the work begun at Fort Myers. Ford remembered the Ogeechee from his earlier forays through that section of Georgia, making his way north back to Dearborn from Florida in his chauffeured Ford limousine. More than that, he recalled the poverty he had seen on Bryan Neck and what he might contribute to the betterment of conditions there. Concomitant with the more tangible aspects of a move to the Ogeechee were the pure aesthetics of the matter—the stark natural beauty of the River, the Neck and the Georgia coast in general struck a chord with Henry and Clara. They also wanted a permanent winter home in a temperate climate.

For Ford, what began as an agricultural experiment of enormous consequence, evolved into something of a social experiment as well, with the Ogeechee providing the centerpiece, the backdrop for all that was to come over the ensuing quarter-century. "Helping people is my religion," Ford is supposed to have commented to a Ways Station resident in the early years of his activities in lower Bryan.

In 1925 Ways Station was a small village in a poor, rural section of tidewater Georgia. Two railroads, the Seaboard Air Line and the Atlantic Coast Line, passed through Ways and shared the trestlework spanning the nearby Ogeechee. The prosperity of the nineteenth century rice growing years on the Ogeechee was a distant memory and the area around Ways Station and Bryan Neck had fallen upon difficult economic times. More recently, the large Hilton-Dodge sawmill at Belfast had closed, putting many of the local residents out of work just before World War I. People now subsisted on small-scale agriculture, turpentine processing and making moonshine. Bryan Neck was one of the poorest sections of coastal Georgia when Ford made his appearance. He quickly realized that he could make a difference and improve conditions for people.

Perhaps even more conclusive testimony as to Ford's intentions in this regard is illustrated by another remembered conversation in 1925. A plainspoken man by any measure, Ford purportedly remarked to R.L. Cooper, a Savannah real estate agent who, on behalf of Ford, began buying up large chunks of acreage on Bryan Neck, "I am not interested in making money. I have made more money from manufacturing motorcars than I could ever spend. I am much more interested in the Martha Berry School in upper Georgia." And, of course, by extension in the natural evolution of things, helping the people of Ways Station and Bryan Neck, as history would demonstrate.

The challenges faced by Ford and his team from Dearborn in the ensuing years would be great. It may be no exaggeration to say that what occurred at Ways Station after 1925 is representative of Ford's greatest social challenge. How successfully that challenge was met and surmounted is the enduring legacy of Henry and Clara Ford in the town that became Richmond Hill.

One should constantly be reminded, however, that this remarkable legacy began with the mystical, magical River known as the Great Ogeechee.

Henry Ford & the Restoration of Fort McAllister

In June 1861, Confederate engineers under the direction of Lt. Alfred L. Hartridge of Savannah began building earthworks and a battery mounting four guns at Genesis Point on Bryan Neck. The battery's primary purpose was to provide for the defense of the lower Ogeechee River and its important communications link with the Atlantic & Gulf Railroad crossing upstream near King's Ferry.

This simple fortification was completed to a point in August 1861 that it could accommodate a garrison of troops, and emplacement of guns. Shortly afterward it was named Fort McAllister in honor of Joseph L. McAllister's late father, George W. McAllister of Strathy Hall plantation in lower Bryan County. Joseph, friend of Lt. Hartridge, made available family-owned lands at Genesis Point on which to build the fort.

Though not rating much more than a footnote in the standard histories of the Civil War, Fort McAllister set a standard for persistence, pluck and endurance that became unique in the annals of American military and naval warfare.

The earthen fort was constructed of sand, river mud and palmetto logs, and featured well-protected magazines that provided protected storage of ammunition and a "bombproof" that offered shelter for the fort's personnel. Submerged obstructions placed in the Ogeechee, along with gun mounts at the battery, covered the river approaches to Fort McAllister. These guns, in tandem with the fort's earthen walls, were to make McAllister an exceedingly resilient defensive work, as events were to prove. Contemporary photographs show Fort McAllister as being completely cleared, and devoid of any trees and the greenery so abundant at today's site. This was intentional—the Rebel defenders wanted a clear, unobstructed view of both the River and the landward approaches.

Fort McAllister successfully repelled, seven different union naval attacks by warships stationed as part of the blockading forces in nearby Ossabaw and Wassaw sounds, and in the nearshore Atlantic waters. The vessels that attacked Fort McAllister featured the latest in naval technology, being *Passaic*-class ironclad warships, an advanced and larger version of the original USS *Monitor*, that had fought the Confederate ironclad CSS *Virginia* in a battle that revolutionized naval warfare in the spring of 1862. *Passaic*-class monitors were the most technologically advanced warships of their time, with superior machinery, armor-plate protection and weaponry. Shells from their artillery were repeatedly lobbed at Fort McAllister during the river attacks in 1862 and 1863, all to little avail. The fort never fell to these assaults as the earthen sand walls of the fort simply absorbed and dispelled the shock and explosions of the Union shells.

In frustration, the Union suspended its attacks; the Federal strategy focused on the subjugation of Charleston by sea later in

1863. It took a landward attack by overwhelming Union forces in December 1864 for Fort McAllister to finally be defeated, near the culmination of William T. Sherman's March to the Sea and the eventual investment of nearby Savannah. This was a crucial factor in the fort's demise as it had been designed and built primarily to defend the river approaches to Bryan Neck, rather than attacks from the land. Nonetheless, the sharp engagement that resulted in the loss of the fort by Confederate was accorded lasting status as being one of the bloodiest engagements of the Civil War, especially so considering its brevity (a 20-minute assault). Major George Anderson, commander of Fort McAllister, famously noted in his report to his superiors, "The fort never surrendered. It was captured by overwhelming numbers…" Casualties among Union General William B. Hazen's attacking force were 24 killed and 100 wounded. Confederate losses were 16 killed and 28 wounded.

The war ended several months after McAllister surrendered, and the fort lay abandoned and all but forgotten for many years, overgrown with weeds, trees and thick underbrush. When Henry Ford arrived on the scene to revitalize lower Bryan County sixty years after the war, the fort had eroded almost to the point of disintegration. Ford, however, proved to be Fort McAllister's salvation. He was fascinated with the area's history and soon began a concerted effort to restore some of the older structures on Bryan Neck. He was especially interested in Fort McAllister.

In 1936, Ford's workmen began clearing the Genesis Point site and built a road to the old fort from the Bryan Neck Road (present day Highway 144 Spur). In a project that eventually cost $14,600, Fort McAllister's bombproof, complete with its chimney, and ammunition and powder magazines were excavated and rebuilt, and the former earthworks restored to their original configuration. Former Fort McAllister superintendent and the fort's leading historian, Roger S. Durham, noted "Ironically [the fort], long neglected by Southern people, was renovated by a son of the North to serve as a monument to all Americans who fought in that conflict."

Ford's restoration of Fort McAllister excited and energized area patriotic organizations and, in 1938, the Savannah Chapter of the United Daughters of the Confederacy acquired the fort's original garrison flag from George W. Castle of St. Louis, a descendant of one of the Union soldiers who had captured the fort in December 1864 and who had carried the flag home as a war trophy. In December 1939, on the 75th anniversary of the fort's capture, the flag was once again raised over the earthworks of Fort McAllister in a special ceremony.

The Georgia Historical Society coordinated a gathering of area descendants of some of the Confederate defenders of the fort with a special program on the site in June 1941, with the principal speaker being Walter Hartridge, descended from Lt. Alfred L. Hartridge, who in 1861 built and commanded the Genesis Point Battery which became Fort McAllister.

When Ford died in 1947 the various agricultural and timber operations he had begun in Bryan County and Richmond Hill twenty years earlier began to wind down. These changes impacted the restored Fort McAllister as well. The cost of maintaining the fort was a mere $440 annually, largely for grounds upkeep. However, the Ford Plantation, which facilitated the maintenance of the site, determined in 1946 that the fort was not a necessary part of its operation. This occurred following the discovery that some of the timbers of the restored bombproof and magazines were deteriorating through moisture and rot and the Plantation was reluctant to incur the cost of repairs.

When Ford's holdings on Bryan Neck were sold in a series of transactions beginning in 1951, the Fort McAllister site became the property of International Paper Company which, seven years later in 1958, deeded thirty acres of the fort site and adjacent property to the Georgia Historical Commission. Thus for the first time, Fort McAllister became a viable site for public visitation and educational programs. In the early 1960s, the much-needed repairs were made to the structures built by Ford, the grounds were cleared and landscaped, and a museum and office facility built. In November 1963 Fort McAllister was officially opened as a state historic site with Alston C. Waylor as the first superintendent. In 1972 the state of Georgia acquired additional property adjoining the site and a state park was developed for public recreation with camping facilities, a boat launching area on the Ogeechee and enhanced interpretive activities and programs. Over the years these outreach efforts have been expanded and improved under the administration and operation by the Georgia Department of Natural Resources' Parks and Historic Sites Division.

One of the most interesting corollaries to the development of the fort by the state was the work begun in 1960 by the U.S. Army Corps of Engineers to investigate the wreck of the Confederate commerce raider CSS Nashville, sunk in February 1863 by Union naval gunfire in the Ogeechee across the marsh from Fort McAllister. Sections of the heavy machinery were brought up from the river mud and put on display on the grounds of Fort McAllister. Periodic marine archaeological investigations of the Nashville remains have been made over the succeeding years, both by local experts as well as the state of Georgia. Many additional artifacts from the wreck have been salvaged and are on display in Fort McAllister's museum exhibits.

Ford & His Detroit Friends in Coastal Georgia

The words of the great Savannah lyricist Johnny Mercer would be particularly applicable to those prosperous, flourishing days of the late 1920s in coastal Georgia—

"The days of wine and roses, laugh and run away like a child at play".

The song lyrics evoke affluence, carefree spirits, and yachting trips along the intra-coastal waterway between the barrier islands.

These were the days just before the stock market crash of 1929, and the ensuing Great Depression that engulfed the American financial and social landscape. Three friends on the coast, who each had as their common bond the automotive industry centered around Detroit, Michigan, were certainly unaware of approaching troubled times.

They were Henry Ford of Ways Station (soon to be Richmond Hill), Henry Norton Torrey of nearby Ossabaw Island, and Howard E. Coffin of Sapelo, a short hop down the coast. Their impact on American automotive development and American industry in general is an essential ingredient in the emergence of the United

States in the late nineteenth century as the world's leading economic power.

The almost simultaneous appearance of Ford, Torrey and Coffin in coastal Georgia during the period 1918-1925 was no coincidence. Ford was the latecomer of the Detroit trio. Ford was from the suburb of Dearborn, site of his Ford Motor Company, and Coffin was from nearby Grosse Point. The three Detroit neighbors came seeking, among other things, sanctuary from the northern winters, a place to find temporary solitude from the demands in their roles as "captains of industry."

What they also had in common was an appreciation and awareness of the Georgia lowcountry, so much so that all three men built lavish homes. Two of them eventually made them their permanent residences.

By 1925, when Ford began acquiring acreage on Bryan Neck, his friends were already well established in Georgia and had begun building their homes on Ossabaw and Sapelo.

Unlike Torrey and Coffin, Ford and his wife, Clara, never made Richmond Hill and Bryan Neck their permanent home. Instead, they made annual winter excursions to the Ogeechee where they spent several months interacting with local employees in the Ways Station community, expanding agricultural operations and gradually putting into place the social and economic dynamic that is still being felt in south Bryan today.

As Ford was developing the mass production processes that would make his company an icon of American industry in the 1920s, one person with whom he frequently consulted was Howard Coffin. One of the nation's leading automotive designers, Coffin was vice-president and chief engineer of the Hudson Motor Car Company of Detroit, a corporation headed by Coffin and his co-partner Roy Chapin.

In 1912, Coffin and his wife Matilda purchased Sapelo Island as a winter retreat. Along with a business partner, Clement Keys, Coffin also acquired nearby St. Catherines Island. During World War I, Coffin served on the War Department's civilian Advisory Board and played a major role in designing tracked vehicles to transport American doughboys on the European war front. Coffin also had significant aviation involvement and was co-founder of a business that eventually became United Airlines. From 1918 to 1925, the Coffins undertook a complete reconstruction of the old Sapelo Island tabby house of antebellum planter Thomas Spalding. This became a home so palatial that National Geographic Magazine did a photographic spread on it in the early 1930s. Concurrent with this project was Coffin's rebuilding of the old Button Gwinnett house on the north end of St. Catherines, the original of which dated to the Georgia colony.

Coffin had numerous distinguished visitors on Sapelo, including two presidents of the United States, Calvin Coolidge and Herbert Hoover in 1928 and 1932, respectively, and the famous aviator Charles A. Lindbergh, the first person to fly solo across the Atlantic Ocean, New York to Paris. In 1926, with much of his Sapelo work completed, Coffin, with his young cousin, Alfred W. Jones, established the Sea Island Company and its signature Cloister Hotel resort, which opened in the fall of 1928.

Ford and members of his family were frequent guests of the Coffins on Sapelo. Ford's signature appears several times in the

Coffins' Sapelo Island Guest Book now on deposit in the Sea Island Company's archives. There are also extant a number of photographs of Ford family members on Sapelo during the 1920s and early 1930s.

Closer to Bryan County was Ford's other Detroit connection, the Torrey family of Ossabaw Island. Henry N. Torrey (1880-1945) acquired Ossabaw in 1924. He and his wife, Nell, moved there from their previous winter residence, Greenwich, on the Wilmington River near Savannah. Torrey was a surgeon affiliated with the Harper Hospital in Detroit, specializing in industrial surgery, which explains both his business and social connections with Ford and Coffin.

From the Torreys' visits to see their friends on Sapelo, the Coffins, evolved the concept for their own expansive residence on Ossabaw. In 1924, they began construction of their beautiful Spanish-Mediterranean style home on the North End of the island near Bradley Point, about the same time the Coffins were completing their Sapelo house.

Like Ford on Bryan Neck and Coffin on Sapelo, Torrey had extensive agricultural operations on Ossabaw. There were farm and cattle activities at several points on the island, including Buckhead, Middle Place and South End.

Among the first visitors to the new Torrey residence in February 1926 were the Fords during one of their visits to Bryan Neck several miles up the nearby Ogeechee River. This was during a period when Ford was engaged in the acquisition of his land holdings in Bryan and Chatham counties.

Several years later, Henry and Clara Ford followed suit with a stylish residence of their own, Richmond, constructed on the banks of the Ogeechee and being completed in 1936. By then, the nation was in the midst of the Depression, and Coffin had been forced to sell Sapelo in order to keep his Sea Island venture solvent.

Both Sapelo and Ossabaw are now managed by the State of Georgia. However, the Georgia coastal legacies of both Coffin and Torrey remain. Sea Island continues to be one of the nation's leading resorts. The Torreys' daughter, Sandy Torrey West (born in 1913) continued to reside in the family residence on Ossabaw's North End until 2016, and is one of the coast's most passionate advocates for the conservation of its natural and ecological resources.

Clyde: A Lost Town of Coastal Georgia

Clyde is the former seat of Bryan County, situated in the central section of the county amid the oaks and pine flatwoods inland from the coastal tidewater. Like other small settlements in the area, the little town was literally removed from the map as the result of land condemnation proceedings related to the establishment by the federal government of the Camp Stewart training base just before the Second World War. Clyde's history is not particularly significant, certainly lacking the attention given by historians to the antebellum rice plantations or that of the Henry Ford era in lower Bryan County. Yet, Clyde represents an aspect of coastal Georgia history that needs to be remembered along with other communities, such as Willie and Taylor's Creek in Liberty County, that disappeared within the vastness of the Camp Stewart initiative.

In early 1797, the Bryan County justices valued two acres of William Clark's plantation at Cross Roads at $24 for the purpose of establishing a county seat and courthouse. Cross Roads was at the intersection of the Savannah-Darien Road (present U.S. 17) and the Bryan Neck Road (present state 144). Later that year, the Georgia legislature authorized the "permanent seat of the public buildings at the Cross Roads about two miles from Ogeechee Bridge (King's Ferry)..."[817] Apparently the Cross Roads, later named Ways Station, and still later, Richmond Hill, was designated as the county seat for

---

[817] "Marbury and Crawford's Digest of the Laws of the State of Georgia, 544, 546, cited in Charles C. Jones, Jr., *Dead Towns of Georgia* (Savannah: Georgia Historical Society, Collections IV, 1878). Bryan County had been created in 1793 from portions of Chatham and Effingham counties.

the convenience of its location, both for the planters of Bryan Neck, and for the increasing numbers of settlers establishing themselves on farms in the central part of Bryan County in the Canoochee River section, and in the sparsely-populated upper part of the county.

In 1814, the legislature responded to the increased need for a more central location for the Bryan County seat, and a new site for a courthouse was purchased at or near Mansfield in the central section of the county. Known simply as "Court House" or "Bryan Court House," the new site is reflected as such on early nineteenth century maps.[818] Adiel Sherwood refers to the chief town of Bryan County as being "Court House" in 1827 and places its location as "four miles west of the Canoochee River."[819] This is Eden, the name which replaced that of Court House, and later became Clyde, the Bryan County seat until its removal to the railroad town of Pembroke in 1937. By the mid-1840s the Bryan County seat was being shown on maps as Eden, in the precise location of "Court House."[820]

Bryan County deed records show that county buildings were not built for at least two years at the new site approved in 1814, for it was in April 1816 that William Harn sold to the county commissioners a two-acre tract for the construction of a courthouse building at the site in central Bryan County that became known as Clyde. Harn had

---

[818] Daniel Sturges, "Map of the State of Georgia" (Savannah, 1818).
[819] Adiel Sherwood, A *Gazetteer of the State of Georgia* (Charleston, S.C., 1827). The 1818 Surges map, cited above, shows Court House as being more west from the confluence of the Ogeechee and Canoochee rivers, and a short distance north of the Canoochee.
[820] William G. Bonner, "Map of the State of Georgia," (Milledgeville, Ga., 1847).

been granted the land in 1815, among other properties in that section.[821]

Typical of the families of upper Bryan County in the antebellum period was that of Remer Jacob (Jake) Wise, born in 1812 in neighboring Bulloch County. Wise was a substantial landowner in upper Bryan, at one time owning a large tract between the Canoochee River and Eden (Clyde), now part of the Fort Stewart Military Reservation, and on which the Wise family cemetery is located. Part of his lands lay on the north side of the Hencart Road, later known as Old Clyde Road (state 144). On his plantation near Eden, Wise cultivated cotton, corn, tobacco and other crops, and also harvested timber on his pine lands. He was one of the leading producers of pine tar, rosin and turpentine before and after the Civil War. Wise was reportedly the oldest citizen in Bryan County at the time of his death in 1891 at the age of seventy-nine.[822] Stories about Wise were passed down the generations and part of them are reproduced here as they provide a contemporary picture of life in upper Bryan County before and during the Civil War.[823]

> ..."Jake was a planter and he and his brothers William and John owned large tracts of pine timber land, as well as cotton, corn, indigo, hay, tobacco and backwater rice fields....Before, during and after the Civil War Jake and his younger brother William (One-Arm Bill), and their sons owned and worked tracts of pineland, backwater creeks and ricelands clear downstream to where the Ogeechee and Canoochee rivers meet. It is said that Jake and William built the first

---

[821] Bryan County deed records, Book D, Clerk of Superior Court, Pembroke, Ga.
[822] *Savannah Morning News*, September 16, 1891.
[823] Author's interview with John F. Wise of Montgomery, Alabama, 1999, a Jacob Wise descendant. John Wise compiled the following anecdotes from stories passed on to him by David Stephen Wise in 1978.

turpentine and pine tar still in Bryan County. One of Jake's many contributions to the county was to provide the land and slaves to build new backwoods roads and a mesh of dirt trails through the thick pine woods on and leading to his property...There were stories about how Jake and his neighbors and a number of slaves desperately barricaded the old Clyde-Pembroke Road, just west of [Eden], not far from the old courthouse, to spoil the Yankees' flanking attach on Fort McAllister and march into Savannah. After skirmishing and blocking the Yankees for four days (6-10 December, 1864), and burning the creek bridges from Eden to the Savannah Road, they were overwhelmed by sheer numbers of Union troops...When the Yankees broke through, Jake and his group hid in the backwater swamps and woods to evade capture. After about two days of hiding they unwillingly came out of the swamps, cold and wet clean through, and walked to the burned and damaged Courthouse to get help for their wounded and to find and bury their dead...At the Courthouse, Jake identified himself and demanded the Yankees help put out the fires they set, and provide medical help for the injured. He defied the Yankee officers by refusing to give them information about Fort McAllister and backroad map markings. He admonished them for their excessive cannonading, ransacking, raiding of home gardens, and for deliberately firing on the Courthouse, homes, outbuildings, churches, and the senseless killing of farm animals...Jake said the Yankees spitefully shot mules, horses, dairy cows and beef cattle, and the deliberate burning of the Courthouse, the jail, corn and tobacco [barns], and the three nearly sanctified churches. Since Jake was the senior Confederate Military District official, he was arrested and carted away in chains. {He] was locked up in a prisoner of war compound inside Fort McAllister. On Christmas Eve Polly, Jake's wife, frantically pleaded with the Yankee commander for the release of Jake and his son from prison. They were successful and Jake and his son were conditionally released on Christmas Day. They walked the road to the area of the present Clyde cemetery where the town's big artesian well was located. The Yankees used this well to water their men and horses and did not contaminate it with dead animals when they left. It was the only uncontaminated well for miles around where people could get drinking water...By the end of January 1865, about a month into his house arrest, the Yankee guards and the [Hencart} Road outposts suddenly packed up and went to their big camp on the other side of the Ogeechee River. Soon as the Yankees left, Jake said he applied some 'Yankee honor' and immediately ignored his parole order. For the next two months Jakes was everywhere in the district. He traveled on mule and horseback, organizing parties of men to rebuild homes, tend to smallpox and typhoid fever outbreaks, and to make sure everyone buried all the dead people and animals found..."

Another story of the Wise family and the little town of Clyde concerns Jacob Wise's younger brother, William Henry Wise (1826-1910). These recollections provide a contemporary look at Eden-Clyde during the postbellum period:

"In 1868, Bill had a new home built on the western side of Clyde. He and his brother Jake purchased and improved a string of wooden buildings across the road from the Clyde courthouse. These buildings were on the main road through town...and were developed into a country store at one end, a county law office, a private law office, a doctor's office and the county tax collector's office. There was a large stable and horse corral at the north end of town, originally operated by Bill's childhood friend John Harn. Later, the Harn family made one of the buildings nearest their barn into a small, ready-made clothing, merchandising and home hardware store...Bill and succeeding family members ran the old Clyde country store for over fifty years, up through the 1930s...Bill was also in a partnership with his friend John Harn to run the only blacksmith shop in Clyde. The Clyde country store was a very important place in the town. It became the post office and the unofficial employment office. Whenever someone was looking for work, they would talk to Bill or post a notice at Bill's store. At one time during the 1880s, Bill complained that this hiring service was out of control and affected his store business so much that he had to have a proper 'Help Wanted' notice board made up and attached to the side of the store, away from the store's front porch...At his funeral his friends talked about how One-Arm Bill was always jokingly chided about burning his home to the ground on his birthday about 1900, along with the Clyde courthouse records. The story was that the judge moved the court records to Bill's home for safety reasons because the old wooden and dried-up courthouse was a fire trap. The court's records were stacked in an unused bedroom...Bill broke in a new tobacco pipe and accidentally dozed off in an armchair while reading the newspaper and smoking his pipe. When Bill awoke the house was in flames. By the time his neighbors came to his rescue they said Bill

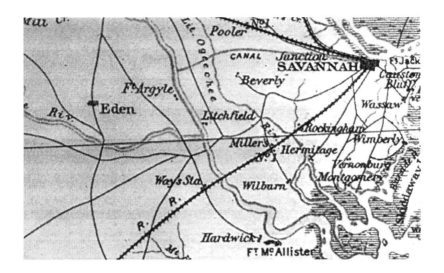

A portion of Bryan County from an 1860 map of coastal Georgia. Eden is at center left near the Canoochee River. Ways Station is at lower center and Fort McAllister is at bottom right. The Ogeechee River flows through the center of the map from top to bottom.

was jumping up and down and yelling 'the hell with the house, save the court records!' It was too late, because it was the court records that fed the big fireball and reduced the house to cinders..."

For the period following the Civil War until the early 1890s, when the railroad was built through upper Bryan County and the towns of Pembroke, Ellabell and Lanier were established and grew, the primary town of the county was county seat of Eden, the town name being in use into the early 1880s. Sholes' *Gazetteer* reported the population of Eden as being only twenty-five residents in 1879; the town, as noted, had a general store, a post office and churches in the area.[824]

---

[824] C.W. Norwood, comp., *Sholes' Georgia State Gazetteer and Business Directory for 1879 & 1880*, cited in David McKivergan and Mildred Fryman, *Fort Stewart and Hunter Army Airfield Historic Preservation Plan*, Technical Synthesis Volume, Prentice Thomas and Associates, 1990.

Eden became Clyde in 1886 as the result of a convoluted process that had begun almost thirty years earlier because of post office considerations. Station Number 2 out-bound from Savannah on the Central of Georgia Railroad in neighboring Effingham County was also named Eden and confusion often arose from references to two Edens in such close proximity in southeast Georgia. The Bryan County Eden was identified as such on maps as late as 1882.[825] The James R. Butts map of 1882 labels the county seat as "Bryan (Eden)" then, seven years later in 1889, an updated version of the same map identified the county seat as Clyde.

Most of this confusion is cleared up through a scrutiny of U.S. postal service records, which note that the post office designation for Eden in Bryan County was dropped in April 1857, and the Eden in Effingham County was then given official post office status. However, the U.S. post office department had no authority to change the name of a town, no matter how small, just its post office status, thus the Bryan County seat continued to be called Eden into the 1880s. For mail purposes, postal authorities changed Eden's designation to "Bryan." In September 1886, John H. Heery was appointed postmaster of Bryan/Eden. About the same time, county commissioners decided the time had come to end the prevailing confusion regarding two Edens in such close proximity, in addition to providing the county seat of government with a designation more original than "Bryan" or "Bryan Court House." Thus in the fall of 1886, a change of name was approved in which the county seat was

---

[825] James R. Butts, "Map of the State of Georgia," Macon, Ga., 1882, revised in 1889.

henceforth to be known as Clyde, to become official on January 1, 1887.[826]

Clyde was named for Sir Colin Campbell, Lord Clyde (1792-1863), noted field marshal of Scotland. A two-story frame courthouse was built in 1901 to replace the earlier structure built in 1860, then restored after being partially burned by federal troops in 1864. The new courthouse served the county until the seat of government was moved to Pembroke in 1937.

Though never incorporated, Clyde continued to serve as the Bryan County seat despite the growth of railroad communities such as Pembroke and Lanier in the upper part of the county. Clyde had the disadvantage of poor communications as the settlement was several miles from the nearest river, the Canoochee, and it was bypassed by the railroads. The new Savannah & Western Railroad was completed through upper Bryan County in 1889-90 and because of the rapid growth of rosin and turpentine production in that part of the county, along with commercial businesses and a railroad to serve them, there were several unsuccessful attempts by business leaders in upper Bryan to relocate the county seat to one of the railroad communities. In 1906, the population of Clyde was about 100 citizens, with the courthouse, county offices, post office and several stores and residences within the township's limits.[827] By 1910,

---

[826] Records of the U.S. Postal Service (Record Group 28), Georgia, Bryan County, Reel 281-30, v. 26 (1857-76), v. 42 (1876-1889), NARA, Washington, D.C.
[827] *Fort Stewart Preservation Plan*, op. cit., 130.

two turpentine distilleries were operating at Clyde[828] and in 1917, the population of the little town was given as 200.[829]

Due to the growth of Pembroke as the primary business and financial center of Bryan County in the first three decades of the twentieth century, as well as the town's ideal location on two major communication routes, the Seaboard Air Line Railway and the Jefferson Davis Highway (U.S. 280), it became apparent by the early 1930s that Clyde's days as the county seat were numbered.

One dilemma faced by the Bryan county commissioners was where to build a needed new county facility in light of the growing support of moving the county seat from Clyde to Pembroke, despite it being at the upper end of an elongated county that stretches from Pembroke over thirty miles southeastward to the salt marshes and Ossabaw Sound. County officials took steps to apply for federal funds to go toward the construction of a new courthouse, regardless of where it went.[830] The federal funds applied for were available for building a new courthouse building at Clyde, however, rather than Pembroke, thus removal of the county seat to the latter would necessarily abrogate the government grant.[831] While these discussions were evolving among county officials in 1935, petitions were circulating in two sections of the county miles apart, one advancing the removal of the seat to Pembroke, and the other supporting it

---

[828] *Young and Company's Business and Professional Directory of Cities and Towns in Georgia* (Atlanta: 1909-10).
[829] Lucien Lamar Knight, *A Standard History oif Georgia and Georgians* (Chicago: Lewis Publishing, 1917), 1248.
[830] Bryan County commission minutes, July 2, 1935; Papers of the late J. Dixie Harn, Pembroke, Georgia (private collection).
[831] J. Dixie Harn Papers.

being moved to Ways Station on the opposite end of the county.[832] Legal wrangling ensued over the issue and two lawsuits soon followed.[833]

A new petition was then circulated calling for an election to determine the location of the county seat; it would require two-fifths of the registered voters of Bryan County to sign the petition in order for a special election to be called. The requirement was subsequently satisfied, and it being noted that

"a number of proposed candidates have been breaking their necks running away from anyone that looks like he might have a petition to be signed...They say they are strong on moving the courthouse but just can't afford to sign the petition...It will be a warm election and we hope that no one gets mad with anyone else, as it is every man's right and privilege to do what he wants and no one should blame another one for wanting the courthouse located near him and property that he may own."[834]

On December 18, 1935, in perhaps the most important referendum ever held in Bryan County, before or since, a majority of voters approved the moving of the county seat from Clyde to Pembroke. To no one's surprise, the breakdown of the vote confirmed the wide disparity of opinion. Voters in the 19th district (Pembroke) were overwhelmingly in favor of the courthouse move by a margin of 408-6. Conversely, in the 1137th district (Clyde), the vote was 132-1 against the move. In the 20th district (Ways Station), the vote was 77-4 against the move and in the 1380th (Ellabell-Blitchton) the vote was 87-17 in favor. The total vote in favor of the move was

---

[832] Ways Station was re-named Richmond Hill in 1941.
[833] *Pembroke Journal*, October 11, 1935.
[834] *Pembroke Journal*, October 18, 1935.

thus 500 to 232, which meant the voters had approved the move by thirty-four votes more than the necessary two-thirds majority required in an action of this kind. Not surprisingly, there were charges of voter fraud and other irregularities in the lower two districts of the county (Clyde and Ways).[835]

Early in 1936, the Bryan commissioners tabled the construction of the new courthouse until the plans for the move of county administration and operations from Clyde to Pembroke could be implemented. Thus, pending formal approval of the move from the state legislature, county operations and court would continue to be conducted at Clyde throughout 1936.[836] The state general assembly formalized the removal of the seat from Clyde to Pembroke on February 11, 1937. The same day, Bryan County state representative Daniel Brooks Warnell of Pembroke announced the ratification of the December 1935 vote, and its being immediately signed into law by Governor Eurith D. Rivers.[837]

The first actions related to the large-scale division of Bryan County, and the resulting disappearance of Clyde township, to be

---

[835] *Pembroke Journal*, December 20, 1935. It is a perception among some that the removal of the county seat from Clyde to Pembroke was occasioned by the federal government's acquisition of the middle portion of the county, including the Clyde area, pursuant to the development of the army training base at Camp Stewart in 1940. Such is not the case. The voters decided the move four years before the land condemnation proceedings in Bryan, Liberty and other counties for Camp Stewart.
[836] Bryan County commission minutes, February 4, 1936.
[837] *Pembroke Journal*, February 12, 1937. The J. Dixie Harn Papers cited earlier contain numerous documents pertaining to the relocation of the county seat, as well as the history of Pembroke and north Bryan County. The new two-story brick courthouse in Pembroke was completed and dedicated on May 18, 1938, a structure still in use at the time of this writing in 2020.

associated with Camp (later Fort) Stewart occurred in September 1940. It was at that time that the first troops began arriving at the new installation near Hinesville in neighboring Liberty County to begin construction of the Army's training center, troop barracks and other facilities. In the ensuing eighteen months, the U.S. government condemned large sections of Liberty and Bryan counties and smaller portions of Long, Tattnall and Evans counties to provide large swaths of undeveloped land for the Camp Stewart military reservation training center.

Fort Stewart research historian Mildred L. Fryman identifies three reasons for the selection by the federal government of this portion of the U.S. southeast for the establishment and expansion of a large military reservation: protection of the port of Savannah; the heavily-forested and swampy lands making up the proposed reservation carried low property assessments, and thus could be obtained at minimal costs; and the "political intervention by interested parties," based on considerations of wartime policy making. "It is appropriate to point out," Fryman noted, that in all probability federal authorities greatly under-estimated the number of families to be displaced in the affected counties by the creation of Fort Stewart. Original estimates suggested three to four hundred family units would be affected; in actuality, there were more than fifteen hundred families and about six thousand people impacted directly by this decision."[838]

---

[838] Mildred L. Fryman, in *Fort Stewart Historic Preservation Plan*, op. cit. In addition to scattered small farm and turpentine tracts throughout central Bryan, Liberty and the other three counties, several small communities would be condemned and their populations resettled. These included Clyde, Letford and Roding in Bryan County, and Taylor's Creek and Willie

Local newspaper editor Frank O. Miller did not mince words in the spring of 1940 when expressing his opinion about the government takeover of Bryan County land:

"The report of appropriating $3.5 million for the purchase of 525,000 acres of land which is supposed to take a strip of land eighteen miles wide and thirty miles long has got all our people on the edge of a nervous breakdown. In fact, this editor has a first class case of the jitters.

"We carried in our paper last week the first published story of anything in connection with this training ground and stated that reports were current that the Government was contemplating all the land in Bryan County between the Seaboard railway on the north and the Coastal Highway on the south for an aeroplane anti-aircraft center.

"There is no way to keep the government from taking the land. If they want it, they will get it. Still, we believe if our people will be reasonable in their price with the government that the government will be fair with them. There is no use of kicking, or cussing or raising hell generally about it. If they want our land, they will get it. Just as well make up your mind and begin to look for a place to move and start life all over again.

"While no official information is available, we understand that within the next few weeks, the government will have men contact the property owners and try to reach an agreement satisfactory to all parties concerned, and if they fail in this that condemnation proceedings will be instituted and the land will go to the government. And it is thought that those living in the territory that the government wants will probably have until January 1st, 1941 to get a place to move to. Just what this will do to us and our county is hard to say. If the government takes a large part of our land off the tax books and our people have to move to some other county to live, it will certainly make things hard with the rest of those living in Bryan County."[839]

---

in Liberty. Willie was in Liberty across the Canoochee River from Letford, while Taylor's Creek was near the Liberty County seat of Hinesville on land that would be utilized as the main operational base for Camp Stewart.
[839] *Pembroke Journal*, May 31, 1940.

Several months later, editor Miller provided his subscribers with additional information and details about the reservation:

"The War Department, through the acquisition facilities of the Soil Conservation Service, Department of Agriculture, is now proceeding with the appraisal and purchase of lands for the site of the large anti-aircraft training center to be located in parts of Liberty, Long, Bryan, Tattnall and Evans counties, described as follows:

"Beginning at a point one and one-half miles north of Hinesville, northwest to the village of Alton (but excluding the villages of Alton and Smiley); thence due north to a point four miles south of Claxton, thence eastwardly paralleling the Seaboard Air Line and approximately four miles south thereof, to the Ogeechee River; thence southeast along, but exclusive of the Ogeechee River to the Atlantic Coast Line Railroad; thence southwest paralleling the Atlantic Coast Line right-of-way to the vicinity but exclusive of the village of McIntosh, thence northwest to the starting point, exclusive of the village of Flemington.

"Appraisals and negotiations with landowners have not yet progressed to the point where any definite westerly boundary can be estimated but, in general, it is believed that all farmers and residents within Liberty and Bryan counties should make preparations to vacate the lands and move all personal property, livestock, etc. not later than March 1st, 1941..."[840]

The official transference of private lands to the federal government began in the spring of 1941, the announcement noting that

"Title to approximately 76,800 acres of land in Liberty and Bryan counties for Camp Stewart anti-aircraft training center near Hinesville was acquired by the United States yesterday when Federal Judge William H. Barrett signed a decree granting immediate title to the government. The property condemned yesterday was the first of a group of tracts which will comprise the Camp Stewart military site. Ultimately the site will take in 360,000 acres..."[841]

---

[840] *Pembroke Journal*, November 14, 1940.
[841] *Savannah Morning News*, March 8, 1941.

On March 27, 1941, the Bryan County commission approved the closing to the public of all roads in the middle section of the county entailing the army training center. With this development, 105,000 acres, about one-third of the land of Bryan County, including the communities of Clyde, Roding and Letford and the smaller settlements of Green Bay and Little Creek, came under the administration of the U.S. War Department; the section was thus closed to the general public of the county. The military reservation separated the upper and lower sections of Bryan County. With the few roads in the middle section of the county, including the dirt road that connected Pembroke to Ways Station, via Clyde, now inaccessible to the civilian public, Bryan literally became two counties in one with no connection between the upper and lower sections. As part of the agreement with Bryan County, federal official agreed to support the development of Morgan's Bridge Road, later designated State 204 (Fort Argyle Road) in order to provide citizens with the lower end of Bryan (G.M.D. 20) access to the county seat at Pembroke and vice-versa. From Pembroke, this road went through Lanier and Ellabell, skirted the northern boundary of the reservation, crossed Morgan's Bridge over the Ogeechee River into Chatham County to a junction with U.S. 17, thence south to Richmond Hill.[842]

The exodus of inhabitants from the middle section of the county began in early 1941 and continued through the end of that year. William W. Speir surveyed many of the lots in Clyde for the federal government in 1940 and 1941 and recalled that the removal of

---

[842] Bryan County commission minutes, September 2, 1941, May 12, 1942, August 4, 1942.

residents and the dismantling of buildings at the former county seat was rapidly expedited.[843] The majority of people in Clyde, Roding and vicinity moved to the lower end of the county, resettling in Richmond Hill, and at or near smaller communities such as Clarktown, Cartertown and Daniel Siding, all proximate to U.S. 17 south of Richmond Hill.[844]

Properties within Clyde itself surveyed and purchased at a pre-determined "fair market value" included those occupied by the former county courthouse, the Bryan Lodge 303 F.&A. Masons, the Bryan County Board of Education, Clyde Methodist Church, American Legion Post No. 27, general stores operated by Preston Wise, P.R. Bacon, W.H. Davis and John Harvey, and residential properties owned by such families as Earl and Emma Shuman, Ruby (Wise) Harvey, John L. Harvey, J.G. Harvey, Mrs. E.B. Wise, W.H. Davis, J.W. Wise, P.R. Bacon, W.L. Rushing, Addie K. Strickland, Robert Harvey estate, H.M. Wise, Bertha Stewart, Ben and Lucille McCallar, R.B. O'Bryan, and Mrs. W.R. Clanton. Outside of Clyde along either side of the dirt road leading to the Canoochee River two and a half miles to the south, the deeded lands included properties in the names of Wise, Goethe, Arnsdorff, Lewis, Shaw, Harvey, Gill, Smith, Sauls, Davis, Warnell, Dukes and the Wise family cemetery.[845]

A useful diagram researched and compiled in 1993 by Wyman May delineates all of the properties in Clyde as of 1941, and

---

[843] Interview by the author with W.W. (Billy) Speir of Richmond Hill, Georgia, December 1, 1998.
[844] Interviews by the author with Mr. and Mrs. W.W. Speir and H.O. Rahn, December 1, 1998.
[845] Diagram of 1941 Clyde compiled from land plats and deed records by Wyman May, 1993; interview by the author with Thelma Wise Speir (Mrs. W.W. Speir), Richmond Hill, Georgia, December 1, 1998.

identifies their public or private owners at the time of the federal condemnation proceedings. All that is left now of the village are the fading headstones in the Clyde cemetery, the dirt roads and trails, and the surrounding oak and pine forest.

Nothing is more symbolic of the passing of a community than the discontinuance of its postal service. Clyde's post office was officially deactivated by the postal service on December 9, 1941. Although most were gone by then, there were still a few people remaining at Clyde, most of them awaiting housing in the Richmond Hill area. Some of the displaced citizens took up temporary lodging at the old courthouse in Clyde and the schoolhouse. By early 1942, all persons had relocated away from the section, many into the housing sections of Richmond Hill being built at that time by Henry Ford.[846]

* * *

Going back to the site of Clyde sixty years after its literally being removed from the face of the earth often arouses conflicting and, to the uninitiated, confusing, emotions. At the site of Clyde, seat of Bryan County from 1816 to 1937, there is simply nothing left except the surrounding woods, a dirt road or two and the old cemetery, to remind one that a community ever existed on the site. That is why the author, in an attempt to adduce some measure of understanding as to the fabric of Clyde's buildings and its environs, but most importantly, a proper sense of the collective lives, values, goals and thoughts of its people, made a daylong visit in late 1998, with the

---

[846] Thelma Wise Speir provided the author with the particulars of the departure of residents from Clyde based on her own recollections and her conversations with other former residents of the community.

permission of the proper Fort Stewart authorities, to the site with some who had actually lived there to feel the place for himself.

Therma Wise Speir (1919-2014) was a native of Clyde and experienced her childhood and adolescence there in the years just before the life of the little village ended forever. She was the daughter of W.C. Wise (1886-1925) and Addie Sikes Wise of Clyde. She was married to William Wiley Speir (1917-2004) , the latter growing up at Green Bay near Clyde and graduating from Ways High School. They were married for more than fifty years.

Access to the site of Clyde from either end of Bryan County—i.e. Pembroke or Richmond Hill—is still by way of the old sand road that once was designated as State Road 63. Accompanied by Thelma and Billy Speir, and H. O. "Buck" Rahn, all of Richmond Hill, we proceeded toward Clyde from the south (Richmond Hill) and crossed the small bridge over the dark, tannic waters of the Canoochee River, relatively narrow at this point, being the head of tidewaters. The Clyde Road, maintained by the military, proceeds for a little over two miles through pine flatwoods, interspersed with occasional oak, bay, hickory and gum, and thickets of saw palmetto and bayberry. Nearing Clyde, on the right side of the road, is the Wise Cemetery, resting place of members of that and other families who once lived their daily lives in the area.

Despite being armed with ample foreknowledge of the site, one's initial impression upon entering Clyde itself for the first time is one of disappointment—there is nothing substantively different about one's surroundings to demonstrate or prove that one is actually *somewhere*. There is the sandy road, and the familiar tree canopy and vegetation, but besides the cemetery, there is nothing to indicate anything resembling prior human habitation, nothing to prove that people once lived and worked in this quiet peaceful setting, that things *happened* here. One is struck by the feeling that these woods, these surroundings, probably are representative of a landscape little different from the rural Bryan County landscape of sixty years ago, a hundred years, a hundred and fifty years previous. The Clyde of today is nothing but pine, oak and scrub, and the dirt road curving away to the northwest to Pembroke fifteen miles away and southeast to Richmond Hill, nine miles distant.

Soon after turning right off the main road down a shaded, sandy lane, one sees the tangible evidence that people once did live here. It is the old Clyde Cemetery, a small, fenced burial ground comprising the graves of the families who lived, and farmed and turpentined these lands for generations, families who represented the essence of the pioneer settlers of middle and upper Bryan County. Their names are Wise, Shuman, Harvey, Gill, Clanton and Harn. The earliest tombstones in this well-kept graveyard, which is maintained by the Army as are others scattered throughout the Fort Stewart reservation, amid a peaceful setting of oak and cedar are those of Henry Wise (died 1888) and Jacob Wise (died 1891). Nearby is where Press Wise ran his general store, and across the road is a huge live oak tree, the "hanging oak," always spoken of by the people of Clyde in muted tones. It is adjacent to a patch of ground where the two-story frame courthouse, built in 1901 and demolished during the government takeover in 1941, once stood.

On the other side of the oak, across the lane from the courthouse site, is where the Masonic Lodge building stood, once an integral part of the social and fraternal life of the little village. We are shown where the wood-frame Clyde Methodist Church once stood, built in 1886 after the Charleston-centered earthquake shook the ground in these parts. In an open area across the Red Bug Road, which took many a traveler to Ellabell and the north part of Bryan County, little Thelma Wise once played ball with her playmates. Here in the underbrush are remains of the artesian well, a free-flowing public fountain with water to slake the thirst of locals and visitors alike, and which has long since ceased to flow.

Down the lane, back towards the main road, is where the Clyde Consolidated School once stood, which Thelma Wise attended as a child. She relates that she and her mother moved to Green Bay, about five miles west of Clyde, a year after her father died suddenly in 1925. However, she attended the Clyde school, which was built about 1927. The children in this section of Bryan County attended the consolidated schools through the middle grades before moving on to the high school in Ways Station.

There were three general merchandise/grocery stores at Clyde, a saw mill and a turpentine still, school, church and post office, in addition to county offices for ordinary, clerk of county and sheriff. It was always relatively quiet. But never as quiet as this day. It is difficult now to imagine that things of substance once occurred here, as still and peaceful as it is where the only sounds are the muted calls of birds, the whisper of the breeze through oak and pine, and an occasional animal scurrying through the underbrush.

Maritime Notes from Coastal Georgia

Coastal Georgia was an important source of live oak timber for northern shipbuilding interests in the late eighteenth and early nineteenth centuries. The frames and hull planking of early United States naval vessels were largely built of live oak hardwood from Cumberland, St. Simons and Ossabaw islands. The wooden warships of the Navy of the early Republic were the most sophisticated and technologically advanced of their type in the world. The emergence of tidewater Georgia as an influence on the development of the early Navy provides, among other factors, credence for the presence of a maritime heritage for the region.

Blackbeard Island south of Savannah was endowed with an ample forest of Southern live oak (*Quercus virginiana*). Over the millennia, many of the trunks and boughs of the gnarled trees had become bent and curved through the ceaseless action of the ocean winds that swept over the little island. The lower parts of the oaks were thus bent into shapes that were particularly suited to molding the knees and bends necessary for the constructions of the hulls of the warships of the era. Thus, the U.S. Navy Department was quick to acquire Blackbeard when it was placed on public auction in 1800 by agents of the defunct French Sapelo Company that had owned Sapelo and Blackbeard islands in the 1790s.

In 1794, under authorization by President Washington and the Congress, America's leading shipbuilder, Joshua Humphreys of Philadelphia, was charged with designing the strongest and most technologically-advanced warships of their class in the world, these being the original six frigates of the early United States Navy. Humphreys sent his ship fitters to survey the southeast coastal islands to mark stands of live oak timber suitable for the construction of the warships. These crews were marking oak stands on St. Simons Island as early as the summer of 1794 precedent to the cutting and molding of the trees to construct the frames of the new ships. Boston shipwright John T. Morgan was contracted by the government to go south and arrange contracts for the cutting of oak on the properties of private landowners. Virginia S. Wood notes:

"In addition to live oak and red cedar from Georgia, a combination of the best timber—white oak, yellow pine, pitch pine, and locust—was to be used. Humphreys specified live oak for futtocks, knight heads, hawsepieces, bow timbers, stanchions, knees, transoms, and breasthooks. It was essential that 'great timbers,' those pieces used in the hulls, be large as well as strong; 'compass pieces,' the curved members used in frames, could be hewn from trees of irregular shape, and live oak met this requirement. For those directing the operation, it was easy enough to sit comfortably in Philadelphia and demand the finest live oak; however, it was quite another matter to drag it from the malarial swamps of Georgia. After all arrangements had been made, Morgan was to superintend the cutting and hewing of timber to see that it was shipped to the six ports where construction on the frigates was to begin...St. Simons and Hawkins islands in Georgia were among the first sites designated for the live oaking. But things got off to a slow start as Morgan was confronted by unexpected problems. He received moulds and oxen in August 1794, but no hands to do the work. Furthermore, as he wrote to Humphreys, 'I have not seen 10 fair days since I left you. The whole country is almost under water and if the rains continue it will be almost impossible to get the timber, for where the live Oak grows is all low Land and Swampy in a dry time, but there was never so much rain known in this Country'"[847]

---

[847] Virginia Steele Wood, *Live Oaking: Southern Timber for Tall Ships* (Boston: Northeastern University Press, 1981), 25-27. This book remains the definitive study in the procurement of south Atlantic live oak for ship construction in the late eighteenth and early nineteenth centuries.

Despite the difficulties, the shipwrights and timber crews prevailed. Using the durable oak hardwoods from the Georgia and South Carolina islands, the American heavy frigates of the 44-gun class—*Constitution, President* and *United States*—and 36 (later 38)-gun class—*Congress, Constellation* and *Chesapeake*—were built between 1795 and 1800. Timber from St. Simons and Cumberland islands went into the construction of USS *Constitution*—"Old Ironsides"—the most famous of the original six with her victorious engagements in three actions against Royal Navy warships in the naval War of 1812.[848]

While no Blackbeard Island timber went into the original frigates, some of the island's oak was cut and transported to northern shipyards for later warship construction. The Navy Department noted that Blackbeard abounded with "large timber as well as small and never having been culled, may by cutting out from time to time be kept in a constant state of improvement, as a nursery." It was also noted that flats of a thousand feet could load at different places and the island afforded ample pasturage for the oxen required to haul out the oak to the molding and loading areas. On March 17, 1800 it was advertised that "The Island of Black beard will be sold in this city [Savannah] on the 5th day of April [the island] Containing about 1,600 acres situated in McIntosh County…it being pointed out by the Executors of Francis Dumoussay to satisfy an execution against the Estate of the deceased Dumoussay. Conditions cash."[849] The Navy Department thus acquired the island for $15,000 for use as a

---

[848] See Tyrone G. Martin, *A Most Fortunate Ship: A Narrative History of Old Ironsides* (Annapolis: Naval Institute Press, revised edition 1997) for particulars on the ship's career and the preservation of the vessel as a national monument in Boston Harbor.
[849] *Georgia Gazette* (Savannah), March 17, 1800.

timber reserve. Rather than harvest timber right away, the Navy leased Blackbeard for cattle range and small-scale agriculture as noted in 1812 when William L. McIntosh secured rights to "...occupy, and to raise stock on the island of Black-beard..."[850]

Marine listings in the Savannah newspaper[851] and a contemporary account in the manuscript holdings of the Navy Department attest to the removal of live oak timber from Blackbeard Island by northern ship-fitters for warship construction after the War of 1812. In the fall of 1816, E. & T. Swift of Falmouth, Massachusetts and Joseph Grice of Philadelphia sent gangs of workers to Blackbeard for oak amid plans to build eight 74-gun ships-of-the-line and nine 44-gun frigates apportioned to the congressional naval expansion act of 1816.[852]

The only account of live oak operations at Blackbeard is a unique document in the naval archives at the Washington Navy Yard in which shipwright James Keen (1781-1860) of Philadelphia kept a record of his crew's activities in 1817-18. Keen's journal is one of the few surviving first-hand sources attesting to the daily routine and rigors of a typical early nineteenth century live oak camp.[853]

The Philadelphia crew first appeared at Blackbeard in the fall of 1816, followed by a second trip a year later. While in Georgia, Keen consulted with Thomas M. Newell of Savannah, a Navy agent and

---

[850] *Republican and Savannah Evening Ledger*, October 24, 1812.
[851] *Columbian Museum and Savannah Daily Gazette*, 1818, 1819.
[852] Wood, *Live Oaking*, 46.
[853] "Journal of James Keen, November 27, 1817-April 5, 1818," Entry 346, Records of Boards and Commissions, 1812-1890 in Record Group 45, Naval Records Collection of the Office of Naval Records, NARA. Keen's journal was published as Virginia Steele Wood, ed., "James Keen's Journal of a Passage from Philadelphia to Blackbeard Island, Georgia for Live Oak Timber, 1817-1818," *American Neptune*, October 1975, 227-47.

liaison officer for private contractors cutting timber on Blackbeard and other islands. Keen also interacted with James Shearwood of neighboring Sapelo Island who was himself engaged in timber contracts with the Navy Department. In his capacity as "Superintendent of Blackbeard," Newell arbitrated labor disputes between the timber-cutting crews comprised of white labor, mostly from New England, and locally-leased slaves. Keen began his journal in November 1817 during the second period of Blackbeard operations by the Philadelphia crew. Virginia Wood offers the following observations about Keen's live oakers:

"We learn that in approximately sixty-nine working days, 12,061 cubic feet of timber was molded for the frame of a forty-four gun frigate, that slave labor was used for building roads and hauling timber, that relationships among the men were often less than amicable and 'demon rum' triggered many an argument, that there was a daily sick list, that certain local inhabitants were very much involved in the business of selling timber or services to the Navy. Of considerable interest is the emergence of facts about Blackbeard Island which enables us to assign it a more prominent role in the history of coastal Georgia. In his journal Keen implied that timber was cut at the island's south end. This was our first destination [on a 1974 visit by Ms. Wood to the island], and en route we passed dense, jungle-like growth typical of the coastal islands. To my surprise there are no live oak trees at the south end of Blackbeard. Instead, there are approximately 180 acres of pine forest and 180 acres of pine mixed with hardwood. Turning our attention northward, we stopped at Nelson's Landing formerly Brailsford's Landing, on Blackbeard Creek where the island narrows. One can easily walk to the beach in a few minutes time, as Keen mentioned doing on occasion. It is conceivable that in 1817-1818 the beach was even closer to the landing than now...Although the original deed conveying Blackbeard Island to the United States in 1800 mentioned 'houses, out houses, buildings, messuages, tenements' today no structure survives to indicate that this landing was once a dock for vessels or the site of live oakers' headquarters.[854] Twice in his journal Keen referred to cotton fields at the north end of the island. Approximately two and one-half and three miles north of the presumed headquarters site, there are two barren fields. Surrounded by thick forest growth (including live oak), these four-and-one-half and two-acre tracts are now referred to as 'Indian fields.' Could these two places have been the sites of Shaddock's cotton fields in 1818?"[855]

While not as high in the national maritime awareness as such regions as Chesapeake Bay and New England, coastal Georgia nonetheless has its own distinct legacy. The natural waterway known as the "Inland Passage" became a commercial transportation route from the earliest days of European settlement. The coastal islands were an ideal buffer against the effects of bad weather often encountered in the rough outside Atlantic waters. The tidal rivers and creeks inside the islands thus provided a protected passage for waterborne traffic.

Georgia was among the leading producers of rice and cotton prior to 1861 and a maritime culture evolved around the transport of these commodities in shallow-draft sloops and schooners from the river plantations and the saltwater islands to the markets in Savannah and Charleston. After the Civil War, the maritime focus shifted to a lucrative commercial timber industry. Rafts of yellow pine timber were floated from the interior down the Savannah, Oconee, Ocmulgee, Ohoopee and Altamaha rivers to the sawmills on the coast. Ships from Europe and the Northeast proliferated local harbors to load cargoes of lumber. Evidence of this activity can be seen today in ballast rock deposits in the marsh along the rivers and

---

[854] The structures noted in the 1800 deed of conveyance are probably attributable to the eleven-year French period of ownership of Blackbeard Island during which there was agricultural activity.
[855] Wood, ed., "James Keen's Journal," 231-32.

sounds and the rotting pilings of loading docks near the former sawmills. Darien became an international timber market— the port was a leading Atlantic exporter of pine from 1870 to just after 1900. Timber cutting and lumber production were the economic engines of coastal Georgia, and people found livelihoods in vocations associated with a maritime culture—boat builders, bar pilots to lead timber ships to anchorages from the open sea and stevedores to load timber into the vessels.

The period 1870-1900 saw the transition of the old coastal agricultural economy into one based on timber, lumber processing and turpentine production. The coast's maritime culture came to full flower around Darien, Doboy Sound and Sapelo Sound, centered around sawmills and the traffic in vessels loading cargoes of Georgia pine products. The enterprising Joseph Hilton of the Darien-based Hilton-Dodge Lumber Co. was, for about thirty years, the leading timber broker on the Atlantic seaboard with branches in New York and Boston. The maritime traffic required large numbers of bar pilots to assist foreign vessels in navigating the often-treacherous offshore shoals and the shallow mudflats and estuaries; ballast islands sprang up along the tidal rivers as European ships unloaded ballast in exchange for cargoes of timber—examples of these are in evidence around Sapelo Sound (Hazzard's Island, Front River, Julianton River), Doboy Sound (Doboy, Rock and Commodore islands), North River (Hird and Union islands), Darien's Lower Bluff and the Long Reach of the Darien River.

The importance of the Altamaha River, particularly in regard to Darien's booming postbellum timber industry, was not lost on Richard Grubb, editor of the town's weekly newspaper, the *Darien*

Timber Gazette. In the spring of 1874, Grubb penned one of his more memorable *Gazette* editorials, in which he compared the vagaries of the Altamaha in circumspect, if somewhat unusual, terms—

"The Nile is said to be everything to Egypt," Grubb wrote. "In fact, without the Nile there would be no Egypt...To a certain extent, the same may truly be said of the Altamaha River and Darien. Without the Altamaha there would be no timber trade and no rice planting, and without these there would be no Darien...For the presiding deity of the former stream, duly regarding his venerable reputation, regulates the movements of the waters under his control...The Jolly God of the Altamaha has lately been cutting such antics [flooding] to the discomfiture of timber cutters as to arouse a grave suspicion that he exacts a toll of Darien whiskey from the bottle of every raftsman who ventures to return home by the *Daisy* steamer. Under these circumstances, we have determined on the interests of our friends...to keep a close watch on the movements of his godship, and to report promptly any future attempt of his to raise a flood...But to do this effectually we must secure cooperation. This consists in every timber cutter and buyer and all of their friends, subscribing immediately to the *Gazette*. When that is done, they must read it occasionally, at least..."[856]

Steamboats on the Inland Waterway

Steamboat traffic in coastal Georgia came into its own in the 1830s and 1840s. By 1850, the inland passage from Charleston to the St. Johns River had increased traffic, both from steamers and coasting sailing vessels. After the Civil War the number of inland waterway vessels expanded as the absence of railroads between Savannah and the Altamaha left water transportation as the only alternative for passenger travel and freight shipment. The low, single-stack steamers were usually built with an oversized deck cabin amidships to

---

[856] Richard W. Grubb in the *Darien Timber Gazette*, May 30, 1874.

accommodate passengers, with the wheelhouse located forward atop the cabin. After 1865, these wooden craft were more prevalent, being built in the boatyards around Charleston, Beaufort and Savannah. According to maritime historian Rusty Fleetwood:

"In the 1870s the shipbuilding industry was in much the same situation it was 120 years earlier. [T]here was little capital to invest in large, oceangoing craft ... the vessel registry lists of the period show an increasing amount of smallcraft construction from 1866 onward in both sail and steam. The majority of these craft were small sloops under forty feet in length, followed by schooners averaging about fifty feet. Steam vessels, which had to be of good size to carry engines, fuel and cargo, were usually over sixty feet in length, but many were built in smaller sizes for towing or harbor duties, as well as the occasional small launch or passenger ferry."[857]

The *Timber Gazette* advertised scheduled steamer service on the inland passage between Savannah and points in northeast Florida from the 1870s into the 1890s. Steamers such as the *Nick King, Lizzie Baker, David Clark, Reliance* and *J.B. Schuyler* ran the inland route several times a week with passage advertised from Savannah to Florida via Thunderbolt, Isle of Hope, Wassaw Island, Romerly Marshes, St. Catherines Island, Sapelo High Point, Commodore Island, Doboy Island, Darien, St. Simons Mills (Gascoigne Bluff), Brunswick, Jekyll, Cumberland, St. Marys, Fernandina, Mayport, Jacksonville, Green Cove Springs and Palatka. The *Schuyler*, Captain L.W. Burns, promised "No Sea Sickness" on its twice-weekly runs, in addition to comfortable passenger accommodations and other amenities. The larger steamers were equipped with sleeping cabins

---

[857] Rusty Fleetwood, *Tidecraft: The Boats of Lower South Carolina, Georgia and Northeast Florida, 1650-1950* (Savannah: Coastal Heritage Society, 1982), 130.

for passengers who chose to pay the higher fares to obtain them. Nicholas King (1819-1889) was one of the most popular steamboat captains on the Savannah-to-Florida route. King arrived in Savannah from New Jersey prior to the war, and became a steamer captain operating between Savannah and Palatka. His Savannah obituary noted that "Captain King was a favorite among travelers, and the boats he commanded were always crowded with passengers."[858] In 1869, King took command of the new steamer *Nick King*, named in his honor:

> "We take great pleasure in writing her down, for the information of the public, as A-No. 1. Her accommodations for passengers are spacious, elegant and entirely new, while her hull and machinery are of the staunchest kind. Captain King, so long and favorably known on the Florida line, is in command, and perfectly familiar with every square foot of water and mud between Savannah and Palatka, and the old traveler always feels safe in his hands. The other officers of the boat are perfect in their respective duties, while among the stewards, waiters, etc., we recognized several old colored friends who have long been catering for the travelling public and are perfectly at home in their business."[859]

The growth of railroads spelled the demise of inland waterway steamboat service in the 1890s. The *Timber Gazette* is devoid of advertisements for the steamer lines after 1891. Apparently, the last steamer making a regular run on the inland passage was the Georgia &.Florida Line's *St. Nicholas* in the early 1890s. An item in the *Brunswick Advertiser and Appeal* has this description of steamboat routine:

---

[858] *Savannah Morning News*, January 8, 1889.
[859] *Savannah Republican*, April 9, 1869.

"The steamer *St. Nicholas*, last Saturday, on her upward passage, parted her rudder chains at lower mills [Frederica River], and proceeded at once to St. Simons dock. Here she quickly repaired damages and was on her way ... with such dispatch as not to lose connection — all due to the tact and energy of her commander, the gallant Captain Usina. On the trip before the last, owing to the severe gale then blowing, he was stove against the wharf at Doboy, smashing his wheel house. Whilst waiting for the tide to rise at Jekyl [sic], he stopped at St. Simons, bought lumber and nails, put all hands to work, and had a wheel house as good as new by the time he could pass through Jekyl creek."[860] .

The *David Clark* was a popular steamboat. In 1885, the *Advertiser and Appeal* noted:

"Captain E.F. Daniels of the *David Clark* is probably the safest and most reliable Captain going out of the port of Savannah. The steamer *David Clark* carries the largest crew of any steamer, either ocean or inland, going out of the city of Savannah. The steamer *David Clark* is twelve years old. It was built in Jacksonville, Fla., in 1873. Her timbers are of our best Southern woods. She is pronounced yet to be as good as new — a compliment to the mechanism of the South. The steamer *David Clark* makes two round trips from Savannah to Brunswick and back each week, and touches for freight and passengers at St. Catherines Island, Doboy, Darien, Broughton Island, Wright's Island, Cathead, Grantley's Wharf, Battery Island, Chapman's Wharf, Frederica and St. Simons."[861] .

Unfortunately, the *Clark* had an unhappy end with this unpleasant news in the fall of 1889:

"The steamer *David Clark* was destroyed by fire while docked at Fernandina. The steamer is almost a total loss, as a strong northwest wind was blowing and the fire spread with great rapidity. Several of the crew barely escaped with their lives. The vessel was built on the St. Johns River in 1873 and put on the inland route between Savannah and Florida in 1877. She was 150 feet long

---

[860] *Brunswick Advertiser and Appeal*, April 12, 1884
[861] Ibid., December 19, 1885

and had cabin passenger accommodations for fifty. She could carry 700 barrels of naval stores or 450 bales of uncompressed cotton. The *David Clark* belonged to the Georgia and Florida Steam-boat Company. A new boat to take her place could not be built for $15,000. A few days ago the *St. Nicholas*, a shorter boat, was appraised at $8,000. The *Clark* was fully insured."[862]

Before the advent of rail connections, several vessels regularly plied between Darien and Brunswick. At his St. Simons boatyard in February 1880, Captain Urbanus (Barney) Dart, Jr. built the small 17-ton steamer *Ruby*, named for his daughter. She was propelled by a 15-horsepower engine installed by E. Briesnick, a Brunswick machinists firm. Piloted by Dart, the *Ruby* was built for the purpose of providing the first regular steamboat service from St. Simons to Brunswick. She began making her twice-daily runs in the winter of 1880, and at the end of six months, had already shuttled more than 5,000 passengers.

In McIntosh County, Captain Bourke Spalding of Sapelo Island operated the steamer *Ogeechee* about this time. The *Ogeechee* shuttled freight and passengers between Doboy Island and Darien as well as to Sapelo and the island sawmills around Darien. In the spring of 1883, the new steamer *Egmont* joined the *Ruby* on the St. Simons-Brunswick route, and in 1884, the first regular service between Brunswick and Darien was established, as the *Egmont* began making daily trips between the two ports. Near the end of that year it was noted, "Already in a former issue we took occasion to announce that Capt. Dart had established a daily line between Brunswick and Darien, touching at many points on the intervening islands. On this he has placed the public's favorite steamer — *Egmont*. Such has been

---

[862] *Darien Timber Gazette*, October 12, 1889.

The steamboat Hessie on the Brunswick-to-Darien inland waterway route.

Capt. Barney's encouragement that he has authorized us to state the route is permanently established, and the *Egmont* is a fixture."[863]

In early 1888 the new steamer *Hessie* would "hereafter run between Brunswick and Darien on Mondays, Wednesdays and Saturdays, leaving Brunswick at 7:30 a.m.; arrive at Darien 11:30; leave Darien 2 p.m.; arrive at Brunswick 6:00 p.m. Stops both ways at St. Simons Mills and Frederica. C.E. Arnold, Captain."[864] About the same time, the *Hessie*'s sister vessel, *Emmeline*, began daily trips from Brunswick to Cumberland Island and Fernandina. In 1890, the *Hessie* began six-day-a-week service between Brunswick and Darien. Captain A.L. Allen succeeded Captain Arnold as pilot of the *Hessie*. Richard Grubb, always a promoter of water-borne travel and the coastal steamboat businesses, noted in 1888 that "Captain Allen of the steamer *Hessie* is making many friends in Darien. The captain is never too busy to favor his customers and friends.

---

[863] Ibid., November 29, 1884.
[864] *Brunswick Advertiser and Appeal*, January 17, 1888.

He is certainly very accommodating."[865] The *Hessie* provided nearly three decades of service, and was a durable local fixture well after Darien's peak timber days had passed.

The opening of rail service between Darien and Brunswick in 1914 marked the beginning of the end for the *Hessie's* daily transit. Steamboat business declined as most patrons preferred the more rapid and convenient train ride on the Georgia Coast & Piedmont Railroad, a short-line from Tattnall County terminating at Darien in 1895, then extended to Brunswick with the construction of trestle-work and bridges over the Altamaha delta from 1912 to 1914.[866] C. & P. between Darien and Brunswick. The steamer line held on for a while as the *Hessie* continued service for over a year after the railroad was opened. As late as the summer of 1915, the *Brunswick News* was reporting the *Hessie* making daily runs to Darien from Brunswick, and the *Emmeline* continuing its route to Cumberland and Fernandina. The line's *Seagate,* a newer vessel, provided service from Brunswick to St. Simons Pier. In mid-1918, Brunswick steamboat agent J.B. Wright suspended service by the *Hessie* between Brunswick and Darien. Once-weekly runs by the *Hessie* were briefly made in

---

[865] *Darien Timber Gazette,* September 29, 1888.

[866] The G.C. & P.'s route in McIntosh County roughly followed the route of the Cow Horn Road (now state highway 99) from Warsaw to Crescent thence to Darien. The tracks from Darien to Broadfield on the Glynn County side of the delta enabled the conveyance of cars from Darien by rail to Glynn, enabling the motorist to then drive to Brunswick about twelve miles further. The Georgia Coast & Piedmont went bankrupt and suspended operations in 1920. The track bed from Darien to Brunswick was converted to a road that was the forerunner to the present U.S. 17. The most detailed review of the operations of the G.C. & P. and its predecessor lines in McIntosh County is Buddy Sullivan, *Early Days on the Georgia Tidewater,* all editions, 1990-2018.

1920 when the G.C. & P. ceased operations.

When calling at Darien the *Hessie's* berth was a waterfront section with 120 feet of river frontage, a site later occupied by the Ploeger Packing Company. The Hessie Dock tract occupied Lots 2 and 3 of Block 1 on the Darien waterfront plat, east of the foot of Northway. This section was conveyed by deed to Samuel M. Street in 1847, then to timber broker Carl Epping in 1869. The two lots were later acquired from Charles H. Townsend by James Walker in 1879. Walker, in turn, sold the lots to C.M. Quarterman in 1880, when the lot became known as Quarterman's Wharf. J.B. Wright of Brunswick acquired the so-called "wharf lots" from Quarterman in 1897 after which the tract became referred to in local records as the "Hessie Dock Property." Wright sold the lots to the city of Darien in 1918, with the city selling them to Atlantic Seafood Packers (Ploeger-Abbott) in 1936.[867]

The coastal steamer life was not always idyllic, as several of the boats met untimely fates: The *Clyde* capsized and sank in Sapelo Sound in the summer of 1874; the popular steamer *Lizzie Baker* was lost on the upper Florida coast on the St. Johns River bar in the winter of 1875 (her captain, Peter LaRose, was one of the best-liked on the route); the *David Clark* caught fire and burned to the waterline in 1889. Regarding the loss of the *Clyde*, the *Timber Gazette* noted:

"It is with deep regret that we announce the loss of the steamer *Clyde*, in Sapelo Sound, on Saturday last. The upsetting of the boat, from Capt. John L. Day's account, seems to have been occasioned by

---

[867] Deed Book B (1879), 425; Book E (1880), 344; Book G (1897), 99; Book R (1921), 178; Book X (1926), 239; Book 7 (1936), 576, RMCG.

one of those sudden squalls incident to this latitude at the present season. We cannot forbear just here a word of advice. The class of boat to which the *Clyde* belongs is safe and well adapted to the inside route but is not constructed to meet the dangers of the open Sounds that must be navigated between here and Savannah. The rescue of the crew without loss of life from so great peril is as remarkable as the catastrophe was sudden and unexpected. The *Clyde* was valued at $15,000 and is a total loss, there being no insurance."[868]

Jack Plane, a Savannah reporter, wrote an interesting account of the steamboat experience in the fall of 1879, including some observations about Darien. The writer was on an excursion on the *David Clark* from Savannah to the St. Johns River:

"…When I awoke, we were rounding Sapelo Island, and in full view of Doboy. When but a boy studying geography, I was often puzzled to find this point off the coast of Georgia, but from the peculiarity of the name, and my difficulty attending my search for the island, it impressed itself upon my mind and created a desire to visit it. Doboy Island is a real place—a place of importance. The Hilton Lumber Company does an immense business, while the rivers reaching up into middle Georgia send down millions of feet of timber, which is carried from Darien and Doboy to the various foreign ports. Sometimes there are fifty to sixty vessels here, all loading with our yellow Georgia pine, Liverpool and South America claiming the largest share. Our stay at Doboy was too short to go on shore, and I had to be content with observations from the upper deck of the *Clark*. I could only see two or three stores, and about the same number of dwellings. From Doboy, we diverged from the direct line to the right, following one of those serpentine streams which penetrate the marshes in every direction. After an hour's run we reached Union Island, upon which is located two extensive saw mills, one belonging to the Hiltons, and the other to Capt. James Lachlison. We rounded about and went back to Doboy. Thus entering another outlet, we hastened off to Darien, twelve miles distant. Darien of to-day is not the Darien of long ago. Her commercial importance has waned since the increased prosperity of

---

[868] *Darien Timber Gazette*, July 4, 1874.

Savannah, and the building of the Atlantic and Gulf and the Macon and Brunswick railroads. Still, she is neither dead nor doomed to annihilation. Darien suffered fearfully from the ravages of war, being almost totally destroyed by the Federal army. But with a spirit unconquered and an energy undaunted, the citizens went to work and rebuilt even more handsomely and more substantially than ever before. The business part of the city is compactly built and some of the storerooms are amply and well-filled with every variety of goods. On the Ridge, three miles distant, where the people summer it, there are many fine residences. Colonel Grubb of the *Gazette* has been very kind and courteous to me since my arrival here and is a strong friend of the News. Since the dethronement of Tunis Campbell, comparative peace has reigned. The colored population of the county is in large excess of the white . . . And notwithstanding every store has a bar attached, I have seen very little drunkenness since my arrival ...The celebrated case involving ownership of Commodore Island was called [in McIntosh Superior Court]. Commodore Island lies seaward of Doboy, and was purchased a few years ago by Messrs. Langdon & Co. Mr. Malcomb and Mr. W. Mitchelson erected each a very nice and comfortable residence on Commodore and greatly improved the property."[869]

Darien's Postbellum Timber Port

Of the several timber firms in and around Darien during this period, the largest was the Hilton Timber and Lumber Company, a concern that also involved the Lachlison and Foster families, all three families being inter-related. The enterprise actually had its origins before the Civil War. Robert Lachlison (1804-1881) came from Lancashire, England circa 1840, settling in Savannah where he was in the machinery repair trade. He was joined soon after by his brother James, and their brother-in-law Thomas Hilton, Sr., also a native

---

[869] *Savannah Morning News*, November 27, 1879. Commodore Island is almost entirely salt marsh, with its highland comprised of several small hammocks of an acre or less of high ground fronting on Back River southeast of Doboy Island. It was upon these hammocks that the small dwellings referenced in the article were built.

Englishman.[870] In 1845, Robert and James Lachlison acquired the Darien Upper Steam Saw Mill on Cathead Creek. They obtained the sawmill at a sheriffs sale "by virtue of a writ of *fieri facia*, issuing from Bryan County Superior Court in favor of Andrew Low, against Henry C. Tunno, Phineas M. Nightingale and Bryan M. Morrell."[871] Thomas Hilton and his son Thomas, Jr. (1825-1904) also joined the venture on their arrival at Darien. Before the Civil War the Hiltons lived at Upper Mill before moving to the Ridge.

Thomas Hilton, Sr.'s youngest son, Joseph, and Robert Lachlison's son, James, were only teenagers during this period, but they saw service in the Civil War, and engaged in the Darien lumber trade afterwards. Joseph Hilton (1842-1920) and the younger James Lachlison (1837-1920) were first cousins.[872] Robert Lachlison and his son James were engaged in sawmill interests at Darien after the war with their cousins the Hiltons and the Fosters. According to a November 1873 deed, the Lachlisons were operators of a steam sawmill, the America Mill on Union Island opposite the Ridge. Hiltons & Foster operated the rebuilt Upper Mill at Cathead and mills on Union Island and Doboy Island. By the late 1880s, the

---

[870] Portions of the following section about the Hilton family are based on the author's Introduction in Buddy Sullivan, ed., *High Water on the Bar, An Operational Perspective of a Tidewater Timber Port, with the Memoir of Thomas Hilton* (Darien, Ga., 2009), 7-37.

[871] Hilton Family Papers, Collection 387, box 1, folder 5, GHS, for miscellaneous documents relating to the early Darien timber activities of the Hilton family.

[872] Thomas Hilton, "High Water on the Bar," privately printed, Savannah, Ga., 1951. Thomas Hilton's memoir of the activities of the Hilton, Lachlison and Foster families and their association with the timber business before and after the Civil War is contained, with annotation, in Sullivan, ed., *High Water on the Bar*, 51-79.

younger James Lachlison had become superintendent of mills for the Hilton-Dodge Lumber Company.

In 1878, the firm of Hiltons & Foster became the Hilton Timber and Lumber Company. Within two years, the firm purchased the sawmill at Lower Bluff east of Darien. Joseph Hilton became president of the firm, and Hilton Timber and Lumber evolved as the leading operation of its kind on the U.S. east coast by the late 1880s. Hilton's son, Thomas Hilton (1885-1958), has provided insights into the timbering interests of his family in his memoir, "High Water on the Bar."

In 1888, Hilton Timber and Lumber merged with the Dodge-Meigs Company of New York and St. Simons Island. Over the next decade, the Dodge interests were not as profitable as the company would have liked; the company had become financially stagnant. A merger thus ensued in 1888 with the region's other large timber firm, the Hilton Timber and Lumber Company, with the latter assuming management of the new firm. Its name was the Hilton and Dodge Lumber Company, and it was from that point the largest pine timber firm in the United States.[873]

"The first member of the family to come over here was Uncle Robert Lachlison, as a representative of an English firm making heavy machinery. Later, his brother James came to join him, then some of the Hilton boys; Jim and Tom on a sailing ship. This was too much for Grandmother Jane Lachlison Hilton, who made Grandfather Thomas Hilton close out his building business in Preston, England and make the difficult journey to Darien, Georgia,

---

[873] Hilton Family Papers, box 1, folder 3, GHS contains deeds for Joseph Hilton for lots in Darien and shares of stock in the Hilton-Dodge Lumber Co; box 2, folder 12 contains the agreement for sale of the St. Simons Mills to Hilton in December 1888; box 2, folder 12 also contains the journal of Joseph Hilton covering a period Oct. 31, 1891 to Nov. 30, 1893..

where by that time we understand, Robert and James Lachlison had a saw mill on Union Island, just off the Ridge. Grandfather started a sawmill venture mill on Cat Head Creek, at the upper ridge of Darien, on a site known as the Upper Bluff close to the point where Cat Head Creek flows into Darien River. This was about 1854 or 1855. The lumber was shipped by small sailing vessels, brigs or brigantines that only carried about half the cargo of the small three-masted schooners in coastwise trade later on. These early cargoes were mostly ship timbers to New England ports. The crews used long poles in working the little vessels upriver to the mill. They came in over Doboy Bar. Timber for the mill was bought on the public booms at Darien, of original growth Long Leaf Yellow Pine — settlers living up the Altamaha drifting rafts down river to Darien.

"When Dad was old enough to hunt one of his favorite sports was going up Cat Head Creek in a bateau, shooting ducks, which were plentiful. Rice was being planted in a big way in the Altamaha River delta, making choice feeding ranges for wild fowl. 'Oasis' was the name of a rice plantation located up the creek from Upper Mill. In the main Altamaha delta were the large rice islands of Cambers, Butlers, Generals, Champneys, Rhetts, Broughton, with Hofwyl, Broad Field and others on the Glynn County side. Darien is only about nine miles from Doboy Sound, but the salt water, pushed back by the big flow of the Altamaha, did not reach these rice fields. The planters gradually gave up rice planting after the war between the states. Labor was more costly, and when a hurricane struck, which was most likely in late August or September, about harvest time, an entire crop could be lost… Rice played an important part in Darien's history. Then the settlers up River shipped cotton and other farm products to Darien on 'flat boats' of various types, some of which were abandoned, and others of a long, narrow construction laboriously poled back up river. At Darien, cargoes were unloaded into warehouses at the foot of the Bluff, where the land was high enough for this purpose. These warehouses were built of 'tabby,' thick walls of oyster shells and lime, tamped into forms.

"During these times a larger saw mill than either of our family mills was in operation at Lower Bluff, about a mile down river from Darien, the site of old Fort King George. The mill had two English type log gang saws. There was much speculation as to the age of this mill, some people believing it to be among the oldest of the steam saw mills in the United States.[874]

"These gang mills cut hewn, or scab timber. Farmers living in the scattered settlements up the Altamaha, cut the timber, squared it with the broad axe as was the custom in those days, dragged it to the river, usually with oxen, making up large rafts. The timber was fine grain Long Leaf Yellow Pine, with only a small amount of sap wood. The long sticks hewn enough to square them roughly, or with about half the amount of broad axe work, leaving considerable bark, but enough flat surface to efficiently put the log through the big gangs. This was known as 'Scab' timber. The hewn timber could be exported, loaded out of the water into sailing ships, for manufacture into the sizes wanted at destination ... The [Altamaha raftsmen] cooked on the raft, generally tied up at night by snubbing ropes to trees on the bank. On tying up on the booms at Darien, their timber was inspected and measured by a public inspector, then sold to a mill man or exporter. The sellers or raft hands purchased such articles as could be carried back home, but the return journey was difficult. As more railroads were built it became easier, but even in my

---

[874] Information among the appended letters at the end of the original booklet "High Water on the Bar" provides insights into early sawmill activity at Lower Bluff. There had been sawmilling on the site since the first English occupation of the area by Carolina rangers who built Fort King George in 1721. In a letter to Thomas Hilton in December 1939, McIntosh County historian Bessie Lewis noted "Concerning the use of 'deals'—I know they were used at Lower Bluff in 1721, fifteen years before the Highlanders arrived there, as the records show that the soldiers' barracks at Fort King George were partitioned with 'thin split deal,' and that the material was sawed in 1721 at what is now Lower Bluff by sawyers from South Carolina under the supervision of Col. John Barnwell." The later possible connection of William Scarbrough with the Eastern Steam Saw Mill at Lower Bluff in the 1820s and 1830s was also mentioned. Census records indicate that Scarbrough was a resident of Darien in 1830. The remains of the water-powered sluice mill alluded to in a letter written November 14, 1939 by R.D. Fox, associated with the lumber interests of Darien and the Hiltons, are still in evidence at the Fort King George Historic Site at Lower Bluff. The steam-powered gang saws were set up near the same site, convenient to the Darien River, when the Eastern Steam Saw Mill began operations at Lower Bluff in 1820. It was this facility that was enlarged and modernized immediately after the Civil War by Young and Langdon, then later by Joseph Hilton. Extracts of the letters of R.D. Fox and Bessie Lewis are contained in Sullivan, ed., *High Water on the Bar*, 68-71, with originals in Hilton Family Papers, op. cit., box 2, GHS.

recollection, some of the so-called 'raft hands' would hire a man to row them across the several branches of the Altamaha, up Hammersmith's Creek on the Glynn County side to a landing, then walking some six or eight miles to 'Old Number One' a flag station on the Southern Ry out of Brunswick. They would get off at Jesup or Everett, or the station nearest their homes, and walk again. Often they had not been to a town for months, so after pocketing their timber money, there was usually celebrating in Darien's ample number of saloons.

"The name 'Timber' was for the English export business, which by this time had grown to large proportions through the Port of Darien. The English correctly used the term 'timber' instead of lumber. At first the timber was squared with the broad axe, then it was found this could be done quicker and more economically with small ground saw mills that were movable from one place to another. The English importers only wanted the hewn timber they had been accustomed to, and no sawn timber, but soon accepted sawn. It was along in these days, probably in the eighteen nineties, that the flow of the golden-hearted timber down the Altamaha reached its peak. This was the 'High Water' point for the little city of Darien, with its homes, custom house, exporters offices, stores and bars. A rather large saw mill, for those days, had been built on Doboy Island in Doboy Sound, by northern interests, and was later bought by Hilton Timber & Lumber Co. This mill, like the others, cut lumber orders for the coastwise trade: Philadelphia, New York and New England ports. The foreign ships were mostly barks, or square-riggers of some sort and drew too much water to load at Darien so used loading grounds in Doboy and Sapelo Sounds. Stories often told around Darien were that seventy-two to as high as eighty-seven ships have been counted at one time in both Doboy and Sapelo sounds, loading, outside, coming or going out over the bar. Our people had loading grounds for foreign ships in Sapelo Sound at Julianton. Steamships soon began to take over this trade.

"The booms began above Darien, continuing on both sides far down river except immediately in front of the town. It was said that one could sometimes walk from raft to raft for a mile or more. The booms extended about three miles along the Darien River. On the next river in the delta, Butler River, were the Hilton Cypress booms. The exporters had their ship cargoes assembled, and towed to the loading grounds in the Sounds. The foreign vessels were chartered under a form requiring a minimum number of thousand feet per day, and the shippers falling short of this paid demurrage; but on the other hand, if time were saved, and loading completed before the time that would have been taken by the fixed amount, then the ship paid the charterers dispatch money. Every effort was put forth to win dispatch money. The boss stevedores were men of brawn and skill. The stevedore 'hands' as all laborers about loading jobs, booms and saw mills were called, were all colored, carefully picked and trained, many being wonderful physical specimens. When the steamships came along, there were steam winches to help, but in sail, it was by hand. There was a winch forward, but turned by men.

"The timber was brought alongside ship in the water. Ports (in the bows) were removed from the wooden sailing ships, the long, heavy timbers, muddy from the river, taken in through the ports, laid on rollers, rolled to the part of the ship wanted, turned by cant-hooks into place. Then the loading was done over the side and through the hatches, with the deck-load to finish. Each gang of stevedore hands had a leader, who sang a line of a chantey song, the others coming in on the short chorus, then with a 'ho' all heaved together on the big stick in perfect time. These stevedore hands lived in different places, some in or near Darien, others at a settlement beyond the Ridge, known as 'Connigan Bridge' and a settlement on the northern end of Sapelo Island, called 'Sapelo High Point.' Most of these square riggers came direct to Doboy or Sapelo Sound, and when they could bring no cargo, so loaded rock ballast. The loading grounds were selected at the deepest water points, some alongside islands, while others were by the marsh, clump piling driven for the vessels to lie alongside. The ballast rock was dumped on the bank or in the marsh. Planks were laid from the vessel's rail, and the rock carted out in wheelbarrows. After this was repeated from many ships, large piles of smoothly washed rocks appeared, and in some marshy places formed small islands. Below the high water mark these rocks are covered with barnacles and raccoon oysters. Large ballast piles are on Union Island on the Ridge River. An old picture shows a brigantine loading there, and she may have gone to England, but I think it unlikely. Craft like this may have brought ballast rock. The Company had a shipbuilding customer in Nova Scotia, and a brigantine could have engaged in this trade, sailing south in ballast.

"When a ship cleared for a foreign port, the papers were carefully drawn up in the Darien office, all done by hand on long sheets of paper, showing the number of pieces of each size and length, as 12 x 12-27/36, meaning 27 pieces 12-12, 36 ft. long. The writing was in smooth, rounded script, and neat. At the bottom of the last page appeared 'E&OE', errors and omissions excepted. A copy was made in an old letter press with a large iron wheel on top ...

"For many years we moved from the Ridge about May, returning in the fall, and sometimes remaining [in New York] through Christmas. We usually took the boat from New York to Savannah ... sometimes the train to Brunswick and the little steamer *Hessie* to Darien the next day or we might take a boat direct from Savannah to Darien, but this was long, and of uncertain schedule. Still another way was to get the train at Barrington Station, edge of the Altamaha swamp, where the same sort of horse drawn outfits would meet us, and drive about twelve miles, much of it through swamps, to the Ridge ...

"The tow boats played an important part around the mills, docking the vessels and towing them in and out over the bar. The Company owned two — the *Iris* and the *Passport,* used in towing timber from the Darien booms to mills or loading grounds. A drift of timber stretched out a long distance behind a tow boat, channels were narrow, and crooked, with sharp turns in strong running tides. On a run to St. Simons or Altamaha Cypress mills, the boat would leave the Darien booms on the right stage of tide, day or night, go down the Darien River a few miles, make a turn sharper than a right angle to avoid a long sand bar, go through 'Three mile cut,' giving the rafts little room on either side. On coming out into a wide branch of the Altamaha, cross almost to the edge of the marsh, then hard aport to 'One mile Point' and so on. Some dark nights in going through 'Three Mile' or close along the marsh, one could hardly see the jack staff from the pilot house window, while mud banks with high marsh grass on top, towered above the boat. The tow boat Captains made the trip so often they knew where they were all the time, seldom getting into trouble. Large alligators lay on mud banks, not moving until the boat came near, then sliding down into the muddy water ...

"The mills had been cutting long leaf Pine and Cypress but [later] the Company was giving attention to the Coast Type Shortleaf as all this variety was called then, to distinguish it from Longleaf and Yellow Slash. There were areas of this Shortleaf or Loblolly in Bryan County, and they bought large quantities extending into Liberty County up to the vicinity of Taylor's Creek, running into some Long Leaf and Slash when getting well inland. A large mill was built at Belfast where vessels could load. The vessels were three or four masted schooners carrying mostly from three hundred and fifty to five hundred thousand feet of lumber. Belfast never settled down with a steady crew, like the old mills, not being very successful. The old growth Shortleaf showed many defects. Lumber prices were low. I believe I am correct in saying that from 1904 until 1912, when our family sold the Company's holdings, that lumber from Belfast brought a lower average price on vessels alongside buyers docks in New York and Philadelphia, than the same timber from which it was cut would bring today [1950] as stumpage.

"The right kind of timber for the large double circular mills at Darien and St. Simons was becoming scarce, and the Company found it necessary to close down and dismantle the mills ... The Doboy Island mill had suffered the same fate. The old mills in good locations, particularly Lower Bluff in Darien, and St. Simons, had crews who had never worked anywhere else. Some of the younger members of the crew sang 'Oh, roll those saws, oh roll 'em roun, what you gonna do when the mill shuts down.'"

Hilton's remarks about rock ballast deposits in local waters bear further scrutiny. Ballast deposits are still in evidence in many places in the local waterways to which the timber ships had access. The increased maritime traffic after the Civil War in response to the rafting of timber to Darien required knowledgeable local bar pilots to assist vessels, foreign and domestic, in navigating the offshore shoals and sandbars guarding the entrances to the sounds, as well as the mudflats and shallows of the tidal rivers approaching the sawmills. Small hammocks sprang up along these waterways as European ships unloaded rock ballast in exchange for cargoes of timber. Examples of these are still in evidence around Sapelo and Doboy sounds, Doboy Island, North River and Lower Bluff. The earlier contemporary accounts about ballast hammocks are the most reliable. The ballast piles were in Sapelo Sound in the great amounts along the Front River east of Creighton Island and northeast to Sapelo Sound at the Hazzard's Island group on the north end of the Creighton marshes where timber loading docks were situated; other ballast piles were in the Julianton River at the south end of Harris Neck at the Hilton docks. There is much evidence of ballast at the north end of Blackbeard Island where, from 1880, ships deposited rock during the disinfection process at the South Atlantic Quarantine Station. From 1890 the preponderance of timber activity occurred in Sapelo Sound as the larger barkentines and square riggers, and later steamships, preferred the deeper anchorages afforded by that inlet. One of the ballast islands on Front River, about a mile and a half below Sapelo Sound, was the J.K. Clarke timber wharf with a post office designated Sapelo, Ga., for the convenience of shipping interests utilizing the Sapelo Sound anchorages. At the Front River junction with the Sound is the ballast deposit and its hammock, Hazzard's Island, actually a grouping of three small, separate hammocks referred to locally by the more familiar appellation "Hazzard's Ballast Pile." Here were the loading docks of Hunter, Benn & Co. of Darien. Hilton & Dodge Lumber Co. had its docks across the Sound on the lower Julianton River not far from the south end of Harris Neck.

In Doboy Sound, ballast deposits are in abundance along the North and Back rivers around Doboy and Commodore islands. Rock piles in the area of the docks at Doboy are still in evidence as are those across North (Ridge) River just north of the Doboy docks on aptly-named Rock Island. There was a smaller sawmill on Rock Island with docks for ships loading lumber. Some of the brick firebox and ironwork foundations can still be seen on Rock Island amid the cedars and cabbage palms, this being the remains of the postbellum Cane Creek Mill, also known as Empire Mill. Several dwellings were constructed on the Rock Island hammocks on either side of Cane Creek. The docks on both sides of the North River were crowded with ships loading timber and lumber from the Doboy and Cane Creek mills.

From late September to mid-spring the local harbors were crowded with ships, both inside loading timber, and outside awaiting entry to the anchorages. The safe movement of shipping about the sounds and connecting rivers to the mills was the work of the local bar pilots. Pilot boats, usually fast-sailing, versatile workhorses of the local sounds, conjure vivid images of coastal Georgia's maritime heritage. The pilot sloops and schooners of McIntosh and neighboring Glynn were often the fastest on the coast judging from results of the annual boat races held in the postbellum period. The vessels were noted for their exceptional speed. The Darien and Doboy boats operated from the Ridge where many of the pilots and their families had homes overlooking the Sound. The importance of the pilots to the rhythm and flow of the Darien timber economy cannot be exaggerated. It fell to these watermen to guide the timber ships across and around the shoals, sandbars and mudflats protecting the entrances to Doboy and Sapelo sounds, then to safe anchorages inside. The boats sailed by these men were designed for speed to enable the pilots to get out to the offshore ships with the greatest expediency possible. It was often timber money that financed the construction of these boats.

"The Darien area's pilot boat owners had a lot of money coming in as a result of the highly-lucrative timber business," notes maritime historian Rusty Fleetwood, "which was the primary reason the Darien pilots were so necessary in the first place. These Darien men would go and get a highly regarded Northern designer to design the best and the fastest pilot boats they could. They were spectacular boats, ninety and a hundred feet long on the waterline and were very, very fast."[875]

Such experienced Darien captains as William H. Patterson, James Dean, and their colleagues, were among the outstanding pilots and won so many races that their rival skippers from Charleston, Savannah and Brunswick became, according to Fleetwood, "really miffed about it, and sometimes fists would fly because the tempers of those losing the races would get out of control. The pilots were out to press on every square inch of canvas they could get. The pilot boat skippers liked to show off a bit before the crowds of race watchers."[876] The pilot boats built locally were constructed on the mainland along the tidal creeks around Savannah, Beaufort and Charleston. However, some the best, and fastest, Georgia boats were acquired from northern builders, particularly those in New England and in the Baltimore and Chesapeake Bay region where vessels with speed had been legendary for generations. As a busier port, Savannah had more pilot boats than Darien or Brunswick. Some of the most reputable Savannah boats were the 71-foot *Mary Odell*, built in 1872 at Bath, Maine, the 62-foot *Neca*, built at Savannah and the New England-built (1868) *Sprite*, a 64-footer. The *Uriah Timmons* of Darien, a workhorse in the 1890s and early 1900s, was a 52-foot schooner built in North Carolina. Brunswick had the 70-foot *Telegram*, built in 1875 at Mystic, Connecticut, and another Connecticut boat, the *Glynn*, a 75 ½-footer built in 1883. The largest

---

[875] Rusty Fleetwood, *Tidecraft: The Boats of South Carolina, Georgia and Northeastern Florida, 1550-1950* (Tybee Island, Ga.: WBG Marine Press, 1995, expanded edition of the original *Tidecraft*, 1982), 149, 152.
[876] Ibid., 148-53.

pilot boat of the area was the 99-foot Brunswick boat *Gracie*, built at Noank, Connecticut in 1884.[877]

The annual regattas featuring the south Atlantic boats were among the premier competitive events of the last two decades of the nineteenth century. Many of the competitions were held near Savannah off Tybee Island and Wassaw Sound, since this area was convenient to boats competing from Charleston, Brunswick and Darien, a day's sail away. Fleetwood notes, "Though the formal races were usually under the sponsorship of a local yacht club, there was an undertone of seriousness usually not found in the yachting set, for these were professional sailors, and the handling of fast schooners was their business. To put one's reputation, and that of the boat and the home port, on the line was not a thing taken lightly...The boats were customarily tuned to the utmost for the races, most hauling out the week before to ensure clean bottoms, and using new sails and running rigging for the event."[878] The Tybee races of the 1880s and early 1890s are regarded as the peak years of the competition.

Speed was important as pilots often had to sail fifteen to twenty miles out into the Atlantic to meet incoming vessels. In an active period, several timber ships at a time might be anchored offshore awaiting a pilot. Offshore, the pilot typically left his sloop, boarded

---

[877] Minutes of the Darien Pilot Commissioners, 1874-1930, original records in City of Darien archives, City Hall, Darien, Ga., contain various entries attesting to the acquisition of pilot boats from northern owners. Information and specifications of pilot boats are from Fleetwood, *Tidecraft* (1995 edit.), 151-53.

[878] Fleetwood, *Tidecraft*, 1995 edit., 152-53.

Towboat and timber ships in Doboy Sound, ca. 1880.

the arriving ship and, while providing navigational instructions to the helmsman and master of the vessel, brought the ship in to a safe anchorage in the sound, being compensated for his services by pilotage—fees established by the Darien Board of Pilot Commissioners. South End Creek near the lighthouse on the Doboy Sound end of Sapelo Island was a favored anchorage and station for pilots awaiting their turn in the rotation to bring ships in to the harbor. For boats on duty at the lighthouse, relief boats often came out from Darien or Doboy with supplies, water and other necessities. In addition to the chief pilot, pilot boats had three or four additional crew members per boat—a deckhand, a cook and one or two apprentice pilots learning the trade prior to obtaining their own pilots' license. The apprentices performed general maintenance and often accompanied the licensed pilots when guiding ships into or departing the harbor.

One of the best known of the Darien pilot boats was the *Young*

America of Doboy, Captain James Dean, and winner of several races in the annual competitions held off Tybee Island. In 1882, this outstanding vessel was lost in a wreck on the Wolf Island shoals, one account noting, "The fine pilot boat *Young America*, of Doboy, which went ashore on Wolf Island shoals on Thursday night last, is a total wreck, having thumped to pieces on the shoals. No one was on board at the time. Her loss is greatly regretted as she was a very fine craft, and her reputation of being the fastest sailer of any vessel of her description in Southern waters."[879] James Dean (1829-1903) was one of the veteran branch pilots of coastal Georgia. A descendant, Faith Dean Gilroy, notes that for two generations "Captain Dean's Place" on the Ridge was held in women's names. Records show that in 1865 Sarah Doyle of Ireland bought six acres from Dr. Joseph Baker. She put the property in trust for her daughter, Mary Dean, wife of James Dean, also an Irishman. Mary Dean died in 1888. In 1895, her three children, Matthew, Frank and Isabelle, deeded the property over to their father, James. After James' death in 1903, the property passed to his oldest son Matthew James Dean (1865-1915), then to a younger son, Frank James Dean (1867-1950). Both of the latter also became pilots.

The governing agency for the bar pilots was the Pilot Commission for the Port of Darien.[880] The first "Rules and Regulations" of the Pilot Commissioners were officially enacted in 1872, and provided oversight for the activities of local pilots, established pilotage (fees),

---

[879] *Savannah Morning News*, February 20, 1882.
[880] Minutes of the Darien Pilot Commissioners, 1874-1930. Annotated extracts of the Minutes are in Part III of Sullivan, ed., *High Water on the Bar*, op. cit., 80-111.

and maintained governance over the masters of incoming vessels.[881] There was a regulatory pilots board precedent to the start of the commissioners' minutes in 1874. The earlier records covering the period 1865 through 1873 were lost, as were virtually all other local public documents, in the 1873 courthouse fire. The Pilot Commission was an appointed board composed of individuals involved in timber and maritime affairs, or associated with the business community. Pilot commissioners were appointed by the county board of commissioners. There apparently was no set term length as several pilot commissioners served for lengthy periods in the 1880s and 1890s. The group established maritime and navigational policy for local harbors and waterways and regulated the operations of both the pilots and the ships utilizing the local anchorages. The Pilot Commission was a clearing house for maritime affairs, ruling on disputes that sometimes occurred among the pilots, and the shipping interests calling on the port; and other matters ranging from installation and maintenance of aids to navigation to implementing channel dredging in concert with the federal government. While ships arrived from South America, Germany, Scandinavia, and New England to load pine, the greatest preponderance of vessels were those of British registry. The pages of the Pilot Commissioners minutes make frequent reference to disputes regarding pilotage and the interaction between the pilots themselves, and the pilots with timber ship captains. Most of the incidents involved the masters of British and German vessels. These incidents reveal the competitive nature of the pilots themselves, and

---

[881] The rules and regulations are listed in Sullivan, ed., *High Water on the Bar*, 84-86.

also the occasionally adversarial relationships the pilots had with ship captains and their agents.[882] An example from the minutes of a Pilot Commission meeting in the spring of 1887, with G.W. Long, Chairman; James L. Foster, H.S. Ravenel, D.S. Sinclair and R.J. Walker in attendance: "The case of M.J. Dean vs. J.W. Patterson was heard. Investigation etc., violation of rules 26 and 27, in boarding schooner *Edward C. Allan True* off steam tug *Leon*. After hearing evidence in the case, it is considered and ordered by the Board that J.W. Patterson be, and is hereby declared entitled to the pilotage and pilot fees of the *Edward C. Allan True,* and that said complaint is hereby dismissed with cost on the complainant."[883]

The Pilot Commission met at regular intervals, typically monthly during the height of the timber era, and occasionally in called sessions as circumstances required, usually to settle contentious disputes. After 1909, meetings of the Board were held with less frequency, testimony to the decline of Darien's timber fortunes and fewer vessels calling on the port. Later, there were gaps of several years between meetings; the last meeting in which the Board transacted any business was in 1924.

The Oyster Fishery of Coastal Georgia

In 1889, the Georgia legislature began establishing guidelines for the developing coastal oyster industry. The state requested federal assistance in

---

[882] Some of the more interesting, and intriguing, disputes as adjudicated by the Pilot Commissioners, and noted in their minutes, are recounted in ibid., Part III.
[883] Minutes of the Darien Pilot Commissioners, April 28, 1887.

collecting bottom samples and other data based on interviews with local watermen to guide state authorities in framing judicious laws relevant to oyster cultivation. The result was a report by J.C. Drake, Ensign, U.S. Navy, who, in command of the Coast and Geodetic Survey schooner *Ready*, conducted a systematic oyster survey of the Georgia coast in the fall and winter of 1889-90. His assessments were provided in a final report with a portfolio of detailed maps released by the Coast and Geodetic Survey in the spring of 1890. In his conclusions, Drake noted that the natural oyster beds of the Georgia coast had been depleted by excessive fishing and that the nearer the markets the more the beds were depleted. Drake went on:

"The recent oyster law of the State does not require a knowledge of the location and area of the natural beds. It very properly permits any one to enter ground for private cultivation on any oyster bed which is not reported to by the public for the procuring of oysters by the use of tongs for consumption or for sale. So few and so small are the oysters which now remain scattered along the shores that it would be to the interest of the State if its citizens were permitted to lease any area, the State selling to the highest bidder the now almost depleted oyster beds. As a means of rapidly depleting the natural beds no more effective method could be instituted than the establishment of factories for the canning of oysters. These in the end will be of great benefit to the State, because the sooner the natural beds are depleted the sooner will the citizens engage in private cultivation, and enact laws that will give inducement to capital."[884]

The Drake survey specifically addressed the inlets and their attendant waterways. Drake's notes from his investigations are enlightening from both an oystering, ecological, geographical and navigational perspective for the coastal waters, and selections from his survey are included here:

"*Wassaw Sound.*–This sound lies between Tybee Island on the north, and

---

[884] J.C. Drake, "On the Sounds and Estuaries of Georgia with Reference to Oyster Culture," U.S. Coast and Geodetic Survey, Bulletin 19, March 1890, 201.

Wassaw Island on the south. It is 2 miles in width at its mouth, and only extends that distance inland to Cabbage Island. With the exception of the deep channel leading into the Tybee River on the north and the Wilmington River on the south, it is for the most part very shoal, and the bottom is generally shifting sand. The adjacent shores are nearly all marshy, and along the Cabbage Island shore there is a narrow streak of the so-called raccoon oysters and many dead shells. Being exposed to the heavy seas, the shoal water, and the shifting bottom, the water itself is entirely too salt. The currents are those produced by the rise and fall of the tides, which are augmented by the northeast winds.

"*Wilmington River.*–This river enters Wassaw Sound at its southern and western side. For the first 8 miles it has a general northwest direction to the village of Thunderbolt, which is the oyster depot of Savannah. For the first 5 miles it lies between Wilmington Island on the north and east, and Skiddaway [sic] Island on the south and west and has an average width of half a mile. It then narrows to one-fourth of a mile, running about 3 miles with this width to Thunderbolt. Beyond this, connecting with the Savannah River, it is too fresh for the propagation of oysters. The depth of water for the greater part of the river is 20 to 40 feet. The bottom is variable, there being several long strips of soft mud where oyster deposits are constantly taking place…Along the wooded portions of Wilmington Island the left bank is washing away, and hence oysters should not be planted very near this shore. A few natural beds were found in this river, principally between Thunderbolt and Turner's Rock, but they are of no consequence, having been about exterminated by excessive fishing, being so near the oyster market…

"*Herb River.*–This is a tributary of the Wilmington River, which it enters about 1 mile below Thunderbolt. From its mouth it leads through marshes in a general southwesterly direction, and separates Dutch Island on the east from the mainland on the west. It is about 4 miles long. In places of small area considerable deposits of mud are going on, and dead shells are found.

"*Skiddaway River* is a tributary of the Wilmington River into which it flows nearly opposite Turner's Rock. It leads through marshes in a southwesterly direction, separating Skiddaway Island on the east from Dutch Island and the Isle of Hope on the west. The character of the bottom is soft mud, with an occasional area of hard and sticky mud and sand.

"*Half Moon River* flows into Wassaw Sound through the marshes of Wilmington Island, just south of the mouth of Tybee River. It averages about 400 yards in width for the first mile, when it narrows and extends through the marshes north and west to the wooded portions of Wilmington Island. The bottom is soft mud and generally unfit for the cultivation of oysters.

"*Turner's Creek* is a narrow winding stream, separating Wilmington Island on the south from White Marsh Island on the north. It is about 4 miles in length, and about 200 yards in width, and is the connecting link between Tybee River and Wilmington River. A few oysters of poor quality were found in this river, but the water is too fresh, or liable to become so, to admit of oyster cultivation.

"*Romerly Marsh Creek* comes into Wassaw Sound near the mouth of Wilmington River. The area of this creek is 250 acres.

"*Odingsell River* begins in the Romerly marshes and flows nearly south for about 3 miles, where it empties into Ossabaw Sound. It separates Wassaw Island from Little Wassaw Island, and averages about one-eighth of a mile in width. The water in this river is very salt.

"*Vernon River* enters Ossabaw Sound to the northward of Raccoon Key. It has a general northwest direction, and is about 9 miles in length. For the first 3 miles it is about five-eighths of a mile in width then it narrows to one-fourth of a mile. Above the mouth of Burnside River the bottom is generally very soft and unsuitable for oyster cultivation. There is also a marl formation opposite the mouth of Little Ogeechee River, which extends more or less to the mouth of Vernon River. With the exception of a heavily-wooded hammock known as Green Island, the Vernon River flows entirely through the marsh as far as Beaulieu, and must therefore contain a large amount of mud brought out of the marshes on the spring tides. In the Vernon River opposite Hell Gate the dredge brought up a quantity of dead oyster shells, most of them being very old and large…The average specific gravity at Montgomery, from 151 specimens, was 1.02. A prolonged local rain would make it extremely doubtful as to oysters living above White Bluff, and for cultivation it is recommended to go no higher than Montgomery and no lower than Hell Gate. The current due to the tide is strong. The total area from Montgomery to the mouth is 1,728 acres; area beyond 1,000 feet from the shore, 1,080 acres. Area of natural oyster beds, 20 acres.

"*Burnside River* is a tributary of Vernon River, coming into it on the northeastern side of Skiddaway Island. It is about one-fourth mile wide, and extends eastwards about 2 ½ miles, when it divides, the principal branch taking the name of Back River. In February 1889, about 4,000 bushels of oysters were planted near the shore in Burnside River, adjacent to the wooded portion of Skiddaway Island. These oysters came from Bradley's Creek, near Ossabaw Sound, and Walburg's Creek, near St. Catherines Sound. They were planted in water from 2 to 10 feet at low tide, and the character of the bottom was part hard sand with dead shells, hard and tenacious mud, and soft mud. In February 1890, one year after planting, I made a haul with a steam dredge over the different parts of the bed. It was found that the oysters had grown rapidly, and in one more year would be marketable.

"*Ossabaw Sound* lies between Wassaw Island on the north and Ossabaw Island on the south, the distance across the mouth being about 3 ½ miles. It extends inland only 2 miles to Raccoon Key. No part of this sound was considered fit for oyster culture by reason of its shoal water, shifting bottom, and exposure to the heavy seas from the ocean.

Ogeechee River enters Ossabaw Sound on the south side of Raccoon Key, and really appears as a prolongation of the sound as far as the Middle Marshes. It is the second largest river on the coast of the State, extending into the interior of the country northwesterly for some 250 miles. By reason of the large volume of fresh water flowing out of this river, only a short portion of it is available for oysters, namely, from its mouth to about 1 mile above the Florida Passage, making a distance of about 5 miles.

"*Bradley's River* comes into Ossabaw Sound from the north end of Ossabaw Island. It is about 5 miles long, and averages about 200 yards in width for the first 3 miles. Only the first 2 miles of this river were examined. It is very natural to infer that the upper and narrow portion of this river is well adapted to the cultivation of oysters as far as concerns the density of the water.

"*The Florida Passage* is a tributary of the Ogeechee and, with Bear River, separates Ossabaw Island from the mainland. It is about 2 miles long and averages about 400 yards in width. The bottom is soft mud where a few oysters of an inferior grade may be found.

"*Red Bird Creek*, a small, narrow stream about 3 miles long, comes into the Florida Passage on the west side, about 1 mile from its mouth. The water in this creek is too fresh for oysters, except near the mouth, and even there, oysters are liable to be killed by the overflow from the Ogeechee.

"*Buck Head Creek* comes out of the marshes on the west side of Ossabaw Island at its junction with the Florida Passage. It is about 2 miles in length. This creek has a total area of 96 acres and contains no natural oyster beds.

"*Bear River* begins at the junction of the Florida Passage and Buck Head Creek, and flows through extensive marshes in a southerly direction separating Ossabaw Island from the mainland. It enters St. Catherines Sound on its north side, being 8 miles in length and at its mouth 1 ¼ miles wide. The natural oyster beds lie along the shores and partly ebb out at low water, and are about depleted by excessive fishing, there now being more dead shells than oysters. The oysters found in this river are small but of a superior quality.

"*Kilkenny Creek* enters Bear River at the west side about 2 miles above its mouth. It is 5 miles in length, and flows westwardly for the first 2 miles with a width of 400 yards. It then narrows to about 100 yards and flows northerly, connecting again with Skippers Narrows into the Florida Passage. The creek has a depth of from 2 to 12 feet, and the bottom changes from hard mud and tenacious mud to clay, and is well adapted to the cultivation of oysters.

"*Skippers Narrows* is well adapted to the cultivation of oysters, the bottom being hard mud and sticky. The area is small though, and can only be cultivated by the use of hand implements. Both Skippers Narrows and the upper part of Kilkenny Creek are liable to be affected by the freshets from the Ogeechee River. Experiments with planted oysters have been carried out in Skippers Narrows and at the head of Kilkenny Creek by Mr. George Appleton of Bryan county. The oysters had greatly improved and rapidly grown, being for the most part marketable after 2 years' planting. A few barrels of Blue Point oysters were brought by Mr. Appleton from the north and planted in this locality. The oysters so planted showed a rapid growth and appeared to retain their peculiar flavor.

"*St. Catherines Sound* separates Ossabaw Island on the north and St. Catherines Island on the south. It is about 1 3/8 miles in width, and extends inland into the marshes about 2 miles. The sound is totally unfit for the cultivation of oysters by reason of the water being too salt, by reason of its exposure to the heavy seas, especially the northeast gales, and also by the large amount of its area being very shoal.

"*Medway River* is the principal tributary to St. Catherines Sound, of which it appears as a prolongation. That part of it examined extends about 7 miles inland. The depth of water in this river ranges from 1 foot to about 30 feet, there being many shoals making out in the middle of the river. Along the shore there is a series of natural oyster beds of the raccoon type, the total area of which is 49 acres. The size of the oysters indicated that the beds are very much depleted by excessive fishing. At one place on the river the shore had changed so that the depth of 8 feet shown on the chart by the survey of 1857 is now dry at low water.

"*North Newport River* enters St. Catherines Sound to the southward and westward. It flows mostly through the marsh for about 9 miles. It has an uneven bottom like the Medway River.

"*Walburg Creek* enters St. Catherines Sound close to the north point of St. Catherines Island. It has an average width of one-eighth of a mile. Its direction is southerly for 2 miles, then westerly for 2 miles where it joins the North Newport River. The bottom is soft mud.

"*South Newport River* enters Sapelo Sound on its northern side. It runs through marsh on both banks in a northwesterly direction for about 7 miles, where it joins with North Newport River. It has a width of 1 ¾ miles at its mouth, but narrows rapidly, and 2 miles above averages one-half mile. The total area is 2,300 acres. Area of natural oyster beds, 32 acres.

"*Wahoo River* enters South Newport River at its mouth on the south side. It runs in a northwesterly direction for about 3 miles, averaging about 300 yards in width. The total area of the river is 256 acres.

"*Sapelo Sound* separates St. Catherines Island on the north from Blackbeard Island on the south. It is only 1 mile in width at its entrance, but extends inland to the westward about 4 ½ miles, with an average width of about 1 ½ miles. The main body of this sound is deep and the bottom hard, but the water is too salty for oyster culture.

"*Sapelo River* is a prolongation of Sapelo Sound in a westerly direction. It is about 1 mile in width at its mouth, but soon narrows to one-half mile, which width it holds for 1 ½ miles to the entrance to Broro River. Beyond this it extends into the wooded country for about 15 miles. The deep water from Broro River to Front River is the only part which is considered favorable for the cultivation of oysters. The total area from its mouth to Broro River is 2,112 acres. Area of natural oyster beds is 17 acres.

"*Barbour's Island River* enters Sapelo Sound about 1 mile west of the mouth of South Newport River. This river was not examined but from native oystermen it was learned that a few scattered oyster beds extended along near the shore.

"*Julienton River* enters Sapelo River on the northern side 1 ½ miles to the westward of Barbour's Island River. It runs a crooked westerly course, has an average width of one-fourth of a mile for about 3 miles, this being the area examined. The total area of the river examined is 630 acres. The natural oyster beds lie along the shores, and are about exterminated by excessive fishing.

"*Back and Front rivers* are two small tributaries of the Sapelo River, coming into it from the southward on either side of Creighton Island. They are only about 2 miles long and 100 yards wide, having a depth ranging from 6 to 20 feet. In Back River there is a total area of natural oyster beds of 3.5 acres. Front River has an area of natural oyster beds of 11.5 acres.

"*Mud River* is a broad and shallow stream which enters Sapelo Sound from the southward and separates Sapelo Island from the mainland. For the first two miles it is about 1 mile in width. The bottom is almost entirely of soft mud, and the only part suitable for oyster culture is a narrow strip along its bank adjacent to the wooded land of Sapelo Island. The marshy banks on both sides are lined with raccoon oysters. The total area of the river is 2,430 acres. Area of natural oyster beds is 40 acres.

"*New Tea Kettle Creek* is a narrow winding stream of about 100 yards in width, having a general north and south direction, and connecting Mud River with Doboy Sound. It is about 4 miles in length, and runs through marshes its entire distance. The total area is 190 acres.

"*Old Tea Kettle Creek* lies to the westward of New Tea Kettle Creek, and also connects the lower part of Mud River with Doboy Sound. It is about 4 miles in length, has a general northwesterly direction, and an average width of about 300 yards. Several small beds of oysters are found along the edges, of an inferior grade, but suitable for planting purposes. Total area of the creek is 608 acres. Total area of natural oyster beds, 25.5 acres.

"*Duplin River* is the first tributary to Doboy Sound on the northward side, into which it empties 1 ½ miles to the westward of Sapelo Light-house. It is a small stream averaging about 150 yards in width, and extends some 5 miles to the northward in the marshes of Sapelo Island. The total area of the river is 355 acres. Area of natural oyster beds is 22 acres.

"*Doboy Sound* separates Sapelo Island on the north from Wolf Island on the south. Extending in a northwesterly direction, it is about 5 miles long, and averages about three-fourths of a mile in width. A large volume of salt water enters and renders almost the entire area unsuitable for oyster culture. Along the shores are strips of oysters and dead shells. Several hauls with a steam dredge were made in this sound between the mouth of Connegan River and Sapelo Light-house, and quite a number of star-fish were brought up in the dredge, which fact would of itself render the attempt to cultivate oysters here a useless undertaking.

"*Connegan River* is a tributary of Doboy Sound. It extends through the marshes to the southward about 3 miles and joins North River by a small branch, thus receiving indirectly a portion of the fresh water from the Darien River. The bottom is variable, but generally hard, and suitable for oyster culture. The total area of the river is 616 acres.

"*North River* enters Doboy Sound on the north side of Doboy Island. It extends through marshes in a westerly direction for about 5 miles, where it joins a small creek connecting with the Darien River, by means of which it receives a small quantity of fresh water. The total area is 528 acres. Area of natural oyster beds is 7 acres.

"*Back River* enters Doboy Sound on the south side of Commodore Island. It is about one-fourth of a mile in width, and bends northward and westward and thence southward, where it is joined by the mouth of Darien River. It is about 3 miles long, and runs entirely through marshes. The character of the bottom is hard and is well adapted for the cultivation of oysters. The specific gravity at the mouth is 1.0189; at the head it is 1.0171. At the village of Doboy the mean specific gravity was 1.0174. The total area of the river is 540 acres. The area of natural oyster beds is 28.5 acres. The maximum current observed at Doboy was 1.7 knots per hour.

"*Rockdedundy River* is really one of the deltas of the Darien River. Samples of oysters taken here show the conditions favorable for a rapid growth.

"*Darien River* is considered unfit for the cultivation of oysters by reason of its waters being too fresh.

"*South River* extends in an easterly direction along the north side of Wolf Island marshes for a distance of 3 miles, where it empties into Doboy Sound. The bottom is generally favorable for the growth of oysters. The total area of the river is 320 acres. Area of natural oyster beds is 20.5 acres.

"(Note.) — Wolf Creek and Beacon Creek, both coming out of the marshes of Wolf Island, were not examined.

"*Little Mud River* is the first tributary to Altamaha Sound on the north side. Extending to the northward about 2 miles and separating Wolf Island from

Rockdedundy Island, it joins the mouth of Rockdedundy River. It has an average width of about 300 yards, disregarding the shoals at the mouth of the river. The water in this river is liable to become very fresh when there is a rise in the Altamaha River. The total area is 321 acres. The area of natural oyster beds, 14.5 acres.

"*Altamaha Sound* lies between Wolf Island on the north and Little St. Simons Island on the south. It is about 2 miles wide at its entrance but the sound is obstructed by a series of shoals and marsh islands, among which the narrow channels run most circuitously. Oysters will not grow in this sound higher up than 2 miles from the mouth, or from the western side of Egg Island to the mouth of the sound. Making out from the northeast point of Little St. Simon's Island there is a narrow reef of oysters. This reef is formed along the side of the channel. It averages about 60 yards in width, and extends into the ocean for about one statute mile. The oysters are all of an inferior quality and at least three-fourths of the mass is composed of dead shells. This reef is formed on hard sand bottom, and the continuous catch and growth of young oysters on it presents a remarkable phenomenon in the life of the oyster. The reef is directly exposed to the heavy northeast seas, and during a portion of the stage of flood tide it would seem natural to suppose the reef to be covered with entirely salt water. On the other hand, during a part of the ebb, the water over this reef must be very fresh, so fresh that fishermen tell me that they are able to drink it.

"*Hampton River* connects with Buttermilk Sound on the east side and flows in an easterly and then in a southerly direction, separating St. Simons and Little St. Simons island, and coming out on the coast 5 miles below the mouth of Altamaha Sound. It is about 12 miles in length, and the depth of water ranges from 8 to 40 feet. The prevailing character of the bottom is sticky. There are a few sand shoals at intervals, but very little evidence of shifting bottom, and so far as concerns the character of the bottom this river is admirably suited adapted to the growth of oysters.

"*Village Creek* comes into Hampton River from the southward about 1 ½ miles above its mouth, winding through the marshes, and separating Long Island from St. Simons Island, and at its head connecting with a narrow and tortuous stream that flows southward between the two islands named, and enters the sea at the south end of Long Island. The oysters are poor and small—poor by reason of the high salt water, and small from being crowded together. The total area of the creek is 352 acres.

"*Frederica River* flows almost entirely through marshes in a southerly direction, separating St. Simons Island from the mainland, and connecting with the fresh water of Buttermilk Sound, flows into St. Simons Sound. It is quite crooked and will not average more than 150 yards in width, except for 2 miles from the mouth. The water in this river is found to be entirely too fresh for the growing of oysters above a point 2 miles from its junction with Mackay's River.

"*Mackay's River* comes into St. Simons Sound about 1 mile to the westward of Frederica River. It is wider than Frederica River, but shoaler in places. The total area of this is 960 acres.

"*St. Simons Sound* lies between St. Simons Island on the north, the marshes making off from the mainland on the west, and Jekyl Island on the south. It is about 1 mile wide at the entrance, has a depth ranging from 5 to 10 fathoms, and therefore contains a large quantity of sea water. The only part adapted to the growth of oysters is the area embraced within one-half mile from the mouths of Frederica and Mackay's rivers, the remaining area being too salt.

"*Brunswick River* is the principal tributary to St. Simons Sound, of which it appears as a prolongation to the southward and westward. It has an average width of about 1 mile for the first two miles, or to Brunswick Point, where it turns to the northward and narrows to three-fourths of a mile, holding that direction for 2 ½ miles to Buzzard's Island, where it divides into two branches, the main branch being called Turtle River. The depth of water in Brunswick River ranges from 15 to 40 feet for about three-fourths of the area. That portion of the river east of the upper mouth of Plantation Creek is considered too salt for the growth of oysters.

"*Turtle River* begins at the southeast point of Buzzard's Island, and extends in a northwesterly direction for about 7 miles, separating Blythe Island on the west from the mainland on the east. Along the shores there is a perceptible deposit. The area covered by deeper water is considerable favorable for oysters.

"*Colonel's Creek* is a tributary of Brunswick River, into which it flows at the junction of Turtle River. It separates Colonel's Island on the south from Blythe Island on the north, being about 8 miles long.

"*Jekyl Creek* separate Jekyl Island on the east from the marshes on the west, and has a length of 3 ½ miles, running nearly north and south, and connects Brunswick River with Jekyl Sound. It has a width of about one-fourth of a mile. The bottom consists principally of soft mud, and is considered unfit for the growth of oysters.

"*Jekyl Sound* is a branch of St. Andrew's Sound, lying to the northward and westward of it, and is about 2 miles long and 1 mile wide. The water in this sound is considered too salt for oyster propagation.

"*Satilla River* comes into St. Andrew's Sound on its west side. Like the Altamaha, this is a fresh-water stream, taking its rise in the interior of the State. The first three miles of this river is the only part need be considered, the water above this becoming too fresh. The river has a width of about 1 mile for the above distance, and has a westerly direction, with marshes on both sides."[885]

---

[885] Ibid., 184-99.

Coastal Georgia had a successful oyster industry from the 1880s through the 1930s. In some years, local harvests rivalled Chesapeake Bay, long-recognized as the leading oyster-producing region on the east coast. As Drake pointed out, however, overtaxing the resource without implementing proper re-seeding and other conservation methods would deplete the resource, similar in concept to the over-cutting of the Altamaha pine forests precipitating the demise of Darien's timber industry. In 1980, Duane Harris researched Georgia oyster trends, basing his investigation on Drake's findings in 1889-90. Harris observed that "as early as 1889, Drake noted a general depletion of oyster beds, especially beds which were located near oyster houses. Drake felt that continued depletion, especially that which was expected as a result of cannery harvest, would ultimately be beneficial to the industry by forcing private cultivation and the enactment of reasonable harvesting/transplanting laws."[886] Drake's advice went unheeded for the most part, although "good laws, especially those which require the harvester to return a portion of the shells harvested to the growing area, have been in the Georgia Code since at least 1889," Harris pointed out. "Judging from Drake's report, however, Georgia's oyster laws were difficult to enforce then, as they are today. Failure to replace shell material to harvested areas is probably the most significant reason for the depletion of Georgia's oyster resources."[887]

The leading Georgia canneries in the early twentieth century were those of Augustus Oemler (1857-1927) and his descendants at Savannah, St. Catherines Island and Harris Neck, the Maggioni family at Thunderbolt, McIntosh County and Brunswick, the Atwood family at Valona and Cedar Point, and Paul Ploeger at Darien. The Ploeger cannery was the last such

---

[886] C. Duane Harris, "Survey of the Intertidal and Subtidal Oyster Resources of the Georgia Coast," Coastal Resources Division, GDNR, 1980, 5.
[887] Ibid., 10.

facility to operate on a large scale in coastal Georgia; it closed in 1960.

In 1890, Oemler obtained oyster rights to the creeks and marshes between Skidaway and Wassaw islands in Chatham County. Later, he built oyster canneries at Wilmington Island and on the portion of Wassaw Island known as Long Island, which operated until 1908. Joseph Parsons, owner of Wassaw, recalled that "as long as my father [George Parsons] lived, Oemler was a frequent visitor at Wassaw and there existed between them an almost filial relationship. Afterwards, when he had his house and cannery at St. Catherines, we saw less of him here, but frequently visited him there, and had many wonderful deer hunting parties with him and the Rauers family."[888]

Some of the local oyster gathering leases specified that shells must be dumped back into the creeks and marsh banks of the islands adjoining Wassaw and Ossabaw sounds, including Skidaway, Wilmington, Wassaw, Green, Ossabaw, and lower Bryan Neck at Kilkenny Creek. Many of the shell banks along the tidal streams in Chatham and Bryan counties are the result of oyster fishermen removing their oysters, and discarding the shells. A state health law enacted in 1943 made it illegal for commercial oystermen to open their oysters except in controlled, sanitary, conditions. Shell piles thus accumulated around the sites of canneries along the coast.[889]

Oemler's most ambitious venture was his cannery on the south end of St. Catherines Island. A sizeable number of Chatham County oystermen harvested oysters in the tidal waters around Skidaway, Wassaw, Wilmington and Tybee islands during the peak period of production from the 1890s to the 1920s. Some of these watermen were under contract to Oemler, or gathered oysters on beds that were under lease rights to him. Oemler's

---

[888] Elizabeth D. McMaster, *Wassaw: The Story of an Island* (privately published, 1974), 82.
[889] V.E. Kelly, *A Short History of Skidaway Island* (Savannah, Ga.: The Branigar Organization, 1980), 70.

Wilmington Island cannery produced 1.4 million cans of oysters in 1905.

Oemler and his family lived at St. Catherines for part of the year. His wife was Frieda Rauers Oemler (1879-1961), daughter of Jacob Rauers (1837-1904), owner of St. Catherines. In 1900, Oemler entered into a five-year agreement with Rauers by which Oemler, for $600 per year, received rights to harvest oysters in the marshes surrounding the island. Oemler developed a cannery on Back Creek with three boilers and hired black workers to operate the cannery with housing provided in dwellings associated with the former South End plantation on St. Catherines. Augustus and Frieda Oemler built a house and lived on the south end of St. Catherines, not far from the cannery and its docks. In 1928, soon after Oemler's death, the Rauers family leased oyster rights at St. Catherines to Savannah oystermen C. Philip Maggione and Joseph P. Maggione. There are deeds and land plats among the McIntosh County records attesting to the oyster activities of both Oemler and the Maggiones in the Harris Neck area.

In June 1926, George A. Morison of Milwaukee, Wisconsin, who owned Barbour Island, sold two acres of marshland on the east side of the Barbour River at Gould's Landing to Oemler, a tract that included "all that certain parcel of marsh land lying on Barbours Island River approximately opposite to Gould's Landing containing two acres more or less." The same agreement included a plat of this small tract opposite the northeast side of Harris Neck across from Gould's Landing. This "Map of a Proposed Factory Site for Capt. Augustus Oemler on Barbours Island in McIntosh County" delineates a two-acre rectangle in the Barbour Island marshes on which Oemler sited his oyster cannery.[890] Eighteen months later, another deed indicates further oystering

---

[890] Deed Book Y (1926), 109, RMCG. The oyster activities of Augustus Oemler are documented in Liberty County Deed Records (1900, 1918), Superior Court, Hinesville, Ga. See also George J. Armelagos and John Toby Woods, Jr., *St. Catherines Island: The Untold Story of People and Place* (Atlanta, 2012), 64-67, 233 (n36); "Capsule

Oyster cannery on Shellbluff Creek, Valona, early 1900s.

activity at Harris Neck. In January 1928 Freda Rauers Oemler sold for $5,000 to the Maggiones a two-acre patch of high ground in the marsh opposite Gould's Landing that

"with the improvements of the above described lot of land consisting of buildings in which was conducted by Augustus Oemler an oyster canning factory known as the Oemler Oyster Cannery, together with all the machinery, tools and equipment located in said factory, including pipes, fittings, tanks, shucking houses, tongs, steam cars, steam chests, boilers, cans and oyster shells, located on said land; also all canning materials, boats, barges, batteaux, belonging to said cannery including one motor boat equipped with one 30-horse power engine, and all equipment, apparel and furniture used in connection with said boat; and four oyster bateaux located on St. Catherines Island."[891]

In 1905, the Shell Bluff Canning Company was in operation in the harvest and marketing of oysters at a factory on Shellbluff Creek at Valona in McIntosh County. Period photographs depict the cannery on the later site of

---

Review of Wassaw Island History, A Compilation of Information from Wassaw Island Logs, Correspondence, Scrapbooks and Recollections," unpub. ms., nd.
[891] Deed Book 1 (1928), 254-58, RMCG.

the Durant shrimp docks. Shellbluff Canning was managed by James L. Atwood, and his partner, Robert A. Strain. The Valona business also had a branch on Florida's Gulf coast at Cedar Key. In 1907, James Atwood's brother, Jules E. Atwood, went to Cedar Key to manage the operation there. J.E. Atwood remained involved with the Valona fishery for many years. Walter W. Atwood constructed clinker-built oyster sloops of excellent design and quality during this period. His boat yard was near J.L. Atwood's cannery on Shellbluff Creek on the later site of the Valona post office. The wood-frame post office building, no longer active, was once the boat house at Walter Atwood's yard.[892]

A 1905 postcard photograph (above) shows the docks, boats and buildings of the Atwood cannery on Shellbluff Creek. Two of the boats moored at the cannery dock, are clinker-built, single-masted oyster sloops with V-hulls. The *Juliet* was one such vessel, built about 1904 by the Atwoods and Charles Burrows, father of Hugh Burrows. The *Juliet* was one of several boats used to gather oysters for Shell Bluff Canning. Rusty Fleetwood notes that these sloops of the turn of the century and shortly afterwards were unique, and native to the coasts of Georgia and lower South Carolina:

"These one-masted sloops were, after all was said and done, slow and hard-to-manage craft. After 1905, oysters were prohibited to be stored below deck. They had to be kept up on deck for health reasons and the vessels, out of necessity, changed a little after that ... The oyster sloops could hardly get out of their own way under sail. They weren't very fast and they more or less went with the tide for steerageway. The oysters would load down the boat considerably. They were primarily operated by black men. The black men in the smaller attendant bateaux would collect the oysters with rakes at low tide; they would fill up the bateaux, and then unload the oysters from the bateaux aboard the sloop which would, when fully loaded, take the oysters to the local

---

[892] *Darien News*, November 1, 1962.

cannery."[893]

The sloops were essentially oversized bateaux, decked over with a centerboard and a small deck house aft for the men. Smaller sloops under thirty-five feet were usually flat-bottomed. Those up to fifty feet were V-bottomed.

"Both types were planked lengthwise on the bottom, it being thought this type of construction with its full framing system gave a stronger craft that would stand up to the heavy loads of oysters when the boats were grounded out on the banks and mud flats. [After the sanitary laws of 1905] ... the already wide craft then became extremely broad to enable them to carry heavy loads piled high on deck with holding boards added along each rail to contain the cargo. The sloops were built throughout the area, not just in the major cities, but also at Daufuskie, Hilton Head, Halfmoon Creek, Wilmington Island, Ossabaw, Belvedere and Doboy. Examples would be the sloop *Envy*, built in 1900 at Thunderbolt with register dimensions of 43.2 by 17.3, or the *Olive*, 35.5 by 15.2 built at Harris Neck, Georgia in 1901. The advent of the engine did not revolutionize the fisheries overnight, for in some cases, such as those of the oyster fishery, the engines were an expense all out of proportion to the cost of the hull itself ... Between 1903 and 1909 only 27 new sloops were built in South Carolina and Georgia, while 75 gasoline-powered craft of all types were constructed. Naphtha, or gas engines, as produced in the early 1900s were massive chunks of iron usually no more than two cylinders which produced formidable amounts of torque at low revolutions per minute, emitting a pocketa-pocketa-pop sound that went largely un-muffled."[894]

In 1911, the Shell Bluff Canning Company of Valona deeded 2,000 acres of marsh land to William H. Kittles for oystering purposes, most of the acreage being around Old Teakettle Creek between Mud River and Doboy Sound. During the period 1910-1920, Kittles accumulated additional marsh tracts for oystering

---

[893] Rusty Fleetwood, Lecture before the Lower Altamaha Historical Society, November 1987.
[894] Rusty Fleetwood, *Tidecraft: The Boats of Lower South Carolina and Georgia* (Savannah, Ga.: Coastal Heritage Society, 1982), 153-54.

rights. The 1911 agreement between Kittles and Shell Bluff Canning is interesting for the geographical details it provides, as well as giving a sense of the activity associated with the local oyster industry in the early twentieth century. Kittles also held title to marshlands in Sapelo Sound. In 1916 he deeded a considerable portion of the marshes to his Atwood River Canning Company of Valona.

William H. Kittles (1880-1928) was one of the most productive oystermen in the history of the McIntosh fishery. His Atwood River Canning Company was on the lower tip of the neck of land comprising the southern section of Valona at the headwaters of Atwood Creek; the cannery was on the site later occupied by the shrimp docks of the Kittles family. Kittles and his wife, May Atwood Kittles (1889-1976), daughter of George and Sophie Atwood, established a home they called Andreleau, at Valona near the cannery. Andreleau was apparently named for the prominent antebellum Savannah cotton factor, Andrew Low whose daughter-in-law, Juliette Gordon Low, founded the Girl Scouts of America in 1912. Later, the Kittles' sons, Peter and George, operated a commercial shrimp business on the point of land where the oyster cannery had been, and kept several shrimp boats at the docks. This activity peaked in the 1960s. W.H. Kittles died in 1928, and five years later his widow, May Atwood Kittles, married Harry Jones of Waynesboro, Georgia. Jones died in 1958. For many years afterward, until her death in December 1976, May Jones was looked upon as the matriarch of Valona.

Neighboring Cedar Point, coastal homeplace of the present author and about two miles north of Valona, had on-again, off-again oystering operations on Cedar Creek between the world wars.

On January 22, 1942, the L.P. Maggione Company of Savannah leased from Henry G. Atwood oystering privileges on marshlands comprising Fourmile Island, bounded by Sapelo Sound, and the Sapelo, Bruro and Julianton rivers. This arrangement also included 3,000 acres of marsh between Sapelo River and Mud River, 350 acres of marsh around Dog Hammock on Sapelo Sound; the land at Cedar Point on the banks of Cedar Creek on which the Atwood cannery stood, "and also the flat marsh land adjacent to and comprising a part of the Atwood Home Place [at Cedar Point] lying north and south of the factory building, provided that the lessee shall not pile oyster shells upon such marsh land higher than three feet above the level of the adjoining high land."[895]

Three years later the Cedar Point Canning Company was under lease to another group—three young men who, like thousands of others in coastal Georgia during the period, were returning home from military service in the Second World War. Good jobs were at a premium, and the potential profits in oystering seemed a good prospect at the time. In September 1945, R.E. Sullivan, H.O. Hunter, and W.D. Hubbard formed a partnership and managed the Cedar Point cannery, shipping processed canned oysters to the Campbell Company in Atlanta, as well as selling oysters by the gallon to local and area distributors.[896] The partners had a shrimp boat, the

---

[895] Lease Book B (1942), 233, RMCG.
[896] Roy E. Sullivan (1921-2016) was the father of the author of the present book. He and his wife, Mary Kate Hunter Sullivan (1924-1954), lived only a few yards from the Cedar Point cannery with his mother-in-law, Mary J. Hunter, grandmother of the author. The Cedar Point house had been built her father, Dr. Henry Herbert Johnson ca. 1925. The author now resides on the same plot of ground at Cedar Point, in a new home built in 2018.

White Rose, supplementing the operation, and an oyster bateau towboat, the *Roma.*

This group ended activity at the Cedar Point cannery in 1949, but it continued to operate on an irregular basis under lease from Mrs. H.G. (Jane) Atwood of Cedar Point until the mid-1950s. The old Cedar Point factory fell into ruins in the 1950s. The author recalls playing amid the abandoned factory with its rusting tin roof, and inside, an artesian well continually flowed fresh water through a lead pipe; shell banks lined the adjacent creek, the shells blanched by years of sun exposure. Eventually, the facility disappeared, its lumber sold for scrap, and the property sold by Jane Atwood. In the early 1980s, a private residence was constructed on the foundations of the factory overlooking the creek.

The oyster-gathering procedure of the turn of the century was about the same as it would be fifty years later; sub-tidal oysters were picked off the bottom of the waterways by long-handled tongs. Many of the so-called "coon" oysters were gathered from the banks of the creeks and rivers by hand — work of the hardest kind for those who labored in this fishery. During the off-season for oysters in the warmer months, many of the coastal Georgia canneries canned the vegetables grown by oystermen in the spring and summer.

Georgia oystermen harvested nearly 500,000 pounds of oysters in 1880. For the next 30 years, Georgia harvests were among the highest in the world. In 1908, the Georgia harvest was a record eight million pounds, with fourteen canneries in operation. There was a dramatic decline two years later with only three million pounds harvested in 1910, following which the industry went into a gradual decline for the next forty years. Harris noted the 1936 state harvest was 330,000 pounds and, by 1951, the total was down to 293,000 pounds. The decline continued until the all-time low was reached in 1978 with 38,000 pounds harvested. A mild recovery was in progress when widespread oyster disease dealt the industry another setback in 1986.

Shrimp Boats & Shrimp Fishing

During most of the twentieth century the maritime heritage of coastal Georgia was most evident in its shrimp fishery. Some families have had several generations involved in the commercial shrimp fishery. Blacks, and later, increasing numbers of whites, pursued oystering, then shrimping to supplement their depressed incomes from declining agriculture on the coast, as well as the demise of a once-lucrative timber industry. The shrimpers of the first two decades of the 1900s were mostly local African Americans, and first-or-second generation Portuguese, Greeks, and Spanish migrating to Georgia from northeast Florida. European shrimpers predominated in Fernandina, long the shrimping capital of the eastern U.S. "Portuguese and Sicilians were among the foremost fishermen of the Old World," notes Rusty Fleetwood. "When the combination of readily available ice, railroads, and mechanical refrigeration came to the northeast Florida area, the market for shrimp increased tenfold."[897] In the early twentieth century, the boats of Mike Salvatore of Fernandina, Florida were a great influence on boatbuilding in Georgia. Fleetwood noted:

"What is interesting about Salvatore's boats is that they led the way from the early open-boat shrimpers to where you started having a raised deck on the boats. Today, of course, you see the bows raised high on almost all shrimp boats. The high peaked bows of the shrimpers helped them more easily weather the heavy seas when

---

[897] Fleetwood, *Tidecraft*, 160-62.

Floyd Atwood and the Sheik, *Cedar Creek, Cedar Point. This rig is typical of the shrimp boats of the 1940s.*

fishing offshore, as the boats began to do more and more. Then, as now, the deckhouses are placed forward in the vessel, not aft. About 1915 the shrimpers began to utilize gasoline engines, or what were called semi-diesel engines which would have run on diesel fuel but were started with gas."[898]

Salvatore and the other Greek boat builders of northeastern Florida became known for the exceptional quality and durability of their vessels. DESCO Marine of St. Augustine became one of the most prolific shrimp boat builders on the Atlantic coast until the domestic shrimping industry began to decline starting in the mid-1970s. Fleetwood explains that "the shrimp boat builders had standards for each size, and the craft were turned out in numbers in St. Augustine, Fernandina, and Brunswick. Many shrimpers still used

---

[898] Fleetwood lecture, op. cit.

the typical vee-bottom construction of the area, but they soon developed (in the 1920s) a shape that approximated the shape of the Greek hull in a chine-built boat. With these boats came an increase in power, and the move to diesel power also began."[899] The boats got bigger in the 1930s. The *Miss Angelina*, built at Thunderbolt in 1934 for Joseph A. Cesaroni, was forty-five feet long with a fifteen-foot beam and a 60-horsepower diesel engine. A similar engine powered the 42-foot *Perry E. Meyers*, built for P.H. Ploeger of Darien in 1938 at Fernandina.

"Descendants of these craft are still built in the area [1980s], both by large commercial yards such as DESCO (formerly Diesel Engine Sales Company) and by the shrimpers themselves, who construct basically the same style of hull whether chine-built or round bottom—in fiberglass or steel as well as wood. The shrimping industry had a great economic impact on the area in the 1930s, helping it through the Depression years. Residents of waterfront communities now were awakened not by the sound of oars against tholepins, but by the ignition of Lathrop diesels as the un-muffled shrimpers cranked up and left for work."[900]

African Americans were in the forefront of the early fishery. Dan Thorpe (1902-1992) of McIntosh County was among the first of the black shrimpers, beginning work in the early 1920s. Thorpe noted that in the 1920s shrimp usually brought about three cents a pound, heads on. Headed shrimp—heading was done aboard the boats as they were netted, or at the local docks before being sent to the markets—brought 3 ½ to 4 cents per pound. In later years, the shrimp brought substantial increases—to 35 cents a pound in the late 1930s and early 1940s, then later, to roughly $400 per box of one

---

[899] Fleetwood, *Tidecraft*, 161.
[900] Ibid., 162.

Shrimp boats at Darien, mid-1950s. The boats are bigger than those of a decade or more earlier, with higher bows to enable trawling in the rougher waters offshore.

hundred pounds.[901] Shrimp were trucked to the processing plants in Savannah, Brunswick and Jacksonville from the local docks in iced-down 100-pound plywood boxes.

Local commercial fishermen—first the oystermen and shad fishermen, then the shrimpers and crabbers, were a tough, hard-working breed. In the first three decades of the twentieth century, their oyster bateaux, and their small shrimp boats plied the tidal waterways, oystermen in late fall and winter, the shrimpers in summer and fall. Their durable craft were built to last, to absorb the constant punishment inflicted by day-after-day service in the nearshore waters in all types of weather. The local watermen had to be as hardy as their craft. These men who pursued their livelihoods on and near the sea—the sounds, and the nearshore waters, and rivers and creeks between the barrier islands and the mainland, had to be thoroughly knowledgeable about local marine conditions, which

---

[901] Author's interview with Dan Thorpe, Crescent, Ga., April 5, 1988.

were always undergoing change. The early *Coast Pilot* navigation guides issued to mariners by the U.S. Coast & Geodetic Survey, which regularly conducted surveys of the nation's coast lines, are instructive, for they serve as a useful geographical template for local conditions in any given era. For example, in the 1959 edition of the *U.S. Coast Pilot*, amid the peak years of the coastal shrimping industry, there is this information for McIntosh County waters:

"**Chart 574.—Sapelo Sound** is about 32 miles southwestward of Tybee Light. About eight miles from the entrance the break in the shore can be seen on a clear day. The tower of the abandoned lighthouse 10 miles southwestward of the sound can also be seen from off the bar and is a good landmark…With the aid of the chart, and on a rising tide and a smooth sea, vessels up to a 15-foot draft should have no difficulty in entering during daylight hours by following the buoys. A comparison of the surveys made since 1859 shows virtually no change in the bar except in the vicinity of the shoalest part of Experiment Shoal…Another unmarked channel south of the main channel had a reported depth of 8 feet and is used by fishing boats. Pilots are not available for Sapelo Sound. No towns or villages of any importance are on the sound or tributaries. In northeasterly weather anchorage can be made in the lower part of South Newport River with fair protection. The mean range of tide is about 7 feet. In the entrance to the sound the average velocities at strengths of flood and ebb are about 2 and 2 ½ knots, respectively…Sapelo Sound is somewhat rough when there are strong east or northeast winds. About a 7 foot draft can be carried 6 miles up the Sapelo River to the landing at Pine Harbor…The Atlantic Intracoastal Waterway enters Sapelo Sound from the northward through South Newport River and continues southward to Doboy Sound through Sapelo River, Front River, Creighton Narrows, and Old Teakettle Creek…A draft of 13 feet can be carried from the deeper waters of Sapelo River into the mouth of Front River, at the head of which a dredged channel through Creighton Narrows offers passage to Old Teakettle Creek and thence to Doboy Sound. Mud River, flowing into the head of Sapelo Sound, is a broad, shallow body of water.

"The coastline from Sapelo Sound to Doboy Sound is formed by the shores of Blackbeard and Sapelo islands. These are separated by Blackbeard Creek, which empties into Cabretta Inlet. From all points of view they appear as a single island and are described as such. Taken together they have a length of 11 miles in a south-southwesterly direction and a width of 4 miles. Large portions of both islands are heavily wooded. These islands present no well-marked distinguishing features, except the usual sand beach backed by dense woods in level outline and the abandoned lighthouse tower near the south point of Sapelo Island. The western part of Sapelo Island consists almost entirely of broad marshes with numerous creeks. Most important of these is Duplin River, which has deep water for several miles and affords means of communications with the island. Sapelo is separated from the marshes lying between it and the mainland by Mud River and New Teakettle Creek. Blackbeard Island is a game refuge under the control of the U.S. Fish and Wildlife Service.

"**Doboy Sound.**—is 45 miles southwestward of Tybee Light and 16 miles northeastward of St. Simons Light. The entrance between Sapelo Island and Wolf Island is about 1 mile wide and obstructed by shifting shoals extending about 4.5 miles offshore... if there is too much sea to cross the bar, vessels are advised to enter via St. Simons Sound and the Intracoastal Waterway. The marked channel over the bar at the entrance to Doboy Sound is not considered safe for strangers with drafts of more than 8 feet and only then under the safest conditions of a rising tide and a smooth sea. The channels are used by local shrimp boats. Pilots are not available. Doboy Sound extends northwestward about 5 miles from the bar with a width of about 0.8 mile. The mean range of tide is about 7 feet in the sound and about 7 ½ feet at Darien. Good anchorage is found anywhere in the channel of the sound upstream from Commodore Island except in the cable area. The Intracoastal Waterway enters Doboy Sound through Old Teakettle Creek and passes southward through North River, Darien River, Rockdedundy River, and Little Mud River to Altamaha Sound. Duplin River, entering Doboy Sound from northward, is a small stream about 5 miles long and good for a reported depth of 10 feet until near its head. A large private dock is on the eastern bank of the river approximately 0.3 mile upstream from the entrance.

Sapelo, a village with a post office on the southerly end of Sapelo Island, is reached by boat going up South End Creek on high tide only. In an emergency some services and supplies can be obtained here. Old Teakettle Creek enters the sound about 1 mile northwestward of Duplin River. It forms a part of the Intracoastal Waterway. A depth of 7 feet can be carried 0.7 mile up Shellbluff Creek to the small packing plant at Valona. The docks are privately owned by a shrimp-boatbuilding yard with a small marine railway for hauling them out. In an emergency, gasoline may be obtained at Valona. Atwood and Hudson creeks are small streams emptying into the head of Doboy Sound from the northwestward. About 10 feet can be taken up Atwood Creek for a distance of 2 miles. Hudson Creek has a depth of 9 feet to the mouth of a small creek leading to a small shrimp packing plant at Meridian Landing. Carnigan Rivers enters the head of the sound and is connected with North River by a branch known as Buzzard Roost Creek. North River enters Doboy Sound west of Doboy Island. It extends westward 6 miles to the village of Ridgeville where it joins May Hall Creek, which, running southward, connects with Darien River 5 miles above its mouth. Doboy Island is wooded and has several buildings on its southwest end. A small private landing is on the west side of the island. Back River, on the southern side of Doboy and Commodore islands, forms another, and little used, entrance from the sound to North and Darien rivers. South River, also little used, empties into Doboy Sound from southwestward about 0.8 mile above the entrance. Darien River runs southwestward for a distance of 11.5 miles were it joins the Altamaha River. The controlling depth from Doboy Sound to Darien is reported to be 8.5 feet. Care is necessary when navigating this river due to the shoals and numerous floating snags. Water is fresh in the Darien River at Darien after the ebb has been running about three hours. Darien is 8.5 miles above Doboy Island on the north bank of the Darien River. It is of little commercial importance. Fishing and pulpwood are the main industries. Shrimp and shad fishermen base here. It has telephone communication and a good highway passes through the town from Savannah to Brunswick, 18 miles away. Gasoline, diesel fuel, ice, fresh water and supplies are procurable. Two marine railways, one owned by a packing company, are capable of hauling our fishing boats up to 55 feet in length and 21 tons in weight. The depth of water alongside the wharves is 7 to 14 feet.

"**Chart 575.**—Between Doboy Sound and Altamaha Sound is Wolf Island, which is about 2.5 miles long in a north-south direction. The island is almost entirely marsh, cut by numerous creeks. Altamaha Sound is 48 miles southwestward of Tybee Light and 12 miles northeastward of St. Simons Light. The entrance and the sound are obstructed by shoals which are dangerous to navigation. It is advisable to enter Altamaha Sound via the Intracoastal Waterway..."[902]

Ice-making was an important factor in the growth of the fishery in the mid-to-late 1940s. It was about that time that Guy H. Amason came to Cedar Point and developed an ice manufacturing plant that provided an immediate lift to the local fishery. Boats could now take on ice to preserve their catches, and thus remain at sea for longer periods of time, trawling for more shrimp when they were "running" as well as conserving fuel by reducing runs back to port. Amason also owned several boats and marketed his own shrimp, and that of others locally, at his Amason Enterprises.

Until the mid-1940s most shrimpers had to haul their nets in by hand using thick manila rope. After the Second World War several innovations emerged to more efficiently facilitate the dragging and recovery of nets, such as powered winches and steel cable. Another technological development was the double-outrigger. By the early 1960s, all of the larger boats were being fitted with double trawl booms to enable them to drag two nets simultaneously rather than one. Like ice-making, these improvements enabled the shrimp fishery to prosper. Also, starting in the 1940s, truck lines began to develop, many being operated primarily for the rapid transport of iced-down boxes of shrimp direct from the docks to processors in Georgia and Florida. Taking the lead locally in the long-distance shipment of local seafood was the Darien firm of L. & W. Trucking Company (Lanasa and Wexler). Starting just after World War II, and managed by

---

[902] *United States Coast Pilot 4, Atlantic Coast, Cape Henry to Key West*, Sixth (1959) Edition (Washington, D.C.: U.S. Department of Commerce, Coast and Geodetic Survey, 1960), 95-96.

Michael W. Lanasa (1912-1967) of Darien, L. & W. Trucking had terminals in Key West and St. Augustine, Florida for a time.

The early 1950s to the mid-1970s was the peak era for the commercial fishery at Cedar Point and Valona, indeed for all of McIntosh County. Burrows acquired wharfage along Cedar Creek in the mid-1950s adjacent to the Amason docks and ice plant. There was a marine railway between the two docks, making this area a center of activity for two decades.

When the Georgia shrimp fishery was developing in the 1920s, two brothers from Valona found themselves in the pioneering forefront. These were Hugh A. Burrows (1903-1975), and Hunter A. Watson (1909-1978), both of whom had become highly-successful shrimpers by the time the industry reached its 1970s peak. Burrows purchased his first shrimp boat at the age of sixteen in 1919. Three years later, he became the youngest towboat captain ever to receive a captain's license in McIntosh County. Burrows, Watson, and Alexander McIntosh Durant (1896-1975) made Valona one of the most prosperous shrimping communities on the southeast coast. It evolved into a community where virtually every family was linked to the commercial shrimping industry.

Meta Atwood (Burrows) Watson (1870-1957), daughter of John McIntosh Atwood of Crescent, was the mother of Valona shrimp fishermen Hugh Burrows and Hunter Watson, and their sister, Lewis Graham. Meta Watson was the matriarch of Valona for the local shrimpers, a mantle that was unofficially passed to her first cousin, May Atwood Kittles Jones, and after 1976, to her daughter, Lewis

Graham.[903] The Valona shrimping influence was further extended by the contributions of Fred Todd, A.M. Durant, and Stuart Atwood, and in the second generation by Lawrence Jacobs, and Peter and George Kittles.

Alexander M. (Alex) Durant was born October 25, 1896 at Meridian, the son of Francis E. and Margaret (McIntosh) Durant. In 1922, he married Mary Virginia Jennings. In 1929 he began shrimping from the docks of Hudson Creek Landing near Meridian. In 1933, Durant began building a fleet of shrimp boats, Durant & Sons, and built a dock and facilities on Shellbluff Creek at Valona. The Durant shrimp docks were built at the oyster cannery formerly on the site, the Shellbluff Canning Company, established at Valona ca. 1905 by Robert and William Strain of Darien. Durant's son, Charles J. Durant (b. 1931), later became the head of Durant Shrimp Company of Valona. After the Second World War, A.M. Durant expanded his business to include operations at Fort Myers, Florida where his son-in-law, Paul Herring, was manager and partner.[904] During the 1950s and 1960s, many of the Durant boats, and other local boats, fished the warmer waters of the Gulf of Mexico; some boats, like those of the Durants, were based out of Fort Myers in the winter season. Other Valona families maintained business interests at Fort Myers, among them the Amason and Hagan families.

Lewis (Burrows) Graham (1898-1995) of Cedar Point, sister of Hugh Burrows and Hunter Watson, and perhaps best remembered for her many years of service as Valona postmaster, recalled the peak years of shrimping in McIntosh County, a livelihood with which she

---

[903] Author's interview with Lewis Graham, Valona, Ga., April 5, 1988.
[904] Author's interview with Charles Durant, April 4, 1988.

Shrimp boats at Durant docks, Shellbluff Creek, Valona, early 1960s.

always had a close connection. She experienced two generations of family shrimpers, and shared her memories with the author:

"They were wonderful days. The days of shrimp fishing when it really meant something in this county. Hugh and Hunter, and all the others, worked awfully hard. They had to work hard to become the successes they were in the local shrimping business. In the early days, the boats stayed out only one day at a time. They didn't have the advantage then of having ice on board to keep their catch cool. Hunter and Hugh and the others would go out in the boats—and they were little boats then—at daybreak. The boats were so small some didn't have a deckhouse. They would haul in their nets by hand, which was terribly hard work. The shrimpers made their coffee and boiled shrimp to eat in little sandbox fires they made on the decks of their boats. They would come home exhausted at the end of the day. Someone on shore would always keep an eye out for the boats in the late afternoon. When the boats were sighted on their way in, someone would drive to Meridian or Crescent or wherever, and pick up the headers. The shrimp would have to be headed and sent out as soon as the boats returned in the late afternoon or the shrimp would spoil. A lot of the heading was done right on the boats on the way in. Valona and Cedar Point were the big ports for the

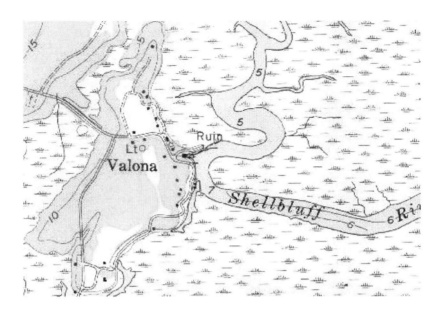

The Valona shrimping community from a 1954 USGS topographic map.

shrimp boats. They always have been—except for Darien, which always had a lot of boats tied up on both sides of the bridge. The creeks going to Valona and Cedar Point out of the sounds were among the few that were deep enough for the shrimpers to use on the lowest tides. Later, the boats started getting bigger. Men began to own more than one boat. The blacks and whites worked together in the industry here and helped each other. Hugh Burrows had all those boats and docks along the creek at Cedar Point. His finest boat was the *Pinta*, 57 feet and about 30 tons, built at DESCO n St. Augustine in the late 1950s. She was the beauty of all the McIntosh County shrimp boats. The *Pinta* was the boat Hugh fished himself, but he had several others.[32] Two of them were the *Franchel* and the *Gaius*, both about 45 feet. Hunter Watson had his own docks at Valona there on the creek across the way from Alex Durant's docks. In the 1950s and 60s, like Hugh, he was at the top of his profession. One of his bigger boats was the *Chief*. It fitted him. He also had the *Mar-Gin*, and the *Adventure*, both close to sixty feet. Those were all wonderful boats. But the biggest shrimp boat anybody had ever seen hereabouts up to that time was probably the *Miss Valona*, a big 62-footer, which Mr. [J.A.] Radford, who ran the store at Valona, had built about 1959 or 1960."

By the late 1990s, there were third-and-fourth generation shrimpers in McIntosh County. By then, however, it was difficult to prosper in the industry due to the rising costs of fuel, maintenance, and marine insurance (for those who could afford it), and worst of all, the growing preponderance of imported shrimp from distant countries, which severely undercut the domestic markets on the south Atlantic and Gulf coasts. By 2000, the industry was only a shadow of its former self—as demonstrated in the statistics. Georgia shrimp landings went from 16 million pounds in 1960, to 2 million pounds in 2003; the number of licensed Georgia trawlers went from a high of 1,500 in 1978 to a mere 246 in 2013—the lowest number of vessels operating since the 1920s.[905]

Charting the Coast of McIntosh County

Any discussion of coastal maritime history must include the role played by the charting of the waters and provision of navigational aids for mariners. The effort to chart America's inland and offshore waters was initiated by the federal government in 1807 with the creation of the United States Coast Survey. By the mid-nineteenth century the government was conducting surveys of the Georgia coast, as witness the 1855 issuance by the Coast Survey of a "Reconnaissance of Doboy Bar and Inlet, Georgia," the earliest government navigational aid for waters in McIntosh County. The reconnaissance chart was a preliminary survey by a hydrographic party under the command of Lieutenant T.A. Craven, USN, and was compiled on a scale of 1:40,000. This chart was preliminary to the

---

[905] Data extracted from annual commercial fishery reports, Coastal Resources Division, GDNR.

issuance of a planned finished chart for Doboy and Altamaha sounds. The Civil War intervened and the first edition of the Doboy Sound chart was not completed until 1871.

The 1855 chart of the Atlantic approaches to Doboy Sound (fig. 13), and the lower section of the Sound itself, demonstrates that the nineteenth century work of the Coast Survey was remarkably accurate, considering the then-limited scientific resources with which the Survey had to work. Soundings were made and recorded with the use of elementary lead-lines heaved by hand by a no doubt poorly-paid leadsman while a Coast Survey official, perhaps Lieut. Craven himself, dutifully recorded the depths as they were announced.[906]

The early Doboy chart, though limited in the area it covers, is nonetheless interesting for the water and land features it delineates. In 1855, the Atlantic approaches to Doboy Sound were such that even the best mariners were tested. The North Breakers and the South Breakers protected the entrance offshore about two and a half miles from the southern tip of Sapelo Island. The pilots had to use caution in their approach by not allowing too much of a northerly drift when nearing the entrance, for a pair of dangerous shoals jutted out from the southern tip of Sapelo to about two miles offshore. These were Chimney Spit closer inshore, and Pelican Spit further out. The Wolf Island beacon is shown as being less than a mile south of the northernmost tip of the Wolf Island beach. "Sandy Plains" are indicated on the lower end of Sapelo's Nanny Goat Beach. The

---

[906] The technical and scientific aspects of the nineteenth century work of the Coast Survey are thoroughly covered in Albert E. Theberge, *The Coast Survey, 1807-1867* (Washington, D.C.: National Oceanic and Atmospheric Administration, np., 2001). Available online at www.lib.noaa.gov/edocs/Bache4.htm

lighthouse is shown on a sand spit rimmed by salt marsh less than a mile from Doboy Sound's entrance. Symbols for buildings are delineated on the south end of Sapelo as well as on Doboy Island. Northeast of the Doboy docks where North River empties into the sound on the point of what later came to be known as Rock Island is "Grass Point." Less than a mile southeast of Grass Point is Shoal Point, shown as being on the Doboy Sound side of Commodore Island.

In 1857, the Coast Survey issued a topographical map of Sapelo Island, followed a year later by a topographical and hydrographic survey of the Sapelo Sound region. While not a navigational chart, the topographic map of Sapelo, aspects of which are discussed in chapter 4, is useful for its delineation of agricultural fields and plantation infrastructure before the Civil War.[907] In 1859, a finished navigation chart for Sapelo Sound, including topographical features, was issued, this being the Coast Survey's first edition of Chart No. 444, for Sapelo Sound. The chart reveals a number of notable features. Mud River is shown as the same, broad, shallow estuary that it is today. Dog Hammock is delineated. Symbols of buildings identified with the legend "Brailsford plantation" are shown at Sutherland's Bluff on the Sapelo River. Front River, east of Creighton Island, is shown tapering out to a dead end in the marsh just below the southern tip of Creighton. Fifty years later, the government would dredge a channel through the marsh and the stream known as "Scott's Creek," the end result being a new route for the intracoastal waterway into the South Sapelo River and the

---

[907] U.S. Coast Survey, *Topographical Reconnaissance of Sapelo Island, Georgia,* 1857, Register No. 678, RG 23, NARA.

Dividings, thus bypassing shallow Mud River. The chart shows the upper section of Sapelo Island, delineating fields of cultivation, Chocolate plantation and High Point. Creighton Island is delineated in the same general configuration that it retains today. The upper third of the island, in addition to a strip along the eastern side and a portion at the southern tip, are all shown to be under cultivation. Creighton was owned in 1859 by William Cooke, son-in-law of Thomas Spalding. Buildings are shown on Creighton's upper end, delineating a slave settlement. Also shown is a short causeway leading to a wharf on the Back River at Creighton's northwest tip.[908]

The Civil War interrupted the Coast Survey's charting of Georgia waters, but after the war, topographic and hydrographic surveys were resumed and maps and charts were issued based on the findings. The Coast Survey issued its first topographical map for Doboy Sound in 1868, features of which will be discussed below. The map is useful for delineating the configurations of Doboy Island buildings, Hird Island, Union Island, and other aspects of the coast and marsh hammocks from Cedar Point southward to the Ridge.[909] Similar surveys were issued in 1869 for Darien[910] and Altamaha Sound.[911] The Altamaha Sound map, discussed earlier, defined the upper half of St. Simons Island, the Altamaha estuary, Wolf Island and Buttermilk Sound. The Doboy Sound survey displayed most of Sapelo Island and the waterways and islands westward to the

---

[908] U.S. Coast Survey, *Sapelo Sound, Georgia*, No. 444, 1859, RG 23, NARA.
[909] U.S. Coast Survey, *Doboy Sound & Vicinity, Georgia*, 1868, Register No. 1080, RG 23, NARA.
[910] U.S. Coast Survey, *City of Darien and Vicinity, Georgia*, 1869, Register No. 1114 bis., RG 23, NARA.
[911] U.S. Coast Survey, *Altamaha Sound and Vicinity, Georgia*, 1869, Register No. 1114, RG 23, NARA.

mainland. In 1871 the first of a series of four harbor charts were issued by the Coast Survey for Doboy and Altamaha sounds, Chart No. 446. The 1871 chart, a companion chart to the Sapelo Sound chart issued a dozen years earlier, was especially timely as it provided information to the increasing numbers of foreign and domestic ships arriving in Doboy Sound during the postbellum period. The chart was based on the two topographic maps of 1868 and 1869 of Doboy and Altamaha sounds, as well as the 1855 reconnaissance chart of Doboy Sound referenced earlier.[912]

The 1871 Doboy Sound chart has some interesting features, especially as it defines the Darien River below Darien as being considerably wider and deeper than it is now. The river is quite wide as it passes Lower Bluff and the Hilton mill at old Fort King George. Timber ships, mostly coasting schooners with less draft than the ocean-going square-riggers, could sail directly to Lower Bluff to load lumber. Pico Cut is shown, but much narrower than today. The passage past Lower Bluff has long since filled with marsh as the tidal course of the Darien River has carved a wider gap through Pico, resulting in the hairpin loop past Lower Bluff to become merely a small creek. Black Island is shown in 1871 to be smaller than on modern charts. Union Island across from Blue and Hall Landing is identified in 1871 as Pumpkin Hammock, and continued to be on government charts and maps into the 1900s. There was another Pumpkin Hammock on the Duplin River on Sapelo Island. Subsequent editions of the Doboy Sound-Altamaha Sound Chart No. 446 were issued in 1875, 1879 and 1897.

---

[912] U.S. Coast Survey, *Doboy and Altamaha Sounds, Georgia*, No. 446, 1871, RG 23, NARA.

The Coast Survey's systematic charting of coastal waters after the war is amply documented. Several references appear in the *Savannah Morning News* in 1869 and early 1870 citing the U.S. revenue vessel *Nansemond* in company with the Coast Survey schooner *Bache* conducting surveys of the Georgia and lower South Carolina coasts. The personnel of the *Bache* were implementing charting and hydrographic surveys of the coastal sounds and rivers. The *Nansemond* is referred to in the McKinley journal as having been in Sapelo Sound for a period of time. It was not until 1905, when timber activity had reached a peak in the Sapelo and Front rivers, that a second edition of the 1859 Sapelo Sound chart was issued. In 1878, the Coast Survey was re-designated as the Coast and Geodetic Survey. Later, the agency revised its chart numbering system. A new harbor chart, future editions of which are still in use by local mariners, was issued in 1927 by the Coast and Geodetic Survey (fig. 68). Entitled "Sapelo and Doboy Sounds, Georgia," the new chart combined the earlier 444-446 charts of Sapelo and Doboy sounds, and was the first of the No. 574 series which evolved into the 11510 series of the same chart in the 1970s. This was the first chart to display all of Sapelo and Blackbeard islands on one chart as well as the first with Sapelo and Doboy sounds together, but it did not have Altamaha Sound, that being issued separately as new chart No. 575.[913]

Another series of Coast Survey charts was issued in the mid-1870s, based on 1860s surveys. The first of these was a chart delineating the upper Georgia coast, "Savannah to Sapelo Island,"

---

[913] U.S. Coast and Geodetic Survey, *Sapelo and Doboy Sounds, Georgia*, No. 574, 1927, RG 23, NARA.

issued in 1874 as coast chart No. 156. In 1876, the companion chart for the lower half of the Georgia coast was issued as No. 157, titled "Sapelo Island to Amelia Island." Subsequent editions of these charts were issued by the Coast and Geodetic Survey in the 1880s, then yet another series of them in 1895 and 1900. New hydrographic surveys of Sapelo Sound were conducted in 1902, preparatory to the issuance of the 1905 harbor chart for that inlet. Additional hydrographic and topographic surveys were made in 1924 and 1925 of Doboy and Altamaha sounds, the results of which provided the basis for the first edition of the 1927 chart for Sapelo and Doboy sounds.

An examination of the charts enables a clearer understanding of how the waterways have played such a crucial role in the maritime and economic development of coastal Georgia, an application that pertains to the lessons of war as well as peace, and perhaps best exemplified by a U.S. Coast Survey chart of the entire Georgia coast, from the Savannah River to the St. Marys River issued in 1861. This overview chart perfectly illustrates the difficult task facing the Union Navy in imposing its blockade in the war years. Confederate blockade runners kept naval officers guessing much of the time as they could choose to depart, or enter any number of the inlets, sounds, rivers and creeks along the Georgia and upper Florida coasts. There were never enough warships adequate to the task of monitoring the embayments and the runners the U.S. Navy did catch was often attributable to good intelligence networks or luck.

Doboy Sound & Vicinity, Georgia, 1868–a topographical map on a scale of 1:20,000–will now be accorded closer scrutiny as its relevance to the discussions in the last several chapters has been made clear. Several features are of interest. The map shows the original causeway to Marsh Landing at the south end of Sapelo Island in the precise position it is presently located. Also shown is a plank walk, or causeway, through the marsh connecting the south end of Sapelo's mainland at the present site of the Marine Institute to the lighthouse island. The causeway is shown as a straight line and generally parallels South End Creek. It is no longer in existence. In 2014, the author walked the area where the causeway began and, via a modern wooden research boardwalk through the marsh, covered about half the distance to the lighthouse island along the same path of the causeway shown on the 1868 topo map. Interestingly, this plank walk-causeway is not delineated on the 1857 topographic map of Sapelo. On the mainland, the 1868 map depicts buildings at the "Thicket" on the site of the antebellum sugar mill, and accessed by "Thicket River" (later Crum Creek). Other features are docks and buildings at Doboy Island and Blue and Hall Landing, the Carnigan River (spelled "Connegan" on the map), connected to North River (fig. 36) by Buzzard Roost Creek, Union Island, Black Island, "Herd" Island "My Hall" River and "The Ridge." "Grass Knoll" is identified as the area later known as Baywood; Atwood and Hudson rivers are identified, as is "Cedar Point" and "Manchester." Shell Bluff Creek is delineated as flowing from the head of Old Teakettle Creek to the eastern side of Manchester. The shoreline has changed in the nearly 150 years since 1868. The south end of Sapelo has an altogether different appearance on the old map. Since 1868, the natural north-south shifting of the barrier island beach has resulted in considerable buildup of sand and mud flats on the south end of Nanny Goat Beach. The map shows Cabretta Island on the seaward side of Sapelo as being an entity to itself. Then, a boater could circumnavigate Cabretta by entering an inlet into Cabretta Creek and going north through the marsh until exiting into Blackbeard Creek at the entrance to Cabretta Inlet. This could be done as recently as the 1930s. Now much of Cabretta Creek has filled in and only marsh separates Cabretta and Sapelo. The 1868 map identifies a similar shifting on the north end of Wolf Island below Sapelo. The upper end of Wolf has undergone considerable alteration, particularly around Beacon Creek.

The Inland Passage—The navigational benefits of the inland waterway have long been recognized. The sheltered passage inside the barrier islands from Charleston to the St. Johns River has always been an ideal conveyor for coastal watermen. As noted several times in the McKinley journal excerpts in the previous chapter the seaward passage outside the islands often had rough seas and was challenging for all but the largest vessels. There are numerous instances of vessels wrecked or disabled either approaching, or inside the exposed sounds separating the barrier islands, embayments that in reality are more like extensions of the open sea. For the movement of commerce and passengers in the nineteenth century, the inland passage was therefore extremely important. Recognizing the importance of the inland waterway, the federal government in the late 1800s and early 1900s began dredging operations and issuing navigational aids to mariners utilizing the passage.

There was much small-vessel traffic on the inland passage between Charleston and the St. Johns in the postbellum period, chiefly cargo-carrying sailing boats, steamboats, and steam tugboats performing a variety of tasks. The larger sailing vessels, and steamships later, utilized the outside route where their size enabled them to better handle the rougher waters of the open sea. Especially helpful to mariners were the coast pilot volumes issued by the U.S. Coast and Geodetic Survey.[914] For Georgia, the 1885 edition of the *Atlantic Local Coast Pilot, Sub-Division 20, Winyah Bay to Savannah,* and Sub-division 21 in the series, *Tybee Roads to Jupiter Inlet* were detailed aids. Sub-division 20 covered the "Inside Passage to Fernandina." In the late nineteenth century, the U.S. Army Corps of Engineers implemented a systematic program of dredging the channels of the Georgia inland passage to meet the demands of increased use by larger vessels.

In 1918-19, a Compilation and Field Inspection by the Department Engineer of the U.S. Army Corps of Engineers resulted in the production in 1920-21 of a series of Grid Zone Tactical Maps of coastal areas. The "five-thousand yard grid system progressive maps" were compiled with overlays of U.S. Coast and Geodetic Survey charts and U.S. Geological Survey maps for the period. Four of the maps entailed areas of McIntosh County, and a number of features bear noting as they define the county's 1920s geography. The Darien Quadrangle map shows the Georgia Coast & Piedmont Railroad running north to south through the county from Oak Hill west of Cedar Point along roughly the route now covered by highway 99. The siding at Broadfield is shown; and a spur track to the Lower Bluff sawmill east of Darien. Just east of Ridgeville is "Pumpkin Hammock" with a benchmark

---

[914] U.S. Coast and Geodetic Survey, *Atlantic Local Coast Pilot, Sub-Division 20, Winyah Bay to Savannah, with the Inland Passage to Fernandina,* 1885; and U.S. Coast and Geodetic Survey, *Atlantic Local Coast Pilot, Sub-Division 21, Tybee Roads to Jupiter Inlet,* 1885 (Washington, D.C.: Government Printing Office), originals in RG 23, NARA. These editions were succeeded by U.S. Coast and Geodetic Survey, *United States Coast Pilot, Atlantic Coast, Section D, Cape Henry to Key West,* first edition, 1913, and second edition, 1922.

noted as "Union Island Chimney." Further east, another benchmark on the north end of Hird Island is identified as "Aikens." Further east, at Rock Island on the North River just northwest of the upper end of Doboy Island is a benchmark labeled "Cane Creek Tank." On Doboy itself is "Doboy Island Stack" and "Doboy White Chimney." On the lower end of Sapelo Island, the abandoned brick lighthouse is delineated with the new lighthouse slightly northeast. A benchmark, "Spalding," is west of Shell Hammock. Artesian wells are marked at Cedar Point, Manchester, Valona, Meridian, north end of Hird Island, Doboy Island, south end of Black Island; and on Sapelo Island at Long Tabby, Marsh Landing, South End Creek, and the lighthouse island. On Wolf Island, the grid map shows the "old tower" of the abandoned Wolf Island beacon. Near the mouth of Beacon Creek are several channel range lights and, on the south end of the beach, the abandoned Wolf Island clubhouse.

The two adjoining Corps maps to the north are the Sapelo River and South Newport River quadrangles, published in 1920. They delineate areas then or formerly under cultivation on the upper end of Harris Neck, Barbour Island, several tracts on the road between Harris Neck and South Newport, Bruro Neck, the upper White Chimney River, part of Creighton Island, and land along the Cowhorn Road between Crescent and Eulonia. "Crescent Sta. P.O." is delineated at the curve of the G.C. & P. as it turns westward. Buildings are shown at Sutherland's Bluff, the upper end of Creighton, the south end of Harris Neck near the Julianton River, and on Front River at the former timber loading hammocks. "Sapelo" is delineated on the bend of the Front River east of Creighton. The town of Fairhope is shown, but not the railroad spur as the tracks were removed before the field inspection was made. Above Eulonia Station, the "Head of Navigation" of the Sapelo River is delineated. West of the "Dixie Highway" the G.C. & P. tracks go northwest from Eulonia to "Warsaw (Old Darien Jc.)" where buildings are shown around the intersection with the Seaboard Air Line tracks. Other buildings are shown at the former site of the Brickstone factory up the Seaboard track, and structures and two artesian wells appear at Jones Station. Between Warsaw and the Dixie Highway is Young's Island where several structures are shown. A tract of land abutting the west side of the Dixie Highway and fronting the marsh at South Newport is shown to be under cultivation.

The Atlantic Intracoastal Waterway

Transportation and economic considerations on the upper Georgia coast in the nineteenth and early twentieth centuries were heavily dependent on navigation of the local waterways. To the west of Ossabaw Island is the inland passage, a natural water conveyor for maritime traffic in both pre-historic and historic times. From south to north the inland waterway transited Ossabaw from St. Catherines Sound into the Bear River thence through Florida Passage, Ossabaw Sound and Hell Gate into the waterways south of Savannah.

In the decades following the Civil War, steamboats and sail-powered craft frequently utilized the calmer waters of the inland passage to and from the Savannah port. One problematic section of the waterway passed through an area known as Romerly Marsh between Skidaway and Wassaw islands in linking Ossabaw and Wassaw sounds. This was a difficult passage for vessels to navigate on much less than a high tide as the route transited shallow sections east of Skidaway through Odingsells River, and then into Ossabaw Sound going south. Deeper draft vessels were compelled to utilize the deeper waters off the seaward sides of the barrier islands. One government report about Romerly Marsh noted that "vessels drawing five feet of water cannot pass through on less than half-tide."[915] In 1880, the U.S. Army Corps of Engineers investigated several alternative routes to facilitate easier passage from Romerly Marsh to and from Ossabaw Sound. The importance of maintaining proper depth of the inland waterway was emphasized in the Corps' Annual Report for 1881:

> "...[T]he inside passage between Savannah and Jacksonville is a valuable water route for the transit of passengers. Properly improved, it would furnish cheap and convenient transportation for the merchandise required and the products of the field and forest produced by a population covering an area of at least 10,000 square miles by affording a sheltered passage to light-draught vessels that could not venture upon the outside passage. The distance between Savannah and the Saint Johns River is over 200 miles [sic], and the route traverses numerous sounds and navigable creeks and rivers, penetrating far into the interior of the coastal district. Its value is emphasized when the United States becoming involved with a maritime power is taken into consideration."[916]

In 1866, George Parsons purchased Wassaw, a barrier island between Tybee and Little Tybee to its north and Ossabaw to the south. Wassaw was bordered on its western (inland) side by Romerly Marsh. West of Romerly Marsh was the south end of Skidaway Island, a sizeable "back-barrier" island much of which at the time was owned by the Waring family of Savannah. There was a dock, Waring's Landing, that provided access through Romerly Marsh to Odingsells

---

[915] Washington, D.C.: U.S. Army Corps of Engineers, *Annual Report of the Chief of Engineers*, v. 19 (1881), "Examination of Romney [sic] Marsh, Georgia," 1160.
[916] Ibid., 1161-62.

River.[917] The federal River and Harbor Act of 1882 opted for a Romerly Marsh inland waterway passage which, by means of dredging a cut through the Wassaw Island marsh, entailed a connection of Dead Man's Hammock Creek with Wassaw Creek north of Odingsells River. This longer, more expensive, transit which bypassed the previous route through Steamboat Cut, was presumably selected to satisfy local commercial interests that preferred improved access to the Wassaw Island beaches that the route provided via Wassaw Creek for the Georgia and Florida Steamship Company, which regularly transported passengers to the island.[918]

In 1884, New Cut was dredged through Long Island amid the Wassaw marshes immediately west of the main island to improve the passage via Wassaw Creek to the Odingsells River, thence into Ossabaw Sound. This route thus bypassed the former route, further west, through Romerly Marsh and Adams Creek at the southern tip of Skidaway Island. During 1885-86 New Cut was again dredged after an acrimonious dispute between the Savannah District Corps of Engineers and the Florida Railway and Navigation Company, which ran steamers from Savannah to Fernandina, Florida via the inland waterway. Supplemented by a contribution from George Parsons, the steamboat company provided $10,000 to facilitate the dredging work. Parsons wished to improve access to Wassaw for his naphtha

---

[917] V.E. Kelly, *A Short History of Skidaway Island* (Savannah, Ga.: The Branigar Organization, 2nd edit., 1994), 90.
[918] William P. Tinkler, *The Atlantic Intracoastal Waterway in Georgia: A Study of Its History, Maintenance and Present Use* (Brunswick, Ga.: Georgia Department of Natural Resources, 1978), 6.

launches going to the island from Savannah, primarily to his family compound at Cedar Landing on the northwest side of the island.[919]

With private interests thus providing the funding and the Corps supervising the dredging, the New Cut project was completed in April 1886. The new passage was given the unofficial name of "Parsons Cut." It was a channel cut 4,117 feet through the Wassaw marshes and Long Island; yet in the two decades of its use as the primary inside route it was never considered a particularly satisfactory, nor convenient, passage.[920]

The utilization of naphtha launches makes an interesting adjunct to this narrative as they were frequently seen on the inland waterways of postbellum coastal Georgia, particularly in the waters around Chatham County. Joseph Parsons of Wassaw, son of George Parsons, recalled these vessels and their operations around Wassaw in the 1880s:

"...These first naphtha boats were not [propelled by] internal combustion engines, but burned naphtha under a coil burner. The same naphtha circulated in the coil and generated pressure on the same principle as the steam engine. They were extremely unreliable and gave a great deal of trouble, but were a very great improvement on sail and oars. Those early motorboats were built on sailing yacht lines, with sterns cut away under water so that the more

---

[919] "Capsule Review of Wassaw Island History, A Compilation of Information from Wassaw Island Logs, Correspondence, Scrapbooks and Recollections," unpub. ms., no date.

[920] Corps of Engineers, *Annual Report*, v. 26, pt. 1 (1886), "Improvement of Romerly Marsh, Georgia," 1103-05. Monitoring and maintenance in the years after the passage opened revealed troublesome deficiencies with the route largely due to frequent shoaling in Wassaw Creek.

power applied the more they settled aft. They could not make more than six to eight miles an hour."[921]

The River and Harbor Act of September 1890 authorized the Corps of Engineers to conduct a survey of "the inside route between Savannah, Georgia and Fernandina, Florida with a view of obtaining a steamboat channel of seven foot depth at mean low water."[922] This survey, which investigated channel improvement along the full length of the Georgia coast, is regarded as the beginning of the federal Atlantic Intracoastal Waterway Project. The 1890 survey proposed a single project for improving four navigationally difficult sections of the existing passage: Romerly Marsh in Chatham County, Mud River and Little Mud River in McIntosh County, and Jekyll Creek in Glynn County. The survey further recommended that an improved—and shorter by about five miles—Romerly Marsh route west of New Cut be dredged through the marsh from Habersham Creek into Odingsells River. The survey added that "had not the opening of the Wassaw Creek route been made mandatory by Congress that route would not have been selected by the engineers" and proposed that the New Cut route be abandoned in favor of the Habersham Creek route.[923] Despite the shorter distance the recommendation was not accepted. The Corps' report reiterated the utility of an improved inland passage along the Georgia coast:

---

[921] Elizabeth D. McMaster, Wassaw: The Story of an Island (privately printed, 1974), 82.
[922] Corps of Engineers, *Annual Report*, v. 32, pt. 2 (1892), "Preliminary Examination of Inside Route Between Savannah, Georgia and Fernandina, Florida," 1309.
[923] Ibid., 1315.

"A regular line of steamers plies the entire route, making semiweekly trips. Another line is established between Savannah, Darien and Brunswick, making three trips per week…The steamers carry passengers as well as freight. There are also a small number of freight steamers making irregular but frequent trips between the Ogeechee, Altamaha and Satilla rivers, and the ports of Savannah, Darien and Brunswick. Other small steamers are engaged in the oyster and fishing business, and ply between the numerous oyster beds and fishing grounds along the inside route…A large fleet of sloops and schooners of from 25 to 50 tons burden bring oysters, fish, rice and shells from points along the inside route to the cities, and a number of barges towed by tugboats, are used in transporting the products of the sea and of coastal plantations to the city markets. Large vessels are often towed from port to port without cargo or ballast by the inside route thus avoiding rough weather at sea. About 25 million feet of lumber are annually rafted and towed from the mouth of the Altamaha River to Sapelo Sound and St. Simons Sound for shipment in deep-draft vessels to foreign ports. The freights carried outward from the cities along the inside route are mainly general merchandise, commercial fertilizers and guano, mill and camp supplies. The freights collected along the route and brought to the cities consist of cotton, rice, naval stores, vegetables, fruit, oysters, fish and shells…"[924]

By the turn of the twentieth century, the navigational problems associated with the Romerly Marsh cuts led to the Corps of Engineers conducting a reevaluation of the Atlantic Intracoastal Waterway (AICW) in the Ossabaw Sound area. The Emergency River and Harbor Act of June 6, 1900 authorized a "preliminary examination and survey of the Skiddaway [sic] Narrows connecting the Isle of Hope with Burnside River for a channel 75 feet wide and

---

[924] Ibid., 1323-25.

6 feet deep at mean low water."[925] Regarding this potential new passage along the west side of Skidaway Island, the Corps' survey noted that "the present navigable route through Skiddaway Narrows consists of an extremely tortuous and very narrow channel, the bottom of which is bare at low water and at high water an ordinary row boat cannot pass through the channel without the oars being interfered with on both sides from the marsh grass growing on the banks." The District Engineer further noted that "local commerce is too small to justify a cut through the Narrows, which would be nearly 2 miles long...Skiddaway Narrows is not worthy of improvement by the United States."[926]

Although the 1900 survey recommended this route not be improved for use as part of the AICW, a resurvey three years later reversed the earlier finding and opted for the dredging and widening of the Skidaway Narrows route. This passage to Ossabaw Sound was much shorter than the route to the Sound via New Cut and Wassaw Creek then in use. The District Engineer recommended on August 12, 1903 that the project be expedited since it provided a passage that

> "is 6 ½ miles shorter than the present route by way of Parsons [New] Cut and Wassaw Creek. It is much further inland and better protected from storms such as interfere with navigation by small boats of the open areas in Ossabaw and Wassaw Sounds. It is capable of being made secure from enterprises of an enemy in time of war, and therefore

---

[925] Corps of Engineers, *Annual Report*, v. 42 (1901), "Preliminary Examination of Skiddaway Narrows, Georgia," 1729.
[926] Ibid.

possesses a valuable military advantage over all other routes."[927]

Congress authorized the project and the contract dredging of Skidaway Narrows began in October 1905. The new route thus provided a secure inside passage between Skidaway Island and the Isle of Hope connecting Skidaway River on the north to Burnside River on the south, thence to Vernon River and into Ossabaw Sound via Hell Gate, a passage that remains a component of the AICW to the present day.[928]

In McIntosh County, the Corps' resurvey of 1908, based on earlier recommendations, proposed an alternative route for a portion of the waterway, this being to bypass the Mud River route west of Sapelo Island altogether, and adopt a new route east of Creighton Island from Sapelo Sound to Front River, thence into Scott's Creek. A channel through Scott's Creek, later designated as Creighton Narrows, would be dredged to connect Front River with South Sapelo River (Crescent River), and thence into Old Teakettle Creek at its juncture with the lower end of Mud River at the Dividings. The passage would be three miles longer than the old route but would cost considerably less to maintain as Mud River required constant dredging. The Creighton Narrows route would provide "a good connection between Darien and the timber wharves on Front River from which a very

---

[927] U.S. House of Representatives, Doc. No. 450, Fifty-eighth Congress, 2nd Session, 1904, "Skidaway Narrows, Georgia" (Washington, D.C.: Government Printing Office), 3.
[928] Corps of Engineers, Annual Report, v. 66, pt. 2 (1906), "Improvements of Skidaway Narrows, Georgia," 1210.

large amount of lumber is shipped."[929]

When the 1908 resurvey was conducted, Darien's timber trade was in decline, although vessels with lumber consigned to European ports still utilized the Front River loading grounds at Sapelo Sound.

There is local documentation relating to this new leg of the inland passage by which the Atwood family granted the Corps of Engineers dredging rights through Scott's Creek and the marsh below Creighton, which the Atwoods owned. In December 1912, Henry G. Atwood, et al. did

"grant unto the United States, under authority of Congress, the right to construct and perpetually maintain a cut or canal four hundred feet in width for the purpose of navigation connecting South Sapelo River and Front River along the following described lines, viz: beginning at low water line on the north shore of South Sapelo River near approximately two thousand feet northwest of its junction with Old Teakettle, commonly known as the Dividings. Together with the right to deposit the soil from the said cut or canal [Creighton Narrows] upon the lands adjoining the cut or canal owned by J.M. Atwood et al. and together with such other rights or privileges as may enable the United States to properly construct and perpetually maintain said cut or canal."[930]

Work on the new route was in progress in 1913. The *U.S. Coast Pilot*, 1913 edition, notes that "Improvements are authorized to dredge a cut from near the head of Front River to Old Teakettle Creek, and this will form the inland passage to Doboy Sound. When these improvements are completed the inland route by way of Mud River and New Teakettle Creek will be abandoned. Mud River enters the head of Sapelo Sound from southward; it is a broad, shallow body of water with a channel depth of 7 feet marked by range beacons, and is important only as a part of the inland passage between

---

[929] U.S. House of Representatives, Document No. 1236, Sixtieth Congress, 2nd Session, *Savannah-Fernandina Waterway,* 1904, GPO, Washington, D.C., 5; Tinkler, *AICW Project,* 18.
[930] Deed Book L (1912), 56, RMCG.

Savannah and Fernandina. When the passage by way of Front River is completed, this route will be abandoned."[931] The Creighton Narrows route was complete and had been in use several years, as noted in the 1922 edition of the *Coast Pilot*: "At the head of Front River a canal 6 feet deep has been dredged to Old Teakettle Creek, and this forms a part of the inland route to Doboy Sound. Mud River: No further dredging will be done to maintain this depth, as the present inland route leads through Front River."[932]

The River and Harbor Act of March 1913 authorized a survey and cost analysis for the improvement of Generals Cut connecting the Butler River with the Darien River. A January 1914 Corps of Engineers report described Generals Cut as being "a small, straight canal, about 2,000 feet in length which, in connection with certain small creeks, constitutes a useful waterway for small boats from Darien across the delta of the Altamaha River."[933] A project to remove logs and stumps from Generals Cut was authorized in March 1919. The River and Harbor Act of June 1938 authorized the last major improvements to the Intracoastal Waterway in Georgia. These included the deepening of the channel from seven to twelve feet from

---

[931] U.S. Coast and Geodetic Survey, *United States Coast Pilot, Atlantic Coast, Section D, Cape Henry to Key West*, 1st edition, 1913 (Washington, D.C.: Government Printing Office, 1913).
[932] Ibid., 2nd (1922) edition.
[933] U.S. House of Representatives, Document No. 581, Sixty-third Congress, 2nd Session, "General's Cut, Georgia," 2; Tinkler, *AICW Project*, 21.

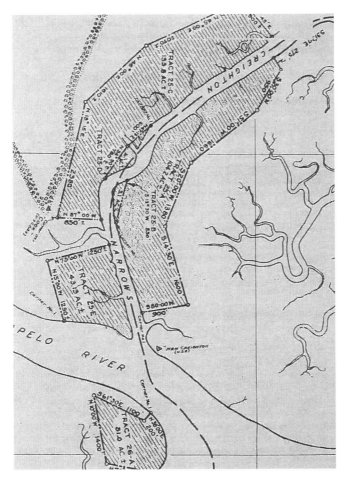

Dredge spoil survey for the shores of Creighton Narrows, 1939.

Savannah to Fernandina, and stipulating that "local interests shall furnish without cost to the United States, all necessary rights of way and spoil disposal areas for construction and maintenance of said Intracoastal Waterway."[934]

The Act provided a uniform twelve-foot inside channel from Norfolk, Virginia to Jacksonville, Florida to facilitate the movement

---

[934] U.S. House of Representatives, Document No. 618, Seventy-fifth Congress, 3rd Session, 1938, *Cape Fear River, N.C. to St. Johns River, Fla., Intracoastal Waterway.*

of bulk cargoes on tugboat-propelled barges which, by then, had become a common method of transporting industrial goods.

In 1939, dredge spoil disposal areas were acquired by the federal government on that portion of the AICW comprising Creighton Narrows. The deed dated September 19, 1939, with an accompanying survey map (fig. 77), noted that

> "Whereas, the Congress has, by the River and Harbor Act approved June 20, 1938, authorized the construction of the Intracoastal Waterway to a project depth of 12 feet from Savannah, Georgia to Cumberland Sound, Georgia, in accordance with the project described in House Document No. 618, 75th Congress, Third Session. Whereas, E. M. and H. G. Atwood, hereinafter called the Grantors, are the owners in fee simple of a tract more particularly described as beginning at Corner No. 1, not monumented, which is on the low water line of the eastern bank of Creighton Narrows; from this point U.S. Engineer Department survey station 'New Creighton' bears S 25 degrees - 00' E, 800 feet distant, thence northwesterly along the low water line of the eastern bank of Creighton Narrows approximately 1850 feet to a point not monumented. The tract or parcel contains 104.2 acres, more or less. [The grantors] release unto the United States of America the right and easement to enter upon, occupy and use any portion of the tract for the deposit of any and all spoil or other matter excavated in the construction and maintenance of the aforesaid waterway and its appurtenances."[935]

Increasing numbers of barges towed by tugs were utilizing the Intracoastal Waterway between Jacksonville, Savannah and the north. The channel deepening enabled deeper-draft vessels to use the waterway and thus enable the more efficient movement of bulk cargoes between Philadelphia and Jacksonville. Shipments of railroad ties, lumber and other naval stores products were transported north on the AICW prior to World War II with shipments south including iron, steel, roofing, and oil. Gus Stein, Jr. (1878-1957) was a McIntosh County pilot at the Ridge who for several years was the captain of R.J. Reynolds' yacht *Zapala*. Stein was an advocate of the

---

[935] Deed Book 9 (1939), 571-72, RMCG.

improvement and increased usage of the AICW in the 1930s and 1940s, and piloted numerous vessels on the waterway in his long maritime career.

A restricted war edition publication about the AICW issued by the Corps of Engineers in 1943 with limited distribution to tugboat pilots and navigators, noted:

"The commerce south of Norfolk is truly that of an intracoastal waterway, carried on towed barges and small freight boats. In 1941 over 3,700,000 tons of freight were transported on the waterway south of Norfolk. The principal commodities so transported were sand, rock, gravel, pulpwood, gasoline, fuel oil, and other petroleum products, lumber, cross ties, and other processed wood products, logs, piling, poles, fertilizers, fish and oysters, coal, iron and steel, tobacco, and groceries. The oil barge program – Under a program approved by the War Production Board the Corps of Engineers is carrying out a project providing for the construction of a fleet of barges, tugs and towboats for use in transporting oil to the east coast. The barges will be used for moving oil from the Texas oil fields, along the Gulf Intracoastal Waterway to Panama City, Florida, across the state by tank car to Jacksonville, Florida, and thence by barge along the Atlantic Intracoastal Waterway to distribution terminals. The fleet will consist of 500 oil barges, 100 tugboats, and 21 river tugboats."[936]

After World War II increasing numbers of pleasure craft utilized the waterway, benefiting from the 12-foot channel. Commercial towing companies reached their peak of activity in the 1950s and early 1960s with the large amounts of pulpwood, freight, heavy equipment and other materials shipped by barge on the waterway. Pleasure yachts, sailboats and shrimp boats also used the waterway. By the 1980s these types of craft were the predominant vessels utilizing the route as barge traffic gradually decreased. The Corps of Engineers has periodically dredged parts of the AICW on the Georgia coast to maintain the project channel depth. Dredge activity in the

---

[936] U.S. Army Corps of Engineers, *The Atlantic Intracoastal Waterway*, special (restricted) publication, 1943.

creeks and rivers of the Intracoastal Waterway has always been in progress, although the average citizen on shore would hardly be aware of it. Areas that require dredging are those behind the barrier islands where the tidal currents converge—divide—and create shoaling, obvious impediment to navigation. These circumstances are prevalent in large tidal rivers and in areas called "narrows." In McIntosh County, for example, periodic dredging is necessary in Creighton Narrows to maintain the twelve-foot channel. Tides meet in the narrows and often create shoaling, thus necessitating dredging.[937]

Dredge spoil is pumped into disposal easements in the marsh. The easements were acquired by the state of Georgia between 1939 and 1942, then awarded to the Corps of Engineers for spoil deposit areas. The easements include some 7,000 acres of salt marsh on both sides of the AICW through coastal Georgia. Numerous small hammocks along the waterway, in which cedar, wax myrtle, marsh elder and other native vegetation adaptable to the salt water environment, has grown up in the marsh, are the result of the Corps' dredge-spoil disposal since the early 1940s.

Dredging in McIntosh County has been conducted by the Corps since the early 1900s. Mud River was dredged in 1906 with 44,665 cubic yards of spoil being removed. In 1929 and 1930, a total of 500,000 cubic yards of spoil was dredged from Mud River, although it was no longer the primary inland route. Over 40,000 cubic yards of spoil was dredged from Front River in 1944. Creighton Narrows has received the greatest amount of dredging of any McIntosh waterway. From 1914 to 1975, the passage was dredged twenty times with 436,000 cubic yards of spoil removed in 1949, and 393,000 in 1974. In 1943, over 112,000 cubic yards were removed from Old Teakettle Creek, and over 13,000 cubic yards were dredged from Shellbluff Creek at

---

[937] Tinkler, *AICW Project*, 49.

Valona in 1944. In Doboy Sound, the AICW channel was dredged eight times from 1943 to 1975 with 241,000 cubic yards of spoil being removed in the busy dredging year of 1949. Other local passages which have received regular dredging have been North River, Rockdedundy River, South River, Little Mud River, Three-Mile Cut, Altamaha Sound and Buttermilk Sound.[938]

---

[938] Ibid., 59-61.

Land Use & Landscape: Railroads and Naval Stores

Throughout much of its history coastal Georgia's population has been concentrated near the tidal rivers. Using Highway 17 as a convenient dividing line, the trend has seen the east side of the route being the most populous, partly dictated by the need of rice planters to be near the tidal estuaries; the same was applicable later for those who followed commercial fishing pursuits. By contrast, the areas west of the highway are for the most part remote with a landscape thickly-wooded with pine forests, sand hills and saw palmetto, broken only by the occasional logging trail. There was a time, however, when these areas were the scene of considerable railroad activity, and a naval stores industry that prospered thanks to the rail shipment of commodities. To illustrate these factors, McIntosh County will serve as a useful case study for the period 1890-1950.

With the railroad supporting the movement of naval stores, particularly turpentine and rosin, sawmills and timber operations, brick-making, and stock raising, half a dozen small communities developed along the stretch of track from Jones Station south to Townsend, thence to Cox Station in the 1890s. Except for Townsend, these communities have largely faded away; some, such as Warsaw and Brickstone, have disappeared entirely. By 1950 the local naval stores industry was in decline, being overtaken by technological developments. Later, the railroads disappeared from western McIntosh County. After almost a century of operation from Jones to Cox, the Seaboard Air Line, later Seaboard Coastline, permanently suspended activity in 1985, emphasized by the removal of track through the county.

Economic development in western McIntosh began in the late 1880s when railroad agents began securing rights-of-way for track that would become part of the new line from Savannah to Jacksonville. One of the first settlements on the route had multiple names in its early history: Ninety-Six, Hilton, and Flotono. In 1893, the name was permanently changed to Townsend, so named for Joseph Townsend, one of those employed by the railroad who rode on horseback to lay out the route of the new line through the pine woods of the western sections of the coastal counties in the early 1890s. In 1893, work was nearly complete on the Florida Central & Peninsular linking Savannah and Jacksonville. The line was initially known as the Florida Northern Railroad, which began the work of laying track. It became the Florida Central & Peninsular in 1893 then, in 1900, the Seaboard Air Line Railway. Passenger service on the new F.C. & P. began in late 1893. The McIntosh County stop on the line was Barrington Station, a small depot less than a mile north of Cox. Later, the Barrington stop was discontinued and the new point for that section of McIntosh County became Cox Station.

The Darien & Western Railroad, which became the Georgia Coast & Piedmont in 1906, intersected with the Florida Central & Peninsular, later Seaboard Air Line, at Theo. The station at Theo later became Darien Junction and, still later, Warsaw. Passengers on either the G.C. & P. or the Seaboard could make connections on the other's route. Darien Junction was on the Seaboard tracks about halfway between Jones Station and Townsend, and was so named because it was the point at which travelers on the "South Bound" could make connections with Darien passengers on the Darien &

Western from 1895 on.

Elisha McDonald Thorpe (1878-1966) was the most prominent citizen in this section in the early-to-mid-twentieth century. Thorpe married Maude Davis whose father, C.H. Davis, had come from Texas to build trestles for the Seaboard Air Line Railroad, and was living at Townsend. Thorpe was postmaster of Townsend and, with his father-in-law, operated a general store in the settlement. Thorpe also operated the McIntosh Naval Stores Company which was among the leading operations of its kind in the early 1900s with turpentine stills at Townsend, Ardoch and Tibet, the latter just across the McIntosh line in what is now Long County.

Along a timber siding, which was east of, and paralleled the Seaboard tracks, the community of Warsaw, formerly Darien Junction, grew up around a saw mill that was built in 1925. The timber siding was known locally as Warsaw Siding. There is ample documentation of sawmill and naval stores activities at Warsaw, as well as the disposal of the rights-of-way when the G.C. & P. ended operations in 1919. An indenture in April 1922 notes the sale of a portion of these lands by F.A. McIntosh of McIntosh County to James Miller of Richmond, Virginia (Georgia Land & Livestock Company) by which, for $10 and "other valuable considerations," McIntosh conveyed to Miller "all that part of the Georgia Coast and Piedmont right-of-way in McIntosh and Long counties beginning at the right-of-way of the Seaboard Air Line Railway at Warsaw Station in McIntosh County and running thence westwardly to the west end of the old station ground at Tibet being a width of 200 feet, more or less."[939]

The Twin Tree Lumber Company acquired property at Warsaw for its sawmill operation, and other activities associated with the Warsaw Lumber Company, including the rail shipment of its milled lumber. The company leased large tracts of timber land in McIntosh, Long and Liberty counties to supply timber for the Warsaw mill. The 1929 *Soil Survey of McIntosh County*, compiled by the U.S. Department of Agriculture, includes a map that denotes buildings and railroad alignments at Warsaw. The map delineates a short railroad siding (Warsaw Siding) running northeast off the main Seaboard tracks, and bisecting the Townsend-Jones road, to the Warsaw Lumber Company's sawmill on the Townsend-Jones Road a little east of the Seaboard track.[940] The 1929 soil map notes a series of longitudinal structures near the siding that are related to the sawmill, perhaps being lumber storage sheds.

In early 1934, a twelve-foot flywheel suddenly disintegrated while in operation and ripped apart the main facility of Warsaw Lumber's sawmill, in addition to causing a fire. It was reported that

"the large saw mill at Warsaw, owned and operated by the Warsaw Lumber Company, was almost completely destroyed by fire. It is thought that the fire originated in the dynamo room. Lights for the mill village are generated by the mill, and there seems to be no other plausible explanation for the origin of the fire. There was a great quantity of lumber on the mill yards, possibly four million feet, but it was saved from the flames. Mr. Waits, manager of the mill, states that the mill will be rebuilt, and new machinery installed, as the

---

[939] Deed Book S (1922), 69, RMCG.
[940] G.L. Fuller, B.H. Hendrickson and J.W. Moon, *Soil Survey of McIntosh County, Georgia*, Series 1929, No. 6, Bureau of Chemistry and Soils, U.S. Department of Agriculture, 1932.

company yet has a good deal of timber to cut at this location."[941]

But the mill was not rebuilt, so costly was the loss. Warsaw Lumber continued to operate for two more years, cutting timber in that section of McIntosh County, then transporting it to sawmills at Eulonia and Riceboro to be milled into lumber for shipment to Savannah. In early 1936, the Company suspended operations at Warsaw completely, the decision largely based on the fact that it had cut virtually all the marketable timber it could on the lands it either owned or leased. Warsaw Lumber later leased its lands on a 99-year lease to Union Bag & Paper Corporation of Savannah.

Nothing remains of the sawmill site, and very little tangible evidence remains of the Warsaw community that grew up around the mill, with the exception of a brick vault just off the isolated dirt road that connects Townsend and Jones near the point where the railroad once passed through. The brick structure on the former site of Warsaw served as a fireproof vault in the 1920s and 1930s, when Warsaw and the Warsaw Lumber Company were active centers of activity in the remote pine barrens and saw palmetto of western McIntosh County.[942]

* * *

The southeast Georgia naval stores industry led the world in the production of rosin, turpentine and other by-products of the pine in the late nineteenth and early twentieth centuries. Workers in the pine flatwoods, usually African Americans, began in spring and early

---

[941] *Darien Gazette*, January 19, 1934.

[942] Author's interview with Mr. and Mrs. Earl McQuaig of Darien, Ga., January 28, 1987. Mr. and Mrs. McQuaig were residents of Warsaw in the 1920s and 1930s when the Warsaw Lumber Company sawmill was in operation.

summer by cutting a V-shaped section of the pine tree near the base, following which a tin cup or box was affixed beneath the cut to collect the gum as it flowed from the cut into the receptacle. The gum flowed most freely in the hot weather months. Periodically, workers collected the gum boxes, pouring the contents into wooden barrels transported by horse-drawn wagons, and later by rickety trucks. The barrels of gum were hauled to the local turpentine still where the gum was transferred to metal vats. The vats were heated; the vapors from the heating rose to the top, then passed through a copper coil. The coil passed through a wooden vat filled with water that cooled the vapors until they were liquefied. The liquid was then drained from the coils in the form of turpentine. What remained in the metal vats after the cooling process was rosin. Turpentine and rosin were shipped to market in barrels.[943] From about 1900, the ports of Savannah and Brunswick were the world-leaders in the export of these products, in addition to tar and creosote. After 1875, Georgia's pine belt south of the fall line became the scene of increasing turpentine production and other naval stores activities.[944] Georgia was the world leader in the industry from 1880 to 1905, when Florida took the lead until 1923. Georgia then regained its premier position which it retains. Dr. Charles B. Herty, a University of Georgia chemist, developed many innovations through his experimentation that revolutionized the naval stores process and

---

[943] *Report of the Secretary of Agriculture*, 1892 (Washington, D.C.: Government Printing Office).
[944] Mark V. Wetherington, *The New South Comes to Wiregrass Georgia, 1860-1910* (Knoxville: University of Tennessee Press, 1994), 118-22.

increased the productivity and potential of the industry.[945]

The Cox Naval Stores Company began operations in 1928 under the management of H.W. Poppell and J.M. Reddish, both of McIntosh County. They leased substantial tracts of acreage from 1928 to 1934 in western McIntosh County's 1514th G.M.D. for turpentine production. In January 1929 Cox Naval Stores acquired turpentine leases from A.B. Poppell, G.M. McIntosh, L.R. Riley, A.C. Anderson, H.A. Holland, E.M. Thorpe and others, as well as "one 16-barrel capacity still and fixtures, 45 clip barrels, cooper shop, tools and fixtures and 60,000 turpentine cups, more or less, with gutter equipment used in connection [with tapping pine trees]."[946]

According to the 1929 soil survey the largest industry in the county then was naval stores production. It was reported that about 7,000 barrels of turpentine of fifty gallons each and 35,000 barrels of rosin of 280 pounds each were being sold annually from McIntosh at values ranging from $400,000 to $450,000, the products being marketed either through Savannah or Brunswick. In its report the soil survey further noted:

"Longleaf and slash pines are the principal trees worked for the crude gum, although a few loblolly pines have been worked but are usually very poor producers. The slash pine is preferred and is reported to produce more gum than the longleaf. Production is based on crops' of trees, 10,000 trees constituting a crop. Production per crop and the quality of the product differ with the size of the trees and the length of time they have been worked, the height of production being about 40 barrels of turpentine per crop. The highest quality turpentine is obtained from freshly-cupped or virgin

---

[945] Kenneth H. Thomas, Jr., *McCranie's Turpentine Still, Atkinson County, Georgia* (Athens: University of Georgia Institute of Community and Area Development and GDNR, 1975), 5 ff.
[946] Deed Book 2 (1929), 404, RMCG.

trees. The stand of trees ranges from 1 or 2 to 50 or more an acre, so that in the better areas 250 acres will constitute a crop and elsewhere from 400 to 500 acres are required for a crop. There is a noticeable difference in the manner in which trees are worked. The better and more conservative method, followed by many producers, consists of putting only 1 cup on smaller trees and working no trees less than 9 inches in diameter. However, it is common, more often on leased land, that trees 5 inches in diameter will have 2 cups and 18 or 20 inch trees 4 or 5 cups, the worked faces completely girdling the tree. It is reported that at least 75 per cent of McIntosh County's mainland area is in the control of turpentine and lumber companies, whose holdings range from a few thousand to more than 50,000 acres. Part of the area is conservatively worked and reforestation is being urged, but elsewhere the methods employed are destructive to the trees, and practically no second growth has developed on account of fires and livestock grazing.

"Most of the trees large enough for lumber have been cut, except on scattered small tracts. One sawmill, which is sawing about 60,000 feet of pine a day, is still operating at Warsaw [Warsaw Lumber]. The company owning this mill has cut both pines and swamp hardwoods but has shipped most of the hardwoods as logs. Another product of the county is deer-tongue, or vanilla leaf (*Trilisa odoratissima*), of which about 240,000 pounds a year are picked, the present price is about 7 ½ cents a pound, at which price the crop is worth about $18,000. The deer-tongue is shipped mainly to New York, Baltimore, Wilmington, and Richmond, from whence three-fourths to seven-eighths of the crop is exported to Germany and France. Deer-tongue grows principally on the Leon soils, but it is found in nearly all parts of the county."[947]

With the breakup of the Hilton-Dodge Lumber Company from 1912-16, many of the corporation's lands in McIntosh and Liberty counties were acquired by two new companies started at the same time, often operating in tandem, and soon thereafter merged under a single corporate management. These were the Newport Company and the Georgia Land and Livestock Company. The Newport

---

[947] *Soil Survey of McIntosh County, Georgia*, Series 1929, 4-5.

Lumber operations in the pine flatwoods, early 1900s.

Company was a land investment and real estate entity incorporated in 1916 with its office of business at Townsend, and Elisha M. Thorpe as president. Also incorporated in 1916 was the Georgia Land and Livestock Company, a real estate firm initially comprised mostly of investors from Virginia. Georgia Land and Livestock was financially supported by the Virginia Trust Company of Richmond. The president of the G.L. & L.C. was J.M. Paschall of Richmond. There was considerable interaction between the Newport Company and Georgia Land and Livestock, and it was no coincidence that the primary offices for both firms was at Townsend.

Deed records attest to a flurry of transactions in February and March 1921 involving both corporations. Much of the activity was associated with the merger of Newport Company's assets with those of Georgia Land and Livestock under the name of the latter. Most of the transactions by which the Newport Company was phased out and absorbed by G.L. & L.C. were completed by the end of March 1921.

Georgia Land and Livestock was starting what its Virginia stockholders envisioned would be a profitable cattle-raising venture on a scale to rival anything in Texas. Thousands of head of cattle were brought in to graze within fenced pasture lands scattered through the western McIntosh pine woods, particularly in areas west of Eulonia and in the Townsend, Jones and Cox areas. In February 1921 Georgia Land and Livestock gained title to a considerable herd of cattle from a corporation based in Atlanta. The herd comprised 4,235 head of cattle, in addition to 160 bulls, 538 calves and 4,963 sheep. In land, Georgia Land and Livestock acquired over 70,000 acres in McIntosh and Liberty counties in 1921 and 1922. Much of the acreage, gained by outright purchase or through lease, was to be used for cattle pasturage in the sparsely-populated sections of McIntosh County.

In 1917, G.L. & L.C. constructed a series of concrete silos in the pine woods for the storage of silage for its cattle grazing. The silos still stand as silent monuments to the grand cattle-raising venture, scattered through the west and southwest sections of McIntosh County near Townsend, Eulonia, Jones and the Long County line, some near existing roadways.[948]

The cattle-raising project by Georgia Land and Livestock was ultimately unsuccessful. Grand in concept, and seemingly well-organized, the idea failed possibly because it simply over-reached and

---

[948] Author's interview with Jim Daniel of Eulonia, Ga., January 28, 1987. At the time, Daniel was a forest supervisor for Union Camp Corporation of Savannah.

was too ambitious. Cattle imported from Texas, Florida and Georgia were unable to adapt to the sandy, pinewoods environment of the coastal Georgia interior. The project lost momentum, and finally failed altogether. In 1925, the Georgia Land and Livestock Company sold or mortgaged 85,000 acres, and the company went bankrupt after having been active only nine years. Many of the lands held by Georgia Land and Livestock eventually came into possession of Union Bag Camp of Savannah in the 1930s and 1940s.

The Altamaha River: A Coastal Legacy

The course of the Altamaha River, from its creation by the confluence of the Oconee and Ocmulgee Rivers in southeast Georgia, to its terminus at the Atlantic Ocean, has been navigated by a variety of boats—dugout canoes, cotton barges, steamboats and commercial fishing craft—for hundreds of years.

The appellation *Altamaha* is Native American in origin. In its most elemental translation, the name is interpreted as "the way to Tama", Tama being a pre-Columbian Indian settlement at the confluence of the Oconee and Ocmulgee. This is a point about one hundred miles inland to the point where the Altamaha River is formed and flows southeasterly to the sea. In the aggregate, the Altamaha-Oconee-Ocmulgee watershed drains slightly more than the eastern third of the state of Georgia, making it one of the most extensive river systems in the eastern United States. The river, originally called *Alatamaha,* was named thus by early Spanish explorers, later being Anglicized to the present "Altamaha" by eighteenth century English colonists. Letters, reports and other documents written by English and Scottish officials from Savannah, Darien and Frederica, ca. 1740-1770, on deposit among the manuscript collections at the British Archives at Kew, London, and the Georgia Historical Society, Savannah, alternately refer to both Alatamaha and Altamaha. The early American naturalist, William Bartram, who documented the flora and fauna along much of the river during the 1770s, often utilized the spelling *Alatamaha* in his extensive notes and journals.

The Altamaha was the primary riverine conduit for successive human populations who utilized the river to transport goods from the interior to the coast and, conversely, from the coast back to the interior of what became Georgia. Archaeological investigations indicate extensive use of the river by Native American groups, largely associated with the Lower Creek nation. In pre-Columbian eras, the river transfer of goods from the coast to the interior is exemplified by the materials native to the coast, such as oyster shells, conchs and whelks, being found well inland, even along the Altamaha's two major extensions, the Ocmulgee and Oconee. Additionally, the transfer of flint knaps and other Indian artifacts from the interior have been identified in the lower reaches of the Altamaha by archaeologists to indicate an active river trade by Indians from the upcountry to the coast.

The use of the Altamaha became more pronounced with the settlement of the southern colonies by the English. With the establishment of the South Carolina colony in 1670, trading posts along the river were developed as the new settlers interacted with Indians upstream. With the arrival of Oglethorpe and his colonists at Savannah to establish the Georgia colony in 1733, river trade became more extensive, both on the Altamaha and the Savannah. English traders and trappers had extensive business activity along the Altamaha and there was an important trading post and settlement at Mount Venture on the river in what later became Wayne County. Based on archaeological findings, as well as manuscript research, the location of Mount Venture, a trading post established by Mary Musgrove in 1739, is known to have shifted several times during the colonial period. However, the primary location of the Mount

Venture settlement, and the site with the most extensive use, was at Sansavilla Bluff on the Altamaha, near the present boundary between Wayne and Glynn counties.

The presence of Mount Venture was in direct recognition of the fact that the Altamaha River was the primary waterway of southeast Georgia, and the major navigable conduit between the upcountry and the Atlantic Ocean. Mount Venture was in a prime position of importance as a river way station for the trading initiatives of colonists throughout the region. Significantly, a key player in the development of Mount Venture was a woman, the well-known Mary Musgrove, half-Indian, half-English interpreter for Oglethorpe and other colonial officials in their dealings with local Indians. Traders usually employed small craft such as wooden bateaux and dugout canoes in their transit of the Altamaha conveying goods from the principal port towns of Charleston and Savannah. Later, after the Revolutionary War, larger craft came to be employed for transportation, including pole boats and flatboats. These were particularly useful following the development of Milledgeville on the Oconee River as Georgia's permanent state capitol starting in 1807.

The development of Milledgeville was the consequence of the migration of settlers away from the seacoast into the interior. State land lotteries and head-right grants after the Revolution provided cheap land to encourage the settlement of the interior of the new state. As was the custom in America during this period, populations tended to establish their trade centers on river systems to provide convenience of communication with the Atlantic seaports. The Altamaha, with its feeder streams, the Oconee, Ocmulgee, and Ohoopee, was a prime example of this. Milledgeville was established at the head of navigation on the Oconee. Later, the Georgia legislature facilitated the development of two additional trading towns at the head of navigation of important rivers, Macon on the Ocmulgee in 1823 and Columbus on the Chattahoochee in 1827. (Augusta, at the head of navigation on the Savannah River, had been founded much earlier, in the first year of the Georgia colony).

In these sections of interior settlement agricultural operations developed as the economic mainstay, bolstered chiefly through the cultivation of inland grown, short-staple, cotton and provision crops. Barges, pole boats and flatboats, were utilized to expedite the transport of agricultural commodities from Macon and Milledgeville down to the major shipping point on the coast, Darien, near the mouth of the Altamaha delta, and only ten miles from the sea. In the 1820s and 1830s, Darien became a major cotton exporting port, rivalling even Savannah for a time. By the early 1830s Georgia was the world leader in cotton exports, and one third of that was being shipped from Darien with the Altamaha River as the conduit for the movement of cotton from the interior.

The primary markets for the central Georgia cotton belt were Macon on the Ocmulgee and Milledgeville on the Oconee. These rivers flowing to their merger as the Altamaha were the only means of navigation to Darien on the coast. This connection was firmly established shortly after the War of 1812. By 1818, local newspaper accounts were regularly reporting the movement of steamboat traffic along the river between the state capital and Darien, including the increasing shipment of cotton down the river to the coast on specially-designed river craft known as "Oconee boxes." For the convenience of the growing amount of steamboat traffic between

Milledgeville and Darien there were a number of river landings at points along the Oconee and Altamaha. These were suitably-located access points by which farmers could load their cotton onto the vessels for shipment to the Darien market and thence to points beyond—Savannah, Charleston, Boston and Liverpool, among other destinations. Boat traffic making the return trips upriver to Milledgeville, and later Macon, would convey freight, supplies, mail and other necessities to the trading towns and settlers along the Altamaha system.

A good example of an important Altamaha River landing point was Doctortown, in present day Wayne County. Doctortown became a river landing in the antebellum era in response to the growing use of the river as an agricultural conduit. It was the principal town of Wayne County prior to, and just after, the Civil War (Jesup, the present county seat of Wayne, was not established until 1870). Doctortown was also situated adjacent to the railroad crossing on the Altamaha, this being the Savannah, Albany & Gulf railroad linking Savannah and southwest Georgia, with its terminus at Thomasville. This railroad was built in the mid-1850s to provide access to the Atlantic coast for cotton and other farm commodities from the southern sections of the state, mainly those lacking convenient waterway access to the sea.

Much of the commercial and agricultural activity as it pertained to the use of the Altamaha system was documented in detail through the various media outlets of the day, including newspapers in Savannah, Milledgeville, Macon and Darien. In the 1820s the weekly *Darien Gazette* had regular columns devoted to shipping news and the arrivals and departures of steamboats between Darien and

Milledgeville. The *Georgia Messenger* of Macon, March 31, 1824, attests to the arrivals at Macon of the ships *Bachelor* and *Rebecca* from Darien with cargoes of iron, salt and other commodities.

Government work to improve the Altamaha's navigability was far more extensive in the postbellum period of the river's use than that even in the heaviest use of the river prior to the Civil War. This is puzzling, considering the degree of river traffic between Macon, Milledgeville and Darien. This activity is amply documented through the marine shipping columns of the 1820s. To cite one example, the shipping news in the *Darien Gazette* of February 15, 1825 lists the vessels in the Darien port, with their points of origin. Several of these are from the interior, including two from Macon and one from Milledgeville, all transporting cargoes of cotton. These were sizeable shipments, specifically being 192, 502 and 234 bags of cotton on the three vessels in question. Cotton bags were roughly equivalent in weight to the more familiar and compactly packaged bales, about 300 pounds.

Another example from the *Gazette*, from the issue of March 8, 1825, notes the arrival at Darien of a boat from Dublin (on the Oconee), and another boat from Milledgeville, both transporting loads of cotton, and again from April 5, 1825 with vessels from Milledgeville and Macon with cargoes of 600 bags of cotton. Up to April of 1825, as indicated by the newspaper article, there had been 12,000 bags of cotton brought into Darien from upriver to that point in the year. Most of the cotton was eventually shipped to the major export centers of Savannah and Charleston for overseas markets, as well as to the New England textile mills. During the 1820s and 1830s Darien was, statistically, one of the leading cotton exporting centers in the American South., a factor solely in consequence of the town's geographical situation near the mouth of the Altamaha-Ocmulgee-Oconee river system.

Darien was also the outlet for much of the locally-produced of rice cultivated on the Altamaha delta plantations between McIntosh and Glynn counties. The most prominent of these rice plantations were Hopeton-on-the-Altamaha, Elizafield and Hofwyl-Broadfield, all in Glynn County, and Cambers Island, Butler Island, Generals Island and Broughton Island, all in McIntosh County, along with several large rice tracts along Cathead Creek, a tidal tributary of the Altamaha west of Darien. The heavy production of rice in the Altamaha delta was due to the unique ecological circumstances of the section, whereby fresh water from upstream was utilized to flood the cultivated fields with the ebb and flow of tides from the nearby Atlantic enabling the operation of a complex system of hydraulics (tidegates, canals, embankments, levees, etc.) by which the fields were alternately flooded and drained during the spring and summer growing cycle. Because of the millions of pounds of "clean" and "rough" rice shipped from the Altamaha delta plantations each year a heavy preponderance of inland waterway coastal shipping prevailed in the lower reaches of the river, calling not only at Darien to take on cargoes of rice, but also at several of the individual plantations, particularly those that had their own threshing and pounding mills.

The prosperity of Darien as a major agricultural market was not to last. The development of railroads, specifically the Central of Georgia connecting Macon, Milledgeville and Augusta to Savannah starting in the late 1830s, proved to be the end of Darien's preeminence as a cotton port. No railroads were to come to Darien until 1895.

Developers were reluctant to build a line to the town because of its supposed "unhealthiness" due to the marshes and rice tracts in such close proximity, these being thought to be the purveyors of malaria and yellow fever. A second factor in the demise of Darien was the national financial panic of 1837, which caused the loss of the charter of the influential Bank of Darien through which a great deal of cotton money flowed both from upriver and locally.

The rafting of pine timber provided the chief economic impetus for the Altamaha River system and Darien after the Civil War. This activity actually began in earnest in the two decades prior to the war. Sawmills were built at Darien as early as 1817-18, and rafts of timber came into the town by way of the Altamaha in steady amounts after that. Mills were built east of town at Lower Bluff, along the Darien waterfront, and on the small tributary of Cathead Creek. Upcountry farmers along the Oconee, Ocmulgee, Altamaha and Ohoopee rivers, cut pine timber during the off-growing season (fall and winter), squared the timber near the river banks, and fashioned substantial rafts of the squared timber to float down the river system, eventually being graded, assessed and sold to the timber buyers and sawmill operators at Darien.

The river traffic connected with timber after the war supplanted agriculture as the major economic activity on the lower Altamaha. Timber cut along the rivers eventually went to the sawmills at Darien and St. Simons Island. Deep-water shipping from Europe and South America, along with coastal shipping from the middle-Atlantic region and New England, converged on Darien to load timber and lumber. This activity reached a peak in 1900, although timber rafting and sawmilling on the Altamaha continued until about 1920. By then, the source of timber began to be so depleted by over-cutting that the industry died out almost overnight.

The Darien newspapers of the 1870s and 1880s attest to the great volume of Altamaha River traffic. Steamboat routes continued to be run between Milledgeville and Darien, and locales such as Doctortown at the railroad bridge over the Altamaha continued to serve as layover points for the boats. Darien was the leading timber port on the south Atlantic coast from 1870 to 1900, a situation that would have been impossible without the Altamaha River providing the direct source of revenue.

Richard Grubb, editor and publisher of the *Darien Timber Gazette,* clearly understood the critical nature of the geographical circumstances of Darien when he wrote on May 30, 1874: "The Nile is said to be everything to Egypt. In fact, without the Nile there would be no Egypt...To a certain extent, the same may be truly said of the Altamaha River and Darien. Without the Altamaha there would be no timber trade and no rice planting, and without these there would be no Darien..."

The U.S. Army Corps of Engineers' survey of the Altamaha in 1883 identified ongoing improvements to navigation on the river, and made a number of useful observations on its map accompanying the report, to wit: Town Bluff is situated just below the Forks, where the Oconee and Ocmulgee converge at Lumber City to form the Altamaha. A sawmill is shown at Town Bluff, with "deep water" clearly marked on the river at the town site to guide boats transiting that section. The Corps' survey identifies other landings along the Altamaha on its progress toward Darien—Piney Bluff, Reddish's Bluff, Oglethorpe Landing, "Confederate obstruction", Yellow Bluff,

Doctortown, Sansavilla, Fort Barrington, Clarke's Bluff, Rifle Cut, Darien River, and Lower Bluff east of Darien. The chart is important since it delineates the various locations along the river where "improvements" had been made in the early 1880s in conformance with the safe conduct of steamboat and other marine traffic between the Forks and Darien. "Improvements" indicates dredging of silted sections of the river and the removal of obstructions, such as snags.

The end of timber rafting and the further development of railroads in the section in the first two decades of the 20th century led to reduced river traffic on the Altamaha. After 1925 use of the river was largely that of commercial and recreational fishermen.

Later in the twentieth century the Altamaha once again served as a conveyor of large water craft. In March and April of 1971 a 700-ton nuclear reactor vessel was transported from Chattanooga, Tennessee to Baxley, Georgia, on the Altamaha River as the key component of the construction of the Plant Hatch nuclear plant by the Georgia Power Company. This unusual, circuitous, river voyage entailed the reactor vessel being powered by two tugboats from Tennessee to Baxley by way of the Tennessee, Ohio and Mississippi rivers, thence to the Gulf of Mexico. The craft then proceeded from New Orleans via the Atlantic Intracoastal Waterway to the Cross-Florida Canal. From Florida's east coast, the reactor moved north along the Intracoastal Waterway to the Georgia coast north of Brunswick, then proceeded more than one hundred miles up the Altamaha River to its final destination at Baxley. This effort entailed a 25-day journey covering some 2,500 miles, the concluding leg of which showed once again the validity of the Altamaha River as a navigable waterway to both large and small maritime vessel use.

Saving a River: William Haynes & Ophelia Dent

Other than Thomas Spalding, the person most readily identified and associated with Ashantilly is Bill Haynes. Haynes spent practically all of the last fifty years of his life residing in the Ashantilly house, and gained considerable professional acclaim for the beautiful documents and images produced from his Ashantilly Press on the grounds of Ashantilly. The devotion toward preserving their home by Haynes and his sisters, Frances and Anne Lee Haynes, was rewarded in 2016 when Ashantilly was placed on the National Register of Historic Places, a singular and highly-prestigious honor.

It was during a sojourn in New York to study art as a young man in the mid-1930s that Haynes began to realize the direction of his professional life. In an autobiographical sketch written shortly before his death Haynes provides clues to the evolving process of his becoming a printer. For a time in the 1930s Haynes "was still wedded to the notion that [he] would become a painter or possibly a sculptor. I had not totally abandoned those first intimations of my awakening drive to create..." Haynes relates that he attended a summer class at Columbia University "under a famous teacher of lettering. From this I formed the habit, as urged, of collecting examples of fine printing...in those last years in New York, it was from a class in the methods and techniques of the Old Masters of the 15th and 16th centuries that my mind was by then firmly devoted to being a painter. In the fall of 1936, I left New York to try my hand as an independent artist. Six months later our house at Ashantilly burned. Two years later a fortunate bequest made it possible to begin restoration of our home [as] the major portion of the walls had survived in good shape."

While in the U.S. Army in the Second World War, Haynes served first at Camp Stewart near Savannah, then later in the south Pacific where he was inspired by the natural beauty of New Guinea amidst the turmoil of the Pacific War. This assignment provided the fundamental basis for his interest in natural history and maritime history. A perusal of Haynes' Ashantilly library by even the most casual observer makes clear his devotion to subjects related to nautical affairs—such as his set of the definitive historical novels of Patrick O'Brian relating to the British navy in the early nineteenth century—and natural history, particularly his enthusiasm for the Altamaha River explorations of John and William Bartram. Other volumes in his collection reflect his interest in far-away, exotic places, and the natural flora and fauna found in distant lands.

Haynes was inspired by the natural beauty of New Guinea and Australia. It was partly the experience of his South Pacific watercolor art that led to his study of commercial art in New York after the war. But his focus was diverted, as Haynes himself recalled years later: "I was guided to Cooper Union and in my second year encountered the printing press and simple typography...I was captured by its possibilities—for creative work, a means of support, and to live a life at Ashantilly. With that goal in sight, distant as it might be, I was filled with the excitement of expectations." Those expectations were fulfilled by his return to Ashantilly in 1954, soon after which Haynes established his Ashantilly Press. Here, he perfected the skills in the art of letterpress printing. Beneath the oaks of Ashantilly emerged the legacies of Haynes and the Ashantilly Press, from books and prints reflecting his interest in local history and the Altamaha River, to the poetic works of Sidney Lanier and the commissioned works of other authors. Haynes' empathy for wildlife is reflected in his advocacy of the preservation of the Altamaha River basin. His attention to coastal environmental issues, and the Altamaha in particular, is an extension of the philosophies refined over the years through his ongoing study of naturalist William Bartram who left his imprint on our present-day understanding of low country ecosystems.

The first piece produced by Haynes at Ashantilly Press also became one of his most memorable and enduring impressions. It was a silkscreen image of Old Fort King George, rendered in 1955 at the request of McIntosh County historian Bessie Mary Lewis. This oversize artistic, visually appealing, work was produced on a 6 x 9 handpress. It was on this press too, that Haynes set to type his first book, *Anchored Yesterdays*, a history of the early years of Savannah originally compiled and written thirty years earlier by Elfrida DeRenne Barrow and Laura Palmer Bell, both of Wormsloe, Isle of Hope, Savannah.[949] Producing *Anchored Yesterdays* was evidently a most laborious task being that the book was rendered, as Haynes

---

[949] Elfrida DeRenne Barrow and Laura Palmer Bell, *Anchored Yesterdays: The Log Book of Savannah's Voyage Across a Georgia Century in Ten Watches*, reissue by William G. Haynes, Jr. in 1956 from the Ashantilly Press, produced from the original book published in 1923. It was reissued in hardcover by the University of Georgia Press in 2001. Elfrida DeRenne Barrow (1884-1970) was descended from the Noble Jones family of Wormsloe, Isle of Hope, Savannah. Her husband was Dr. Craig Barrow (1876-1945), chief surgeon of the Central of Georgia Railway hospital in Savannah. The Barrows lived at Wormsloe, as have their descendants to the present day.

recalled, on his small hand press, a page at a time, taking a year to produce.

In 1962 Haynes completed his separate press building, then expanded that facility in 1974. There, he continued to produce award-winning books and pamphlets. One of the most popular of his Press publications was a booklet embracing the enduring poem, *The Marshes of Glynn*, originally composed in 1878 by Georgia poet Sidney Lanier. Issued from Ashantilly Press in 1957, this award-winning work was highlighted by Haynes' use of his own woodcuts and the ornamental textual embellishments that had become his trademark. *Marshes of Glynn*, reprinted several times, remains the largest selling publication from the Ashantilly Press.

By the 1970s, some of the work of the Ashantilly Press began to reflect Haynes' emerging interests and energies on behalf of the preservation and conservation of the Altamaha River basin of coastal Georgia. In this regard, he prepared two important documents, *Rally for the Protection of the Altamaha River Basin* (1971) and *Conference: Man in the Landscape* (1976).

In his later years, Haynes became a passionate advocate for the protection of the Altamaha, an effort reflected in his co-founding the Lower Altamaha Historical Society in 1979, an organization devoted to the study and dissemination of the history and culture of both its namesake river as well as McIntosh County. A catalyst for the subsequent creation of the Society was his organization in 1976 of the "Man in the Landscape" conference held in Darien as the local participatory event in the United States Bicentennial observance. The purpose of the symposium that featured lectures by historians and environmentalists was the fulfillment of a collaborative inquiry "into man's relationship to his natural environment through the history and culture of the lower Altamaha River region."

In the mid-1960s, Haynes was instrumental, with Darien mayor James A. Williamson, Dr. William Tailer and Bessie M. Lewis, in local efforts to establish Fort King George as a state historic site. The initiative began with museum construction and grounds improvement, followed by the building of a blockhouse replica in 1989. As reflected in his advocacy of Fort King George and his co-founding the Lower Altamaha Historical Society, Haynes was an authority on the history of Darien and McIntosh County. His collection of books and manuscripts accumulated over years of research, and grew quite large, particularly concerning the colonial history of Georgia and South Carolina, a particular interest of his. Haynes' Altamaha River advocacy and support of coastal environmental issues in general is reflected by the gradual reduction of publications from the Ashantilly Press. The conservation of the river became paramount in his life, both professionally and personally. Haynes' energies regarding protection of his beloved river were shared and fueled through his close association with friends and fellow advocates, particularly Miss Ophelia Dent of nearby Hofwyl-Broadfield, Dr. William Tailer and Derby Waters of the Altamaha Conservancy.

Ophelia Troup Dent (1886-1973), named for her grandmother Ophelia (1827-1905, wife of George C. Dent), worked especially closely with Haynes in the movement to protect the Altamaha delta. She was the fifth generation of a rice-planting family at Hofwyl

Ophelia Dent as a young woman.

dating back to the early 1800s. Although rice production had long since ceased at Hofwyl, Miss Dent continued to live with her sister Miriam Gratz Dent (1883-1953) at Hofwyl, in the lower Altamaha about five miles south of Darien and Ashantilly. With frequent correspondence to all who would listen, she passionately urged local and state civic leaders and lawmakers to place stringent protections of the river of her ancestors. When she died in 1973, her will stipulated that Hofwyl become a protected state property for the perpetuation of cultural education and environmental preservation advocacy. Hofwyl-Broadfield state historic site is perhaps the greatest legacy of Ophelia Dent, as Ashantilly was to become for Bill Haynes years later.[950]

---

[950] Ophelia Dent memoirs, Hofwyl-Broadfield State Historic Site archives, Brunswick, Ga.

Ophelia Dent's legacy on the Altamaha spanned four generations earlier beginning with William Brailsford. Brailsford (1760-1810) was the son of English merchant Samuel Brailsford and had moved to Charleston after the Revolution. In 1786, Brailsford married Maria Heyward (1767-1837),

The 1825 McIntosh County tax digest shows the estate of William Brailsford as possessing 160 slaves and 1,602 acres on Broughton Island, which may not have included his holdings at Broadfield on the mainland, that tract being in Glynn County.

In addition to Broughton Island, Brailsford cultivated rice at Broadfield, directly across the Altamaha from Broughton. Broadfield was on the tract originally known as Broadface, previously owned by Henry Laurens McIntosh, son of Lachlan McIntosh. Brailsford died in 1810, and the management of Broadfield plantation fell to Maria Brailsford and her daughter, Camilla. In 1814, Camilla Brailsford (1794-1847) married James McGillivray Troup (1786-1849), Darien physician, and a man of growing influence in the region. James Troup assumed management of Broadfield and other Brailsford holdings. A daughter, Ophelia Troup (1827-1905), was born to the Troups at their Darien home on Cathead Creek.

In 1916, Charles S. Wylly noted that the "Broadfield plantation in north Glynn County was devoted to the culture of rice, and not until the death of Mrs. Maria Heyward Brailsford did it become the residence of the Troup family. Until then they resided in Darien in the winters, and in the summers at Baisden's Bluff overlooking a wide and beautiful river; the place is now a station called Crescent, from the horse-shoe bend of the river." Troup died at Broadfield in 1849, two years after his wife Camilla.

Troup left a heavily-mortgaged estate comprising some 7,300 acres, two residences, and 357 slaves on several Glynn and McIntosh county tracts. In 1847, Ophelia Troup married George Columbus Dent (1821-1884) and inherited a part of the family's holdings at Broadfield. In 1856, the Dents moved to the part of Broadfield plantation that they renamed Hofwyl, for the Hofwyl school in Switzerland where Dent had been educated. Hofwyl comprised the lower half of the Broadfield tract given to Ophelia Troup Dent as her dowry.[951] Their son, James Troup Dent, planted at Hofwyl after the Civil War.

The post-Civil War story of Hofwyl is highly interesting. In 1880 James Troup Dent (1848-1913), son of George and Ophelia Dent, married Miriam Gratz Cohen (1850-1931). The joining of the Dent, Troup and Brailsford families with the wealthy Cohen and Gratz families was significant financially for Hofwyl, and also represented the joining of two powerful, but culturally different, Jewish and Christian families at a time when even intermarriage between different protestant denominations often raised eyebrows. The propitious infusion of capital saved Hofwyl from bankruptcy, and enabled James T. Dent to reclaim much of the previously lost Brailsford and Troup properties. Dent continued to grow rice at Hofwyl-Broadfield until his death in 1913. He was never able to return the plantation to its previously profitable status. The combination of high labor costs, migrating "rice birds" and two hurricanes proved costly. Dent's son, Gratz Dent (1881-1932), converted Hofwyl-Broadfield from a failing rice plantation to a

---

[951] Ophelia Troup Dent memoirs, 1902, Hofwyl archives, GDNR.

moderately successful dairy farm. Gratz Dent managed the dairy until his death in 1932, whereupon operation fell to his two sisters, Miriam and Ophelia. Until the dairy closed in 1942, the two sisters personally prepared and delivered between 100 to 150 bottles of milk daily to customers in Glynn and McIntosh counties. Neither sister ever married but they hardly led spinster lives. Though of reduced means compared to earlier times, the family name still carried social standing and prominence. Margaret Mitchell, author of *Gone With the Wind*, was a frequent visitor to Hofwyl, and Ophelia often travelled with her close friends, Alice and Pierre DuPont. Miriam died in 1953, leaving Ophelia as the last heir to the family estate that spanned five generations. On a morning in September 1973, in the ladies parlor of the Hofwyl house, "Miss Ophelia" Dent quietly finished her morning coffee and then passed away. It has been told that, before they took her away, Rudolf Capers (1902-1982), her friend and beloved butler for many years, carefully set out a full place setting of her finest china and silver one last time, "for Miss Ophelia, the grand lady of Hofwyl."

One work Haynes composed and intended to issue through the Ashantilly Press was his own statement on the urgency of preserving the Altamaha. This thoughtful document is "The Altamaha: Two Decades in the Life of a River," the metal typeface for which he set at Ashantilly Press, and a work on which he was completing final editing. "The Altamaha" is a very personal account, an exposition by which Haynes charts the unyielding efforts by himself and others on behalf of the preservation of the River during the 1970s and 1980s. Declining health in his later years prevented the completion of this document. Portions of the paper are cited here for the words penned by Bill Haynes reveal much about Haynes the man. As Thomas Spalding of Sapelo was very much the local philosophical conscience in the nineteenth century, so Bill Haynes was in the twentieth. Beyond the Ashantilly Press and the Ashantilly Center, his thought-provoking and penetrating thoughts about his beloved Altamaha may arguably be Haynes' greatest legacy:

"There are rivers which capture the imagination that are as familiar to us as household words far beyond the limits of the lands through which they flow. The very origins of their names are shrouded in mystery. Legends built around them have developed an aura of magic that is palpable, and irresistible to man. The Altamaha is one of these. The Altamaha has been the patron of man from time beyond knowledge, and is a good reason for Darien being where it is. It has the distinction of a name known to the world through literature, history, and the botanical brethren, because of a single book. The work of William Bartram, artist and naturalist, and of a rare and lovely flowering shrub or small tree, the *Franklinia Alatamaha*, the Bartrams, father and son, made known to the world and named in honor of Benjamin Franklin. From my childhood the Altamaha was for me a source of imagination, although the extent of my contact with the river was limited to what could be seen from the bluffs at Darien, and in crossing the four streams of the Delta. I do remember the dwindling days of the timber rafts until they ceased altogether...It was a new idea to grasp when I returned home, that the great Altamaha River might be vulnerable. I saw the ruined nets of the fishermen, a jellied glue-like substance discharged by the paper mill upriver, and on contact the nets became a congealed unusable mass. And other chemicals from that source found their way too frequently into the river for easy assimilation. I had not realized so soon as this, 1954, that the Altamaha was also being polluted by runoff of pesticides from cultivated lands, and sewage waste from communities along its banks...William Tailer, that strangely interesting and independent individual, was a medical man who settled in Darien...I admired Dr. Tailer, and he influenced me to become involved in these community efforts on which we worked closely together. He was also a sportsman, [and] was alone on the River near Fort Barrington, we assume there was a diabetic seizure, causing him to fall overboard and drown. So in the end it was the

Altamaha who claimed him for her own...There is Miss Ophelia Dent who expressed her opposition to destruction of the River, from the viewpoint of a family who planted rice in the Altamaha Delta for many generations, and who regarded the rice fields and River as an inseparable resource, for the future feeding of people...Dr. Eugene Odum, the principal advocate for preserving the Altamaha as a free-flowing stream, presented a series of cogent arguments supporting his position on the Altamaha as a more important resource in its natural state...For a time, tranquility reigned, no one was making overt attacks on the River. The fishermen in their boats were up and down its length as usual. I felt frustrated, there was no visible adversary to strengthen our response—but I suspected the worst, that someone was making plans secretly against our river, for it was too quiet. But the smooth flow of the Altamaha was undisturbed. I had my work, too long neglected in thinking about the river...An example which best expresses the close relationship between river and coast by its thoughtful simplicity is a comment by Lillian Dean, formerly with D.N.R., 'In many respects I feel that the Altamaha is more of a unique and important natural area than individual coastal islands. The fact that the river is intertwined with coastal life in so many different ways is part of the reason, I think.' And again, 'While the river does not contribute a great deal in new nourishment to the coastal marshes and the food chain each year,' says Dr. Don W. Kinsey, Director of the University of Georgia's Marine Institute at Sapelo Island, 'the little it does give to them is critical to their functioning'...In May, 1980, the first meeting of the Lower Altamaha Historical Society was held in the Courthouse in Darien where the Rally to protect the Altamaha was held in 1971. How strongly its members would rush to the Altamaha's defense was unknown but a relationship was established, and the future will determine its value...It was a decade [1975-85] of intense activity on the river by all kinds: scientists, environmentally-oriented persons, or those simply enjoying a day's boating. Magazine articles were drawing attention to the unique scenic beauty and resources for recreation of the Altamaha. It was rediscovery, as the great prize that all wished to possess and control, each for his own selfish use, regardless of the host of claimants...Hans Neuhauser of the Georgia Conservancy told of experiencing the reality of the Altamaha, seeing what Bartram surely must have seen in his day, a river comparatively untouched, always the same, and yet changing all the time. The River has a way of cleansing Man's intrusion."[952]

As Haynes aged and his concerns grew about the future of Ashantilly beyond his death, he began studying his options. In some ways, Ashantilly and the Altamaha were conjoined, at least from his visionary perspective, thus the consequence of these deliberations was the donation by Haynes and his sister Anne Lee in 1993 of Ashantilly to the newly created Ashantilly Center, Inc. In creating the Center with the assistance and input from supportive local citizens, Haynes was able to establish the future of Ashantilly (with the conservation of the River always a priority) as a venue for educational training in an array of restoration skills to preserve the history, culture and native crafts of the area. A conservation easement for Ashantilly in September 1994 noted that the property be "preserved in substantially its existing state in accordance with open space and values, thereby furthering the conservation and protection of a relatively natural habitat of fish, wildlife, plants, and similar ecosystems." Bill Haynes died August 24, 2001 at the age of ninety-three.

---

[952] William G. Haynes, Jr., "The Altamaha: Two Decades in the Life of a River," n.p., no date.

Afterword: A Low Country Legacy

To describe growing up in the low country, I would have to take you to the marsh on a spring day, flush the great blue heron from its silent occupation, scatter marsh hens as we sink to our knees in mud, open you an oyster with a pocketknife and feed it to you from the shell and say "There. That taste. That's the taste of my childhood." And I would say, "Breathe deeply" and you would breathe and remember that smell for the rest of your life, the bold, fecund aromas of the tidal salt marsh, exquisite and sensual, the smell of the South in heat, a smell all perfumed with seawater. My heart belongs in the marshlands. The boy in me still carries the memories when I lifted crab pots out of the river before dawn, when I was shaped by life on the river, part child, part sacristan of tides.

Pat Conroy, *The Prince of Tides*[953]

Coming home…

Simple words, yet they represent far more than meets the eye in my case.

Truly, I have always been at home wherever I have been in my native tidewater Georgia, but in 2018, I *literally* went home, likely—hopefully—for the last time. Going home is a fundamental instinct all of us have but which, in later life, few of us can ever hope to attain however much we may yearn for it. I am one of the lucky ones. I began at Cedar Point and, God willing, I will end at Cedar Point amid the tides and marshes.[954]

---

[953] Pat Conroy, *The Prince of Tides* (Boston: Houghton, Mifflin, 1986). Used with permission. Pat Conroy (1945-2016) had a low country upbringing contemporaneous to my own, and we always shared a mutual appreciation for, and understanding, of the coastal ecosystem. He is recognized as a leading figure of late twentieth century Southern literature.

[954] In mid-2018 I completed the building of my Cedar Point home on ancestral waterfront property going back to 1911.

My first conscious memory as a child very likely was that of the smell of the salt marsh. That thoroughly distinctive aroma must have indelibly—and permanently—etched itself upon my lifelong awareness long before I attained any particular notion of its import or significance.

I share my affinity for, and memories of, the marshes with an abundance of sentimentality to any and all who will listen to me, whether in my lectures, teaching or casual conversations with family and friends. The salt marshes are inextricably attached to my unending romance with the low country coast, along with its oak, pine and palm forests, the restless dunes of the island beaches, the endless fluidity of the tides and winds, the egrets, herons and pelicans, those and other familiar denizens inhabiting our extraordinary ecosystem. But the ecological signature of our coastal country is undeniably the marshes, and the floods and ebbs of the tides that nurture them.

The late Pat Conroy is almost poetic in evoking the truest sense of the marshes, the aromas and beauty of which quicken the pulse of native coastal Southerners. Like Conroy, my life too was "shaped by life on the river" and I too have always embraced the endless vicissitudes of the marshes with their pervasive aromatic pungency—particularly amid the mudflats at low tide on a warm, languid summer afternoon. There is nothing earthly comparable to the marvelous, majestic marshes of the Georgia and South Carolina low country. Small wonder then, and with no exaggeration, that from an early age we have always called this "God's Country."

I have always encouraged my children to "breathe deeply" and savor the alluring aroma of the marshes. One of the last things I said to my daughter Amanda as she went away to the University of Georgia for her freshman year of college was, "No matter what you do in life, or where you are on this earth, you will always be drawn home by the smell of the salt marsh, and its association with the best memories of your childhood." Eventually, I think we all come back home to the marshes—certainly so in spirit, if not always in reality. We children of the low country always sense the gentle allure of the marshes wherever we are. We are drawn back, somehow wanting to come full circle to reside again amidst the ambient sensuality of our adolescence, to again embrace the securities and remembrances that are uniquely associative to those verdant green blades of *Spartina* that comprise the miracle of the marshes. My children and I get all this honestly. All the generations of our family have experienced similar feelings of the need to be drawn home to the seaboard at various stages in life, myself included, of course. We are infused with the infectious lure of the marshes, the mudflats, the sea and the tides, the blue heron ever in search of the elusive fiddler crab.

The quiet little tidewater settlement of Cedar Point, in McIntosh County in coastal Georgia, was where, in the nineteen fifties and sixties, I spent a great deal of my childhood and adolescence experiencing the supposed affecting innocence of youth. It was also a time when I acquired, through my family and their friends, a growing appreciation for coastal history and culture. Much of the early tradition of the local oyster and shrimp fisheries is related to the Atwood family, descendants of Henry and Ann McIntosh Atwood. Simple advice given by Meta Atwood Watson is as applicable today as it was when she expressed her thoughts in the early 1900s, and fits perfectly within the theme of this book: "Never move away from the coast because you'll never starve here," the family matriarch told her children.[955] Her father, John McIntosh Atwood, taught his family equally deep allegiance to the tidewater, but for a different reason—he knew his children might leave temporarily but they would always return to "smell the marshes."[956]

With the acquired—and often painfully gradual—maturity that came in those adolescent years, I found myself embarking on a growing love affair with my native land-and-seascape, amid the pleasant associations of our little tidewater communities and neighbors, all familiar names, some not even on a map—Cedar Point, Crescent, Belleville, Manchester, Valona, Hudson and Meridian, most with sandy roads with shell that were so hot to one's bare feet in the summer, the coast all hugged and buffered by the local barrier islands a few miles in the distance—Sapelo, Doboy, Blackbeard and Creighton. In my mind's eye I can still see the greenish-blue tree line of Creighton in the distance, directly across the marsh from Cedar Point, reposing placidly a mile eastward.

It was an exposure to which I related countless times sitting on the steps of the "big house" at Cedar Point. Creighton was long, low and always to my vivid childhood imagination looking much like a long passenger train racing along the tracks towards its terminus by the sea. And always the smells, the omnipresent aromas associated with my youth, not only those of the marsh, but also of burning oak leaves in the early spring, deer tongue plants drying in the sun, and the familiar iodine scents experienced around the shrimp docks with

---

[955] *Altamaha Echoes* 1 (1), September 1986, Lower Altamaha Historical Society.
[956] Ibid.

their blends of fish and crab, salt air and the mudflats at low tide, these in harmony with the mix of diesel fuel and tarred shrimp nets. There was, and remains, a sublime pleasantness about these olfactory associations of my youth.

I have wonderful childhood and adolescent recollections of Cedar Point—roaring fires, loud conversation and laughter amid a house full of people at Christmas, a rope swing in the big live oak tree out front, swimming in the shallow "tide pool" at the Point, feeding the chickens in the back yard on cold mornings, building a pirate ship out of an old brick barbecue pit, beach excursions to St. Simons and Jekyll with cousins, aunts, uncles and friends; and the memorable occasion in the summer of 1964 when we rode out Hurricane Dora at Cedar Point, with the terrifying wild run of the winds uprooting hundred-year-old live oaks, and the surging waters of the nearby creek rising ever closer to the front doorstep.[957] It was that time span from 1957 through 1967, covering my ages 10 through 20, that were truly the most memorable years of my adolescence. They were the balmy, palmy days of summer in coastal

---

[957] Hurricane Dora approached shore off the Atlantic as a Category 3 storm during the day on September 9, 1964, making landfall that night north of St. Augustine, Florida. Although Dora came ashore some distance south of McIntosh County, the lower Georgia coast was in the path of the hurricane's northeast counterclockwise winds of greatest intensity. There were 90 mph winds on the barrier islands from Sapelo to Cumberland. We stood on the bluff at the abandoned Cedar Point oyster factory and monitored the tide rise with flashlights in the dark. It broke the bluff and got into the lawn. High winds, with higher gusts were experienced in the coastal areas of McIntosh, with heavy rain. US 17 was closed to traffic south of Darien due to flooding, the county was without electrical service for days, and many oak and pine trees were uprooted, damaging homes and vehicles. It was an altogether unnerving experience even though where we were it was only a minimal hurricane. The county saw nothing like it again until Matthew and Irma in 2016 and 2017.

Georgia, carefree, footloose days. We were typical "river rats," as my friends, cousins and I wandered like nomads about Cedar Point and Valona, sometimes with a "plan," but more often than not simply acting upon the spontaneity and impulses that are the inevitable companion of youth.

Occasionally we would ride our bicycles the two miles along Highway 99 from Cedar Point to Crescent, for the simple expedient of purchasing a Coke and a nickel bag of salted peanuts. More often than not we could be seen swimming off the dock in the creek at Manchester, impatiently awaiting high tide and slack water—the best time for enjoying the creek; or roaming about the sandy roads of Valona, sometimes crunching through the oyster shell lane leading down to Alex Durant's shrimp docks there on Shellbluff Creek. No purpose in mind whatsoever until, spotting (and enjoying the invigorating aromas) the big rusting steel drums full of Atlantic blue crabs caught by the nets of the local boats. We all had the thought simultaneously—let's get some chicken necks, lines and a peach basket and go crabbing. And just like that, three or four of us would be pulling an old pine bateau out from the marsh, down the muddy bank, and off for an afternoon of crabbing in the nearby creek.

This often occurred in our ramblings around Cedar Point as well. The constant proximity to fresh seafood was like an aphrodisiac—it precipitated a natural inclination to indulge in the bounty of the waters all around us. The aromas of the marshes amid the creeks at low tide, with the hot breath of the July sun bearing on sun-reddened backs, dipping crab lines close to a mud flat, luring the Atlantic blues toward their impending date with a steam pot later that afternoon. Meeting the incoming shrimp boats in late afternoon was always a highlight. Many were the days I eagerly sprinted down the sandy lane paralleling Cedar Creek to Hugh Burrows' docks to meet Cap'n Bobo (Hugh Burrows) bringing in the *Pinta* from twelve or more hours of trawling in the Sound or offshore of Sapelo. The fragrances of the docks have never left me—a mixture of the smells of nets, dried-out shrimp and fish, salt water and marsh wrack, diesel fuel and tar. As a lad of twelve and thirteen, Bobo paid me fifty cents every Saturday morning to clean the deckhouse of the *Pinta*. Starting in the galley, I hand-washed pots, cutlery, and crockery, including those heavy coffee mugs that were so thick you could almost drive a nail with one; scrubbed down the table and floor, stocked the groceries for the coming week in the cupboards and the below-deck freezer, tidied the stateroom, and swept out and cleaned the windows of the wheelhouse. I'd have done it all for nothing it was so invigorating. But Bobo always gave me a half-dollar piece upon the completion of my labors, and in those days, fifty cents was like a small fortune to a kid. For instance, it could cover the Saturday afternoon matinee in Darien with my friends, including a fountain Coke and popcorn.

Darien and McIntosh County had long had a maritime tradition. People relied on the waterways for mobility, roads being of poor quality and connection before the arrival of railroads and highways. Boats of all sizes and description were to be found on the waters of tidewater Georgia and lower South Carolina. Boat builder and small-craft historian Rusty Fleetwood of Tybee Island said it best: "To tell the story of this region, it is necessary to tell of boats. Not necessarily fancy or large craft, just plain, get-from-here-to-there boats that could live with the mud, the oyster rakes, the narrow creeks, and the short,

Lazy summer days of our youth on the McIntosh County tidewater: Shellbluff Creek, Valona.

choppy seas of the sounds and would be simple and cheap to build and operate."[958] I understood this at a very early age, obviously due to my proximity to tidal waters and shrimp fishermen and my own explorations on the local creeks and rivers, blessedly free from the constraints and diversions of "the hill"—the high ground of our environment.

This was thus a time when my curiosity and interest in our coastal geography manifested itself. By the age of twelve I was devouring the Coast and Geodetic Survey navigational charts of local waters. I also had topographic and hydrologic maps of our land and water areas spread over the floor and table where I memorized every place name, learned every nuance of the waterways, the tide ranges, the location

---

[958] Rusty Fleetwood, *Tidecraft: The Boats of Lower South Carolina, Georgia and Northeast Florida, 1650-1950* (Savannah: Coastal Heritage Society, 1982), v.

of every sandbar, shoal and mudflat, the depth of the creeks we regularly explored in our little skiff. These investigations awakened my historical awareness and a growing interest in learning more. The abandoned oyster factory and docks in front of my grandmother's house at Cedar Point were always a source of interest. This operation thrived in the 1930s and 40s, and here my father and two friends managed affairs during the period right after World War II. There were a couple of summers where Quiz Forsyth and I cataloged the names and owners of all the shrimp boats at Valona, Cedar Point, Belleville and Meridian. We cycled to the docks in these communities, plus hitch-hiked into Darien several times, to compile our lists of the boats there, and even sketch pictures of the boats on ruled notebook paper, however crude and amateurish these drawings turned out to be looking back on them now. The ballast islands along the waterways near the sounds were also intriguing to me. Often, in the four summers from 1960 through 1963, I made solo exploratory forays by boat to these areas, taking notes and photographs of such places as Hazzard's Island, Creighton, Doboy and Commodore islands, the old lighthouse on the tip of Sapelo, Hird Island, the tabby ruins on Carnochan Creek at the Thicket, and the shrimp docks at Meridian, Valona, Cedar Point and Belleville. There were many boat excursions in my little aluminum boat with the 10-horsepower kicker, going from Cedar Point to Valona, cutting through the marsh on high tide to Kittles docks on the lower tip of Valona, thence to Doboy Sound and Blue and Hall, all being south of Cedar Point; or in the other direction, along the Crescent river to Creighton and Baisden's Bluff, Belleville, via Rattlesnake Cut, then to Pine Harbor and Fairhope via Roscoe's Cut that connected both sides of

Belleville on the Sapelo River. As river rats we spent a lot of summer time in those days around Belleville and Pine Harbor. We never thought we'd grow up—or needed to—and have to give up those carefree days on the river.

Years later, when my children were still young, I realized the urges had never waned, the pull of the water was just as intense as ever. We graduated to a bigger craft, and the girls and I made longer trips—to exotic, isolated places like Blackbeard and Cabretta islands, going "outside" and navigating south along the shores of Sapelo, swimming on the inside section of the south tip of Nanny Goat Beach with the abandoned lighthouse tower across the way on a sparkling sunlit summer afternoon. Then there were my historical investigations by water to the Darien River, the rice islands of the Altamaha delta—Butler's Island, Cambers Island, Hopeton, Altama and Broughton—and northward into Sapelo Sound to the ballast islands along Front River, and across the Sound to Julianton on the south end of Harris Neck. It was important to me to be able to physically "experience" the locales I was writing about in my history books. Along the same lines were the many auto trips to the remotest sections of the county, such as the Harris Neck wildlife refuge, Jones, Townsend, Cox and the lost settlement of Warsaw.[959]

---

[959] My earliest ancestor in McIntosh County was my maternal great-grandfather, Thomas Marshall Hunter (1870-1937), who as a young man served as the pastor of the Darien Presbyterian church, 1894-97. He and his wife, Sallie Owen Hunter of Charleston, lived at Ashantilly during his Darien pastorate, where a son was born, Howard Owen Hunter (1895-1964), my maternal grandfather. My mother, Mary Kate Hunter Sullivan (1924-1954), lived with her mother, Mary J. Hunter (1893-1968) in the Cedar Point waterfront home built by her father, Henry Herbert Johnson (1862-1937), in the mid-1920s on property he acquired from the Atwood family in 1911. It was on this tract that occurred the foregoing remarks regarding my childhood and adolescence in McIntosh County.

INDEX

Adler, Emma Morel, 75, 653
Adler, Leopold, 75, 653
Altama plantation, 338-40, 592
Altamaha River, 21, 54, 58, 79, 213, 244, 251, 258, 314-16, 320, 341, 343-445, 351, 694-95, 788-801, 806-09
Altamaha Sound, 67, 580, 728, 744, 745-46, 754, 755, 776
Amason, Guy H., 740, 743
Anderson, Rachel, 327
Appleton, George L., 369, 388-89, 389n, 725
Appleton, Louisa Arnold, 389
archaeology, 87-122
Arnold, Louis Gindrat, 367-68, 374, 375, 377, 388
Arnold, Richard James, 227, 247, 360, 367-89
Arnold, Thomas Clay, 369, 375, 379, 380, 386, 388
Arnold, William Eliot, 370, 375, 388
Ashantilly, 193, 195, 280, 798-802, 809
Atlantic Intracoastal Waterway, 762-76
Atwood family, 103, 734, 737-38, 747-50, 770, 812
Ayllon, Lucas Vasquez, 88, 88n, 89

Bailey, Cornelia Walker, 187, 543, 546, 548, 551, 621, 625
Baldwin, Loammi, 344-45, 348
Barnwell, John, 106, 110, 258
Barrow, Dr. Craig, 800n

Barrow, David Crenshaw, 503, 504, 506, 511, 522
Barrow, David C., Jr., 544, 571
Barrow, Elfrida DeRenne, 800, 800n
Baruch, Belle W., 51
beach and dune systems, 15-20
Beaulieu, 629, 640, 723
Behavior Cemetery, 543-46
Belfast, Ga., 382n, 657, 711-12
Bell, Malcolm, 262, 266, 274, 295, 297, 300, 310, 323, 497n, 553-55
Bell, Muriel Barrow, 497n, 553-55
Belvedere Island, 400, 424, 425-28, 433, 444, 466, 735
Berolzheimer, Philip, 57
Bilali, Mohammad, 184-89
Blackbeard Island, 16, 41, 68, 80, 132, 535, 537, 580, 608, 688-93, 713, 725, 744, 756
Blue, Alexander, 287, 288, 289
Bourbon Field, Sapelo I., 93, 128, 132, 136-38, 491, 513, 539, 571
Brailsford, William, 803
Brower, David, 83
Brown, Katie, 187, 544, 546
Brunswick, Ga., 10, 44, 70, 114, 265, 342-45, 349-52, 579, 585, 590, 591, 641, 691-96, 703, 705, 709-10, 723, 734, 736, 740, 761, 779
Brunswick-Altamaha Canal, 330, 343-46, 348-52
Bryan County, 227, 341-42, 348, 353, 354, 357-89, 396, 654-87, 662n

Bryan Neck Presbyterian Church, 361, 366, 390
Buckhead, Ossabaw I., 629, 634, 644, 646, 649, 666
Burnside River, 642n, 723, 767, 769
Burrows, Hugh A., 734, 747-50
Butler, John M., 227, 285, 298
Butler, Major Pierce, 151, 198, 228-29, 236, 244, 249-50, 298, 329, 357
Butler, Pierce M., 227, 266-67, 267, 274, 275, 282, 297-302, 304-05, 310, 316
Butler, William, 357
Butler's Island, 71, 205, 206, 210-57, 266-92, 297-324
Buttermilk Sound, 274, 275, 728, 754, 776

Caldwell, Sheila K., 106-12
Cambers Island, 151, 154, 183, 329, 330, 794, 819
Campbell, Tunis G., 306-07, 464-65, 487, 493-94, 521, 521n, 640-41
Candler family, Cumberland Island and, 61, 61n, 84, 588
Cannon's Point, 55, 68, 70, 122, 282, 328, 331, 337, 338, 502
Canoochee River, 200, 348, 354, 358, 362, 371, 669, 669n, 670, 680n, 675, 683, 685
Carnegie, Lucy Coleman, 60-61
Carnegie, Thomas, 56, 60-61
Carnegie family, 63, 82-84, 587
Carnochan, William, 114, 116, 173, 174, 180
Cathead Creek, 325, 330, 428, 705, 794, 795, 804
Cedar Point, Ga., 104, 736-38, 737n, 746 passim, 754, 758, 760, 810-19, 814n, 819n
Central of Georgia R.R., 299, 343, 348, 353, 355-56, 674

Champneys Island, 162, 242-44, 314, 320, 566, 567, 707
Chatham County, 41, 64, 140-41, 183, 227, 341-42, 346-48, 352-56, 404-07, 413, 449, 476, 629-30, 635, 638, 642n, 721-24, 731-32, 762-69
Cherry Hill plantation, 359-60, 364, 368, 370-71, 373, 374, 376, 379, 381-83, 387-88
Children of Pride, The, 198, 293
Chocolate, Sapelo I., 93, 137, 139, 144-45, 149-51, 150n, 190, 192, 496, 536, 539
Clay, Eliza Caroline, 359, 362, 363, 365, 386, 388
Clay, Joseph, 358-59
Clay, Mary Anne Savage, 358-60
Clay, Matilda McAllister, 360, 365, 366
Clay, Robert Habersham, 365, 366, 388
Clay, Thomas Carolin, 365
Clay, Thomas Savage, 227, 247, 359-65, 367, 380, 396
Cloister Hotel, 36, 70, 71, 586, 591-94, 665
Clyde, Ga., 668-87
Coastal Marshlands Protection Act, 35-37, 81, 82n
Coffee Bluff, 635, 643
Coffin, Howard E., 57, 64-72, 80, 569-98
Colonel's Island, Glynn Co., 729
Colonel's Island, Liberty Co., 41, 199, 203, 206-10, 291, 292, 440, 447, 457
Confederate States Navy, 638-40
Conference on the Future of Marshlands, 35-37
Conroy, Pat, 810, 819n, 811
Constitution, USS, 690
Coolidge, Calvin, 585-87

821

Corbin, Francis P., 337-38
Corps of Engineers, 23, 351, 356, 581, 662, 760, 763-75
cotton cultivation, 154-62, 214, 228-33, 404-08
Coulter, E. Merton, 113-15, 149, 165. 168, 173, 175-77, 182, 193, 196
Couper, James H., 56, 215, 221, 225, 227, 247-48, 289, 299, 328-39
Couper, John, 160, 247, 328, 331, 337, 338, 407
Cox, Ga., 326, 777-78, 786
Creighton Island, 102-05, 183, 397, 402, 446, 536, 601, 712, 726, 753-54, 761, 769
Creighton Narrows, 22, 23, 743, 769-73
Crescent, Ga., 173, 747, 749, 761, 804, 813, 815
Cumberland Island, 35, 56, 58, 60-61, 63, 80, 82-86, 89, 141-42, 418, 641, 688, 690, 696, 700, 701, 773

Dallas, Moses, 640
Darien, Ga., 52-54, 280, 324-26, 693-95, 699-720, 791-97
Darien Timber Gazette, 693-94
Darien Presbyterian Church, 390-93, 451
deer tongue, 784, 813
Delta plantation, 408, 415-17
Demere, Raymond P., 360, 374
Demetre, Anne Harris, 397-99
Demetre, Daniel, 397-99
Dent, James Troup, 261, 317, 805
Dent, Miss Ophelia, 317, 802-06
DESCO Marine, 740, 741, 750
dividings, 21-23, 754, 769-70
Doboy Sound, 16-21, 24, 507-08, 514, 521, 521n, 529, 694, 707, 717, 726-27, 743-44

Doctortown, Ga., 380n, 792, 796, 797
Dodge, William E., 53-54
Drake oyster survey, 721-30
Drums and Shadows, 184-85, 324-27, 473-75, 553-55
Duplin River, 23-25, 531, 581, 607, 617, 726, 744, 745
Durant, Alexander M., 748, 749, 750, 815

ecology, of coastal Georgia, 10-11, 13-45, 46 *passim*
Eden, Ga. (Bryan County), 341, 669-74
Eden, Ga., (Effingham County), 674
Effingham County, 341, 342, 564, 568, 668n, 674
Elizafield plantation, 106, 112, 113-14, 242, 262, 330, 344-46, 351, 567
Ellabell, Ga., 673, 677, 682, 687
environment, of coastal Georgia, see ecology

Five Pound, 246, 274, 275
Fleetwood, Rusty, 696, 714-15, 716, 734-35, 739-41, 816
Floyd, Marmaduke H., 113, 173-74, 176-77
Folly Farms, 370
Ford, Henry, 58, 73, 364, 367, 370, 570, 588, 654-67, 684
Fort King George, 106-12, 115, 118, 120, 258-59, 800, 802
Fort McAllister, 358, 360, 486, 658-63, 671, 673
Fort Stewart, 670, 679-83, 680n, 686
Fraser, Charles, 83-84
Freedmen's Bureau, 303, 387, 464, 464n, 487-91, 493-94, 641

Generals Island, 277, 290, 290n, 315, 316, 794
Genesis Point, 358, 366, 658, 660, 661
Georgia Coast & Piedmont Railroad, 117, 701, 701n, 760, 778
Georgia Land & Livestock Co., 442, 784-87
Georgia's Disputed Ruins, 113-14, 173-76
Glynn County, 73, 106, 126, 130, 132, 227, 328-40, 342-46, 348-52, 591-92, 793, 728-29, 766, 804
Gould, Thomas K., 416, 419, 423, 435
Goulding, Rev. Francis R., 188-89, 390-91, 392, 451
Graham, Lewis B., 747-49
Grant, Hugh Fraser, 227, 239, 242, 262, 344-45, 346, 351
Green, Allen, 549, 551-52, 620
Grubb, Richard W., 470, 566, 694-95, 700, 704, 796
Guale Indians, 88-94, 101-02

Habersham, Robert, 227, 237-41, 363, 373-74
Habersham, William N., 639
Halfmoon Bluff, 206, 207
Hall, Basil, 236, 260
hammocks, 29-30
Hampton plantation, 208, 216, 229, 236, 238, 238, 249, 251, 270, 272, 276, 281-82, 287, 289, 301, 313, 318, 319-20
Harris, John, 400, 416, 420-23, 439-40, 443, 444, 445, 462
Harris, Margaret Harper, 420-23, 435, 444, 439, 441, 444, 445, 446, 447, 464-66, 464n
Harris, Reid W., 36, 37

Harris, William Thomas, 397-400, 438, 443
Harris, William Thomas, Jr., 400, 404, 417, 419-22, 457, 462
Harris Neck, 397-485
Harris Neck Airfield, 478-82
Haynes, William G., 798-802, 806-09
Hazzard, Liverpool, 305, 310, 325
Hell Gate, 723, 762, 769
Hillery, William & Co., 498-99, 535
Hilton, Joseph, 694, 705-06, 708n
Hilton-Dodge Lumber Co., 118, 657, 694, 706, 784
Hines, John Pray, 375, 376, 377, 378, 379, 379n
Hines, Lewis, 376, 379, 379n
Hinesville, Ga., 200, 679, 680n, 681
Hobcaw Barony, 51
Hoffmann, Charles and Tess, 371, 374, 380, 389
Hofwyl-Broadfield, 261, 317, 707, 794, 802-06
Hog Hammock, 192, 496-502, 539-43, 547-48, 551-59, 606, 611, 618-26
Holmes, Dr. James, 263-65, 275, 280, 305,
Hopeton plantation, 215, 221, 225, 234, 247-48, 285, 289, 328-40, 794, 819
House, Albert V., 225, 242
Houstoun, James E., 429, 430
Houstoun, James E., Jr., 429, 430, 433-34, 436, 453, 454
Howell, Clark, 72, 588, 596
Hunter, Rev. T.M., 819n
hurricanes, 44-45, 57, 180, 235, 249, 256-57, 312, 337, 481, 500, 508, 531-32, 535, 544, 643, 707, 814, 814n

Huston, Tillinghast L., 58, 58n, 71, 253, 320-22, 323-24

Irene period, 91, 94, 103, 105
Isle of Hope, 375, 696, 722, 767, 769

James, Thomas C., 287, 289, 297, 298
Jekyll Island, 35, 49, 56, 58, 61-63, 77-78, 79, 82, 84, 125, 130, 132, 139, 148, 157, 297, 608, 696, 729
Jekyll Island Club, 49, 56, 59-60, 61-63, 77-78, 470
Jenkes, Ebenezer, 341-42
Johnson, Dr. Henry H., 737n 819n
Jones, Alfred W., 69, 70, 72, 111, 340, 575, 579, 582, 591-92, 595, 600, 665
Jones, Rev. Charles C., 197, 198, 207, 293, 295, 362, 393-94, 395
Jonesville, 199, 199n
Judy, slave, 246, 275, 279
Julianton plantation, 401-15

Keen, James, 691-93
Kelso, William, 118-21
Kemble, Frances Anne, 243, 243n, 246, 254, 266-84, 285, 297, 300-01, 304, 305, 312-13, 316-17
Kenan Field, 91, 93, 95, 102, 491, 498, 505, 537, 559
Keys, Clement M., 57, 76-77, 582, 587, 588, 665
King, Barrington, 203, 204
King, James Audley M., 202-03, 208, 290, 291
King, Julia Rebecca Maxwell, 202, 203, 207-08, 279-80, 451
King, Julia Rebecca, 208-10, 295-96

King, Roswell, 226, 235, 248, 254
King, Roswell, Jr., 197-98, 201, 202, 203-10, 213, 216-17, 223, 227, 228-30, 246-47, 248, 267, 269, 274, 284-96, 299, 310, 326
King, Roswell, III, 202, 203, 205n
King, William John, 415, 416, 421, 422, 423, 434, 443, 444, 446, 449-53, 455, 468
King Savannah, 137-38, 497, 551
Kollock, George J., 632, 634-39, 642, 643

Lachlison, Robert, 353, 382-83, 704-05, 706
Lamar, Charles A.L., 297-98, 298n
Larson, Lewis, 88, 100-01, 103, 104, 105-06
Leigh, Frances Butler, 304-18
Leigh, Rev. James W., 307-18
Levett, Francis, 401-12
Lewis, Aunt Jane, 324-26
Lewis, Bessie Mary, 107, 110, 112, 258-59, 321, 800, 802
Lewis, Eugene W., 72, 588, 592
Liberty County, 41, 126, 131, 197-210, 227, 235, 257, 287, 290-96, 395-96, 403, 404, 404n, 437, 440, 447, 449, 451, 456, 668, 679, 711
Lindbergh, Charles A., 587-88
Little Cumberland Is., 58, 80
Little Sapelo Island, 25, 29, 41, 123, 127, 150n, 488, 492, 502, 506, 513, 529, 547, 572, 576-77, 585
Little St. Simons Island, 57, 58, 67, 80, 229, 257, 275, 728
live oak (*Quercus virginiana*), 37-38, 68, 688-93
Lorillard, Pierre, 56, 469-72

824

Lower Bluff, 52, 107-21, 694, 706-07, 712, 755, 760, 797
Lyell, Sir Charles, 252-53, 336

McAllister, George W., 227, 360-61, 365-67, 375, 658
McAllister, Joseph L., 366, 658
McDonald, Alexander, 633
McDonald, Daniel, 285, 337, 446
McFeely, William S., 85, 184, 185, 499, 535, 621
McKinley Archibald C., 503-05, 510-24, 529 *passim*, 530-31, 535
McKinley, Sarah Spalding, 503-05, 529 *passim*, 531, 534, 535
McMaster, Elizabeth, 63-64
McPhee, John, 83, 85-86
Maggione family, 436, 447, 732, 733, 737
Marengo plantation, 425, 426, 428-33, 436-38
marshes (*Spartina alterniflora*), 24-37, 810-12
Maxwell, Audley, 202, 207-08
Maybank plantation, 197, 201, 207, 364, 393, 447
Medway River, 200, 204, 207, 362, 725
Middleton, John M., 369, 375, 386, 388
Midway Congregational Church, 198-99, 202, 293, 390, 395, 452
Minda, slave, 280, 310
Mississippian period, 91, 93, 94
Modena plantation, 57
Montgomery, Chatham Co., 642, 642n, 723
Moore, Clarence B., 88, 93, 95-100, 102-06, 468
Morel, Amos, slave, 383-86
Morel, John, 628-29, 631
Morel, John, Jr., 629-31

Morgan's Bridge, 682
mosquitoes, 257-66
Mud River, 22-23, 90, 98, 726, 737, 743, 744, 753-54, 769, 770, 771, 775
Mulberry Hill tract, 367, 376-77, 379
Musgrove, Mary, 627, 789, 790
Myrtle Grove, 367, 368-70

naval stores, 777, 781-84
Nightingale, P.M., 227, 330, 705
Noble, Edward, 77

Ocean Steamship Co., 355
Oden, Thomas, 210, 267, 273, 285, 286n, 337
Odum, Eugene P., 26, 31, 36, 80, 613-15, 808
Oemler, Augustus, 476-77, 730-33
Ogeechee River, 241, 342, 347, 352-53, 357 *passim*, 654-62
Oglethorpe, James E., 121-22, 147, 259, 398, 627, 789, 790
Old Teakettle Creek, 21, 22, 735, 743, 744-45, 758, 769, 770, 771, 775
Olmsted, Frederick Law, 212, 372-73, 373n, 383, 393
Ossabaw Island, 36, 56, 74-76, 93, 627-53, 666, 724, 762
Ossabaw Sound, 635, 639-40, 648, 723-24, 731, 762-69
oyster fishery, 720-39

Parrish, Lydia, 187, 189, 310
Parsons, George, 55, 63, 731, 763, 764, 765
Parsons, Joseph, 63, 731, 765
Pembroke, Ga., 669, 673, 675-78, 678n, 682
Peru plantation, 422, 424-26, 436, 444-48, 462-63, 467
Pin Point, 642, 642n
Pinkey House tract, 369-70

825

Poppell, Tom H., 482-83, 610
Psyche (Sack), slave, 274, 274n, 282
Possum Point, 326-27
Priester, John N., 442, 442n
Priester tract, 442-43

Raccoon Bluff, 129, 132, 136, 141, 151, 492, 496, 497-500, 535-37, 546-53, 572, 618-20
Raccoon Key, 639, 723, 724
railroad development, 343, 348, 673, 675-76, 777-78
Renty, slave, 289, 299,
Reynolds, R.J., Jr., 34, 70, 72, 594-95, 598-614
Riceborough, 200, 203, 207, 240, 395, 437, 781
Richmond Hill, Ga., 58, 73, 326, 357, 376, 588, 654-58, 661, 663, 668, 682-84, 685, 686
Richmond plantation, 359-65
rice cultivation, 210-28, 248, 256 passim, 328 passim
Roebling, Robert C., 57
Romerly Marsh, 723, 762-64
Rose Dhu Island, 635, 643

St. Catherines Island, 17, 76-77, 89, 115, 125, 464, 476, 582, 632, 725, 730-33
St. Cyprian's Church, 308, 313, 318, 563, 567
St. Simons Island, 55, 70, 72, 120, 147, 154-55, 157, 158, 208, 216, 236, 281, 328, 502, 602, 689, 706, 728
St. Simons Sound, 728-29, 767
Sampson, slave, 246
Santo Domingo de Talaje, 106-10, 114-15, 119-21
Sapelo Island, 90-102, 123-96, 486-559, 569-626
Sapelo Sound, 88, 88n, 536, 709, 712-13, 725-26, 737, 743-44, 753, 756-57, 770

Savage, Mary Butler, 357-58
Savage, Thomas, 357-58
Savage, William, 368, 376, 379
Savannah, Ga., 4, 22, 53, 63, 64, 73, 75, 76n, 77, 89, 113, 121, 122, 122n, 125, 129, 135n, 139, 140-43, 150, 156, 167, 180, 181, 182, 194, 212, 221, 225, 226, 227, 237-42, 264-65, 269, 294n, 297-301, 311, 341-42, 352-56, 358, 365, 373, 375, 376, 380n, 382, 384, 386, 398, 405, 406, 412-13, 426, 428, 448, 449, 461, 476, 486, 526, 546, 558, 564, 622, 624-25, 628-34, 636, 636n, 640, 641, 642, 647, 655, 673, 690-92, 697, 705, 709-10, 716-18, 725, 726, 736, 756-63, 767, 772, 777, 778, 779, 780, 785, 786, 787, 788, 791. 799, 799n
Savannah-Ogeechee Canal, 341-42, 346-50, 352-56
Sea Island, see Cloister Hotel
Sedgefield tract, 376-77, 379
Seven Mile Bend, 369, 388
Shadrach, slave, 275, 300
Shell Ring, Sapelo I., 98-102
shrimp fishery, 739-751
Silk Hope plantation, 357-58, 368, 376-77, 379-80, 379n
Sinda, slave, 278
Six Mile Creek, 330, 344-46, 350, 351
Skidaway Island, 41, 57, 63, 155, 405 passim, 416, 570, 722-23, 763, 764, 767-68
Skidaway Narrows, 762-69
slavery, conditions of, at Butler's Island, 244-57; at Sapelo Island, 180-92
soils, 39-44
South End Place, Ossabaw I., 634-38

South Hampton plantation, 198, 201, 203-06, 205n, 235
Spalding, Charles H., 429, 503
Spalding, Ella Barrow, 503-04, 522, 525-26, 529, 534, 542
Spalding, Randolph, 192, 193, 194, 447, 490-92, 527, 529
Spalding, Thomas, 146-96
Spalding, Thomas II, 503-04, 506-10, 512 *passim*, 526-28
Spalding, Thomas B., 503-04, 506, 513, 518 *passim*, 523-25
Speir, W.W., 682, 685
Speir, Thelma W., 685-87
Starr, Charles H., 374, 382
Stebbins, Charles Austin, 436, 437-38
Sterling Bluff, 358
Stevens, Charles, 237, 239
Strachan, Frank D.M., 646, 646n
Strathy Hall plantation, 360, 365-67, 368, 374, 379
sugar cane, 166-71, 233-36
Sullivan, Roy E., 737-38, 737n
Sunbury, 200, 204, 440, 456

tabby, 166-67, 171-80
task system, 216-17
Taylor's Creek, Ga., 200, 668, 679n, 680n, 711
Thicket, 113-14, 171, 173-74, 176, 180, 758, 818
Thomas, Edward J., 424, 444, 445-48, 450, 459, 467
Thomas, John A., 426, 436, 446, 447-48, 468
Thomas, Jonathan, 421, 424-26, 429, 431-33, 436-37, 438, 443
Thomas, Mary Ann, 425, 429, 431-34, 436-37, 438, 454
Thompson, Victor, 101-02
Thorpe, Elisha M., 415, 417, 434, 460-61, 478, 779, 785
tides, 23-24
timber industry, 107-21, 706-07
Tivoli plantation, 362-64

Thunderbolt, Ga., 696, 722, 730, 735, 741
Torrey, Nell Ford, 57, 73, 588, 647-51, 663, 666
Townsend, Ga., 777-79, 785
Tranquilla, 357, 359, 362-63, turpentine production, 781-84
Tybee Island, 716, 718, 721, 731, 816

University of Georgia Marine Institute, 24, 31-34, 613-17

Valona, Ga., 22, 104, 733-36, 745, 747-50, 761, 813
Vernon River, 640, 723, 769
Vernon View, 642, 648
Wahoo Island, 430, 434-35, 452, 454, 455, 475, 477
Waldburg, Jacob, 201, 202, 487
Walker Mound, 104-05
Walthour, George W., 201, 202, 227, 449
Walthourville, Ga., 199, 203, 447, 447n, 448
Wanderer, slave ship, 297-98
Wannamaker, John, 56, 644-46
Waring, Antonio J., 88, 99-101, 104
Warsaw, Ga., 762, 779-81
Wassaw Island, 55, 58, 63-64, 80, 476, 722-23, 731, 762-66, 768
Wassaw Sound, 659, 716, 721-23
Waterbury, James, 56, 632, 644
Water Witch, USS, 639-40
Watson, Hunter A., 747 *passim*
Ways Station, 326, 588, 654-58, 664. *See also* Richmond Hill
Weed, Henry D., 634, 646
Weeping Time, auction, 298-301
West, Eleanor Torrey, 74-76, 645, 651-53
White Hall plantation, 367-76, 384, 385, 387, 388-89, 389n
Williams, Joseph, 391-92

Willie, Ga., 668, 679n
Willink, Henry F., 638-39
Wilmington Island, 405, 722, 731, 732, 735
Wilmington River, 666, 722-23
Wise, Jacob R., 670-73
Wister, Owen (Dan), 284, 310, 318-20
Wister, Sarah Butler, 284, 301, 305-06, 310, 313, 315, 318
Wolf Island, 58, 266n, 607, 718, 727, 745, 752, 754, 759, 761

Woodville, 206-10, 295-96
Woolford, Cator, 340, 592
Wylly, Alexander C., 539-40
Wylly, Charles S., 185, 534, 804

Yellow Bluff, 206, 207-08, 292
yellow fever, 257-66